Singing Is A Gift --

A Gift You Develop To Share With Others!

-- L.A. Peterson

Published by
Total Research Publishers
Music Publishing Division -- Verity Music
P.O. Box 637, Taylor, MI 48180

ISBN 1-878459-00-7

Book printed in the U.S.A.
Cassette Tape manufactured in the U.S.A.

First Printing, December, 1989
Second Printing, September, 1990

YOU CAN SING GREAT

-- At Any Age --

By Rick Wiesend
In Cooperation With *Vocal Instructors and Professional Entertainers*

HELLO

Thank you so much for ordering my singing improvement program. I know it will work for you if you try. I tried to create a fun and interesting program that will help you develop a great voice, no matter what your age. It's never too early or too late to develop your voice.

If you feel you need specialized training consider one of my advanced tapes. If you find singing as enjoyable and fulfulling as I do, you will find the advanced tapes both rewarding and fun.

Once you develop your voice, share it with others -- just as God has intended.

Rick

P.S. Use the following tips to help you get started on the cassette tape.

"How To Sing Great"

1. Use Dolby on your cassette player, if you have it, for the best sound reproduction.
2. Play at a medium to low level. *Do not blast the tape too loudly when you listen and practice with the tape. It's best not to strain your ears or your voice when you practice!*
3. Build your practice sessions. Start with 10 minutes. Build to an half hour...or longer, if you have the time. Do not strain your voice when you practice. This cassette tape, *the only one of its kind -- YOU HAVE THE ORIGINAL -- has been scientifically planned to build your range, endurance and vocal strength gradually; without vocal damage!*

QUANTITY SALES

"You Can Sing Great -- At Any Age -- How To Sing Great" is available at special quantity discounts when purchased in bulk by corporations, organizations, schools, vocal and music teachers, and special-interest groups. For details write:

Verity Music
Attn: Special Music Sales Dept.
P. O. Box 637, Taylor, MI 48180

Or call 1-800-922-1666 and ask for the
Special Music Sales Department.

INDIVIDUAL SALES

You can get additional copies of *"You Can Sing Great -- At Any Age -- How To Sing Great,"* the complete vocal improvement program directly from us. You can buy the book or the cassette tape as a package or separately.

The package price (for the book and cassette tape) is $16.95 plus $3.00 for shipping and handling.
That's a savings or $5.95 over the individual prices!)

Extra copies of the cassette tape, *"How To Sing Great,"* are $9.95 plus $3.00 for shipping and handling for each tape.

Extra copies of the book, *"You Can Sing Great -- At Any Age,"* are $9.95 plus $3.00 for shipping and handling for each book.

Send payment to:

Verity Music
P. O. Box 637, Dept. SIB, Taylor, MI 48180

Or call 1-800-922-1666 for Visa and Mastercard orders only.
Ask for the *Sales In Book Department.*

A SPECIAL THANK YOU!

I've been very fortunate over the years to have been associated with some great singers and other music business professionals who have enhanced my professional and personal life. I owe much to the influence of these people. I just want to say *"Thank You, Again."*

THIS BOOK IS DEDICATED TO THEM:

Barbra Streisand, it seems like only yesterday when you were belting out songs in that club in Detroit. Actually it was 1961, who would believe it. Barbra, you showed me that faith in oneself is more powerful than any force on Earth.

Johnny Mathis, you have proven over and over again that nobody can hold those high notes as long as you! Try as I might, you're still the master.

Mahalia Jackson, you brought out in me some very heavy soul I never thought I had. God Bless You.

Berry Gordy, for your deep wisdom and advice.

Martha and the Vandellas, for the free before-concert, dressing-room harmony lessons. They were great!

The Temptations and the Four Tops, for teaching a bunch of *"white"* boys some real *"soul-stepping"* routines. We would have been lost without your help. Thanks again.

Smokey Robinson and the Miracles, I still recall those amazing stories you shared -- *about how your early songs were born* -- before our television appearances a number of years ago. Smokey, I'll never forget your unique voice and your great songs.

All of the Motown family, you did the leg-work making Detroit *"the place"* for music and records. Thanks for paving the way and making it a little easier for me to break into the tough music business.

Marvin Gaye, you made me realize that the family should come first; the career next; personal gratification last. May God ease your burden and pain.

Jackie Wilson, I still remember you singing *"You Better Stop Your Doggin' Around"* to the *"nervous"* taxi cab driver when we were almost late for a show in Detroit. I'll bet you and Marvin are singing a duet up there. God Bless!

Sonny and Cher, I won't forget our concert at the Detroit Masonic Temple. Cher, you've come a long way from the days when you were shy backstage and let Sonny do all the talking.

Rich Becker, the best engineer in Detroit. Thanks for the free studio time in the early days. I'm so proud of you; I knew you had what it takes!

Palmer Records and Handlman Co., all the people -- *like John Kaplan and Tom Schleshinger* -- behind the companies that gave me my break and kept my records on the racks. Thanks, again!

Johnny Williams, for sharing your knowledge of music and conducting me through many recording sessions.

Bobby Darin, for teaching me how to *"Scat."* We all miss you, God Bless!

Bo Diddley, who taught me to play the guitar in an open key chord -- *unorthodox, but very effective.* Your music inspired my own songs.

Eugene Dyer, my most dedicated school choir director, thanks for the encouragement. I'll never forget how nervous I was singing *"Mary's Boy Chile"* --my first solo -- in front of all those people.

John Benkleman, a vocal instructor and friend. You instilled in me a love for musical theater, for that I will ever be grateful. You will never see the fruits of our labor; but -- *somehow* -- I know you would approve.

WITH SPECIAL THANKS AND LOVE TO:

Lucy, my wife, few of my dreams -- *both our dreams* -- would ever have been realized without your help.

Wendy, Natalie and Tiffany, my daughters, for patiently waiting for my attention as I lovingly but unrelentlessly *"slaved"* in my recording studio and on my word-processor to produce and write *"How To Sing Great."* This one's for you!

John J. and Dorothy Wiesend, my mom and dad, thank you for instilling in me your love of music and song.

Jacky and Danny, my brothers, for the fun harmony sessions we have.

Roger Neuman, my close friend who's brilliant in business. Thanks for believing in me and telling me to stick to singing.

Tom DeAngelo, my close friend who lights up my daughters' eyes.

Louise Peterson, who sang beautiful Polish folk songs to me. And *"picked"* my musical spouce, long before I did! We'll always be there when you need us!

Anthony Peterson, who taught me never to give up until a new skill is mastered and a job is well done. And who gave to me his incredible common sense. *"Na Sdrovia...Goodbye...We Love You!"*

So you like to sing. Or you don't feel you can carry a tune. *Or you would like to learn to sing better so that you can become a lead singer in a band...or a soloist in the choir.* Or you want to learn how to make money with your voice...or with a song you have written. *Or you just want to be able to take the voice you use in the shower and build the confidence you need to sing in front of others.* Or you may want to help someone else learn to sing. Whatever your reason for wanting to improve your singing, *you have made the right decision with this fun and exciting vocal improvement program.*

Singing and songs should be a part of everyone's life. Singing comes naturally! Everyone knows how to sing! Or do they? You may feel you know how to sing, but unless you have learned how to bring the most out of your vocal cords you are *only tapping a small portion of your potential!*

Some people have a natural talent and a good voice, but most great singing voices belong to people who have learned how to develop their vocal muscles to do the right thing. They have learned how to avoid all the musical pitfalls. They have learned how to enhance their natural talent and create a voice others only dream about.

You don't have to dream any more. You don't have to listen to any of the great singers -- *in Folk, Gospel, Country, Religious, Blues, Rock, Jazz, Pop, Contemporary or Musical Theater* -- and wish you had their talent. You can learn how to sing better than you ever dreamed possible with this innovative cassette tape and book program for vocal improvement. You can use this program for your own betterment, or you can help someone else -- *your child or grandchild* -- to maximize their vocal potential.

In all the years he has been involved in music, education and entertainment, *Rick Wiesend* has discovered a real void in educational material on teaching adults, teens and children how to sing. The only educational material available is written for vocal and music teachers and is far too technical in language and approach to help the average person. *Rick Wiesend has changed musical history!* He has tapped the combined knowledge of hundreds of vocal instructors, professional entertainers and musical stars from across the country to create a program that is simple enough for a beginner but advanced enough for a professional to sharpen their skills. It's written for children -- *as young as three* -- and teens interested in rock and adults -- *up to 103* -- who can reap great rewards after developing their natural talents.

This new book and corresponding cassette tape is so necessary and obviously lacking in the educational field, it's hard to believe someone hasn't written it before. Of course, there are very few vocal instructors with the qualifications and expertise in so many diverse types of singing who could conceptualize and bring to life such a book and tape.

You will find that this cassette tape and book -- *written for you* -- are stimulating and interesting and full of singing tips it would take a life time to accumulate. Above all, you will find that this singing improvement program is fun and IT REALLY WORKS!

-- *Johnny Williams.*

Rick Wiesend is an author, vocal instructor, singer, professional entertainer and record/video director/producer. He wears many professional *"hats"* and despite his varied background and education, his first love is still singing.

Long ago he realized that there was a gap in information and educational material on vocal improvement for the average person. So over the past 25 years he interviewed professional singing instructors, coaches and professional entertainers and researched at university musical libraries with the intent of someday creating a program everyone -- *both novice and professional* -- would benefit from and enjoy.

Unlike some contemporary vocal instructors, he does not feel that individuals should box themselves into voice or style classifications.

He has trained his voice to sing bass, baritone, second tenor, first tenor, alto and soprano and he never limits himself to one type of singing. He performs Folk, Country and Western, Gospel and Religious, Rock, Blues, Modern Jazz, Pop or Contemporary songs and is involved with Barber Shop Quartets and in Musical Theater. Recently he added Rap to his repertoire.

While attending college, he wrote and recorded his first No. 1 hit record -- *"Wait A Minute"* -- using the alias *"Tim Tam"* of *"Tim Tam And The Turn Ons."* Also making *"Cash Box"* and *"Billboard"* magazine's top hits chart were the follow-ups called *"Cheryl Ann"* and *"Kimberly."*

Concert performances followed with stars like Stevie Wonder, Charlie Pride, *"Mitch Ryder And The Detroit Wheels,"* Sonny and Cher and *"Paul Revere And The Raiders,"* and many, many more. And television appearances with Simon and Garfunkle, Jackie Wilson, *"Smokey Robinson and The Miracles,"* *"Martha and The Vandellas,"* and most of the other Motown groups, to name but a few.

Entertainment and education always have been in his blood. He finds great satisfaction in guiding individuals to their vocal potential and excels in group harmony training.

To find what the average person knows and wants to learn about singing, he asked editor L. A. Peterson to interview hundreds of people from across the United States and Canada. The consensus of their remarks have been incorporated with his text.

You'll find that consensus -- *in the form of comments and questions* -- in the darker print throughout the book. L. A. Peterson is the former *Entertainment Editor* of *The Ypsilanti Press,* and has served as *News Editor* and *The Editor* of *Associated Newspapers.*

Notes of Interest

Here are a few quick tips to help you almost immediately improve your singing and help you develop your own style. *First,* practice with the cassette tape, *"How To Sing,"* as often as you can. You will actually feel and hear an improvement in your voice the first time you do the exercises. And after the first session, your confidence will build.

Second, read the book and put it away for a few weeks. Reread the book again. You'll find that on the second and third reading you will retain much more. The terminology will make more sense. Reread specific areas if you are going to be looking for a job; if you are going on an audition; if you have a concert or club date to rehearse. You will be able to relate to the performance, star tips and other vocal tips and utilize them in your own singing.

Third, tape yourself singing songs and exercises. You will be able to hear your mistakes and the improvement in your voice. It's a good idea to tape yourself because the voice others hear when you sing, isn't the voice you hear. That's why most people are shocked and embarrassed the first time they hear themselves on tape -- *a cassette tape or a video recording. Get used to hearing yourself the way others do.*

Tape the practice sessions and after a week, play them all back. Listen for the improvement...you will hear it! Save the first session on tape, keep taping your practice sessions and a month later play the first tape and your latest tape. You will amaze yourself! Save the first tape...listen to it a year later. If you continue with this vocal improvement program, you will continue to hear progress.

Fourth, memorize some songs you like -- *it doesn't matter if they are Folk, Rock, Rhythm & Blues, Gospel, Show Tunes, Jazz, Rock or Religious.* Then tape yourself singing the songs.

Fifth, listen to some great singers you admire in any musical style. Learn some of the songs and then tape yourself singing with the great singer. Listen for the difference in your voice and in the other singer's voice. Listen to what you do differently that you like...that you don't like. Don't try to copy the style another singer uses, but use the tapes to compare and improve upon your voice and style.

How do I teach you or your child or grandchild to sing with this book? The answer's a simple one. *I need your help.* I need you to read and to listen. I need you to put your best effort forward as you practice. If you have purchased this program for a young child, I need you to help them. They will need adult supervision and guidance with this program.

I can't teach you or your child or your grandchild to sing with this book alone. There's no book in the store or in the library that is going to teach you to sing. *To learn to sing you must hear the notes and the music. You must hear sounds to imitate them!*

Rick Wiesend

This book is designed to give you the background ammunition you need to help develop your voice into a great one. *It is filled with tips and suggestions accumulated over the past few decades from vocal teachers and professional entertainers across the United States. Many are professional secrets carefully guarded by the stars! Secrets that would take you a life-time of performing to unveil.*

The cassette tape, "How To Sing Great," gives you the foundation you need to improve your voice. It includes exercises which are designed to work on specific aspects of your voice. It includes some fun songs to sing. And it shows you *how to sing Pop or Contemporary, Folk, Blues, Country, Rock, Jazz, Religious, Gospel, Patriotic and Show Tunes.*

If you do your homework and practice the vocal exercises, you will:

  1. Stretch your vocal range both octaves higher and octaves lower.

  2. Enhance your vocal tones.

  3. Strengthen your voice dramatically.

4. Stay in perfect key with the music.

5. Learn to follow many difficult rhythm patterns.

6. Learn breath control as you sing.

7. Learn to sing falsetto effectively.

8. Learn to yodel.

9. Learn to "Scat" (phrasing made popular by the great Ella Fitzgerald and Scatman Cruthers).

10. Learn to harmonize with other voices.

In this book, you'll learn what it takes to become the lead singer of a band. And you will learn ways that *you never imagined to capture the attention of your audience.*

"You Can Sing Great -- At Any Age -- How To Sing Great," the complete vocal improvement program, will teach you how to sing better than you ever dreamed possible. It will give you the confidence you need to sing in front of other people. It will teach you the skills you need to make your voice great. And it will teach you the tricks of the trade to help you present your song *LIKE A PRO!*

You'll also learn how to create or perfect your own singing style; and make a mediocre song sound great or a great song sound phenomenal!

You'll learn where and how to begin if you want to try to make money with your voice. And as an added bonus for singers who write their own songs, you'll learn how to protect the song from pilfergers; how to contact record producers and recording companies; how to decide which recording artists are best suited for your song, and so very much more!

The best way for you to learn to sing is to take private vocal lessons from a QUALIFIED teacher; the second best way -- *the most affordable and often the only means available to the vast majority of people* -- is this vocal improvement program.

THIS PROGRAM WAS CREATED FOR YOU!

If you have just developed an interest for singing, and don't know what musical style is your forte, try folk or blues. And even if you have another preference, you'll find that folk music is a big favorite no matter where you sing. Your family, friends or audience can relate to folk songs. *Here's a tip, if you want songs to go over big with your audience, sing songs they are familiar with.* That's why it's a real good idea to put folk and blues songs in your repertoire --*most everyone knows them.*

Musically speaking, folk and blues, can be sung effectively by most anyone -- even a novice. Folk and blues are written simply. If you can sing on key, you can sing folk and blues. *If you can't sing on key, you'll learn how if you keep reading!*

You will be able to sing any song better if you know and understand the words. If you learn a little about the background of the songs you are going to sing, you will bring them across more effectively because you'll understand the motiviation behind them.

To be a great singer you must sing from the heart. You can't have the same experiences as the original writers did, but you can learn to project their feelings when you sing their songs.

Folk and blues come from our roots. They are songs about people and places of the "good old days." Folk songs have power. They are effective even with a novice voice because they originally weren't written to be sung with an instrument -- you don't need a guitar or a piano or even a banjo to sing folk.

Folk songs originally were written to the beat of such things as marching boots or clanking pickaxes or shovels in mother Earth. These songs mostly were written anonymously and passed on from generation to generation by word of mouth.

In order to put more feelings into a song, imagine what the people of that time would be doing.

Imagine hearing the British Redcoats marching after the Boston Tea Party as they sang *"Yankee Doodle."* Those Redcoats were trying to belittle the Colonial soldiers with:

Yankee Doodle keep it up,
Yankee Doodle dandy,
Mind the music and the step and
With the girls be handy.

Yankee Doodle went to town,
Riding on a pony,
Stuck a feather in his hat,
And called it macaroni,

Yankee doodle, doodle doo,
Yankee doodle dandy,
All the lads and lassies are
Sweet as sugar candy.

Aren't you glad we had the last laugh! It's a fun song that both adults and children in the United States and England love to sing.

Or imagine rough American seamen hauling lines as they sang *"Shenandoah."* They were home sick as they sang:

> *"Oh Shenandoah, I want to hear you!*
> *Away! you rolling river!*
> *I'll come to you across the water.*
> *Away! I'm bound away across the wide Missouri.*

Or imagine Julia Ward Howe in 1861 being appalled as she heard Union troops singing a song about bawdy women and easy liquor in a song called *"John Brown's Body."*

She took the melody and changed the words. Think of her when you sing *"Mine Eyes Have Seen the Glory of the Coming of the Lord:"*

> *Mine eyes have seen the glory of the coming of the Lord.*
> *He is trampling out the vintage where the grapes of wrath are stored,*
> *He has loosed the fateful lightning of his terrible swift sword.*
> *His truth is marching on*
>
> *Glory, glory, Hallelujah!*
> *Glory, glory, Hallelujah!*
> *Glory, glory, Hallelujah!*
>
> *His truth is marching on!*

Some popular folk songs had their roots in historic folk. The original "Scarborough Fair" is an old English folk song. The updated -- *and rewritten* -- version is now a classic from the movie, *"The Graduate."* The original went like this:

> Where are you going? To Scarborough Fair?
> Parsley, sage, rosemary and thyme,
> Remember me to a bonny lass there,
> For once she was a true lover of mine.
>
> Tell her to make me a cambric shirt,
> Parsley, sage, rosemary and thyme,
> With out any needle or thread -- work's in it,
> And she shall be a true lover of mine.
>
> Tell her to wash it in yonder well,
> Parsley, sage, rosemary and thyme,
> Where water ne'er sprung nor a drop of rain fell,
> And she shall be a true lover of mine.

I've wanted to interrupt, but this has been so interesting I didn't want you to stop. *(Remember who I am? I'm a consesus of the average singing enthusiasts across the country. You'll find me popping up here and there asking the questions and making the comments you yourself will probably be making as you read this book and practice with the cassette tape. And now on to my comments.)* Just think, Simon and Garfunkel took an old English folk song, updated the words and had a million seller. I can't write music, but I sure could take an old song and change the words! There's still hope for me. But on to my question. What is the difference between folk singing and The Blues? You seem to lump them together, here.

Folk music is traditional music of a people expressed in songs. You'll find *English* folk songs and *American* folk songs and *Italian* folk songs and *French* folk songs and *Polish* folk songs and *Russian* folk songs and *German* folk songs. The lists could go on and on. Every nationality has their own folk songs -- their heritage.

Every nationality around the world has its own folk songs. Using folk songs -- from the United States or from your own heritage -- is a fun and easy place to start learning to sing. You already know many, many folk songs!

The Blues also are folk songs -- *American Negro folk songs.* (For those musically inclined, the third or seventh note in these songs are flatted.)

The Blues are dynamic songs of hardships, hopes and disappointments. Blues is essentially vocal music and in the early days it was sung *a cappella* (without musical accompaniment). Today a guitar commonly is used to accompany Blues singers. Of course, complete orchestrations can be effective, too! Some of the great Blues singers you should listen to are Bessie Smith, B.B. King, Louis Jordan, Muddy Waters, Clyde McPhatter, Joe Turner, Roy Brown, Howlin' Wolf and Little Walter.

Listen to the greats to help you sing great. Try to be like a sponge and absorb the feelings they put into their work. If you listen to a wide spectrum of music --*everything from folk to rap* -- you will be able to capture in your voice the excitement and the emotions needed to impress your audience.

In order for you to most dynamically come across when you sing any type song, especially The Blues, try to choose songs which best express your feelings.

Over the years some Blues songs have been updated. Many of the original blues came from prison gangs, work gangs and poor farm workers. Remember *"I've Been Working on the Rail Road"* and there's always:
the *"Lonesome Blues:"*

> *I woke up this morn-in', feelin' sad and blue,*
> *Baby done quit me, what am I gonna do?*
>
> *You know I'm lonesome, and the blues is in my way.*
> *I may be down and out today, but I'll be up some day.*

Or how about this one:

> C. C. Rider, just see what you have done
> You made me love you now your woman's come.
> You made me love you now your woman's come.
> You made me love you now your woman's come.

You caused me, Rider, to hang my head and cry,
You put me down; God knows I don't see why.
You put me down; God knows I don't see Why.
You put me down; God knows I don't see why.

Do you recall another version sung by Elvis Presley? One of the first songs he sang at his concerts and on television appearances was "C. C. Rider." Elvis sang folk songs and The Blues and Gospel and Religious songs and rock. He was so loved by so many people because he didn't squeeze himself into one classification. He wasn't just a rock singer!

It's not a bad idea to take a tip from the master. Learn to sing in as many styles as you can. Be able to give something to everyone you are performing for.

You know, I never thought of that before. I thought of a singer as being a folk singer -- like the group Peter, Paul and Mary -- or a jazz singer -- like Louis Armstrong -- or a pop or contemporary singer -- like Bing Crosby. I always thought of Elvis Presley as a rock singer. He WAS so much more! It sure makes a lot of sense to fill your repertoire with all styles of music.

Most of our musical styles have their roots in folk and The Blues. Gospel reflects the blues and early Negro spirtuals. Country and western has it's roots in folk singing of the early settlers of the United States. Jazz is an uniquely American music style mixing African rhythms, Blues and even a touch of church music.

To be a great singer you have to sense the beat of the music. You have to feel the rhythm pattern and the melody of the notes and translate those feelings to your audience in words. That's why Gospel and Jazz singing is so moving. And why it's so hard to do.

The best training grounds for Gospel singing is the Black church. The Gospel style that you hear today is almost 60 years old, but it's nothing new to generations of poor Black people. It's simply a celebration of *"Old Time Religion"* in song.

So what to do if your not poor or Black? Listen to the Gospel greats. Absorb what they have to offer. If you think of Gospel music, you

"Silent Night Holy Night All Is Calm All Is Bright." Some of the greatest voices belong to Gospel singers. To develop a great voice, sing in church...sing in your car...sing whenever you get a chance!

think of Mahalia Jackson singing *"Amazing Grace"* or The Edwin Hawkins Singers' version of *"O Happy Day."* These great performers have taken Gospel from the church and performed it on stage in concerts and on television for all of us to appreciate.

Gospel normally is sung a cappela *(which means without musical accompaniment).* But organs, drums, piano, guitar and tambourines are being used to supplement the sound.

When you compare music styles, you'll find that the most outstanding voices -- *outside of opera* -- sing Gospel. Aretha Franklin started in Gospel with her father, The Rev. C. L. Franklin, in Detroit's New Bethel Baptist Church, and still sings Gospel today; even though she makes her living singing rhythm and blues. One of her top albums was the 1972 *"Amazing Grace"* with James Cleveland. It was a musical and spiritual triumph and even though it was a Gospel album, it found its way to the top ten album charts.

If you sing Gospel, fill your presentation with as much emotion as you can muster. Make your audience feel every note and every word...move them!

The spiritual, *"Sometimes I Feel Like A Motherless Child"* is a song filled with emotions.

Sometimes I feel like a motherless child,
Sometimes I feel like a motherless child,
Sometimes I feel like a motherless child,
A long ways from home, A long ways from home,
O Lawdy, A long Ways from home.

Sometimes I feel like I has no friend,
Sometimes I feel like I has no friend,
Sometimes I feel like I has no friend,
And a long ways from home, a long ways from home,
O Lawdy, a long ways from home.

Sometimes I feel like I'm almost gone,
Sometimes I feel like I'm almost gone,
Sometimes I feel like I'm almost gone,
And a long way from home, a long ways from home,
O Lawdy, a long ways from home.

Great singers gather up all their feelings of loneliness and despair and translate those feelings to the audience. Even if you haven't lived the experiences you are singing about doesn't mean you can't relate the feelings to others. It takes proper phrasing, feelings and timing to bring Gospel across effectively!

Other religious singers can take a lesson from Gospel. If you sing in church, learn the words to the songs you are to sing. Learn the melody. You won't be able to belt out the songs like you would in a Black church, but put your heart and soul into it. *You'll walk away from church with that song in your heart, a smile on your face and peace in your soul!*

Amen! Maybe if a few people would start belting out some songs in "White" churches, music would become a more important aspect of the service. I'd love to go to church and see the people FEEL THE MUSIC.

Also filled with feelings and spirit and emotional drive is Jazz. Jazz is a musical style that first appeared in the United States around the 1900's. As I have said it was a mix of African rhythms, Blues, church music and even a little rag time. Jazz changes continually, but the pulse -- *the beat -- remains constant. Jazz evolved from Negro folk music to the art it is today.*

Jazz seems to have such a mystique about it. It's definitely unique and alluring, but it shouldn't be frightening -- even to a novice singer.

Jazz songs start with a melody and end with a melody. *The middle melody is improvised. (It's composed during the performance; and not rehearsed.)* If you listen to Jazz, you're listening to active creation. A Jazz singer changes the melodies of a song as he (or she) sings.

You mentioned Louis Armstrong as a Jazz great. The list is exhaustive. Others include Bessie Smith, Miles Davis, Herbie Hancock, Billie Holiday, Ella Fitzgerald, Sarah Vaughn and Mel Torme. Their contribution to Jazz is indescribable!

To be able to sing Jazz

1. You'll have to have great confidence in yourself.

2. You'll have to sing with a big, full voice.

3. You'll have to develop an intense vibrato.

4. You'll have to stretch your range. Learn to hit real high notes!

5. You'll have to be creative.

6. You'll have to learn to Scat.

7. You'll have to develop a rich timber (or tone guality).

This vocal improvement program -- *the book and cassette tape --* is giving you the ammunition you need to sing Jazz. And to sing folk, Gospel, religious, country and western, popular and contemporary, rock and rap songs.

If you let me quote from your cassette tape: ''Do you like coun-

try music; good old country music!'' **Yes, I do. I like to sing that "Old Time Religion," but I also like to sing country. Give me some tips.**

Country's easy and fun to sing. It's also a music deep from our roots. This time it's a mixture of folk and fiddle tunes and African and Irish and German and Cajun and Gospel and honky-tonk and western swing and blue grass and old-time singing cowboy and Nashville and boogie and rockabilly.

Notice the picture I have built? Each music type has been layered upon another. Each has borrowed from and embellished on the musical style that came before. I'm not writing a musical history book -- *I'm writing on how to sing the songs* -- or I could delve more deeply into the history of each of the styles. It's very interesting and enlightening!

The country you hear today is direct and powerful. To sing country you must develop the same skills you need to sing Jazz, but you also should learn how to yodel. Country yodeling is borrowed from the

When you think of Country singing, what do you think of? Cowboy hats & boots, bandannas & guitars. Swiss mountaineers! Yes...that's right. Swiss mountaineers. When you learn to yodel, you are learning an art passed down from the moutain folks in Switzerland.

Swiss and Tyrolean mountaineers. It's characterized by falsetto tones interspersed with regular chest tones. So you'll have to develop your falsetto (which is a very high vocal tone) to sing country.

Again, I am giving you the ammunition you need to do it. Practice the falsetto exercise on the cassette tape. Practice the yodeling exercise. Make up some of your own. Yodeling is fun!

Listen to all the country and western singers. Learn the different subgroupings under the catchall title -- *country.* The singing cowboys were Gene Autry, Roy Rogers and Tex Ritter. And let's not forget the singing cowgirl -- *Dale Evans.* Hard country sometimes called honky tonk country music was sung by Ernest Tubbs, Hank Williams, Ray Price and George Jones. And then we get to rockabilly -- *from whence rock was born!*

Rockabilly is a mixture of country, swing, black rhythm and blues and Gospel. Who comes to mind when I mention rockabilly? Elvis Presley, of course. And also Carl Perkins, Jerry Lee Lewis, Johnny Cash, The Everly Brothers and Buddy Holly.

"Home, home on the range." Most people don't associate country singers with horses and the open range anymore. Could you imagine Dolly Parton -- with her mighty wig flying -- on a horse? Country has changed over the years. But when you think of country, you still think of the cowboy hat and boots!

And what about country rock with Patsy Cline and Eddy Arnold.

We can't leave country until we mention Willie Nelson, Roger Miller, Kris Kristofferson, Tom T. Hall, Dolly Parton and Loretta Lynn. And what about the country-pop music of today. Songs by Glen Campbell, Charlie Rich, Anne Murray, Kenny Rogers, Barbara Mandrell and The Oak Ridge Boys. These are the "cross-over" recording artists on the record charts. They are loved by country and popular music aficionados, alike.

Ricky Skaggs is even bringing back bluegrass. And he's loved by modern country listeners and the traditionalists.

How do you sing country? You practice the vocal exercises on the cassette tape. You perfect all the skills. You listen to all the greats. And you decide what type of country you want to sing. It's a difficult choice. Country is fun. It's challenging. People never tire of country...there's a whole wide field just waiting for you. It's easier to break into country than into any other field in the music business today. You'll find bars and clubs all across the United States who employ country singers and bands. And, of course, Nashville is where you should go if want to get a recording contract. You'll have to have unusual talent, a lot of ambition, patience and determination to succeed!

So as I have already established, out of folk and out of country and out of rockabilly, ROCK EVOLVED. Rock pioneers were Fats Domino, Bill Haley, Little Richard, Chuck Berry and Bo Diddley.

Rock then evolved in waves. There was the British Invasion with The Beatles, *The Rolling Stones, The Who,* and the *"Kinks"* and *"Animals."* Then came the tiny boppers groups like *"Gerry and The Pacemakers,"* Herman's Hermits, *"Gary Lewis and the Playboys,"* "Paul Revere and the Raiders" and the *"Monkees."* Also coming into popularity at the same time was *"Mitch Rider and the Detroit Wheels."*

Of course, there was Folk Rock with Bob Dylan, the *Byrds,* Simon and Garfunkel, the *"Mamas and Papas,"* Sonny and Cher and *Donovan.* And soul from James Brown, Jackie Wilson, Marvin Gaye, the *Supremes, "Martha and the Vandellas,"* Temptations,

Rock around the clock.

Rockers gets you up dancing.

Miracles, "Jackson 5" and little Stevie Wonder. And then came the hippie music with the *Grateful Dead, Jefferson Airplane, Jefferson Starship,* Janis Joplin, *"Sly and the Family Stone,"* Buffalo Springfield, Steppenwolf, Jimi Hendrix, Joe Cocker and Led Zeppelin. Rod Steward gave us folk/jazz mixed with rock. As did Elton John, Pink Floyd and Jethro Tull.

A softer more natural country rock came from Emmylou Harris, the *"Nitty Gritty Dirt Band," "Crosby, Stills, Nash and Young,"* Dan Fogelberg and Bob Dylan. Southern rock came from the *Allman Brother Band,* Marshall Tucker, *Charlie Daniels Band* and Jimmy Buffett.

Contemporary rock forms followed with Bruce Springsteen, Boz Scaggs, Steve Miller, *Hall and Oates,* Bob Seger and Peter Frampton.

And then the hard rock or heavy metal bands. From Britian came *Deep Purple, Foreigner,* Ozzy Osbourne, *Def Leppard* and *Queen.* From the United States came *Z.Z. Top, "Grand Funk Railroad,"* Ted Nugent, *Aerosmith, Journey,* Pat Benatar, Van Halen, *"REO Speedwagon," J. Geils Band* and *Kiss.*

And you can't talk about rock without talking about the glitter concerts by David Bowie and *T-Rex.* And then came punk with aggressive rock by the *"Sex Pistols," "Clash," Patti Smith,*

"Plasmatics" and *"DMZ."* If you want to know what the latest craze is or who's on top just turn to *"MTV" or "VH-1"* if your television is connected to a cable system. Or you can turn the radio to soft or hard rock stations. Most middle-aged people tend to find soft rock a little easier to the ear; while teen and young adults still flip for heavy metal.

Rock, today, is a major commerical and artistic force. There's money to be made in rock'n'roll!

If you're a rock star, you're a hero.

Rock combined traditional European ballads with irregular Afro-American rhythm. Lyrics -- *when they make sense at all* -- capture little experiences in the lives of the songwriters. Rock melodies are simple but the band plays with as much force as it can muster.

Lyrics in rock today usually aren't very important. If you sing rock, you needn't worry about singing out too loudly. You'll be miked for amplification and your engineer will control how you come across.

Don't get me wrong. I love rock. I had a couple of rock records in the late 60's. I sang a part of *"Wait A Minute"* and *"Kimberly" on the cassette tape. (You also heard Kimberly sing on the cassette tape. Kimberly's my niece who was named after the song.) Along with "Cheryl Ann,"* all three songs made it on the charts of *"Billboard Magazine "* and *"Cash Box"* magazine.

You can love rock and still learn how to sing. Rock singers occasionally do perform pop ballads. And if you sing rock -- *or contemporary* -- songs you should learn to harmonize.

Harmony was a very important ingredient to the group's sound. Doing harmony with the *Turn Ons* was fun. The *Turn Ons* included my brother Dan Wiesend and Earl Rennie, Nick Butsicaris, Don Grundman and John Ogen.

You may no longer be doing the Doo Wop harmony *--or the street corner soul of the 1950's and 1960's* -- as your soul brothers did. But harmony enhances any song. Even singers like Tiffany and Debbie Gibson use harmony backgrounds. Most singers who perform on *"The Tonight Show"* with Johnny Carson bring their own backup singers to do harmony. Harmony is beautiful.

When you harmonize a number of voices combine to create a

united sound. Each singer is singing on a different key, but the sound blends so well you feel the wholeness...the results can be moving.

Harmony is very hard for some people to learn. But if you listen carefully to the demonstration and practice with the exercise on the cassette tape, *"How To Sing Great,"* you will be able to master the skill.

How about Pop and Island Calypso? I do love the sound and feel of this type of music. Got some tips on singing Pop songs and singing to the Calypso beat?

Pop is the contemporary music of a mostly all-white audience. Old time pop recording stars included Bing Crosby, Nat King Cole, Pattie Page, Dean Martin and Frank Sinatra. Some of pop's stars today are Barbra Streisand, Bette Midler, Lisa Minelli, Bernadette Peters, Neil Sedaka, Andy Williams, Robert Goulet and Ann Margret.

Lyrics to pop songs uphold high standards and are not racey or off-color. Pop songs are mostly slower ballads with nice musical arrangements.

To sing pop you need to master the exercises on the cassette tape. You need to use a full, powerful, rich voice. You need to stretch your range and develop an effective falsetto to add variety and class to your presentation. And you need to perfect your own unique vibrato. Master the exercises on the tape -- *even the fun exercises* -- and you'll steadily build a better, cleaner voice.

You should listen to other pop stars, but here is where you can excel in creating your own singing style. How do you do that? Easy. You use your God-given voice -- *enhanced by proper exercise* -- and you put yourself into your songs. You're the lead singer, whether or not you have a group behind you. Keep reading and follow the tips I give for lead singers. *You need to put class and flash into your performance!*

It's relatively easy to be accepted as a pop singer and to make money with this style of singing. These old standards are very popular in dinner clubs and small lounges. And you'll find pop stars headlining in Las Vegas and Atlantic City. There's still a vast audience for pop because of its smooth and pleasing style.

Many Broadway and musical theater presentations use pop lyrics as a basis of the presentation. But rock and jazz and blues and soul also have found their way to Broadway. To be accepted in musical theater you not only have to be able to sing the songs, but you also have to act. Many of today's pop stars take show tunes and put them in their acts. The songs have good, solid lyrics and magnificent arrangements and can be dramatically sung. The audience can easily identify with the numbers which adds recognition and instant approval to your performance!

Let's leave the Broadway stage and find our way to a tropical paradise. If you think of the islands, you think of the island master --*Harry Belafonte.* He put warmth and sex appeal into his performances. To sing Calypso try to perfect the island accent -- *it's a proper British English.*

Island music has a Reggae beat. And Reggae changes all the time. Caribbean and Jamaican music has played a very important role in the internationalization of rock. Calypso songs have topical or humerous lyrics. Some Raggae songs have political overtones. Most Reggae has an old-fashioned, slow and soulful feel.

Reggae enthusiasts should listen to Bunny Wailer, Jimmy Cliff, *Toots and the Maytals,* Yabby You, the *Congos,* Horace Andy and Barrington Levy.

What about the latest craze in singing? You've taken me from Folk to Rock; with a little Pop and Raggae thrown in. What about rap?

Would you believe that the *"latest"* craze in singing is over 1,000 years old!

Most songs are poetry being sung. Rap is poetry being said to a beat. Rap's recent popularity germinated from Harlem, New York. Top rappers included Millie Jackson, Kurtis Blow, the *Sugarhill Gang,* Grandmaster Flash, Timex Social Club, *Run D.M.C.,* Boogie Boys, Fat Boys, *"Dough E. Fresh & the Get Fresh Crew,"* Whodini, UTFO and *"Rockmaster Scott & The Dynamic Three."*

Rap is particularly popular among Black performers and is slowly spreading into "white" music. J.J. Walker, formerly the star of "Good Times" has joined the ranks of record artists with his rap records. He even had comedienne and talk show host, Joan Rivers (a Jewish American), rapping on a recent show. Pop singer Andy Williams uses Rap in his concert. He introduces the piece by saying something like this: "Did you ever hear a white man sing rap."

Some performers -- *Black and White* -- are using a little rap as a part of their songs. Instead of singing the entire song, some performers are breaking up the singing with rap -- *as a tasty addition and neat transition from the sung verses.*

Rap can be fun...and it's not all that hard to do.

To rap you need a steady beat. You can do it with hand clapping, or finger snapping or a constant drum beat. If you want to rap to a drum beat but don't know a drummer, invest in a drum machine. It's a marvelous little device that can be programmed to play an untold number of drum beats. You can even program cymbals and bells to the drum sound. But remember to keep the beat simple; not too melodic.

Or you could simply record yourself saying something like *"bom she bom she bom she bom"* over and over again on your tape recorder. That will give you the beat with which you need to rap.

The next step is to compose a simple poem. Or you could listen to some of the famous rappers and use their lyrics to teach yourself the proper feel.

Here's an example of a verse you can practice with:

I met this girl at a party last night.
We were having a good time, then we got in a fight!

I couldn't understand why she was being so mean.
Until she hit me over the head with a tamborine!

The key to rapping is to have wordy verses to say in a sing-song way. When you make up your rap verses make sure the last words of each phrase rhyme. Like the night-fight and mean-tamborine.

There's nothing more to rapping. It's effective. It's easy. And you'll be sure to get your audience's attention if you add a touch of rap to your repertoire. *Rap is leaving the streets in Black neighborhoods and finding its way to radio and televison, on the "white" concert stage and even into commercial advertising!*

I really did get a lot of tips about how to sing different types of music. I can't wait to start experimenting. What else are you going to teach me in this book?

Are you going to learn to be a great singer from reading a book? You already know the answer to that question, don't you? *Of course not!*

But that doesn't mean you should stop reading.

You can learn an enoromous amount about singing by reading about voice development, the best technique and proper care of your voice.

As an added bonus you also will pick up *secret tips* on voice and song presentation that I have compiled for you through years of experience -- my own and those of other vocal instructors and professional entertainers across the country. *Tips it would take YOU a lifetime to accummulate, if ever!*

You'll also learn about what songs you *should and should not* sing in public -- *information most entertainers will never divulge to you.* And you'll learn about song protection and how to sell a song, if you are a songwriter.

Although you'll gain a lot from reading this book, the key here is that you can learn ABOUT singing, by reading. The only way you will learn TO sing, is by singing!

I'm glad you said that first. When I was attracted to this vocal improvement program, I wondered how you were going to teach me to sing with a book. Now it makes more sense. There's no way I can learn to sing better just by reading!

Part of the process of learning to be a great singer is learning to listen to sounds with your ears and learning to imitate those sounds

You should expose your children to all kinds of music. You should teach them how to sing. It's fun and easy to do with this vocal improvement program.

with your voice. And it's not a secret that you can't learn to imitate by just reading -- *you have to hear to imitate.*

And when I discuss imitating here, I'm not talking about copying the style of another singer. I'm talking about imitating a specific sound to improve your vocal range and quality. *(I'll discuss imitating the styles of other singers later in this book.)*

You can become a great singer. And in as little as seven days, you can learn to do amazing things with your voice. *Things that you never before thought were possible.* Of course, seven days marks just the beginning of your singing improvement program. Great singers never stop working on their voice. They continue practicing and working with vocal instructors to perfect their sound.

Once you see what you can do with your voice in just seven days, you will want to continue to improve. You will be so proud of what you have accomplished that you will just beam when someone notices how well you sing. The improvements will come quicker than you ever imagined!

I've been practicing with your cassette tape. In fact, I've had this program for about four days and this is the first time I picked up the book to read. I've already noticed a difference in my singing. The cassette tape is fun and I enjoy doing the exercises, especially the exercises on side two.

In order to become a better singer -- *even a great singer* -- you must practice every day. When singing the sound originates from the throat. Not everyone uses the proper inner throat muscles when they sing, but with the exercises on the cassette tape, you will learn to relax the outer throat muscles -- *which only hinder your sound* --and flex the inner throat muscles. This will free your vocal cords to stretch and thin which will result in a great voice and sound.

Aside from thinking of your voice as a muscle that you must develop, think of it as a tool. You must take proper care of that tool to get the best use from it. And you will be learning how to develop your vocal muscles and how to care for them as you read on.

I'm in my 40's and I have never had formal voice training. I wasn't even in the choir in high school. Is there any hope for me. Is it too late to develop my throat muscles?

No...it's never too late. It may seem to you that great singers are born, but that is not necessarily true. All the great singers have learned to develop their talents. Even though some people seem to have more inherent talent than others, everyone can teach the proper inner throat muscles and their vocal cords to do the right thing.

Some people will have an easier time learning to sing well if they have an *"ear for music."* They will have an easier time and they may learn faster; but even if you do not feel that you have an *"ear for music,"* it doesn't mean you cannot develop a beautiful voice.

After you have mastered the cassette tape which came with this program, and the advanced tape which is available, you may decide you are ready to find a *"professional instructor"* for private lessons. I highly recommend that you do. But I am concerned about who you pick. Just about anyone who can play the piano can call themselves a *"professional"* voice instructor. You will have to be very careful that you are choosing a qualified person. Through years of experience, I have compiled some tips on how to pick the right person. You will find these tips later in this book. Please do yourself a favor and read the tips before you pick an instructor.

Everyone is different. Everyone is learning to sing --*learning to improve his or her voice* -- for different reasons.

You may want to improve your voice so that you have more confidence in your ability. You may want to take the voice that you keep to yourself in the shower and share it with others.

You may want to gain more confidence in your voice so that you can sing better in church...better in the car when you have passengers...or you may just want to be able to sing "*Happy Birthday*" at the next party without embarrassment!

You may be a drummer of a heavy metal band who wants to become a lead singer. You feel the lead singer gets all the attention from the audience; drummers are not appreciated, and you want to get some of the glory for yourself.

Or you may want to develop a career for yourself around your voice. You may want to become a recording star. You may want to be able to entertain others. You may want to do commercials on radio or televison. Or you may be a songwriter, unsure of your talent, who wants to be able to sing on a demo tape to send to song publishers or a record producer.

Or you just may be a proud grandparent or parent who feels their grandchild or child has potential! And you bought this voice improvement program for them.

Do you want to know the truth? Actually I bought this program for a number of reasons. I want to learn to sing better because I am a shower singer and a little intimidated about singing in front of others. My wife has a pretty good voice but she feels that she needs more practice. And my daughter sings around the house all the time. I tried to find a vocal instructor in my area for her, but there was no listing in the "yellow pages" for vocal instructors!

You all have different reasons for trying to improve your voice. Each

Songwriters can make lots of money on record and tape sales if they learn how to do it!

of you has his or her own motivation. That motivation for singing will determine your motivation for practicing. *And with three people using this program, you certainly will be getting more than your money's worth!*

But you all should practice every day. Start slowly with the exercises. Just work with the first two or three exercises the first few days. Gradually build your exercise sessions until you are practicing roughly for half an hour a day. You already have a good start. *Sing in the shower. Sing in the car going to and from work. Sing everytime you get a chance.*

Read what other professionals have to say:

"I try to vocalize every day," soprano Martina Arroyo said. *"The voice gets stiff if not used. I always sing around the house...it's part of my life."*

Ms Arroya is known for her appearance at the Metropolitan Opera, Carnegie Hall and even the *"Tonight Show"* with Johnny Carson on televison. She said that she sang scales at least one-half hour a day.

Another soprano who has performed at the Metropolitan Opera feels the same. *Licia Albanese said she sang every day.* She also said she made a point of singing on Saturday and Sunday -- even if she was not performing.

Tenor Placido Domingo, another Metropolitan Opera great, has a little different idea. He only vocalized for 10 minutes at a time. He said he believed in vocalizing in small segments.

This great tenor said he believed that half-hour sets were too much. He said: *"You get tired without any good reason."*

As you can see, different performers have different ideas about how much to practice. I believe that if you are not sick -- *you don't have a cold, allergy or sinus problem* -- you should vocalize at least one-half hour a day. Your motivation and the time you have available to practice, will determine what is right for you.

Although it may seem a boring way to learn to be a great singer, you should practice with exercises. It is not enough to just sing songs. Each exercise you learn and each scale you do properly takes you one step closer to a better voice. *The exercises on my tape were designed to perfect another skill to make your voice great.*

My wife knows that she has an alto voice -- she was in the high school choir -- but I don't know what classification I am. In the tape you say: "And now it's your turn -- basses, baritones, tenors, altos and sopranos." How do I know when I should sing?

Your wife may feel she is an alto. But using the exercises on my cassette tape she should be able to expand her range. She should be able to hit both tenor and soprano notes. Tell her not to lock herself into any category.

She may have had a very good choir instructor, but choir instructors are trained to develop the voices of the assembly as a whole. They usually do not give individual vocal instructions and they usually do not try to help each individual expand his or her range. I'm not criticizing the work of choir instructors, they have a very difficult job to do. But many choir instructors do not teach privately because their expertise lies with bringing out the best from a whole group to create a beautiful, unified sound. Not to bring out the best of one individual! Some choir instructors do teach privately and have perfected good individual teaching techniques, but they are in the minority.

Initially in the tape I tell you to sing when you feel comfortable and begin singing in the middle of your range. When you are singing you will be able to feel if you are straining to hit a note. After using the cassette tape for a while, you'll know what basic range you are in.

If you are a beginner singer, it's a mistake to try to classify yourself as anything. You will be able to expand your range -- *both higher and lower* -- as you continue with the exercises on the tape.

Even if you are a professional, voice classification usually is unnecessary. And you, too, will find that vocal exercises will help you expand your present ability.

As I have demonstrated, I have developed my voice so that I can comfortably sing bass, baritone, second tenor, first tenor, alto and soprano. As a male, I don't have the highest soprano voice around -- *but I can hit soprano notes.*

Parents who have purchased the tape and book for their children should work with them at first. I work with all my children, even with my 3-year-old daughter, Tiffany. She's had music around her all her life, and when I play the exercises on the tape she sits down at the piano hits keys and sings along with the tape.

I get the biggest charge out of hearing her sing "Do...Re...Me."

My two other daughters have sang all their lives. We use the cassette in the car on short or long trips. We all sing together as we drive and I can hear the improvement in the childrens' voices on a daily basis.

I wouldn't classify a child in any of the categories. I don't think anyone who is just learning should lock themselves into any classifications.

Thinking about my children, makes me remember my own upbringing. My father played the accordian and piano. He used to play and sing at weddings and parties and also entertained on the radio. He especially liked honky-tonk music.

My mother always sang to me. She always encouraged me to sing. Whenever my parents had family or friends over, I was encouraged to sing.

And I did. The attention and adoration I got from my parents and the rest of the company was infectious. I wanted to keep getting that attention. I kept singing so that I could keep performing. And I found my calling at a very young age.

You can do the same for your children. As unusual as it may seem, my wife and I have surrounded our children with music from the day they were conceived! That's right -- *not born; but conceived.* I sang to my unborn children and we played music for them. Scientific tests have proven that a fetus can hear and be stimulated by the outside world.

Now you tell me. I didn't start with my daughter before birth. Does that mean she won't be a great singer?

Start right now no matter what your daughter's age is. It's not necessary to start before birth, but do start surrounding your children with music soon after birth. Sing to them. Get them a musical mobile. Play records or cassette tapes for them. Encourage them to sing as soon as they are speaking words.

Here's another tip to interest children in music.

Replace popular songs with your child's name and sing the "new" song to them. I did that with Tiffany. When she was born I used to replace the words to the Disney classic *"Zip A De Do Da"* and I would sing *"Tiff A Ne Do Da."* Now whenever Tiffany hears the Disney classic on television, she gets the biggest smile on her face. She thinks they are singing just for her. When we drive someplace, she'll sing her song, *"Tiff A Ne Do Da,"* all the way through, over and over again. She associates the car with singing, and she just loves to sing. Of course, you can sing to and with your children

Make singing fun for your child. Let the little ones dress up and pretend to play the piano when they sing. Tiffany loves to sing. And she loves to play dress up. She loves when we sing to her. Your child will too!

anytime -- *night or day.* We sing a lot in the car because we can easily pop the exercise cassette into the player. You have a captured audience in the car and it's really fun and interesting to sing together. It does bring the family together.

I encourage you to sing together with your children, but, above all, encourage your child or children to sing in front of others. *By singing in front of others at a young age, your children will overcome the fear of performing for a crowd.* This will not only help them when they sing, but will help them when they go to school. They will have the confidence to raise their hands in class to answer a question. And they will not be afraid to give a speech in front of the class...or the whole school!

I cannot stress enough how important it is to support and encourage your children to sing. When I was growing up, my best friend used to sing with me occasionally when I performed for my parents' company.

He liked doing it and he had a good voice. But he never did anything with his voice. I believe the reason he stopped singing was because he was never encouraged at home.

His parents were embarrassed when he tried to sing for their friends and relatives. They felt the adults would be bored by the show. They told him that he was not allowed to sing at their family functions.

Frankly, I don't give a darn if the adults are bored. And I'm glad my parents didn't either. Actually most adults, enjoy listening to children sing. And, if they don't, sitting through a few minutes of song won't hurt them one bit.

Most great singers aren't born that way. They developed a love of music and song. They sang whenever they got a chance. And they developed their own special vocal ability.

Going back to great singers, don't all of the great opera singers classify themselves as something? You are the one who wrote about soprano Martina Arroya and Tenor Placido Domingo.

Although classifications aren't necessary for the average singer, you'll be able to classify yourself after you train your voice with the exercises on the tape.

When that time comes, and if you do play the piano or know someone who does, use the piano chart which follows to see what range you fall in to. If you don't have a piano, simply listen carefully to the cassette tape. I give you general starting points for each classificiation and you will know which you fit into.

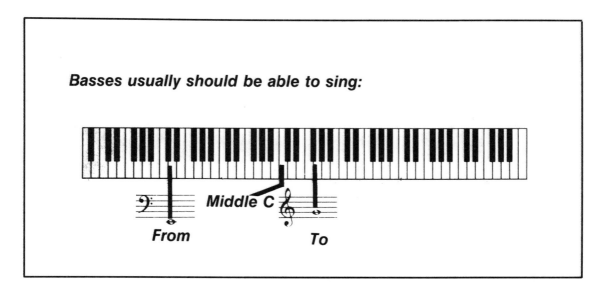

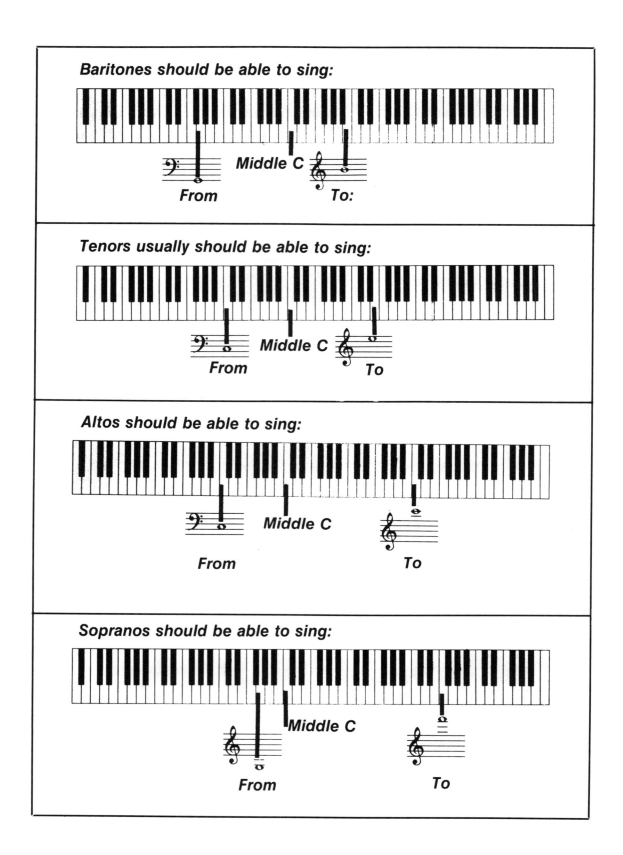

Remember, every voice is different. Your voice is unique because of the tone and resonance that you create. And your voice can only get better if you sing with the exercises, specially chosen to perfect another skill towards making your voice great!

Each of the foundation exercises on the tape will help stretch your range. As you increase your range you also improve your tone and strengthen your voice.

I realize that every voice is unique. I wish my voice was as unique as Kenny Rogers' or Robert Goulet's. My wife would give her eye-teeth to sound like Bernadette Peters. And, believe me, I am practicing every day to increase my range. But you threw a new word at me. What is resonance?

Tell your wife to keep her eye-teeth. She has her own unique voice and should work with the vocal exercises to produce the best sound she can.

"Voices are like fingerprints; there are no two alike in the world," said singer John Alexander. He is a great tenor who performed at the Metropolitan opera. Alexander is known for his remarkable stamina and youthful sound.

"God gave us our own unique sound," he said. *"If we can build on that, then we have built on a firm foundation."*

Work on developing your own unique voice. Unless you want to become a professional imitator, it may even be injurious to your voice to strive to imitate someone else. A sound and style that are appropriate for one person's voice may not be for anothers.

Here I go editorializing again. Sorry. I just know that each and every one of us can develop something beautiful with our voices!

But, now back to your original question. *Resonance is the process which transforms the sound which begins in your vocal cords to the full tone that emerges from your mouth when you sing.* The tone from your vocal cords, which are in your throat, pass through resonating chambers (kind of like echo chambers). The resonating chambers are the pharynx, oral cavity and nasal cavity.

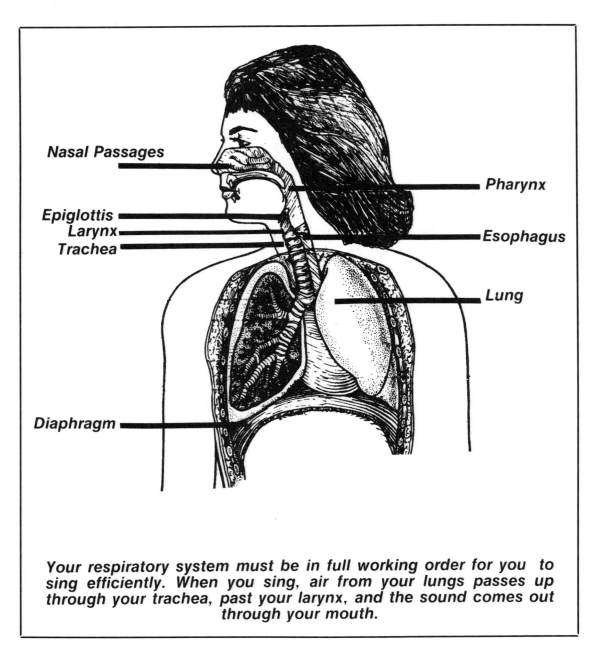

Nasal Passages

Pharynx

Epiglottis
Larynx
Trachea

Esophagus

Lung

Diaphragm

Your respiratory system must be in full working order for you to sing efficiently. When you sing, air from your lungs passes up through your trachea, past your larynx, and the sound comes out through your mouth.

The *pharynx is the cavity which connects the nasal passages and mouth with the esophagus.* The esophagus is the tube which passes food to your stomach but also contains the *trachea, or respiratory passage leading from the larynx or voice box to your lungs.*

When you sing, air from your lungs passes up through your trachea, past your larynx, through your oral cavity and out your mouth.

As the tone passes through the resonanting chambers it enhances, strengthens and beautifies the sound which emerges from your vocal cords.

To be a great singer your voice must sound natural and flowing. You should not have to strain when you sing and you should sound and look comfortable. You should develop a ringing, rich quality to your voice and you should develop vibrato. *The foundation exercises on the cassette tape are designed to accomplish just that!*

Vibrato...vocal cords...please explain. Do I really have to know all this to be a great singer?

No you don't. But it's not all that hard to understand. The same mechanism which allows you to speak, allows you to sing. But when you sing you push more air up through your resonating system to sustain the sound longer.

Your vocal cords are located at the top of the trachea in your throat. Without vocal cords there would be no voice. *The vocal cords are similar to rubber bands. They make pitch, furnish timbre and initiate vibrato.*

The 1/2-inch or so vocal cords or bands are a set of muscles and ligaments. They open and close in wave-like motion. They vibrate when drawn together and when air is passed up from the lungs.

Men usually have vocal bands which are large and make lower pitches, thus men are classified as *basses, baritones and tenors.* Women have smaller vocal bands and sing in higher ranges -- *alto and soprano.*

The combination of the shape, size and tension of your vocal cords determines the pitch and timbre of your voice. *The normal goal of vocal exercises is to work at thinning and shortening the vocal bands.*

When you thin the bands you are stretching them. When they are stretched as far as they can be, a process called shortening takes place. The cords themselves don't shorten in actual length, but the vibrating length is shorter.

Don't forget the bands and the muscles around them control your sound. Muscles that are properly exercised will perform properly. As you thin the bands you will be able to reach both higher and lower notes. You will thin the bands by doing the vocal exercises on the tape. Thinning the bands improves your tone, helps you form vowels and consonants correctly and helps increase your range!

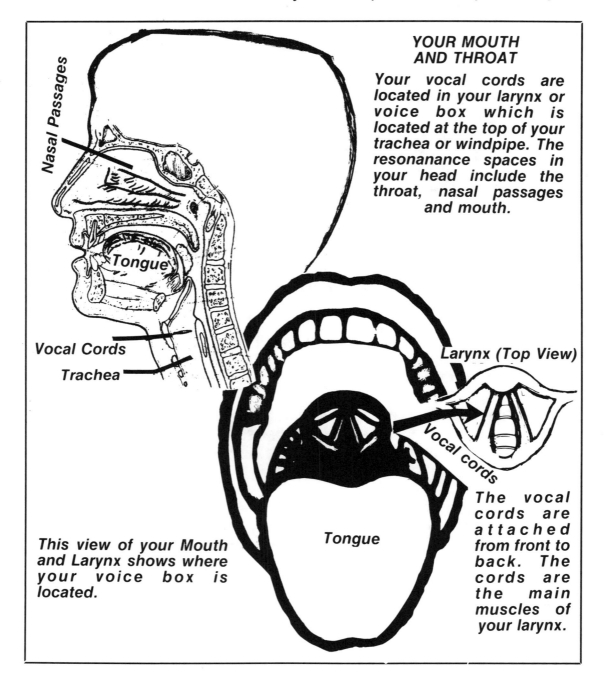

YOUR MOUTH AND THROAT

Your vocal cords are located in your larynx or voice box which is located at the top of your trachea or windpipe. The resonanance spaces in your head include the throat, nasal passages and mouth.

Nasal Passages

Tongue

Vocal Cords

Trachea

Larynx (Top View)

Vocal cords

Tongue

This view of your Mouth and Larynx shows where your voice box is located.

The vocal cords are attached from front to back. The cords are the main muscles of your larynx.

So that's why vocal exercises are so important. When I bought your cassette tape on singing, I assumed I would get songs to sing. I do the vocal exercises now, and I also sing with you at the beginning and ending of the tape. I do feel my voice is getting stronger and my range is expanding. I don't think I'm great yet!

To help you become a great singer you do have to develop some vibrato. Listen to singers such as your wife's favorite *Bernedette Peters or Cher or Natalie Cole or Michael Jackson or Julio Iglesias or Tony Bennett.* They use a lot of vibrato when they sing.

I'm glad you mentioned Bernedette Peters. She's great. I recently saw her concert in Las Vegas and she blew me away. It's hard to believe that such a small person can develop such a big voice. Not one person in that large audience walked away from the concert without raving about her talent!

Yes, she's really talented. And it's quite obvious that she has worked to develop her tremendous voice. She has maximized her rich vibrato. *But don't confuse natural vibrato with the echo you hear on some records. Singers like Michael Jackson and Julio Iglesias use machine-created echo to enhance their sound. Jackson has great vibrato naturally and really accentuates it with echo!*

Vibrato is the slight fluctuation of pitch and intensity. You create vibrato by the normal relaxation and contraction of the vocal muscles when you sing. Good vibrato gives a performance energy and is attained through practice and good breathing.

The best vibrato sound is one that is stable and even; not jerky or shaky. Some singers have no problem creating vibrato. Others find it almost impossible. Vibrato usually can only be achieved with a mature voice -- *children will develop it as they get older.*

Some children do have a great vibrato at a young age. Listen to the young *Judy Garland.* You can hear her rich vibrato on *"Somewhere Over The Rainbow."*

Or listen to *Aileen Quinn* who played the part of Annie in the motion picture *"Annie."* Listen to her sing *"Tomorrow"* or *"I Think I'm Gonna Like It Here"* or *"I Don't Need Anything But You"* in the 1982 hit by *Columbia Pictures Industries, Inc.*

If you do not naturally have vibrato in your voice, you can develop it with the exercise on the tape. In order for you to achieve vibrato, your vocal cords must by very flexible and free from tension. *All the foundation exercises work towards vocal cord flexiblity.* The evenness of the vibrato depends on breath control.

If you work on proper beathing when you sing your vibrato will be good. You will find that the better the abdominal muscles work together, the better the support and more acceptable the vibrato sound you will produce.

Breath control. I think a lot of singers have a problem with breath control, don't they? How do I develop good breath control to help develop good vibrato?

Most people have a misconception of what good breath control really means. Recently a young rock drummer with an up-and-coming Detroit-area band started talking to me about breath control.

"Man, I'm having a big problem with breath control," he said. *'I can really sing but I just seem to lose it."*

After I had him demonstrate *"losing it,"* I realized he didn't know when to take a breath to finish a long phrase. That has nothing to do with proper breath control in singing.

Now you're losing me. Please explain. Isn't that breath control?

Yes, but breath control doesn't just mean being able to sing a long phrase. Good breathing is the basis for all good singing. *Good breathing provides the energy a singer need for phonation, resonance and articulation.*

Proper breath control prepares the vocal mechanism for singing. Respiration opens the vocal bands or cords and the proper deep breathing:

1. Widens the throat;

2. Lowers the larynx into the best position;

3. Lifts the soft palate in the mouth for the best annunciation.

Exercises will help with breath control.

One of the biggest skills a singer must master is keeping his throat open while singing. With proper breathing and proper enlargement of the pharynx in the throat, a singer will achieve tones which are warm, deep and rich.

Being able to sing long phrases will come naturally as you continue to train your voice. But for those singers who are really having a problem with breathing for long phrases, I have devised an exercise to quickly help you. Following also are tips on breath control and proper stance and exercises to help you develop a warm, deep and rich tone.

Even if you don't feel you have a problem with breath control, I can't stress enough how important it is for you to please read on. The exercises are easy and the tips have been accummulated from my own research and experience and from discussions with other vocal instructors and professional entertainers. *They are invaluable!*

I'm trying to do the singing exercises for at least an half-hour a day. Sometimes for an hour when I have more time. I don't have time for more exercises! Singing isn't going to be my full-time job. I'm doing it for fun.

These exercises are easy and can be done at any time night or day. Just read on and you'll see. After doing the exercises for a while, I promise you that you'll see a difference. *These exercises are easy enough for a three year old to learn. Parents who are helping their child with this vocal improvement program should learn these simple exercises and work with their children to teach them to breathe easily and properly.*

BREATHING EXERCISE # 1

1. Breathe in as fully as you possibly can to the count of 4.

2. Breathe out to the count of 4.

3. Do this count of 4 breathing twice more.

4. Breathe in as fully as you can to the count of 8.

5. Breathe out to the count of 8.

6. Do this count of 8 breathing twice more.

7. Breathe in fully to the count of 12.

8. Breathe out to the count of 12.

9. Do this count of 12 breathing twice more.

10. Breathe in as fully as you can to the count of 16. (You may not be able to achieve holding your breath this long the first few times you do this exercise. But you will build to it. Don't be discouraged if you can't do it right away. You will!)

11. Breathe out to the count of 16.

12. Do this count of 16 breathing twice more.

As you can see, you can do this exercise any place at most any time. You will be inhaling and exhaling more air over a longer period of time each time you progress in the exercise. *You will be increasing your lung capacity and breath control.*

Learning to hold your breath as you do in this exercise will help you increase your chest size and strength. It will help you keep the proper muscles taunt and stretched. Keeping your muscles stretched for as much as a minute at a time, as you do with this exercise, will increase their resilience and allow you to be able to sing longer phrases.

Remember our young rock star? He wanted a quick fix. This exercise will give him the air capacity in his lungs to sing those long rock phrases so he doesn't *"lose it"* again!

You're right. That's simple enough. So give me some more quick exercises I can do to improve my singing and breath control.

If you put constant pressure on the muscles of your abdomen and on your back you will cause them to stretch properly to help you breathe correctly, thus giving you the proper muscle support necessary for efficient vocalization.

Some singers find that using a simple elastic belt or elastic shorts helps them. Tenor Placido Domingo recommends this type of belt, which can be purchased at orthopedic supply stores or pharmacies, to give you proper support on a temporary basis. If you can't find one locally, look in the back of this book for more information.

You will find after doing the breathing exercises that with proper breathing the sternum (long, flat bone which supports the ribs) moves out; the chest moves up, and the rib cage expands. This will just happen naturally; you won't actually be conscious of it.

"When I breathe, my diaphram goes out, the whole rib cage fills and the back muscles are absolutely engaged to their fullest," said mezzo-soprano Marilyn Horne. Also a Metropolitan Opera great, Ms Horne believes that if you stand straight you automatically put yourself in a position to have the maximum support for proper breathing.

More on stance coming up. Here's another breath control exercise.

BREATHING EXERCISE # 2

1. Lay on the floor. Put a large, heavy book on your stomach. Breathe deeply. Hold your breath for 20 seconds.

2. Continue breathing deeply with the book on your stomach for a total of 15 minutes.

BREATHING EXERCISE # 3

1. Pull your stomach in to look as thin as you possibly can.

2. Hold that pose for 20 seconds.

3. Push your stomach out to look as fat as you possibly can.

4. Hold that pose for 20 seconds.

5. Repeat this thin-fat exercise at least three more times.

6. Repeat this exercise periodically whenever you get a chance. You can do it when you are driving in a car or truck...watching television...in the shower...or just doing the dishes.

Children get a real kick out of this exercise. They love to see how skinny they can look and how fat they can become.

Hey, I've been doing some of these exercises. My flabby abdomen muscles hurt a little. I'm going to continue doing these breathing exercise. Feels to me like I'll get an added benefit -- I'll trim my abdomen and stomach, too.

Any exercise which requires deep breathing will help you improve your heart and circulation. Exercise promotes good health, which creates a feeling of well being. If you feel good and feel good about yourself you will be able to do a better job no matter what you do...sing...or drive a truck...or teach a class...or make corporate decisions...or study if you are a student.

Exercises which require deep breathing include walking at a quick pace or jogging -- *in the open air or on a stationary machine.* Bike riding, tennis, volleyball, aerobics or dancing -- *square dancing, ballroom dancing or the latest teenage craze.* Simple things such as gardening, or horse-back riding or even walking up and down stairs can give you a good workout!

Breathe deeply when you do any of these exercises. You will be building endurance and more lung capacity. And you will be creating better muscle support.

Any exercise which requires deep breathing is good for your singing.

One word of warning about another popular sport -- *swimming.* Be careful when you swim that the water or chemicals in the water (if you are in a pool) do not irritate your ears, nose or sinuses. Take care that you do not develop an infection from the water. Try using ear or nose plugs when you swim.

Here's one more simple exercise before I discuss how to breathe and proper stance. It's simple and one my doctor suggested I do for tight neck muscles.

BREATHING EXERCISE # 4

1. Sit up straight. Put your chin on your chest. Clasp your hands behind your head. Gently pull down. Breathe deeply as you hold that position for up to one minute.

2. Relax.

3. Repeat the exercise twice more.

If your neck and shoulders are relaxed your voice will flow more freely when you sing. This exercise will relieve tension in the neck and relax both your neck and shoulders.

Just as I had a misconception about what to expect with a vocal improvement program, I also didn't realize the importance of proper breathing. Should I breathe through my nose or my mouth when I sing?

That's a good question. You must be reading my mind because next on my agenda is discussing how to breathe when you sing. Different vocal instructors and performers feel different about it.

Some feel you should breathe through the mouth on short phrases or rests and breathe through the nose during long rests. Others wouldn't even think of breathing through their noses when they sing.

"I am strictly a mouth breather," said Kurt Baum, a Metropolitan Opera tenor who was still singing when he was 80. *"If you take air gently through the mouth, you have an open throat. The nose is only there to avoid germs. You have to learn to sing on a minimum of breath."*

TV singer and Metropolitan opera soprano Gilda Cruz-Roma also inhales through the mouth when she sang.

Stop for a second. I've got a question that has been bugging me for a while as I read this book. Why do you always quote opera stars?

Simple. Opera stars have the best trained voices. Many other singers just sing on instinct. Opera singers have extensive training and they know technique. If I were to quote from a pop star would you be impressed? You might be if you enjoyed pop singing, but would you be if you loved jazz or religious singing. I think not. Opera singers know what they are doing. This type of musical theater is the most difficult style to master. Opera singers know proper stance, proper breathing and proper vowel formation.

I believe the most efficient way to breathe when you sing is through your mouth and a little through your nose. You do have to be careful when you breathe that you do not dry the velum (the soft back part of the palate (roof of the mouth) and pharynx.

Here's a tip, if you are singing professionally, or if you will be singing for a long period of time in front of friends or relatives, have a glass of water or another drink handy. *Periodically take a sip to keep your mouth and throat from drying out.*

Now on to proper stance. Good posture when you sing will help you breathe properly and will enhance your tonal qualities.

Don't stand with your knees locked. If you stand too rigidily you will cut off circulation and get tired quicker. If you do get tired, move a little when you sing. The simple movement will help ease some of the fatigue.

Your legs should be free to move, when you sing. You could stand with one leg slightly in front of the other. This will help you sway back and forth when you perform if you feel like it.

If you prefer to sit when you sing, use a stool not a chair. The stool will force you to sit up straight. Do not lean forward when you sing. It will hamper proper breathing.

If you are going to stand try this stance:

1. Place one foot several inches in front of the other.

2. Stand tall. Your spine should be straight, but not rigid.

3. Lift your chest so that it is in a nice, natural position.

4. Let your arms hang naturally at your side. Or hold a microphone with one or both hands if your singing will be amplified.

With this stance you will be able to swing back and forth to the music, if you wish, without losing your balance.

Now, if you really want to get dramatic and decide to jump on the piano for effect, make sure you don't slouch. Keep your spine straight, but not rigid, so that your breathing is not hampered.

I know it's really important to warm-up your voice before you begin a performance. I've heard singer Kathy Lee Gifford of the "Live with Regis and Kathy Lee," TV talk show, talk about her

warm-ups. She apparently warms up her voice with exercises for days before a performance. Why are warm-ups so very important?

Singers face an occupational hazard.

Didn't know that...did you? It does seem like such a benign occupation. But if you misuse or abuse your speaking voice, you will be in trouble with your singing voice. You also can misuse your singing voice and find yourself with a problem.

Notice my warnings on the cassette tape. I advise you to start singing in your middle range. I always advise my students to begin singing in their middle range and then begin stretching their range as they warm up their voice. You should never warm-up your voice in the lowest or highest part of your range.

Misuse and abuse can occur to your speaking voice if you:

1. Speak loudly in competition with a radio or television;
2. Yell at sports events -- *at a football, hockey or baseball game;*
3. Speak loudly to be heard over the noise at a party, on a plane, in a car or on a bus;
4. Yell so that small children will listen to you.

Misuse and abuse also can occur in your singing voice, if you:

1. Try to sing too loudly;
2. Sing for too long of a time;
3. Try to imitate a singer or a singing style which is unappropriate to your voice;
4. Sing in a range well above or well below your abilities.

Kathy Lee probably is in trouble all the time. She's got to compete against Regis Philben; and that's got to take some loud talking! Don't get me wrong. I love the show and love Regis and Kathy Lee. I wouldn't miss it!

Kathy Lee is careful with her voice. She's a professional singer and has to be. She'd be in real trouble if she didn't. Carnival Cruises certainly wouldn't hire her as a singing spokeswoman if she couldn't sing!

If you do abuse your voice, you may find your singing affected in one of the following areas. You may find problems with pitch, tone, quality, breath support or volume. Some conditions can be treated simply by resting the voice and curtailing the activity which caused the problem. Other conditions may necessitate a visit to the doctor.

The usual approach to voice problems are antibiotics, other pills, vocal rest, steam or hormones.

Occasionally vocal rehabilitation may be necessary to correct problems. A vocal clinician has the expertise to guide an individual back to their best voice, according to *Morton Cooper, Ph.D., a speech therapist in Westwood, CA.*

Some physicians use ultrasonic vibrator treatments to reduce swelling in vocal tissues. The treatment provides temporary relief.

I have found that one of the best treatments for voice problems is humming or sighing. *That's right simple humming can do the trick!* Doing an exercise of humming or sighing will thin and soften the vocal cords and ease swelling.

Humming is a very good conditioning exercise that you can do at any time. Hum with songs on the radio or just hum a tune that you like. Humming can be done just about anyplace -- *even at work* --without getting a critical eye from your co-workers!

Mothers often hum to their children because it's a pleasing sound. They don't realize that they are helping to develop a better singing voice with the hum.

Sighing also is a good exercise. Take a deep breath in and let it out in a sigh -- *like in an ahh.* The sigh relaxes your vocal cords. Give it a try.

You're right! And it feels good too. I wouldn't have too much of a problem humming when I work. I'm a truck driver. I can sing or hum to my hearts content and there's no one to criticize me. That's why I wanted your singing improvement cassette. I barrel down I-75 doing my E's and Ah's and singing with the harmony exercise. No one gives me a second glance. Most everyone sings with a radio or cassette player in the car now-a-days!

Professional singers do not have the luxury of being able to take the day off because of a cold. But if you just sing for the fun of it, it's best not to vocalize when you have a cold, a sinus condition or a throat problem.

Sing to your heart's content on the road, but don't practice your exercises or sing if you have a cold. It may develop into a bigger voice problem. Also your voice quality could be affected if you are suffering from emotional problems such as depression, anxiety or mental tension. Or physical problems such as exhaustion, fatigue, or an upper respiratory infection.

As you progress in your vocal improvement program, you should become much more concerned about your overall health and you will become more conscious about the condition of your nose and throat.

If you do not work at maintaining a healthy body -- *eating the right foods and doing exercises* -- you will find that you do not have the stamina to perform and your performance will suffer -- *Even if your performance is just for your family or for your own enjoyment.*

Rock singer Mick Jagger of the Rolling Stones runs. His onstage performance, which equals a 5- to 10-mile run, required him to start working out so that he is ready for the road two months before a concert tour.

"I still run abut seven miles a day when I'm working, lift weights and play as many team games as I can," Jagger said. "I do a lot of boring exercises and I lay off the goodies."

You also will become much more concerned about your physical condition, sinus, hoarseness, laryngitis and assorted tumors which can cause trouble. Any one of these conditions could put a road block in your presentation.

Any of these conditions probably won't stop you from performing, though, if you become a professional singer. *(Amateurs, please DO STOP SINGING while you have any medical conditions which affect your voice or vocal cords.)*

Exercise, no matter what kind you prefer, will help you with breath control and with your vocal efforts.

For professionals, the show must go on! You don't see professional performers canceling shows because of hoarseness or a cold. At a recent show in Las Vegas, the singer who was impersonating Elvis Presley had a bad cold. His performance did suffer. But the audience was there to see his impersonation of Elvis and accepted the bad performance. *Audiences usually feel a bad performance is better than no performance at all.*

Here's a singing tip, if you are performing, don't be afraid to explain your problem to the audience. They will be able to accept you, and they will have sympathy for the way you feel.

Singers must take great care when they are vocalizing not to strain their vocal cords or damage their throats. As I have said, something as simple as yelling at a sports game or a boxing or wrestling match can cause hoarseness.

Hoarseness actually is a symptom and not a disease. It can be caused by yelling or abusing the vocal cords in some other simple way. It also can be caused by chemical irritants, tobacco or alcohol.

So if you smoke -- stop. You'll not only help save your throat; but you'll help save your life. You'll also save your loved ones from suffering. Smoking causes cancer. Please excuse me...I'm editoralizing here, but a few puffs of *"enjoyment"* isn't worth your life. I've known a few people who have died from lung cancer because of their smoking habit. It's not a pleasant way to die! And their families suffered even more watching their loved one suffer so much.

I'll excuse your editoralizing. I don't smoke. I agree!

Back to my medical lesson. Hoarseness also can be caused by a cold or congestion of the throat from a sore throat. *Aside from my vocal humming and sighing technique, probably the only home treatment for hoarseness is rest of the vocal cords. Put simply -- be quiet, don't talk, don't sing!*

If you have hoarseness that lasts longer than three weeks contact a doctor.

If your larynx or voice box becomes inflamed, you have laryngitis. You know if you have laryngitis. You can't speak above a whisper.

You can develop laryngitis by straining or overusing the voice; or it can result from an infection.

Singers are highly prone to laryngitis. So are mothers who shout at their children, children who scream a lot, or anyone else who uses their voice for a long time, loudly.

You also can get laryngitis with a cold, nose, throat or bronchial infection.

The best treatment for laryngitis is to rest your voice. Stay out of smoky or dusty places which will just irritate your injured larynx. And if the condition persists see a doctor who may prescribe drugs or suggest heat treatments.

Tumors of the larynx are not uncommon. Most of these -- *polyps, cysts or fibrous growths* -- are benign, or non-cancerous. Nodules may form on your vocal cords if you abuse them. These nodules are not unlike a corn or callus on your foot caused from an ill fitted shoe. Except in your throat the nodule is caused by irritating your vocal cords. Sometimes a doctor will recommend removal of the benign tumor. Results usually are excellent.

Cancer of the larynx also can occur. Early cancer of the throat causes a huskiness of the voice. It does not cause pain or bleeding. *If the cancer is caught at an early stage it is curable.*

I never thought I would get a medical lesson when I bought a book on singing. You're right. I am becoming more concerned about my health.

Remember...all the usual diseases of the throat or the voice box have the same symptom -- *hoarseness.* If you have hoarseness which persists see a doctor.

Sinusitis or a cold may cause problems for singers, too. Everyone knows what a sinus infection is. Thick, pus-containing discharges from the sinus can cause local pain and tenderness in and around the nose and eyes.

The most important thing to do if you have a sinus problem or cold is keep your sinus secretions draining freely. You may need to use antihistamine drugs in the form of pills, nose drops or sprays. In some cases a doctor may prescribe an antibiotic. Warm packs and steam humidification helps ventilate the sinuses and aides in drainage.

Another problem singers must face are nasal polyps. They are soft, moist outgrowths from the mucous membranes which line the nose. The polyps may obstruct the nasal airways and severe obstructions should be removed by a doctor. Nasal polyps are almost always benign. The polyps may grow back after they are removed. Severe obstruction forces a singer to breathe through his mouth, which may cause a problem when he sings.

Just as a recap: *Remember to take good care of yourself physically and mentally and to avoid abusing your body and your voice.* You already have read my no-smoking warning; but it's important not to abuse your body and your vocal cords with alcohol or other drugs, either. Stimulant drugs like amphetamines and cocaine and depressive drugs like alcohol and *Valium®* can distrupt your neuromuscular sytem which will affect your ability to sing. Your ability to remember! And your equilibrium! *Elvis Presley allowed himself to get involved in drug abuse and it did show. He got fat and lazy and he lost touch with reality. During one of his last performances I saw in the Detroit area, he walked off stage and had back-up singers take the lead. The performance was no longer of "the King's" caliber. It was quite a disappointment!*

Aside from drug abuse, things like excessive coughing, forced throat-clearing and trying to sing too loudly will cause damage. It will lead to hoarseness and directly affect your singing.

If you find that you have to perform, but your throat is sore you can use commercial throat sprays and lozengers available at drug stores and pharmacies to soothe your irritated throat. You also can drink hot liquids like tea. Hot drinks and sprays won't help you to sing better; they will just make your throat feel better. And even if you don't have a sore throat, it's not a bad idea to keep your mouth and throat moist by drinking water or another non-alcoholic drink during a performance.

You are still a little ahead of me. I don't have to worry about my performance being affected by a sore throat. I haven't walked in front of an audience yet. I don't know if I ever will. I don't think I have the nerve to do it!

I feel fear before each performance. If I didn't, I would get worried because I have learned to use my fear -- *I channel that fear into excitement which enhances my performance.*

Very few performers don't get nervous or feel fear before a show. Believe it or not, most entertainers are basically shy people who have learned to channel that fear into creativity and deliverance.

Do you think Johnny Carson doesn't get nervous before his monologue? Or Barbra Streisand? She refuses to do concerts because her fear and nervousness are so overwhelming. Singer Carly Simon didn't do concert work for years because she could not overcome the anxiety of live performances. She suffered from extreme stage fright!

Lets face it -- *its scary.* But if you are ready to do the show (well rehearsed, etc.), that fear will subside once you get started.

Probably the biggest hurdle in front of any singer -- *a novice or a professional* -- is fear. It's easier to jump that hurdle than you think. I know you are thinking that it's easy for me to say that because I sing professionally, but anyone can learn to use their fear to enhance their performance.

I've gotten letters over the years from people just like you who are ''shower'' singers but are afraid to sing in front of other people. *Or who like to sing but are too self-conscious because they are heavy or have acme or walk with a limp.*
Here are a few tips:

My first tip to help you face the anxiety and fear of performing in front of others is *to practice relentlessly with the vocal exercises on the cassette tape.* Feel your voice improving. Know that your range has expanded. Take comfort in the fact that you have improved your tone and the quality of your voice. When you feel confident in your vocal ability, you naturally will do better. You will feel more at ease.

My second tip is *practice the songs you want to sing.* Learn the words. When you are sure you know the songs, you will sing them better. You will feel more at ease performing them.

My third tip is to video tape your practice sessions to see how you come across.

My fourth tip is *to concentrate on your strengths when you perform -- not your weaknesses.* Don't choose material you are unsure of. Don't allow any member of your audience to talk you into singing a song you don't know well enough. Think of some excuses before hand and don't get railroaded into singing the *"Notre Dame Fight Song"* if you are only vaguely familiar with it. Give the audience your best material only!

My fifth tip is *to start small.* Your goal may be an audience of hundreds at Carnegie Hall, but start with one. Sing in front of your husband or wife or a friend. When you feel really comfortable performing in front of a single person, move on to include more of your immediate family and friends.

A great way to help you face your fear is to invite a small group of people over for a dinner or party and have a little song session. You'll see by the reaction of your guests how you are coming across.

When you feel at ease and confident in your singing ability for a small group, expand the scope of your audience.

The more you perform, the more you will realize that the initial fear you feel usually subsides as you sing. The appreciation you get from your audience gives you an adrenalin high that spurs you on to your best work.

The feeling that you are loved; that your talent is being recognized; that you are enriching the lives of others with your songs is a tremendous ego booster. Your self-esteem will leap by quantum measures and you will not be able to wait for your next performance.

Sure...the adoration of the crowd...the boosted ego...that sounds great to me. But the initial fear is a killer! I'm not ready to take that step.

Tips From The Stars

Don't box yourself into categories.
"I can sing ballads...church hymns, all kinds of songs. Plus, I can write, act, and think. I'm multidimensional, and I don't want to be known for just one thing."
-- Donna Summer to *Ebony Magazine.*

Taking the first step, getting started, is the hardest thing to do. Don't try to fool yourself into thinking you have to be relaxed. That's impossible to do. You already recognize that fear. Take it another step further and accept that you are afraid.

It is very important for you to read and reread my next statements. Make a copy of it and REREAD it before you go on stage. Make sure you understand it. Here goes:

As you stand in the wings waiting to sing, recognize that you are afraid. Accept that fear. Don't try to fight it. Don't try to wish it away. Don't try to pretend it isn't there. Sorry...but it's there. If you exert your energies trying to wish it away, you'll just make yourself more nervous and anxious.

Once you face the fact that you are afraid...that fear no longer will be a catastrophic feeling. That fear will not master you. Despite the fear you will do what you love to do -- you will sing. That fear will not control you to submission! You will control that fear and you will gain both self-confidence and self-respect!

You will take the anxiety that the fear created and turn it into excitement. Put that excitement in your performance and you will be a knockout.

While discussing anxiety and tension, singer, actress and comedienne *Carol Channing* said: *"Tension can be an asset if you make it work for you. It keeps you on your toes!"*

Are you telling me that once I take the first step and stage my first singing performance, I'll be able to overcome my fears? I'm still not convinced.

Yes...you will be able to overcome your fears. Your fears won't go away. Say to yourself: *"Wow, am I afraid,"* and then take a long, slow deep breath. Concentrate on your breathing.

Think about the worst thing that could happen to you when you sing. What is it -- *you forget the lines?* Fine, what have you learned on the cassette tape -- *Scat your way through the song, until the lines come back.*

What's the second worst thing that could happen to you. The crowd doesn't like you. That's not the end of the world. And most audiences you encounter aren't crass enough to boo you off the stage. Unless you are Kathie Lee Gifford, that is! Let me relate a little story here. Kathie Lee sang ''The Star Spangled Banner'' before an audience of thousands on one of the Monday night football games. She *''sang her brains out,''* as she likes to say. When she finished and started to walk off the field the crowd started clapping and then booing. That's right -- *BOOING!*

Now, talk about shooting down your confidence and self-esteem. She felt terrible; she wanted to find a place to hide. And then she realized that the crowd wasn't booing her. They were booing the opposition team coming onto the field at the same time she was leaving.

Nothing worse than that could happen to you! Just remember to forget about the bad things that *''might''* happen and replace the negative thoughts with the positive things that WILL happen. You won't forget the words and the crowd will like you.

Use your fears -- *turned into excitement* -- as a positive force towards success. Your new venture into entertainment will help you grow as a person. You will experience a great feeling of power because you have attained your goal and you realize that your potential has no limits!

I really do feel a little excitement. I sure would like to get lucky in the big dollars music business.

People get lucky in the music business by being ready and being in the right place at the right time. How do you help yourself to be ready? Aside from working on your voice:

1. You learn to build your self-respect.
2. You learn to build your self-esteem.
3. You learn to build your strengths.
4. You learn to appreciate yourself.
5. You learn to like yourself.
6. You learn to trust yourself.

Get my drift? Get on your side! When you think positively about yourself, you realize that you have the potential to get lucky. If you practice, stretch your mind and your vocal abilities, and if you have the desire to work for a greater goal, you have the magic ingredients necessary to motivate yourself. You will be lucky...you will succeed...you will sing in front of that crowd...you will make them like you!

I still have one other question. You have taught me how to build my self-esteem and confidence here, but what about the overweight person...or the person with acme...or with the limp that you first wrote about?

The weight, the acme and the limp don't mean much. Don't look in a mirror and see your fat belly. You'll clobber your self-esteem. Look in the mirror and focus in on your inner beauty and strengths. After all, this inner beauty is what you are conveying in your singing and that's what your audience will pick up and be left with when you walk off the stage.

OK...at first, they may see your physical flaws, but that's soon forgotten as you replace it with the power of your performance.

Think about your positive traits, when you face your audience and then knock them dead with your beautifully developed voice and confident personality.

Your looks aren't the main thing. They aren't going to think about your beer-belly or your zit, they are going to leave your performance in awe of your songs and talent. Or course, I'm not telling you not to try to improve your appearance. If you lose weight you will look better and above all sing better. You also will develop more self-esteem which will show in your presentation. And if you have a bad complexion -- if you are a man or a woman -- make-up does wonders to smooth out your skin. If your hair is thin or balding, or if you have embarrassing bald spots, there is a product on the market that fills in the thin and balding spots. See the cosmetic secret of the stars, *Formulox*™, in the back of this book. It's for men and women. Try to be the best that you can be no matter what you do.

Here's one more tip that will help you build confidence and also help you polish your performance. It's a technique major singing (and acting) stars have been using for quite some time. Video tape your practice sessions or rehearsals -- *especially your complete dress rehearsal.*

Rock and country groups, *particularly,* will find video footage very helpful. You will be able to see for yourself how you are coming across. You will be able to critique your performance and correct any mistakes before you go in front of an audience.

I use video taping all the time. I found it an especially effective technique to help my daughter overcome nervousness; and we have used it to determine the best outfit for her to wear for a vocal recital. My wife chose a very pretty dress for Wendy to wear for her second recital and when I did a dress rehearsal for Wendy, we realized that the dress buckled up on her when she moved on stage.

We quickly had her change her outfit and continue the rehearsal until we found the perfect costume to compliment her act.

Video taping is very helpful for young children to teach them hand, arm and body movements and to help them learn how to walk or dance on stage. Proper movements enhance a performance. Movements add life to the singer's act. Some singer's who don't move on stage give the appearance that they are afraid. Movements can even mask a shaky hand. Rehearsing with a video camera also helps you overcome awkwardness on stage. You will find that if you use this technique *"secretly" used by many stars you will take the "kinks"* out of your act before you are embarrassed in front of a crowd.

Rock groups should tape rehearsals. You will be able to see how the whole act goes together. You will be able to see if you or another band member is making inappropriate movements. And if your costumes look and feel right. You'll also be able to do mini sound checks of the instruments and the voices

If you do not have a video camera, record your performance on a cassette tape. At least you will be able to hear how you will come across to the audience. Seeing and hearing the performance on video tape is better than hearing alone; but hearing on the cassette tape is better than going on stage *"cold."*

Tips From The Stars

Keep your act and your costumes up-to-date. Mick Jagger of the Rolling Stones has changed with the times.

The early sixties found him in a white shirt, tie and vest. In 1972 he wore an Elvis-inspired jump suit. For the 1989 concert tour, Jagger wore raunchy, royal clothes. He said: *"A bit o'swank never hurt a flashy act."*

Now that you know how to build your confidence to perform, it's the perfect time to get you out in front of the band to show your stuff. Here's the information every young rock hopeful bought this book for. I'm going to teach you what you need to know to become the lead singer!

I would love to see my daughter as the lead singer in a band. Or better yet, the headliner in a Las Vegas or Atlantic City show! And I don't mean as a top-less dancer. I mean as a TOP singer.

Usually the term lead singer refers to the member of a rock or country band who does most of the singing and is right up front. To be a lead singer of a rock band, you don't have to have a phenomenal voice. Listen to the lead singers of many of the rock and heavy metal bands. Without all the loud music behind them, they wouldn't have a chance of making a living with their voices. The lead singer of a country band better know his stuff. Country singers don't have the luxury of having super loud music mask their voices.

It certainly helps to have a great, distinctive voice. But the most important asset you must have to be a lead singer in a rock band is showmanship. You must be a better showman than the other members of the group. You have to be able to control the other members of the band without them resenting your authority. They won't resent you if you prove to them that you are the best and you can weave the group's sound together better than they could by themselves. You have to prove that you can *"sell"* the group's sound to the audience.

Here are my TEN GOLDEN RULES for singers who want to become the lead:

1. You must develop total confidence in your voice and in yourself.

2. You must know your voice limits and never strain for too long.

3. You must be able to channel your stage nervousness or stage fright into performance excitement.

4. You must be in total control on stage -- *almost to the point of appearing "cocky."*

5. You must know how to capture the attention of your audience.

6. You must be able to keep the audience in *"the palm of your hand"* for your ENTIRE show.

7. You may want to create a gimmick that makes you outstanding.

8. You must sing songs that your audience will appreciate and enjoy hearing.

9. You must keep your act polished and updated.

10. You must be able to illicit the support of your band and not let resentment build up because of your up-front position.

If you are a young rock hopeful, hopefully you began reading this book from the start not just from here. If you started here, go back to the beginning. Your chances of taking the lead depends on your ability to create the best performance and you need to know everything that I have taught in this book so far.

If you have read from the beginning, you know by now if you strain your voice you will damage it. If you try to push your voice further than it is capable of going, you may blow your voice and not be able to effectively complete your show.

That's why the exercises on the tape are so invaluable. And why you should continue to do them every day. You will gradually build your range with the exercises. You will strengthen your voice.

The performers who seem to abuse their voices the most are rock singers. They are the least trained in voice development and they do not build their voices to have the stamina they need to sing so loudly for such a long period of time. Rock singers constantly battle the loud instruments behind them to be heard. They usually do not have good amplification equipment and good sound engineers that should be doing the job for them. They continually strain their voices as they scream above the roar of the electric guitar, bass, keyboard and drums!

You may not be able to afford better speakers and microphones, so what can you do? As boring as it may seem to you, you should vocalize with the foundation exercises on the cassette tape.

The exercises are designed to build the proper muscles around your voice box which will enable you to sing lounder and for a longer period of time. I find that if I vocalize with Exercise 1 to 7 everyday, my voice continually gets dramatically stronger. Yours will too!

I get your drift. Like I said, I am practicing with the exercises. They really aren't boring if you get into them. If you just listen to the piano accompaniment without singing, you may get bored. But if you sing along with the exercises and concentrate on the sound you are producing, the exercises are fun to do. I still am a little unsure of myself, I am trying. How in the world can I get cocky?

Please don't get cocky. I just want you to appear cocky. To be cocky is to be conceited. To appear cocky is to bring across to your audience an attitude of complete confidence in your ability and in your presentation.

The wrong attitude on stage can kill a performance. Your audience doesn't want to feel that you love yourself. They want to love you for what you are doing. They want to love your voice and your performance. They want to be entertained; not repelled by your attitude of self-love.

Look at the degree of success and the different attitudes of superstar Michael Jackson and rock star Prince. Jackson appears cocky, and the audience loves him. Prince is cocky.

You will naturally appear cocky if you have confidence in your voice, in the band, in the songs you are singing and in the show you have thoroughly rehearsed.

Be thoroughly rehearsed -- *leave little to chance* -- and you will capture the attention of your audience. You will keep them in *"the palm of your hands"* if you give them what they want.

Most up-and-coming rock or country bands always want to do their original material for the audience. And that's fine if you are *Kiss* or Billy Joel or Cher or Dolly Parton. New bands should rehearse

Probably one of the easiest things to do once you have mastered the vocal exercises and developed your voice, is create your own style. How? Easy! Put your personality into your singing. Put your own feelings into your songs. Listen to other great singers. What do you remember about their style? You may remember his or her voice if it is outstanding, but most likely you will remember the singer's personality or stage presence.

"When you sing about being in love, you must have love on your face," said soprano Licia Albanese, another opera great. *"Expression and quality of voice go with the meaning of the words."*

Foreign pop singer Julio Iglesias doesn't even think an individual has to have a good voice to sing. He did not start singing until he was in his mid-twenties and he believes singing has nothing to do with voice. He said that singing is personality and what you put into your deliverance. Think about it, do women remember Julios' voice. No, they remember his sex appeal.

How do you create your own style? *Sing from the heart.* Put as much emotion into your presentation as you can muster. Put your personality into the song. There are no two people on earth with the same personality -- *not even identical twins.* Put your personality into your singing and you are creating your own unique style!

The type of songs you sing also will help determine your style of delivery. The style is written right into the music. As you already have learned Country has a style and feel of its own; as does Rock and Jazz and Calpyso and Pop and Contemporary and Rhythm & Blues and Gospel and Religious and even Rap. When you sing songs in any of the style classifications, you create your own style by the way you deliver the songs.

You should always concentrate on what you can do best when you are performing before others. Also always remember to put all you have into the ending of a song. Even if you *"screw up"* the beginning or the middle of a song or your delivery isn't up to par; if you put a little extra *"something"* into the ending that is what your audience will remember. If you recall, I sometimes use a falsetto ending to some songs. It can be impressive.

That's what you want to work on -- *impressing your audience.* Leave them wanting more...think of the feeling you have when you are watching a great movie and it ends. You don't what it to end. You want to see the sequel. Leave your audience wanting to see the sequel!

songs made popular by the big rock or country groups. Throw in a little original material, but don't make the original material *"the show"* until you have developed your own following.

You will be giving the audience what they want if they can identify with the music and songs. Music identity adds to the enjoyment the audience will get out of the show. It will add to the excitement the audience will feel because they will be able to sing along with the songs. Very few songs are hits the first time they are heard. The more air play a song gets on radio and *MTV,* the better it's chances are. The same for concerts. Most big stars don't introduce a song for the first time in concert. They perform songs the audience already knows and loves.

Aside from singing the songs the audience wants to hear, to be a lead singer and to lead your group to the top, you should find a gimmick.

What kind of a gimmick? It could be your voice. Or your music. Or your personality. Or the personality of the band. Or your costumes.

Look at the gimmicks the biggest stars have used in the past or are using today. Improvise. Don't copy. Create your own style.

The shock-rock group, *Kiss,* comes to mind when I talk about gimmick. Their gimmick was costumes that totally masked their identities. Members of *Kiss* wore bizarre stage makeup. Singer Gene Simmons dressed like a fire-breathing, vampire-costumed ghoul. He became known for the way he would lap his snake-like tongue at his audiences. He wore 12-inch-high platform boots, each shaped like a demon's mouth, complete with bladed teeth.

Part of the group's gimmick meant its members were never seen in public without makeup. So whenever group members ventured out, they would cover their faces with handkerchiefs to mask their identities.

Little did people know that behind the masks, Simmons was a former 6th grade teacher who was a brilliant and confident businessman and an outstanding rock 'n' roll merchandiser.

The public loved it.

They also love Cher. There is no question that aside from her phenomenal voice, Cher's gimmicks are her wigs and her costumes -- *or lack of them* -- and her personality, her lovers and her life-style. The publicity about her everything-revealing costumes does nothing but sell more albums, CDs and videos! The public never gets enough of Cher.

Country singer Willie Nelson's gimmicks include his long, braided hair, head bandanna, beard, boots, jeans, plaid shirt or T-shirts, and down-home country stage personality. When he first started out, he used to be clean-shaven, wore his hair neatly cut short, and wore conservative clothing. He went nowhere! His musical *"ship came in"* when he changed to his scruffy image.

Dolly Parton's gimmicks include her outstanding voice and songwriting talents, her wigs and her stage personality. And just like TV giant Oprah Winfrey, she has used her weight-loss (and gain) to muster public interest and support.

Another lady with a gimmick is k.d lang.   k.d. (Kathy Dawn Lang) is an up-and-coming Canadian-born country-rock singer who's unbelievable and refuses to be classified. She changes her style and presentation with each song. Her gimmicks include her voice, with it's rich and emotion-packed timbre, and her appearance *--short, punkishly modish hairdo; and unusual wardrobe from ripped hose, funky skirts and suede western jackets to men's stylish suits to full white wedding regalia.* Using the lower case letter in her name and album titles like *"shadowland"* also is a part of her gimmick.

Want to be a lead singer? Create an ORIGINAL knock-out gimmick!

That sounds pretty tough for the average person to do. But, I guess rock stars aren't average. You really do have to have a lot of confidence in yourself to put on one of those costumes and sing.

Actually, you are wrong there. It's easier to perform in a disguise than as yourself. Most popular or contemporary, rhythm and blues, jazz and Gospel singers use no costumes -- *they use refined talent.*

Country and rock singers have the option of hiding behind or enhancing (which every way you want to look at it) their performance with costumes and gimmicks.

Once you have created a gimmick -- *if you feel you need it* -- you still have to be able to take command of your audience. Here are some tricks I have used to keep my audience enthralled. I like to make each audience member feel I am singing to and for them. Elvis Presley was the master at this. One of his gimmicks was choosing ladies or little girls in the audience to give his neck scarfs to. He also kissed these adoring fans. This was one of Elvis' secrets to working his audience up into a frenzy. As was his vibrating hips in the beginning of his career. And his white, skin-tight, beaded costumes.

I usually try to make eye contact with people in the audience. I smile at them. I make them feel I am singing just for them. Walk around the stage when you sing. Don't just stand in the center. Make sure you will be able to carry your microphone to the remotest section of the stage. Say *"Hi"* to the different individuals. Thank them, individually, for coming. Shake their hands. Male lead singers can give the women a peck on the cheek. Female lead singers may want to find a handsome guy in the audience and give him a kiss or a hug.

It's not a bad idea to talk to the audience; not just sing for them. Tell them little stories -- *even if you have to make them up.* Share secrets with the audience. Make them feel they are *"in on something." Keep your stories brief, but funny and entertaining. Make the stories appear to be spontaneous. Don't make them sound rehearsed. Here's where video taping can really come in handy. You will be able to polish your "unrehearsed"* stories.

Many comedians who appear on *"The Tonight Show"* actually have a script of jokes prepared, although the audience doesn't know it. Johnny Carson is in on it. He is given questions to lead the comedian into a joke. Carson and the guests are so good at what they do that the conversation appears to be spontaneous.

They had me fooled. I'll watch for that when I turn on Carson tonight. Hope he has a comedian on. Your tips sound great. What other tips do you have for lead singers?

Tips From The Stars

If you do get some level of success, don't let it go to your head.

"Even though I appreciate fame, I remember once I used to pick cotton, and I feel like even then I was somebody...I have the same feet, hands, and heart as everybody else. I'm just blessed with a good voice."

-- Country singer Charley Pride

Thanks. Here's another one. I like to get the audience involved in the songs. You can do this in different ways, depending upon if it is a club or concert performance.

In a club you can have individuals in the audience sing with you. You can sing a part of a song and have them answer you in song. You can bring them on stage and do a little skit with them. You can go right out in the audience and sing to different individuals -- *pick a pretty girl...or a matronly grandmother.*

When you are first starting out you may be a little afraid of audience participation. You may be afraid of dealing with the audience on a one-to-one basis. If you have this fear then *"plant"* a few people in the audience. Pretend that you have picked them spontaneously and have them sing with you. You may feel more comfortable knowing the response you will get from your *"plants."* Once you get the knack of this art, you won't need *"plants"* anymore.

Comedians *"plant laughers" in their audiences all the time. Laughter is contagious. It won't hurt for you to use the same technique; except your "plants"* will sing.

Performing before a large concert audience you can break the audience up into singing sections. You can have all the women sing with you or have them answer you in song. You could then pick on all the men...all the teenagers...all the blondes...all the mothers...all the children.

Or you could break the audience up by aisles. Have different sections compete against the others for the loudest response. Always tell your audience participants: *"I can't hear you."* Encourage another round of singing at a louder pitch.

Most people have a little *"ham"* in them and love to become a part of your show. Make sure you compliment them on their efforts. Getting the audience to participate with you probably is the easiest way to leave them soaring with an energized spirit and a terrific memory of your performance.

Work out routines with members of the band. Spotlight them on songs they can sing well. Or on a great guitar *"riff"* or piano run. One of the members of the *"Turn Ons,"* Earl Rennie had a great bass voice. He could hit unbelievably low notes. During a show I always would try to signal him out and had him show the audience how low he could go. He actually would rumble the stage with his low notes. The audience ate it up -- *they loved it.* And so did Earl.

Introduce the band by name to the audience. Don't just name the drummer and the guitarist and the keyboard player and the bass player. Introduce them with a little story or anecdote. Let your audience and the individual band member know how important he (or she) is to you and to the group as a whole.

Give them credit for a song they wrote or a melody line they created. Make them feel as important as they feel you are! Playing up their importance will help *"keep the peace"* in the band and will help keep you in control of your group. Too many good bands break up because of ego problems; never to be heard of again! Develop the grounds for mutual trust and admiration and you'll help keep the group together and you on top as the lead singer of your band!

Little need be said about keeping your act fresh and updated. The singers and groups which have the longest careers are the ones that constantly refresh their acts. That's just what the Rolling Stones have done over the years. That's why they are still on top. *"People"* magazine recently said of the Stones: *"The Rolling Stones have proved that they are the oldest, grayest, richest and quite possibly Greatest Rock and Roll Band Ever."* The reason is simple. They stay up to date!

I can see that the tips from the stars which you are giving me are invaluable. Everything from video taping rehearsals to keeping the audience in the palm of my hands to keeping the show modern. I do want my daughter to learn everything there is to be learned about singing and stage presence. Could we back-track a little though? I have never been real musical -- I don't play a musical instrument. When I listen to my daughter vocalize with the cassette tape, how do I know she is on?

The biggest problem for children and even for adults who have never had voice or music training is to be able to start singing on the right note and continue to be in perfect pitch with the music.

You can learn how to sing on the right note more easily than you can imagine even if you are an adult and have trouble getting started...or if you are working with a child who is just learning to sing.

The problem with pitch is that your ear hears the note one way, but it comes out of your mouth another way. Your mind has translated the note wrong. The best way to conquer this problem is to use the "Do Re Me" exercise on the cassette tape. Instead of singing the Do Re Me, hum the exercise up the scale.

If you change this exercise into a humming exercise, it will teach your brain to tell your vocal cords how to hit the notes in perfect pitch. You will be learning to flex and/or relax the right muscles in your throat to do the job right.

Don't be discouraged if you have a little trouble with this exercise at first. You may not feel that you or your child are hitting the right notes. Try taping this exercise on another cassette recorder or on video tape. Listen to your voice in the recording and you will be able to tell if you are on key.

Using this technique, adults usually can teach their brains to tell their throats what to do quickly. It takes longer for children, so be patient. All three of my daughters can hit notes on key -- *even the three year old!*

By now you realize how much importance I place on singing as a part of family life. Singing can become an integral thread that helps hold the family and extended family together. All the members of my family from Grandpa Wiesend to the newest member of the clan, Tiffany, look forward to get-togethers -- *they all end in a family sing-a-long.* My two brothers also have made singing an important aspect of their family life. My niece and nephews all enjoy singing and take musical instruments. Singing is an activity every member of your family can enjoy -- *from the oldest to the youngest.* Age is no barrior.

Recent research in *Alzheimer's,* a baffling disease of the brain, has found a surprising link between the ailment and music as therapy.

Even most *Alzheimer's* patients, who sometimes no longer communicate with the family, can identify with beautiful music and songs from their past. It is very comforting to them.

As I have said, newborns respond to music and the sound of their mother's voice. So mothers...talk to your baby...sing to your little ones. And if you have an aging grandparent or friend...talk with them...and sing to them, even if they don't respond in turn.

Everyone can and does benefit from music and learning how to sing. From the old to the young, it's never to late to develop your singing voice.

So how do you teach a child to sing?

The job used to be done for you. And if you still live in a progressive school district and rich neighborhood, your child probably can get all the vocal stimulation he (or she) needs in school. But with massive millage defeats in so many areas, and the constant restraints put on local school boards because of budget cuts, many school districts can no longer afford a full-time music instructor. Classroom teachers try to fill the void by including singing in their curriculum. But they don't have the time nor the music education necessary to help a child develop vocally.

Churches take up some of the slack. But most organists and choir directors also cannot allocate the time necessary to develop individual voices.

So where does your child learn to sing? *At home, of course...from you.* There have been reams of material written on vocal development over the years. But they were written for the musical educator; not the average parent.

I'm here to make your job easier. I will teach you how to teach your child to sing. Even if you feel that you do not have an *"ear for music,"* you can do it. And, as an added bonus, you will improve your own voice as well!

In order to teach your child to sing, you must teach him (or her) to differentiate between notes. The basic *"Do Re Me"* exercise on the cassette tape is your starting point. Sing the notes -- *one note at a time* -- to your child. Use a soft, quiet, light voice. Most children from toddlers to ninth graders can hit notes in a high alto to low soprano range. The notes in that range are the ones you should be singing to your child.

A child will mimic your voice. That is why you should use a light voice in your upper range to teach your child how to sing. Your child can not mimic you if you use your full, rich voice.

But, by all means, do use your best voice when you are practicing the vocal exercises by yourself. The more you vocalize with the exercises the better your voice will become.

Another tip is don't blast the tape for your own vocal sessions, or those of your child's. Play the tape especially low for your child during his vocal sessions. Your child's efforts should not be confused by a loud piano.

Sing the first three notes and have your child mimic you. Add three more. And then the last two until your child can sing the whole musical scale by themselves.

Keep vocal sessions short at first. Attention spans of toddlers, preschoolers and first and second graders are short. A bored child will not learn and you will just become frustrated. Make the vocal sessions lively and fun!

Once your child has learned *"Do Re Me Fa So La Te Do"* progressively up the scale, you can begin adding some more fun to the exercises. Start singing and skip a note; let your child fill in the skipped note. Alternate skipping notes. For example, you sing *"Do;"* he sings *"Re;"* you sing *"Me,"* etc. Your child will gleam with pride when he (or she) can fill in the missing notes correctly.

You also can use the *"Do Re Me"* exercise but replace those sounds with a word or words. Just do it in *"La's"* up the musical scale. Or with the child's name -- *Crys - tal...Crys - tal...Crys - tal* --up the scale.

Three-year-old Tiffany can sing *"Do Re Me"* progressively up the scale by herself. I do not limit her to just the *"Do Re Me"* exercise, though. I work with her on all of the foundation exercises on the

Children of all ages can learn to sing. Six-year-old Natalie (right) and her 3-year-old sister Tiffany vocalize with the cassette tape, "How To Sing Great," every day. Along with older sister Wendy (you'll meet her on Pg. 112), all three girls have been exposed to music since before birth and continually after they were born.

cassette tape. (She also sings with me whenever I sing on the tape. Except, of course, when I sing:

"*Tiffany...Oh...Tiffany...Tiffany, I love you so*"

in the beginning of the tape. She just smiles from ear to ear.

I even change the words to some of the exercises to make them more fun for her and her sisters -- *Natalie and Wendy.* They really enjoy the *"Lolly"* exercise. But we change the words to *"Lolly Pop"* instead of *"Lolly Ah."* They love it. Your child will too!

Also sing with your child working down the musical scale to add variety to the vocal sessions and to teach them that note progression goes both ways.

Have you noticed that I didn't interrupt you once? I don't know of one parent who isn't interested in teaching their child how to sing. We should leave our children with a legacy of song. That's more valuable than all the jewels on Earth!

Always praise your child's efforts. Even if he (or she) sings a little off-key or flat, criticism is counter-productive.

You will be surprised how quickly your child will learn how to sing progressively up the musical scale. All singing is based on different note patterns. It is not necessary to teach your child difficult patterns or to force him (or her) to strain to reach notes. No one should strain their voices when they vocalize with the exercises or when they sing songs. Straining is unnessary. Singing range is a by-product of vocal exercises. It will come with time and practice.

You also could teach your child to sing little phrases. Sing *"Good Morning"* to them, instead of saying it. Make up a little pattern: *"Good Morning, Randy!"* And have Randy answer using the same note pattern you made up: *"Good Morning, Mommy."*

Or sing: *"What do you want for lunch, Hollie?"* As she sings back, using your same pattern: *"I would like hot dogs for lunch, Mommy?"*

Of course, it could be Daddy, too. Mothers and fathers should try to take an equal role in teaching their children to sing.

Daddy sing: *"I love you, Robert."* As Robert responds: *"I love you, Daddy."*

If you use this singing-answer technique you may even help your child develop into a great songwriter. Singer-songwriter Carly Simon says that she feels she learned to write songs because her mother used to have her sing answers to questions. You will help your child associate words with music which may make the art of songwriting a little easier.

This singing-answer technique is fun for you and your child.

It's also very effective to have your child sing a song with you and then stop singing and let the child continue. You can pretend that you can't remember the words and your child will be thrilled because he (or she) does. This technique helps a child not only learn the words to a song, but also the melody. It also builds their confidence.

Another avenue for vocal improvement is singing Folk songs. The lyrics usually are simple. The note progression is simple and the rhythm and melody are simple. Simple enough for children -- *and adults* -- of any age to learn. As I have said, children are great mimics. They mimic TV characters, and their sisters and brothers and they mimic you -- *their parents.*

Children learn by copying. Teach them to sing by copying you and also teach them proper enunciation and breath control at the same time.

Teaching a child breath control sounds too rough? Actually, it's as simple as teaching *"Do Re Me."* Even simpler. Proper breath control is achieved through good posture. If you use good posture and teach your child to sit up or stand straight when they sing, you are teaching them breath control. Your child should be erect, but relaxed when he (or she) sings. Proper posture habits learned now will last a lifetime.

Most children do not start slouching until they reach junior high school. But, if you have taught them proper stance while singing, they will automatically stand erect to sing. They have learned the right way!

One small problem you may encounter with first through third graders is lost teeth. Lisping with lost teeth will soon pass when the permanent teeth replace the little baby teeth.

As you start working with an older child, you will find that the volume of the tape can be increased and the length of the sessions can be lengthened.

Children in the fourth through sixth grades will be able to hit higher notes. They will be able to sing more progressions on the cassette tape of vocal exercises. And they will be able to sing more difficult songs. Folk songs, Negro spirituals and hymns are still good training grounds for young voices.

You might be surprised to learn that both a girl's and a boy's voice will change as she (or he) near her (or his) teens. Girls and boys voices will deepen. At any age, children should be encouraged to sing within their range -- *but their range will start to widen as they get older.*

I didn't know a girl's voice changes. That isn't something that is real noticeable, is it?

A girl's voice usually will only drop a little. She may start singing a lower soprano or a little lower alto.

A boy's voice probably will change from his soprano or alto voice to a tenor, baritone or bass. The process doesn't happen overnight, either. You should continue to encourage your son (or daughter) to vocalize with the cassette tape as his (or her) voice changes. Just reassure him (or her) that the change will only make his (or her) voice better. Your child will develop a deeper, richer range. The process is a natural one of maturation.

A child in his (or her) teens should be able to work with the cassette tape and vocalize by themselves. Encourage half-hour sessions, if possible. Listen to the child's progress. Continue your praise. Always encourage your child to use an easy, free style of singing. No straining! No difficult note patterns until he (or she) is ready. Again, recording the exercises would prove to be invaluable. You could have an older child record the exercises and then listen to them when you have more time.

Stress to your young singer that they should continue good posture; that they should sing with a pure, clean sound; and that they should enunciate vowels and constonants correctly.

Watch for any of the following problems as your child vocalizes:

1. Tight jaw.

2. Lips that are tense and too close together.

3. Singing with a raised head.

4. A head that moves up and down with the notes or pitch.

5. Rounded shoulders.

6. Slumping of the body.

Don't criticize your young singer when you try to correct these bad habits. Teach your child to do the breathing exercises you find in this book if they are having problems with tightness and tenseness. Humming the "Do Re Me" exercise on the cassette tape also will

Tips From The Stars

Pay attention to what your child listens to. Parents should guide a child's music listening! When rock singer Jon Bon Jovi's video, *"Living In Sin,"* had trouble with *MTV's* censors, he said: "If you've got your 5-year-old watching MTV and you're not paying attention to what he's watching, then whose fault is it? Pay more attention to your kid. Put on Sesame Street and have them learn something."

help relax throat muscles. Emphasize proper posture and breathing if there are problems with stance.

You will not be able to steer your young teen away from heavy rock music. Don't try. But continue to encourage them to sing good, simple songs. Sing with them. Play cassette tapes with good music on them when your child has no choice but to listen -- *like in the car when you are driving them to school, the store or on a trip.*

Don't criticize their favorite rock musicians, but don't enourage them -- *at this age* -- to strain their voices. There is no reason for them to try to sing too loudly. Just keep trying to encourage good music listening and appreciation. Tell them if they learn how to sing these good songs, they will be able to sing rock 'n' roll better. Explain to them if they strengthen the right muscles, they will be able to sing better and longer without going hoarse, if they decide to become a rock star. Once your child has mastered the foundation exercises on the cassette tape, you might consider getting my advanced, specialized tape for him (or her). There's a whole tape for the lover of rock music!

Expose your child to as much good singing music as you can get your hands on. Here's a personal example. Ten-year-old Wendy was in the stage where she just wanted to listen to recording star *"Tiffany"* and *"Debbie Gibson."* That's what 12-year-old cousin Jaime listens to. Debbie Gibson and Tiffany are good, but we wanted to broaden Wendy's scope of music.

So on goes a tape by k.d. lang. As I have explained, k.d. is an up-and-coming country-rock singer with a tremendous range and power. She could *"blow"* traditional female country singers off the stage. After seeing her on *"The Tonight Show"* with Johnny Carson, my wife, Lucy, fell in love with k.d.'s voice. So did I.

Well, after Debbie Gibson, you can imagine the looks we got from Wendy and her sister Natalie. Mom and Dad can't possibly expect them to listen to this singer.

But after a few days of k.d. in the car, what did we hear but a chorus of *"Ran and way...ran a way...with a will of its own,"* from Wendy and Natalie and Tiffany from the back seat. That's from k.d.'s tape!

Guess what. The kids love k.d. now! To save face, they pretend they don't like her singing in front of Jaime.

I can't stress enough the importance of exposing your child to as much good singing music as you can get your hands on.

Probably the biggest damage that can be done to a young voice is forcing limitations on it. In range, style and musical preferences. There is no need to force classifications on your child; just as classificiations are unnecessary for adult voices.

The best voices are the most versatile ones. No one has to be locked into any one vocal classification -- *bass, baritone, second tenor, first tenor, alto, soporano.* As you -- *and your child* -- stretch your range up and down the musical scale, you are training your muscles to produce the best, most pleasing sounds. Singing vocal exercises on my cassette tape is the best way to improve your voice and your range. Expose your child to music all his (or her) life and he (or she) will develop his (or her) own love of singing.

One day my daughter may be the next Debbie Gibson or better yet Bernedette Peters. She could make a lot of money with her voice as a recording and concert star. But what I really would like to know is how can I make money with my voice, now? I'm practicing with the vocal tape and I am getting more confidence in myself. I think I'm almost ready to try my hand at entertaining.

Making money with your voice can be as simple as collecting a few dollars going Christmas caroling or more difficult like establishing a career for yourself as a bar or restaurant entertainer. *Or you could really make a bundle as a commercial or jingle singer.* If you can write music and play an instrument, it will help you break into this very lucrative field.

If you are really good and if you are really lucky, you may even establish a career for yourself as a recording artist. *It's not a very easy field to break into, but others with less talent than you, have done it.*

Let's start with something easy first. No one starts at the top. If you decide you want to go Christmas caroling, get together with a group of friends or relatives and practice. Then go around your apartment building, your street or neighborhood and sing your heart out. *Don't be offended if everyone isn't thrilled by your attempt.* You will still be able to make a few dollars and have fun at the same time.

Christmas is a good time to also check with your local shopping mall. If you are good enough, you might be able to convince the mall association to hire you or your caroling group to entertain shoppers while they stroll through the mall area.

Sounds like a pretty good idea. But what if it's not a holiday season. I don't want to wait until Christmas to try to make money. Where can I get my start NOW? I want to be another Willie Nelson and my wife wants to be another Streisand!

This may not have been the way *Barbra Streisand* started, but here's another suggestion for you to get your voice heard by others and make a little money along the way. Check with small restaurants in your area. They may be willing to pay you to sing and entertain diners a few hours each evening.

A small mall restaurant in *St. Petersburg Beach, Florida* does just that.

While walking through the mall recently, I heard the sound of a woman singing old standbyes drifting through the halls. Upon further investigation, I found her singing in a small restaurant. She accompanied herself on a keyboard and was dressed to the hilt. I was impressed! The owner of the small restaurant said that his dinner business had doubled since he hired the singer.

And it wasn't even his idea!

She approached the owner with the idea and he was very resistant to it. He felt that he couldn't afford to pay for an entertainer when business was usually so slow. But she persisted and offered to do the first week for free.

She now makes $75.00 a day for singing three hours a night. And the restaurant owner wouldn't think of doing without her. Not bad for a senior citizen who otherwise would be filling her hours with televison. Now she has a chance to do what she loves and make money at the same time.

Come up with an unusual costume to wear when you sing in front of others. Your audience will be impressed!

Do me a favor and don't tell the restaurant owner. She would be willing to sing for free. It's so much fun!

If you decide to go the restaurant route, you could accompany yourself with a small keyboard, guitar or other instrument if you play; or a cassette tape recorder with your music on it, if you don't.

If you opt for a cassette recorder, make sure you have a good speaker system and a microphone to amplify your voice. Also you could add things like a tambourine or a set of chacha's to add life to your performance.

Other places to check to get jobs include:

1. Your local cable television station;

2. Convalescent homes for the aged in your area;

3. Elementary and junior high schools;

4. Preschool and nursery schools in your city;

5. Local civic organizations like the Kiwanis, Lions and Jaycees;

6. Organizations like Veteran's of Foreign Wars (VFW) and Knights of Columbus. Or even your local YMCA or YWCA.

7. Local government agencies or your city or township recreation department. You may be able to entertain at concerts or festivals or banquets, ethnic festivals or county fairs.

8. Churches who sponsor fairs or festivals as fund raisers.

9. Scout functions.

Any other suggestions? I'm about ready to give my singing abilities a try, but I'm a little bit afraid of this challenge.

You could advertise in your local newspaper and entertain at birthday parties, graduations, weddings and anniversaries. Make sure you specify in your ad the many different types of functions you are capable of entertaining at. A sample ad could read like this:

LET ME ENTERTAIN YOU...or your children
Planning a party? I can help you entertain people of all ages from children to senior citizens. Call me for your next birthday party, graduation, wedding, anniversary or family reunion. Also available for corporation functions, civic groups and for Cub Scouts, Brownie, Boy Scouts and Girl Scout get-togethers. No party too small. Call me and make your job easier.

You may find some groups resistant at first to hire you. You will have to build a name for yourself. Offer to perform for free in the beginning.

Try entertaining at a children's party. Parents often are at a loss what to do with their little darlings. Choose appropriate songs for the children's ages and get the kids involved with the songs.

Parents -- and the children themselves -- will sing your praises if you do a good job. You soon may find yourself turning down jobs because you are too busy.

One local Motown singer goes to a neighborhood pizzeria every Friday night and performs for free. Friday night is a big night for pizza and many parents come in with their children. The singer hands out business cards and gets lots of jobs. The parents see how much the children enjoy the entertainment. *The one free night brings in lots of business.* And the restaurant brags about the entertainment and encourages patrons to hire the singer for birthday parties, anniversaries, weddings and family reunions.

A few hours of work on a Friday night brings in lots of free advertising, lots of business and lots of fun.

Now that sounds like a good suggestion. Free advertising. Even running an ad in my local newspaper wouldn't be too expensive. I would imagine that it is pretty hard for parents to entertain children at a birthday party. And everyone likes to sing. So that would be a fun and easy way to entertain kids. I know some parents who hired a clown and a magician to entertain, but the children weren't too involved in the show. A singing show would be fun. I'm going to run that ad right now and start making some money.

As you start making money, invest some of that cash into better equipment -- update your sound sytem, update your clothing and buy colorful accessories. Even consider buying a lighting system to add to your performance.

Here are some tips to help you with your performances:

1. Choose songs that interest you. You can bring them across better.

2. Choose songs that capture attention and will gain approval of your aududience.

3. Choose songs that are appropriate for the age of your audience. Children's songs for young ones. Oldies for people in their 40's. The old standbys for senior citizens.

4. Put yourself in a good mental state before, during and after your performance.

5. Make sure you get proper rest before an auditon or the actual performance.

6. Dress appropriately for the audience. Wear an unusual outfit if you have one. You don't need expensive costumes, but you should stand out as the entertainment. Get flashier as you gain confidence and make a little money singing.

7. Use the best sound system that you can afford. The only way to capture and keep the attention of your audience is to be heard.

Is there anything I need to know legally to make money with my voice?

Always protect yourself. Stay within the law. Get a separate checking account to keep track of your income and expenses. Some bands may find they have to join a musical trade union in their state to perform at bars and clubs. If you perform on televison, there is another trade union you must join to get paid. Be sure to get the proper licenses to do business (Check with your city or state to see if you need some type of license; usually you don't.) and be sure to declare your income to the *Internal Revenue Service (IRS)* come tax time. You do not want to get into trouble because of unreported income if you are ever audited.

It may even be to your advantage to declare income from your voice; remember you will be able to write off expenses you incur to produce that income. Expenses such as your sound system; costume and make-up; advertising; and maybe even the use of your car or truck. Check with your tax advisor or the *IRS* to see what you can legitimately write off.

Sounds to me like making money with my voice could develop into a full-time job. I certainly will see to it that I take all the advantages allowed by law! But what if I start writing and composing my own songs? How can I make money if I write music?

"I write the words," sang Barry Manilow -- *and got rich.*

Yes...some songwriters do get rich. *You can make money if you write songs in a number of ways:*

1. You could record your song, sell it to a major record label and make money off the record sales, the cassette tape sales, the CD sales, and the sales of the music video inspired by your words. You also could make money touring the country in concert singing your hit or by making the rounds of the television talk shows plugging your music.

2. You could sell your song to a major recording star who would pay you outright for your music and then he would cut the record; and you would make money from radio and television air play. (More on this later.)

3. You could sell your song to a record publisher, sign a contract and get an advance.

4. You can make money on print royalties as the writer. These are royalties for the sale of the printed copies (sheet music) of your composition. Royalties is the term used in the music business for compensation you receive for granting someone the right to use your work.

5. You can make money from mechanical and performance rights. (An explanation of this later on, keep reading.).

6. You can make money from foreign royalties. (I've got a little story to tell you about foreign royalties a little later on. You should get a kick out of it!

If you are a songwriter, what are your chances of making it big? I hope I don't discourage you when I say slim. If you are discouraged, you're trying to get in the wrong business. *If you are a dedicated songwriter, you won't be discouraged, will you?* You'll just keep writing and keep hoping and sending your demo (demonstration) tapes to song publishers and record companies.

And please don't get sucked into the ads that solicit poems and songs. The companies usually are just out to get money from you. They will sell you a list of song publishers or record companies for a fee. You could get the same list with a little legwork. Song producers and record companies don't have to advertise, they are approached with good material hundreds of times a week in person or through demo tapes in the mail.

I'm so glad you mentioned those little classified ads. You see them all over. So the ads aren't placed by anyone in the business that actually can get a song off the ground. That's good to know. Poets and songwriters should read this and save their money!

Why do I paint such a bleak picture for songwriters? *Simple.* Many song publishers can't find outlets for the material they already have. And many of the biggest recording artists today, write their own songs. Recording artists are becoming more and more self-contained. They write their own material and record at their own studios. Singers like Lionel Richie, Neil Diamond, Debbie Gibson, Michael Jackson and Prince usually write their own material. So do the heavy metal bands.

But there is hope if you write genuinely great songs and you're lucky. Some big recording artists -- who do not have the talent to write and are at a real disadvantage in the very competitive music business today -- look for good original material written by others to record.

If you write songs, you may be looking for an outlet for your talents. It's a rough business, only the best will survive and thrive! But if you have talent, commitment and perserverance, you may see your name or at least your song *"up in lights."* So...where to begin?

First, study this book from cover to cover and keep it as a reference. (Among other things, you'll need to refer to the section on copyright many times in the future if you plan to write songs.) Practice with the cassette tape, *"How To Sing Great."* A songwriter who can perform his own work has an edge over a writer who is not able to sing. The reason? The least expensive way to make a demo (demonstration) tape to send to a song publisher or record company is to do it yourself.

Then you have to decide if you want to be a songwriter or a singer/songwriter. If you want to be a songwriter and have others perform your work you will want to contact song publishers and record companies who may be able to sell your song to a name recording artist. If you want to be a singer/songwriter (sing your own material on a record) you probably will have to do the same work as a songwriter does to get noticed. But you will have to have an especially unusual sound or some connections to make it!

I could print a list of publishers for you to contact, but the list probably would be outdated before this book gets to the printers. If you don't want to travel to the music centers -- Los Angeles, CA; New York, NY; or Nashville, TN -- your best bet is to go to your local record store and find a recording star or group that sings material similar to your songs.

Check the record jacket, or cassette tape to see if the group or individual takes total writing credits for the songs on the tape or album. If they don't, they probably don't write their own material, and there is a chance they might like your songs. In making record deals, performers sometimes take partial writing credits -- *even though they have not written a song. To make the recording artist and the writer feel better, sometimes the star will change a word or two in the composition.* That is one of the concessions you may have to make as a songwriter.

You do the work, but split the glory and the money with the artist. May not sound fair, but -- *in some cases* -- if you are not willing to split writing royalties, you just won't be recorded!

Well...now back to your local record store, write down the name and address of the record company. Go home, call telephone information and try to get the phone number for the song publisher or record company listed on the album jacket or cassette tape.

When you call, explain to the receptionist that you want to send a demo tape and find out who you should address it to. If you get a chance, talk with the person who will be listening to your tape.

Record the demo tape (a good-quality cassette tape is fine), write a cover letter and mail the material personally addressed. Don't send the tape certified. There's a good chance no one will sign for it and it will be returned to you. You'll just waste the postage and certified fee. *Publishers and record companies often won't sign for a package because of a fear of a copyright infringment suit.*

If you do not address your demo tape to the right person, you may find it returned to you unopened. Some record publishers and record companies will not listen to unsoliciated material. It will be returned to you marked *"Return To Sender."*

I've got an idea. Couldn't a prospective songwriter check his local directory to see if there are any song publishers or record companies in his area?

Yes, that's a good idea. If you live in or near a big city you may find a record company listed in the local directory. If you do not live near a large metropolitan area, you probably won't have any luck in your search.

Detroit used to be a music center when Motown recording company recorded in their studio on Grand Blvd. -- *Hitsville, U.S.A.* There still are a number of hit songs recorded in and around the Detroit area today. Bob Seger occasionally records at Ambience -- a recording studio in Farmington Hills, a Detroit suburb. And many others stars record at Richard Becker's *PAC-3* recording studio in Dearborn, another Detroit suburb.

If you do have the means to travel to New York, Los Angeles or Nashville, bring your material on cassette tapes and start knocking on doors.

You'll find listings of song publishers and record companies in local phone books. Make sure you don't waste your time by presenting the wrong material to the companies. Find country-oriented song publishers for country songs. Seek out Jazz people, if you write Jazz. Find the rock publishers and recording companies if you are into rock 'n' roll, etc.

You also should look into making contact with business managers and attorney's who have recording artists and writers as clients. Publishers will listen to material on cassette tape submitted to them by these professionals.

You will boost your chances of becoming a success in the record business if you can write your own songs and sing them. If you tire of seeing the rejection notices for your songwriting efforts from publishers and record companies, you could check out the local bar bands in your city. Ask if they would do your material. Or join an established band, or form your own.

If you find that your material goes over real well with the audience, you might consider professionally recording your material. Then you could submit the finished work to record companies. If they don't accept your efforts as a songwriter, they may as a recording artist.

A demo for a songwriter can be simple -- *a piano and voice on cassette tape.* Present at least four to six songs on the cassette; with your best song first.

A demo for a record company you hope will sign you to a record contract, has to be polished. Book time at a 16-track or 24-track professional recording studio and be prepared to do your best.

One great song isn't enough, either. Keep writing.

A record company doesn't want to hear just one song. They have learned from experience that it is very expensive to get a record off the ground with a new singer or group. They will not outlay the hundreds of thousands of dollars necessary to produce and promote your song, if they do not feel you have back-up material in the wings.

What if I start writing and composing my own songs? How can I get protection?

You'll probably be surprised to know that just the act of writing automatically gets you copyright protection. The instant you create an original song, you are protected under *the Copyright Act of 1979 (title 17 of the United States Code).*

It is not necessary to register your copyright with the government, but you do gain certain advantages in the enforcement of your rights, if you do the proper paperwork.

I do advise you to register your work; it's not that expensive and the paperwork isn't that complicated. Contact the *Copyright Office, Library of Congress, Washington, D.C. 20559.* You could call (202) 287-8700, the *Copyright Public Information Office,* for forms and additional information about laws. Or if you need application forms for registration of a claim to copyright, you may call (202) 287-9100 at any time, day or night, to leave your request on a recorded message on the Forms HOTLINE. To use the HOTLINE you must know the application form you need. Use *Form PA* for published and unpublished works prepared for the purpose of being performed directly before an audience. *Form SR* is for sound recordings.

If you write songs you will want to join one of the performing rights organizations. This is another way songwriters get paid. You will get checks for radio air play and if others perform your songs.

The organizations are the *American Society of Composers, Authors & Publishers (ASCAP) and Broadcast Music, Inc. (BMI). ASCAP is* at One Lincoln Plaza, New York, NY 10023. You could call the New York office at (212) 595-3050. Or check with your local telephone directory to see if *ASCAP* has a local office in your city. BMI is at 320 West 47th Street, New York, NY 10019. You could call the New York office at (212) 586-2000.

If you sell a hit song -- *or even a mediocre hit that gets air play* --you will be getting checks from the organization you have joined. I still get quarterly check for air play on many of my records. Some of the records are over 20 years old!

If you write songs it's not a bad idea to start your own publishing company. You will be able to make more money that way. Both songwriters and publishers make money when songs are recorded and played. When you sell a song to a publisher they own the copyright. Check with your local state or county to find out how to start your own publishing company. It usually is as simple as registering a company name (doing business as) with your county. Then you will be able to negotiate a better deal with a publisher who picks up your song; you will split publishing royalties with them.

You also will want to get acquainted with another organization. The *Harry Fox Agency,* is a mechanical rights society and syncronization licensing agency operated by the *National Music Publishers's Association. The agency deals with the licensing of actual records and records used in connection with motion pictures, commercial, television films and video tapes. It acts as a watchdog for song publishers. You can contact the agency by calling (212) 370-5330.*

You mentioned something about a foreign royalty story. What was that all about?

Oh...Yes. In my early teens I wrote and recorded a rock song called *"Hold Me."* It never went big in the United States, but boy did it go over in Japan. A Japanese group heard it, had it translated, and recorded the foreign version. To my big surprise *"Hold Me"* was a hit and I received writing royalty checks to boot!

Songwriting can be fun and rewarding.

If you want to be a songwriter or a singer/songwriter you are going to have to do a lot of work. You are going to have to learn the music business. My purpose here isn't to write a book about how to write songs or how to get those songs recorded. My purpose here is to give you a little overview on the recording business as another avenue or market for your singing talents.

If you really are interested in getting more information about songwriting and recording, there are many very good resource books on the market written by experts. You'll find a list of those book in the back of this book.

And be sure to get a subscription to one of the music trade publications, *"Cash Box"* or *"Billboard Magazine."* They will be invaluable. Following I have included the phone numbers and addresses of these publications and a few others that may be helpful to you in your quest for stardom and big bucks:

Cash Box Publications -- 1-212-586-2640
157 West 57th ST, Suite 1402, New York, NY 10019

Billboard Magazine -- 1-212-764-7300
1 Astor Plaza, New York, NY 10036

Billboard Directory -- 1-201-363-5679
1695 Oak ST., Lakewood, N.J. 08701

Songwriter's Resources -- 1-213-463-7178
National Academy of Songwriters (NAS)
6381 Hollywood Blvd., Suite 780
Hollywood, CA 90028

Just a few words about *NAS.* According to a spokesman the academy is a non-profit membership organization dedicated to educating, assisting and protecting songwriters, in addition to fostering the art of composition. The academy serves as an information clearinghouse on the art, craft and business of songwriting, music publishing and the record industry. *NAS* holds song seminars and even evaluates songs through the mail.

Members of the organization receive detailed song critiques by music industry professionals. New songwriters may find this service an invaluable way to improve their songs. Other services include discounted legal services; and if you have had at least one song commercially released you will be able to take advantage of the organizations *"Pro"* services. With these services you will be able to pitch your songs to select producers and artists each month through the mail or in person at the *NAS* office.

You're in good company if you join *NAS,* the spokesman continued. The great Lamont Dozier is involved; patrons include Paul Simon, Lionel Richie, *BAM Magazine* and *Black Music Association.* Members include Burt Bacharach, Phil Collins, Jimmy Webb, Boz Scaggs, Barry Mann, Carole King and Kenny Loggins -- *just to name a few.*

A real exciting opportunity for songwriters are song contests. *Billboard Magazine* has been sponsoring a *Song Contest* for the past few years. In the contest *Billboard* is searching for new creative songwriting talent. The magazine gives away over $100,000 in cash and prizes. Song categories include Rock, Pop, Country, Jazz, Latin, Gospel and Rhythm & Blues. In the past, the winning Country and Rhythm & Blues songs were recorded by Capitol Records. The Latin winners were recorded by EMI Latin and the Jazz winners were recorded by Blue Note recording company. To find out about the contest write to *Billboard Song Contest,* P. O. Box 35346, Tulsa, OK 74153-0346. Or check *Billboard Magazine* for details.

One last reminder if you are sending your cassette tape away for a song contest, to a song publisher or to a record company: Don't forget to put your name, address and telephone number on the cassette and cassette case. If your letter or contest application are lost in a paper shuffle, at least your tape will be identified.

I wish you luck! The songwriting/record business is a hard nut to crack; but the rewards -- in hard cash, prestige and self-esteem --are phenomenal!

This really has nothing to do with songwriting, but I was wondering why you picked the songs you did at the end of the cassette tape?

Actually it has a lot to do with songwriting. There are a number of reasons I decided on singing those songs. First, they were songs most people would recognize. Second, the songs teach your voice to be versatile because of the note progressions and the difficult rhythm patters on some of the numbers, especially the last song. Third, the songs I picked demonstrate how one singer can change song styles and tempos and sing in different ranges.

Throughout the tape I have demonstrated how it is not necessary to force yourself into one range or into one style. And fourth, the songs are in *Public Domain* and I can record them without infringing on anyone's copyright.

If you decide to perform songs that were written by other people, you have to be sure that you do not infringe on copyright laws. Either you have to get permission to record the songs from the copyright owner, or you have to get a performance license from *ASCAP* or *BMI,* or you have to write the songs yourself; or you have to be sure the songs are in *Public Domain.*

Some copywritten songs are in *Public Domain* and can be performed without a license, according to an *ASCAP* spokesman.

Public domain (PD) works do not enjoy copyright protection for a number of possible reasons:

1. They were created before copyright protection was available.

2. The copyright may have expired.

3. Under the old copyright law, the copyright owner may have failed to observe a formality and lost his right to protection.

Some songs which are at least 75 years old, are in public domain because the original copyright and any extensions have expired.

Some such songs are *"After The Ball"* by Charles K. Harris (1892); *"Sidewalks of New York"* by James W. Blake and Charles B. Lawlor (1894); *"My Wild Irish Rose"* by Chauncey Olcott (1899) and *"Give My Regards To Broadway"* by George M. Cohan (1904).

Old folk songs also are in *Public Domain.* They belong to no one person; but to everyone. *"London Bridges"* is an example of one such song.

The definitive expert on what is or is not in Public Domain is the Copyright Office in Washington, D.C. If you decide to record check carefully on the copyright status of any song you want to sing to make sure that you are not infringing on anyone's rights. You do have to be careful that you pick the original version of a song in public domain. *Songs in public domain can be re-copywritten with a new arrangement.* If you perform the new arrangement, you would be infringing on the newer copyright.

Don't be fearful of performing copywritten songs; just be safe. Authors created the works and deserve to be paid by others using their creations. *Wouldn't you want to be compensated if you wrote a song? This is another one of the ways songwriters make money!*

I may try songwriting, but in the mean time I still want to work to develop that great voice. I do plan on getting one of your advanced exercise tapes on country music for myself, on rock for my daughter and on pop for my wife. They sound like fun and I am sure they will be as rewarding as the cassette tape that came with this package, but how do I go about finding a vocal coach or instructor if I decide my daughter needs more training?

Unfortunately there is a real need for good vocal instructors. There aren't many teachers trained in voice and the good ones have more students than they can handle. That's why this program was created. There is a real void in good material on *How To Sing!*

If you are trying to find a vocal instructor, the first place -- *of course* -- is the friendly *"yellow pages"* as you *"let your fingers do the walking."*

If you live in or near a big city you probably will have more luck in locating an instructor. If you live in or near a college town you also may find an instructor listed in the phone directory. Or you could check with the local college's music department to see if any of the professors give private lessons.

If you live in or near New York City, NY or Los Angeles, CA you probably won't have any trouble locating an instructor.

You are never too young or too old to learn to sing. This vocal improvement program will teach you most everything you need to know to develop a great voice. Or to help your child maximize his (or her) vocal potential!

If you live in a rural area or a small town or city, you may have no luck in your search for a teacher. You could check with instructors who give lessons on musical instruments to see if they know any vocal teachers.

Or you could check with your local church to see if the organist or choir director gives lessons. Or your local school, to see if a music teacher offers private sessions.

If you are lucky enough to find someone who says they will be willing to give you lessons; you may not be that lucky after all.

Don't feel so lucky to have found a teacher, that you blindly pay for the lessons. You probably will be paying upwards of $10.00 in a small town or $15.00 in a larger city for a half-hour vocal session.

Don't feel intimidated by the term "vocal" instructor. And don't be intimidated by the person. Find out the individual's qualifications. Know what you are paying for!

To make your job easier, I have prepared a list of questions for you to ask the teacher. After the list, I'll explain why these questions are important. Here are a few of the questions you should ask the teacher:

1. How much do you charge?

2. How long have you been teaching voice?

3. What are your qualifications to teach voice?

4. What other credentials do you have?

5. Did you sing professionally?

6. Do you teach technique?

7. Are you primarily a voice coach?

8. Do you treat vocal instructions as a science?

9. Do you play the piano to accompany your students during lessons?

10. Do you have someone else play the piano during lessons?

11. How do you conduct a vocal session?

12. What are your musical preferences?

13. Are there any books I am going to have to buy? Or are there any other supplies I will need to take lessons?

14. Are you or were you ever a professional singer?

15. Do you have any famous students? Who are they?

16. Will you give me the telephone number of at least four of your students so that I can call them?

OK. I ask the questions. I get the answers. How do I evaluate what the teacher tells me?

The first question -- *How much do you charge?* -- probably isn't the most important question. But the answer could save you and the teacher valuable time.

If the teacher wants more than you can afford, simply thank her (or him) and say goodbye. You don't have to waste time asking the other questions.

You also could end the conversation early, if the teacher can't really communicate with you. Do you understand what the teacher is telling you? Is he (or she) trying to talk above you? Is he (or she) trying to impress you with their knowledge of the human anatomy (talking about the larynx, trachea, soft palate, esophagus, epiglottis). Or throwing things like *"chest voice," "head voice," "singing from the diaphragm"* or *"singing with more support"* at you.

If the teacher can't communicate with you over the telephone, you'll have a problem with the lessons. If the teacher tries to impress you with big words or confusing terms, he (or she) is setting himself (herself) up as musically superior. And the superior-inferior relationship will permeate your lessons.

Does he (or she) tell you that you have to take an instrumental lesson, too. A piano lesson and the vocal lesson together. A violin lesson and a vocal lesson.

Stay way from this teacher for sure.

You don't have to learn a musical instrument, nor do you have to read music, to be able to sing great. (Of course, it doesn't hurt if you can read music, but it is not a prerequisite to a good voice.)

That reminds me of a little story. My sister-in-law wanted to find a vocal instructor for her daughter, Sheri. Sheri has a very nice singing voice. She sings along with recording artists Tiffany and Debbie Gibson all the time. She sings in school talent shows and wins! Well, back to the story. They live in a rural, lake area and there were no vocal instructors to be found.

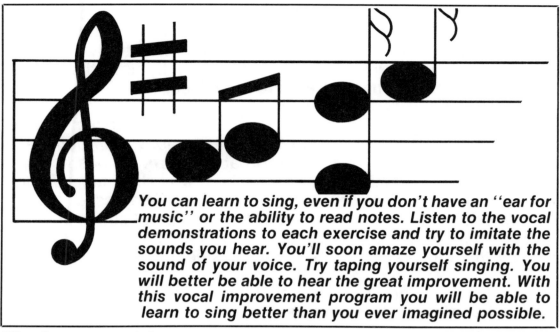

You can learn to sing, even if you don't have an "ear for music" or the ability to read notes. Listen to the vocal demonstrations to each exercise and try to imitate the sounds you hear. You'll soon amaze yourself with the sound of your voice. Try taping yourself singing. You will better be able to hear the great improvement. With this vocal improvement program you will be able to learn to sing better than you ever imagined possible.

The instrumental music teacher said he would love to throw in vocal instructions for Sheri if she took piano lessons. It didn't matter that they didn't have a piano. He could sell them one!

Unfortunately, I hear the same story all the time. You must find an instructor who is willing and qualified to teach voice.

And now on to the importance of some of the other questions. There is a difference between a *"vocal coach"* and *"a voice technique teacher."* *A vocal coach is just that. A coach to cheer you on and show you what to sing. A technique teacher can show you how to sing it.*

Don't be impressed or confused if the teacher says they teach the "scientific" approach to singing. That doesn't mean much. The *"scientific"* approach just means the teacher is concerned about how your throat produces the sounds. They'll be the ones talking about the larynx, trachea, etc.

He (or she) should be giving you exercises (such as the exercises on my cassette tape) and listening to make sure you hit the notes properly and make the correct sounds. He (or she) should be able to know what aspects of your voice needs work and give you the proper exercises to do the job.

Be very wary of a *"vocal teacher"* who plays the piano for you, listens to you sing and gives you a series of songs to learn. You don't need a teacher to make you learn the words to a song. You can do that on your own. As you have learned by now, the core of any voice improvement program are exercises.

My cousin's daughter, Jennifer -- who lives in Minnesota -- takes singing lessons. He told me he was really happy with Jennifer's teacher. The teacher was a former Broadway star. He has her sing an "E" exercise and then has her sing Broadway show tunes for the rest of the half-hour session. Boy, is my cousin impressed. I didn't want to criticize the Broadway star's methods, but I suggested that he ask for more exercises. My cousin was aghast. He didn't take Jennifer there to learn exercises...he takes her there to learn songs!

As I have said before, the general public has a real misconception about what vocal instructions are!

It's OK if a vocal instructor plays the piano for you as you sing exercises; but an instructor who utilizes another pianist will be better (and more expensive). He (or she) will be listening to you exclusively; not worring about the next note he (or she) has to hit on the piano.

It also doesn't matter if the teacher has had famous students, although it is fun to impress others by saying *"My vocal instructor worked with Stevie Wonder and Frankie Valli and Jimmy Rogers and Lionel Richie."* At least your friends will be impressed!

Since a good instructor teaches with vocal exercises, it doesn't matter what their musical preferences are. But, on occasion, you may want to sing specific songs for your teacher if you are having a problem with them. If you love country music and your teacher loves jazz; you may not get an accurate critical appraisal.

Also it doesn't matter if your vocal instructor ever sang professionally. The instructor should be able to sing, though. Have the instructor sing for you. If he (or she) has a good voice you will feel better about taking lessons from that person.

And normally you shouldn't have to buy any books or manuels to take lessons. You already know the basics of the body anatomy as it relates to singing. This book teaches you most everything you need to know about the mechanics of singing. And you really have a head start on voice improvement if you have been doing your breathing and vocal exercises.

The only supplies you should need is a cassette tape recorder to record your lessons for practice later.

If the teacher does give you the telephone numbers of some of her students, be sure to call them and ask the intelligent questions. Don't ask them if they like the teacher. Of course they do. You wouldn't have been given their telephone number if they didn't.

Ask them, instead, how the lessons are conducted. Find out about the type of exercises they sing. Find out how long they have taken lessons and if they have had any other instructors. Find out if the teacher helped them with any specific voice problems and what they were.

It isn't easy to find a good vocal instructor. If you do decide to take lessons, try it for a couple of weeks. If you don't feel you are improving don't waste any more money. Just keep doing your vocal exercises on the cassette tape. You will continue to see improvement if you do!

You have absolutely amazed me. I wasn't sure what I was getting when I bought this vocal improvement program. I made a lot of incorrect assumptions. I assumed the cassette tape, ''How To Sing Great,'' would include a whole bunch of songs for me to learn to sing. I assumed I would get nothing out of this book, ''You Can Sing Great -- At Any Age.'' I did not think a book would help me learn how to sing.

I'm glad I was wrong. You have accomplished all that you promised...AND MORE.

You gave me the background ammunition I need to help develop my voice into a great one. *The tape and book are filled with tips and suggestions accumulated over the past few decades from vocal teachers and professional entertainers across the United States. Many are professional secrets carefully guarded by the stars! Secrets that would take me a life-time of performing to unveil.*

The cassette tape, *"How To Sing Great,"* gave me the foundation I needed to improve my voice. It includes exercises which are designed to work on specific aspects of my voice. It includes some fun songs to sing. And it shows me *how to sing Pop or Contemorary, Folk, Blues, Country, Rock, Jazz, Religious, Gospel, Patriotic and Show Tunes. The book even showed me how to Rap.*

I did my homework and am practicing the vocal exercises. I have:

1. Stretched my vocal range both octaves higher and octaves lower.
2. Enhanced my vocal tones.
3. Strengthened my voice dramatically.
4. I have learned to stay in perfect key with the music.
5. I have learned to follow many difficult rhythm patterns.
6. I have learned breath control as I sing.
7. I have learned to sing falsetto effectively.
8. I have learned to yodel.
9. I have learned to "Scat.".
10. I have learned to harmonize with other voices.
11. And I have learned so many more things to help me sing better than I ever imagined possible.

I have learned what it takes to become the lead singer of a band. And I have learned ways that I never imagined to capture the attention of MY audience.

"You Can Sing Great -- At Any Age -- How To Sing Great," the complete vocal improvement program, did teach me how to sing better than I ever dreamed possible. It has given me the confidence I need to sing in front of other people. It did teach me the skills I need to make my voice great. And it did teach me the tricks of the trade to help me present my song *LIKE A PRO!*

I also have learned how to create and perfect my own singing style; and make a mediocre song sound great or a great song sound phenomenal!

I have learned where and how to begin if I want to try to make money with my voice. And as an added bonus, I have learned how to protect the songs I write from pilfergers; how to contact record producers and recording companies; how to decide which recording artists are best suited for my song, and so very much more!

Best of all I have learned how to teach my child how to sing and I also have learned how to find a vocal instructor if I decide to continue her training. You came across, as you promised, in this vocal improvement program and I now know how to maximize my child's vocal potential.

This program was for me...and my wife...and my child...and my grandchild -- if I had one. Thank you.

Unfortunately, our time has come to an end. It's been my pleasure to present to YOU almost everything YOU need to know to develop YOUR voice and become a great singer. I just don't know how to stress enough the importance of doing the vocal exercises *--especially the foundation exercises. The SMART person (adult, teen...particular the up-and-coming rock hopeful...or child) will follow this program and develop his (or) her voice to the fullest.*

I can't give YOU a great voice on a silver platter. It's up to YOU. YOU can not maximize YOUR singing potential or that of a loved one if YOU do not take the time to do these exercises which are designed to perfect another skill towards making:

YOUR VOICE GREAT!

YOU may also want to look into one of my specialized tapes as a means of continuing YOUR progress in Rock, Pop, Jazz, Rhythm & Blues, Gospel and Religious, Country and Westen, Folk, Popular or Calypso music. And believe me, the children's sing-a-long is a real winner. YOUR child -- *three to 12* -- will love it. My children do!

Just in closing, I have a few more quick *Thank YOU's:*

To the staff at *ASCAP, BMI, Harry Fox Agency, The National Association Of Teachers Of Singing,* and the *Copyright Office* for all their advice. To all the vocal instructors and coaches and professional entertainers who have honored me with their wisdom over all my years of research; to my editor, and to Kimberly and Wendy for singing with me on the cassette tape.

Dear Reader, I've given YOU the ammunition in this book and on the cassette tape that YOU need to develop a great singing voice. THE SKY'S THE LIMIT! One day YOU will be the SINGING STAR or the COUNTRY or ROCK GROUP or the SONGWRITER others will want to emulate.

Wendy

Kimberly

Bibliography

Allen, Bob, *"Waylon & Willie: The Full Story In Words And Pictures Of Waylon Jennings & Willie Nelson,"* Quick Fox, New York, 1979.

"ASCAP Hit Songs," American Society Of Composers And Publishers, New York, NY, 1980.

Bacon, Tony, *"Rock Hardware,"* Crown Publishers, New York, NY, 1981.

Baer, Hermanus, *"Establishing A Current Basic Technique For Singing,"* The National Association of Teachers of Singing, *Bulletin 28,* 1972.

Belz, Carl, *"The Story of Rock,"* Oxford University Press, New York, NY, 1969.

Brodnitz, Friedricks, *"Keep Your Voice Healthy"* C. C. Thomas, *Springfield, IL,* 1973.

Brown, Oren, *"Causes Of Voice Strain In Singing"* The National Association of Teachers of Singing, *Bulletin 15,* 1958.

Burgin, John Carroll, *"Teaching Singing,"* Scarecrow Press, Inc., *Metuchen, NJ,* 1973.

Busnar, Gene, *"Super Stars Of Rock: Their Lives and Their Music,"* Julian Messner, New York, 1980.

Campbell, E. And J. Moran, *"The Respiratory Muscles And The Mechanics Of Breathing,"* The Yearbook Medical Publishers, Inc., *Chicago, IL,* 1958.

Chapple, Steve and Reebee Garofalo, *"Rock 'N' Roll Is Here To Pay,"* Nelson-Hall, Inc., Chicago, IL, 1977.

Christy, Van A. *"Expressive Singing"* (3rd Edition), William C. Brown And Co., *Dubuque, IA,* 1974.

Coker, Jerry, *"Listening To Jazz,"* Prentice-Hall, Inc., *Englewood Cliffs, NJ,* 1978.

Cooper, Morton, *"Modern Techniques Of Vocal Rehabilitation,"* Charles C. Thomas, *Springfield, IL,* 1973.

David, Andrew, *"Country Music Stars: People At The Top Of The Charts,"* Domus Books, Northbrook, IL, 1980.

Dwyer, Edward J. *"Concepts Of Breathing For Singing,"* The National Association Of Teachers Of Singing, *Bulletin 24,* 1967.

Eggar, Robin, *"Not Fade Away,"* US, Straight Arrow Publishers, Inc., New York, NY, 1989.

Escott, Colin And Hawkins, *"Sun Records,"* Music Sales, New York, NY, 1980.

Fields, Victor A., *"Training The Singing Voice,"* King's Crown Press, *New York, NY,* 1947.

Fisher, Hilda B., *"Improving Voice And Articulation,"* (2nd Edition), Houghton Mifflin Co., *Boston, MA,* 1975.

Garcia, Manuel, II, *"The Voice And Its Disorders"* (3rd Edition), J. B. Lippincott Co., *Philadelphia, PA,* 1972.

Goldman, Albert, *"Elvis,"* McGraw Hill Book Company, New York, NY, 1981.

Goldrosen, John, *"Buddy Holly: His Life And Music,"* Popular Press, Bowling Green, 1975.

Groia, Philips, *"They All Sang On The Corner,"* Edmond Publishing Co., New York, NY, 1973.

Heilbert, Tony, "The Gospel Sound: Good News And Bad Times," Simon And Schuster, New York, NY, 1971.

Hines, Jerome, "Great Singers On Great Singing," Doubleday And Co., Garden City, NY, 1982.

Hirshey, Gerri, "Nowhere To Run: The Story Of Soul Music," Penguin Books, NY, 1985.

Hopkins, Jerry, "Elvis," Simon And Schuster, New York, NY, 1971.

Hopkins, Jerry, "The Rock Story," Signet Books, New York, NY, 1970.

Hubbard, Donald J., And Carol Kaleraloha, "The Role Of Rock," Prentice-Hall, Inc., Englewood Cliffs, NJ, 1983.

Husler, Frederick, And Yoonne Rodd-Marling, "Singing, The Physical Nature Of The Vocal Organ," October House, New York, NY, 1965.

Ingram, Madeline D., And William C. Rice, "Vocal Techniques For Children And Youth," Abingdon Press, New York, NY, 1962.

Jackson, Richard; Selected And Introduction Notes By: Steven Collins Foster, "Steven Foster Song Book," Dover Publications, New York, NY, 1974.

Kawashima, Dale, "Singers Must Take Care Of Speaking Voice, Doctor Says," "Cash Box," Bulletin 38, 1979.

Leeder, Joseph A., And William S. Haynie, "Music Education In The High School," Prentice-Hall, Inc., Englewood Cliffs, 1958.

Livingston, Robert Allen, "Music Industry And Law Reference Book," La Costa Music Business Consultants, Cardiff By The Sea, CA, 1981.

Marsh, David, "Paul Simon," Music Sales, New York, NY, 1978.

Miller, Douglas, and Marion Nowak, "The Fifties," Doubleday, 1975.

"Mix, The Recording Industry Magazine" NBB-Acquisitons, Inc., Emeryville, CA, 1987-1989.

Oermann, Robert K., With Douglas B. Green, "The Listeners Guide To Country Music," Facts On File, A Quanto Book, New York, NY, 1983.

"Occupational Outlook Handbook," United States Department of Labor, Bureau of Labor Statistics, Washington, DC., 1983.

Paul, Ouida Fay, "Working With Singing Problems Of Adults," Choral Journal, Bulletin 7, May-June, 1967.

Proctor, Donald F., "The Physiological Basis Of Voice Training," Annals Of The New York Academy Of Sciences, Bulletin 155, 1968.

Rice, William, "Basic Principles Of Singing," Abingdon Press, Nashville, TN, 1961.

Rosewall, Richard, "Handbook Of Singing," Summy-Birchard Co., Evanston, IL, 1961.

Rachlin, Harvey, "The Songwriter's And Musician's Guide To Make Great Demos," Writer's Digest Books, Cinncinnati, OH, 1988.

Seeger, Peggy, "Folk Songs Of Peggy Seeger," Oak Publications, New York, NY, 1964.

Sharp, Cecil J., Editor, "One Hundred English Folk Songs," Dover Publications, New York, NY, 1916.

Silverman, Jerry, "Folk Blues," The MacMillan Co., New York, NY, 1958.

Stambler, Irwin, and Grelun Landon, "Encyclopedia Of Folk, Country, And Western Music," St. Martin's Press, New York, NY, 1983.

Sundberg, Johan, "The Accoustics Of The Singing Voice," Scientific American, 1977.

"Taber's Cyclopedic Medical Dictionary," F. A. Davis Co., Philadelphia, PA, 1981.

Thompson, Roy, Fred Dellar and Doublas B. Green, *"The Illustrated Encyclopedia Of Country Music,"* Harmony/Salamander, New York, NY, 1977.

"The Merck Manuel Of Diagnosis And Therapy, (15th Edition), Merck, Sharp, And Dohme Research Laboratories, 1987.

"Up On The Roof" and *"Takes A Backseat," People Weekly,* Time Inc. Magazines, New York, NY, 1989.

Vennard, William, *"Developing Voices,"* Carl Fischer, Inc., *New York, NY,* 1973.

Vennard, William, *"Chest, Head, And Falsetto,"* The National Association of Teachers of Singing, *Bulletin 27,* 1970.

"Vocal Suicide In Singers," The National Association of Teachers of Singing, *Bulletin 26,* 1970, pgs. 7-10, 31.

Warner, James A., *"Songs That Made America,"* Grossman Publishers, *New York, NY* 1972.

"Webster's Music Dictionary," Compiled By: M. H. Guandala, Ottenheimer Publishers, Inc., 1953.

Whitall, Susan, *"Way-Out West: Singer k.d. lang Can't Be Lassoed Into Any Category,"* The Detroit News, Detroit, MI, 1989.

Whitlock, Weldon, "Profiles In Vocal Pedagogy," Clifton Press, *Ann Arbor, MI,* 1975.

Williams, George, *"The Songwriters Demo Manual And Success Guide,"* Music Business Books, *Riverside, CA,* 1984.

Williams Roger, *"Sing A Sad Song: The Life Of Hank Williams,"* Ballantine, New York, NY, 1973.

"Willie Nelson Family Album" Lana Nelson Fowler, H. M. Poirot and Co., Amarillo, TX., 1980.

Woodward, Bob, *"Wired: The Short Life and Fast Times Of John Belushi,"* Simon And Schuster, New York, NY, 1984.

INDEX

In Alphabetical Order -- For Convenience Names Are in Alphabetical Order By First Name

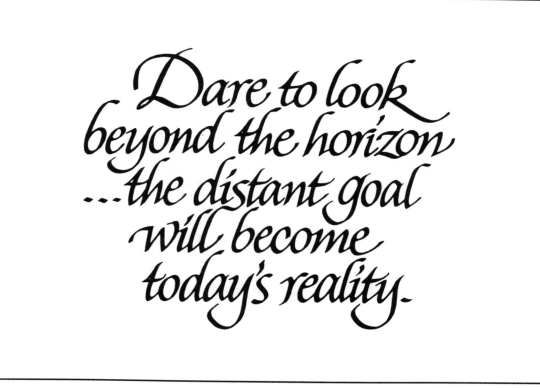

Advanced Singing Programs:
Learn To Specialize In YOUR Favorite Style!

Individual Cassette Tapes Show YOU The Way!

(SPECIAL) Now that YOU have learned the basics, YOU can advance YOUR vocal skills in any one (or all -- a separate tape for each catagory) of the following singing styles:

* **Rock 'N' Roll**

* **Country & Western** *(Also Has Advanced Yodelling)*

* **Rhythm And Blues**
* **Gospel And Religious**
* **Folk**

* **Jazz** *(Also Has Improvisation & Advanced Scat)*
* **Calypso Or Reggae**
* **Pop Or Contemporary**

* *There also is a special SING-A-LONG tape for children three to 12.*
* *Because of all the recent requests, an advance tape on HARMONY.*

YOU will learn to excel beyond YOUR wildest dreams and actually become a SPECIALIST in any one or more of the above styles. Each of the specialties is available on cassette tape. *YOU will learn most everything YOU need to know to sing like a PRO in each field.* Among other things, YOU will:

* Learn complicated beat patterns.
* Enhance YOUR vocal tones.
* Powerfully strengthen voice.
* Make good songs sound marvelous.

* Develop YOUR singing potential.
* Continue mastering YOUR style.
* Make mediocre songs sound great.
* Make your voice sound phenominal.

These are advanced cassette programs developed specifically to enrich YOUR singing ability. *YOU will find each and every one fun and rewarding.* And because they are on cassette tapes, YOU will have the luxury of enjoying them in the privacy of YOUR own home or car. YOU will be saving hundreds of dollars on vocal lessons and gaining a wealth of information on singing.

The children's SING-A-LONG is specially geared for the busy parents who does not have a lot of time to work on a child's singing. It includes fun songs, sung by children and adults, which are easy for a youngster to learn with/or without supervision.

YOU have gotten just a taste of harmony on *"How To Sing Great."* The interest in harmony by both adults and young adults who love rock, pop and contemporary music has skyrocketed. A tape devoted exclusively to harmony can take YOU so much further in mastering this beautiful skill!

YOU have come a long way towards YOUR great, new voice with the basic vocal tape, *"How To Sing Great."* **YOU won't want to stop with the basics. Order one or more of the advanced tapes today!**

ORDER FORM ON NEXT PAGE

Advanced Singing Cassette Tape ORDER FORM

Order as many of the cassette tapes as YOU like for hours of singing enjoyment and improvement. I can offer YOU a savings on shipping and handling if YOU order more than one tape at a time. See the SPECIAL SAVINGS OFFER below.
YOU can enhance the skills you have learned with *"How To Sing Great"* with these advanced tapes. YOU can use them in conjunction with the original tape to add variety to your singing improvement sessions.

Mail Order To:

Verity Music
Dept. TIB
P. O. Box 637
Taylor, Michigan 48180

( ) **Specialize In Singing Rock 'N' Roll** *for only* . . . . $ 9.95 (plus $3.00 S&H)
( ) **Specialize In Singing Rhythm & Blues** *for only* . . . . 9.95 (plus $3.00 S&H)
( ) **Specialize In Singing Gospel & Religious** *for only* . . . . . . 9.95 (plus $3.00 S&H)
( ) **Specialize In Singing Country & Western** *for only* . . . . . 9.95 (plus $3.00 S&H)
( ) **Specialize In Singing Folk** *for only* . . . . 9.95 (plus $3.00 S&H)
( ) **Specialize In Singing Pop & Contemporary** *for only* . . . . 9.95 (plus $3.00 S&H)
( ) **Specialize In Singing Calypso & Raggae** *for only* . . . . 9.95 (plus $3.00 S&H)
( ) **Specialize In Singing Sing Jazz** *for only* . . . . 9.95 (plus $3.00 S&H)
( ) **Children's Sing-A-Long Fun** *for only* . . . . 9.95 (plus $3.00 S&H)
( ) **Specialize In Singing Harmony** *for only* . . . . 9.95 (plus $3.00 S&H)

SPECIAL SAVINGS OFFER: If YOU order more than one tape; just add $3.00 for shipping and handling. We will assume the rest of the shipping costs to
SAVE YOU MONEY.

Name _____

Address _____

City, State, Zip _____

Certified check or money order must accompany orders over $25.00 in value.
No C.O.D.'s ☐ **Visa** ☐ **MasterCard**

Card No. _____
Exp. Date _____
Signature _____

Specialized Books For Singers And Songwriters
(That YOU Probably Won't Find In YOUR Local Library Or Bookstore.)

Here are the books that I wrote about. YOU will find that most of these books will not be in YOUR local library or in a local bookstore. The books are easy-to-read and give YOU a wealth of information on different aspects of the music business which YOU will not be able to get anyplace else. *When I was first starting out in the music business I would have given my eye-teeth for any one of these books. They are an absolute must for singers, songwriters and hopeful rock singers and other entertainers!*See the order form for details. Good Luck in the music business...and happy and informative reading.   -- Rick Wiesend

"Make Money Making Music (No Matter Where You Live):" Author James Dearing shows you how to build a successful music career in your own community -- playing clubs, performing radio and TV jingles, operating a recording studio, teaching and selling lyrics through the mail, plus he shares proven methods of getting a record contract. 320 pages. $17.95. (plus $3.00 shipping and handling).

"The Basic Guide To How To Read Music:" Author Helen Cooper give you a quick and painless guide to the principles of reading music in staff notation. It contains all the terms and symbols you are likely to come across when studying music and explains them fuly. If you are learning to sing or learning to play an instrument, this book becomes absolutely essential. It includes sections on pitch, rhythm, transposition, and more. 80 pages. $7.95. (plus $3.00 shipping and handling).

"If They Ask You, You Can Write A Song:" One of America's top songwriting teams and winners of two Academy Awards tell you everything you need to know about writing and selling a song. By Al Kasha and Joel Hirschhorn. This is the definitive book on songwriting according to the great Marvin Hamlisch. 352 pages. $ 9.95. (plus $3.00 shipping and handling).

"The Craft Of Lyric Writing:" Author Sheila Davis, a successful lyricist, composer and teacher, analyzes more than 30 successful lyrics to show you why they caught the music industry's attention. You'll learn how to select the most effective song form for your lyrics, handle rhyme, meter and beat; edit and re-write your songs and choose titles that will help your songs sell. 252 pages. $19.95. (plus $3.00 shipping and handling).

"The Craft And Business Of Songwriting:" A powerful, comprehensive, up-to-date book about songwriting and the music industry. Author John Braheny, co-founder of the *Los Angeles Songwriter's Showcase,* shares his experience and insight into the entire music industry to help you create artistically and commercially successful songs. $19.95. (plus $3.00 shipping and handling).

"Instant Piano:" Breakthrough "music minus one" cassette that lets you do fool-proof improvising at the keyboard. Accompanying book guides you through country, classical, jazz and rock while giving valuable tricks of the trade that will help you should like a pro. Perfect for absolute beginners who want to let loose on the keyboard before they've had a single lesson, or for experienced players who want to forget technique and just plan. By Les Horan & Linda Ekblad. $10.95. (plus $3.00 S&H).

"How To Pitch And Promote Your Songs:" This is a great guide describing how one man went from being an unknown to setting up his own songwriting business. This easy-to-read volume gives you direct and interesting information on how the business works and how you can make it work for you where ever you are. $12.95. (plus $3.00 shipping and handling).

"The Songwriter's Guide To Collaboration:" The first book for songwriters devoted entirely to information on sharing writing responsibilities to splitting the costs and royalties. Top name songwriters tell how they worked together to get their songs published and recorded. By Harvey Rachlin. 12.95. (plus $3.00 shipping and handling).

"This Business of Music:" A practical guide to the music industry for writers, publishers, record companies, producers, artists and agents. This is the revised, expanded and updated new Copyright Act edition of a book that has become established as the most relied-upon guide to the music/record/tape industry. It 38 chapters and more than 200 additional pages of law, regulations, forms, licenses and contracts cover recording companies and artists, music publishers and writers and general music industry aspects. By Sidney Shemel and M. William Krasilowsky. 575 pages. $24.95. (plus $3.00 shipping and handling.)

MORE GREAT BOOKS ON NEXT PAGE;
plus ORDER FORM information

"More About This Business of Music:" A practical guide to five additional areas of the music industry complex not treated by *"This Business of Music"* including *serious music, background music and transcriptions, tape and tape cartridges, production and sale of printed music and live performances.* 36 appendices supply examples of agreements, licenses, copyright statutes and regulations, organization lists; *ASCAP* and *BMI* background music service license agreements; an analysis of the current employment outlook for musicians, music teachers, singers and singing teachers -- *to name only a few of the helpful items. By Sidney Shemel and M. William Krasilowsky. 204 pages. $16.95.* (plus $3.00 shipping and handling.)

"How To Make And Sell Your Own Record:" Termed a "bible and basic text," this book by Diane Sward Rapaport has helped revolutionize the recording industry. It answers all the questions about making, packaging, distributing, selling, copyrighting and, in fact, even enjoying records. This newly reviwed and enlared edition adds 30 pages of valuable information about cassette duplication, new technologies and foreign licensing. Costs and prices have been updated and the directory of trade and music magazines has been revised. The introduction highlights the small label renaissance of the last decade and the networks that serve it. 183 pages. $14.95. (plus $3.00 shipping and handling.)

"The Complete Handbook Of Songwriting (An Insider's Guide To Making It In The Music Industry):" The book details how to take a song from concept to contract. Covers demos, copyright, publishing, recording and writing for commercials, film and theater. By Mark and Cathy Liggett. 338 pages. $9.95. (plus $3.00 shipping and handling.)

Specialized Books For Singers And Songwriters
ORDER FORM

☐ "Make Money Making Music (No Matter Where You Live)"	**$17.95 each**
☐ "The Basic Guide To How To Read Music"	**$ 7.95 each**
☐ "If They Ask You, You Can Write A Song"	**$ 9.95 each**
☐ "The Craft Of Lyric Writing"	**$19.95 each**
☐ "The Craft And Business Of Songwriting"	**$19.95 each**
☐ "Instant Piano"(cassette tape and book)	**$10.95 each**
☐ "How To Pitch And Promote Your Songs"	**$12.95 each**
☐ "The Songwriter's Guide To Collaboration"	**$12.95 each**
☐ "This Business of Music"	**$24.95 each**
☐ "More About This Business of Music"	**$16.95 each**
☐ "How To Make And Sell Your Own Record"	**$14.95 each**
☐ "The Complete Handbook Of Songwriting (An Insider's Guide To Making It In The Music Industry)"	**$ 9.95 each**
Shipping And Handling Per Book	**$ 3.00 each**

Visa And Mastercard orders call:
1-800-922-1666 *ask for Sing Book Sales Department*
Check or money order customers send payment to:
Verity Music, Sing Book Sales Dept., P.O. Box 637, Taylor, MI 48180

Name: _____

Address: _____

City, State & Zip: _____
If you want to send in a Visa or Mastercard order, also fill out the following:

Card Number: _____ Card Exp. Date: _____

Cardholder's Signature: _____

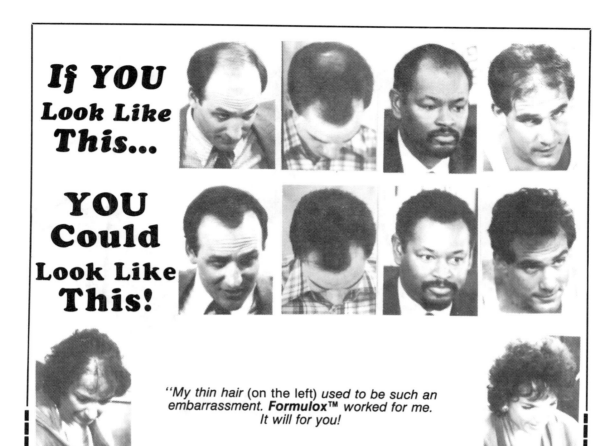

If YOU Look Like This...

YOU Could Look Like This!

"My thin hair (on the left) used to be such an embarrassment. Formulox™ worked for me. It will for you!"

It's Simple. *YOU Can Do It.* It's Not A Hairpiece!

By JOHN PETERS

I promise you that if you use *Formulox™* according to the easy-to-follow directions, you can achieve the same dramatic results as the people you see here, or I'll send every penny of your money back.

Simply apply a little *Formulox™* to the spots that are thin or balding. *Formulox™* eliminates the appearance of hair loss. It works for men and women. It works on permed or color-treated hair; or hair damaged by processing. It works if you are losing your hair naturally, or if your hair is just thin. Order *Formulox™*, you'll be glad you did. Remember, YOU have nothing to lose, but the look of baldness! My list of satisfied customers is growing each day and I want YOU to be one of them.

For more information write to me, at the following address:
Formulox™ For Your Hair, Dept. YCS, Box 366, Taylor, MI 48180.

Xcode® 4

Richard Wentk

WILEY

Wiley Publishing, Inc.

Xcode® 4

Published by
Wiley Publishing, Inc.
10475 Crosspoint Boulevard
Indianapolis, IN 46256
www.wiley.com

For general information on our other products and services or to obtain technical support, please contact our Customer Care Department within the U.S. at (877) 762-2974, outside the U.S. at (317) 572-3993 or fax (317) 572-4002.

Library of Congress Control Number: 2011929798

To Zofia

About the Author

Richard Wentk is one of the U.K.'s most reliable technology writers, with more than ten years of experience as a developer and more than fifteen years in publishing. He covers Apple products and developments for *Macworld* and *MacFormat* magazines and writes about technology, creativity, and business strategy for titles such as *Computer Arts* and *Future Music*. As a trainer and former professional Apple developer returning now to development on the iPhone and OS X, he is uniquely able to clarify the key points of the development process, explain how to avoid pitfalls and bear traps, and emphasize key benefits and creative possibilities. He lives online but also has a home in Wiltshire, England. For details of apps and other book projects visit www.zettaboom.com.

Credits

Acquisitions Editor
Aaron Black

Project Editor
Martin V. Minner

Technical Editor
Brad Miller

Copy Editor
Gwenette Gaddis

Editorial Director
Robyn Siesky

Editorial Manager
Rosemarie Graham

Business Manager
Amy Knies

Senior Marketing Manager
Sandy Smith

Vice President and Executive Group Publisher
Richard Swadley

Vice President and Executive Publisher
Barry Pruett

Project Coordinator
Katie Crocker

Graphics and Production Specialist
Carrie A. Cesavice

Quality Control Technician
Rebecca Denoncour

Proofreading and Indexing
Christine Sabooni
BIM Indexing & Proofreading Services

Media Development Project Manager
Laura Moss

Media Development Assistant Project Manager
Jenny Swisher

Media Development Associate Producers
Josh Frank
Shawn Patrick
Doug Kuhn
Marilyn Hummel

Contents

Preface

After a few years with Xcode 3, my first impressions of Xcode 4 were mixed. At first, I thought the redesign was unnecessarily rigid and proscriptive. I missed Interface Builder's floating windows and object palettes, and I couldn't find a convincing reason for the enforced three-way window split in the editor.

Over time, I realized my first impressions were wrong. Software tools for developers, like software tools for users, should work hard to make life easier. The venerable old GCC compiler toolchain that ran under the hood of Xcode 3 was developed at a time when the command line was the only available UI. Although some developers still love the command line, it's an unforgiving environment that penalizes simple mistakes. It can be powerful, but it's also literal-minded and not at all transparent.

Many development environments, including Xcode 3, have taken this same approach but applied it in a visual environment. The test of a good tool is that it anticipates your needs to the point where it disappears, leaving you with a clear canvas for your imagination.

Xcode 4's designers have taken a step toward this by asking how to simplify or eliminate some of the tedious and repetitive work that was necessary in the past. Xcode 4 doesn't accomplish this aim completely—some promising early ideas were removed in the final release—but many of the features are simpler and more responsive than their equivalents in Xcode 3. As a result, the development process is faster, simpler, and more productive.

The first goal of this book is to introduce the new features to users who were used to older ways of working and to bring new users up to speed with the essential features of Xcode. Newcomers should start at the front of the book and work their way through it in order. The sequence of the earlier chapters is designed to be a practical primer for Xcode development, not just a list of features and changes.

A second goal is to introduce some of the more complex features in more detail. Many newcomers use Xcode in a simple click-bang way, missing out on the power and flexibility hidden under the surface. The less-obvious features are easy to skip, but exploring them can open up new possibilities for testing, debugging, project management, and build control. Some tools, such as Instruments, have further hidden layers of their own that would require a further book the size of this one to explore fully.

Because space is limited, this book doesn't dig into every feature to the deepest possible level. But new Xcode 4 users and experienced Xcode 3 users should find creative inspiration here, as well as a good store of tips and techniques that can push them through the essentials of basic development and into the deeper possibilities of managed testing and build design.

Every author works hard to make his or her books as helpful as possible. Comments and feedback are welcome at xcodedr@zettaboom.com.

Acknowledgments

Although book publishing has become digital, book writing hasn't. A book continues to be a team effort.

My thanks go to acquisitions editor Aaron Black for suggesting the project when Xcode 4 was barely a gleam in Apple's eye and to project editor Martin V. Minner for his continuing support and extended patience. Sincere thanks are also due to the rest of the team at Wiley for their hard work behind the scenes.

Alexa, Rachel, Hilary, Michael, and the Eurotribe (*sans pareil*) all helped with support, entertainment, and occasional suggestions, some of which were helpful.

Software development has become a communal activity, and particular appreciation is due to the countless bloggers, experimenters, developers, and problem-solvers on the Web whose generosity and creativity have made so much possible in so many ways.

Finally, love as always to Team HGA. I couldn't have written it without you.

Introduction

This book is about developing iOS and Mac projects using the Xcode 4 development toolchain. You'll find this book useful if you have experience with Cocoa or Cocoa Touch and have used Xcode 3 in the past or if you have worked with other development environments and are curious about how to work productively with Xcode 4.

This isn't a book about languages or frameworks, and the only loose prerequisite is some basic experience with a C-family language. However, this isn't a book about theory. You'll get the most from it if you download and install Xcode 4 for yourself, work through the examples, and experiment with it as you read.

If you're new to Apple development, you also may want to read the Objective-C, iOS, and Cocoa Developer Reference titles. A few framework features are mentioned in the text, but you don't need to be familiar with them to use this book successfully, although you need to be familiar with them to develop iOS and Mac apps that can be sold through the App Store.

Chapter 1 looks back briefly at previous Mac development tools and introduces some of the core differences between Xcode 3 and Xcode 4. It introduces the essential elements of the Xcode UI and explains how it's possible to create iOS and OS X projects.

Chapter 2 explains how to choose a Mac for development, how to sign up as a paid developer, and how to install and customize Xcode. It's a feature of Xcode development that while the installation process is simple, it has hidden options that are easy to miss. Also, there are important differences between installing a single version of Xcode and using multiple versions across multiple platforms to develop production projects while also experimenting with beta OS code.

Chapter 3 introduces the Xcode templates. It demonstrates how you can use the templates to get started with app development, but also explores some of the more specialized templates available for both iOS and OS X projects, and it explains where to find the templates so you can make simple modifications to them.

Chapter 4 looks in more detail at the new editor features, including the new navigators that collect project information in a single switchable pane. This chapter explores the many new project navigation features and support tools, and it introduces time-saving features in the new enhanced code editor.

Chapter 5 explains how to organize and manage files and projects. It examines groups in the project navigator, demonstrates how to add and remove files from a project, and explains how Xcode 3's tools for managing supporting frameworks have been moved to the Xcode 4 build settings.

Chapter 6 is a guide to the Apple Documentation built into Xcode. Apple has structured the Documentation in specific ways, and you'll progress more quickly and with less effort if you understand what this means in practice. Understanding and using the Documentation and searching it in Xcode are key skills. Don't skip this chapter, even if you already have experience in other environments.

Chapter 7 introduces the key features of Interface Builder and explains how you can use IB to build complete applications, because IB isn't just for interfaces. It explains the purpose of the File's Owner and First Responder objects, and it builds a simple iOS app that responds to a button tap.

Chapter 8 explores IB in more detail. It shows you how to manage media and other resources and how to control OS compatibility. It also explains how to localize your project so it can support foreign languages.

Chapter 9 takes a closer look at the new time-saving features in Xcode, including the structure management tools that can help you move sections of code to their most appropriate location, manage indentation intelligently, and add or remove comment blocks. This chapter also introduces code completion and explains how you can customize the code snippet and code completion macros with your own most-used blocks of code.

Chapter 10 introduces the Xcode Organizer, a multi-purpose tool for managing supporting files and other project information that doesn't belong in the code editor. It introduces device provisioning and profiles and explains how you can manage your test devices.

Chapter 11 takes a comprehensive and detailed look at the Xcode provisioning process, which is necessary for device testing, beta distribution, and App Store distribution for both iOS and OS X projects. It takes you step by step through the provisioning process and explains the principles of provisioning so you can understand what certificates, identities, and profiles do and why they're necessary.

Chapter 12 introduces the Xcode build system. It introduces project and target build settings and explains the relationship between them. It also looks in detail at build setting management, explaining how you can use build configurations and the new schemes feature to create flexible, multi-target builds for more complex projects.

Chapter 13 goes deeper into the build system. It introduces a list of common and useful build customizations, takes you step by step through the different build processes needed for iOS App Store, iOS Ad Hoc, and OS X App Store builds. It also explains how you can use Xcode to submit projects to the App Store. Finally, it introduces the internals of the build system and explains how you can use custom scripting in the build phases and build rules to satisfy almost any build requirement.

Chapter 14 explores the new version control features. It introduces the different ways in which you can manage project versions in Xcode and illustrates their strengths and weaknesses. It ends with a practical example of using Xcode with the GitHub collaborative online code repository and explains how GitHub can be used for solo and group projects.

Chapter 15 introduces the Xcode debugger. It explores the different ways in which you can view and use console, and it demonstrates how you can add, remove, and manage breakpoints; view variables; and monitor them as they change. It also introduces command-line debugging for low-level control.

Chapter 16 explores Instruments and demonstrates how you can use them to profile almost any aspect of your code, including memory use, performance, and impact on the surrounding system. It includes a profiling example that demonstrates how you can use Instruments to check for memory leaks.

Chapter 17 introduces the Unit Test features and explains how you can use them to create and check automated test cases in your code, to help you guarantee that when you make changes to existing code, it continues to function as it should.

Appendix A lists the many extra tools and utilities included in the Xcode toolchain, including powerful supporting editors such as Quartz Composer and Dashcode.

Appendix B introduces plist editing and explores the new Core Data editor.

Appendix C explains the differences between the old GCC and new LLVM compiler technologies, both of which are included in Xcode.

Code appears `in a monospaced font`. Items you type **appear in bold.**

Projects and examples were developed with various versions of Xcode 4, from the first developer release to the final GM seed, on OS X 10.6.6. Current graphics and features may differ slightly from the illustrations and feature descriptions in this book.

Supporting code is available on the book's Web site at `www.wiley.com/go/xcode4 devref`. See the readme there for the most recent system and software requirements. Code is supplied as-is with no warranty and can be used in both commercial and private Cocoa projects, but may not be sold or repackaged as tutorial material.

Getting Started

Introducing Xcode 4

X code is Apple's free suite of developer tools; it is used to create applications for iOS mobile devices and for Mac OS X. Xcode 4, shown in Figure 1.1, is the most recent version and is a radical update with many new features.

Developer tools are complex, and Xcode has always tried to hide much of that complexity from novice developers. You can use Xcode in a very simple click-to-build way, but this simplicity can be misleading. Many developers never explore Xcode's more advanced features and never discover how they can use them to save time, solve problems, or extend their projects with original and creative features.

Xcode also includes an unexpectedly enormous selection of helper applications and developer tools. A complete guide to every element in Xcode would require a shelf of books. This book concentrates on beginner- and intermediate-level features, but also includes hints and pointers for advanced developers.

1 In This Chapter

Understanding the history of Mac development tools

Developing Xcode

Moving to Xcode 4

Comparing iOS and OS X development

Figure 1.1

Xcode 4's simplified interface hides familiar old features and some unexpected new ones.

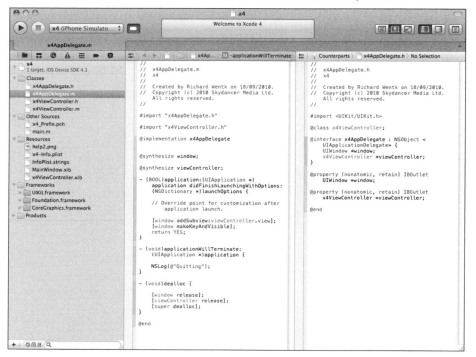

Understanding the History of Mac Development Tools

Before OS X, Apple's IDE (Integrated Development Environment) was MPW (Macintosh Programmer's Workshop). As shown in Figure 1.2, MPW, which is still available today, was in competition with a commercial product called CodeWarrior. Both CodeWarrior and MPW were expensive, and many would-be developers were put off by the initial start-up costs.

Looking back at early IDEs

CodeWarrior was based on the Metrowerks C compiler and environment. It smoothed the transition from the 68k processors to the PowerPC and helped make the new PowerPC Macs a success. As an IDE, CodeWarrior provided complete support for the PowerPC architecture; MPW took longer to catch up with Apple's own new hardware. CodeWarrior also compiled code more quickly than MPW and created faster and more efficient binaries.

Figure 1.2

The MPW IDE is available on Apple's FTP site, and users of antique Macs can download and use it.

NOTE

Early versions of MPW were famous for their error messages, which included "We already did this function," "This array has no size, and that's bad," and "Call me paranoid, but finding '/*' inside this comment makes me suspicious." Later Apple IDEs reverted to more traditional messages.

Developing Xcode

With the move to OS X, Apple decided to retain control over the developer environment. An IDE called Project Builder had been developed as part of the NeXTStep project. A free copy of Project Builder was bundled with every copy of OS X. In fall 2003, an updated and enhanced version was shipped and named Xcode 1.0.

Xcode has been updated with every major new release of OS X. Xcode 2.0 shipped with OS X 10.4 "Tiger." It included improved documentation, better support for Java, and the Quartz Composer visual programming tool, which is described in more detail in Appendix A.

Xcode 3 shipped with OS X 10.5 "Leopard" and introduced improved debugging tools. Xcode 3.1 added support for early versions of iOS.

Xcode 3.2 is shown in Figure 1.3 and was released with OS X 10.6 "Snow Leopard." Prior to this release, Apple supplied separate builds of Xcode for iOS and OS X development. With version 3.2, Xcode became a unified development environment that could target both platforms. This widened the developer base, but also made Xcode more difficult to download. The Mac version was around 800GB. The combined version is typically around 3GB.

Figure 1.3

The Xcode 3 IDE was productive but limited by obvious UI inefficiencies, such as poor support for editing multiple files simultaneously.

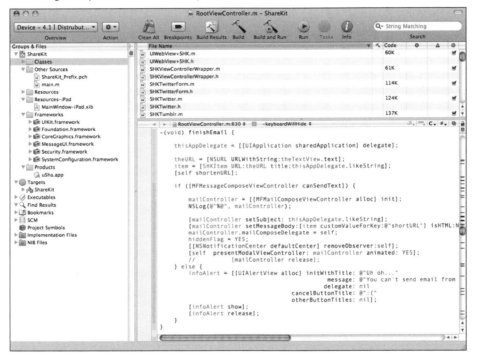

CAUTION

Strong Java support was a feature of earlier Xcode versions, but that has been downgraded in recent releases. Apple has moved Xcode toward supporting C-family development, including C, Objective-C, C++, and Objective-C++. These are now the officially supported languages for iOS and OS X development.

Alternatives to Xcode

Xcode is optimized for visual development of Objective-C and Cocoa projects. In practice this means the Cocoa and Cocoa Touch libraries and documentation are tightly integrated into Xcode. Xcode 4 has moved toward improving support for C++, but there are still limits to how easily it's possible to mix Objective-C, Objective-C++, and C++ code, Apple's own libraries and example source code are a combination of traditional C and Objective-C. C++ and Objective-C++ aren't widely used.

If you are used to developing in a different environment, you may feel that Xcode works in ways that don't match your requirements. If you plan to create windowed applications with official Apple UI elements, building Objective-C and Cocoa code in Xcode is likely to be your most efficient choice. If you prefer to create UNIX applications with command line or X11 features, you may prefer an alternative. Although OS X is based on Darwin/POSIX rather than Linux, it's relatively easy to create a cross-platform application core that can be extended with platform-specific features.

It's possible to use Xcode from the command line in Terminal with your own make files (build management and configuration files). If you're used to GCC and GDB on other platforms, you can run them directly from the command line, bypassing most of Xcode's features.

Java and C/C++ developers may prefer the free Eclipse IDE available at `www.eclipse.org`. Eclipse can be extended with a C/C++ IDE. Cocoa isn't supported, but Java and mixed development are.

For multi-platform support, Mono remains a popular choice. Mono compiles C# rather than Objective-C or C++, but is designed to support cross-platform output, running similar code on Windows, OS X, iPhone, Android, and Linux platforms. Mono also supports ASP.NET web projects.

MonoMac and MonoTouch versions include bindings to key OS X and iOS APIs. A version for Android is also available. The main IDE is called MonoDevelop and is available at `monodevelop.com`. Although Mono has obvious advantages, Apple's support for the competing platform isn't reliably enthusiastic. At times, Apple has barred from the App Store apps developed in languages other than C, Objective-C, and C++. But some MonoTouch applications have been approved for sale. Mono may be a better choice for developers coming from a C# and Windows background who don't want to learn a completely new language.

On the iPhone, Flash developers can package Flash projects as iPhone applications with Adobe's Packager for iPhone. Originally included in various versions of Adobe CS5, Packager was withdrawn when Apple restricted iPhone applications to native Objective-C and C++ code. Apple subsequently lifted the restrictions later in 2010 and at the time of writing Packager is available as a free beta project from the Adobe Labs site at `labs.adobe.com`. Future production versions are likely to have their own URL and product pages.

iPhone game developers may also want to consider Ansca's Corona, which is a simplified scripted development environment for iOS and Android available from `ansca mobile.com/corona`. Corona currently costs $349 per year, but claims faster development times than are possible with Xcode and native Objective-C.

Understanding Xcode 4's Key Features

For developers who are beginning Xcode, Xcode 4 includes the following features:

- A project navigator that lists and groups related project files.
- File and project templates for both OS X and iOS projects.

- A code editor that includes static code checking, code completion, and dynamic hints and tips.

- A visual UI design tool called *Interface Builder,* also known as IB, which can prototype visual interfaces, but can also be used to manage and preload other application objects.

- Further integrated editors for class management and for Apple's Core Data database framework.

- A debugger that supports expressions and conditional breakpoints.

- Support for direct access to various online code repositories.

- A minimal but useful *iPhone Simulator* that runs iOS applications on a Mac.

- A collection of *Instruments*—tools that can profile speeds, monitor memory allocations, and report other key features of code as it runs.

- Support for both visual development and low-level command-line compilation.

- An impressive selection of further helper applications that aren't built into the main Xcode interface but are installed with Xcode and can be run independently, as needed. The tools include a packager for building installable OS X applications, hardware monitoring and testing, an animation design tool, a tool for building JavaScript widgets that can be distributed commercially, and others.

CROSS-REFERENCE

For a list of helper tools and applications, see Appendix A.

Xcode doesn't support or include the following:

- **Editors for graphics, sounds, fonts, 3D objects, or other media types:** External editors must be used.

- **Built-in support for languages other than C, C++, and Objective-C:** You can extend Xcode to work with other languages, but Xcode is optimized for C-family development. (This does not include C#.)

- **Development tools for other operating systems:** OS X is similar enough to BSD UNIX to allow for some code sharing. But Xcode cannot be used to develop applications for Windows, Android, or Linux, or for web languages such as Perl and PHP.

- **Unlocked open development for iOS:** Applications for iOS hardware must be code signed and linked to a time-limited certificate. In practice, this means that even if you use Xcode, own an iPhone, and are a registered developer, your own applications will cease to run after the time-limited certificate expires.

- **Development on non-Apple platforms:** Currently, Xcode requires a Mac running a recent copy of OS X.

NOTE
Rumors surface regularly of a merger, or at least a relationship, between Xcode and Microsoft's Visual Studio series of development tools. There would be obvious commercial benefits to allowing Windows developers access to iOS and the App Store, but Apple's culture tends to be closed and proprietary. A formal link is possible, but at the time of writing it seems very unlikely.

Moving to Xcode 4

Xcode 4 marks a significant change, because the aim is no longer to produce code, but to simplify the developer experience. Many developer tasks are repetitive chores that have become embedded in the development process for historical reasons. Developer tools typically assume a workflow and mindset that date back to the very earliest days of computing, more than half a century ago.

The designers of Xcode 4 have begun to rethink some of these assumptions, adding features that can streamline and simplify the workflow. Some of these features are specific to Cocoa and Objective-C development, while others are more general improvements in code management and debugging. Compiler technology has also improved, and Xcode 4 is moving toward the latest and fastest compiler tools.

CROSS-REFERENCE
For details of the compiler technologies available in Xcode 4, see Appendix C.

Compared to Xcode 3, Xcode 4 has a completely redesigned interface and a selection of extra features:

- A unified interface in a single window
- Integrated editors for all main code and data file types
- Integration of *Interface Builder,* the Xcode visual UI design tool
- Simpler and faster navigation between files
- Integrated code management with version control, repository access, and a code library to simplify reuse of code snippets
- Improved debugging and code testing with more informative error messages, static code testing, support for multiple log files, and better Code Completion (formerly Code Sense) hinting
- New code analysis features, which offer hints about basic coding errors
- Improved and simplified code and symbol searches
- Simplified management of build targets and products

- Support for *Schemes,* which offer fine control over how projects build, and support different build options for different applications (for example, testing, debugging, packaging for distribution, and so on)
- Support for *Workspaces,* which make it easy to manage and work on multiple related projects
- Backward compatibility with Xcode 3.*x* project files
- Improved compiler technology
- Various other time-saving features, such as automatic unprompted file saves before a build

CAUTION

If you load a project made with an older version of Xcode 3 into Xcode 4, you sometimes see an error message reporting a "Missing SDK." You can't build the project until you fix this. For details, see "Selecting the Base SDK" near the beginning of Chapter 13.

Moving from the Xcode 3 to the Xcode 4 editor

The new features of the editor are described in more detail in Chapter 3, but this chapter includes a simple orientation for impatient developers who are already familiar with Xcode 3. In outline, almost all the familiar features have been retained, and there are some new arrivals. But the UI has been reorganized, and features may be in unfamiliar locations.

NOTE

Xcode 4 is backward compatible with Xcode 3. You can load Xcode 3.*x* projects and save them again, and Xcode 3 should still be able to open them. Naturally, you can't open Xcode 4 projects in Xcode 3.

In Xcode 3, floating windows could proliferate uncontrollably, making them difficult to work with. Xcode 4 gathers every feature into a single window with multiple work areas and panes. The active areas can be shown, hidden, split, or resized as needed. Every Xcode feature, including Interface Builder (IB) and the debugger, can appear in this window. Features can be hidden when you're not using them. Hiding and revealing features adds a small overhead, but is much more efficient and productive than a chaotic mess of windows. You can also create your own *workspaces* to save and restore complete window layouts.

TIP

Compared to Xcode 3, Xcode 4 becomes more efficient with a larger monitor. Xcode 3 often wasted screen real estate; for example, the right side of a code window was usually empty. With Xcode 4, you can have a console/debugger, editor, file list, and IB open simultaneously in tiled panes. With a large monitor, these panes become large enough to be truly useful without scrolling, resizing, or switching.

At the top of window, the toolbar area includes a new summary panel that displays project status. This gives progress updates as a project builds and displays a count of warnings and errors after each build. The toolbar has been simplified. Only build/run and stop buttons are available.

In the first release of Xcode 4, it's no longer possible to customize this area with your own selection of build/run/stop/clean options, as it was in Xcode 3.

Working with tabs

Xcode 4 introduces *tabs*—editor sub-windows that work like the tabs in a browser, allowing single-click switching between selected files, as shown in Figure 1.4. Tabs replace the file list that appeared above the editor pane in Xcode 3. The file list was an inefficient way to select files for editing. With tabs, you can add your choice of files to the tab bar as you work and then save the tab bar with the project. You can also delete files from the tab bar when you are no longer working on them.

Figure 1.4

The new tab bar replaces the project file list and appears under the main toolbar near the top of the Xcode 4 window.

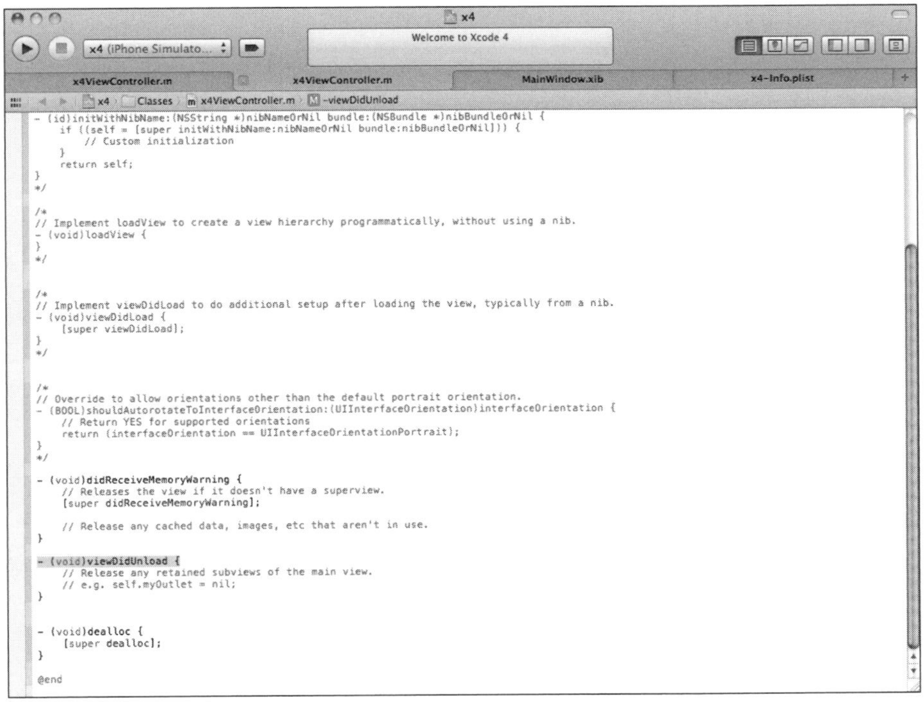

TIP

Tabs save the current cursor position, so you can use them to switch quickly between different sections of the same file. It's often useful to open multiple tabs that show the most significant methods or functions in a file.

Working with multiple windows

Not every developer is enthusiastic about single-window development. Fortunately, you can open multiple windows into a single project and select a different collection of editors and features in each window. A key goal is flexibility; you can arrange your workspace how you want it, with the features you want to see. As shown in Figure 1.5, you can still create a separate floating window to edit a single file by double-clicking the file.

Figure 1.5

In Xcode 4, you can still float individual files from a project in separate windows. But there are usually more efficient ways to work.

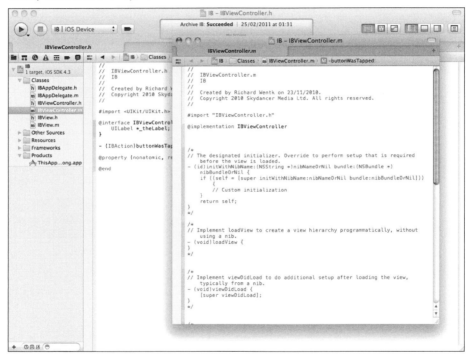

Selecting and navigating files

Xcode 3 included a pair of file and symbol navigation menus above the main editing pane. Xcode 4 extends this idea and displays a hierarchical *navigation bar* that generates a menu tree from your project files, listing the files and symbols. As shown in Figure 1.6, you can select any file almost instantly.

Figure 1.6

The navigation bar drastically speeds up access to any file in your project, by presenting them all in a single unified menu tree.

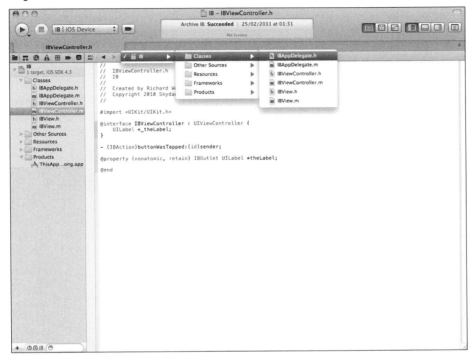

NOTE

In beta versions of Xcode 4 you could use the menu tree to navigate to the methods in each file. This feature was removed in the final release. It was a *very* useful feature, so it may return in future updates. Symbols still appear in the navigation bar in a separate menu, much as they did in Xcode 3.

You also can select files in the traditional way using Xcode 4's version of the Groups & Files pane, which is now called the Project navigator. But the navigation bar is very much faster. As shown in Figure 1.7, it includes a separate menu that lists other relevant items including header files, includes, related classes, and categories. Click the boxes icon to the left of the left-pointing arrow to view this menu.

Figure 1.7

At the left of the navigation bar, a separate menu shows files and items that are more loosely related to the currently selected file.

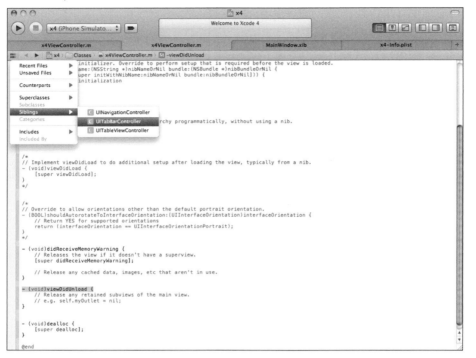

Using the Assistant

Xcode 3 included a *counterpart file* selector that switched an editor window between a class header and its corresponding implementation file. Xcode 4 introduces *Assistant*, which is designed to work with a new vertically split double-pane view. When you select a file for editing, Assistant makes an informed guess about a useful counterpart and displays it automatically, as shown in Figure 1.8. By default, this means that selecting a header displays the implementation file in the second pane, and vice versa.

Figure 1.8

The button for selecting the Assistant option is in the grouping at the top right and looks like a light bulb. It splits the editor into two panes and automatically displays a counterpart file whenever a file is selected.

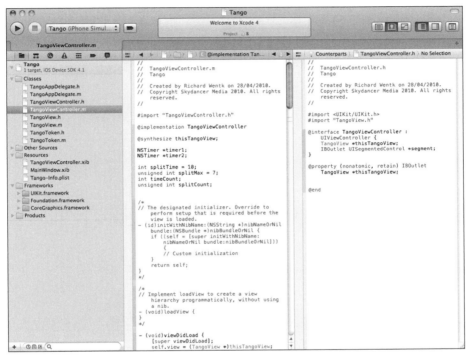

With the vertical split view and Assistant, you no longer need to manually switch between counterparts or to work with the less efficient horizontal split view available in Xcode 3. This feature is one of the most useful timesavers in Xcode 4. You also can manually a select a counterpart or other file using a new contextual right-click menu, as shown in Figure 1.9.

Figure 1.9

You can change the behavior of Assistant to select a specific type of counterpart file, which can include an object's superclass as well as its headers and includes. This is useful for newcomers who may not be aware that Cocoa and other OS X headers are available in Xcode and can be used as a reference.

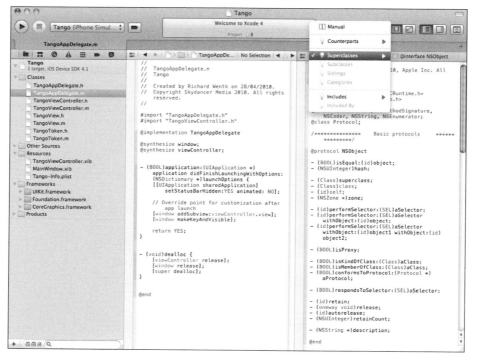

Working with Interface Builder

IB is now built into Xcode 4. It launches at the same time as Xcode, and you can edit a nib file simply by selecting it. IB in Xcode 3 had the same poor window management as the main editor. IB's windows would often hide behind other windows for no reason.

In Xcode 4, you can use tabs, the navigation bar, and other new editor features to work with multiple files more efficiently. Linking and symbol editing have also been drastically simplified. You can drag links directly from a control or object in IB to a code window, as shown in Figure 1.10. Xcode inserts appropriate code for you in both the header file and the implementation. It also synthesizes outlet variables automatically. For detailed examples of creating links among outlets, actions, and IB objects, see Chapters 7 and 8.

Figure 1.10

Creating outlet code automatically in Xcode 4. This is a very powerful time-saving feature.

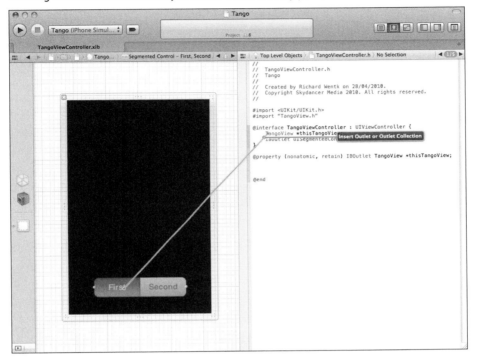

Exploring code and file management

Xcode 4 includes two new panes at the left and the right that can be revealed or hidden as needed, using a pair of buttons near the top right of the toolbar. As shown in Figure 1.11, the left pane, known as the *navigation pane*, includes a simplified but familiar version of the Groups & Files pane from Xcode 3. This pane also includes symbol lists, search options, and log listings.

The Get Info feature in Xcode 3 has been replaced by an info view in Xcode 4. As shown in Figure 1.11, you can display the filename, type, and location in a right pane, which is known as the *utilities pane*. This pane gathers miscellaneous information that previously appeared in various floating windows. For example, IB's inspector panes appear here. It also shows build target and localization information. When you select a file, the contents of this pane are updated automatically. This saves time over Xcode 3's Get Info pop-up menu feature, which presented this information in a less accessible way.

Figure 1.11

New left and right panes in Xcode 4 display ancillary information and manage optional features that may not be needed while editing.

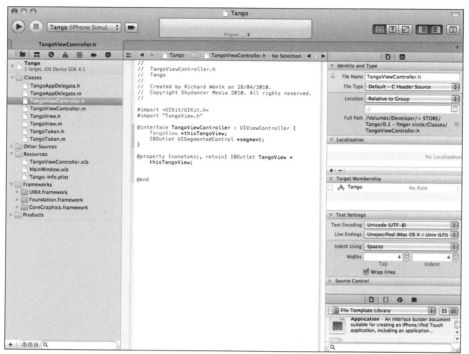

The utilities pane is also shown in Figure 1.11. It includes a new Library sub-pane that can display file templates, standard code snippets, standard system objects that include both UI and data classes, and project media files.

The Code Snippet feature in the Library is shown in Figure 1.12. It's often useful to reuse the same code between projects, and the Code Snippet makes it easy to do this. To add code to a project, drag it from the library and drop it in the editor window. You also can view previews of each snippet by selecting it before dragging. By default, this pane includes a small selection of standard snippets, but you can extend it indefinitely by adding your own. For more details, see Chapter 9.

Figure 1.12

The new Code Snippets feature makes it easy to reuse code and is a partial replacement for Xcode 3's Code Sense macros.

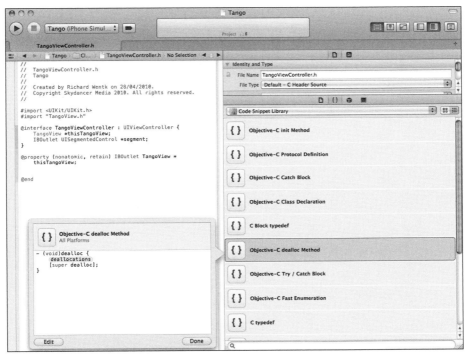

Exploring the debugger

As shown in Figure 1.13, the debugger now appears in a new pane at the bottom of the editor window. To reveal it, select View ⇨ Show Debugger Area. Both console output and debugger output appear in this area. You can choose to view either or both by clicking the new buttons that appear at the top right of the area. The debugger now supports multi-threaded debugging. You can set breakpoints by clicking in the gutter area to the left of the editor.

Figure 1.13

The new debugger area no longer appears in a separate window, although for convenience you may decide to launch it in one. On a smaller monitor, the debugging and console area can feel cramped.

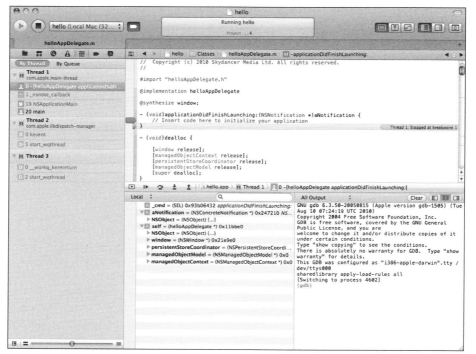

Comparing iOS and OS X Development

Although Xcode supports OS X and iOS development equally and it can be used to develop apps for both the iOS and Mac App Stores, there are significant differences between the two platforms.

Developing for OS X

OS X development in Xcode 4 is build-and-go. There are no restrictions on development, testing, or distribution. You can create applications that run in a debugging environment on your own Mac and package them as applications that you can run independently, sell from a website, or prepare for network distribution. You can also create Mac apps for the App Store—but this is one development option, and not an obligation. Figure 1.14 shows a simple OS X application using a template as a starting point.

NOTE

Xcode doesn't include network deployment features. But it does create application binaries that can be handed to network deployment tools.

Earlier versions of Xcode supported universal binary development, which was backward-compatible with PowerPC hardware. Although OS X 10.6 Snow Leopard was the first Intel-only version of OS X, Xcode supports universal binaries for Mac development and can still be used to develop applications for PowerPC targets. It continues to support AltiVec hardware acceleration. The commercial market for PowerPC applications is tiny, but PowerPC applications remain interesting in specialized media and scientific computing.

Figure 1.14

Create a very simple OS X application using a template as a starting point and adding a text label in IB. The application runs in its own window and replaces the OS X menu bar (not shown here). Although it appears to run independently, it is in fact controlled by Xcode and can be debugged while it's running.

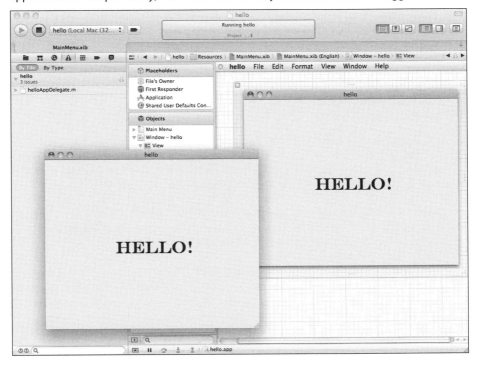

Developing for iOS

iOS development is more complicated than OS X development. Development is controlled by *provisioning,* an Apple-generated security control, which is built into Xcode and manages access to hardware testing and App Store distribution.

iPhone, iPod touch, and iPad platforms all use iOS, but these platforms are significantly different and may not always run the same version of iOS. Even when they do run the same version, not all hardware features and UI options are available on very device.

In extreme cases, conditional code is required to check which device an app is running on and which version of iOS it supports. Code paths may need to be selected accordingly with manual checks at runtime.

Apple is unlikely to simplify this process in future releases of Xcode. It's more likely that the iOS device range will expand, and apps will need to manage an ever-increasing selection of screen sizes, hardware features, and operating systems.

The Xcode Simulator, shown in Figure 1.15, includes separate iPhone and iPad testing options, but it is suitable only for apps that don't use any of the iOS hardware features, such as the GPS and the accelerometer. All but the very simplest commercial apps should be tested on real hardware.

The extra requirements of provisioning and multi-platform support can make iOS development feel challenging and complex. A further complication is the need to produce high-quality supporting graphics and screen designs for maximum buyer impact in the App Store.

To date, Apple's beta cycle for iOS has been more aggressive than for OS X, and it's usual to have a new beta preview of iOS available almost as soon as the most recent version has been made public. Beta development requires a parallel version of Xcode and beta firmware for every test device. It may also require an updated version of iTunes and OS X.

So although the iPhone and iPad are simpler than a Mac, and app code can be very much simpler, you should allow extra time to work for projects to support all the different possible targets, versions, and security options.

Xcode supports these extra possibilities, but it doesn't simplify them. Developing and testing a universal iOS app—a single app that can run on an iPhone, an iPod, and an iPad—remains a challenge.

Figure 1.15

Create a very simple iOS app, and test it in the Simulator. The Simulator is best considered an educational rather than a production environment. It's adequate for apps with simple text and graphics, but it doesn't fully implement the GPS, accelerometer, gyroscope, or other hardware options in iOS devices.

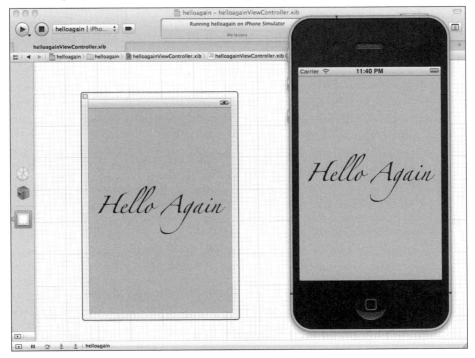

OS X and iOS cross-development

In theory, you can migrate projects between platforms. In practice, Cocoa on OS X and Cocoa Touch on iOS have so many differences that dual-platform development of a non-trivial application is either challenging or unrealistic.

Currently iOS and OS X applications have distinct markets and partially distinct distribution models. Although a few applications have appeared on both—social networking tools and games are the most popular choices—Xcode does little to simplify the development of multi-platform projects.

The development workflow is almost completely distinct. The two platforms have these features:

- **A separate collection of classes for UI design and for data management:** Many of the more creative and sophisticated classes in OS X are either absent or only partially implemented in iOS.

- **A separate testing and debugging environment:** iOS applications can run in a Simulator or on a hardware device. OS X applications run in a debugging sandbox.

- **A different core programming model:** iOS supports task switching with very limited multi-tasking, and limited access to the device file system. OS X supports a wider range of multi-tasking options, and less restricted access to files.

- **Separate documentation suites:** iOS and OS X have separate collections of documentation and distinct source code examples.

- **Different accelerated graphics frameworks:** OS X implements OpenGL in full, iOS implements the simpler OpenGL ES framework.

- **Different project templates for separate bare-bones starter application sketches:** iOS includes a set of sketches for simple UI-driven handset apps. OS X includes a more complex collection of templates that support the development of plug-ins, screen-savers, and other libraries.

- **A partially distinct set of supported instruments for testing:** Limited overlap exists, but some instruments remain unique to each platform.

Apple's Model-View-Controller design pattern implies that applications should keep UI designs, UI management code, and underlying data collections distinct. OS X includes controller classes that make it easier to manage data and create UIs to work with it. Most of these classes are absent in iOS. This makes it difficult to use MVC effectively when attempting dual-platform development.

If you plan to develop across platforms, try to package the underlying data model into its own collection of classes. You may be able to reuse these classes without major changes. Keep UI and UI management code elsewhere.

Generally, combined iOS and OS X remain possible but difficult. It's more realistic to think of Xcode 4 as two separate development environments with a common frontend than as a single unified environment designed to produce code for either platform.

Summary

This chapter explained how previous Mac development tools led to Xcode, listed the key design goals of Xcode 4, and summarized the key differences between Xcode 4 and Xcode 3. It introduced some of the practical differences in more detail and looked at some of the new features. Finally, it explored the fundamental differences between iOS and OS X development and briefly discussed how those differences affect the development workflow.

Getting and Installing Xcode

X code is free and runs on any Intel Mac. However, hobby developers and professionals have different hardware and software requirements. A system tuned for maximum productivity may be very different from one used for experimentation or hobby coding.

Selecting a Mac for Xcode

If you own an Intel Mac, you can run Xcode on it. But understanding the differences between a streamlined and productive working environment and a slow and informal one is useful.

Choosing a processor

Surprisingly, processors have less influence on productivity than other factors. A faster processor can speed up compilation times, but unless you're working on industrial projects with hundreds or thousands of source files, you'll find little obvious benefit to running Xcode on a high-speed multi-core Mac Pro.

Xcode compiles incrementally, which means that only updated files and their dependencies are recompiled after an edit. Compared to Xcode 3, Xcode 4's improved compiler technology cuts compile times even further. iPhone projects compile relatively quickly, even on a Mac mini, shown in Figure 2.1

However, other Xcode features such as code completion and source control can be noticeably faster on a faster Mac. Xcode 4 does more behind the scenes while you edit. It checks code for errors as you type it, and it can also display live help. The faster your Mac, and especially the faster your Mac's disk system, the more speedily these features work for you. On a slow Mac it can take a few seconds to check a file for errors, so there are obvious benefits to working on a faster Mac.

In This Chapter

Selecting a Mac for Xcode

Signing up for development

Getting started with Xcode

Figure 2.1

You do not need the latest, fastest, and largest Mac to use Xcode. You can create professional iPhone apps on a MacBook or Mac mini.

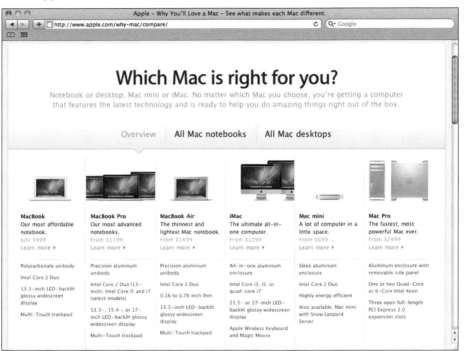

Selecting memory

Xcode 4 uses memory more efficiently than Xcode 3. Even on larger builds, it's unlikely that 2GB will feel restrictive on a Mac that's used exclusively for development. If you create artwork as well as code, you're likely to have some of the applications in Adobe's Creative Suite running at the same time as you use Xcode. Previewing graphics in Bridge, editing them in Photoshop and Illustrator, and importing them into an Xcode project is a standard workflow. Creative Suite and Xcode can work together in 2GB, but 4GB is a more realistic minimum to prevent disk thrashing and delays.

Choosing a monitor

A monitor, or monitor bank, can be the biggest influence on overall productivity. The less time you spend rearranging screen content, the more quickly you can create code. Although you can develop projects successfully on a monitor with a resolution of 1024x768, a minimum resolution of 1680x1050 is very much more productive. At this resolution, you can see the entire Xcode 4 workspace at once and use it as it was designed to be used. Larger monitors are even easier to work with, and a dual monitor system provides a significant speed boost because you can work on multiple projects or multiple files simultaneously.

After you've mastered the essentials of iOS, Xcode, and OS X, you'll spend significant time reviewing class references in the various frameworks and exploring message boards looking for code samples and developer tips. The most efficient way to view the references is to create a set of bookmarks with the most useful class references and view simultaneously in tabs in a web browser. You can then switch between them instantly as needed.

TIP

You can use Spaces to create a separate developer Space that's dedicated to Xcode and its supporting windows. Day-to-day apps such as Mail can be kept in a different Space, minimizing clutter.

Exposé can be another timesaver. When you have many Xcode windows open at once, Exposé is by far the easiest way to switch between them. You can set up Exposé and Spaces in the System Preferences.

The most luxurious and productive development environment has at least two monitors for code and at least one further monitor for online browsing. The extra monitor may be on another machine, but it's more efficient to use a three- or four-monitor Mac; it's often useful to copy and paste code directly into your project from the documentation or other online sources.

Working with disk storage

Disk space and disk features can make a big difference to Xcode performance. Ideally, you should install Xcode on your main Mac hard drive, allowing at least 20GB for a full install of two separate versions (active and beta) with all documentation and your own project code.

Although it's not immediately obvious from the install options, Xcode can be installed and run on an external drive. However, OS X support for external USB drives is temperamental, and external drives are likely to be slower than internal disks. You should use a tool called SpindownHD in a tool collection called CHUD (Computer Hardware Understanding Developer Tools) to control disk idle and sleep modes. SpindownHD isn't a complete solution, but you can use it to extend spin-down times. Without it, Xcode sometimes crashes when it accesses a disk that is sleeping or when a Mac wakes up after hibernating. CHUD and Spindown are installed with Xcode. You can find Spindown in `<Macintosh Hard Disk>/Developer/Applications/CHUD/Hardware Tools`.

CAUTION

The spin-down problem makes it difficult to keep folder and application shortcuts in the Finder window, where they're most useful to you. For example, if you drag Xcode to Places so you can run it quickly and the disk it is installed on hibernates or sleeps, the link may disappear. If you have enough free space, installing on your Mac's boot drive avoids this problem.

A Mac with an SSD (Solid State Drive) for OS X and Xcode can be a significant timesaver. Xcode 4 loads projects quickly but takes much longer to boot than Xcode 3. You can speed up the initial boot by running Xcode from a faster-than-average conventional disk, a RAID 0 system (Redundant Array of Independent Disks), or an SSD. This is a luxury option but is well worth considering for professional development.

Choosing peripherals

Peripherals can make a significant difference to your productivity. It's good practice to choose extras that feel comfortable to work with and don't have quirks, design features, or extras that distract you.

Selecting a printer

A printer isn't essential and is discouraged for environmental reasons, but may be useful for occasional debugging. It can be easier to trace execution through a paper listing than to view it in sections on a monitor. There are no special requirements for printing from Xcode. Any standard inkjet or laser printer works.

Choosing a pointing device

There's no lack of choice in the mouse market, and if you intend to develop professionally, getting a professional mouse with extra features can be well worth the extra money. You'll use it every day, and it's important that you're comfortable with it, that its shape doesn't leave you with RSI (Repetitive Strain Injury), and that it doesn't have extra or missing features that break your concentration. Extremely expensive mice with extra buttons may not be more productive than cheaper models. A good cordless mouse with a smooth scroll wheel can save significant time, particularly if it includes inertia for faster scrolling.

Opinions are mixed on Apple's own Magic Trackpad and mouse models. Some developers feel very comfortable with them, but others don't like them at all. Because pointing devices are a matter of taste, be sure to spend time trying out the various alternatives as thoroughly as you can. You can literally save hours or even days over a year with a cheap upgrade to a pointing device that you feel comfortable with.

Choosing your Mac keyboard

Keyboard action is a matter of personal taste. Some developers love the Apple wireless keyboards, but others find them impossible to work with. Be sure to visit a computer store to try some alternatives. Logitech PC keyboards offer a much wider range of actions and feels, and can easily be customized to create Mac mappings. Although some Apple enthusiasts may be horrified by the idea of using non-Apple peripherals, keyboard feel has a measurable influence on typing accuracy and comfort, so you must pick a feel that works for you.

Depending on your location, your Mac keyboard may have unhelpful character mappings. For example, in the UK, the critical # (hash) character isn't available, and you can type `#import` only by copying and pasting it from an existing import directive. It's a good idea to consider a free character mapping tool such as Ukelele (`scripts.sil.org/cms/scripts/page.php?site_id=nrsi&id=ukelele`), which sacrifices nonessential characters to create a custom layout that includes all the essential characters used in C-family programming.

TIP

You may want to consider using a U.S. keyboard for development. This can be a practical choice if you have a Mac dedicated to development, but is less practical if you also use for Mac for browsing and e-mail. You can buy a U.S. keyboard from the United States using a site such as amazon.com or newegg.com. Beware of import duties and VAT—the final cost may up to 25 percent higher than the order price.

Choosing supporting software

Although Xcode seems self-contained, in practice you're likely to use it with other software. For example, if you choose to view documentation online, your choice of web browser becomes a significant limiting factor. Safari and Google Chrome are reasonably well behaved, but Firefox 3.x is notorious for memory leaks and lock-ups, and for running Flash and Java plug-ins with 100 percent processor utilization. Both can slow Xcode to a crawl. In extreme cases, it's impossible to edit code without a noticeable delay. This may change in future versions of Firefox, but currently Firefox 3.x can't be recommended. Debatably, Chrome provides the best overall browsing experience. It supports Flash and ad blocking, loads pages quickly, and can handle many open tabs—a useful feature when you may have many class references open simultaneously.

Xcode typically requires the most recent version of OS X. If you are a member of the Mac Developer Program, this is included in the program cost. Minor upgrades are free, but iPhone developers may need to buy a major update when it becomes available.

Other tools can be added as needed. Unless you outsource graphic design, you need an editing suite to create start-up graphics, icons, buttons, and other images, as shown in Figure 2.2. This is an essential requirement for the iOS projects, where graphic design is extremely important, and a very useful extra for OS X development. Adobe's Creative Suite is the de facto standard, but it's expensive. Free or cheap alternatives include Gimp for OS X (`www.gimp.org/macintosh`) and Pixelmator (`www.pixelmator.com`).

A small number of helper apps are available for developers. Xcode 3 supported various plug-ins, but these are no longer compatible with Xcode 4. The Mac App Store includes a selection of other apps that have been updated. For example, Accessorizer (`www.kevincallahan.org`) adds boilerplate setter and getter code. More apps are likely to appear in the App Store as Xcode 4 matures.

Figure 2.2

Although it isn't integrated directly into Xcode, Adobe Photoshop works well as an external editor for graphics.

CROSS-REFERENCE

For more information about selecting editors and helper applications for various file types, see Chapter 8.

Signing Up for Development

Xcode 3 was free. It was supplied on every Mac's OS X installation disk in the Optional Installs folder. You can also download the latest version by registering as a developer for free.

Apple has changed this policy for Xcode 4. You can buy Xcode 4 from the Mac App Store for $4.99 without registering as a developer, as shown in Figure 2.3. This allows you to experiment with Xcode 4. It doesn't allow you to create apps you can sell through the store, but currently you can use this option to create Mac apps you can sell from your own website.

You can also register as a developer. This gives you a "free" copy of Xcode 4 and also gives you access to the extra features you need to create apps you can sell, and upload them to the stores.

Figure 2.3

You can buy Xcode 4 from the Mac App Store.

Registering as a developer

To register as a developer, visit the Apple developer home page, which is currently at `developer.apple.com`, shown in Figure 2.4. The design of this page changes regularly, but recent designs have included a selection of sign-up links for the various developer programs.

Figure 2.4

Begin the sign-up process at Apple's developer portal. This image shows the bottom of the page, with a list of programs. Selecting a link takes you to the sign-up page for each program.

Choosing a program

Table 2.1 lists the current developer programs.

Sign-up is straightforward. You must supply an e-mail address for the free program, and you must provide personal details including an address and contact phone number for the paid programs. If you do not already have an Apple ID, you need to create one. If you already have an Apple ID for personal use, creating a separate company ID is useful if you are incorporated; this can simplify taxes and accounting.

Table 2.1 Apple Developer Programs

Layer	Cost	Comments
Mac Developer Program—Individual	$99/year	This program Includes the current production SDK and future seed releases of OS X for a solo developer. Registration typically takes 1 to 2 weeks. With this program, you can sell Mac apps through the Mac App Store. It does not give you access to the iPhone App Store.
Mac Developer Program—Company	$99/year	This program includes the current production SDK and future seed releases of OS X for one or more developers working as a team for a corporation or small business. Proof of incorporation must be faxed to Apple during sign-up. Registration may take a few weeks. With this program, you can sell Mac apps through the Mac App Store. It does not give you access to the iPhone App Store.
iPhone Developer Program—Individual	$99/year	This program includes the current production SDK and future seed releases of the iPhone SDK for a solo developer. It includes access to the App Store. It allows local and remote beta testing on the Simulator and up to 100 devices. Registration typically takes 1 to 2 weeks. With this program, you can sell iOS apps through the iOS App Store It does not include access to OS X seed builds (preview versions of OS X) or to the Mac App Store.
iPhone Developer Program—Company	$99/year	This program includes the features above, but is intended for small companies and corporations. It supports team management features that can allow or deny access to the program for individual developers. Proof of incorporation must be faxed to Apple during sign-up. Registration may take a few weeks. With this program, you can sell iOS apps through the iOS App Store This program does not include access to OS X seed builds (preview versions of OS X) or to the Mac App Store.
iPhone Developer Enterprise Program	$299/year	This program is for corporations developing in-house apps for their employees. Apps must be distributed internally and cannot be sold through the App Store. It requires a Dun & Bradstreet number, which is an international business identification number that is made available only to larger businesses. It includes access to future versions of the SDK and iOS.
iPhone Developer University Program	Free	This program is for accredited degree-granting academic institutions. It allows testing on hardware devices and the Simulator, and it includes access to the current SDK, but not to forthcoming beta versions. It does not include access to the App Store, in-house distribution, or Apple's technical support.

The iOS developer programs

The chief benefits of the iOS developer program, whose portal is shown in Figure 2.5, are access to the App Store retail program and the ability to test apps on real hardware. Testing requires the generation and installation of *certificates* and *profiles*—files that allow you to develop and test apps but don't allow you to copy them freely—on a special area of the developer site. This is a complex process and is described in Chapter 11.

CAUTION

Keep in mind that although the iOS program seems cheap, you need at least an iPod touch to test apps, and an iPhone is strongly preferred. Adding an iPad to your hardware collection can push the total initial cost of app development during the first year to over $1,000. Many developers do not earn this back from sales.

Business sign-up requires proof of incorporation. Documents must be faxed, not sent, to Apple's HQ in Cupertino. If you are a solo developer with an incorporated business, signing up as a company can take an extra week or so, but it simplifies foreign tax accounting for App Store sales. Without a company, a portion of foreign earnings can be withheld for tax reasons until local tax authorities receive paperwork that proves country of residence. With multiple territories (sales regions) in the App Store, this can create a small mountain of paperwork for individual developers and may also hold up payments.

Figure 2.5

Beginning enrollment in the iOS Developer Program can take up to three weeks for companies. Enrollment for individuals is sometimes processed within 24 hours, but may take a couple of weeks.

Enrolling for the iOS Developer Program also provides potential access to the Apple's add-on services for iOS, including the iAD network, the GameCenter network, the in-app purchase scheme, and the push notification service. To use these services, you must enable them individually after enrollment. You also may need to authorize or sign further legal contracts.

The Mac developer programs

The Mac developer programs shown in Figure 2.6 give developers access to the App Store and the opportunity to install and develop for versions of OS X before they're made available to the public. OS X develops more slowly than iOS, but beta updates are made available regularly. These updates may not be completely stable, so it's a good idea—although an expensive one— to install them on a separate development machine.

Because it's possible to sell Mac applications independently from a website without using the App Store, and because anyone can buy and install Xcode for a nominal fee, the incentive to sign up as a full Mac developer may not be completely compelling. It can be worth buying Xcode 4 first to experiment with it, and then signing up as a full developer when you have developed a commercial app.

Figure 2.6

The supplied tools and developer resources for those enrolling in the Mac Developer Program are almost identical to those available to iOS developers, with the difference that Mac developers get access to beta versions of OS X.

NOTE
Having a combined program for both OS X and iOS development would be useful. Unfortunately, Apple doesn't offer one. In practice, either program gives you access to a full version of Xcode with both iOS and OS X development tools and supporting documentation. The programs differ in access to beta versions for their respective platforms, and to the two App Stores.

Accessing developer resources

Developer resources include the online reference libraries, a selection of developer videos, and the developer message boards.

Using the online documentation and references

The iOS and OS X reference libraries, which include documentation described in Chapter 6, are freely available and do not require registration. The URLs change regularly, but currently you can find the iOS library at `http://developer.apple.com/library/ios/navigation/` and the OS X library at `http://developer.apple.com/library/mac/navigation/`. If these URLs no longer work, search for "OS X Reference Library" and "iOS Reference Library."

Viewing developer videos

The developer videos, an example of which is shown in Figure 2.7, include keynotes and background talks, often taken from Apple's WWDC (World Wide Developer Conference) series. In the past, Apple charged $500 for access to these videos. Now they are available via iTunes to anyone who registers for a paid program. The keynote speeches from each year's WWDC remain free and can be downloaded by anyone.

Some developers find that the hands-on examples in the videos offer a more successful introduction to key technologies and essential development techniques than the slightly chaotic explanations in the documentation.

The Mac and iOS Developer Programs allow access to different video collections. Only Mac developers are given access to the Mac Development Foundation Videos. Similarly, only iOS developers are allowed to download the iOS Development Videos.

CAUTION
Video sizes can up to 400MB, and the complete video collection is around 10GB. You can watch them online, but if you have slow- or medium-speed broadband, downloading them may be your best choice. As of version 10.1 of iTunes, batch downloading isn't available. You can mark any number of videos for download, but iTunes unmarks them after it completes two downloads. The remaining videos must be reselected manually.

Figure 2.7

If you download developer videos from iTunes, you can back them up to an alternative location and play them in alternative players, which may be on other machines.

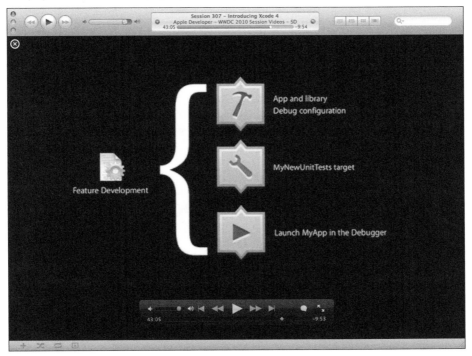

Using the Apple developer discussion boards

The Apple Developer boards are perhaps the least useful developer resource. Alternative developer boards such as stackoverflow (www.stackoverflow.com) have built up a larger collection of questions and answers, discussed in more depth. They're also indexed by Google, which simplifies topic and keyword searches.

The chief advantage of the official developer boards is that Apple employees sometimes read and comment. Otherwise, you can typically get more detailed and more helpful comments from elsewhere, from developers who may have worked through a problem and posted the code for a full solution.

Asking for technical support

Both the iOS and OS X Developer Programs offer developers up to two code-level support incidents per year. You can use these to discuss your code with an Apple technical support engineer. The engineers won't be able to understand a huge project instantly, so technical support incidents are best used for mysterious but localized issues that resist conventional debugging and are beyond the insight of other developers.

Many of the internal features of iOS and OS X are undocumented, and code doesn't always work as you expect it to. For example, UI code may create extra ancillary views while managing transitions, or UI objects may have complex features that can't be accessed externally. Apple engineers are more likely to be aware of these quirks than external developers. But Apple doesn't guarantee that engineers will solve a problem, only that they will look at it. Developers who find the service useful can buy two extra incidents for $99 or five for $249.

CAUTION

Only public non-beta versions of iOS and OS X are supported. You won't be able to ask questions about bugs or features in beta releases.

Getting Started with Xcode

When you enroll in a program, you are allowed to access a page like the one shown in Figure 2.8. The design may differ, but the page includes a download link to the latest SDK (Software Development Kit).

Xcode is packaged as a standard Mac .dmg file, which is typically around 2 to 3GB. You must download the complete SDK with each new update; there's no incremental install or upgrade option.

A complete upgrade cycle may require extra downloads. A new version of iTunes is often released around the same time as Xcode is updated. OS X also may go through an incremental update.

iOS developers need to update the firmware in all their devices—or at least, in all the devices that need to run the current version of iOS. Documentation may need to be downloaded separately.

TIP

If you have a spare older device, it can be useful to keep an older version of iOS on it and use it for compatibility testing. Conversely, if you have a single device such as an iPhone, you may be reluctant to upgrade it to beta firmware for testing. Older apps typically work on newer firmware. However, apps developed for new beta firmware don't work on devices with older versions of iOS, unless you deliberately make them compatible.

A full update can easily require 5 to 8GB of files, including Xcode, firmware, documentation, iTunes, and OS X. This is impractical over dial-up and can be difficult with slow broadband. If you don't have 10MB/s or faster broadband, it's useful to plan updates so you can leave the download running overnight.

Mac developers have a more straightforward experience. OS X is updated less frequently and doesn't usually require extra downloads. Individual OS X beta releases are released approximately monthly, but are much smaller downloads than a full iOS beta. The differences between minor versions—for example, OS X 10.7.1 and 10.7.2—are often so small that you can develop apps without keeping up to date with them.

Figure 2.8

In this example, the download link appears at the bottom left. This location often changes.

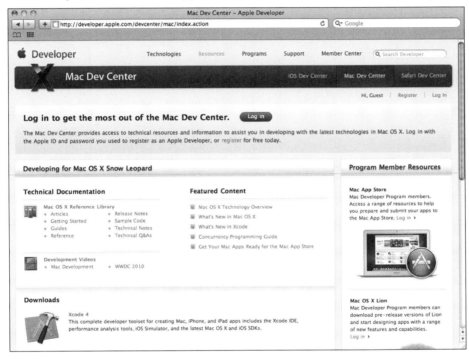

CAUTION

If you're limited to dial-up, Xcode may not be a practical solution for you. At best, you can try to find someone with faster broadband willing to download updates and burn them to a DVD or copy them to a memory stick. Unfortunately, the Xcode documentation is tightly integrated within the SDK, so this is only a partial solution.

Installing Xcode

After downloading, double-clicking the .dmg file mounts it in the usual way. The opened mounted image is shown in Figure 2.9. Double-clicking the .mpkg file starts the installer. If a PDF file is included, it lists the latest release notes.

After displaying the legal agreements, the installer tries to force you to install Xcode on your main system disk, as shown in Figure 2.10.

Figure 2.9

The Xcode dmg package is completely conventional. You can mount it and run the installer in the usual way.

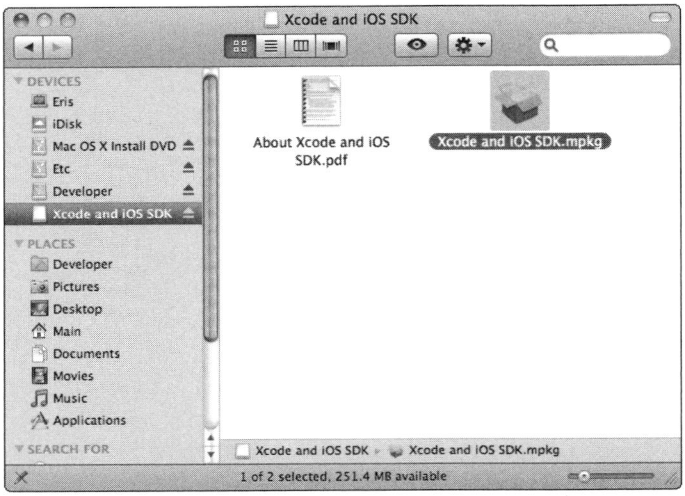

Figure 2.10

The installer doesn't appear to give you a choice of destination. What if you want to install to a different drive?

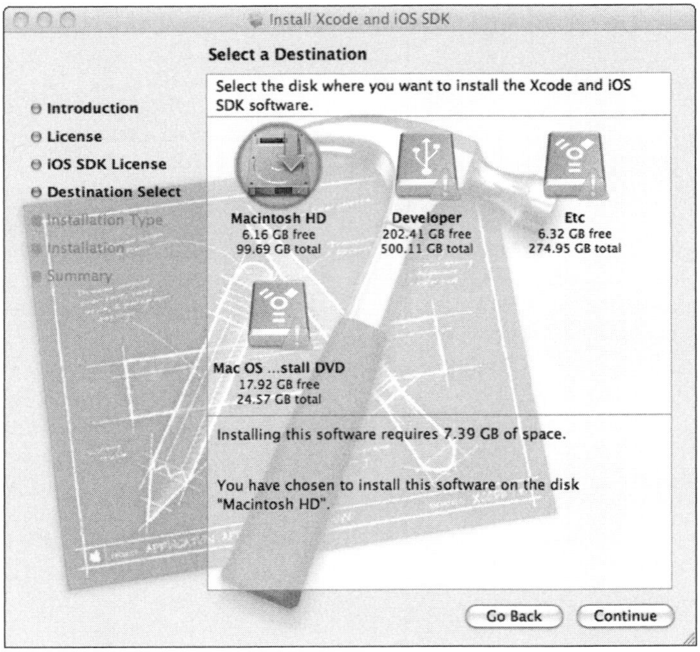

If you click Continue and then click the folder under the Location tab, you can select Other as the location. This opens a drop-down dialog box that allows you to select a drive and folder anywhere in your Mac, as shown in Figure 2.11. You also can create a new folder, if you choose to. Traditionally, Xcode is installed in a root-level folder named /Developer.

Figure 2.11

A hidden option makes it possible to choose Other and then select or create your own destination folder.

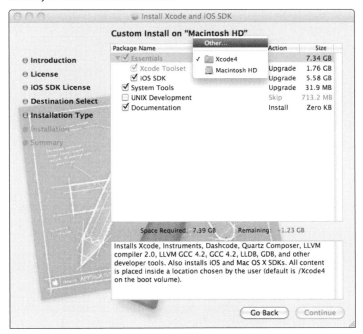

Installing to a different folder or disk creates a split installation. Around 900MB of key features, including some of the system tools, are always installed to the /Developer directory on the main system disk. The rest of Xcode can be installed in any folder you specify.

Typically, you see a list of optional features in the main install dialog box. The UNIX Development tools are of interest only to developers who want a separate set of compiler tools that can be accessed from Terminal using the command line. If you're not interested in UNIX development, you can leave this option uninstalled.

In the past, the documentation was downloaded and installed with Xcode. Now it's downloaded separately after you run Xcode. You can ignore the internal documentation and use Apple's web documentation exclusively, but there are good reasons to use both if you can. For more details about installing and using the documentation, see Chapter 6.

Depending on the current version of iOS or OS X, you may see more than one SDK listed here. In Xcode, an SDK is a collection of code libraries that build code for a specific version of either OS X or iOS. For example, Xcode uses different two iOS SDK libraries to build apps for the Simulator and for hardware devices.

In Xcode 4, Apple typically bundles all legacy versions into a single combined SDK for a given platform. You're no longer given a choice about which versions are installed, and all supported legacy versions are made available. This may change with future updates.

CROSS-REFERENCE
For information about creating applications that can run on legacy versions of iOS and OS X, see Chapter 10.

After you have selected a destination folder, the rest of the installation process is automatic. It can take from half an hour to two hours to install Xcode, depending on the speed of your Mac and its hard disks. You can leave your Mac unattended or continue working on something else. If you have to install Xcode, update iTunes, and change the firmware in one or more devices, the complete process can take up to half a day. If you also need to update OS X, it takes even longer.

CAUTION
Close Xcode and iTunes before you install a new version. The installer pauses if Xcode or iTunes are running.

Creating and organizing project folders

After installing Xcode, you can create supporting folders for your projects. *Do not save your projects inside a* /Developer *folder.* This is critically important. When you update Xcode, the contents of /Developer can be overwritten without notice. For similar reasons, don't install extra helper applications inside /Developer.

If you have installed Xcode into a separate partition, you can keep a project folder elsewhere on the partition. The exact location or name of your projects folder is arbitrary, but it's useful to choose a location that is only a few navigation clicks away from /Developer.

Figure 2.12 shows one possible folder workspace for Xcode and associated project folders. It's useful to have a scratch folder for quick trials and experiments, and a production folder for commercial projects. You may also want to have further separate folders for Apple sample code, template examples, downloaded code, shared or collaborative projects, and so on. Try to keep the main production folder dedicated solely to production code, which includes your own applications and any spin-off frameworks you create. The /Provisioning folder shown here stores certificates and downloaded provisioning profiles used in iOS development. It's good practice to store these in a separate folder to make them easy to find and to avoid misplacing them.

TIP

Prefixing project folders with a plus sign (+) lists them alphabetically in a separate order from the tool and support folders.

Figure 2.12

One possible /Developer folder layout is shown here. +Projects hold test and experiments and +Store hold code used in App Store projects.

Figure 2.13 shows one possible project folder structure. You often reuse graphics and fonts between projects, and it's helpful to keep them in a single shared folder. Similarly, even if some projects are abandoned, it's useful to keep them out of the way in a graveyard folder in case you need to refer to them again.

Figure 2.13

This is one possible projects folder layout. You may want to spend some time organizing your project workspaces before you begin coding. Your ideal layout may look very different, but it's important that it works smoothly for you.

Working with multiple versions of Xcode

SDKs are updated regularly, and you often need to have more than one version installed and available simultaneously. For example, you may have:

- A production version of Xcode for production code
- A newer beta version, used to explore the features in a forthcoming OS update
- An optional alternative or preview SDK with broader changes

Apple doesn't force you to install beta SDKs, but it's commercially useful to offer updated or new apps with new features as soon as the latest version of iOS is released to the public. Apple typically asks for new apps up to two weeks ahead of the release, to allow for review time.

Xcode is modular, and it isn't difficult to work with multiple versions. The core tools change very slowly. The biggest changes happen in the SDK folders and their supporting headers and binaries.

In practice, this means you can install multiple versions in separate folders. Use the /Developer folder for your production version. Other folder names are arbitrary. In theory, you should reinstall your production version of Xcode after installing a beta, but in practice, the order of installation rarely matters.

One caveat is that Xcode projects always run the most recently installed version of Xcode when you double-click them. It's often easier to start the production version of Xcode manually and select a project for editing than to load projects with a double-click in Finder. Xcode maintains a recent files list, so this isn't usually a hardship—and it may be more convenient.

Uninstalling Xcode

In theory, you should uninstall Xcode using an Apple-specified script. Open Terminal, and type the following:

```
$ sudo /Developer/Library/uninstall-devtools --mode=all
```

This removes most Xcode files and the /Developer folder. If you have Xcode installed in a different folder, you can find the script in the corresponding /Library folder.

C A U T I O N
There's no undo for this operation, and the files aren't moved to the Trash. Once Xcode is removed, it is gone, and everything in /Developer goes with it.

In practice, you can often drag the /Developer/Applications folder to the trash, and then install a new version of Xcode on top of the remains of the current one. This method isn't foolproof; it can sometimes lead to duplicated or misplaced frameworks, but it is lazy, quick, and simple. If you haven't customized the other contents of /Developer, you can drag the entire folder to the trash.

Summary

This chapter explored the hardware options you should consider to use Xcode productively, and it introduced the various Apple Developer Programs for iOS and OS X. It explained how to register as a developer, how to download Xcode, and how to create both a default install in the standard locations and a custom install in a selected folder or disk partition.

It also examined multi-version installations with simultaneous production and beta development systems, and it explained how you can remove Xcode from your system if you no longer need it.

Building Applications from Templates

Assembling the ingredients of an application by hand in Xcode isn't a trivial process. It's faster and more convenient to start from a ready-made template, extending it as needed.

Xcode includes templates for different types of iOS and OS X applications, including plug-ins and other special projects for OS X developers. Getting started with a template is easy. All templates include a bare skeleton of essential code and are guaranteed to build and run successfully.

You can make development more efficient by adding your own templates to Xcode's collection. The standard templates are very simple and limited. Some include features that you may not need, and most leave out useful features that can simplify development.

You can use the template system to create complex skeleton apps with almost any amount of code. For example, you could create a game template for iOS that includes a custom framework for graphics management, collision detection, and user input. This template could be reused as the starting point for a series of game projects.

In This Chapter

Using the OS X
Application templates

Using the iOS
Application templates

Customizing the
standard templates

Getting Started with Templates

You can access Xcode's template screen in two ways. Figure 3.1 shows Xcode's startup window. By default, this window appears when you launch Xcode. To show the templates, select the Create a new Xcode project option from the list at the left.

TIP
You can stop Xcode from showing this window by unchecking the Show this window when Xcode launches option near the bottom of the window. The Recents pane at the right is useful, so typically you'll want to see this screen.

Figure 3.1

Xcode's initial boot screen shows recent files, access to Open Other for not so recent files, and the Create a new Xcode project option that gives access to the templates.

You also can select File ⇨ New ⇨ New Project at any time, as shown in Figure 3.2.

Either option displays the drop-down panel shown in Figure 3.3. This is the unified list of templates for both iOS and OS X. The list of categories at the top left separates the two target operating systems and groups templates for each into categories. The Application category is the most useful, but many developers also use items from the Framework & Library collection. Application and System Plug-ins are more specialized, and the Other category includes a complete blank project for iOS and OS X, and an External Build System template for OS X only that can work with an external makefile and command-line compiler. Table 3.1 summarizes the categories.

TIP

You can ignore the categories and show every template for an OS by clicking the iOS or Mac OS X headers.

Figure 3.2

To show the templates after you've started working and the boot window is no longer visible, select the New Project option from the Xcode menu tree.

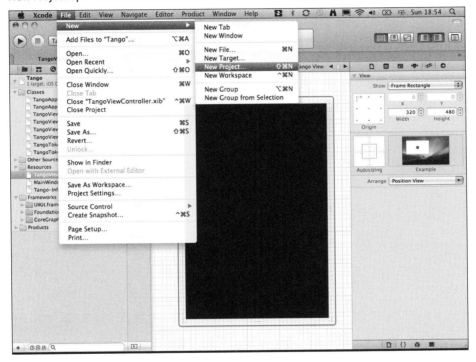

Figure 3.3

The list of standard templates is long, but typically you start with an Application template. The other templates are for more specialized projects.

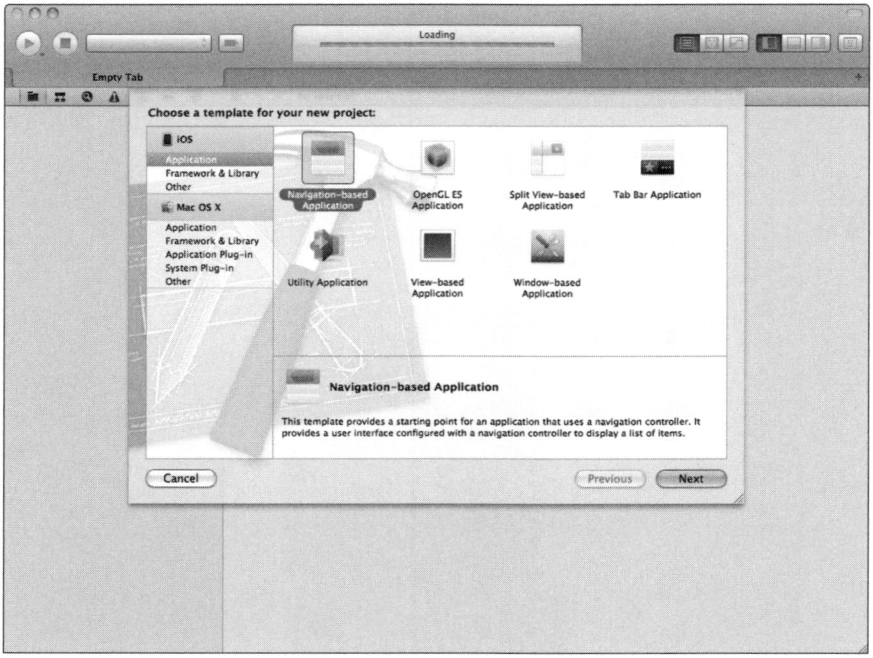

Table 3.1 Xcode Template Categories

Applications	iOS and OS X	Application skeletons. iOS offers a selection of standard application starting points. OS X offers a standard Cocoa application, an AppleScript application with access to Cocoa, and a command-line tool.
Framework & Library	iOS and OS X	Custom frameworks. iOS supports static Cocoa Touch libraries only. OS X supports custom Cocoa frameworks and libraries, project bundles, and C and C++ libraries.
Application Plug-in	OS X only	Plug-ins for specific OS X applications, including Automator, Address Book, Installer, WebKit, Quartz Composer, and Interface Builder.
System Plug-in	OS X only	Low-level plug-ins that extend the features of OS X, such as AU Instruments and Effects, IOKit drivers for hardware support, custom screen savers, and so on.
Other	iOS and OS X	A blank template. OS X also offers an external build system template.

Building a project from an application template

Application templates are guaranteed to build successfully. For example, to build a simple iOS application for the iPhone or iPad, start by selecting the iOS application page in the templates pane, and select the View Based Application template. Click Next, and select a target device using the Device Family pop-up menu in the bottom third of the panel, as shown in Figure 3.4.

Type a name for the App into the Product Name box. This name is used as a prefix for the main source files in the project, and it also defines the name that appears under the app when it's installed in Springboard This is called the *product name*. You can change it later using the build settings described in Chapters 12 and 13. You can also rename the files, but this is a more complex process, and isn't usually helpful or necessary.

CAUTION

Although most of the iOS templates include options that can create either an iPhone or an iPad app, only the Window-based template includes complete support for a truly universal app that can run on either platform without further changes. The other templates require extra manual effort, which includes a conversion stage that is discussed in Chapter 8. It's unfortunate that the templates don't support universal apps more consistently.

NOTE

Leave the Include Unit Tests option unchecked. This option adds features you can use to add automatic tests to your code. It's described in Chapter 17.

Figure 3.4

Most iOS templates include iPad and iPhone variants, but they're not presented in a consistent way, partly because the two device families support different UI features.

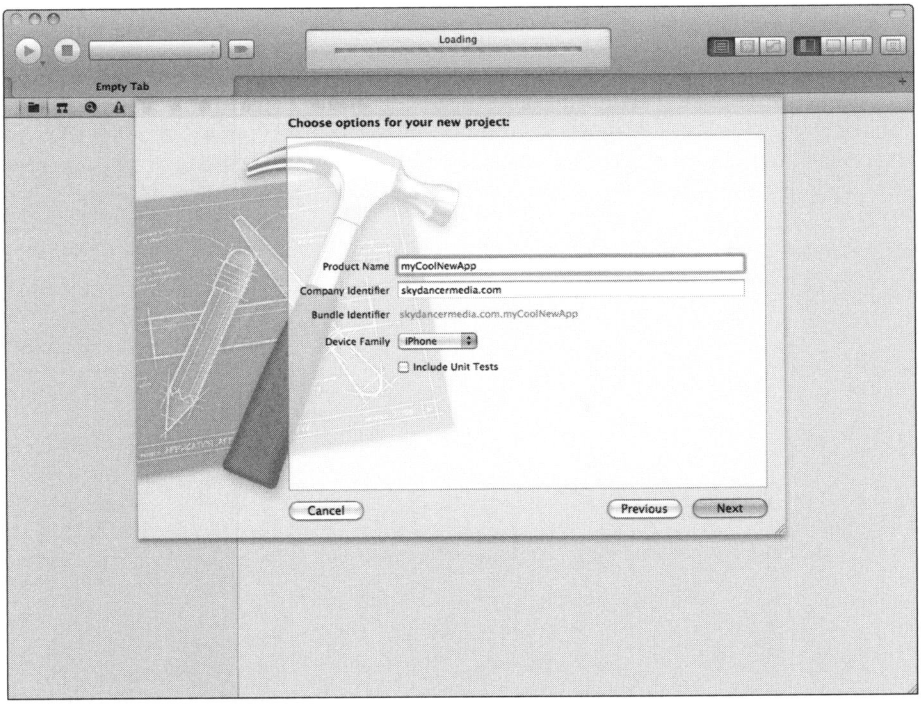

When you create an app from a template, a name and a copyright field that matches the company name are added to the top of every code file in the project. The easy but unexpected way to set the defaults for this content is to create a card with personal details in Address Book and choose Make This My Card from the Card menu. Xcode reads the information from Address Book when it creates a new project. You also can enter the following in Terminal on a single line:

```
defaults write com.apple.Xcode PBXCustomTemplateMacroDefinitions
        '{"ORGANIZATIONNAME"="<OrgNameHere>";}'
```

The *bundle identifier* is used as a file access tag by iOS and OS X and by code in your project. It's calculated automatically by Xcode. You can ignore this field for now. It's used when submitting apps to the App Store, and is described in later chapters.

TIP

Keep iOS app names short: Eight characters or less is ideal. Longer names are truncated with ellipses (…), which look bad and don't help the user. The app name isn't fixed, so you can change it later.

Select Next again, and click Create as shown in Figure 3.5. By default, Xcode automatically creates a new project folder, with the name you gave your app. Select the New Folder option at the bottom left only when you want to create a new enclosing folder for a number of related projects.

CROSS-REFERENCE

The Source Control at the bottom of the dialog box is described in Chapter 14. This is another feature you ignore for now.

Figure 3.6 shows the initial new project page. There's a list of items that look like folders at the top left and various project options, including the supported versions of either iOS or OS X, at the right. The folders are called groups, it's important to understand that they *do not exist on disk*. They're for Xcode's internal use and to help you keep project files organized efficiently.

Figure 3.5

Create a new project folder. The New Folder option is used only when you need to create a new folder one level up from the project folder. The project folder itself is created automatically.

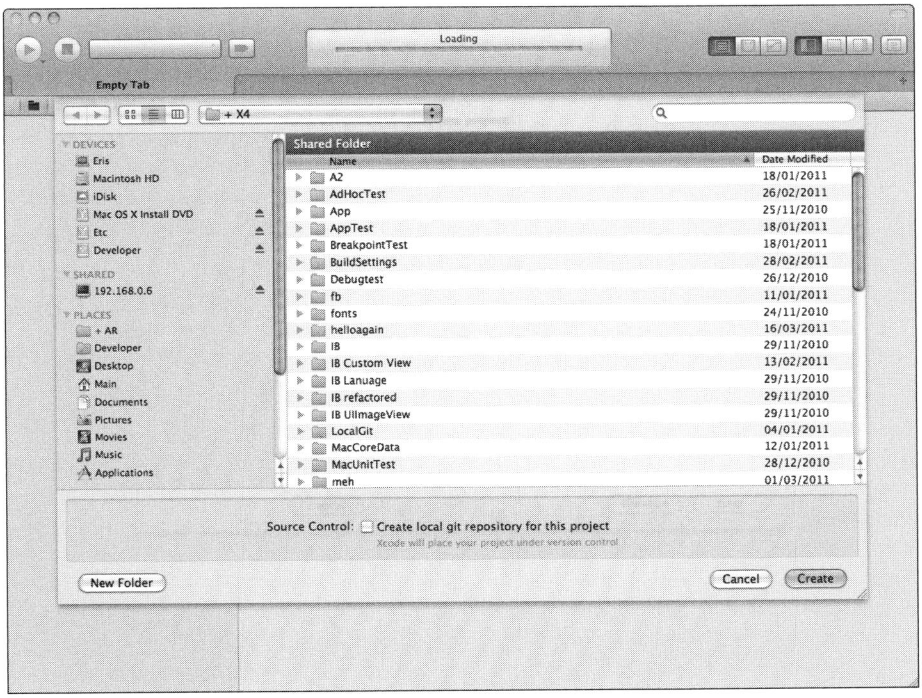

Figure 3.7 shows the files and directories that have been added and how they're arranged on disk. The folder structure is completely different. This seems confusing—and sometimes it is confusing.

Figure 3.6

The new project appears in Xcode. The virtual folders have been opened so you can see the files inside them.

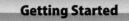

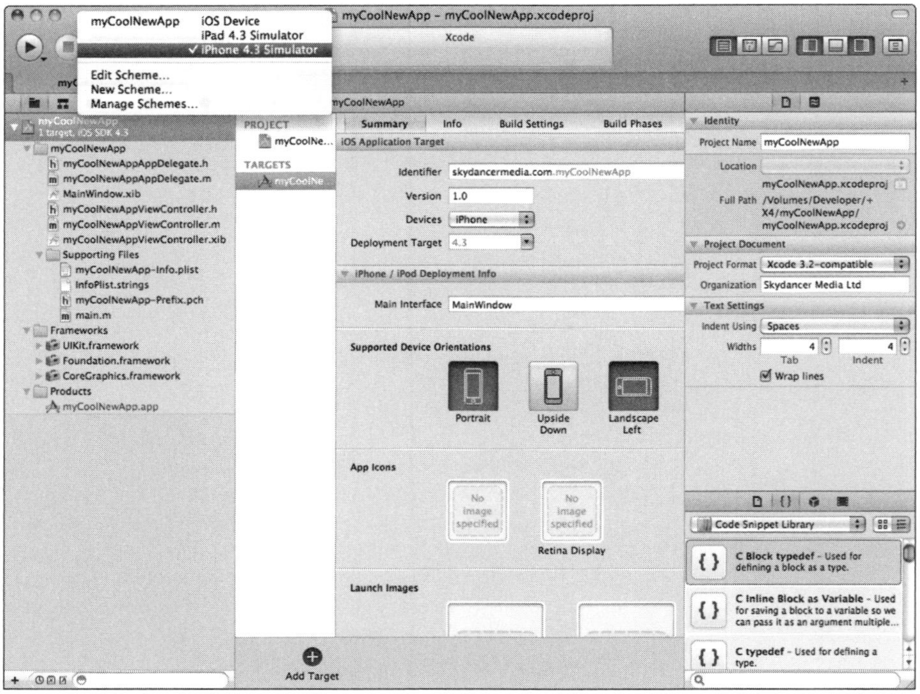

The pane with the folder-like icons at the left of Xcode is known as the Project navigator. It *does not show* a standard directory listing.

In earlier versions of Xcode 3, the items listed in this pane were similar to web links; they looked like a directory and folder listing, but in fact they were loose symbolic links to items on disk. They were so loose you could rename them without changing the files on disk.

This created almost limitless confusion, especially when the links became broken—which they often did. So in later versions of Xcode 3 the relationship was simplified. If you renamed an item in this pane, it was also renamed on disk. If you deleted an item, you could choose to move it to the trash or to remove it from the project but leave the file on disk. Xcode 4 uses the same system.

The folder-like icons remain entirely abstract. They're included to help you keep related files together in the Project navigator, but they don't exist on disk.

Figure 3.7

The new files as they appear on disk. Although the arrangement of files and folders is different, you don't usually need to access this folder directly; typically, you can use the more abstract view available in Xcode without worrying about the differences.

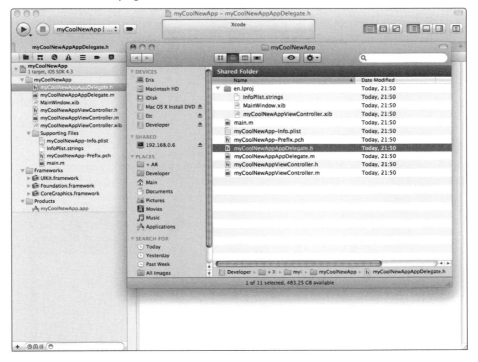

The symbolic link system may seem counterintuitive, but it makes it possible to add files to a project without copying them. For example, you can create a library or framework in a folder on disk, and import it into various projects as a collection of symbolic links that access the original files in their original source folder. Similarly, you can keep image files or fonts in a single folder and import them via links into multiple projects without having to create multiple copies.

CROSS-REFERENCE

For more information about using the Project navigator and the other new navigators in Xcode 4, see Chapter 4.

The other key element to notice in Figure 3.6 is the Scheme/Destination menu near the top left. The Destination sets the platform—for example, the Simulator, or a hardware device for iOS, and either a 32-bit or 64-bit environment for OS X. Schemes manage the internal features of the build process. They're introduced in Chapters 12 and 13.

You can't test apps on a hardware device until you follow the provisioning steps described in Chapter 11. So for now, use this menu to select the Simulator, as shown in Figure 3.6.

You can now click the Run button at the top left of Xcode to build and run your skeleton app. Xcode takes a while to pre-compile the project's headers, build the app, and load it into the Simulator. The first time you build an app or an application for a new target, the build and install process takes some time because Xcode must perform various one-time operations to complete the build. Subsequent builds happen more quickly, because Xcode has much less work to do. Builds also take time to install, so the first time you run an app in the Simulator you see a black screen. The screen usually persists for 10 seconds or so, but occasionally it can last for up to a minute.

Eventually the app loads and runs, as shown in Figure 3.8. The empty gray window isn't very exciting. It does nothing at all, but internally it is a complete skeleton app. You can now go back and begin editing the source files shown in Figure 3.6 to create the UI for the app.

Figure 3.8

Run the template application in the Simulator. As a skeleton application, it does nothing except paint the window gray.

C A U T I O N

The Simulator is a separate application. Xcode launches it and disappears into the background. The Simulator menu replaces the Xcode menu while the former is foregrounded. Typically you float the Simulator window on top of Xcode, so you can re-foreground Xcode by clicking anywhere around the Simulator. You can also use the Dock to switch between Xcode and the Simulator.

Although this example creates an iOS application, the steps for an OS X application are almost identical, with the difference that an OS X application runs in a new window—not in the Simulator. The features of the different OS X and iOS templates are listed in more detail below.

C R O S S - R E F E R E N C E

For more about editing, see Chapter 4. For an introduction to UI design, see Chapter 7.

Looking inside the Application templates

Most applications are built using Cocoa or Cocoa Touch. You can start with a minimal windowed application, or you can select a more complex template that includes one or more supporting views. The Cocoa and Cocoa Touch templates always include the following:

- **Class implementation files that define the basic elements of the application:** For Cocoa and Cocoa Touch applications, the elements always include an application delegate that receives and processes application management messages from the OS—for example, one message is sent when the application finishes loading, another when the application is about to quit, and so on. Depending on the template, the default classes may also include at least one UI view controller, which receives and processes user actions generated by the UI.

- **Class header files to support the implementation files:** The headers include `#import` directives for the essential UI framework on each platform. In templates with more than one class, the headers are imported correctly complete throughout.

- **One or more *nib files* with a .xib extension:** Nib files are OS X and iOS resource files that define the basic properties of a window, and optionally of a UI view. These files have a dual purpose. They define the look and feel of the application UI. You can edit them to add UI objects such as images, buttons, sliders, and other controls. OS X applications include the menu tree in their nib files. Internally, nib files are treated as a general purpose inventory of objects to be loaded and initialized when the application runs. It's one of the open secrets of Cocoa development that you can add any object or class to a nib file.

C R O S S - R E F E R E N C E

For more information about creating, editing, and using nib files, see Chapters 7 and 8.

- ***Links* between the nib files and the class files:** In Apple development, code can control and respond to UI objects only when these links are defined. They appear in two places: in the nib file, and in special directives within the class headers and the implementation code.

- **A *prefix header* file with** #import **directives for the essential application frameworks:** When you build an application, the headers added to this file are pre-compiled only once.

- **A *plist* (property list) file that includes a dictionary of application settings:** You can edit this dictionary to implement standard user preferences for the application. For details, see Appendix B.

- An English *localization* folder. This includes a ***strings* file that is used to *localize* the application so it supports other languages in addition to English:** The strings file includes pairs of strings. One string is used as a key in the application. The other string defines the text that appears when that string is used. Each language you support has its own strings file, with different output strings for each key. The templates contain English localization only.

- **A *main.m* file:** This is a short block of boilerplate startup code that loads the application and creates a memory pool for it. You can usually ignore this file.

NOTE
OS X projects can also link code to the UI using bindings—indirect links between properties and UI elements. The standard OS X templates don't include any bindings; if you want to use them, you have to add your own. Bindings aren't available in iOS.

Using the OS X Application templates

Although there are only three OS X Application templates, all include extra options.

Using the Cocoa Application template

The Cocoa Application template includes the ingredients listed earlier. The two options are shown in Figure 3.9.

You can create a *Document-Based Application,* which is designed for multi-document applications. Each document loads and creates an instance of the same nib file. The template uses Cocoa's NSDocument class to implement the document's features. It includes extra set-up and tear-down features that aren't needed in an application that uses a single window, but it isn't a full implementation of a complete document-based application. You need to add file save/load features, recent file support, and undo code.

The Use Core Data option creates an application with support for Core Data storage. The code implements automatic archiving and loading of the data, but it doesn't implement specific editing features. It also doesn't define a data model. For a brief introduction to Core Data, see Appendix B.

Figure 3.9

Select a Cocoa Application template, and set the two options. The grayed-out Spotlight Importer option isn't available, and you can ignore it.

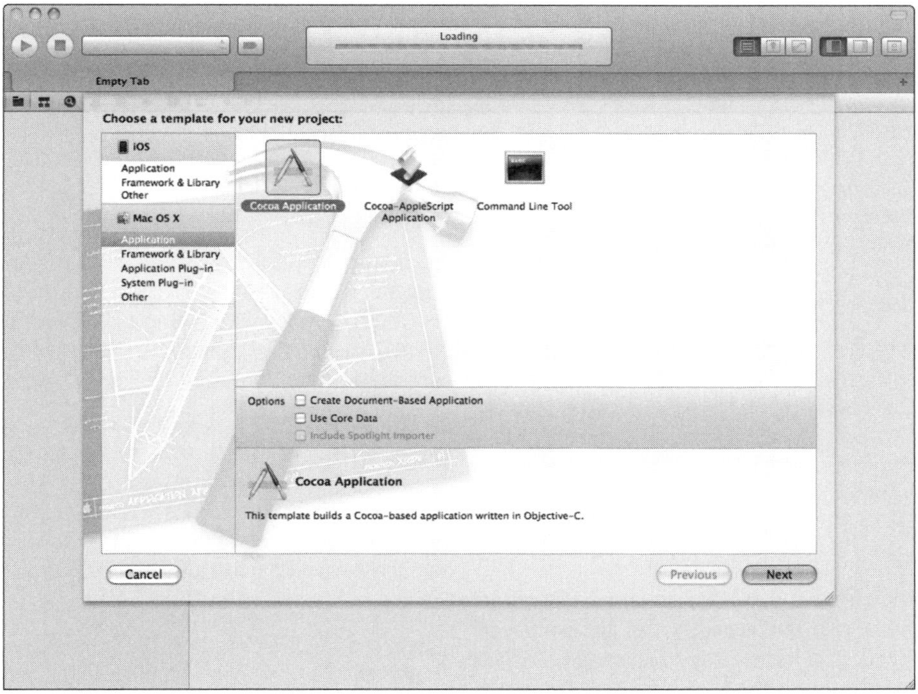

NOTE

Core Data *isn't* a full relational database. Its features are more limited, but it can still be a useful way to manage data objects that can include multiple attributes.

Using the Cocoa-AppleScript Application template

The Cocoa-AppleScript Application template, shown in Figure 3.10, creates a minimal AppleScript application. It's effectively a drastically simplified version of the standard Cocoa Application template, rewritten in AppleScript instead of Objective-C. Only two methods appear here: `applicationWillFinishLaunching` and `applicationShouldTerminate`. Real applications are likely to need more in the way of set-up, so this template is a prime candidate for replacement with a more advanced template of your own design.

Understanding Views in Apple Development

The word *view* has more than one meaning in Apple development. It can mean a complete UI design that defines all the elements in the UI: the buttons, images, and other features. But it also can mean individual UI elements within that configuration. For example, a button may include a *text view* that defines the text. A label may be called a *label view*. And so on. This seems inconsistent, but in general if an object is visible on the screen, it can be called a view. Individual UI items can also be called *controls*.

There's no doubt that the terminology could be simpler and clearer, especially for newcomers. It becomes easier to understand when you look at the classes used in Cocoa and Cocoa Touch. `UIView` and `NSView` are generic containers for on-screen content. Controls are usually subclasses of these top-level elements. The class relationships are easier to understand from the code level than from the top-down design level.

Apple is somewhat evangelical about a design pattern known as Model View Controller (MVC). This aims to split on-screen content from underlying data models, bridging the gap with *controller objects* that can abstract the underlying data from the UI. Done properly MVC can create applications that are efficient and easy to maintain, because the UI only needs to load and display a small subset of the underlying data, without having to make a separate working copy.

But confusion can occur because some classes that work as controllers also implement a complete view. For example, iOS has a class called `UIImagePickerController`, which not only accesses an iPhone's photo library and controls the camera, but it also displays its own complete UIs for both. Technically this still fits the pattern—the controller abstracts the data and manages the UI—but it blurs developer expectations about what a controller class is likely to do.

It's best not to get hung up on these apparent inconsistencies. MVC is an influence, not a religion, and as long as you understand how to use the classes and what a view is in approximate terms, you have all the information you need to work with views successfully.

In iOS, navigation is managed by *view switching*. Typically, a top-level window object is associated with a navigation or view controller. When the user requests a new page, the controller loads the next view and displays it. Usually, it also deletes the previous view after it's no longer visible, to save memory—a process known as *lazy loading*.

Practical UI design is a combination of object and control layout and view switching code. Usually, you create subclasses of views and view controllers to run your own UI-specific code, and you design the view layout in Interface Builder (IB). But you also can add and remove objects from a view under code control, and some developers prefer not to use IB at all.

OS X design is simpler, because views are more static. They may change as the user works with them, but view swapping is an optional refinement and not a key navigation feature.

TIP

For a guide to developing AppleScript applications, see the companion *AppleScript* in Wiley's Developer Reference series.

Figure 3.10

The Cocoa-AppleScript template creates a very simple AppleScript application, which launches and… does nothing.

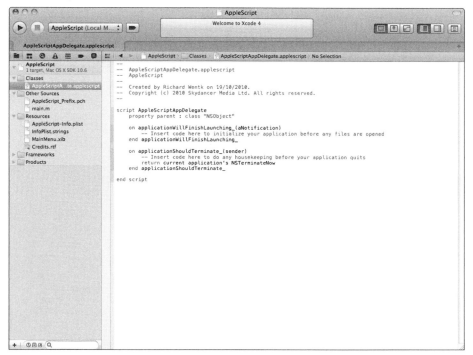

Using the Command Line Tool template

In a Cocoa application, main.c loads and runs the application, and you can ignore it. In a command-line application, main.c *is* the application. As you might expect, the Command Line Tool template creates a C or C++ file designed to run from the command line. Parameters are passed in `argc` and `argv[]` in the usual way. After building, the tool runs in the Console window, which is introduced in Chapter 4. You also can run the tool from Terminal.

As shown in Figure 3.11, you can select one of six templates for the tool. This is less flexible than it sounds. The different variations link against the named OS X libraries. In practice, this means they differ only in the `#include` directive at the top of the file. For example, if you select the Core Foundation option, the template's code looks like this:

```
#include <CoreFoundation/CoreFoundation.h>

int main (int argc, const char * argv[]) {

    // insert code here...
    CFShow(CFSTR("Hello, World!\n"));
    return 0;
}
```

Figure 3.11

Create a Command Line tool, a text-based application that doesn't use a GUI (Graphical User Interface). The menu simply preselects different headers in a `#include` directive.

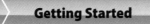

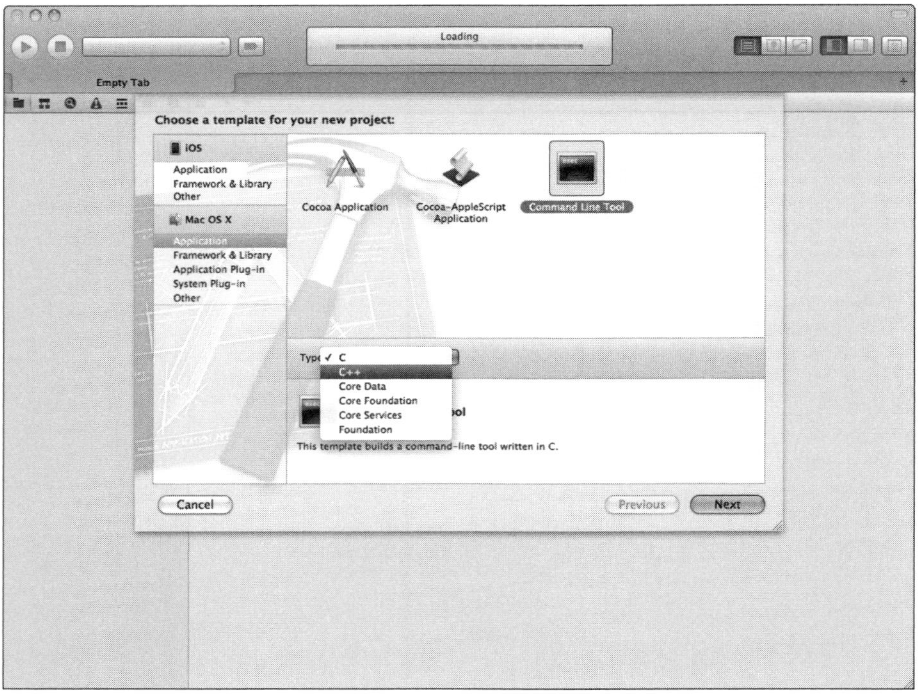

Understanding the iOS Application templates

The default iOS templates include bare-bones examples of various possible iOS UI configurations. Understand that these outlines are a starting point, not a definitive guide to UI design. Real iOS applications rarely have much in common with the templates. As you become more experienced, the limitations of the templates become more obvious and more restrictive, and you'll almost certainly want to modify them or create new templates of your own.

TIP
You'll find it useful to build and run each of the templates in turn. Be sure to save a version of each template to a special templates folder so you can explore each template again later without having to re-create it.

Using the Navigation-based template

The Navigation-based template, shown in Figure 3.12, includes a window that displays a single instance of the `UITableView` class. iOS doesn't support drop-down menus. Instead, you build menu-like navigation trees by combining a Navigation Controller object with one or more of these table views. Selecting a *cell*—an item in the table—is similar to selecting a menu item. Your code can respond by displaying the next table in the tree, or it can perform some other action.

Figure 3.12

Run the Navigation-based template. The navigation controller creates the gray bar at the top of the UI, and the table view generates the table cells under it. You need to add code to set the title, fill in the contents of the cells, and respond when the user taps a cell.

Navigation is managed by an instance of `UINavigationController`, which handles movement through the tree and displays a title and back/forward buttons. As a top-level item, the navigation controller is included in the main window nib. Although it's not entirely obvious from the code, you typically modify the code in this template so it loads another table view when the user taps a cell.

The Navigation-based template is iPhone only. For iPad projects, use the SplitView-based template—it has similar features but supports the iPad's more complex navigation options.

Using the OpenGL ES template

The OpenGL ES template, shown in Figure 3.13, includes set-up and tear-down for an application that uses the OpenGL ES graphics subsystem. OpenGL ES is used for games and for complex custom UIs. It's a specialized high-performance graphics environment, and you can ignore it unless you need to create complex 3D or 2D animations.

The graphics are wrapped inside a class called `EAGLView`, which selects and runs one of the two rendering classes—`ESRenderer1` and `ESRenderer2`—which support OpenGL ES 1.5 and OpenGL ES 2.2 code, respectively.

Figure 3.13

The code of the OpenGL ES template animates a moving shaded square. Significant set-up and tear-down code is needed to make this animation possible.

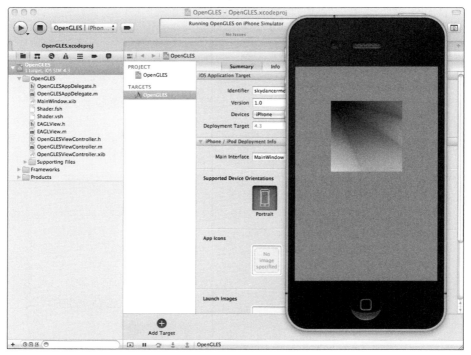

Older models of the iPhone—the 2.x, 3G, and the iPod Touch second generation support OpenGL ES 1.5 code only. In practice, you add your backward-compatible code to ESRenderer1.m and current code to ESRenderer2.m. Alternatively, you can comment out the renderer selection and force your project to run the older code, which is supported on all hardware but lacks some of the powerful features in the OpenGL ES 2.2 specification.

The default code in both renderer files draws a colored square and also maintains an animation counter. The wrapper view includes an animation timer that calls each renderer repeatedly. Your rendering code is responsible for calculating the updated view at each animation frame.

Using the SplitView-based template

The SplitView-based template illustrated in Figure 3.14 is the iPad equivalent of the Navigation-based template. The iPad's larger screen makes it possible to view a list of menu items in a *split* view, which is next to a *detail view* that can display relevant information for each item or for the application as a whole. Navigation code is similar to that used in the Navigation-based template.

When the iPad is vertical or in *portrait mode*, the split view appears when the user taps the naviga-tion button at the top left, floats above the detail view, and disappears when the user taps outside it. When the iPad is horizontal *landscape mode*, the split view always appears at the left.

TIP

You can change the rotation in the Simulator by selecting Hardware ⟳ Rotate Right or Rotate Left. You can also scale the iPad simulator by selecting Window ⟳ Scale 50% or 100%. The 100% view requires a monitor with a width or height of at least 1200 pixels.

Using the Tab Bar Application template

The Tab Bar Application template shown in Figure 3.15 can create an iPhone or iPad applica-tion. You can choose the hardware target using the menu in the Options bar above the tem-plate description. The user taps the buttons on the Tab Bar to select different views.

Figure 3.14

This illustration shows the iPad Simulator window with 50 percent scaling in portrait mode using the SplitView-based template.

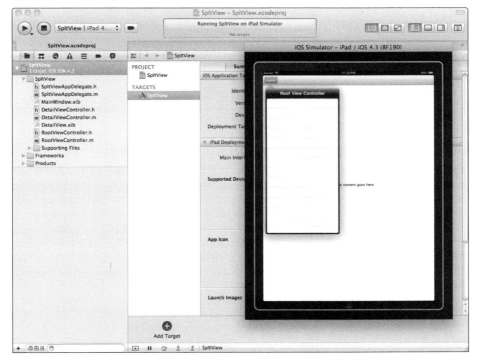

Figure 3.15

The Tab Bar Application template displays and switches views automatically, using the UITabBarController class to manage the switching and UITabBar class to display the buttons and respond to user taps.

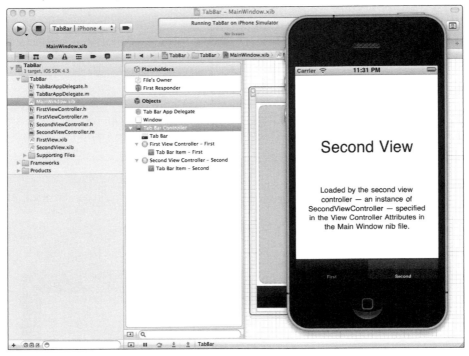

This is one of the more confusing templates, because the code doesn't appear to do anything. In fact, the Tab Bar Controller manages view switching for you automatically. The template includes two view controllers and their associated nib files and code. You can use Interface Builder to add further views—pages—to the template by adding further view controllers to the list inside the Tab Bar Controller in the MainWindow.xib file. There isn't space in this chapter to include a full step-by-step guide to this process, but once you've explored IB in the next few chapters, you can return to this template and experiment with copying view controllers in the MainWindow.xib file, creating new view controller classes, and assigning them to the duplicated view controllers.

Using the Utility Application template

The Utility Application template shown in Figure 3.16 creates an iPhone application with an info button at the bottom right. Tapping the button reveals a flip-side view with a navigation bar and a Done button. The two views have separate controllers. The flip view is typically used for preferences and other application features that don't need to be permanently visible. There is no iPad option for this template.

Figure 3.16

Think of the Utility Application template as a design example than a practical application starting point. Many apps use the main/flip view design idiom, but it's often implemented in simpler and more flexible ways.

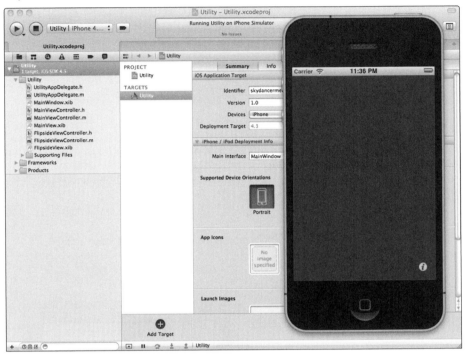

Although you can use this template as is, it has some nonessential features. The navigation bar on the flip-side wastes space. Note that it's simply a navigation bar—a holder for a button, and not a navigation controller. Often, you'll replace the bar and the button with a single return button at the bottom of the screen, perhaps with a custom graphic.

TIP

For Cocoa experts, the flip code triggered by the Done button uses a protocol method call to the superview. Replacing this with a simpler call to `dismissModalView: animated:` in the flip view works just as well. You can use `self` as the modal view parameter. The call automatically finds the superview, so you don't need to specify it.

Using the View-based Application template

You can create either an iPad or an iPhone view-based application with this template, which is shown in Figure 3.17. This is the standard vanilla template used by most developers. It includes a window, a view controller, and a view. The view controller is already subclassed, so you can start adding code to it immediately. The view isn't subclassed, so you can't add code to it. But typically you only need to subclass it if you plan to add custom drawing code for animations or unusual graphics. Otherwise, use the view controller to manage user interactions and to control updates. Add items to the view controller nib to lay out your interface.

Note that this template produces iPad or iPhone applications. If you want to create a universal iPhone *and* iPad application, use the Window-based template.

As a lazy shortcut, all iPhone applications run automatically on the iPad using the built-in emulation mode, which displays them in a half-sized sub-window. The sub-window can be zoomed to fill the screen, but this doesn't increase the resolution—it simply makes iPhone apps look large, but fuzzy.

There's no iPad emulator for the iPhone; iPad apps don't run on an iPhone at all.

Using the Window-based Application template

The Window-based application template is a minimal template with just a window that contains a single label, as shown in Figure 3.18. This is the only iOS template that includes a full universal option and can create a single app that runs on both the iPhone and iPad.

Figure 3.17

The View-Based Application template is the most useful starting point for app design.

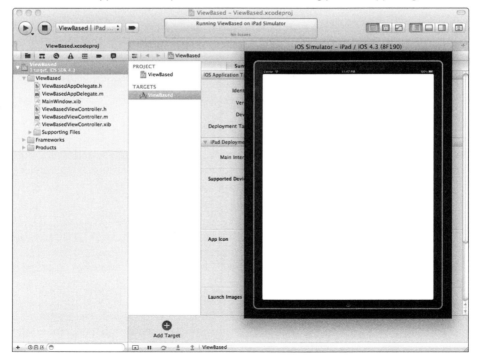

In fact this template simply creates two separate apps, with two separate nibs, and two app delegates The iOS app loader automatically selects the appropriate nib for each platform at run time.

The template *doesn't* create any view controllers. So to create a true universal app you typically add two separate view controllers, each with a nib that defines a unique UI, and perhaps some shared data classes. You have to add links between each view controller and its window in IB.

Introducing the Framework and Library templates

iOS supports only static libraries. You can't create or add a framework to an iOS project. As shown in Figure 3.19, OS X is less limited. You can create a Cocoa framework, a Cocoa library, a BSD C library, or a Standard Template Library (STL) C++ project add-on. The Bundle option groups together a collection of Objective-C files into a format that can be used to create extensions for languages such as Ruby. It can reference the Cocoa or Core Foundation (Carbon) frameworks.

Figure 3.18

Although the Window-based template includes a universal option, in practice, it simply creates two separate nibs with supporting code classes. There's some overlap between the platforms, but creating a dual platform app from this template requires lots of time, thought, and effort.

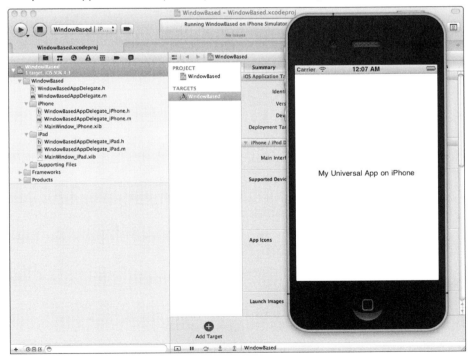

Figure 3.19

You can used the Framework & Library option in the OS X templates to create a range of supporting frameworks and libraries for your projects—and potentially, for the projects of other developers.

NOTE

A *library* is usually just a collection of code, with source files. A *framework* typically builds a single binary and supplies a list of headers for a #import directive. Frameworks can include media content, property lists, and other information as well as code. The framework's folder structure is fixed. In theory, frameworks include a complete class architecture, with implied usage patterns and relationships, while libraries are more likely to contain isolated discrete components. In practice, the distinction is sometimes less clear-cut.

Introducing Plug-in templates

The plug-in templates are specialized, and the details of plug-in design are outside the scope of this book.

In outline, the Application Plug-in templates are designed to add custom features to existing Apple applications, such as Address Book, Automator, and so on. These applications are designed with a standard interface, and the plug-in templates generate code and resource files that match their specific requirements. Experienced developers can use them to add new features to these applications. For example, you can use the Interface Builder plug-in to define your own collection of UI objects and add it to the standard list already built into IB.

The System plug-ins are more low level and can work with more than one application. For example, the Quick Look Plug-in can implement a preview of a custom data type used in your applications. Some of the plug-in templates are minimally complex. The IOKit driver plug-in creates a complete empty C++ file and links it against the Kernel framework. If you're a newcomer to Apple development, you can ignore these more advanced options.

NOTE

The plug-in templates support only Apple-standard APIs. If you want to develop a plug-in for some other application, such as an Adobe Photoshop 8BX plug-in or a VST (Virtual Studio Technology) music synthesizer or sound processor, you typically need to download a suitable SDK or framework and add it to Xcode by hand.

Changing the Standard Templates

It's important to understand that no template is complete. Templates include a bare minimum of features and are designed to eliminate repetitive set-up chores. They're not tutorials, and they're certainly not examples of best practice.

Many useful methods from these classes are missing from the templates, and you should review the class reference documentation, described in Chapter 6, to learn more about them. Typically, your applications rely on methods and properties that don't appear in the standard templates. The most productive templates are likely to be the ones you create yourself. Custom template creation is an advanced topic and is introduced in Chapter 12. But editing the existing templates is relatively easy and can save you time even on simple projects.

Finding the template files

Currently, you can find the iOS template files in /<Xcode Folder>/Platforms/ iPhoneOS.platform/Developer/Library/Xcode/Project Templates

The OS X templates are in /<Xcode Folder>/Library/Xcode/Project Templates

For both platforms, the application templates are in /Application, and the others are in correspondingly named folders.

CAUTION

If you are developing with multiple versions of Xcode, by default they all load their templates from these directories—usually. These locations may change without notice in future versions of Xcode.

Figure 3.20 shows a view of the template file structure, with a list of files. The contents of each template are a standard Xcode project. You can open the project in Xcode by double-clicking the .xcodeproj file.

Figure 3.20

Locating the iOS template files

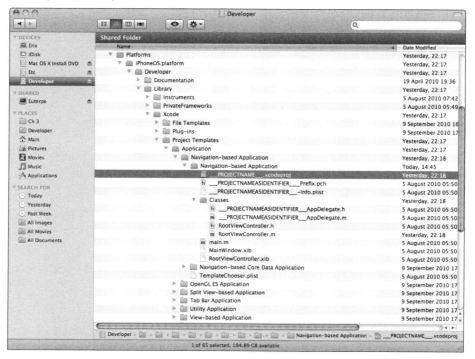

Note that some of the templates have multiple versions; for example, the Cocoa Application template is really a group of six different templates with optional Core Data, Document, and Spotlight features. You can ignore the templates you never use. But understand that if you change one template, the others aren't updated automatically. To create a complete set of modified templates, you must add the changes to every template you plan to use.

N O T E

Each group of templates, such as Cocoa Application, includes a `TemplateChooser.plist` file. If you're comfortable with plists and Cocoa dictionaries, you can open this file to explore how the different options are organized and selected, and how the plist controls the options that appear in Xcode's templates pane.

Customizing the template files

When Xcode uses the files to build a template, the filenames with their underscores are interpreted as macros and replaced with the Save-As name you choose. But if you open the project directly, as shown in Figure 3.21, you can edit the files as if they were a standard project. You also can build and run them. This means you can modify any template as if it were a standard project and save it in the usual way. The next time you use that template, it loads with all your changes.

Figure 3.21

Modifying an OS X template. This trivial change adds a comment, but you have complete freedom to change each file in a template to suit your needs.

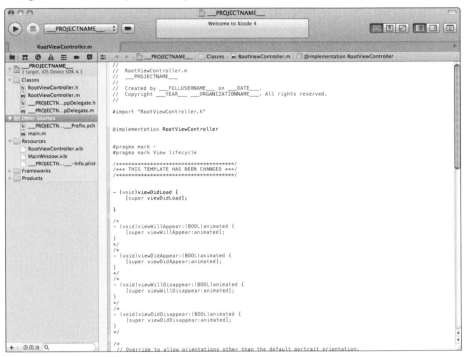

Because the templates are limited, customization is highly recommended. After your first few projects, you can review your code, see which features are reused regularly, and add them to the equivalent template.

CAUTION

Whenever you update Xcode, the standard template directories are overwritten. Whether you're using edited templates or a collection of custom templates, you *must* keep copies in a folder outside the `/Developer` directory and copy them back by hand after every update. If you don't, your edits are destroyed. (In theory you should be able to keep custom templates in `~/Library/Application Support/Developer/ Shared/Xcode/ Project Templates`, but this feature isn't working the first release of Xcode 4.)

Summary

This chapter looked at the Xcode templates and introduced a simple template-based build sequence. It examined the features of the different template types and explored the application templates for both iOS and OS X in some detail. It also explained how to modify the templates to improve them and create useful and full-featured starting points for further development.

Navigating the Xcode Interface

Earlier versions of Xcode made liberal use of floating windows. Xcode 4 gathers together all its features into a single window that is split into working areas. You can choose to hide and reveal different features as you work. Understanding which features are available is one of the keys to maximizing productivity.

Understanding the New Interface

Figure 4.1 shows one view of the new interface. From left to right, the UI is split into navigation, editor, and utility areas. This mirrors Apple's official UI guidelines; all Apple applications follow a similar layout. However, it's a good idea not to take the area names too literally.

For example, the navigation area includes debugging features that are only very distantly related to code navigation. A more accurate description for the left area might be "finding and building." It not only lists files and objects but also reports build issues, supports searches, and simplifies error checking and debugging.

NOTE
Xcode includes a separate console and debugger, which is described in detail in Chapter 15.

The right area is most often used as a code and object library, but it includes extra features that reveal key information about selected items, such as file paths and other miscellaneous settings. This area also includes a built-in help feature.

The editor area is more tightly focused and is used for editing almost exclusively. But you also use it to define critical project-wide build settings and to add frameworks to your project. For example, during iPhone development, you can use this area to select the app icons and launch images for an app.

In This Chapter

Using the navigation area

Using the utility area

Working with the editor area

Getting started with code editing

Introducing build settings

The editor area is always visible, but you can hide and reveal the navigation and utility areas. Click the buttons near the top right of the Xcode 4 window, as shown in Figure 4.2. Each button toggles when you click it, hiding or revealing its corresponding area.

Figure 4.1

Look again at the Xcode interface and its three-way split.

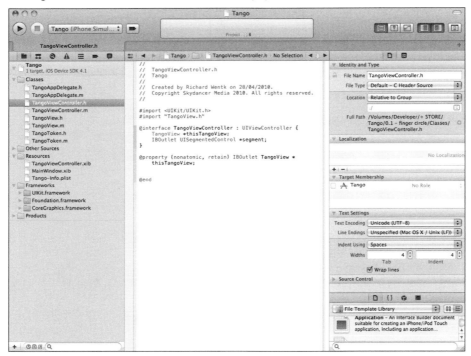

Figure 4.2

The show/hide buttons for the navigator and utility areas

Using the Navigation Area

At the top left of the navigation area is a toolbar with seven icons, as shown in Figure 4.3. Selecting an icon changes the content that appears in the pane under the toolbar.

Figure 4.3

The selection icons for the navigation area

From left to right, the icons select these toolbars:

1. The Project Navigator
2. The Symbol Navigator
3. The Search Navigator
4. The Issue Navigator
5. The Debug Navigator
6. The Breakpoint Navigator
7. The Log Navigator

C A U T I O N

With a couple of exceptions, the images on these icons are perhaps best described as "abstract"; they're not a good guide to the features they select. The best way to learn what they do is to experiment with them.

The Project Navigator

If you have experience of Xcode 3, you'll recognize this as the old Groups & Files pane. It lists the files and other resources used in a project. When you select a file that Xcode can edit, its contents are automatically loaded into the editor area. If Xcode can't edit it—for example, if it's an image file, or a font—the editor area shows a preview.

The file list in this navigator looks like a Finder directory listing. But this is misleading. The "folders" that appear here are called groups. They don't exist on disk. You can use groups to collect related items together. The default list of groups for a project includes Class, Other Sources, Resources, and Frameworks, but you can create new groups of your own and organize the files in your project using any system that works well for you.

To add a new group, right-click in the navigator area and select New Group from the menu that appears, as shown in Figure 4.4. You also can rearrange the order of both groups and files by dragging them to a different position in the list.

Figure 4.4

When you create a new group, it is always added to the next highest level in the group tree.

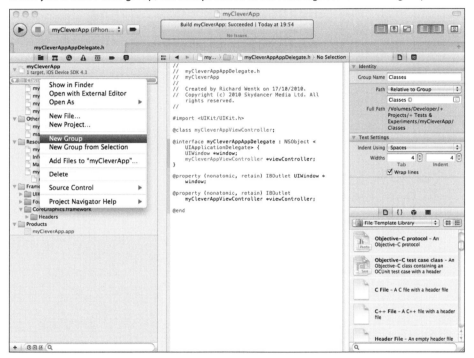

Earlier versions of Xcode 3 maintained a distant connection between the filenames shown in Groups & Files and the files on disk. The filenames were more like bookmarks, aliases, or symbolic links. Renaming a file in the Groups & Files pane didn't modify the name of the file on disk. When you deleted a file from a project, it remained on disk. Newcomers typically found this baffling.

In later version of Xcode 3 and in Xcode 4, the connection between files and links is stronger and more intuitive. When you rename a file in this navigator, the name on disk is updated for you. But it's critically important to understand that the filenames that appear here are still symbolic links to real files. The navigator displays a list of files in the project. It *doesn't* display the files and folders in the project directory. If you open the project directory with Finder, you'll see a different file structure. This makes it possible for the navigator to display project files wherever they're located on disk. To delete a file, you can either use the right-click menu shown in

Figure 4.4, the Backspace key, or the Delete key. Deleting a file displays the dialog box shown in Figure 4.5. You can choose to move the file to the trash, which deletes it from the project and from disk. Or you can remove the reference, which leaves the source file on disk but deletes it from the project.

Figure 4.5

When deleting a file, you can leave it on disk or move it to the trash. Leaving a file on disk can be useful if you want to keep an older version or move it to another project.

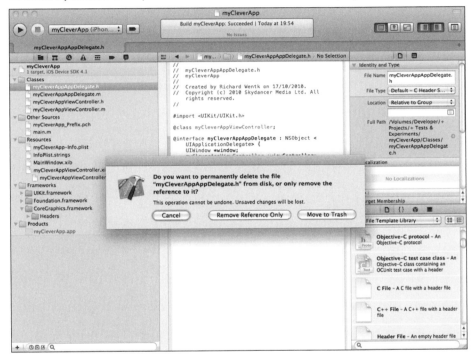

TIP

If the Utility area is visible when you select a file, you can view the file's disk path. Real projects may gather files from many different directories, so this can be a useful memory jogger. You also can use this feature to find framework header files.

The Symbol Navigator

The Symbol Navigator, shown at the left of Figure 4.6, performs two tasks. You can use it to browse the symbols—classes, methods, and other code features—in your project. Selecting a symbol from the lists that appear in this navigator locates and loads the corresponding code into the editor. You also can use it to list and access the internal features of OS X and to view the relevant headers.

Figure 4.6

Selecting a symbol in the Symbol Navigator displays it in the editor window and highlights it.

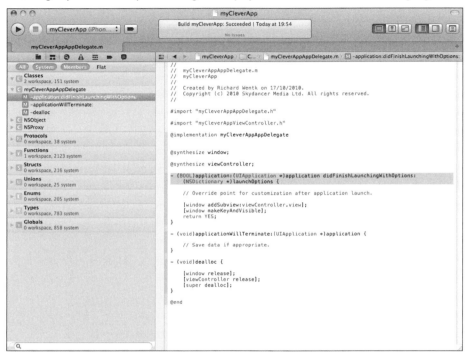

Selecting symbol views

The mini-toolbar at the top of this navigator is the key to understanding it and using it effectively. It has four buttons: All, System, Members, and Flat. You can use these buttons to filter the list of symbols so only the symbols in your code appear. You also can choose to view all the symbols in every framework included in the project. Here's what these buttons do:

- **All** toggles between two views. When All is deselected, only classes are listed. When selected, all other entities appear: classes, protocols, functions, structs, unions, enums, types, and globals. The display shows a useful count of items in the project ("workspace") and items in associated linked frameworks.

- **System** hides and reveals the system symbols. When deselected, only the symbols in your project are listed. When selected, the full set of symbols in all linked frameworks appears. This can be a very long list.

- **Members** hides and reveals internal symbols. When deselected, only classes are listed. When selected, the classes can be opened with a reveal triangle to show methods, functions, and all other code features.

- **Flat** controls whether symbols are organized into a hierarchy. When selected, symbols are listed alphabetically. When deselected, class relationships are shown. For example, when Flat is selected, `NSObject` appears in strict alphabetical sequence near the middle of the class list. When Flat is deselected, `NSObject` appears at the top of the list, because it's a root Cocoa class and contains an entire hierarchy of subclasses.

Using the symbol views

You can use the symbol lists in various ways. Three suggestions follow, but other applications are possible:

- To find a specific method or code feature in your own code, select All and Members and deselect System and Flat. You see a list of the classes in your code. Clicking the reveal triangle next to each class shows the list of methods and other features in that class.

- To remind yourself of the list of methods in a Cocoa class, select all four buttons and scroll down the list to find the class. Select it to view the list of methods and other features in its interface. This literally shows you the original headers from the Cocoa source code, as shown in Figure 4.7. Copy method signatures from the headers into your code, or review the method list to remind yourself of the features supported by the class.

Figure 4.7

Use the Cocoa headers to remind yourself of class features and to check or copy method signatures. It's also a useful starting point for "I've never seen that class; what does it do?" explorations.

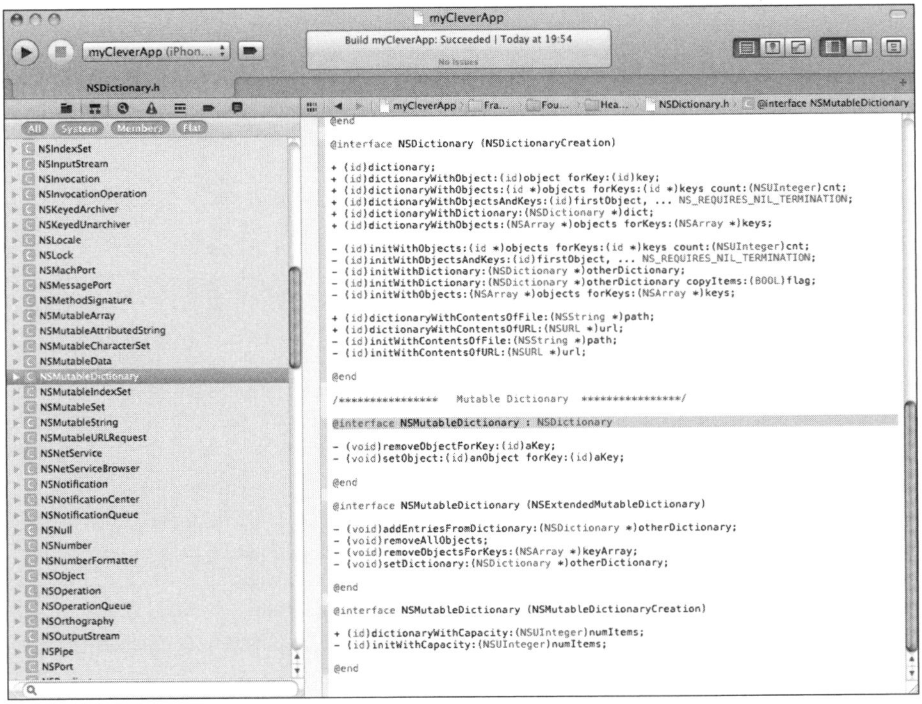

To select a class for editing from a list ordered alphabetically, deselect all buttons. Optionally, use Flat to show and reveal hierarchies. You see a list of project classes, without groups or any of the supporting files that appear in the Project Navigator.

CAUTION

For simple projects, it's usually easier and quicker to navigate to specific classes and methods using the navigator bar introduced in Chapter 1. Symbol navigation can be quicker when the list of classes is very long and your monitor is large enough to display the complete list without scrolling.

The Search Navigator

The Search Navigator is a simple string search tool. To use it, type a full or partial search string into the search field, as shown in Figure 4.8. You can search your project files only or the full list of linked framework headers. You also can select string matching for the start of a symbol name or for any position inside the symbol name.

Figure 4.8

Preparing to search a project for a matching string

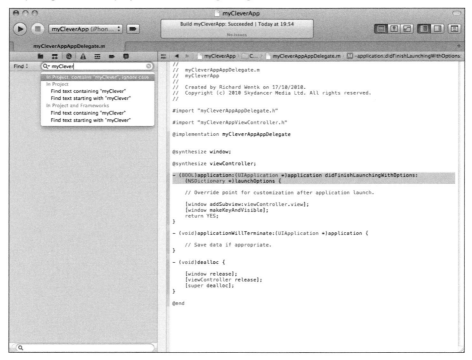

As shown in Figure 4.9, the search isn't aware of context or meaning. It simply searches the source files for a string match. Comments, code, headers, and implementation files all count as hits and are given equal weighting. If you don't specify your search string with care, the result can be a jumbled list of possible hits arranged by file order. It's not helpful to search for a class name, because the search returns every `#import` directive that matches the class name in every class, as well as every other occurrence of the name.

Figure 4.9

Because the results of a search lack context awareness, they can contain unwanted matches.

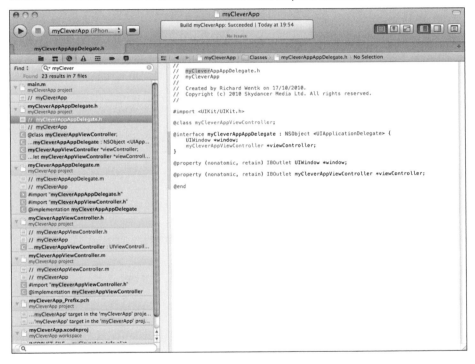

To the left of the search area is the Find/Replace toggle. Select Replace when you want to replace the target string with an alternate string throughout the text. The Replace All button is dangerous and lacks intelligence. But the Preview option can display a list of hits similar to the one shown in Figure 4.10. The area in the middle of the list displays toggle switches that enable and disable replacement for each hit. In a large project, it can take a while to scan through every hit, but this option does allow you to use Replace selectively.

TIP

If you click the magnifying class icon, you see further advanced search options that control case matching and make it possible to use regular expressions in searches.

Figure 4.10

Using the selective replace feature, you can toggle each switch to enable or disable replacing that hit.

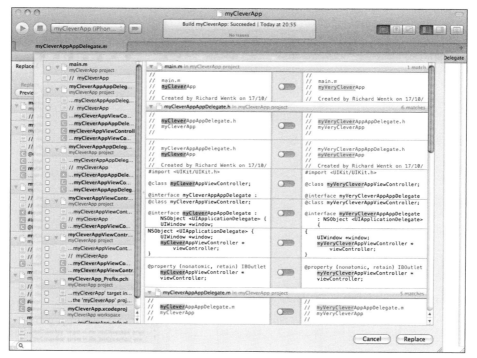

The Issue Navigator and the Log Navigator

The Issue Navigator, shown in Figure 4.11, lists fatal errors and warning messages after a build. Selecting an issue shows it in the editor window, with an adjacent red highlight and description. An icon also appears in the gutter to the left of the code editor. After a build, you can use this navigator to jump directly to problem code; if there are issues, this navigator appears automatically, even when the navigator pane is closed before the build. (This isn't always the behavior you want, but currently there's no way to disable it.)

Although this seems like a simple feature, there are hidden complexities. First, the gcc and llvm compilers produce different error messages. If you've used previous versions of Xcode, you're used to the quirks and limitations of gcc. The llvm compiler option takes a different approach to error reporting, and you see unfamiliar error messages, sometimes in unfamiliar locations.

Figure 4.11

Clicking any warning or error in the build results list displays related code in the editor window.

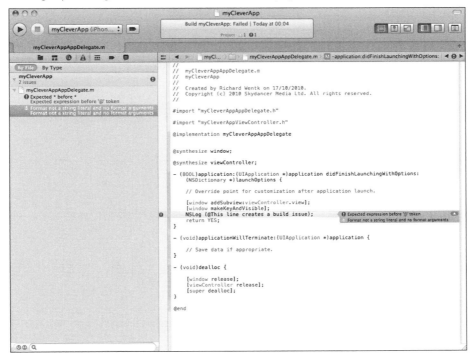

CROSS-REFERENCE

For more information about selecting and using different compilers, see Appendix C and Chapters 12 and 13.

Second, if you're new to development, it's important to understand that errors don't always appear on the correct line of code. For example, if you remove or comment out the closing curly bracket from a method definition, you create a cascade of errors in the rest of the file, but the missing bracket isn't flagged correctly. Some errors require experience and guesswork. Problems in code can often create multiple errors at the same location.

Finally, there are many different possible warning messages, and you can select the ones you want to see. In the Project Navigator, select the project, and then select Build Settings. Select All under it, and scroll down to show the Warnings panel, as shown in Figure 4.12. Many of these options assume intermediate or expert level experience, so it's best to leave them unchanged unless you know what they're for. As you gain experience, you can start to use this feature to choose the warnings you want to see.

Figure 4.12

You can enable or disable each warning message generated by the compiler. You also can disable all warnings, which is usually a bad thing to do.

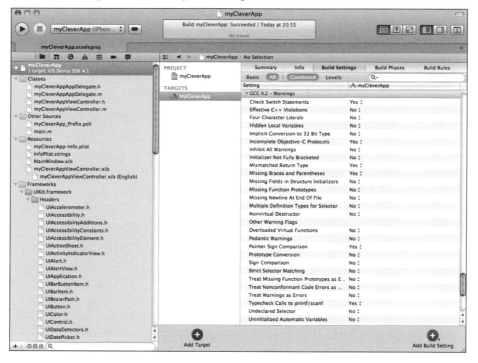

The Log Navigator, shown in Figure 4.13, is an alternate way to display build issues. It's similar to the Build Results window in Xcode 3, with the difference that it can show a list of build results for the project. You can refer to previous builds to compare errors. Double-clicking an issue in the editor window takes you to the code that caused it.

Figure 4.13

Where the Issues Navigator shows issues for the current build, the Log Navigator shows issues for previous builds too.

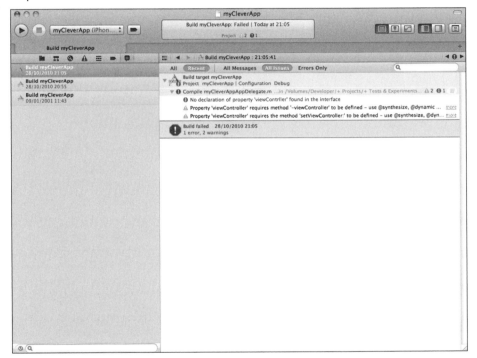

The issue listings here can give you more information than is available in the Issue Navigator. For a full untruncated view of each message, click the more link at the right of each message string. You also can select the message icon that appears next to the message/error count to view the raw compiler output, as shown in Figure 4.14. This isn't usually necessary, but it can be helpful when checking file paths and library locations on disk.

Figure 4.14

Viewing raw compiler output

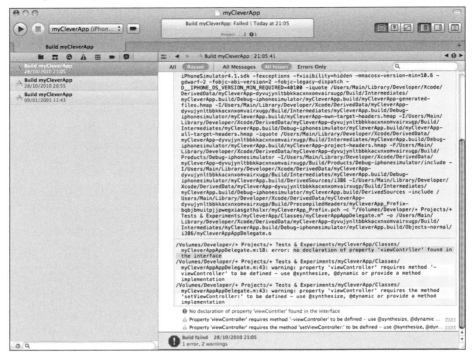

The Breakpoint Navigator and the Debug Navigator

You can add a debugging breakpoint—a feature that stops code execution at a certain line for testing and review—in the main code editor. Breakpoints remain in the code but are only active when *breakpoint mode* is enabled. Click in the breakpoint gutter to the left of any line of code. A blue arrow appears when the breakpoint is active. To disable a breakpoint, click its arrow again.

The Breakpoint Navigator, shown in Figure 4.15, lists all the breakpoints in a project. You can move to any breakpoint by clicking the list at the left. You also can set up conditional breakpoints that are triggered only after a certain number of repeats. Breakpoints are a powerful debugging aid, with many features and options. For details, see Chapter 15.

N O T E
When you add a breakpoint, Xcode switches to breakpoint mode automatically. You can toggle breakpoint mode manually by selecting the arrow icon to the right of the active scheme selector.

Figure 4.15

Setting and listing breakpoints

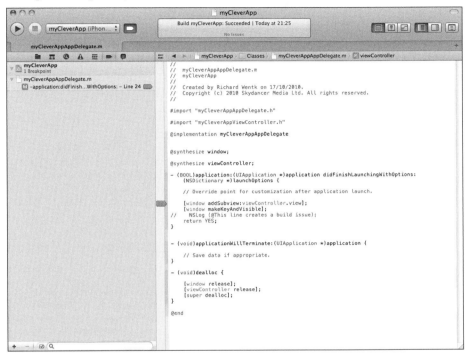

The Debug Navigator, shown in Figure 4.16, lists active threads after a breakpoint is triggered. A separate debug area at the bottom of the screen appears automatically and displays relevant values and objects. For a detailed example of debugging with breakpoints, see Chapter 15.

Loading the navigators from menus and keyboard shortcuts

You can access all the navigators from Xcode's menu tree or via keyboard shortcuts. The Navigators are listed under View ⇨ Navigators. To select them from the keyboard, use ⌘+1-7. ⌘+0 shows/hides the navigator area.

Figure 4.16

Viewing breakpoint and thread information in debug mode, with the Debug Navigator

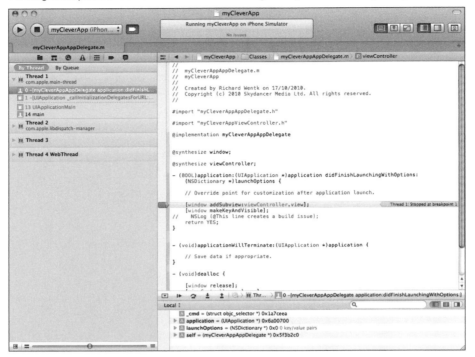

Using the Utility Area

The utility area at the right of the UI has two sub-panes. The top sub-pane displays file information and quick help. The lower sub-pane is a code and object library. You can hide the lower sub-pane by dragging its divider down until only the four icons on its top toolbar are visible.

Displaying file information

When viewing code files, the top sub-pane displays two icons. The icon on the left displays file information, as shown in Figure 4.17. To rename a file, type the new name into the File Name text field. To change the file type, select a new type from the File Type menu.

NOTE

Nib files are treated as a special case. When you select a nib, the top sub-pane shows a more extensive collection of icons that can be used to set the size, properties, and other key features of nib objects. For details, see Chapters 7 and 8.

Figure 4.17

This option displays file path details and extra settings such as the text format.

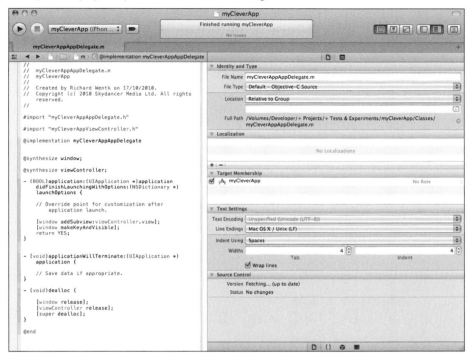

The Location menu sets the root file path reference. The default Relative to Group option is the most useful. It creates a file path relative to the main project directory. You can copy the project directory to a different disk location without breaking this reference.

You also can change the file path to an absolute reference or to a path relative to some other disk folder, such as the /Developer directory. Use this option with care. If you copy or move a file with an absolute reference, Xcode can't find it again. If you do this by accident and lose a file from a project, you can use this pane to reset the path so the link works correctly. Click the tiny folder-window icon to the right of the area under the Location window to select a directory.

TIP
You can use the arrow icon next to the Full Path listing to reveal a file in Finder.

This sub-pane also displays supporting information about the file:

- **Localization** displays foreign language support. Some files can be *localized*, or created in different versions that support non-English languages. For more details, see Chapter 8.

- **Target Membership** sets the build target for the file. Simple projects have a single build target, and you can ignore this option. For more complex projects, see Chapter 12.

- **Text Settings** defines the text encoding for the file. The default is UTF-8 (Unicode Text Format - 8 bit), which supports non-English characters. By default, Xcode creates indents with spaces. If you need code indented with tabs, select that option with the Indent Using menu. You also can set the number of spaces for each indent.

- **Source Control** is used for collaborative development, or development that uses a code repository. For information about repositories, see Chapter 14.

Using Quick Help

The second icon at the top of the sub-pane displays a Quick Help window. In Xcode 3, you could link directly to documentation by highlighting an item, right-clicking it, and selecting a link to the documentation. Quick Help, shown in Figure 4.18, is the Xcode 4 equivalent. Highlighting an OS X object or method displays a list of relevant help information: You can also option-click an item to view help information when the Utilities pane is hidden.

- **Name** is the item name.
- If the symbol is a method, **Declaration** shows the method signature.
- **Availability** lists the OS X or iOS versions that first supported the symbol.
- **Abstract** describes the symbol's purpose.
- **Declared** links directly to the header file in which the symbol appears.
- **Reference** links directly to reference documentation; for more details, see Chapter 6.
- **Related API** shows related methods and objects, where relevant.
- **Related Documents** shows the related programming guides, where available.
- **Sample Code** lists a selection of sample projects that use the symbol or illustrate how it works.

Quick Help can be sluggish on a slow Mac, so even though it's supposed to display useful information as you type, it doesn't always keep up. Because it runs continuously when this pane is open, it can slow down other "live" Xcode features, such as the error checking.

But it also provides quick access to key help documentation. If your Mac is fast enough, it's worth leaving it enabled.

NOTE

Custom objects—objects you have created yourself—display only a link to the class in which they're declared. You can use this feature to move straight to the relevant declaration. Full Quick Help definitions aren't available, and the Quick Help system isn't set up to allow custom additions.

Figure 4.18

There's a surprisingly large amount of useful information in the small Quick Help window.

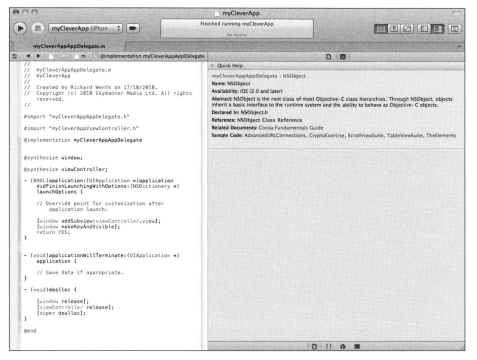

Using the library area

The library area, shown in Figure 4.19, displays four types of files and objects. You can select them with the icons that appear in the toolbar at the top of the sub-pane:

- The File Template Library is a list of file types that you can add to a project. There's some overlap with the file templates introduced in Chapter 3, but the list that appears here is longer and includes files that are used with Interface Builder (IB) and the Core Data editor. To add a file to your project, open the Project Navigator, drag a file from the list in this library, and drop it into a group.

- The Code Snippet Library was introduced in Chapter 1. You can use it to add boiler-plate code to your project. For details, see Chapter 9.

- The Object Library is used with Interface Builder. Use it to select a standard OS X or iOS UI or data object and add it to your project. For details, see Chapter 7.

- The Media Library manages media files you add to the project. For details, see Chapter 8.

Most library use is drag and drop: You can drag objects from the library and drop them into the project's file list or in a suitable editor. iOS and OS X support different object and class libraries.

CAUTION
This library area allows you to drop OS X objects into an iOS project, and vice versa. This isn't usually a useful thing to do.

Figure 4.19

Explore the File Templates in the library area to learn how to add files to your project by dragging them from this area and dropping them into the Project Navigator.

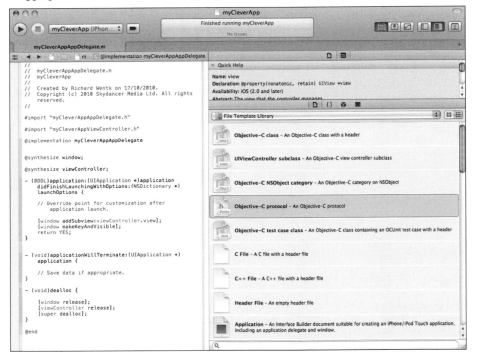

Working with the Editor Area

The key features of the editor area, including basic class and file navigation and the new Assistant feature, were outlined in Chapter 1. In this area, you can do the following:

- Edit code. In addition to simple typing, the code editor includes hidden features such as *code completion,* which automatically suggests code as you type.
- View two associated files simultaneously—typically an implementation file and its associated header, or a nib file and its related source code.
- Create a visual UI layout for your application.
- Design the schema of a Core Data database.

- Compare previous and current versions of a file side by side.

- Define *build settings,* or the list of switches, options, files, and other elements that define how source files are converted into one or more binaries.

TIP

The forward and back arrows at the top left of the editor are easy to miss, but they're an essential timesaver. They work like the forward and back buttons on a browser. For example, if you are currently viewing code but you were previously viewing a UI layout in Interface Builder, the back button switches the editor back to IB for you automatically.

Getting started with code editing

Although code editing seems simple—start typing and stop when you're done—it can take time to get accustomed to the hidden features in Xcode, which include the following:

- **Code completion:** This is a fairly sophisticated feature that makes educated guesses about possible code as you type. You can insert the suggested code with the Tab key or select a different educated guess from a floating menu.

- **Auto-indentation:** This indents the cursor position automatically, taking into account preceding code.

- **Bracket matching:** When you type a closing bracket or move the cursor over it with the right arrow key, the matching open bracket flashes yellow. If there is no matching bracket, Xcode plays a short warning sound.

- **Bracket generation:** Type a new a method signature and an opening curly bracket, then type Return. Xcode adds a closing curly bracket and positions the cursor on the first blank line of the method.

- **Square bracket balancing:** For square brackets only, Xcode adds an opening square bracket when you type a closing square bracket. While this feature can be useful, it lacks intelligence, and sometimes you need to remove the brackets it creates.

The easiest way to master these features is to experiment with them. They're often very helpful, but occasionally you may need to use them in a lateral way. For example, the simplest way to insert a new line of code is to click with the mouse at the end of the previous line and type Return. Xcode inserts a blank line and indents the cursor as needed. Placing the cursor before the insertion position doesn't do what you want.

Using code completion

If you've used Code Sense in Xcode 3, Xcode 4's code completion works slightly differently. The easiest way to illustrate it is with an example.

Create a new project using the iOS View-based application template. Save it with any name; in this example, I use myCleverApp. Open the Project Navigator, and select the `myCleverApp AppDelegate.m` file so the code appears in the editor.

Click with the mouse at the end of a line of code in any method. In this example, I use the `application didFinishLaunchingWithOptions:` method. But code completion isn't limited to any one method or class; it works throughout a project.

Type [UIVi, as shown in Figure 4.20. Code completion pops up the menu shown in the figure. UIView is highlighted to indicate that this is code completion's best guess. To accept the guess, type the Tab key or the Return key. Either inserts UIView in full.

Figure 4.20

Xcode 4's Code Sense feature has been redesigned. But if you're used to Xcode 3, you'll find much of it remains familiar.

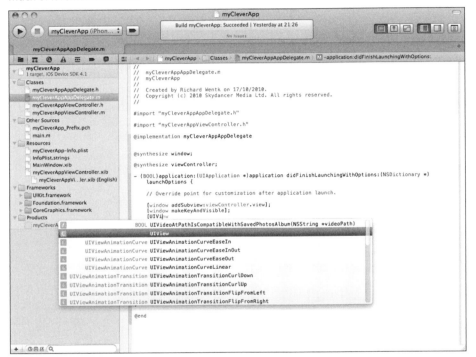

What if I meant to type UIViewController? To select a different guess, you can scroll down the menu with the mouse or the cursor keys. UIViewController appears at the bottom of the list, and you can insert it with Tab or Return, as before. Similarly, you can select any of the other options.

Code completion is a fast symbol listing tool. It has some very basic intelligence and context awareness, but it can't read your mind, and it can't tell whether you want to add a class, a function, or an enumerated constant, so it shows you all the options that fit your clue string. To use code completion efficiently, type enough characters to allow it to find an unambiguous match. The full extended list of pop-up guesses is less useful, although it can be a good memory jogger—for example, when you can't remember a list of constants.

If you add a method that takes parameters, code completion highlights the parameters for you and allows you to tab between them. In the example shown in Figure 4.21, you would fill in the first NSString parameter by typing over it, tabbing to the NSKeyValueSetMutationKind parameter, typing over it, and tabbing again to the final NSSet parameter.

Figure 4.21

Use tabs to skip between parameter fields. The tab key skips the cursor from one field to the next, jumping over the intervening code. The current type-over area appears highlighted in blue.

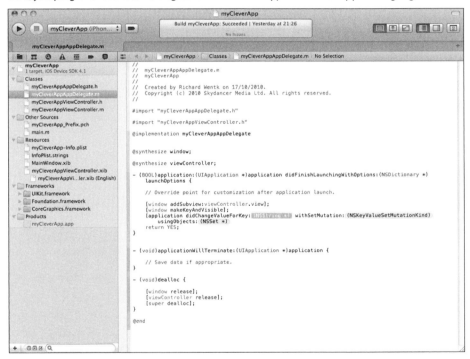

If you're getting started with Xcode, it's a good idea to spend enough time practicing with this feature to make it second nature. Although you can use the arrow keys to move between parameters, this tab-type-skip feature is a significant timesaver.

Using auto-indentation

Auto-indentation works as you'd expect, moving the cursor to the correct horizontal location in the code. It's smart enough to keep track of nest brackets and other features. If you auto-indent a line and the cursor doesn't appear where you expect it to, it's likely there's a missing bracket on a preceding line. This is a useful feature, not a bug. You can indent with spaces or tab characters and select the number of indentation spaces using the File Information area introduced earlier in this chapter.

Using the Structure pop-up menu

Select a few of lines of code inside a method, right-click, and select Structure from the menu that appears, as shown in Figure 4.22. This menu has some extremely useful features. You can move the code left or right as a single block manually, re-indent it automatically to its ideal indentation level, or convert it into a comment.

Figure 4.22

Use the Structure pop-up menu; it's a powerful timesaver.

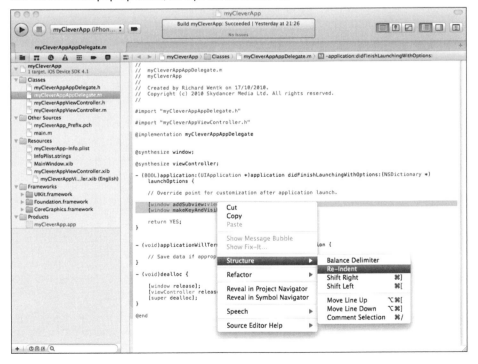

The Balance Delimiter feature highlights the code between matching brackets. Use it to confirm that your brackets are balanced correctly. Move Line Up and Move Line Down swap the code block with the line above it or below it.

This menu is another essential timesaver. Getting into the habit of using it without thinking about it can save significant development effort.

Introducing build configurations

Build settings define build sequences and compiler options for a project. In Xcode, build settings are grouped into *configurations*. Table 4.1 summarizes the differences between the default configurations included in every new project.

Table 4.1 Default Build Configurations

Category	OS	Comments
Debug	iOS	Used for testing and development.
Release	iOS	Useless on its own, but can be edited to create builds for the App Store and for Ad Hoc app release.
Debug	OS X	Used for testing and development.
Release	OS X	Can be used to create an application that can be used as is or packaged with an installer. Also can be edited to create a special build for the OS X App Store.

Understanding project build settings

Xcode makes a distinction between project and target build settings. In Xcode, a target is a set of instructions for building a single binary. A project is a file container that supplies build defaults and also holds the files that can be compiled into binaries. For example, a universal iPad/iPhone project has two targets—one for each platform. A Mac OS X project might create an app and a framework as separate targets.

Project settings are useful defaults for every possible target. Figure 4.23 shows an example of project build settings. You can view this editor by selecting a project in the Project Navigator and clicking the PROJECT icon in the gutter area.

Looking at target build settings

Target settings can override the project defaults. They also define extra runtime details for the target, including icon files, *plists* (property lists), and other specialized features used to create one particular binary. These settings also define some of the possible interfaces between

applications. For example, on the iPhone, you can use them to define a *URL scheme*—an inter-application interface—that allows other apps to launch and run your app and to pass it data. Figure 4.24 shows some of the target settings.

As with the project build settings, you can leave most of the target build settings unchanged. A handful are critical and are described below and in Chapters 12 and 13. Most can be left as defaults.

Figure 4.23

Look again at project build settings; there's so much to see here, but you can leave most of it unchanged.

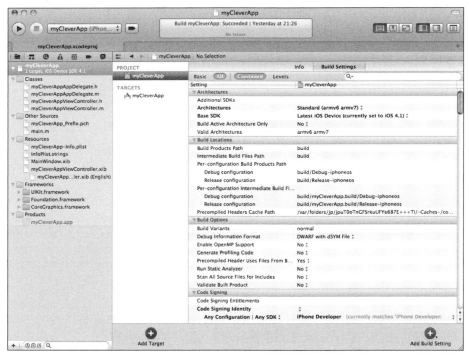

CAUTION

Although you can ignore most of the build system for simple app development, you must know how to make standard changes to the settings before you can sell apps through the App Stores. The full build system is complex and includes projects, targets, schemes, configurations, actions, phases, rules—and more. Chapters 12 and 13 introduce it in detail, and also explain how to avoid most of the complexity when you need to make simple changes.

Figure 4.24

Look at target build settings, which define how all the elements in a project are combined into one or more binaries.

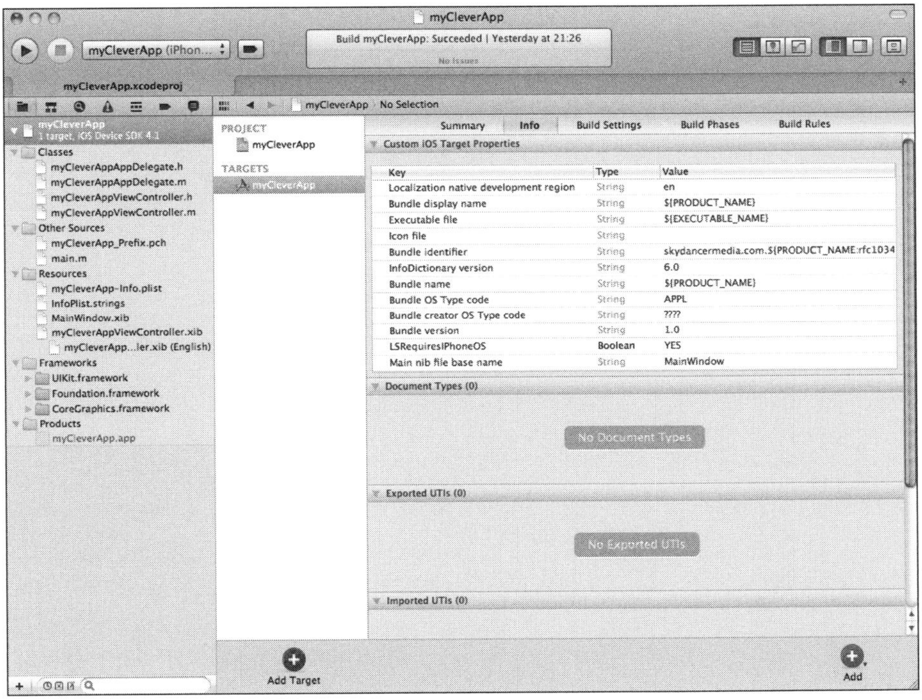

Adding frameworks

One of the critical settings in the Build Settings section is the framework list.

The framework management system in Xcode 4 is completely different from that in Xcode 3. It's no longer related to the Add files… menu option. Instead, it's buried in the Build Phases page of the target build settings, as shown in Figure 4.25.

To add a framework, select your project in the Project Navigator, select the TARGETS icon in the gutter, and select Build Phases. Click the Link Binary With Libraries reveal triangle, and then select the plus (+) icon at the lower left.

You can now select a framework from the list that appears, as shown in the figure. Note that the framework is added to the project root, and not to the Frameworks group. Although the location doesn't affect compilation, you may want to move it for clarity.

To delete a framework from the project, select it in the Link Binary With Libraries table and click the minus (-) icon.

Figure 4.25

Framework management in Xcode 4 has nothing in common with the menu options used in Xcode 3.

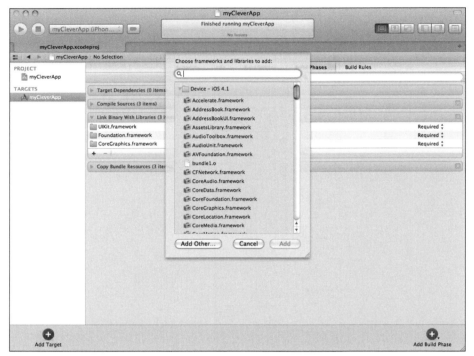

TIP

While you can't use the Add Files option to add system frameworks, you can use it to add third-party frameworks. When you use this feature to add a third-party framework to a project, it's automatically added to the link list.

Summary

This chapter looked at the key features of the new Xcode 4 interface. It detailed the new navigator area and listed the various navigator panes used to move through the code and other resources in a project. It explored the utility area and outlined the file information and quick help features. It also introduced the editor area and explored some of the essential shortcuts used to simplify code editing. Finally, it introduced build settings, listed the differences between project and target build options, and explained how to add frameworks to a project.

Working with Files, Frameworks, and Classes

X code projects include a list of constituent files. When you build a project, Xcode processes each file in turn. Source code files are compiled into binaries and linked together. Resource files are copied to the project's output folder, also known as its *bundle*.

Each step in the process is known as a *build phase*. If your project has special requirements, you can customize the build phases or create custom build phases—for example, to compile source code in a specific sequence, allowing for dependencies. More typically, you can use the default build phases as they are.

You can define the files included in a project in two ways. The simple way is to use the file management features built into the Project navigator. For more advanced management, you can use the features introduced in Chapter 13 to customize Xcode's default build phases. For simple apps, you can usually ignore this option, because the build phases "just work."

CROSS-REFERENCE
For more information about custom builds and build phases, see Chapter 12.

In This Chapter

Adding new files to a project

Working with groups

Working with frameworks

Working with Files and Classes

The Project Navigator includes all the features you need for basic file and class management. The Navigator is easy to work with, but it's worth emphasizing again that there is an indirect relationship between the files and *folders* (or groups) that appear in the Navigator, and the contents of the project folder on disk.

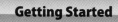

When you create a new Xcode project, the new files are added to a single folder. But this is a convenience, not a necessity.

You can create a working project where the "official" project folder is empty, and every file is in a different physical folder. Project files don't have to be local; they can be anywhere on disk or on a network. This makes it easy to reuse source code and create libraries. The same library code can be referenced from multiple projects without copying.

This applies equally to C/C++ source code, Objective-C class definitions, and resources such as graphics files. If you use a library of custom icons or button graphics, you can keep the image files in a single folder and import them into multiple projects as needed.

There are advantages and disadvantages to keeping files in multiple locations. The advantage is that you can keep single copies and reuse them in multiple projects. The disadvantage is that it becomes harder to keep safety copies of the files in a project. It also becomes harder to use the source control management (SCM) features introduced in Chapter 14.

CAUTION

Typically after you build a project, Xcode copies graphics files into the application bundle. OS X allows your applications to create and access a common resource folder outside of the bundle. iOS doesn't. Be careful about adding files to an iOS project. To minimize the size of the finished app, add only files that are used. Don't add complete folders or resource collections.

Adding new files to a project

To save time, Xcode includes a selection of file templates that add prewritten content, including classes with headers and implementation files that include minimal but useful boilerplate set-up and tear-down code.

The templates are similar to the application templates introduced in Chapter 3. Instead of creating a complete application, they add a useful building block to an existing application. The templates for iOS and OS X are slightly different, but they overlap significantly—much more than for the equivalent application templates.

You can add new files to a project in two ways: using Xcode's New File menu option or by dragging and dropping the file from a template in Xcode's Utility area.

Using the New File menu option

You can select the New File menu option from the main Xcode menu via File ⇨ New ⇨ New File. You can also right-click in or on a group and select New File from the contextual menu that appears when you right-click on a group, as shown in Figure 5.1.

Figure 5.1

Adding a file using the New File option

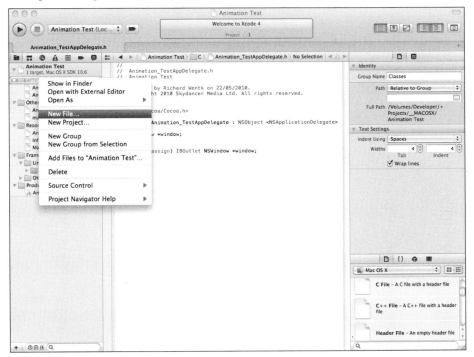

Selecting New File displays the file template list, shown in Figure 5.2. You can select OS X or iOS templates from the list and then choose sub-types from the two panes at the left.

Figure 5.2

Selecting the file template from the iOS and OS X panes

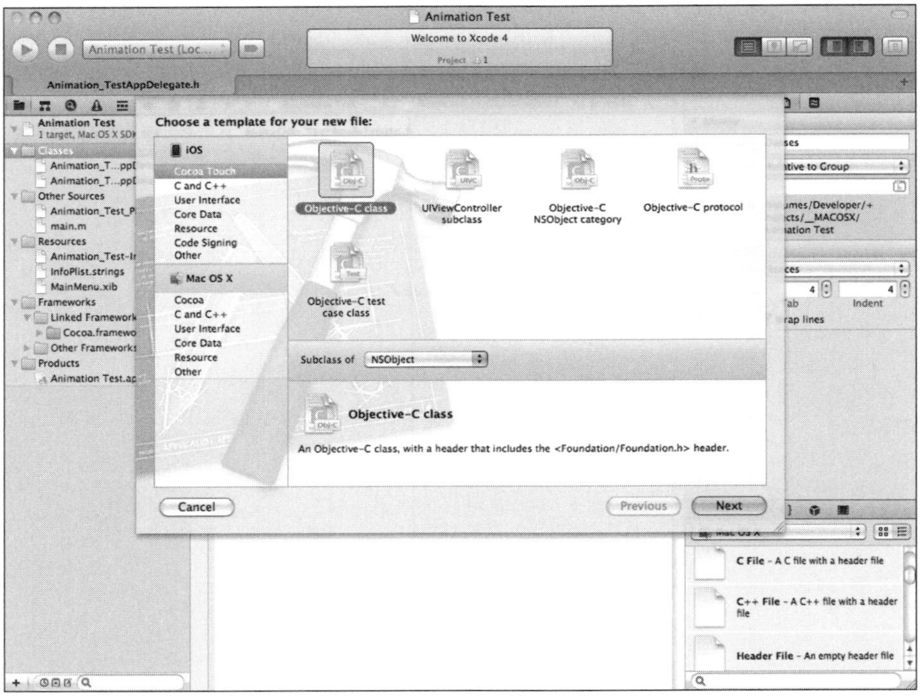

Use the Save dialog to name the file, as shown in Figure 5.3. By default the file is added to the project folder. Optionally, you can choose to save it to a different location. After this dialog box disappears, the file is added to the Project Navigator inside the group that you right-clicked.

NOTE

To emphasize again, the file always appears in the Project Navigator, no matter where you save it on disk. For practical reasons, it's a good idea to save project files to the project folder. You don't have to do this, but if you don't, you may have to keep track of file locations by hand. If you move the project folder to a different location, Xcode may not be able to adjust its file references, and the project may not build.

Figure 5.3

Naming the new file before saving it

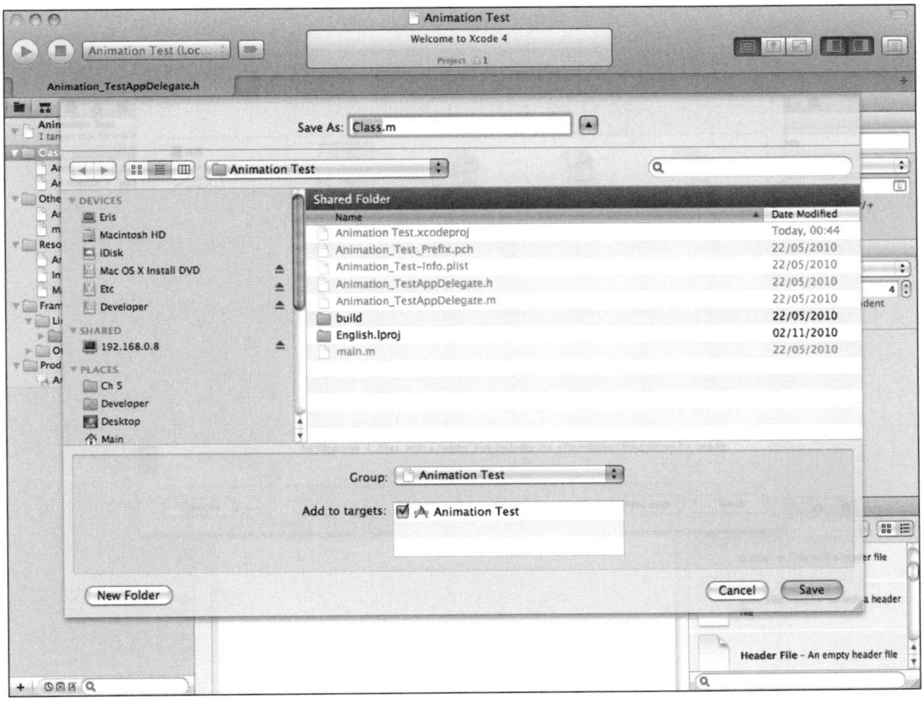

NOTE

You can use the Add to targets option to define which targets the file will be added to. Simple apps typically have a single target, so you can ignore this feature. For more information about targets, see Chapters 12 and 13.

Using drag-and-drop from the Utility area

To use the drag-and-drop feature, select the File Template Library icon if it isn't already selected. Optionally, you can select the iOS or OS X sub-libraries, as shown in Figure 5.4. This is a recommended step. If you don't select a sub-library, the menu lists the iOS templates, followed by the templates for OS X. Although the templates for both platforms appear similar, most are incompatible, and you should filter them to ensure that you're making a selection from the correct list.

Figure 5.4

Selecting iOS or OS X file templates

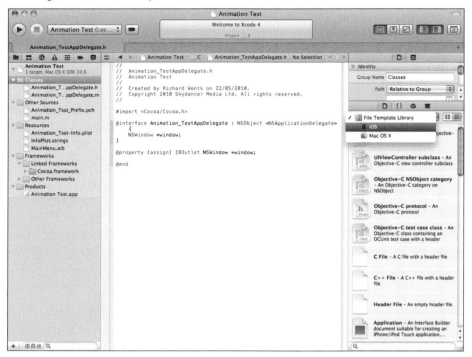

With the drag-and-drop option, you can select a template and drop it directly into any group, as shown in Figure 5.5. The naming/saving step is identical to that shown in Figure 5.3.

Figure 5.5

Adding a file with template drag-and-drop

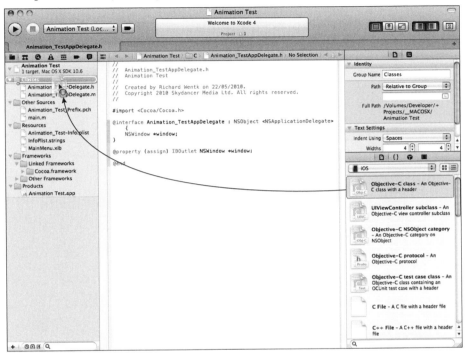

Comparing the New File and drag-and-drop options

The drag-and-drop option is quicker and simpler than using New File, because it skips the two steps shown in Figures 5.1 and 5.2. However, for certain file types, the New File option reveals extra features that aren't available with drag-and-drop.

For example, Figure 5.6 shows the extra check boxes that appear if you use New File to add a view controller to an iOS project. In this example you can use these check boxes to create an iPad-compatible class, with an associated nib file. If you use drag-and-drop, these options don't appear.

Figure 5.6

These extra features available when using the New File option don't appear when using drag-and-drop.

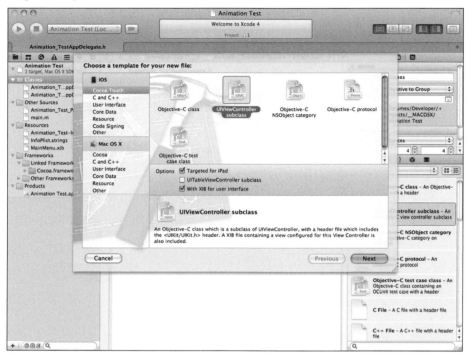

Naming new files

Xcode doesn't enforce a naming convention for new files, so it's up to you to name files using a scheme that works for you. By default, the class files are named `class.m` and `class.h`, which is unhelpful, especially if you use more than one class.

It's good practice to include both the project and functional class name in every new class; for example, a new view controller for the flip view in an iOS project might be called `Flipside ViewController`. Terse and obscure names such as `AClass` or `MyClass` will confuse you later and are best avoided.

Adding a new class

When you add a new Objective-C class, Xcode automatically adds a header file to the project. Where needed, it also adds a matching implementation file to the project. There are five templates for iOS classes and four templates for OS X classes, with significant overlap, as shown in Table 5.1.

Table 5.1 Objective-C File Templates

Template	Availability	Comments
Objective-C class	iOS/OS X	This is a minimal Objective-C class with a header file. By default, this creates a subclass of `NSObject`. You can edit the header to create a subclass of any other Cocoa object.
`UIViewController` subclass	iOS only	This creates a subclass of `UIViewController` with a header, an implementation with sample code. If you add this template with drag-and-drop, you can choose to create a default nib file and select iPhone or iPad screen sizes. The sample code is commented out, but you can remove the comments to create your own implementations of some of the standard `UIViewController` methods. There's no OS X equivalent that creates an `NSWindow` or `NSView` with an associated nib.
`NSManagedObject` subclass	Both	This is a subclass of `NSManagedObject`, with a header, for use in Core Data applications. This template doesn't include sample code or method definitions.
Objective-C `NSObject` category	iOS/OS X	This creates a header and implementation file for an empty category on `NSObject`. You can edit the class name to create a category on some other Cocoa class, and you can add custom methods to extend that class with your own features.
Objective-C protocol	iOS/OS X	This creates a header file with a protocol declaration. Depending on the context, it's sometimes easier to ignore this option and add the protocol code directly to a class.
Objective-C test case class	iOS/OS X	This creates a header and implementation file for an OCUnit test case object. This is used exclusively for automated testing. For more details, see Chapter 17.

CAUTION

You can add iOS templates to OS X projects, and vice versa. For example, Xcode 4 allows you to add an OS X menu to an iOS application. The menu doesn't do anything because it isn't referenced by the code, but it's included—as a waste of space—in the app bundle. When you add new items, be careful to have the correct OS selected.

Adding new resources

Although it's often useful to add new windows and views to a project, the templates make this unnecessarily complex. It would be useful to add nibs and supporting source code in a single step, but the templates don't support this. Instead, you must add a suitable nib from a list of resource files and then add supporting classes manually.

The one exception to this is the `UIViewController` subclass template for iOS, which creates source code files and an associated nib. For other tasks, you must add and edit the nib files by hand, add supporting class files separately, and then reclass the nibs so they're linked to the source code. For more details, see Chapters 7 and 8. Table 5.2 lists the nib files that are available.

Table 5.2 Nib File Templates

Template	Availability	Comments
Application	iOS/OS X	The OS X nib includes a Font Manager, a Main Menu, a Window and View, and an Application object. Note that there's no App Delegate. The iOS version of this nib includes an App Delegate object and a `UIWindow`.
Window	iOS/OS X	The OS X nib includes an `NSWindow` with an associated `NSView`. The iOS nib includes a `UIWindow` only.
View	iOS/OS X	The OS X nib includes an `NSView`. The iOS nib includes a `UIView`.
Empty	iOS/OS X	On both platforms, this is a plain, empty nib. Only the File's Owner and First Responder placeholders are included.

Adding miscellaneous other files from the templates

The templates include a selection of other files. You can add them to a project in the usual ways.

- The C/C++ templates add a standard C or C++ pair of header and code files. You can import these into Objective-C code in the usual way. For more about working with these languages, see Chapter 12.
- The Shell Script and Assembly File templates support shell scripts and assembly code, respectively. You can run a shell script as part of a custom build. Assembly code is used for very specialized hardware-level coding.
- The Core Data templates include a Data Model file and a Mapping Model file. You can add these to projects that support Core Data. If your project doesn't use Core Data, you can ignore them. For details, see Chapter 13.

- Use the Rich Text File (RTF) and Strings File templates to add text-based data. The Strings file is used for *localization*—non-English language support. For details, see Chapter 12. The RTF file is a standard text file. You can use it to hold any string- or text-based data. For OS X applications, you can use an RTF file to define the information that appears in an application's About box.

- Settings and Property Lists (plists) include an empty XML plist file for general property preferences and settings. Both iOS and OS X applications already include an info.plist file with basic application details. The iOS templates include a separate Settings Bundle, which uses an iOS-specific format to define an app's settings and preferences.

- Resource Rules and Entitlements are signed certificates that can be used to lock your application to specific hardware or software environments. For example, on iOS you can use these features to create an *ad hoc build* that runs on specific handsets for beta testing, bypassing the app store. Entitlements and code-signing are complex topics. For practical details, see Chapter 11.

- You can use a Configuration Settings File to create your own list of build settings for a project—for example, to create your own build setting defaults. For information about custom builds, see Chapter 12.

Deleting and renaming files

You can delete a file with the Delete key, or by right-clicking a file and selecting the Delete option from the contextual menu, as shown in Figure 5.7. When you delete a file, a dialog box appears asking you if you want to remove it from the project and leave it on disk ("Remove Reference") or move it to the trash. If you leave it on disk, you can re-import it later if you change your mind about the deletion. This can be a good safety net for small projects, but on large projects, it's likely to clutter up the project folder with unnecessary files.

To rename a file, click once to select it in the Project Navigator and type in the new name. You also can enter the name in the File pane of the Utility area. Figure 5.8 is a composite that shows both options. Renaming a file changes its name in the project and also renames it on disk.

CAUTION

File extensions are significant, but changing the extension isn't enough to change how Xcode processes the file during a build. If you need to change the type of a file and modify how it contributes to a build, select a new type from the list in the File Type drop-down menu in the File pane of the Utility area.

Figure 5.7

Deleting a file using the right-click contextual menu

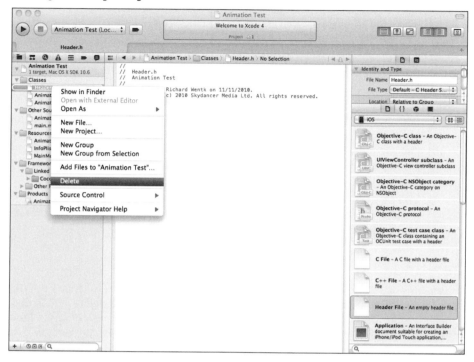

Figure 5.8

The two ways to rename a file

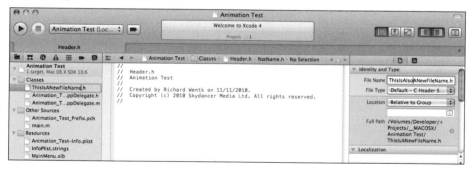

Note that there's no way to rename an entire project. The project name is embedded in the project folder, the class names, the header files, the project nib files, and may also be embedded in various security options including the code-signing features.

You can work on projects with identical names in Xcode, as long as the main Xcode project files are in different folders and you don't try to edit shared files (if there are any) simultaneously in two different windows. If the files are independent, it doesn't matter what the project is called.

Generally, the project name is for your convenience. It has no effect on the final application name, and duplicated project names don't cause problems.

Importing existing files

Because Xcode's file templates aren't exhaustive, you often need to import into a project files created with other editors, such as graphics, sound files, HTML web pages, PDF documents, and so on. During a build, these non-standard file types are copied to the application folder without processing. Xcode includes preview features for a small selection of file types, most obviously for graphics. But you must edit and prepare these files using other tools.

To import a file or folder, right-click a group and select the Add Files to… menu option. You'll see the dialog box in Figure 5.9. Navigate to the folder with the files, and then select the import options using the check box and radio button.

Figure 5.9

Adding an image file to a project from the Pictures folder

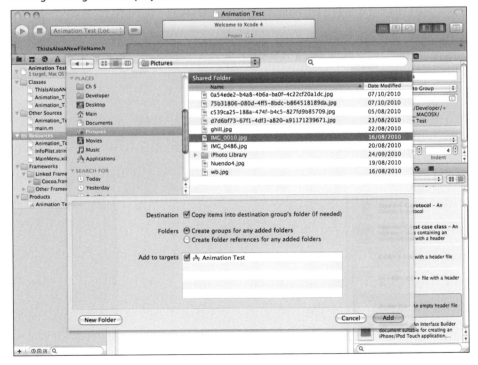

Optionally, you can copy files from the source folder into the project folder. If you leave the Destination box unchecked, files are left in their original location and accessed via a reference. Generally, it's good practice to copy files that are unique to the project, but to use references for files that are reused by many projects.

You can also create groups or folder references for added folders. Although I've emphasized that groups aren't necessarily mirrored in a project's folder structure, you can use this option and the group management features introduced in the next section to create folders on disk that match the groups in the Project Navigator. This step isn't essential, but it can make a project easier to navigate if you're reusing its classes and resources.

Reimporting missing files

As long as you leave a file's Location option set to Relative to Group in the File pane of the Utility Area, you can move a project folder to a different location on disk without breaking the file references.

However, Xcode does occasionally glitch and lose files from a project. If you move items that are referenced indirectly in a different folder, Xcode may not be able to find them. And if you import a project created by an older version of Xcode, the Location option may not have been set correctly.

Broken references appear in the Project Navigator in red. As long as you can find the original file on disk, you can fix a broken reference by hand. Click the window-like icon to the right of the text box above the Full Path string in the File pane. You'll see the folder selector shown in Figure 5.10. Use it to navigate to the folder that holds the missing file, and select it when done. Xcode repairs the reference.

CAUTION
In Xcode 3, you fixed a broken reference by selecting the file on disk. In Xcode 4, you fix it by selecting the folder that holds the file.

Figure 5.10

You can change the path of a file to fix a missing reference or to substitute one version of a file in one folder with a different version in another, although there are better ways to manage version control in Xcode.

Working with Groups

Groups are cosmetic, for your convenience. You can use any group structure, nested as deeply as you like. The default structure with separate class and resource folders is only one of many possible arrangements. You also may create a separate group for each class or (less usefully) a single group for every file in the project.

Moving groups and files

Files are compiled more or less in descending order through the Navigator. Circular class references are handled automatically, so there's no significant speed advantage to reordering the groups. But it's sometimes useful to modify the group order for clarity.

You can drag and drop groups in the Project Navigator, but dropping a group on another group nests it, which may not be what you want.

To move a group to the top of the list, drop it on the Project item at the top of the Navigator. To rearrange all groups into a new order, you need to do this repeatedly. This can be a tedious process, especially if you have many groups.

Moving files is much easier. You can simply drag a file from one group and drop it in another. Any file can be moved to any group.

Creating a new group

To add a new group, right-click the Project item and select New Group from the menu, as shown in Figure 5.11. You also can select multiple items in the Navigator using any of the standard Mac multi-select options and collect them into a single new group by selecting New Group from Selection.

Figure 5.11

You can add a new group from the floating menu or use File ⇨ New ⇨ New Group in the main Xcode menu.

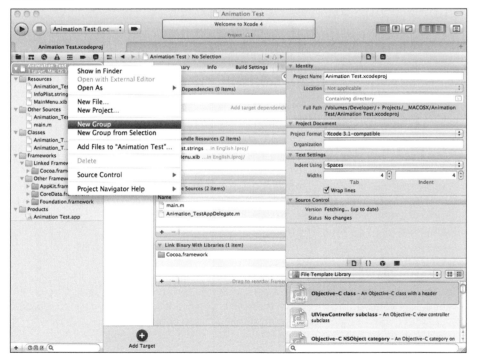

TIP
To create a new group inside an existing group, right-click the existing group instead of the Project item. You can nest groups almost indefinitely.

Organizing groups

Because groups are completely free-form, you can organize your project however you like. There's no need to use the default organization, with separate class and resource groups. For example:

- For an iOS project, collect each view controller and its associated nib into a separate group. This is usually easier to navigate than keeping classes and nibs separated.

- If your project uses many supporting graphics files, group them into a separate Graphics folder to keep them distinct from other resources. This simplifies graphic previews and makes it easier to find the project nib files.

- Similarly, you can keep other project resources such as plists and code-signing files in a separate group to keep them out of your way.

- Source code for frameworks and libraries should have its own separate groups, especially if the files are imported from a standard location on disk. It's a good idea to keep these items separated from project source code.

Working with Frameworks

Apple's frameworks are prewritten libraries that can be imported into any project to add specific features, such as support for video, sound, data management, or various hardware features.

When you build an OS X or iOS project, you may need to add one or more of Apple's frameworks to your project before you can use them. A selection of default frameworks is included in every application template; for example, OS X projects always include the Cocoa and AppKit frameworks, and iOS projects always include Cocoa Touch, UIKit, and CoreGraphics. All projects include the Foundation framework.

Other frameworks are optional, and you must add them manually. For example, you must add the GameKit framework to use the classes and methods built into GameKit. If you don't, the compiler can't find the symbols included in the framework, and your build fails, sometimes spectacularly, with hundreds of errors.

TIP
If you do get hundreds of errors while building, it usually means you've forgotten to import a framework. Typically, most of the errors disappear after you add the framework correctly. Don't forget that you also need to import the framework's header file into every file that references it in your project.

Using frameworks

Although you could add every framework to every project, this would slow build times to a crawl. Depending on the build options, including every framework might also create huge binaries. So it's standard practice to add only the frameworks that are referenced by your code.

TIP

You'll often use at least one of the standard graphics frameworks and perhaps also one of the animation frameworks. It's easy to forget to add frameworks, and adding the headers by hand is a chore. You can save time by creating a default project that already includes a more realistic and useful selection of frameworks than are included in the standard Apple templates.

Apple frameworks include a binary with associated header files, as shown in Figure 5.12. When you add a framework, Xcode adds both the header and the binary to its build list. The header is referenced during compilation, and references to the binary are added while linking.

Figure 5.12

The framework header files include useful comments that often add extra detail and insight that isn't available in the more formal class reference documentation.

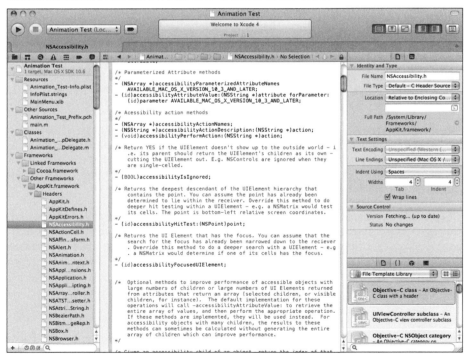

You also can add third-party frameworks. Some frameworks are supplied with full source code. You can add these by importing all files into your project, as described earlier in this chapter. Other frameworks are supplied in a binary/header format. To add these to a project, see the section below.

Adding existing frameworks

The framework management system in Xcode 4 is completely different to that in Xcode 3. It's no longer related to the Add files… menu option. Instead, it's buried in the Build Phases page of the target build settings, as shown in Figure 5.13.

Figure 5.13

Adding an Apple framework to a project in Xcode 4 has nothing in common with the menu options used in Xcode 3.

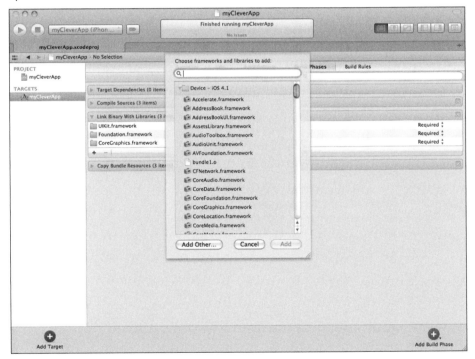

To add a framework, select your project in the Project Navigator, select the TARGETS icon in the gutter, and select Build Phases. Click the Link Binary With Libraries reveal triangle, and then select the plus (+) icon at the lower left.

You can now select a framework from the pop-up list that appears (refer to Figure 5.13). To delete a framework from the project, select it in the Link Binary with Libraries table and click the minus (-) icon.

To add a precompiled third-party framework, select Add Other… and navigate to the framework folder on your disk.

Summary

This chapter introduced file and group management. It explained how to add new files to a project using the standard templates and sketched the key features and applications of each file type, including classes, nib files, and other resources.

It listed the different ways in which files can be deleted, renamed, and re-imported, explored how files can be organized within groups, and outlined some of the ways in which groups can simplify project management.

Finally, it introduced frameworks, explained how frameworks are added to Xcode 4 projects, and contrasted this with the different framework management options used in previous versions of Xcode.

Using Documentation

T he iOS and OS X development tools are supported by Reference Libraries, documentation that provides orientation information for new developers and describes specific features in detail.

Newcomers often assume it's trivially easy to use the documentation. In fact, the organization and content are complex, and using the files effectively is a key developer skill.

The contents are vast. In paper form, they would require many feet of shelf space. To simplify access and to guarantee that the details are always up to date, the documentation is now stored online. You can access it using a conventional web browser, as shown in Figure 6.1, which illustrates the main iOS Reference Library access page.

CAUTION

The URLs for Apple's online documentation change regularly. Use a Google search to find the current location.

You can also access it via the streamlined and expanded documentation tools built into Xcode 4, which are described in the rest of this chapter.

TIP

When you begin with iOS or OS X, you often return to the same documentation pages over and over. The Xcode documentation viewer includes a bookmark feature to help with this. But it also can be useful to load your favorite pages into a separate tabbed browser and keep them open while you work. You can use the OS X Spaces feature to give the browser its own desktop.

In earlier versions of Xcode, the documentation files were downloaded as a single .docset file for each library. Xcode 4 continues to use docset files, as shown in Figure 6.2. When you first install Xcode 4, none of the docsets are available. You must open the Documentation tab in Xcode ⇨ Preferences and select each GET button to download them. Allow between 2GB and 5GB of disk space for a full download.

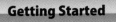

Figure 6.1

You can access the Reference Library using any browser, but Xcode 4 offers more streamlined and efficient access to key information with Safari.

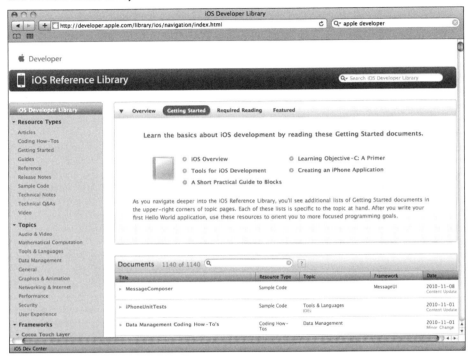

Figure 6.2

You can use the reveal arrow at the left above the documentation details pane to view or hide information about the base documentation.

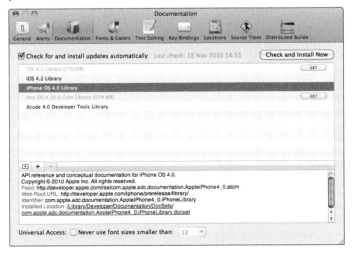

Understanding the Apple Documentation

Accessing the documentation from the web for the first time can feel overwhelming. The organization seems haphazard, and it's not clear which elements are essential, which are useful, and which are irrelevant. The contents are organized by OS and also by *resource types*—different kinds of information. Confusingly, there's significant overlap between the OS X and iOS documentation and also between different versions of each OS.

Comparing iOS and OS X and their different versions

If you access the documentation from the web, the organization online doesn't distinguish between different versions of iOS and OS X. The iOS and OS X portals always show the most up-to-date content. This can be a beta version of the OS, which may not be what you want.

Xcode's own documentation viewer, shown in Figure 6.3, makes the differences between OS versions explicit. Each OS has a separate library header, so you can find the information you need without ambiguity.

Figure 6.3

Using Xcode's documentation viewer is built into the Organizer section of Xcode, but it can be accessed directly from the main menu.

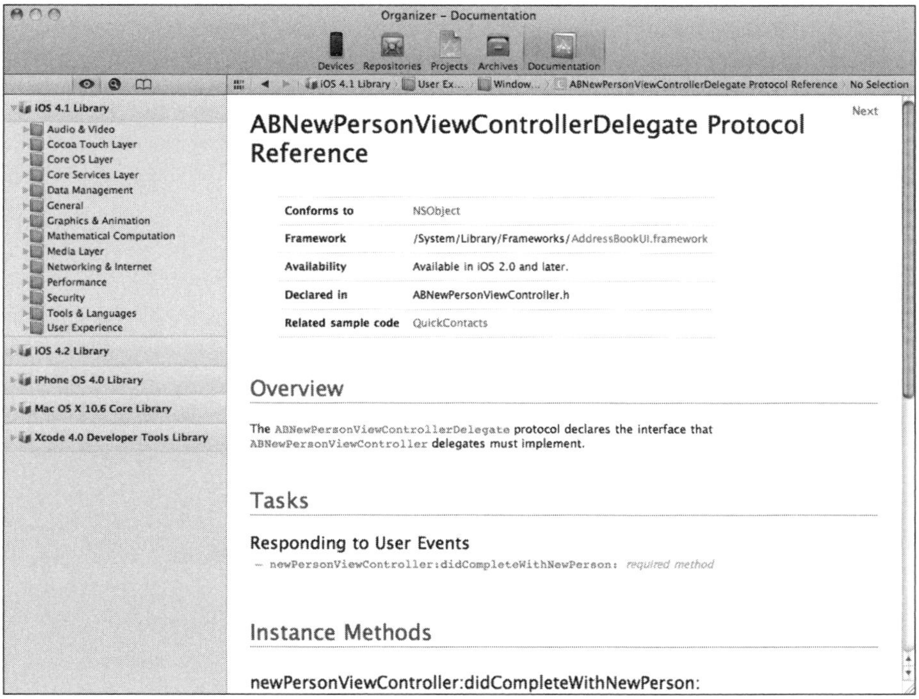

NOTE
You can access the viewer using Help ⇨ Developer Documentation in the main menu or with the (option)+⌘+? keyboard shortcut.

Some elements of Cocoa appear to be in both iOS and OS X. For example, iOS and OS X both include a class called NSArray. Most classes with identical names are genuinely identical on both platforms, but some have significant differences. You should always read the version for the correct OS.

In a beta version of an OS, the documentation may not be finished. You may find yourself reading about an OS X class even though you have followed a search trail looking for iOS classes. This doesn't often happen, but when it does, assume that the OS X details are also correct for iOS.

Understanding resource types

If you explore the web version of the documentation, you'll soon discover that topics are grouped in different ways and that there's significant redundancy and irrelevance in the libraries. Some elements in the documentation are more than 15 years old, and they describe features and techniques that are no longer in use.

To use the documentation effectively, you must understand these limitations and know how to find what you need without being distracted by irrelevant information. You also must understand the different resource types, which are listed at the top left of Figure 6.4. Whenever you view a collection of documents about a broad topic, you can sort them alphabetically or group them by resource type.

The resource types are less prominent when you view the documentation in Xcode. The content has been filtered so only the most relevant details appear. This makes the Xcode viewer easier to work with, especially when you're looking for specific information about a named class. But it does mean that some of the supporting details available on the web don't appear in the viewer.

Figure 6.4

The resource types are listed at the top left of the Developer Library web pages. You're more likely to search for specific topics and references than for resource types.

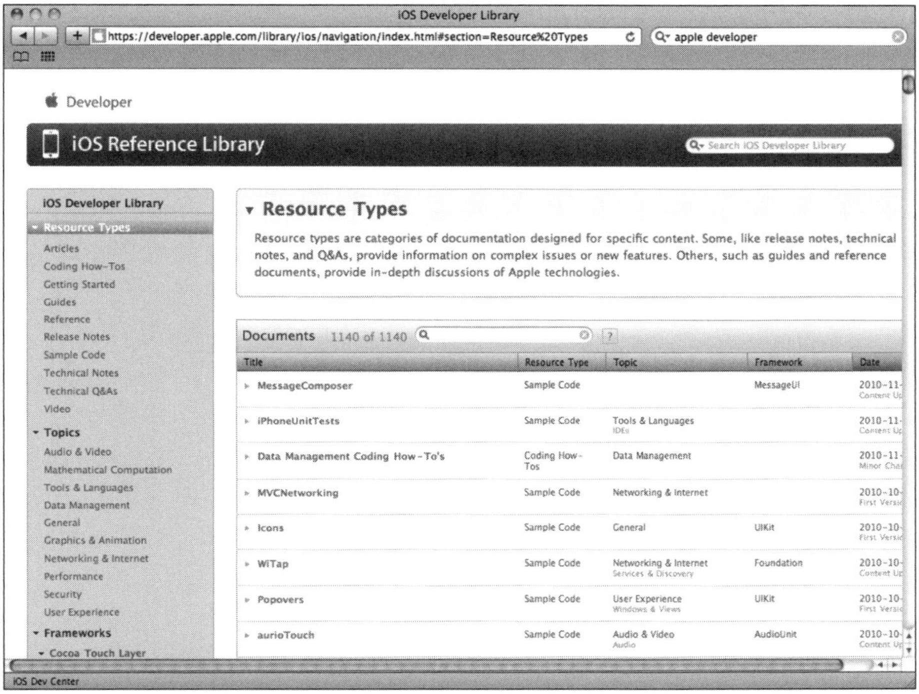

Articles

Articles, shown in Figure 6.5, are a grab bag of essays and features. Many are highly specialized and of little interest. A few are more useful. For example, Maximizing Mac OS X Application Performance is a good guide to performance optimization. Generally, articles are more useful to developers who have some understanding of the essentials of Apple development and are looking for slightly more advanced information.

Figure 6.5

Articles can provide useful extra information for more experienced developers. Beginners can avoid them, unless they're looking for information about a specific topic that is covered in an article.

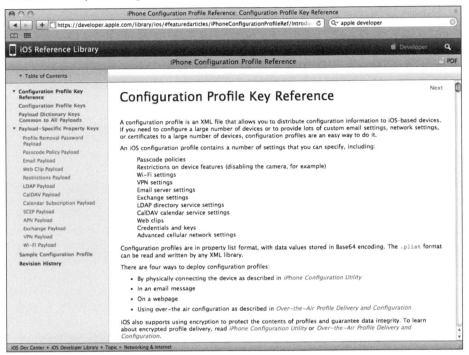

How-To's

How-To's, shown in Figure 6.6, attempt to answer "How do I…?" questions for new developers. The information is of variable quality and often leaves out key facts. For example, the Graphics & Animation Coding How-To document explains how to obtain a graphics context for 2D drawing, but doesn't include full sample code and doesn't explain what a graphics context is or why you might need one. Experienced developers can use how-to's as memory joggers. New developers are likely to find they need extra help to understand the jargon and concepts described in these documents.

Figure 6.6

It's a good idea to be slightly skeptical of the information in the how-to's. For example, you quickly discover that there are easier ways to find out which version of SDK is installed than are described here.

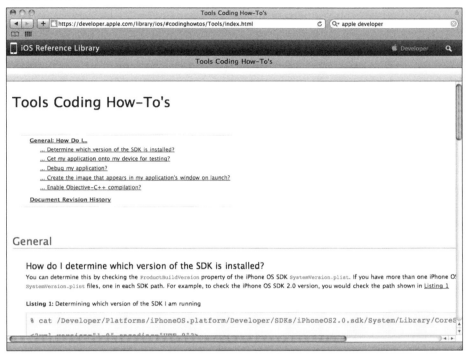

Getting Sarted

The Getting Started guides aren't an ideal place to get started. In spite of the name, most guides are collections of links to the more detailed programming guides, surrounded by sparse extra information. These guides are factually accurate, but they gloss over many of the details and techniques used in actual programming practice. You can use them as orientation material that introduces key concepts and mentions useful classes, but you usually need to dig deeper and wider to fill in the gaps while coding. Figure 6.7 shows the Getting Started with Graphics and Animation document.

Figure 6.7

Don't think of the Getting Started guides as introductions to practical coding. But you can use them as outline orientations, and as very brief and abstract introductions to key OS features.

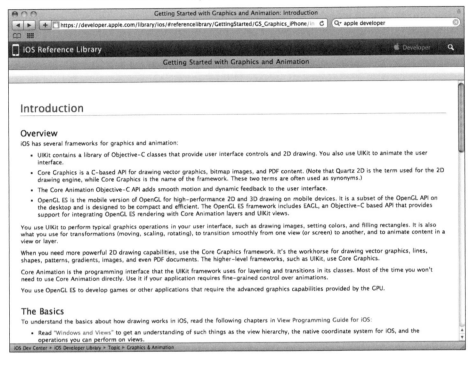

Guides

The Guides include detailed information about development and coding topics. These are the key orientation documents. Some guides, especially the human interface guidelines for iOS, iPad, and OS X, are essential reading. Part of the iPad Human Interface Guidelines document is shown in Figure 6.8. However, the guide contents are often terse, and important practical points may be glossed over or missing. In practice, you sometimes need to look for successful working code in independent developer forums or in the code samples included with the documentation.

Figure 6.8

You should certainly read the Human Interface Guidelines for your target platforms before you begin developing. But you'll find it equally useful to look at the interfaces of popular and successful applications for a more practical view of application design.

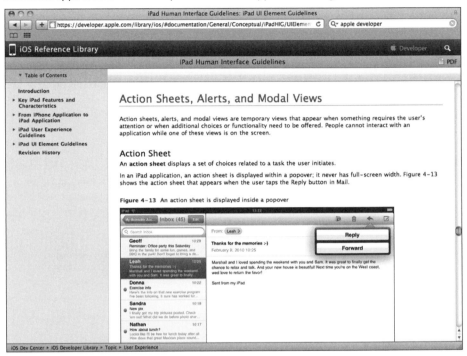

References

The references are the most useful documents, and you'll spend most of your time reading them. The key references are listed below, and there's more detail about the structure of the references later in this chapter:

- Class references detail the properties, methods, and constants used in a class. This is key information: You won't be able to code without it.

- Protocol references are similar to class references, but list useful methods that you can build into your own subclasses using the Objective-C protocol mechanism. (For detailed information about protocols, see the companion *Cocoa* Developer Reference.)

- Framework references list the classes, functions, and protocols used in each framework. You should view the framework reference page for every framework you use in a project before you begin coding. Figure 6.9 shows the Foundation Framework, which is one of the most critical frameworks for Apple development. If you don't review the frameworks, you may miss useful functions, data types, and constants that aren't listed elsewhere. Don't consider this optional: You'll save lots of time if you review the features of each framework before you use it.

- Services references list extra OS interfaces that typically use C rather than Objective-C, and they work at a lower level than the main Cocoa libraries. These references are useful for specialized audio and graphics programming, but beginners can usually ignore them.

Figure 6.9

Because the frameworks aren't prioritized, it's not obvious that some frameworks are more important than others. The Foundation framework, AppKit on the Mac, and UIKIt on iOS are key, and you should review their reference documentation before you start working with them.

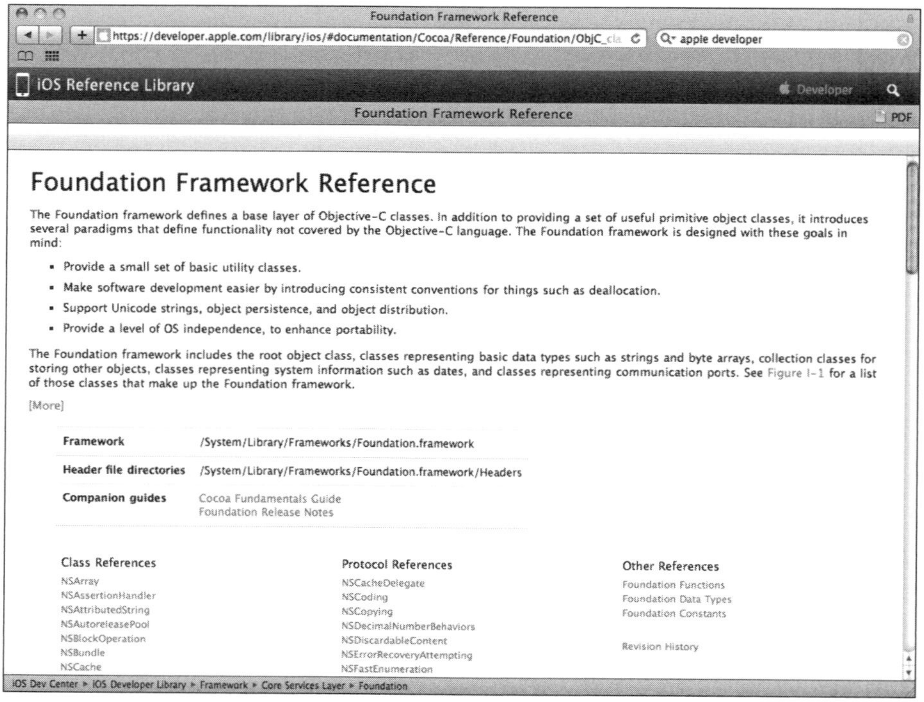

Release notes and API diffs

Release notes are short summaries of the new features and changes in an OS update. API diffs are a more formal list of changes that detail new classes added, old classes removed, and changed features within each class. API diffs are more useful, but it's worth reviewing both before you begin working with an OS update. Figure 6.10 shows part of a typical API diff file.

TIP
Note that each entry in the API diff file is a clickable link that takes you to the reference file for the class or method that has changed.

Figure 6.10

This API diff file lists the differences between iOS 4.0 and 4.1.

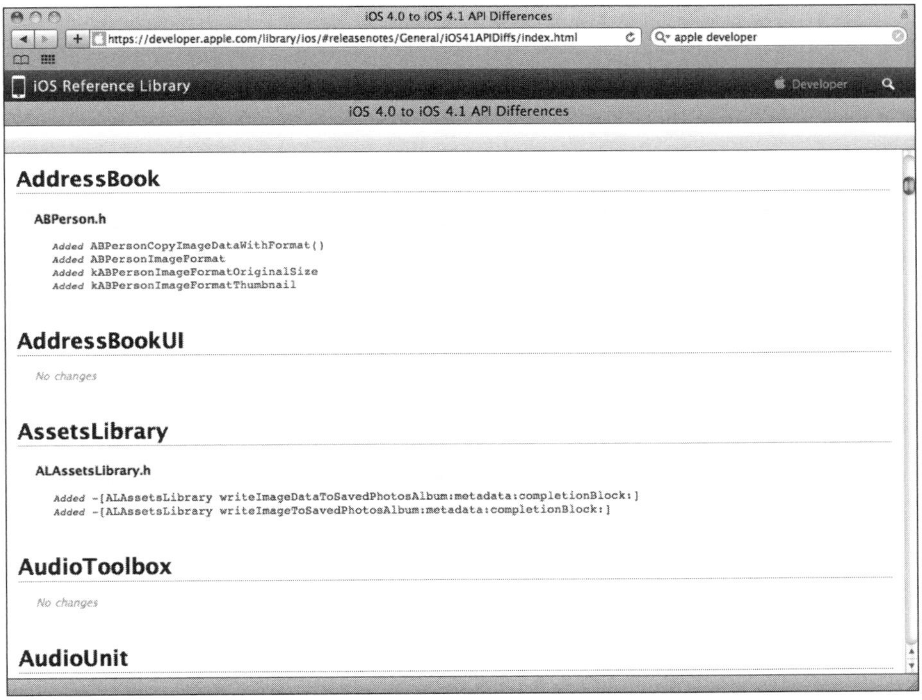

Sample code

The sample code section of the documentation is a library of sample projects that demonstrate key features and techniques. Many code samples are fairly complex and can be difficult to follow. Some are overly complex; they use advanced techniques and solutions when simpler code would work almost as effectively. Try reviewing the sample code for specific solutions and reverse-engineering it or using it with minor modifications. You can also find alternative solutions from other sources online, and they often illustrate useful techniques in a simpler and more accessible way.

If you view the sample code in a browser, you list each file in a browser window and you have the option to click a Download Sample Code button at the top left of the window to download a complete zipped project file. For example, Figure 6.11 shows a project called CryptoExercise that implements a selection of cryptographic features.

If you view the sample code in Xcode itself, you can click an Open Project button that loads the sample project with all of the source code.

Figure 6.11

With sample code, you can view the files individually or download the complete project, unzip it, and build it.

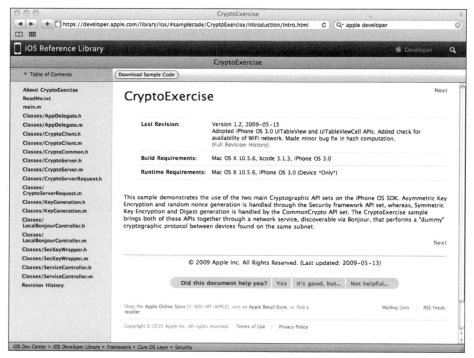

 CAUTION

Sample projects almost always build successfully, but if you load a project for an older version of OS X or iOS, some elements of the code may occasionally be deprecated or no longer available. If you find this, try to find a more recent version. You can also work through the errors by hand. (This is likely to be educational, but time-consuming.)

Technical notes and Technical Q&As

Technical notes expand on topics that aren't typically based on specific frameworks or code features. Technical Q&As deal with specific reported issues and common error messages; they also answer frequently asked questions. Both may include small samples of useful code and discuss solutions to common problems.

In practice, notes and Q&As are a grab bag of assorted unrelated programming and development topics. They could be included elsewhere in the documentation, but for somewhat arbitrary reasons each has been given a unique reference number. For example, Figure 6.12 shows Technical Q&A QA1620, which explains how to animate a `CALayer` object.

The notes and Q&As are far from comprehensive. You'll find a wider selection of useful—even essential—examples, FAQs, and background information on independent developer message boards.

Figure 6.12

A technical Q&A document, from a collection of at least 1,620

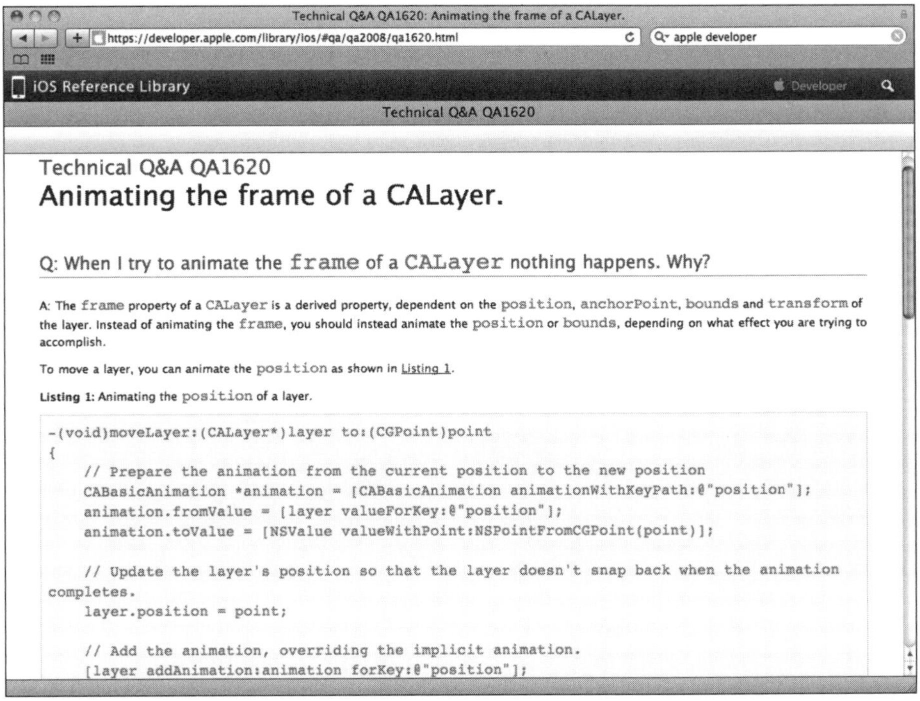

Videos

Videos are now included in the documentation. Figure 6.13 shows an example. The initial selection is sparse, but it may grow in future. Videos can be a helpful resource, but the most useful videos are available separately on the home pages of the OS X and iOS developer portals. Even though video is a slow and lightweight medium compared to text, take time to view the walkthrough videos that demonstrate key techniques and skills; they're more practically focused than the abstract text documentation.

TIP
Registered developers can download and view a further selection of useful demonstration and orientation videos from the latest WWDC pages. For example, the 2010 WWDC (World Wide Developer Conference) videos are available at `developer.apple.com/videos/wwdc/2010`. The videos and slideshows are designed to play in iTunes. They're not listed in the main iTunes content listings, and you can only access them via special WWDC-specific URLs. Search for "WWDC video" for the latest updates.

Figure 6.13
This is one of the small selection of videos that are included in the current documentation. Future updates of the documentation will include more video content.

Using topics

The list of topics organizes the documentation by subject. From one point of view, the topics are self-explanatory. As you'd expect, the Audio & Video topic lists resources relevant to audio and video applications.

What's less obvious is that each of the headers in the Documents list can rearrange the data to emphasize different elements. For example, clicking Title lists all elements alphabetically. The result is an arbitrary jumble of different resource types, as shown in Figure 6.14.

Figure 6.14

Sorting a topic alphabetically by title creates a jumbled list of content that doesn't prioritize the documents in any way.

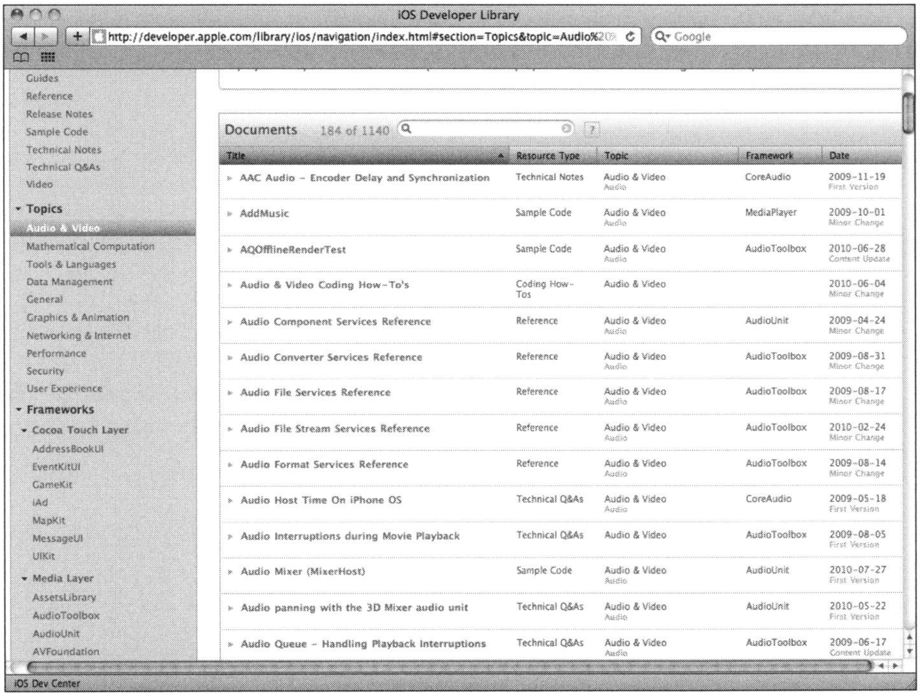

Because titles are somewhat arbitrary, it's often more useful to sort by resource types. Clicking the Resource Type header creates the list shown in Figure 6.15. This helps prioritize the documents and organize them in a more useful way. Note that each resource type list is alphabetized separately.

You also can sort by Framework, which is described below, and by Date. Sorting by date is a useful way to eliminate out-of-date information. Some of the help documents are historical and no longer relevant. Sorting by date can tell you which documents are out of date.

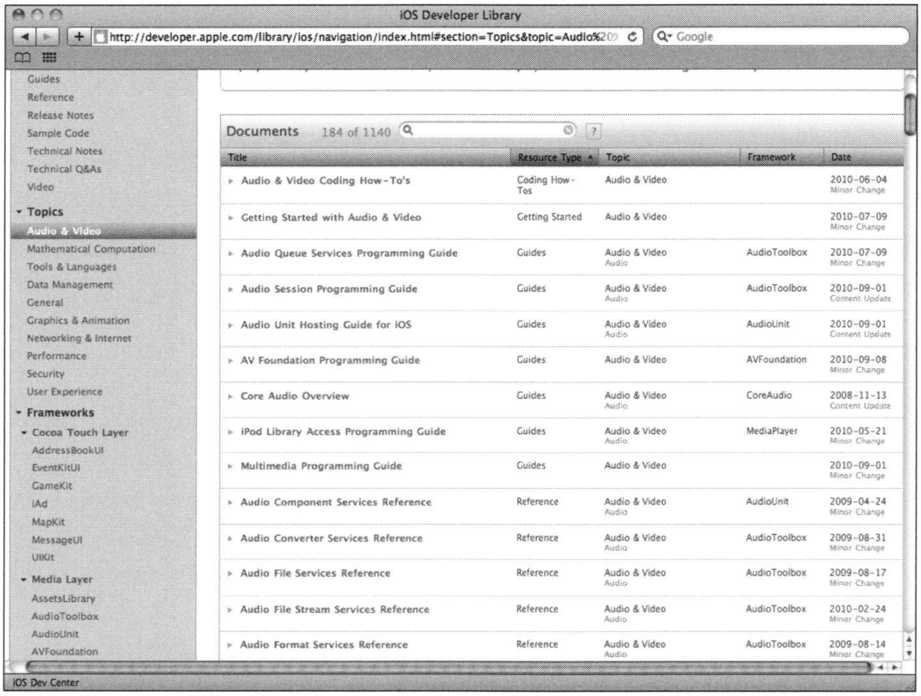

Figure 6.15

Sorting by resource types gives you a more useful view of the content, grouping orientation information, class references, and technical notes into separate lists.

Using frameworks and layers

Although iOS and OS X have different frameworks and layers, the principle is similar for both. A *framework* is a code library with an API that implements one or more useful features. A *layer* is a broad group of frameworks collected together.

The layer groupings are rather arbitrary and can be misleading. For example, in OS X, the Foundation framework includes functions such as `NSMakePoint` and `NSEqualPoints` that are critical for graphics programming. But the Foundation framework is a grab bag of utility features and appears in the Core Services Layer; these critical functions aren't listed in the Media layer, even though it appears to be a complete reference to OS X graphics.

Here as elsewhere, the documentation doesn't distinguish between critical, optional, and barely relevant information. To save confusion, ignore the full list of frameworks and concentrate on the three frameworks used in the default application templates: AppKit, Foundation for OS X; UIKit, Foundation, and CoreGraphics for iOS. In addition, you often need to use the Quartz frameworks and CoreAnimation framework on both platforms, and you may need to use Core Data.

Other frameworks add optional features. You can ignore them unless you want to add specific features to a project.

NOTE
The Cocoa framework that appears in OS X projects is a simple header file that imports the AppKit, Foundation and Core Data frameworks. There is no stand-alone Cocoa framework, and the documentation describes Cocoa as a layer.

Searching the online documentation

A search field is available at the top left of the main Reference Library pages. You can use this to run a simple word-match search. The results show each match, grouped by resource type. For example Figure 6.16 shows the results of searching for the NSMakePoint function.

Figure 6.16

Search for a specific function name. Searching for a vague topic such as "video" doesn't produce useful results. The search feature is best used for specific named features, such as classes, constants, functions, and so on.

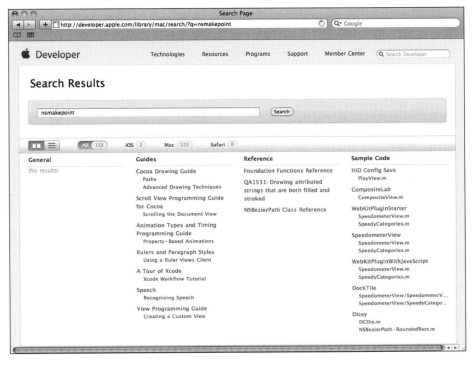

The word-match search isn't intelligent, and it doesn't attempt to group results by relevance. For best results, search for a specific function or class. The results will then show you the guides and related classes which use or mention the item. If sample code appears, it's well worth taking the time to explore it, because it can use related functions and classes that don't show up in a direct search.

Using the Xcode Documentation Viewer

The documentation browser is built into the Xcode Organizer. You can access it in four ways:

- Open the Organizer window from the main menu with Window ➪ Organizer, and select the Documentation icon in the top toolbar.
- Select Help ➪ Developer Documentation.
- Use the Quick Help feature to highlight and search for a symbol in a code listing.
- Use option/alt clicks on symbols to load it directly from your code.

CAUTION

The Search feature in the Help menu *doesn't* search the documentation. In fact, it only provides help for Xcode features. You can't use it to search the rest of the developer library.

Confusingly, the Xcode browser shows two different documentation sets in the same window. The view at the right is a standard web view showing the information that appears when you access the documentation using a web browser. The view at the left is an independent set of quick access links. There are three icons above the list:

- **Explore:** Use this to browse the document hierarchy.
- **Search:** Perform a word-match search.
- **Bookmark:** Create your own list of bookmarks.

There's some overlap between the documents listed in the web view, and in the hierarchical list. For example, both include links to the same class references.

But the two collections aren't identical, even though they're both grouped into similar topics. As shown in Figure 6.17, there are significant differences between the topic list at the left and the web view at the right.

Although this design seems counterintuitive, it eliminates some of the redundancy and irrelevance of the web help, and it creates a more focused environment for searching and browsing. These are the key differences:

- Different versions of each OS have separate documentation files.
- There are fewer optional and tangential elements such as Technical Q&As. When these elements are included, they're more likely to be relevant and useful for a specific topic.

- Class references, functions, and constants are listed alphabetically under section headers. This makes it easier to review and browse the class references.

- The documentation includes *code snippets,* short code examples that illustrate classes and features but aren't part of a complete project.

- The search features display a wider selection of sample code and are generally more likely to produce useful hits.

Figure 6.17

Both of these lists show the documentation for the Audio & Video topic. But the list of items in the left pane differs substantially from the list in the web view on the right.

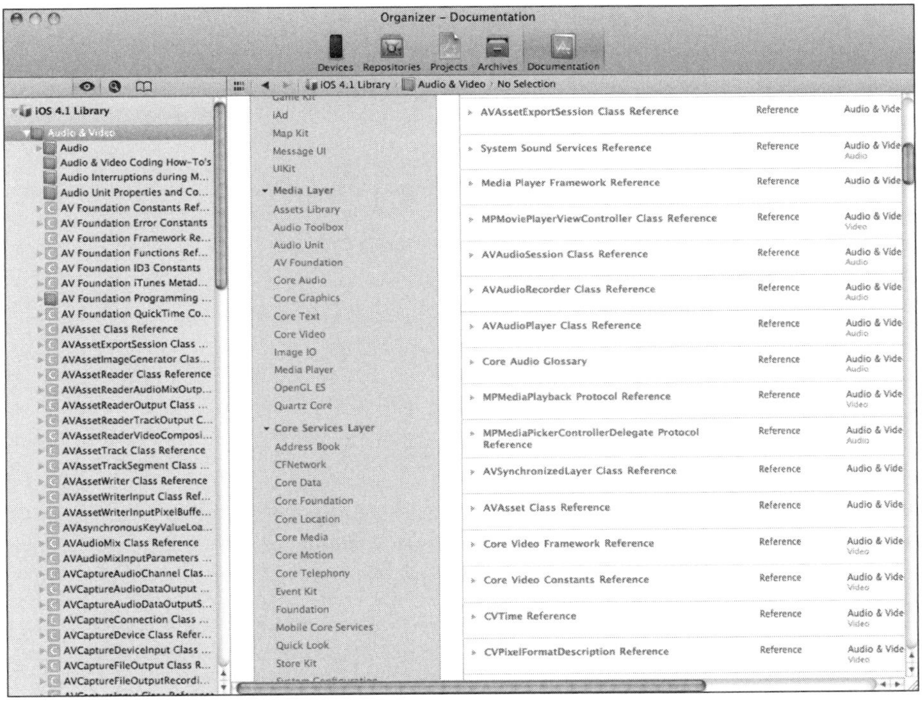

Browsing the documentation

Figure 6.18 shows a typical topic list. To view the documents for each topic, click the reveal triangles at the left. The list shows all items alphabetically: class references, code snippets, and other resource types. There's no way to group the resource types together. Topics may include subtopics; for example, the Audio & Video topic lists common classes and other features, and includes further separate Audio and Video subtopics with documentation that's unique to each.

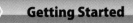

Figure 6.18
This is the topics list in one version of iOS; these lists are relatively static.

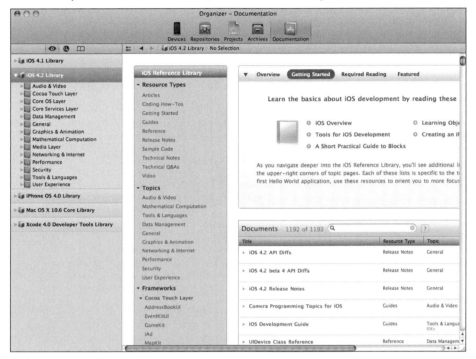

CAUTION
Some items appear under more than one heading. For example the MapKit Constants Reference appears under the MapKit subtopic in the Cocoa Touch layer and also in the User Experience topic. The duplication seems arbitrary.

Generally, topic browsing is most useful if you already have a basic understanding of a topic and need quick access to reference material about specific features. The topics include the same introductory guides that are available online, with the same limitations: They can be useful reminders, but they're heavy going if you're looking for a good, practical hands-on introduction to entry-level coding techniques. Otherwise, the organization is slightly haphazard. You can use browsing to discover and explore OS features that may be lost online, but you need to explore the code samples, code snippets, and independent developer discussions to develop a good working knowledge in practice.

TIP
The viewer includes a hierarchical menu navigation tree in the space above the document window. It's very similar to the hierarchical project view in the main Xcode editor. In theory, you can navigate to any document directly. In practice, some menu levels include hundreds of documents, and the extra scrolling needed to reach them makes this feature less useful than it might be.

Searching the documentation

To perform a word search, click the search icon and type the target word. The viewer lists all documents and resource types featuring that word. Class references typically appear at the top of the list.

The word search is very literal and doesn't attempt to find matches based on content or context. For example, if you search for a specific function or class, as shown in Figure 6.19, the search returns every Sample Code project that uses that symbol, irrespective of prominence or relevance. This can be useful because it gives you many different examples to review and understand.

If the symbol is used in more than one version of the OS—which is usually the case—you see duplicate listings in the search results. For example, you find three documents called "A Tour of Xcode." This looks like unnecessary duplication, but each document is included in a different docset: one for iPhone OS 4.0, one for iOS 4.1, and one for iOS 4.2. Depending on the differences among the OS versions, these duplicated documents may or may not be identical. To avoid inconsistencies, always read the document for your project's target OS.

Figure 6.19

This figure shows a search for a function. All these matches are correct because they contain the function, but some are more useful and relevant than others.

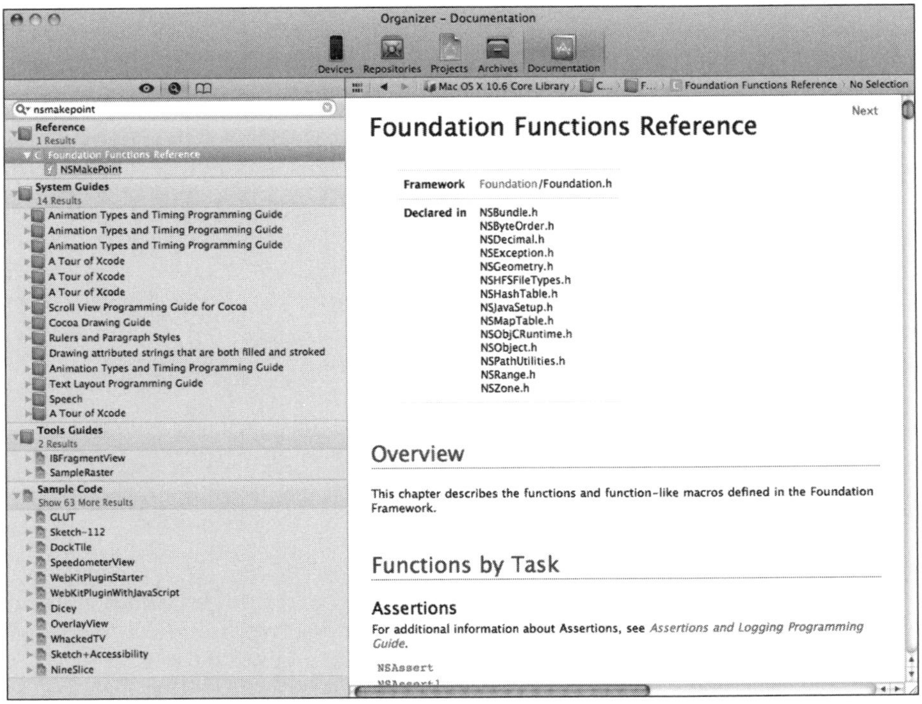

TIP

When searching for code symbols, each symbol has a different icon: C for class, F for function, K for constant, G for a global constant, T for a `typedef`, and E for an `enum`. The search feature finds the containing class reference. To display the specific sub-symbol—a function, a constant, and so on—click the reveal triangle next to the class, and then click the sub-symbol. The documentation window shows the correct item in the class.

For more accurate searches, you can select the target docset, the relevant language, and the match type, as shown in Figure 6.20. When you begin typing a search word, a pop-up menu appears under the search bar. To view the options shown in the figure, select the Show Search Options… menu item. By default, searches look for features in all programming languages. It can be useful to limit results to Objective-C, C, Java, or C++, or some combination of these languages.

Figure 6.20

Limiting the search by OS version. This is a useful way to minimize search clutter.

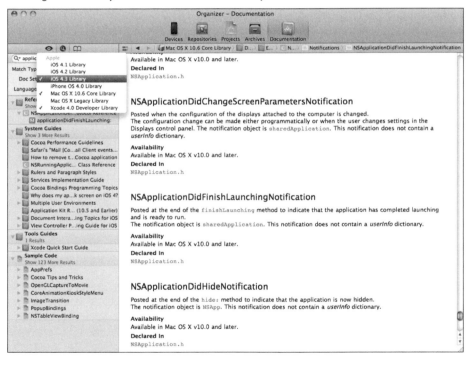

CAUTION

Both OS X and iOS are built from two layers of code: one written largely in Objective-C and another low-level layer that uses C. If you ignore the C layer, you miss some of the more useful features of both versions of the OS. For non-specialized application development, it's usually best to ignore the language filtering and view all results.

Using class references

The Reference section takes up the bulk of the documentation. Most are code references, with formal lists of properties/variables and code interfaces. This group includes Objective-C object references, and C function and struct references for all layers of OS X and iOS. Code references are grouped into the layers introduced earlier. The class references follow a fixed format, part of which is shown in Figure 6.21. A small number of class references include an extra Class at a Glance overview summary:

Figure 6.21

The Class References are long documents; use internal links to drill down through the references.

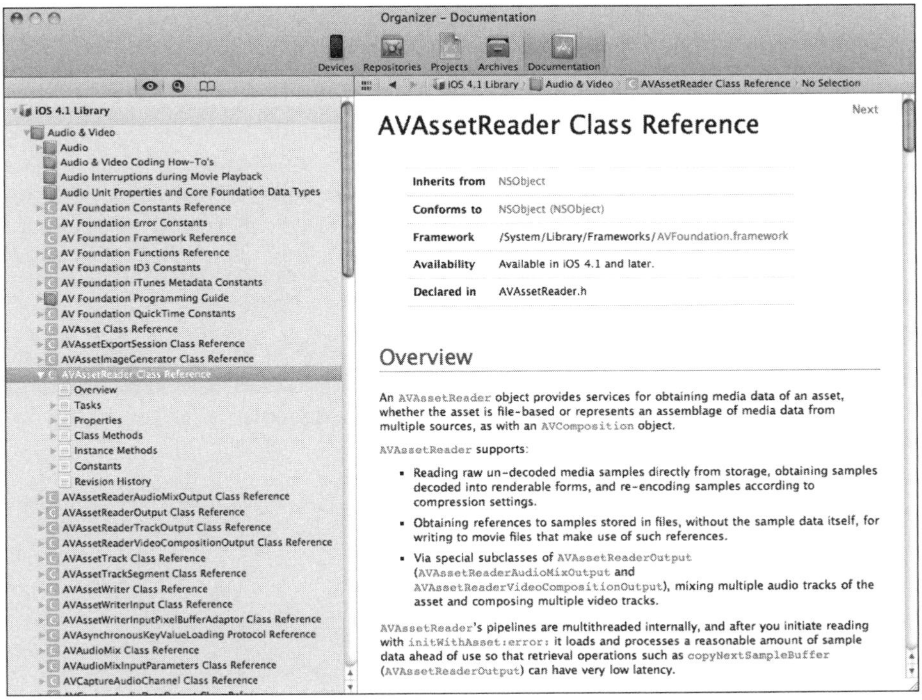

1. The Overview is a short text article that sketches the function of the class and how it should be used.

2. The Tasks section provides a plain list of methods grouped by function. Each method is a link; you can click it to display more information.

3. The optional Properties section lists the class properties and briefly sketches their features. Not all classes include a Properties section.

4. The Class Methods section lists class methods in more detail, with a sketch of their features and function.

5. The Instance Methods section lists the instance methods, using the same format.

6. A final optional section lists other information that may include constants, further optional methods, or information about notification messages generated by the class.

Items in blue are clickable links. For example, the sendEvent: method in UIApplication includes a link to the UIEvent class. To view the reference for UIEvent, click the link.

TIP
In previous versions of Xcode, the forward and back link features didn't always work correctly. Xcode 4 handles forward and back linking much more successfully. The buttons in the bar at the top left of the documentation viewer not only navigate between pages correctly, they also navigate between different items on the same page. You can save time by using these buttons regularly.

TIP
The browser versions of the class references include a useful Table of Contents with direct links to each section—Tasks, Properties, and so on—at the left of the window. The Xcode viewer doesn't display these links in the document area, but you see them if you click the reveal triangle next to a class reference while browsing. They don't appear in search results.

Accessing documentation from code

The documentation browser is ideal for general background searches and for browsing support documents. While coding, you typically want to find the documentation for classes, methods, and other symbols as quickly as possible.

The search feature in the browser is an inefficient way to do this. Xcode includes three faster options:

- Quick Help
- Command-click
- Option-click

Using Quick Help

When the Utilities pane is open at the right, you can display a Quick Help tip for any symbol by clicking it. When the symbol is part of the OS, the tip includes live links to the documentation. For example, if you select a class and click to the right of the Reference item, Xcode opens the documentation browser—if it isn't already open—and displays the class reference.

This feature is Xcode's version of contextual help. In addition to reference and definition links, it also lists related APIs, related documents, and useful sample code. You can use it for a bottom-up, in-depth exploration of any symbol. This is almost always more efficient and productive than top-down browsing. It's also a quick way to check method parameters.

TIP

Quick Help works as you type. As soon as Xcode recognizes a class, the Quick Help window displays the relevant links. This feature is more obvious and more useful on faster Macs, because the help content appears almost instantly.

Using command-click

If you command-click a symbol, Xcode jumps directly to the symbol definition. If the symbol is defined in a framework, Xcode displays the corresponding item in the framework header file. This feature is identical to the Jump to Definition feature described in Chapter 9—but quicker and more intuitive.

Using option-click

If you option-click a symbol, Xcode displays a pop-up that duplicates the quick-help information, as shown in Figure 6.22. This can be a slightly quicker way to access the same information. It's always available, even when the Utilities pane is hidden. The two icons at the top right link to the symbol definition in the documentation, and to the header or code definition.

Figure 6.22

Using option-click to view Quick Help. This pop-up appears even when the Utilities pane is hidden.

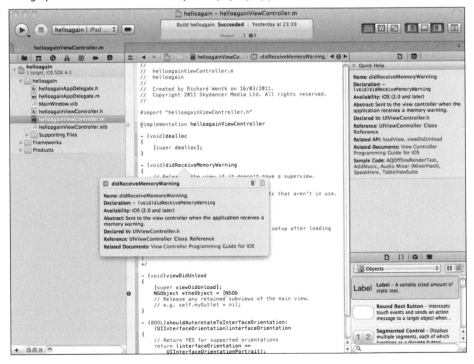

Using Other Documentation

The Internet is a vast resource, and you can find useful tips and code samples by searching for specific classes. But some of the classes use names that are used in other contexts. For example, searching for UIView returns hits that aren't relevant to iOS. You can narrow searches by adding extra keywords such as "iOS," "OS X," and "iPhone." Figure 6.23 shows the results of a combined search. All the hits are relevant, and the results include a good selection of tutorials, discussions, and examples.

Figure 6.23

The web is invaluable for general searches that fill in the gaps in the official documentation. A simple web search returns a jumble of potentially relevant information, but you usually find something of value.

Developer forums offer a tighter focus with more obviously relevant examples. Apple's own developer forums are at `devforums.apple.com`. The conversations are grouped by topic and are often lively. By default, topics are listed chronologically, but you can search for keywords.

Alternative forums include those at `stackoverflow.com` and `iphonedevforums.com`. The former is a useful resource, with a vast community of developers and regular discussions at all levels of expertise. Figure 6.24 shows an example topic search.

Figure 6.24

The equivalent search on `stackoverflow.com` returns a good selection of useful beginner-level hits, mixed with more advanced discussions.

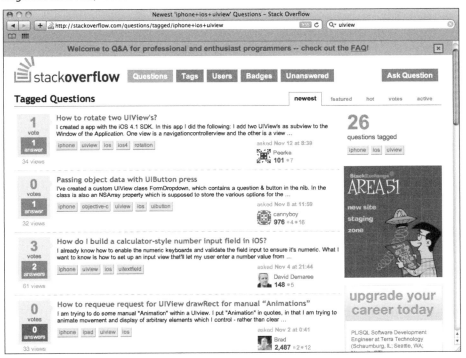

Summary

This chapter explored both official and unofficial sources of documentation. It introduced Apple's online documentation and explained how to view it in a web browser. It also introduced the documentation viewer built into Xcode and explained the differences between the two sources of information.

Resource types and class references were reviewed in more detail, and search strategies were suggested. Finally, the chapter discussed web forums and explained how they can provide useful supporting information that can fill in some of the gaps in the official help files.

Getting Started with Interface Builder

Although Interface Builder (IB) can be used as a UI editor, you must understand that it's a more general object management tool.

Understanding IB

In Xcode, IB has five functions:

- You can use IB to design your application's UI. The UI design includes one or more windows and views, with associated controls—objects such as buttons, sliders, text boxes, and so on. The design process presets the properties of these objects. For example, you can set the default position of an OS X window and control whether it has a drop shadow. Similarly, when you add a button to a UI, you use IB to set its position in the window or view, set its color, and so on. Optionally, you can define custom graphics and other more specialized features.

- You can use IB to pre-instantiate objects in your application. Any object you add to a nib file is created in memory when the file is loaded. This option is completely general: Objects do not have to be visible on screen or be part of a UI. The standard application templates for both iOS and OS X rely on this feature to load the core application classes.

- You can use IB to create your own kit of UI objects. Very advanced developers can create a complete external library of custom UI objects, with associated code. This is a major project and outside the scope of this book. But simple customization is relatively easy. For example, the layout of a standard table cell can be designed in IB as a stand-alone object, and then loaded and repeated as needed in one or more tables. In this mode, you use IB to create useful nib files with collections of objects that can be loaded as needed. These objects can be fragments of a UI, or they can be data collections.

- You can use IB to link code features to UI objects. User actions and events are sent to your code using *actions*—

methods that are triggered in the code when the user interacts with a view or a control. UI object properties such as size, position, color, state, text, and so on are set with *outlets*. Outlets link Objective-C properties to corresponding properties in UI objects. Objects that have custom features are *subclassed*, which tells IB that a UI object has been modified with extra code that you define.

- In OS X only, IB objects can include *bindings*. Bindings link objects and properties indirectly, with semi-automated format translation. In outline, when your code sets a bound property, the UI is updated automatically. Similarly, user interactions are copied to a bound property automatically. Bindings are an alternative to outlets, with extra features that make them ideal for use with data collection objects such as arrays. Bindings are not available in iOS.

Understanding nib files

The files created by IB are called *nib files*. Both iOS and OS X applications load a single default nib file when they launch. This file is specified in the application's plist. But nib files are often linked and nested, so this nib file may (and usually does) load another nib file, which may load yet another nib file, and so on.

CAUTION

An important feature missing from IB is an overall view of the hierarchy, showing how nib files are nested and chained. IB tells you that an object will load another nib, but it doesn't try to show you a complete load tree.

As the nib files load, the objects defined inside them are created automatically. If they're part of the UI, they appear on screen. If they're not, they're loaded into memory. It's important to understand that you can use IB to instantiate objects in this way.

Objects created by the IB loading system are identical to objects created using the standard Objective-C alloc and init methods. There are two critical differences. The first is that nib files include preset default properties, such as size, color, and position. The other is that the object's init method isn't called, so you must add extra code to allow for this.

In practice, you can create a complete UI without using IB at all, by calling alloc and init to create a list of objects in your code as the application starts, setting up useful defaults, and linking the objects into the application's view hierarchy.

Some developers prefer to use this approach, and it's a valid option for UIs with unusual features. For example, if you want to add custom pop-up menus with unique animations and other special features, it's easier to create them in code.

IB is ideal for simpler interfaces that use Apple's standard kit of UI objects. Beginners typically create simple interfaces that use these objects as is, using IB as a layout and preview tool that controls the aesthetic elements of the interface—object justification and alignment, centering, and so on.

More advanced developers use IB to customize objects. Some objects are easy to customize; for example, it's fairly easy in iOS to replace the standard button graphics with custom button art.

Other objects are more challenging. But it's a key feature of the nib system that it has two possible applications. In addition to the default nib files loaded at launch, you can also use it to create independent nib files that can be loaded on demand by any object that needs them. For example you can load UIs on demand as you swap views, or load different object collections at different stages in a game.

N O T E

The extension of nib files is `.xib`. Historically, `.nib` was an acronym of *NeXT Interface Builder*. From IB 3.0 on, nib files were implemented with XML. The extension was changed, but the old name remained.

Using nib files

Manual nib loading is similar to automatic nib loading, with the difference that objects defined in a nib can be loaded and flushed from memory as needed, using a variety of standard loading methods. This is called *lazy loading* and is a standard Apple technique used to minimize an application's memory footprint.

It's especially critical for iOS apps, which have to work with very limited memory. *View swapping* is a related iOS technique that relies on lazy loading. When the user selects a new view by swiping a finger or selecting it from a navigation control (a tab bar, navigation controller, or button), the code loads a new view from a nib file, displays it, and deletes the old view from memory.

The swap can be animated as a special effect. The `UIViewController` and `UIView` classes include methods that create simple animations and delete the old view automatically. For more advanced effects, you can create more complex animations with custom code and delete the view manually.

The view-based application template is a good starting point for view swapping, but it has some quirks and subtleties that can make it difficult to understand. In outline, it works like this:

- Every application has an instance of `UIWindow`, which is the main app window. This is loaded when the application boots and isn't usually modified. This window object is included in the `MainWindow.xib` file.
- A `UIViewController` object is included in the same nib file, together with the `UIWindow` object.
- The `UIViewController` includes a placeholder for a separate `UIView` nib file, which also is loaded automatically when the application starts. This placeholder points to a separate nib file, which is called `<appName>ViewController.xib`.
- The `UIViewController` is subclassed to include code features that manage the UI. The `UIView` object also may be subclassed to create specialized graphics.
- When the user requests a view swap by tapping a navigation object such as a toolbar or navigation bar item, a new view controller is loaded from a nib file. The `UIView` linked to the new controller is swapped into the `view` property of the original view controller. The old view is released from memory. The swap may be animated.

- There are now two view controllers and one view loaded in memory. The new view controller manages UI interaction for the new view, which draws the contents of the window. The old view controller remains in place and is used to manage further swap events.
- The last two steps are repeated whenever a new view is requested.

Figure 7.1 shows the initial nib hierarchy. Bafflingly, the `appViewController.xib` doesn't include a view controller object. Instead, it includes a view object that is loaded *by* the view controller. In IB-speak, the view controller *owns* its nib file. It isn't created by it.

But the `mainWindow.xib` file *does* include a window object. This isn't a logical arrangement, but it's how view-based iOS apps are constructed. It's difficult to use IB effectively unless you take the time to understand it.

Figure 7.1

The initial nib hierarchy of an iOS view-based application

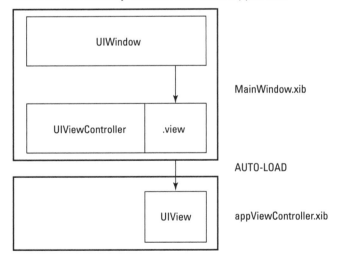

Figure 7.2 shows the hierarchy after a view swap. The window remains in place, as does the original view controller. A new controller object is created in code and initialized with a nib file. A separate swap operation in code swaps out the old view, releases it from memory, and plugs in the newly loaded view. The new controller handles user events for the new view. The old controller manages further view swaps, if there are any. Optionally, it can run further code in the background in a separate thread.

It's important to understand these relationships because IB doesn't make the nib hierarchy explicit. There's no automated feature that tells IB to create the classes and features needed for a view swap. Instead, you must add view and view controller classes manually and organize them correctly.

Figure 7.2

This shows the new hierarchy during and after a view swap operation. Creating a new view controller object loads its nib file. The swap operation has to be done manually, using further code.

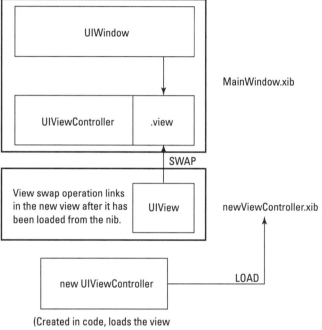

In general, you can use the iOS application templates to get started with app design, but the templates provide a small sample of many possible alternative app architectures. You can create simple applications by working with them as is, but to create more complex apps, you need to understand how to modify, customize, and extend the default nib files.

So it's important to think of IB as an object manager and not just as a UI design tool. You use IB to define an object hierarchy, with optional elements that can be loaded when needed. If you think of IB as the equivalent of a desktop publishing package for UI design, you'll miss this key feature, and app design will remain more challenging than it needs to be.

TIP

A good rule of thumb for a custom hierarchy is to put the main navigation controller object in the `MainWindow.xib` file with the UIWindow and create separate nibs for other views and view controllers as needed. Remember to set subclasses correctly in IB and create links, and the application should work as expected. Subclassing is explained in Chapter 8.

Getting Started with IB

To begin exploring IB, create a new project using an OS X or iOS application template, as described in Chapter 3. In this example, I use the iOS view-based application as a starting point. Save the application as "IB." Open the Resources group, and select `MainWindow.xib`, as shown in Figure 7.3. IB loads and displays the file as a graphic preview of the UI.

Figure 7.3

Unlike the text editor used for code, the IB editor works graphically.

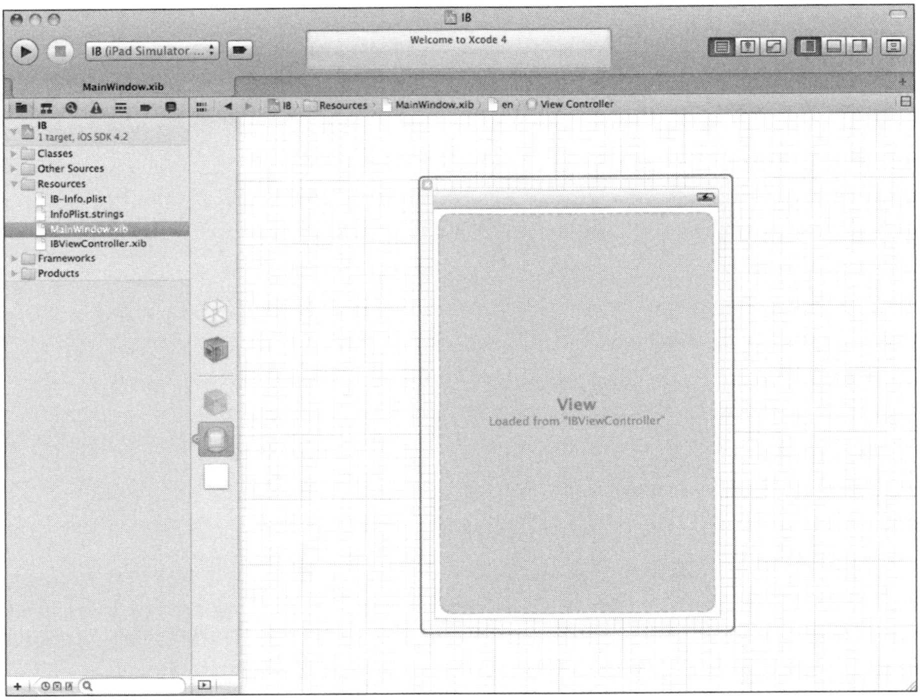

Introducing key features of the editor

Note these key elements of the IB editor:

- The cryptic column of icons to the left of the main editor area represents objects in the nib file. These objects are described in more detail in Chapter 8.
- A reveal triangle at the bottom of this column displays a more detailed list of the objects with text descriptions, as shown in Figure 7.4. You can use this feature to show or hide the detailed view as you work, making space for other IB features.
- The hierarchical navigation menu above the editor area gives you quick access to the objects in the nib and to other nib files.

Figure 7.4

Using the reveal triangle to display an extended view of the objects in a nib, with their names

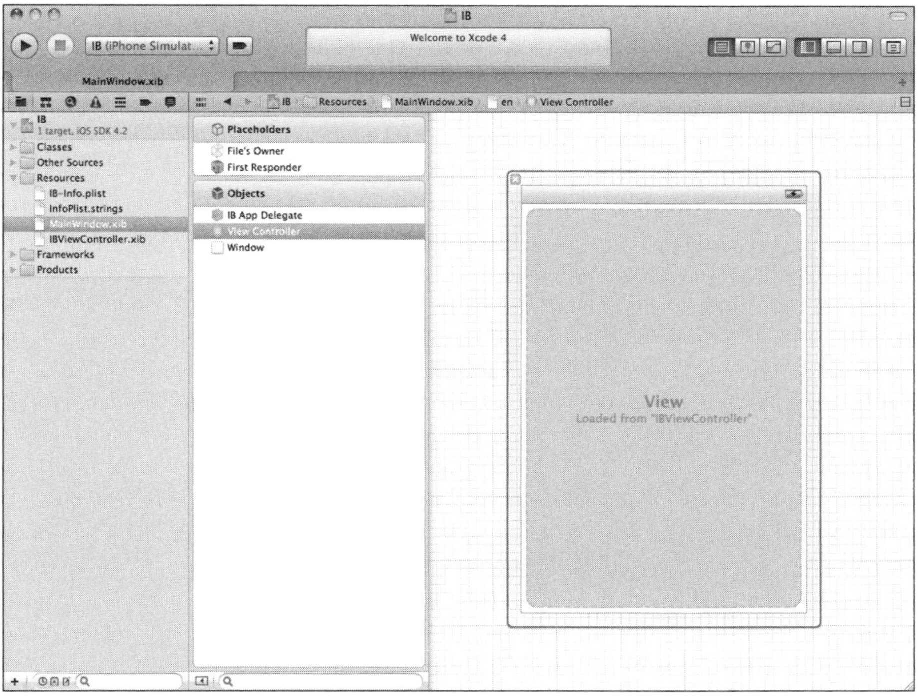

- The navigation menu includes another cryptic item, labeled "en," which is short for English. You can support non-English languages by creating separate nib files with non-English content. This must be done manually. By default, the templates create English-only nibs. Projects created in older versions of Xcode may have no localization features at all.

- In the editor area, the default UI—the placeholder view inside the navigation controller object—is surrounded by a transparent border. You can click this border to close the preview or to drag the object to a different position. For an iOS project, moving the object doesn't change how it appears in the iPhone/iPad display; it's purely a convenience while editing.

- If an object loads another nib—for example, when a view controller loads a view—the editor displays a plain placeholder message that says "the contents of another nib go here." It doesn't attempt to display those contents.

CAUTION
The graph paper background suggests that you can use it as a precise layout grid. You can't; it isn't calibrated accurately in pixels.

Viewing the template nib files

If you click the Window object in `MainWindow.xib`, you see two items in the editor, as shown in Figure 7.5. One is the `UIWindow` object; the other is the `IBViewController`. They may appear layered, as shown in the figure. You can hide either or both by clicking the window close crosses at the top left. You also can drag them apart to make them easier to work with.

If you select `IBViewController.xib`, you see another object—an empty view. The template uses the application architecture that was introduced earlier in this chapter, and these examples illustrate how it appears in IB in practice.

Objects appear ready for editing when you select them. If a nib file contains more than one object, the editor may show more than one object at the same time. Selecting an object in the left column brings it to the top of the editor and draws a highlight box around it in the column. In single-column mode, tool tips show each object's name.

Figure 7.5

Objects appear ready for editing when you select them.

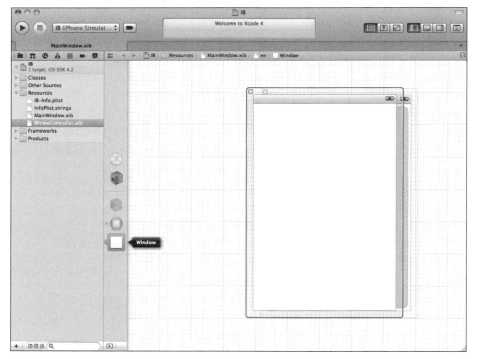

Figure 7.6 shows how you can view both objects at the same time if your monitor is large enough. For an iOS app, the relative position of the objects doesn't affect the appearance of the application when it runs. The default layered orientation is confusing and unhelpful, so it's often

useful to move objects apart like this. However you arrange the objects, it's important to leave room for the Utility pane at the right because it's a critical element in IB.

NOTE
Mac app windows ignore the grid too. You can set the initial launch position of a Mac window in IB using a feature called the Size Inspector, which is introduced later in this chapter.

Figure 7.6

Move objects apart to simplify editing.

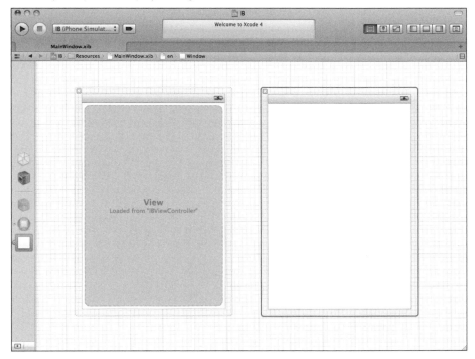

It's worth taking some time to explore these different options. Although you typically use custom views to define separate pages in a UI, you may need to edit the background window as well—for example, to change the color so it doesn't flash white when you swap views with a flip transition.

Introducing the utility area

When the IB editor is in use, the utility area displays extra icons and features that support nib editing. Figure 7.7 shows a typical display. The IBViewController.xib file has been selected, and the Utility area lists some of its attributes. There are six icons in an iOS nib file and eight in an OS X nib, as listed here:

- The File and Quick Help panes are identical to those for the code editor. For details, see Chapter 3.

- The Identity Inspector lists the object's class, includes an optional text label, and features accessibility information. When you subclass an object—for example, when you create a customized copy of a `UIView` or an `NSWindow`—you must select the new class name in the drop-down menu. Otherwise, IB won't know that the `UIView` or `NSWindow` in the nib file is supposed to run the code in your modified version.

- The Attributes Inspector is a list of default properties. This pane has different contents for every object in IB. For example, the UIView shown in Figure 7.8 includes background color, drawing mode, and interaction properties, which enable single- or multi-touch control. The Simulated Metrics options preview navigation features (areas at the top and bottom of the view) so you can design the rest of the view with the correct dimensions. For iOS apps, you can use this Inspector to preview different UI orientations: landscape and portrait. You also can set the default orientation for the app.

Figure 7.7

In IB, the Utility area lists a selected object's properties and options, and displays them for editing. Use the icons at the top of the area to access different sets of properties.

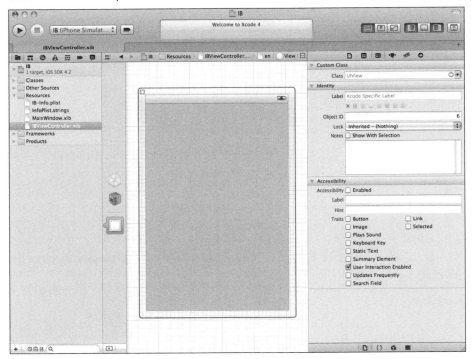

T I P
Almost every property that appears in both lists can also be set in code. But it's easier to preview the results in IB.

● The Size Inspector, shown in Figure 7.9, sets the dimensions and alignment of an object. It also controls *autosizing:* an object's ability to follow a window or view's size and position after rotation or a manual resize. Autosizing is off by default.

● The Connections Inspector, shown in Figure 7.10, lists an object's outlets and actions. When properties and methods are linked to code, you can review and change them here.

Figure 7.8

The Attributes Inspector sets an object's default properties.

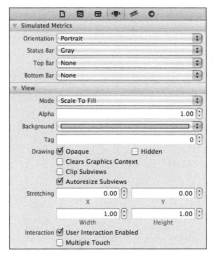

Figure 7.9

The Size Inspector defines an object's position, size, and alignment options.

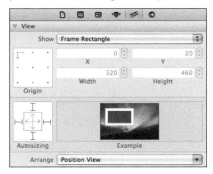

Figure 7.10

The Connections Inspector defines the links between an object's outlets and actions and supporting code. You also can define a delegate object, where relevant.

Two more icons appear in OS X projects, as shown in Figures 7.11 and 7.12.

Figure 7.11

View the Bindings Inspector in an OS X project. Bindings are optional and are best left for intermediate and advanced projects.

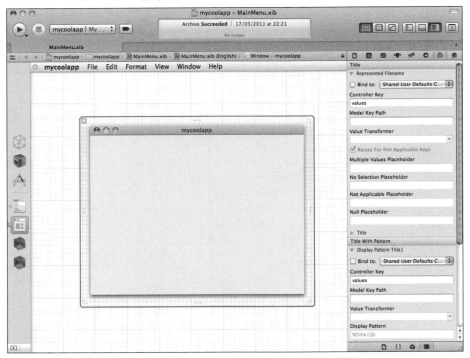

- The Bindings Inspector displays an object's bindings—properties that can be linked using the Key Value Observing (KVO) system built into OS X.

● The View Effects Inspector defines the filters and transitions that are applied to a visible object. You can use this inspector to add blur and sharpen effects, color adjustments, tilings, and so on. This is an easy way to apply one or more standard filters to a view, similar to those available in Adobe Photoshop or GIMP. Filter effects can be animated with custom code.

Both of these icons add optional features that aren't critical to basic app design. For a detailed explanation, see the companion *Cocoa* in Wiley's Developer Reference series.

Figure 7.12

Explore the View Effects Inspector in an OS X project. To view a list of filters, click the Add (+) icon under the Content Filters tab and select the Filter menu.

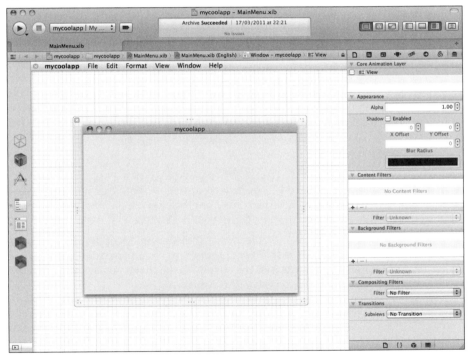

Creating a Simple iOS Project with IB

In Xcode 3, adding objects and linking them to code was a repetitive chore. With IB in Xcode 4, the process has been simplified. This section demonstrates how to use IB to create a very simple app, with a text label and a button. Tapping the button triggers code that reads the text from the label and changes it. The code uses one action, which is triggered by the button, and one outlet, which connects the label in the UI to a corresponding instance of `UILabel` in the code.

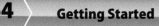

When you create a UI, you drag objects from the *Object library* and drop them onto a view. The Object library appears in the area at the bottom right of the Utility pane. By default it's partially hidden, but you can drag a divider above the icon bar upward to show more of it. The larger your monitor, the more of the library you can see without scrolling.

CAUTION

If you have a small monitor, this feature can be difficult to work with because you continually have to scroll through it, and move the divider to show object properties so you can edit them. You can save time by creating one tab in which the Object library fills the right hand area, and another in which only the properties are visible.

The Object library shares this lower area with other libraries, including a File Template library, a Code Snippet library, and a Media library. To select the Object library, click the cube icon, which is third from the left. Objects in the library are pre-filtered by the project OS; you can't add iOS objects to a Mac project, and vice versa.

NOTE

Because this isn't a primer on Cocoa Touch, the code is very simple. For more information about app design, see the companion *Cocoa Touch* in Wiley's Developer Reference series.

These are the basic rules for UI design:

- When you want to read or write an object's properties from the UI, you must add the corresponding class to your code. For example, if the UI includes a label, you must use IB to add a UILabel object to your code.

- The code is usually placed inside a view controller object, and the object that appears in the display is included in the corresponding view nib file. This isn't an absolute rule—other arrangements are possible—but it's a typical starting point.

- After you have code for a UI object you can define an outlet that links them together. When your code changes an object's properties (its size, position, text label, or some other attribute), the link copies the change to the UI manager and the visible representation of the object is updated on the display.

- If you want your app to respond to user events, you must define an *action* for each event. An action is a special method added to the code to handle user events.

- UI objects can support outlets and actions at the same time.

- You can create "dumb" objects that support neither outlets nor actions. Use dumb objects to decorate the UI—for example, to add a fixed graphic as a background to a view. A dumb object doesn't respond to the user, and it can't be changed from your code.

NOTE

Technically, actions rely on the Target-Action model in Cocoa and Cocoa Touch. You can define actions in IB, but you can also define them in code, and for advanced effects, you can redefine them dynamically. A full discussion of Target-Action is outside the scope of this book. For details, see the *Cocoa* companion title in Wiley's Developer Reference series.

In previous versions of Xcode, objects, outlets, and actions were added manually. In Xcode 4, the process is semi-automated, and it's much simpler, faster, and more productive than it used to be. It's also more reliable, because the automation eliminates many common errors.

Adding objects to a view

Using the IB project from earlier in this chapter, arrange the Xcode interface as shown in Figure 7.13. Select the `IBViewController.xib` object for editing, and click the Assistant editor to split the window as shown in the figure. The editor shows the default view, which is the default UI that appears when the app runs.

The Assistant should show the `IBViewController.h` header file. If it doesn't, select it manually. In the bottom right of the Utility area, select the Object library by clicking the box icon. If the icons are at the bottom of the area, drag the divider up to show the contents of the library.

Figure 7.13

When setting up IB for editing, it's useful to have at least one of the code files open at the same time. The Utility area at the right is essential.

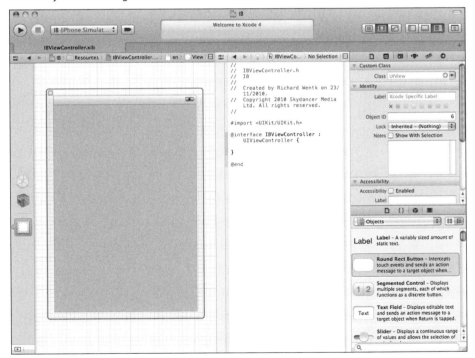

NOTE
If your monitor is wide enough to show the Project Navigator at the left without hiding the other areas, you can leave it in place. It's not critical for this project.

Drag and drop a Round Rect Button object from the Object Library onto the view, as shown. Xcode does two things as you do this:

- When you select any item in the Library, a large tool tip appears to the left with a description of the object. You can dismiss the tool tip by clicking the Done button or by clicking elsewhere in the editor area.

- When you drag an item onto a view, guidelines appear, as shown in Figure 7.14. You can use the lines to center an object in the view or to align it with other objects. In the figure, the button is centered in the view.

Figure 7.14

Add a button using IB's automatic guidelines to center it in the view.

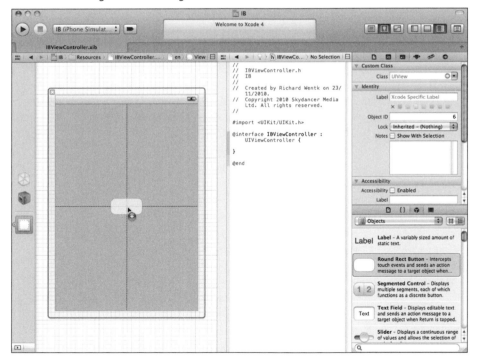

Add a Label object in the same way, as shown in Figure 7.15. The guidelines indicate when the label is centered. If you move the label around the view before releasing it, you see that you can also left- and right-justify the label with respect to the button. Similarly, if you drag to one side of the button, you can align it with the top, bottom, or vertical center of the button.

Figure 7.15

Add a label. The guidelines automatically show top, bottom, left, right, and both vertical and horizontal center lines for other objects in the view.

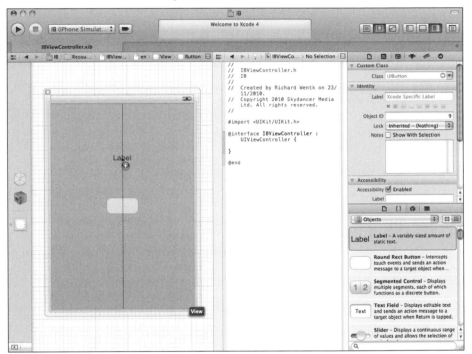

Setting object contents

Setting the contents of UI objects remains a chore. Although both labels and buttons are simple, you typically need to follow these steps:

1. Set the text label.

2. Optionally, change the font, text size, and color.

3. Change the text justification and line breaks.

4. Optionally, add a drop shadow.

5. Resize the object to make sure the text displays correctly.

6. Realign the object after your changes.

Similar steps are needed to set the contents of other objects, such as image views. See the example later in this chapter.

To change the label text, double-click it. The label edge and interior are highlighted. Type "This is off," as shown in Figure 7.16. When you press Return, you see that the label is no longer centered.

Figure 7.16

When setting text in a label, the label doesn't remain centered after editing.

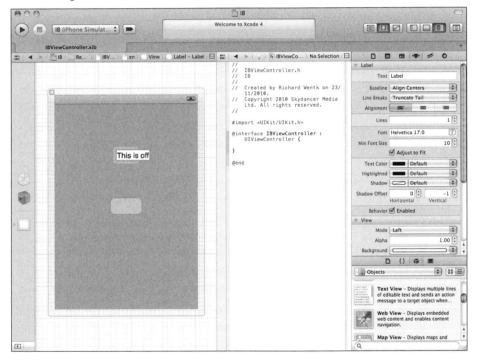

Setting font attributes

Select the Attributes Inspector if it isn't already selected, and click in the Font box. You see the Fonts window, as shown in Figure 7.17, a separate floating window used to set fonts and text styles. Set the font size to 24. Click the center Alignment selector above the font box to set center justification.

Figure 7.17

When setting font sizes, fonts, and other text attributes, the font manager appears in a separate floating window.

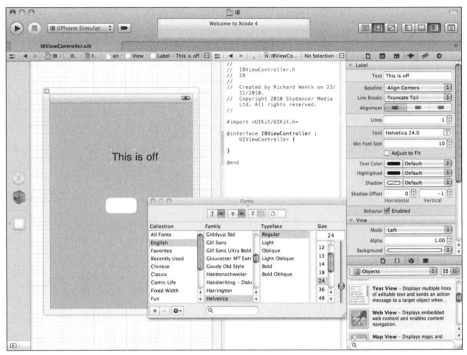

Setting fonts

You can change an object's font, but only to a very limited selection of default fonts. The universal iPhone/iPad project in Figure 7.18 shows a default list that is known to work in IB and on devices. (The project is available for download at `http://www.wiley.com/xcodedev ref`.) Your Mac has a wider selection of fonts installed, but you can't use them in an iOS project, and Xcode 4 doesn't allow you to preview them in IB.

NOTE

The supported font list is updated regularly, and other fonts may be available in later versions of iOS. You may also find that IB doesn't preview some fonts correctly even though they're supported on a device. For a more optimistic list of supported fonts, see `http://iOSFonts.com`. Note you can add any third-party font to an iOS or Mac project, but this requires some build customization. Chapter 13 includes an example.

Figure 7.18

These fonts are supported in iOS 4.2. The selection may change in future updates.

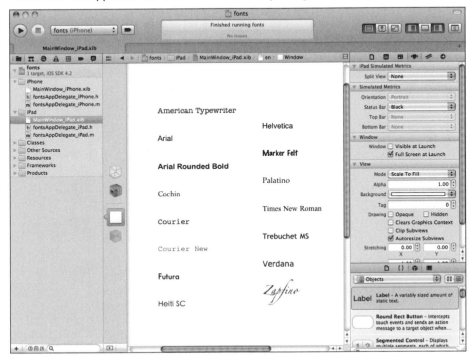

CAUTION

Don't be confused by the fact you can set other fonts temporarily while editing a text field. When you confirm an edit, Xcode 4 replaces any non-standard font with one of the defaults.

TIP

You can use non-standard fonts in an iOS project, but you must import them into the project bundle and load them with special code. Non-standard font support isn't an IB feature, and the code can become complex, so it's outside the scope of this book.

Adding drop shadows and other text effects

The drop shadow effect in iOS is unimpressive. Because Core Image filters aren't supported, the drop shadow isn't blurred, which makes the effect useless. However, you can use the Shadow feature to add a deboss (chiseled) effect. Select the Shadow color picker, and use the default white color with 100 percent opacity, as shown. Set the Shadow Offset settings as shown in Figure 7.19. This creates the extreme effect shown in the figure. For a more subtle effect, set both offsets closer to zero. To eliminate the effect, set the Opacity to 0 percent.

Figure 7.19

Creating a chiseled (deboss) effect with the Shadow color and Shadow Offset settings

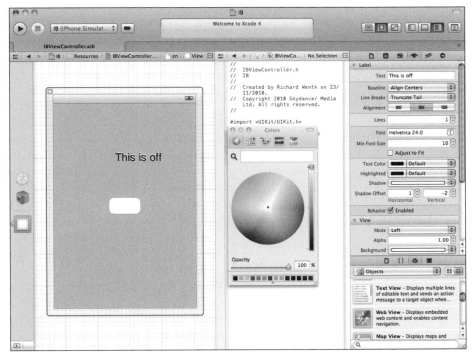

Resizing objects with the mouse

To resize an object, select it. Drag handles (small blue circles) appear at each corner and at the centers of each edge. Drag a handle to resize the object, as shown in Figure 7.20. While you're changing the size, you see a pop-up window with the object's dimensions. Guidelines also appear, as shown in the figure.

Labels, buttons, and editable text fields can be set to shrink text so it fits into the available area, with the Adjust to Fit check box in the Attributes. But this is usually less useful than making an object wide enough to accommodate the largest possible label or message.

For a simple UI, you often drag the left edge of a text area object until the left guideline appears, and you drag the right edge to the right guideline. This sets the width to the maximum available.

For a more complex UI, you have to trade off the dimensions and positions of the various items for maximum clarity, keeping in mind that the UI may need to rotate to a different orientation. In extreme cases, you may need to design separate UIs for different orientations or use code to move objects when the orientation changes.

NOTE

The left, right, top, and bottom guidelines indicate the edge of the usable area in the UI, as defined in Apple's Human Interface Guideline documents. While Apple likes to emphasize these documents, in practice they're suggestions and not absolutes. As long as your UI is clear, intuitive, and aesthetically appealing, you can usually bend the rules.

Figure 7.20

Setting object dimensions by dragging with the mouse

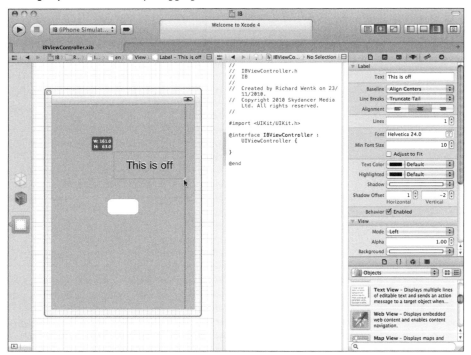

Resizing and aligning objects numerically

The top sub-pane of the Size Inspector includes an Origin box and four number fields. You can use these to set the size and position of an object with pixel precision.

The Origin box selects the reference point used to determine the object's position. The dots in the box correspond to the drag handles around the object. If the origin reference point is set to the top left of the grid in the box, as shown in Figure 7.21, the number fields refer to the object's top-left corner. If the origin is at the center, the numbers refer to the object's center, and so on. If you click the dots in the box, the X and Y coordinates are updated to show the new reference.

The Width and Height boxes set the width and height, as you'd expect. You can use the up/down arrows next to each box to increment and decrement each field. As you do this, the object moves and its dimensions change. You also can type numbers into each box to set it directly.

TIP

When this Inspector is visible, the numbers update automatically when you move or resize an object with the mouse. You can use this feature to create very precise edits. The 0,0 point is at the top left. Numbers can be negative when an object is outside the top or left of the object that contains it. (For more information about containers, see the section about the IB Object Hierarchy later in this chapter.)

TIP

You can move selected objects by single pixels with the arrow keys. You can also view display absolute pixel offsets by option-clicking an object. These can be *very* useful options.

Figure 7.21

Set a top-left origin reference for the label. The X and Y numbers show the coordinates of the top-left point.

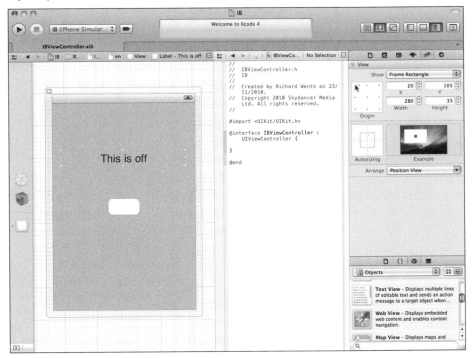

Resizing and aligning objects and object groups

Figure 7.22 shows the contents of the Arrange menu. You can use this menu to align an object with another. The most useful options are Center Vertically in Container and Center Horizontally in Container, which do what you'd expect; they move an object's center to the center of its containing object. In this example, if you select the label object and select Center Horizontally…, the label appears center-justified in the view.

CAUTION

If you set the left and right edges to the left and right guides, centering does nothing. Try changing the width of the object and centering it again. You can also center it vertically, but this moves the label so it covers the button.

Figure 7.22

Selecting options from the Alignment menu

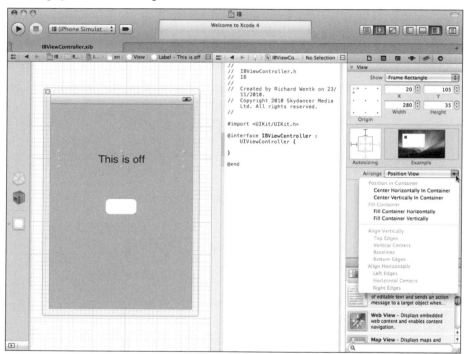

You can select multiple objects by dragging a rubber band box around them or by shift-clicking in the usual OS X way. When you click the reveal triangle at the bottom of the vertical icon bar, you can group objects by name in the list that appears.

Centering multiple objects moves the group to the common geometric center. The best way to understand the other alignment options in the menu is to experiment with them. For example, you can align a group of objects along their top, bottom, or center edges. You also can expand an object so it fills its container, which can be useful when you're using an image view as a background.

N O T E

In Xcode 3, the Alignment options appeared as a group of cryptic geometric icons. This was useful for quick single-click access to the centering function. In Xcode 4, the icons have gone and you have to select the alignment functions from the menu.

Controlling autosizing

By default, autosizing is enabled. If your app supports multiple orientations, you'll find that autosizing breaks the layout after a rotation.

Full support for multiple orientations can become complex in a busy UI and may require custom code. But you can create a simple autorotating UI by disabling autosizing. Click all the anchor tags and the arrows in the Autosizing box to toggle them. They should appear dashed. This disables all autosizing features for that object, and it's likely (but not guaranteed) that the object will now support a different UI orientation.

The four anchor tags around the outside of the autosizing box fix the pixel distance of each edge of an object from its container. The two autosizing arrows inside the box control whether the object's dimensions change. For some applications, you may need to set these to create more complex behaviors—for example, to lock an item to the bottom-right corner of a window so it stays in position when the window is resized.

T I P

In Xcode 3, IB had a useful orientation preview feature. You could rotate a view in IB to check for correct alignment. This option has gone from Xcode 4. However, you can simulate by using the Editor⇨ Simulate Document menu option in Xcode. This loads the nib into an iPhone or iPad Simulator window, without compiling the code. You can check rotation with the Simulator's Hardware⇨ Rotate Right/Left menu options.

To finish the UI, double-click the button and set the text to CHANGE IT. Optionally, you can experiment further with the alignment features. The button's attributes are more complex than a label's and there are more options to experiment with. For example, you can replace the default graphic with a custom image by importing an image file into the project and selecting it in the Background drop-down menu. For a full guide, see the UIButton Class Reference in the documentation. This example uses the button as is.

The finished UI is shown in Figure 7.23. The layout is complete, but it isn't yet linked to active code.

Note that although the design process can seem complex when you encounter it for the first time, it soon becomes more straightforward. With practice, you'll find that it becomes automatic. After you master the features of the different Inspector panes in the Utility Area, you've made a good start with IB.

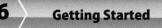

Figure 7.23

The finished UI, before it's linked to active code

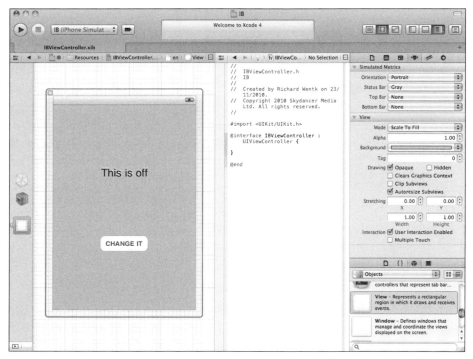

Linking objects to code

Creating actions and outlets is a relatively simple process. Unlike previous versions of Xcode, Xcode 4 *adds the correct code automatically*. It creates suitable properties, synthesizes them, and adds method code stubs. Of course, you must fill out the method stubs with your own event handler code, but the essential elements that support your code are added for you.

Adding an action

The button should do something useful when it's tapped. In iOS, this means adding code to create an action method that handles button events.

The `IBViewController` class manages the UI. So the code is added to this class.

In theory, all controls in iOS can send any of the event messages that are predefined in iOS. Whenever you create an action for a control, the list of events shown in the Connections Inspector in Figure 7.24 appears.

In practice, not all controls implement all events. For example, a button isn't editable, so it makes no sense for it to send an Editing Did Begin message.

The Touch Down message does make sense; it's sent when the user taps a button. To add code that can handle a Touch Down message, drag a line from the circle next to Touch Down in the Connections Inspector, and release it in the area under the curly brackets in the header code.

As shown in the figure, you see a floating location line that marks the insertion point and a tool tip labeled Insert Action.

CAUTION

Don't create the action inside the curly brackets or above them. Add it to the area beneath them, but above the @end directive. Although you can add an action to an implementation file, it's easier to add it to a header file, because the header holds a simple and clear list of every action, without supporting code.

Figure 7.24

When adding an action, the line between the Connections Inspector and the code appears automatically.

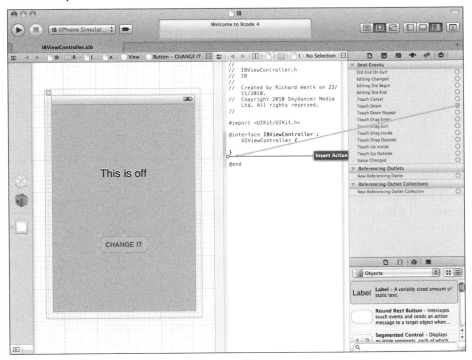

Naming and initializing the action

When you release the mouse, the pop-up dialog box shown in Figure 7.25 appears. To finish adding the action, you must give it a name. Optionally, you can define the parameters that are passed to the method.

The *Name* field sets the name. It's best to give each method a clear and descriptive title. Otherwise, the name is arbitrary, but it must be unique to the class it appears in. This example uses buttonWasTapped.

NOTE

Class and property names use camel code. The first letter is lowercase. For clarity, subsequent words begin with a capital letter.

The *Type* option selects id, or the class of the object sending the message—UIButton, in this example. Use id when you use the same method to handle messages from multiple different objects. You can then add extra code that determines the class of the object that sent the message. You also can use id if you don't need to read the object's properties. Use a specific class when you need to read information from the button or change one of its properties.

In this example, we need to know that the button was tapped, but we don't need to know its color, position, or anything else about it; the default id setting is fine.

NOTE

In Objective-C, id is a catch-all class label. It means "this object is some class, but we either don't know or don't care which one."

The *Event* option duplicates the standard list of possible events. If you change your mind about the event that should trigger the action, you can select a different option here. Usually, you won't.

The *Arguments* option selects one of the following: None, Sender, or Sender and Event. Choose None when you don't need to know anything about the sender object. Choose Sender when you want to read the sender object's properties. Choose Sender and Event when you also want to read information from an optional UIEvent object that arrives with the message—for example, if you want to find the event timestamp.

TIP

To save time, you can leave the default options in this dialog box as they are. You'll get an action method that includes an (id) sender parameter. Your code can ignore this parameter if it doesn't need it.

CROSS-REFERENCE

The File's Owner icon in the dialog box is explained in Chapter 8.

Figure 7.25

When adding an action, add a name and ignore the rest, unless your code demands the extra features.

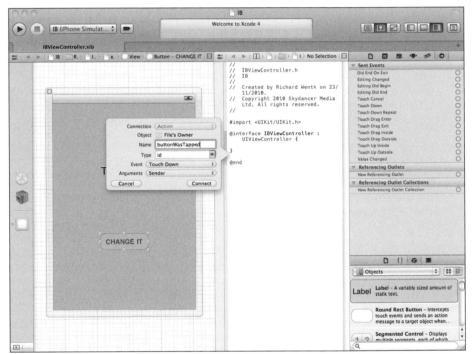

To finish creating the action, select Connect. Figure 7.26 shows the result. An action signature is added to the header file. If you look at the end of the implementation file, you see that a corresponding stub has been added. If you build and run the app now, the action method is triggered if you click or tap the button. It doesn't do anything because there's no code inside the stub, but a button handler is now part of the app.

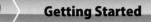

Figure 7.26

To help you complete the action, Xcode adds suitable code to both the header and the implementation file.

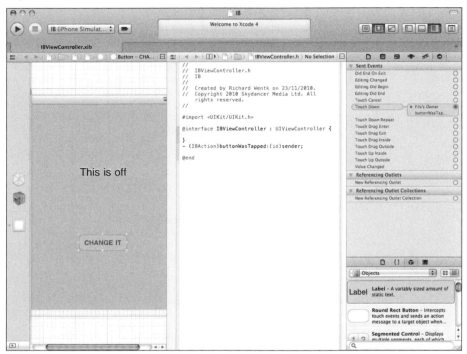

Adding an outlet

The handler should have a visible effect. In this example, it changes the label text. To do this, we need to connect the label to an outlet so we can read and set its properties with code.

Select the label, as shown in Figure 7.27. The Connections Inspector changes to show a Referencing Outlet subpane and a Referencing Outlet Collections subpane. Ignore the Collections option, and drag a line from the circle next to New Referencing Outlet. Add the outlet below the curly brackets.

CAUTION

You can also add an outlet between the curly brackets, but this has a different and less useful effect, as described below.

Figure 7.27

When you add an outlet, a floating location line and a tool tip appear to confirm the operation. Always add an outlet below the curly brackets.

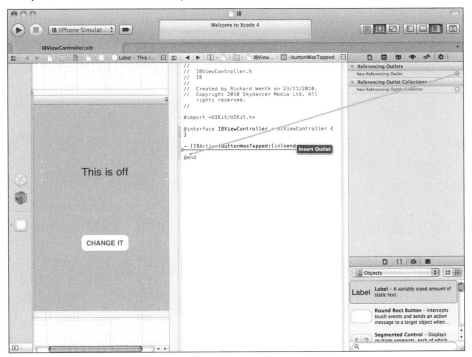

Naming and initializing the outlet

When you release the mouse button, you see the dialog box in Figure 7.28. Type a useful and descriptive name. In a simple app, you can leave the other options set to their defaults.

NOTE

Technically, the Storage option sets how the object's memory is managed. Occasionally, you may need to `assign` (make a pointer copy of) an object. Usually, it's better to `retain` it. A full description of iOS memory management is outside the scope of this book. The Type option is simply the class of the UI object. Occasionally, you may want to select a subclass here.

Figure 7.28

For the second step in adding an outlet, the options other than Name can be left with their defaults.

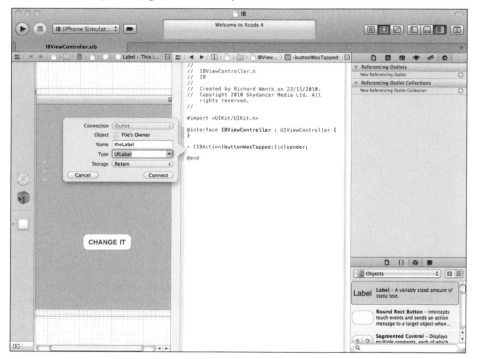

The result is shown in Figure 7.29. Note that IB adds the outlet in two places. A property pre-fixed appears inside the curly brackets, and a separate `@property` declaration with an `IBOutlet` directive appears below them.

Figure 7.29

The complete header file, with the added outlet and action code

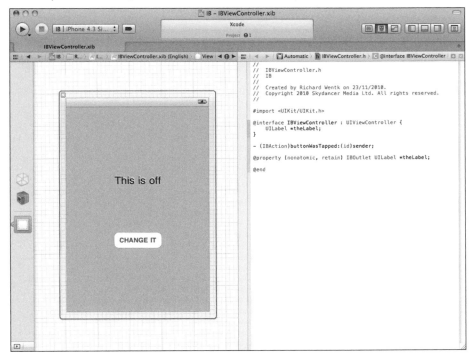

Figure 7.30 shows the bottom of the implementation file. You can see that Xcode has generated supporting code in four places. (For clarity, the new code is marked in the figure with breakpoint arrows. The arrows don't appear in a real project—they've been added by hand as illustrations, so you can see which lines have been modified.)

- A new @synthesize directive has appeared. It synthesizes access to the label property.
- The label object has been included in the dealloc method. This ensures that the memory used by the label object is released when the controller class is released from memory.
- The label has been added to the viewDidUnload method. Code is included to set the label to nil.
- The buttonWasTapped: method has been added as a separate stub.

NOTE

If you drop an outlet between curly brackets, the @synthesize and @property directives aren't added. This is usually a bad thing, but you can use this option when you want to add your own custom setter/getter code.

Figure 7.30

This is the complete implementation file. IB makes changes to this file at the same time as it updates the header file.

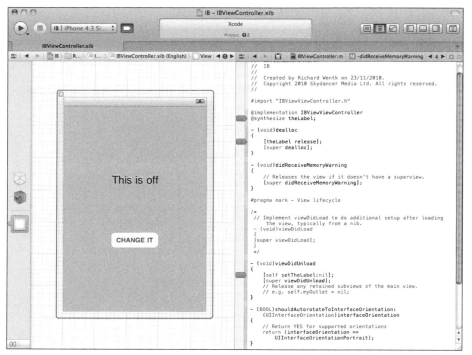

Filling out an action stub

The app is nearly finished. The missing feature is custom code in the action stub that updates the label when the button is tapped.

In the implementation file, add this code between the curly brackets in the IBAction stub, as shown in Figure 7.31:

```
if ([theLabel.text isEqualToString: "@This is off"])
        theLabel.text = @"This is on";
else
        theLabel.text = @"This is off";
```

This code reads the current label text and updates the text to an alternate message when the button is tapped. The key point is that the outlet allows the label text to be read and written.

You can read and write any property. For example, you could change the label's position or the size or color of the text. This example makes a trivial change to the label text, but more complex objects work in the same way. For example, you can read a block of text entered by a user from a more complex text field object. You also can read or write image data to an image view.

Testing the app

Select the iPhone Simulator, and click the Build & Run arrow at the top left of the Xcode toolbar. The app should build and run in the Simulator window. Clicking the button in the UI toggles the label text between "This is off" and "This is on."

TIP

There's more than one way to create a link in IB. You can hold down the control key, and drag links directly from objects in the UI or the object list, to the Connections Inspector, or to the code. You can even type your own outlet code and make connections to it. IB doesn't allow you to make links that are meaningless. Dragging links from the Connections Inspector to the code is usually the fastest, simplest, and clearest option.

Figure 7.31

The finished app, running in the Simulator

NOTE

As of iOS 3.2 you can create an *outlet collection*—a group of outlets held in a standard `NSArray`. Use this option when you want to collect a single object—often a controller—to multiple UI elements. To create a collection, drag a link from the New Referencing Outlet Collection item to your controller. Collections are optional, but they can be useful when you need to update multiple objects. For example, you can use NSArray's `makeObjectsPerform Selector:` method to update every object in a collection with a single line of code.

Understanding the IB object hierarchy

Select the label in the UI, and use the Arrange menu in the Size Inspector to center it vertically. Do the same with the button. The two objects overlap, as shown in Figure 7.32.

Objects are drawn top down, which means that objects lower down the list in the IB object side panel at the left cover objects higher up as they appear on the screen.

Use the reveal triangle at the bottom left to show the items in the view, and swap the position of the label and the button. You'll see that the label covers the button in the UI editor.

Figure 7.32

Changing the order and position of the label and the button demonstrates what happens when one object covers another in the hierarchy.

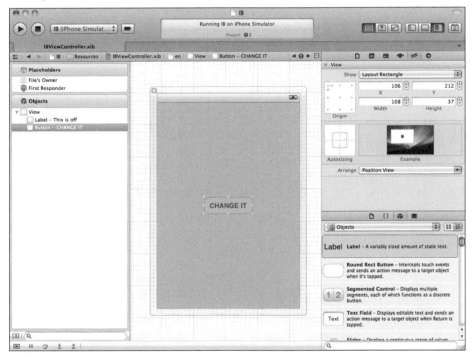

The objects in a nib file are arranged in a tree. Some objects, such as `UIViews`, can contain other objects. In the example, the label and the button are both inside the main `UIView`. The structure is rather like a folder in Finder. You can use reveal triangles to open and close objects, showing and hiding the objects inside them. An object inside another appears indented in the list. When you change the physical position of an object in the hierarchy, all the objects inside it move with it.

You could in theory add a separate `UIView` to the UI, resizing both to create a split UI with two panes. Some commercial apps use this split format to create designs with multiple active areas that respond to the user in different ways. For example, a game might have a control panel with fixed buttons and a display area with animated scrolling graphics.

In complex apps, the hierarchy can become deep, with many objects. For example, Figure 7.33 shows the hierarchy of a minimal OS X app. The nib includes a window, a view, and a deep hierarchy of menu items. You can rearrange the menu headers and menu items by dragging them. For example, you can swap the position of the File and Edit headers. This isn't a useful thing to do, but it demonstrates how the hierarchy is organized and how you can modify it to create your own menu and UI designs.

Figure 7.33

The default OS X application nib is more complex than the iOS equivalent, and it illustrates how objects can be arranged in a tree structure.

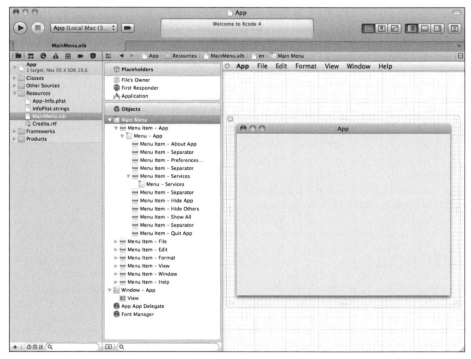

TIP

Note that the minimal OS X app includes a Font Manager object. This object doesn't appear immediately in the app's UI, but it handles font changes for applications that use text. It's another example of an object that's pre-instantiated in a nib file so it doesn't have to be created in code. For information about the other objects in this nib, see Chapter 8.

Comparing IB in Xcode 4 with Xcode 3

If you're used to the version of IB in Xcode 3, this section contains a summary of the changes in Xcode 4.

Xcode 4 can feel very different. In fact, it's recognizably similar, but the features have moved to different locations. Here are the key differences:

- Integration within Xcode means that IB no longer runs as a separate application. This simplifies window management—you no longer need to keep IB and Xcode windows organized on the same desktop—but it means that the IB editor takes time to load when you use it for the first time.
- Links now create supporting code features automatically, and you can drag links directly to a code window. This is a major improvement over Xcode 3, where creating outlets and actions was unnecessarily complex, repetitive, and error-prone.
- The Document window now appears as the icon column to the left of the editor area. You can expand this column to show text labels, or you can leave it unexpanded to save space. You can drag links to objects in either mode.
- The Inspector panes are now embedded in the Utility area.
- You no longer need to remember to save a nib file manually before building. Edited nib files are included in the save dialog box. This is another major improvement.

If you prefer to keep code and nib files in separate floating windows, you can use the tab tear-off feature to float the IB editor in one window while leaving the code editor in another. You can drag links between the two windows in the usual way. But if you have a larger monitor, it's usually more productive to keep the IB editor and the code editor in two split panes. With a very large monitor, you can have a three-way split with an IB file, a class implementation, and a class header visible at the same time, creating links between them as needed. It's a very productive option that was impossible in Xcode 3.

Summary

This chapter looked at Interface Builder in detail. It outlined the key features of nib files and explained how to get started with the Inspectors and the object lists in IB.

It worked through a sample iOS project and explained how to add objects to a UI, how to set their external and internal attributes and contents, and how to align them manually and automatically.

It introduced outlets and actions and demonstrated how to add them to a project and how to link them with active code.

Finally, it sketched some of the features of the IB object hierarchy and summarized the key differences between IB in Xcode 3 and Xcode 4.

Creating More Advanced Effects with Interface Builder

C reating outlets and actions is a key step in application design with Interface Builder (IB). More complex applications require more advanced skills, which are discussed in this chapter.

Using File's Owner and First Responder

The top two objects in the list at the left of the IB interface are *placeholders*. They make it possible to link to objects that are outside the nib file.

Using File's Owner

File's Owner is a placeholder for the object that loaded the nib. It represents a different object in every nib. For example, in `MainWindow.xib` in the sample project in Chapter 7, File's Owner is a placeholder for the `UIApplication` object. In `IBViewController.xib`, File's Owner stands in for the `IBViewController` object.

This may seem complex the first time you encounter this feature, and it's certainly not an intuitive feature, because the true class/object name isn't displayed next to the icon.

However, if you select the File's Owner icon, you can check the class name in the Identity Inspector. It appears in the Class field at the top of the Utility Area.

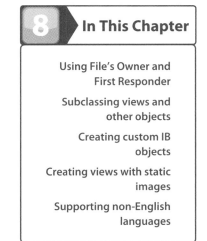

CAUTION
These placeholders can seem confusing, but it's critical that you take time to experiment with them until you understand them. It's very difficult to use IB correctly if you don't.

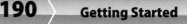

In practice, you use File's Owner as a source and destination for links and actions. If you follow the instructions in Chapter 7, IB is intelligent enough to link to File's Owner automatically. In a more complex application, you may need to create links to a wider selection of objects.

You can use the File's Owner placeholder in two ways:

- To create links to the object that loads the nib file
- To review a complete list of existing links

When you link item by item, it's easy to forget which links have been made. Opening the Connections Inspector and selecting the File's Owner icon shows every link placeholder object in a single display, as shown in Figure 8.1.

TIP

It's often useful to view this list and create links to it rather than linking object by object, because the File's Owner pseudo-object displays all its outlets at the same time. This can be a significant timesaver.

Figure 8.1

Viewing the links to File's Owner with the Connections Inspector

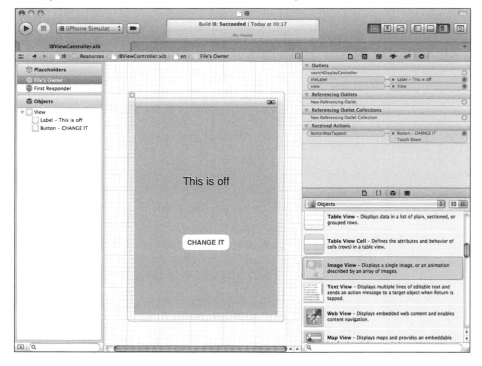

NOTE
The `view` property is pre-linked for you in the view-based application template. Most of the other templates include pre-linked outlets. It's useful to review them; they can give you insight into how the nib hierarchy is organized and how the templates have been engineered.

Using First Responder

At first sight, the First Responder placeholder can seem even more abstract than File's Owner. But the principle is simple.

All iOS and OS X applications include a *responder chain*—an implied hierarchy of objects that dispatches user events. Here's what to expect:

- Windows, views, and certain other objects are subclasses of an abstract event management class (`UIResponder` in iOS and `NSResponder` in OS X).

- This class includes a prewritten selection of methods that can handle standard user events such as copy, paste, undo, and so on.

- You can add your own custom events to this list.

- Unlike a standard action, these messages are passed from object to object until a matching event handler method is found. A common test sequence is view ⇨ view controller ⇨ window ⇨ application, but this may vary, because it depends on the design of the application.

- The First Responder icon is the connection point for this chain. It lists *all* the valid handler methods, in all objects that are part of the responder chain. It's the central event handler for an application, and provides a convenient single access point for responder methods that may be scattered across multiple objects.

- Events without a handler are ignored.

In practice, you link objects that generate messages to the responder chain in the usual way. For example, in the sample IB application, shown in Figure 8.2, you can drag a link between one of the button events, such as a Touch Up Inside, to a responder handler, such as Copy.

A critical difference is that *this doesn't generate code for you*. IB doesn't know which object you want to add the handler code to, so it doesn't try to guess. Instead, you must add the code by hand to whichever responder object suits your needs.

Typically, this means copying a method signature from the `UIResponder` or `NSResponder` class—for example, for the `copy:` method—and creating your own full implementation.

CAUTION
The methods you need to implement aren't mentioned in the UIResponder Class Reference. They're defined in the UIResponderStandardEditActions Protocol Reference, which is part of the UIKit Framework Reference. You won't find them unless you know this document exists. It's worth repeating again that you should review all the references used in a framework; otherwise, you may miss critical features. To add custom methods to the responder chain, define them as an `IBAction` and add them to a nib object. They appear in the responder list automatically, and you can link to them in the usual way.

Figure 8.2

Viewing the First Responder actions in an iOS application

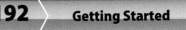

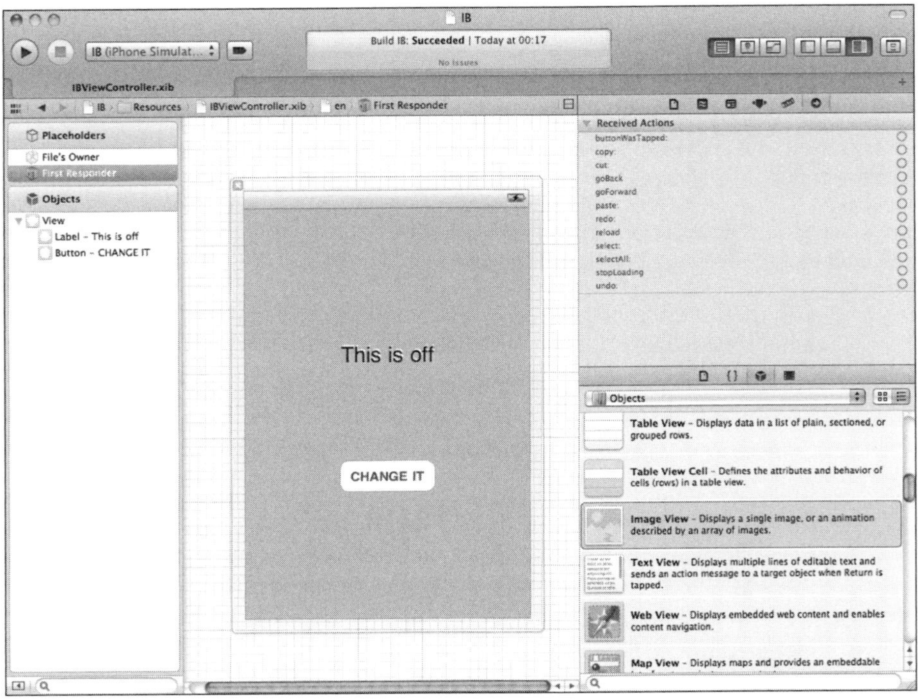

CAUTION

Before this works correctly, you need to let IB know that you're using a subclassed version of the window object. This assignment process is described later in this chapter.

For comparison, Figure 8.3 shows the First Responder list created by the standard OS X application template. iOS includes a handful of standard responder methods. OS X supports nearly 200.

In the application template, many are pre-linked to menu items. None of the methods are implemented, not even with stubs. But you can easily add code to your own subclasses to make them "live."

NOTE

An OS X application includes an extra placeholder object called Application, which stands in for the main application object. It includes a selection of predefined actions, most of which aren't implemented. For information about handling these and other related application events, see the companion Cocoa Developer Reference title.

Figure 8.3

OS X supports many more First Responder actions than iOS.

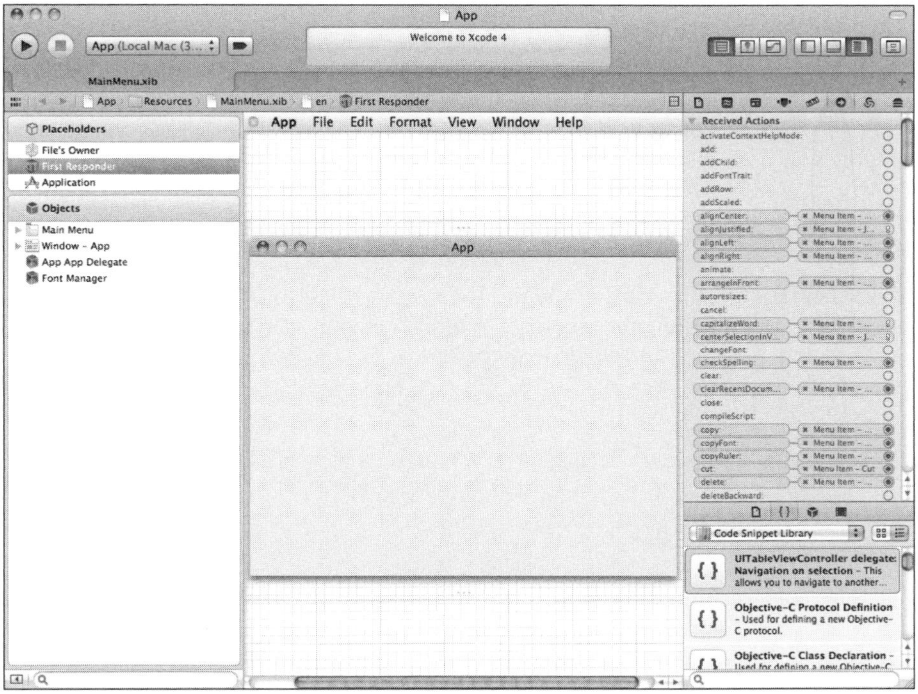

CAUTION

Some very important events don't appear in IB. For example, iOS and OS X touch messages—`touchesBegan:`, among others—aren't listed anywhere in IB. They're hardwired into the responder chain, and you can't redirect them in IB. You can only respond to them with code. If you want to copy and redirect them to multiple objects, you must add code to implement this.

Subclassing Views and Other Objects

A key feature of object-oriented development is *subclassing*—the ability to copy an existing object and extend it with custom code and new features. IB supports subclassing, but the steps required to replace a standard Cocoa/Cocoa Touch class object with a subclassed version of the same object aren't immediately obvious.

To subclass an object, follow these steps:

1. Add a new subclass to the project in the main Xcode editor, and add custom code to implement new features.

2. Assign the subclass to an existing object in IB.

After you have completed Step 2, you can continue to develop and debug your custom code and the new code will be active in your UI.

Any IB object can be subclassed; you can create completely new or substantially modified buttons, sliders, map views, Web views, and so on.

In practice, the UIView class in iOS and the NSView class in OS X are subclassed regularly, because it's often useful to add custom graphics or event management code to a view. Other controls and views are subclassed less frequently.

TIP
You can subclass any object in a nib. It doesn't have to be visible or part of the UI.

CAUTION
Customizing Apple's own subclasses of UIView and NSView—map views, Web views, image views, and so on—can be a frustrating experience. The more complex subclasses include undocumented features and properties, and it's often impossible to add new features without tricks and workarounds. For example, in some situations, animated view swaps are handled by "invisible" views that aren't part of the officially documented view system. Always check unofficial online developer forums to see if other developers have experienced problems—and if they may have already solved them.

Adding a new subclass in Xcode

In this example, we add a new subclass of UIView to the IB project from Chapter 7 and assign the subclass to the background view of the project.

Begin by copying and pasting the project folder in Finder. Rename the folder. The new name is arbitrary, but it must be unique. In the sample code for this project, the new name is IB Custom View. Open the folder, and double-click the .xcodeproj file to load it into Xcode 4.

CAUTION
The project file is still called IB.xcodeproj. This doesn't matter. As explained in Chapter 2, it's very difficult to rename the working files used in an Xcode project, and it isn't usually necessary to do so.

When the project loads, right-click the Classes group and select New File... Select the Cocoa Touch templates, and then select the Objective-C Class template. Select UIView in the Subclass menu, as shown in Figure 8.4. Save the file as IBView.

Figure 8.4

Adding a new subclass of UIView to an iOS project

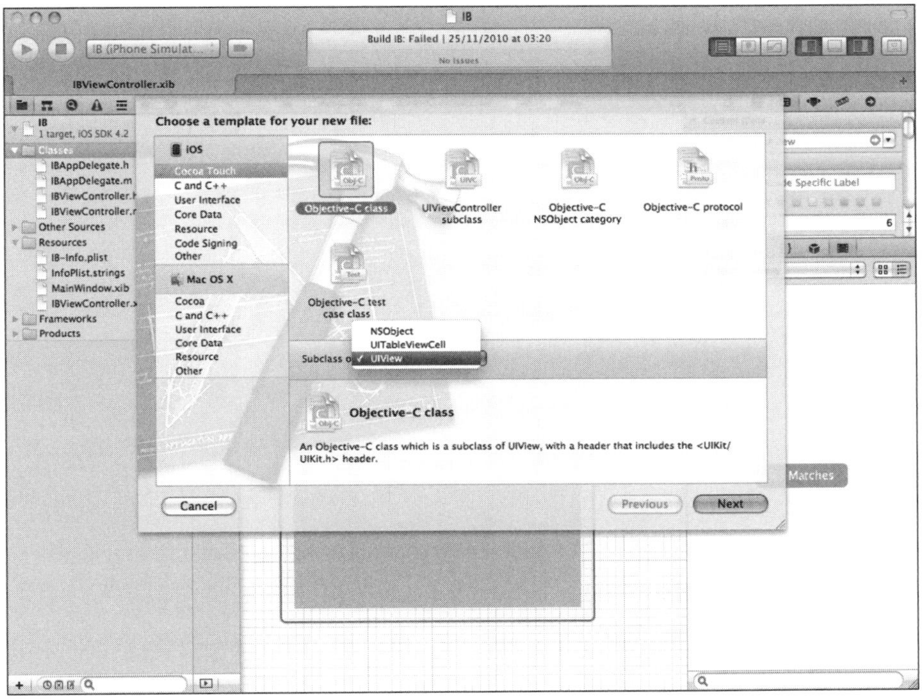

You see two new files: `IBView.m` and `IBView.h`. `IBView.m` includes a sparse selection of extra code that provides a minimal starting point for further customization. It also includes a method called `drawRect:`, which draws custom graphics in the view. By default, this method is commented out. Before we add code to it, we need to take a closer look at the iOS UI.

Figure 8.5 shows the dimensions of the background view as they appear in the Size Inspector. At the top right, you can see that the view is 320x460 pixels. The iPhone screen is 320x480 pixels. Why are 20 pixels missing?

In fact, the default view allows for the status bar at the top of the UI, which is exactly 20 pixels high. The y coordinate of the view is offset by 20, and the view is 20 pixels smaller to compensate.

When you use a background view of any kind in an iOS UI, you must adjust the dimensions to allow for other visible objects. This can affect the calculations used to create custom graphics.

In this example, the view's internal top-left coordinates remain at 0,0. The bottom-right coordinates are adjusted to 320,460 to allow for the smaller view size.

If the UI included other items such as a navigation bar, toolbar, or tab bar, the view's dimensions and coordinates would have to be changed accordingly.

Figure 8.5

Checking the size of the view with the Size Inspector

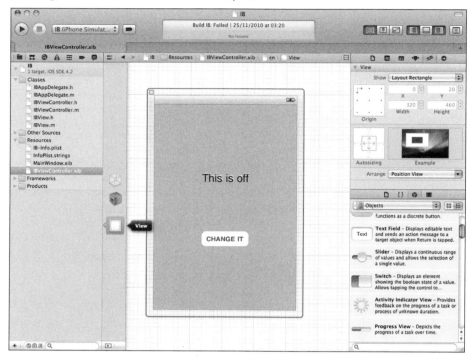

TIP

It's not always easy to remember the dimensions of the various possible navigation and status features. Fortunately, you don't have to, because IB snaps a background view to the correct size when you create a new project from a template. If you add and resize further custom sub-views, IB's snap feature helps you resize them correctly. Note that you can extend a custom sub-view outside the screen area or hide parts of it under navigation objects. This isn't usually a useful thing to do, but the option is there if you need it.

TIP

View management for iPad UIs includes similar features. OS X UIs include related view snapping features, but the design is more open-ended. You don't typically need to shrink a view by a fixed size, unless your application always runs full screen and you need to compensate for the menu bar, in which case you should read the screen dimensions dynamically without assuming a set size. In theory, iOS apps should also make no assumptions about screen dimensions, but this makes UI design very difficult. It's easier to assume the standard screen sizes are valid—for now.

Adding code to the subclass

The `drawRect:` method in a `UIView` is called whenever the screen is refreshed. A refresh happens automatically on launch, so adding code to `drawRect:` is a good way to create a custom background.

N O T E
While it's possible to load an image from a file in `drawRect:` and use the contents as wallpaper, there are easier ways to achieve this result; more details are provided later in this chapter. Similarly, there are easier ways to create a single color static background. `drawRect:` is ideal for more complex effects.

In this example, `drawRect:` code creates a static three-color gradient fill, using C functions from the Core Graphics framework. The code illustrates how a subclass of `UIView` can be customized to create a specific effect. In practice, you can add extra features to any of the existing methods defined for `UIView`, or you can add your own custom properties and methods, as needed.

The code does the following:

- It creates and clears a *context,* an area of memory used for graphics.
- It creates a *color space* object, which holds information about colors.
- It creates an array of three colors from RGB components.
- It creates a color-gradient object using the array.
- It draws a rectangle in the view, allowing for the 20-pixel status bar.
- It draws a gradient fill from the top left to the bottom right of the view.
- It cleans up by restoring the original graphics state and releasing used memory.

```
- (void)drawRect:(CGRect)rect {
    CGPoint startFill, endFill;

    CGContextRef aContext = UIGraphicsGetCurrentContext();
    CGContextClearRect(aContext, rect);
    CGContextSetShouldAntialias(aContext, YES);

    CGColorSpaceRef myRGB = CGColorSpaceCreateDeviceRGB();
    size_t num_locations = 3;
    CGFloat locations [3] = {0.0, 0.5, 1.0};
    CGFloat components [12] =
        {1.0, 0.0, 0.0, 1.0,
         0.0, 1.0, 0.0, 1.0,
         0.0, 0.0, 1.0, 1.0};
    CGGradientRef myGradient =
    CGGradientCreateWithColorComponents(myRGB,
                                        components,
                                        locations,
                                        num_locations);

    CGContextSaveGState(aContext);
    CGContextAddRect(aContext, CGRectMake(0,  0, 320, 460));
    CGContextClip(aContext);
    startFill = CGPointMake(0, 0);
    endFill = CGPointMake(320, 460);
    CGContextDrawLinearGradient(aContext,
                        myGradient,
                        startFill,
```

```
                                        endFill,
                                        kCGGradientDrawsBeforeStartLocation+
                                        kCGGradientDrawsAfterEndLocation);

            CGContextRestoreGState(aContext);
            CGGradientRelease(myGradient);
            CGColorSpaceRelease(myRGB);
        }
```

NOTE

This is lots of code for a simple effect; the Core Graphics library in iOS isn't outstandingly easy to work with. This chapter isn't a primer on Core Graphics, so don't try to remember the details. The key point is that `UIView` can be customized to suit your application's requirements. Subclassing isn't limited to graphics. For example, you also can customize how `UIView` responds to touch events or other user actions. In a more complex application, you might copy touch events, process them in your subclass, and resend them to other objects for further processing. In practice, subclassing is almost infinitely flexible.

Assigning the subclass in IB

If you build and run the application now, you get the result shown in Figure 8.6. The code has been added. But it doesn't run.

Figure 8.6

In subclassing UIView, the first step is to create subclass files and edit their code, but this step on its own isn't enough.

Figure 8.7 shows why. If you select the view in the nib file and look at the entry in the Class menu in the top pane of the Identity Inspector, you see it's set to UIView. When the application launches, it ignores the new code because *the nib file still creates an instance of the original unmodified version of* UIView.

Figure 8.7

In subclassing UIView, the final step tells IB that the view is now an instance of the new IBView subclass. This runs the code in the subclass and enables your new customized features.

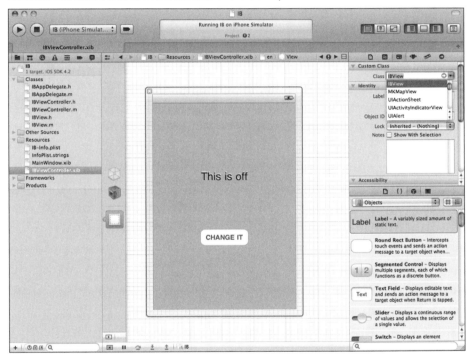

To fix this, we tell IB to create an instance of the new subclass, also known as assigning the subclass. Click the top-right menu as shown in the figure, and scroll down until you find IBView in the list. Click it to assign it. Now the nib file is set up correctly, and it loads the new subclass on launch.

Figure 8.8 shows the result. The UIView draws a colored gradient behind the other items.

TIP

Whenever you select an object in the IB editor, the class identity list is updated to show all its valid subclasses. This listing is indiscriminate, and you can do nonsensical things such as assigning UIWindow as the designated subclass of your new UIView. In most applications, you can ignore most of the items in the list and simply look for your newly added subclass.

Figure 8.8

Running the subclassed view. The code added to the subclass creates a gradient fill.

Working with more advanced subclassing techniques

The following techniques are more specialized. You may not need to use them at all, but it's useful to know they're available.

Adding User Defined Attributes to a subclass

If you subclass an object in the IB library, it automatically inherits that object's attributes. For example, a subclass of UIViewController includes options to set a default orientation and a status bar, a top bar, and a bottom bar. You can't change these attributes, and you can't add further attributes of your own.

But not all Cocoa and Cocoa Touch objects have IB attributes—in fact most objects don't. How can you set initial values for these objects?

One option is to use code. But IB includes a User Defined Runtime Attributes feature, illustrated in Figure 8.9. Objects without "official" attributes include a general purpose keypath, value, and type editor in the Identity inspector. You can add initial values/types here, and they're loaded and set when the nib loads.

Each item is equivalent to running the `setValue: forKeyPath:` method on an object. In the figure, the example has the same effect as adding

```
[self setValue: @"Initial string" forKeyPath: @"myKeyPath"];
```

to an `init` method in the application delegate. Supported types include strings, localized strings, Booleans, numbers, and `nil`.

Figure 8.9

Adding custom attributes to an object

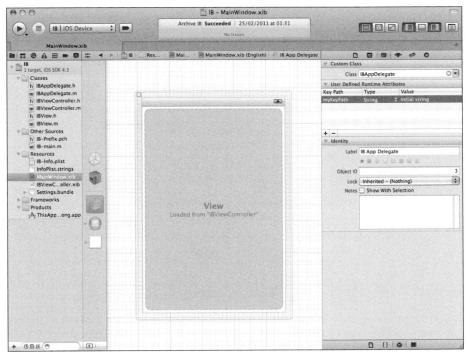

CAUTION

In the first release of Xcode 4, this feature wasn't working correctly. In Xcode 3 it was available for OS X only. It's likely to be fixed in a future release—but check it before you use it.

Subclassing File's Owner

Note that you can follow the steps given above to subclass File's Owner. Typically, you don't need to do this unless you want to add features to the NSApplication/UIApplication classes, or you have a complex nib hierarchy and you need to add code to an element buried in the view hierarchy. For simpler apps, you can leave the default File's Owner class assignments unchanged. But it's useful to remember that even though File's Owner is a placeholder, you can still set its class using the Identity Inspector.

Creating Custom Objects

Sometimes you want to reuse custom objects in other projects. To simplify this, you can add your own objects to the Object Library in IB. But it isn't usually necessary to do this. Even if you reuse objects, it's often simpler to import them again and subclass them again than it is to create a stand-alone plug-in.

A plug-in has two advantages: The object can be added quickly with drag and drop, and it can include a custom Inspector pane for properties. You should consider a plug-in if the following conditions exist:

- You plan to sell or distribute it as part of a library of custom objects.
- You are working with a development team and need to prepare one or more objects independently, but you aren't responsible for their use in applications.
- The objects require significant initialization, which is more easily done with a custom Inspector pane than in code.
- The objects will be reused over and over in many applications.

Creating custom objects is a project for intermediate and advanced developers and is outside the scope of this book. If you have experience with custom frameworks you can find the official documentation by searching online for Interface Builder Plug-In Programming Guide.

Creating Views with Static Images

Subclassing is a very powerful technique, and you can use it to customize any of the standard views and controls. For example, by subclassing `UIButton` and adding custom drawing code controlled by a timer, you can create buttons with pulsing dynamic color animations. As mentioned earlier in this chapter, some classes are easier to modify and extend than others. But as a rule, subclassing is more likely to be limited by your ability to imagine creative effects than by the limitations of iOS or OS X.

However, subclassing takes time. It's often useful to create simpler results such as a UI with a static fixed background. IB includes features to help you design and preview these less complex effects.

To create a static background to an iOS project, use a `UIImageView` object. Drag and drop it on the UI as shown in Figure 8.10. Then drag its position in the object list so it's behind the other objects and higher up the list. If you don't do this, the image view hides the other objects, which usually isn't what you want.

By default, the image view doesn't fill the UI. You can resize it manually by dragging the edges and corners, or you can use the Fill Container Horizontally and Fill Container Vertically options in the Arrange menu in the Size Inspector to expand the image to cover the available background space in the view.

Figure 8.10

Adding an image view to a UI is ideal for wallpaper and for static colored backgrounds.

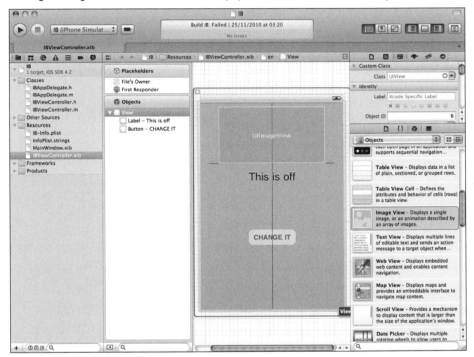

Creating a colored background

The image view doesn't have to contain an image; you can use it to create a static colored background. To select a preset color, click the blue up and down arrows at the right of the Background menu. You see the list shown in Figure 8.11, which displays standard system colors.

While black, white, and gray appear as you'd expect, some of the background colors are more or less obviously textured. For example, the Group Table View Background Color includes vertical stripes, and the Simulator may not always display this accurately.

To set a custom color, click in the area to the left of the menu's up and down arrows to reveal a standard OS X Color Picker. Use the controls to select a color for the image view in the usual way. You can change the opacity for special effects.

CAUTION
Some of the textures look good, but textures may be OS dependent, and they may not appear correctly in the Simulator. If you build an app that supports an older version of iOS, users may not see what you expect them to. To test this, keep one or more hardware test units running older versions of iOS. Differences aren't usually critical, but it's useful to be aware of this issue.

Figure 8.11

Setting a static background color

TIP
To make the image view transparent, select the Clear Color from the default list or set the Opacity to 0 in the Color Picker. Occasionally, you may want to include a dummy view that collects and processes events before passing them on to other objects. To do this, use a transparent view managed by its own subclass code.

Importing an image file

For more complex static effects, you can import an image file. This example demonstrates how to import a file for a full-sized background view that creates a wallpaper effect. The procedure for customizing button graphics is very similar.

You also can extend the procedure to create custom objects such as radio buttons or game tokens. Active features require extra code.

To add a media file, right-click the Resources group in the Project Navigator and select Add Files to <Project Name>… When the dialog box shown in Figure 8.12 appears, navigate to a suitable file. In this example, the project uses a PNG file prepared in Adobe Photoshop and pre-trimmed to 320x460 pixels.

TIP

You can use a file with almost any reasonable dimensions and rescale it manually in IB by dragging the edges and corners. For best results, create a file with the correct dimensions. You can even align the image view outside the boundaries of the UI to show one corner or side.

You can add the contents of one or more complete folders from this dialog box and optionally create a group for each folder. You also can choose to copy the file into the project or to create an indirect reference. For this project, select the Copy option.

Figure 8.12

Use this procedure to import any media file, including graphics, sounds, HTML content, text, and so on.

After import, you see the file in two places, as shown in Figure 8.13. It's added to the Resources group in the Project Navigator. It also appears in the Media Library, which is selected by the icon at the top right of the Library area. If you add further files, they appear in both locations.

In a complex project with many media files, it can be useful to create new groups to collect related media files into one location. You also can create a group for each class and include any associated media files, perhaps in a sub-group to simplify navigation.

Figure 8.13

After import, the new file appears as a Resource and is added to the Media Library.

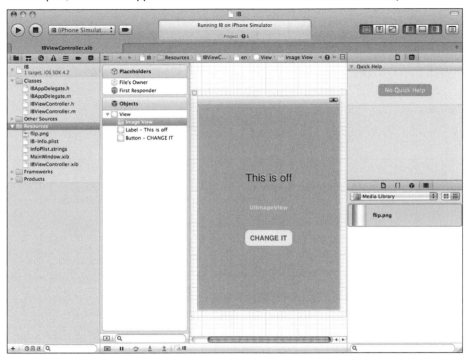

TIP

Although Xcode doesn't include an image editor, it does include a raw hex file editor. Select the Open As↷ Hex option to view any file's raw hex data.

If you click the file in the Resource group, you see the preview shown in Figure 8.14. Xcode doesn't support internal editing of media files, but you can right-click any file and select Open with External Editor to load an editor that isn't built into Xcode. If you save the file afterward, Xcode reloads the new content automatically.

Figure 8.14

Previewing a media file, and selecting an external editor for changes

Assigning an image file

Figure 8.15 shows how to assign the image file to the image view. In the Attributes Inspector, select the image from the Image drop-down menu. All compatible images loaded into the project appear here.

Figure 8.15

Assigning an image file to the image view

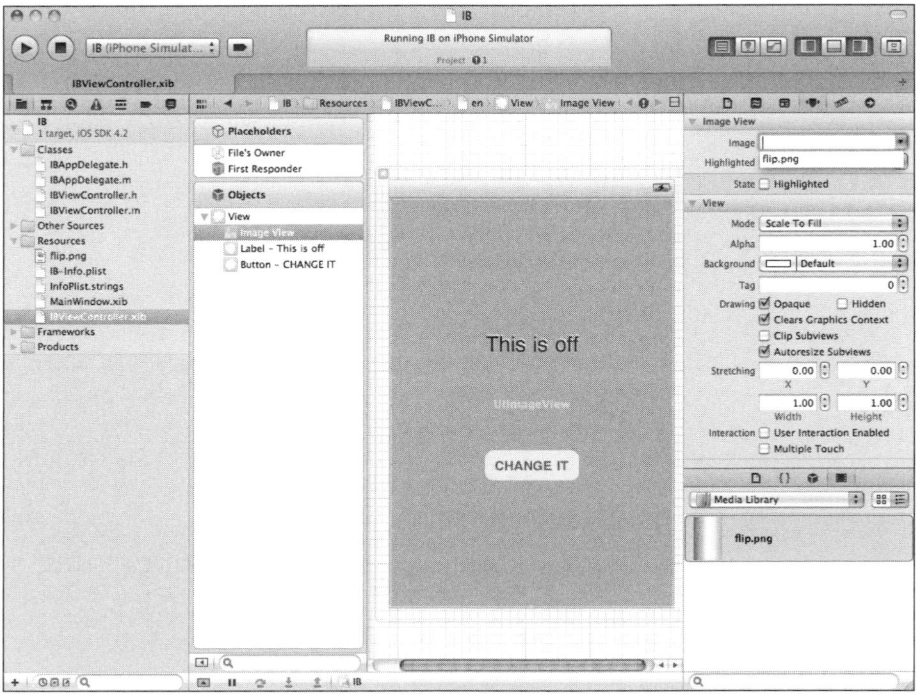

Once assigned, the image view loads the file automatically when the app runs. No further code is needed. You also can preview the image in place in the UI, although certain features such as PNG transparency may not work reliably. Figure 8.16 shows the result.

TIP

To assign a custom image to a button, set the button type to Custom in the Attributes Inspector and assign the image file to the Background property—*not* the Image property. This is enough to implement basic highlighting, and the button darkens when tapped. Buttons have four potential states, but you can ignore the other states unless you're creating complex effects. The Background property defines the button's default look. You can layer the Image property on top of the button for more complex effects.

NOTE

Although OS X supports an `NSImageView` class that is similar to `UIImageView` in iOS, OS X applications are less likely to use background wallpaper. Images are usually used as decorative icons. The iOS Media Library is empty by default. The OS X Media Library includes a selection of standard icons and sounds that you can drag into your application without having to import them. Use the Image Well object with no border to duplicate the effect of an iOS image view.

Figure 8.16

The modified UI with background wallpaper, which Xcode correctly previews in the IB editor

Supporting Non-English Languages

Translating labels and messages into languages other than English is known as *localizing* an application. Localization improves an application's sales prospects, but it can be time-consuming and should be done selectively. Dialects of French and Spanish cover much of the non-English world and should be considered essential. Chinese is becoming an important market. Germany, Japan, and Korea have enthusiastic technology markets and are worth considering. Other languages can be supported as needed for specific applications and locations.

IB supports localization in two ways:

- Each supported language has a separate nib file, with custom labeling.
- Each language also includes a .strings file with a dictionary of text strings, each of which has an associated key.

Creating these extra files is easy in IB. In the Project Navigator, select the main project tab at the top of the pane. Select Project in the adjacent pane, and select the Info tab in the main settings panel.

To add a language, open the Localizations sub-pane and click the Add (+) icon, as shown in Figure 8.17. Scroll down the long list to select the new language.

Adding a new language duplicates the current collection of nibs. It *doesn't* translate the contents. You must update the labels and other features of each nib manually. This may require expert input.

The new nib files are bundled with the application, and the nib loader reads a user's localization settings to select and load the correct nib for each country automatically.

Figure 8.17

Adding support for a non-English language

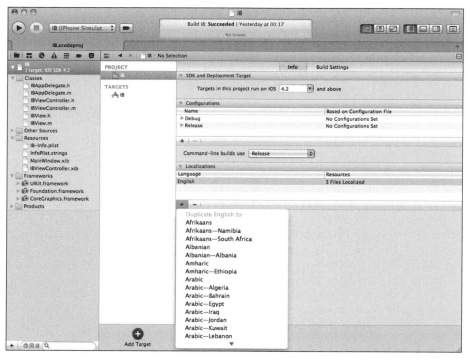

TIP

Adding too many languages bloats the project with many almost identical nib files. Although Apple promotes multi-language support, realism suggests it's more practical to support the smallest possible selection of languages. As a workaround, you can use a single nib file and set the labels on launch with text loaded from the .strings file. This option takes longer to code, but is easier to expand and creates a much smaller final bundle.

IB doesn't support non-English text unless you're already using a non-English keyboard. Use the Character Viewer utility shown in Figure 8.18 to add accents, special symbols, and letters from non-English alphabets. To open the Character Viewer, select the Keyboard item in System Preferences and enable the Show Keyboard & Character Viewer in menu bar option. Click the flag icon that appears in the menu bar, and select Show Character Viewer from the menu. Select special characters as needed, and use the Insert button to add them while editing text.

Figure 8.18

Using the Character Viewer utility to add non-English characters to a nib

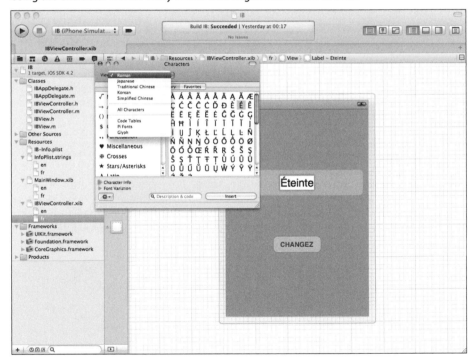

CAUTION

Not all fonts support all characters. You may need to use special non-English fonts for languages such as Chinese, Japanese, and Korean.

TIP

Managing localization strings can be painfully time-consuming. Xcode includes two command-line tools to simplify the process. ibtool can read through a nib and create a list of visible strings. You can then send the strings to a translator. When done, ibtool can fold the translated strings back into another "translated" nib. genstrings is a similar tool, but it works on source code files. For details see the man pages or search for examples online.

Working with Advanced IB Techniques

IB is a deep application with many hidden features. There isn't room to explore them all—in fact, hardly anyone uses IB to its fullest possible extent. But it's worth becoming familiar with some of the more accessible advanced techniques.

Using tags

Many IB objects include a Tag field, as shown in Figure 8.19. You can use this field to search a nib—or more usually, a view in a nib—to find a matching object. For example, to find the button in the figure you might add the following code to the view controller:

```
UIButton* theButtonImLookingFor
= (UIButton *)[self.view viewWithTag: 101010];
```

Typically you *wouldn't* do this for simple object updates—outlets are a better option. But tags can be very useful when you work with table views. You can create cells dynamically and use tags to define how they're displayed—for example, to create cells with alternating colors. Tags can also be a good way to manage UI elements when you generate them in code without using IB at all.

Figure 8.19

Defining a tag for a UI button

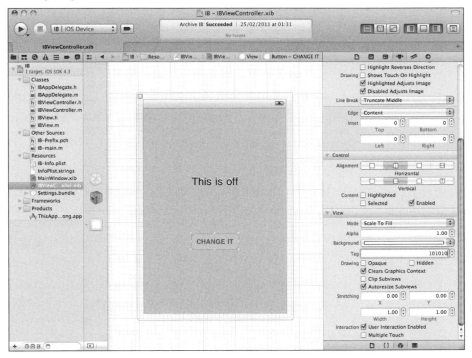

Sending messages between nibs

It's often useful to send messages between objects in different nibs. It isn't trivially easy to do this—some setting up is always required. But it's not a difficult problem.

One common solution is to pass messages through First Responder. Optionally, you can add custom methods to First Responder by clicking it, selecting the Attributes inspector, and adding an action as shown in Figure 8.20. Add the action code to one of the classes in the responder chain. You can then link the custom action to buttons, menus, and other IB message-generating objects in the usual way.

This can be a useful way to leapfrog across objects in the responder hierarchy. For example, if you want to create a button that sends a message to a window rather than a view controller, subclass the window and add a responder method to it.

NOTE

There's only one First Responder item in an application. Although it appears in every nib, it's the same item. (File's Owner is different for every nib.)

CAUTION

Objects with custom methods must be plugged into the responder chain correctly—otherwise messages disappear and are ignored. It can take longer to add the code that ensures an object supports first responder status correctly than to create the responder methods.

Figure 8.20

Adding a custom action to First Responder

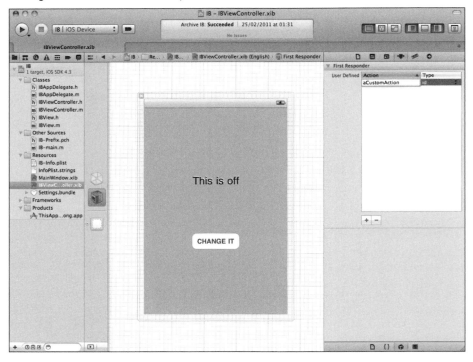

Converting iPhone projects to the iPad

Because there are so many differences between the two platforms, there's no simple automatic way to convert an iPhone project into an iPad app. However, Xcode includes a minimal transitioning feature that can help you begin the conversion process.

The converter relies on the fact that iPad and iPhone apps load different nib files at launch. It takes an existing iPhone launch nib and creates a new launch nib from it for the iPad. This is enough to create a basic universal app that runs on both platforms.

N O T E

The Window-based template creates two separate app delegate files and two starting nibs. Converted iPhone apps also have two nibs, but the main window is controlled by a single shared app delegate which remains unaltered. This is usually easier to work with; app management code is shared, not duplicated. Similarly, it's possible to create a single shared controller that's aware of which platform it's running on. This is more efficient than creating two controllers with similar code.

The best time to convert an app is when it's finished. Figure 8.21 shows a dummy iPhone app UI that stands in for a finished app for this demonstration. You can start with an existing app of your own, or you can load any of the templates. The exact contents of the app don't matter.

In this example there are two nib files. One defines the main window, and the other defines the UI and also instantiates the view controller.

Figure 8.21

Getting ready to convert an iPhone app to the iPad

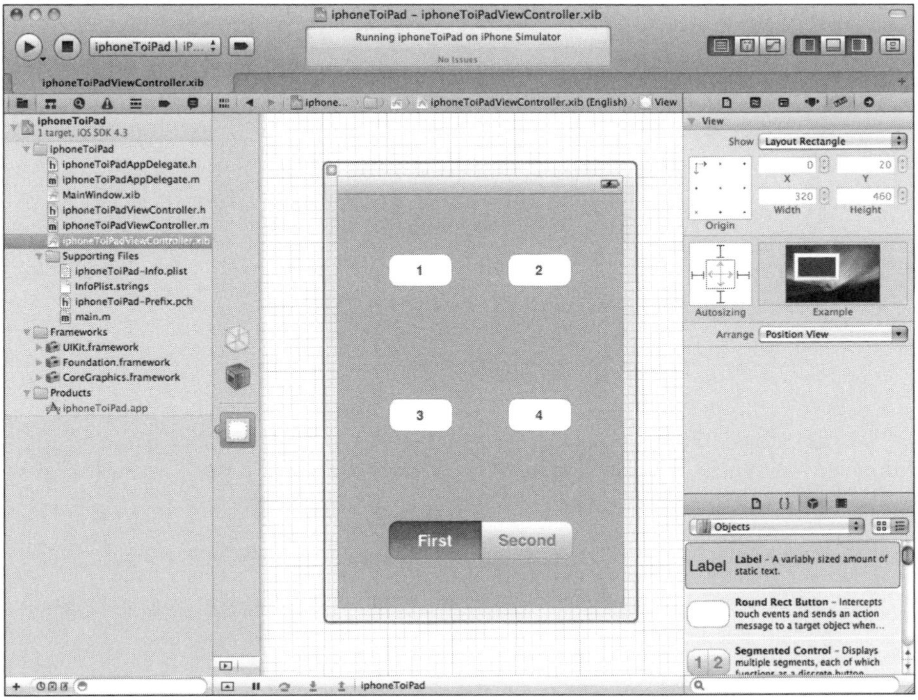

To convert an app, click the project name at the top left of the Project navigator. Select the app under the Targets icon. Select Universal from the menu, as shown in Figure 8.22. (You can also select iPad, which creates an iPad-only version.)

Note that this feature isn't prominent. In Xcode 3, you could select a conversion option from the Project menu. In Xcode 4, you have to know that this feature exists, and where to find it.

Figure 8.22

Selecting the new format

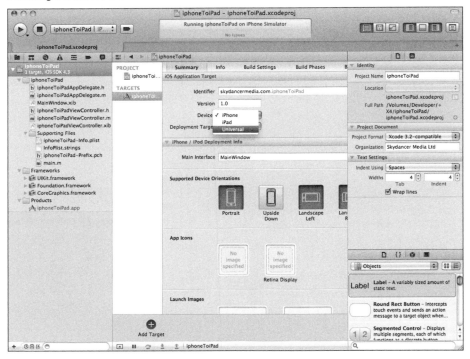

Select Yes in the confirmation dialog. Xcode creates a new group called iPad and adds a new file called MainWindow-iPad.xib to it. This nib is formatted and tagged as an iPad launch nib. You can now run the app in the iPad Simulator, as shown in Figure 8.23.

CAUTION

There's more to an iPad nib than larger dimensions. Nibs contain device information, so you can't simply resize an existing iPhone nib by hand. The converter handles the hidden details for you.

Figure 8.23

Running the converted app in the iPad Simulator

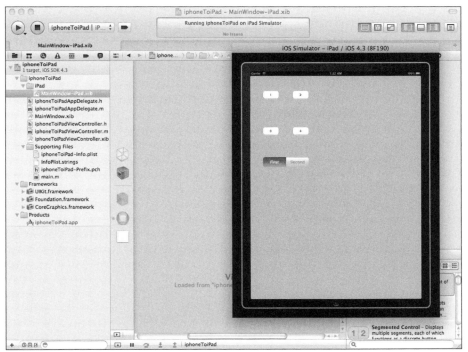

You can see from the illustration that formatting is haphazard. Given the extra space, it's usual for iPad apps to have more features than their iPhone equivalents. A minimal UI that works well on the iPhone can look comical on the iPad, unless you redesign it.

Note that if you run in the iPhone Simulator, the original app loads as before. Only the main window has changed. The view controller remains the same, but you can now extend it with iPad-specific features.

Summary

This chapter introduced the File's Owner and First Responder placeholder objects and explained their role in UI design and event management. It demonstrated how to customize objects by subclassing them and how to assign subclasses to visible objects in IB. It showed how to create simple static background images in IB with flat colors or image files and introduced IB's localization features, with support for non-English nib files. Finally it explored some more advanced applications of IB, including universal iPhone/iPad development.

Going Deeper

9 Saving Time in Xcode

Many editing operations are repetitive, while others can help you organize your code more effectively to simplify development and maintenance. Xcode 4 includes features that can automate many of these operations, saving you time and effort. The key features include the following:

- Code folding
- Structure editing
- Refactoring
- Code snippets
- Jumping to a definition

Using Code Folding

Code folding is a simple feature that can hide code while it isn't being edited. It's a display-only feature that makes it easier for you to concentrate on one section of code without being distracted by surrounding elements.

C A U T I O N

It's easy to activate code folding by accident. If you're not familiar with this feature, you'll wonder why most of your code has disappeared and whether you deleted it by accident. It's important to understand how code folding works, even if you never use it. The code folding gutter described below is very thin, and it's adjacent to the gutter used for debugging. It's easy to select one when you're trying to select the other.

To fold a section of code, hover the mouse cursor in the gutter at the left of the editor, as shown in Figure 9.1. The selected code is highlighted with a white background, and the surrounding code is grayed out, as shown.

Figure 9.1

Selecting a block of code to hide. Code within the nearest matching curly brackets is highlighted and selected automatically.

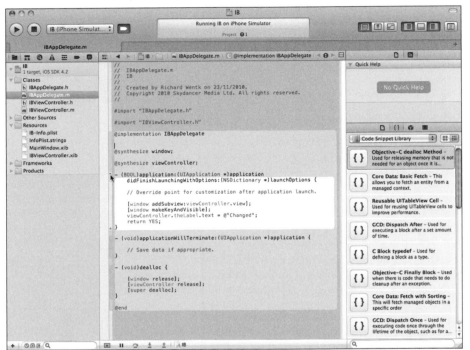

Click on the disclosure triangle in the gutter. Xcode hides the selected code and replaces it with a placeholder {…} graphic, as shown in Figure 9.2. To unhide the code, double-click the place-holder or click once on the disclosure triangle.

Code hiding selects paired curly brackets, so you can hide entire methods or specific code segments. If you hide a complete method the signature remains. If you hide a smaller segment, such as the contents of an `if` statement, the first line of the statement remains as a guide and the contents are hidden.

For convenience, you can also fold all of the code in a file. Select Editor ⇨ Code Folding and choose one of the following options:

- **All:** Folds/unfolds everything between two matching delimiters.
- **Methods & functions:** Folds/unfolds methods and functions only.
- **Comment blocks:** Folds/unfolds comment blocks only.

You can use this feature to hide the large comment block that Apple always includes at the start of sample code.

Figure 9.2

You can unhide code by clicking in the gutter or clicking the placeholder graphic.

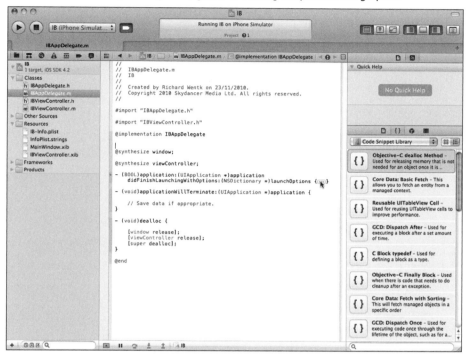

CAUTION

Xcode's code folding is simple and limited compared to the equivalent feature on other platforms. It's delimiter-based and has no syntactic intelligence. You can't do useful things such as hiding long property lists.

Editing Structure

It's often useful to comment or uncomment blocks of code, clean up indentation, check delimiters, move lines up or down within a method, and so on. Xcode's editor includes a contextual right-click menu that implements these features, as shown in Figure 9.3.

TIP

Newcomers to Xcode sometimes miss this menu or ignore it because there's so much else to learn. But it's one of the keys to improving productivity in Xcode, and it's the best way to avoid wasting time on manual code tidying chores.

Figure 9.3

Viewing the Structure editing menu, an unglamorous but very useful timesaver

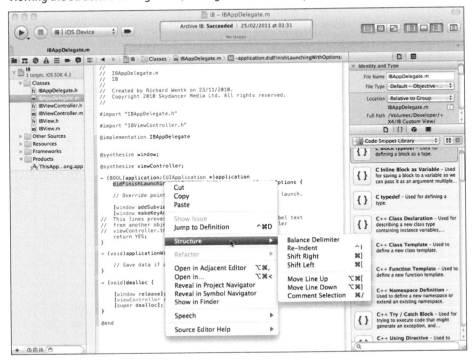

To display the menu, right-click anywhere in the editor area. Some options in this menu require you to select a block of code. The following features are available:

- **Balance delimiter:** This is a display-only feature that helps you fix delimiter mismatches. When you select it, Xcode highlights the matching delimiters nearest to the edit point. Select it again, and it highlights the next matching pair. And so on. You also can double-click any delimiter to find its partner and highlight the code between them.

- **Reindent:** This corrects the indentation within a selected block of code. Code features within matching delimiters are indented by the same number of spaces. This is a good way to clean up a messy edit.

- **Shift Right/Left:** These options move a selected block of code by the number of spaces used for an indentation step. You can use this feature to correct indentation after a major change to a method, but it's often easier and quicker to use the Reindent option after editing.

- **Move Line Up/Down:** In spite of the name, these options can move a single line or a selected block up and down. The line above or below the selection changes position.

- **Comment Selection:** If the selection is uncommented, this option inserts two slashes before each line. If it's commented with two slashes on each line, the slashes are removed. This feature isn't intelligent enough to recognize / * ...* / comment blocks and doesn't uncomment them correctly.

TIP

To make code structures easier to follow, you can change the fonts and colors used by Xcode. Although the changes are cosmetic, they can have a significant impact on productivity, because a good color scheme can make structures stand out clearly. Select Xcode ⇨ Preferences, and choose the Fonts & Colors tab. You can change the font globally by selecting every item that appears in the list and choosing a new font or font size in the Font box.

Refactoring Code

The Structure menu is used for relatively simple edits, but the Refactor menu, shown in Figure 9.4, can create more complex changes. Some changes affect every file in a project.

Figure 9.4

In the Refactor menu, some or all of the options typically are grayed out.

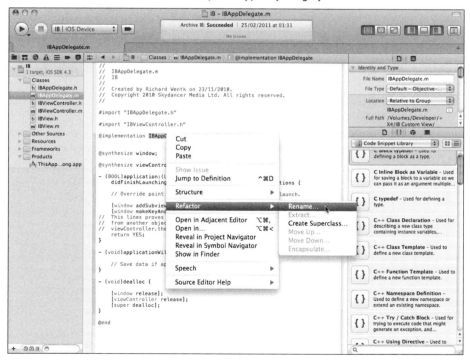

Refactoring is a powerful but sometimes tricky feature that changes or renames structural features in your project. The aim of refactoring is to create clearer organized code that is easier to extend and maintain. Edits shouldn't change basic behavior or introduce bugs. You can refactor code with the options shown in the Refactor menu. You also can use a feature called *Edit All In Scope* to rename symbols within a file.

Using the Refactor menu

In Xcode, you can use the Refactor menu to do the following:

- Rename classes, methods, and other symbols within a class
- Rename classes, methods, and symbols across a project
- Create new superclasses
- Move code into a superclass
- Move code into a subclass
- Create new setters and getters for a symbol

Refactoring can seem mysterious because the options that appear in the Refactor menu are context- and selection-dependent. Xcode displays only the options that make sense; for example, you can't create a superclass for a property.

N O T E

Xcode's refactoring features are based on ideas introduced by developer Martin Fowler. For more information, see http://martinfowler.com. Refactoring has been hotly debated, but you don't need to be familiar with the debate to use the Refactor menu to work with your code.

C A U T I O N

Refactoring can make drastic, wide-ranging changes to a project. It's a good idea to back up a project using one of the options introduced in Chapter 14 before you use this feature. Note that some refactoring options, such as rename, can be very slow.

Refactoring typically works in two stages. First you select an operation and type a parameter, such as a new name, into a dialog. Next, Xcode displays the preview and confirmation dialog shown in Figure 9.5. The preview shows a list of proposed changes in various files at the left, and before/after views of the code at the right.

Clicking Save actions the changes. You can also deselect one or more of the check boxes at the left to leave those items unchanged. For some operations, the proposed changes can be complex and may be spread across multiple sections in multiple files.

The following options are available:

- **Rename:** This works on classes, properties, and method. Select a feature and the Rename option from the menu. Type a new name into the dialog box. Xcode searches every file in the project—this can take a while—and shows the preview/confirmation dialog.

- **Extract:** This works on methods or code sections. You can move a section of code into a separate method or function. Xcode automatically creates a new signature for you. You can edit this before you confirm the change.

- **Create Superclass:** This works on class names. It creates a new superclass. The definition code can be written to a new file, which is the most useful option, or it can be added to the current file, which can be confusing and isn't usually useful. You typically need to fix included/imported headers manually in the superclass definition.

- **Move Up/Down:** This works on methods and properties. Move Up moves the item to the superclass; in other words, it removes the code from the current file and moves it to the superclass definition file. Move Down moves it from the superclass to a subclass.

- **Encapsulate:** This works on properties. It creates code for a getter and/or a setter. You don't need to use this feature if you're already using @synthesize for your properties.

Figure 9.5

Using the preview/confirmation dialog while renaming a class. Xcode searches every file in the project and lists the possible edits here.

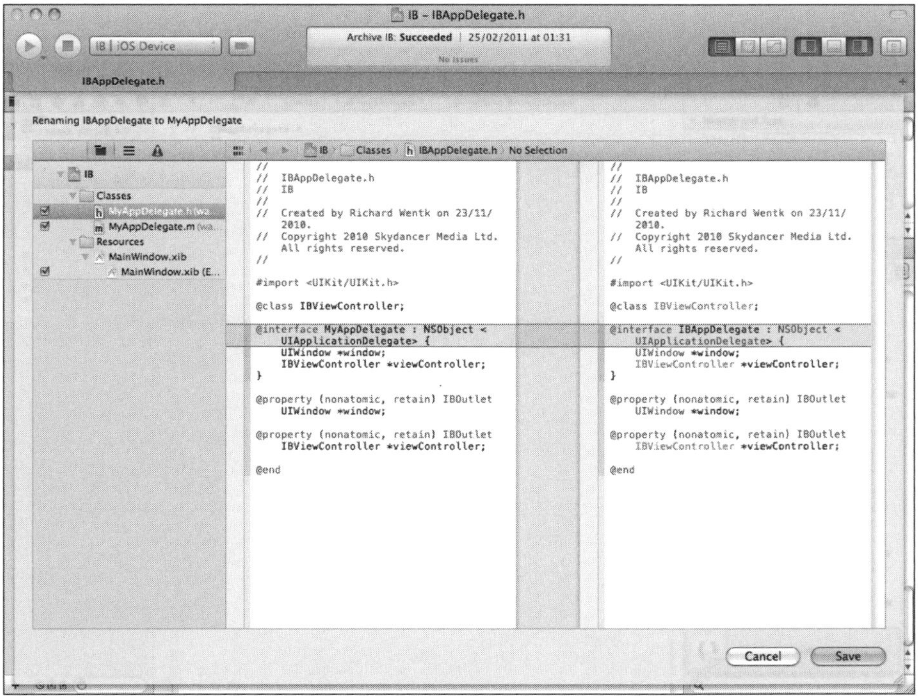

NOTE
Some of the refactoring options modify project nib files. You can confirm or cancel edits using the same split before/after view used to display code files, but the panes show the XML (eXtended Markup Language) data inside a nib. This may appear unfamiliar if you've never looked inside a nib with a text editor. There's no way to view the changes graphically; typically, it wouldn't make sense to show them in this way.

Using the Edit All In Scope feature

It's sometimes useful to rename symbols used in a file. You can use the global find/replace feature in the main menu to rename a symbol in a project, but sometimes you need to limit the changes to a single class, method, or function.

With the Edit All In Scope feature, you can rename one instance of a symbol, and your edit is copied to all matching symbols within the selected scope. Typically you use this within a method or function, but you can also use it to change local variables in a class.

It can be easy to miss Edit All in Scope. To use it, select any object and hover over it with the mouse cursor. Xcode displays a floating selection triangle to the right of the property. Click the triangle, and Xcode displays a right-click contextual menu with the Edit All in Scope entry (and nothing else), as shown in Figure 9.6.

Figure 9.6

Using Edit All in Scope is an easy way to rename a group of objects, but it's easy to miss this feature!

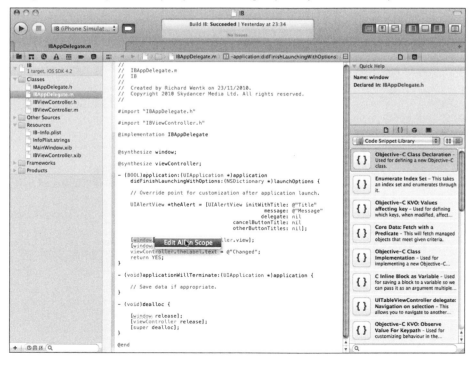

Select this entry, and Xcode highlights all instances of that object in the file. You can now type a new name, and all instances of the name are changed at the same time. Press Return to make the change permanent or Escape to cancel.

CAUTION
Don't use Edit All in Scope to change properties/ivars. If a symbol is accessed from outside a class, use one of the refactor options to rename it.

Using Code Snippets

With earlier versions of Xcode, many developers realized that it was useful to create a dummy file with boilerplate code that could be copied into an active project. Xcode 4 replaces this ad hoc file with a *code snippets* feature, creating a simple but productive new feature. Code snippets add complete sections of code to a project. Xcode includes a small selection of default snippets, but you can expand the library with your own code.

A code snippet can be a line or two of code such as an alert generator or timer initializer, a more complex section of code that implements a standard feature such as animation, or a complete method. Potentially, you can create snippets that implement an entire class with complex default code.

TIP
Code snippets are built into Code Sense, making a very powerful feature. When you create a new snippet, you can define a custom auto-completion string. When you type that string in the editor and press Return, Code Sense copies the snippet code from the library and inserts it. You can add your own placeholder tokens.

Inserting a snippet

To insert a snippet, select the Code Snippet ({}) icon in the Library area of the Utility Pane. Optionally, select an OS or your custom snippets from the pop-up menu, as shown in Figure 9.7. Select a snippet from the list, and drag and drop it into the code editor.

The code is copied and added as shown at the top of the figure. Placeholder variables appear in gray. To complete the edit, select and rename them. You can skip between them with the Tab key.

A preview window with the code appears to the left of the snippets. You can use this window to edit snippets in the library.

CAUTION
By default, the library shows snippets for all platforms. The OS platforms include snippets with different code for each, but some snippets have common names. Always select the platform before using snippets. Xcode allows you to add an iOS snippet to an OS X project, and vice versa.

Figure 9.7

In this example of adding a code snippet, the `tableView:` method has been copied from the snippet library and added to the top of the editor. The floating preview window displays the snippet so you can review it before you add it.

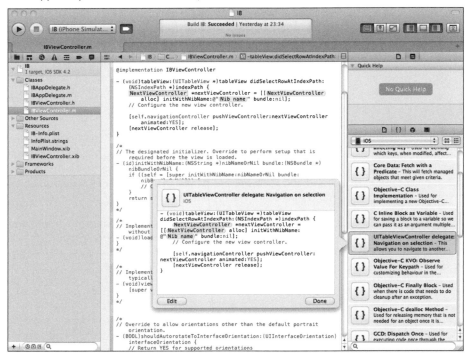

Creating a new snippet

Creating a new snippet is easy after you understand how to do it, but until you do, the process is unintuitive.

Creating a snippet with drag and drop

It's unexpectedly easy to miss this feature, and it has some hidden subtleties. To create a snippet, drag-highlight the code you want to include, click the highlighted area, and *hold down the mouse button until the cursor changes to a pointer*. If you don't hold down the mouse button, Xcode assumes you're attempting to highlight a different section of code.

Drag the snippet to the Code Snippet Library and release it anywhere. The snippet is added as the last item in the User library with a default name—My Code Snippet.

In the first release of Xcode 4, you can only add a snippet when the Code Snippet Library or User items are selected. This means that when the snippet list is filtered to show iOS or OS X snippets, adding a snippet seems to have no effect. In fact, the snippet is added to the User list—which is invisible.

Similarly, you also can't see or insert user snippets when viewing iOS or OS X items. You can only use them when you select the User list or the unfiltered Code Snippet Library list.

This may change in future releases—the current implementation is inconvenient for developers who want to create and use snippets on either or both platforms.

Once you have created a snippet, you can edit the name and add optional symbol placeholders, as described below.

Editing a snippet

To edit a snippet, click anywhere on it in the Library to view the code, and click the Edit button at the lower right. You'll see the dialog shown in Figure 9.8.

Figure 9.8

Editing a snippet

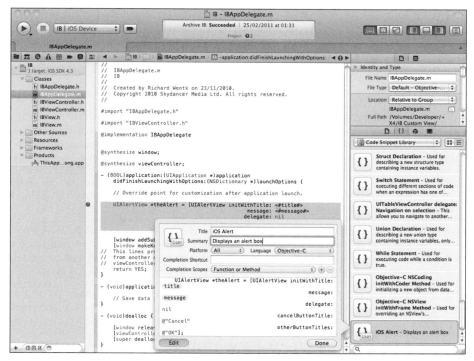

NOTE

Currently, you can only edit User snippets. To create your own version of one of the existing snippets, copy and paste the code into a User snippet and save it with a new name.

You can now edit the following settings:

- **Title:** This defines the name that appears in the Library list.
- **Summary:** This defines the short description that appears in the Library list.
- **Platform:** Select iOS, OS X, or All. Currently this feature does nothing—all snippets are user snippets—but it may be more useful in future versions of Xcode.
- **Language:** This defaults to Objective-C. You can select a different language manually.
- **Completion shortcut:** You can leave this empty or fill it with any unique string to provide a quick-access keyboard shortcut for Code Completion.
- **Completion scope.** You can control how widely Xcode searches when looking for completion matches. The default is Function or Method.

Snippets often need placeholder tokens, which can be filled in later when you use the snippet. For example when creating an alert, you can use a placeholder for the message text.

To create placeholder tokens, type the following:

```
<#placeholderName#>
```

The `placeHolder` name string is arbitrary and doesn't have to be unique. It appears in the snippet code as a highlighted placeholder, and you can edit it and tab over it in the usual Code Completion way.

In the figure, the snippet includes two placeholders: `<#title#>` and `<#message#>`. The choice of the number and placing of the placeholders is up to you. Optionally, you can create different versions of the same snippet with different placeholders; for example, you can create one for an alert that uses standard text and another in which the labels are placeholders and can be filled in as needed.

N O T E

The snippet feature in Xcode doesn't support open development; there's no way to share snippets across a team or make them available online. Public alternatives are available, such as snipt at `http://snipt.net` and Willow at `http://wingsforpigs.com/Willow/Willow.html`. Public snippet sharing may not be ideal for your project, but it can be a useful option to explore, especially for scripted languages such as Python and Ruby.

Jumping to a Definition

It's often useful to jump to a method signature or symbol definition. You can find definitions by searching for them, but it's much quicker to use the Jump to Definition feature.

To use it, highlight a symbol, right-click to show the contextual menu, and select the Jump to Definition option.

If there's a single definition, Xcode displays it in the main code window. Note that the definition may be in one of the Cocoa or Cocoa Touch header files, and not in your code—in which case you'll see a method signature, and perhaps some supporting comments from Apple.

If there are multiple definitions—for example, when there are multiple classes with `dealloc` methods—Xcode displays a new menu with a list of definitions. You can select one to view it.

Note that definitions *don't* appear in the Assistant window when it's open—they take you away from your original editing location into a different file, or a different part of the same file. To move back to the original location, use the back arrow at the top left of the edit window.

Summary

This chapter explored some of Xcode's time-saving features. It introduced code folding and explained how you can use it to hide distracting code while you're not working on it. It described the editing utilities available in the Structure menu and listed the ways in which they implement common code clean-up chores.

Next, it introduced the Refactor menu and explained how refactoring can create code that is easier to update and maintain. Finally, it described Code Snippets and demonstrated how this powerful new feature can be used to create a custom library of code that can be inserted into a project by hand or integrated into Xcode's Code Sense system.

Using the Organizer

10

The Xcode Organizer, shown in Figure 10.1, appears in a separate window and contains an "and the rest…" collection of miscellaneous features. The Organizer is used for project and device management, and it includes a browser for the Xcode documentation library.

To display the Organizer, click the file-cabinet icon, at the right of the icon bar at the top of the Xcode editor window. The Organizer appears in a separate window that isn't integrated with the main editor.

You can use the Organizer's features to manage:

- Provisioning certificates
- Development devices
- Code repositories
- Active projects

The window uses the standard OS X layout. To select the main features, click the icons at the top. Sub-features appear in groups at the left. The active area fills the rest of the screen. Some features include a separate toolbar at the bottom of the screen, with icons for specific options. Because the Organizer is a grab bag of miscellaneous unrelated options, the UI of each page is different.

CROSS-REFERENCE

The Organizer includes the Documentation Browser, which is described in Chapter 6. The Repository and Snapshot features are described in Chapter 14. Provisioning is described in more detail in Chapter 11. This chapter introduces the remaining features that aren't discussed elsewhere.

In This Chapter

10

Working with devices

Using device logs

Managing individual devices

Working with projects and archives

Working with Devices

You can—and usually should—test iOS apps on a number of devices. You don't often need to set up devices manually. When you plug in a new device, Xcode downloads the relevant details and makes it available for testing. This can take a few seconds but isn't a complex process.

Figure 10.1

The Xcode Organizer

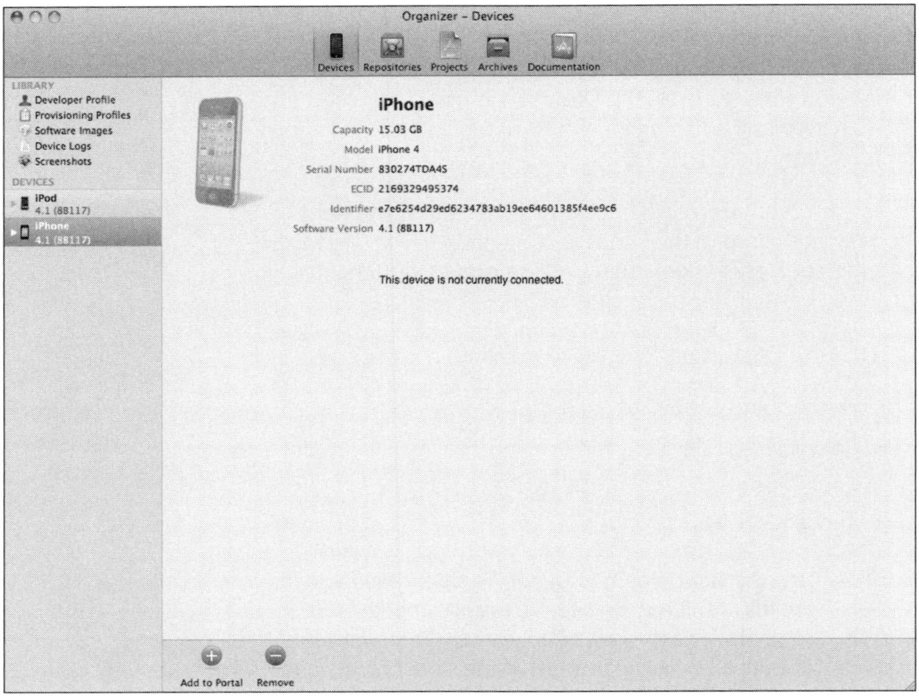

The Device Manager, shown in Figure 10.2, includes useful but optional features that make device testing more productive. The Library subpane at the top left is a menu of general device-related features. The Devices subpane is a list of devices. Each displays a similar list of options.

CAUTION

Some options are available only when a device is connected. For example, you can always see stored screenshots and device logs. But the Console, Provisioning Profiles, and Applications options are visible only for the currently attached device, if there is one.

You can use the Manager to perform these tasks:

- Review and manage provisioning profiles and developer certificates. Use this feature to check the status of profiles and certificates. It includes an option to copy a complete set of profiles and certificates to another Mac.

- Review and manage OS updates. You can check the current installed OS on each device, and update or restore to other versions.

- View device logs. Logs include stack dumps collected during crashes, and process listings that can help diagnose memory errors.

- Create and manage app screenshots. Screenshots can be saved for reference or collected for use in a new App Store listing.

Figure 10.2

A view of the Device Manager, showing the list of devices at the left, device management options at the top left, and an active display and management area in the rest of the screen

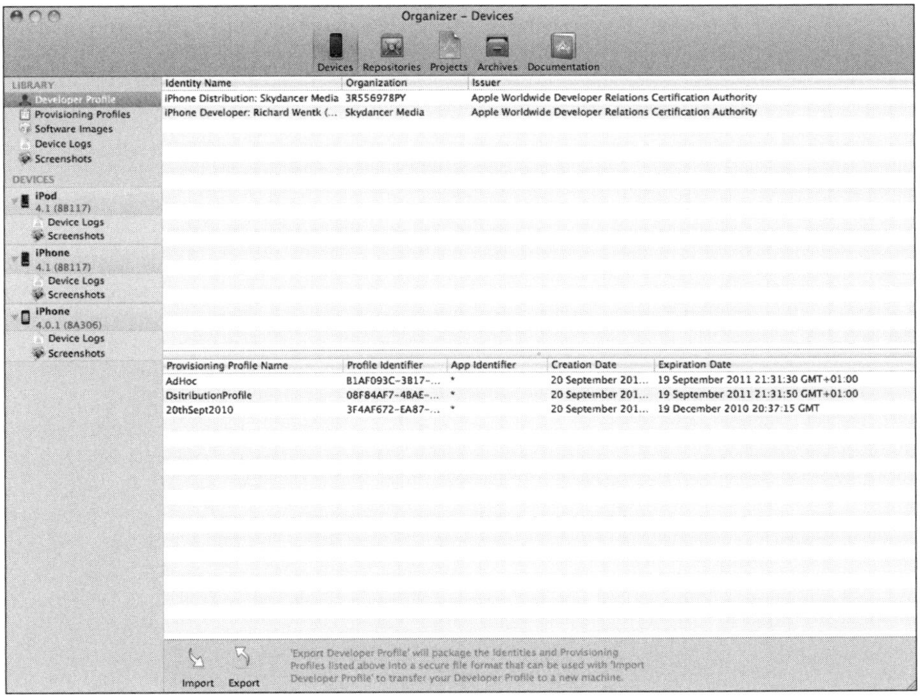

Reviewing and managing profiles

The top half of the Developer Profile window (refer to Figure 10.2) displays developer certificates. The bottom half displays provisioning profiles. Certificates and profiles can't be opened or edited, so this list is purely for review.

However, they can be copied to another Mac. Before Xcode 4, provisioning multiple Macs required manual copying and installation of individual certificates and profiles. In Xcode 4, you can use the Import and Export feature at the bottom of this page to duplicate these files and install them on another Mac with a single operation.

Figure 10.3 shows the Export dialog box. To use this feature, you must specify and confirm a password. Use the same password when you Import the profiles on a different machine.

The Export dialog box creates a file you can copy to other Macs. To recreate the provisioning, run the Import option on the other Mac. You need to specify the same password again.

Figure 10.3

When exporting provisioning information, forgetting the password isn't an option.

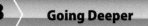

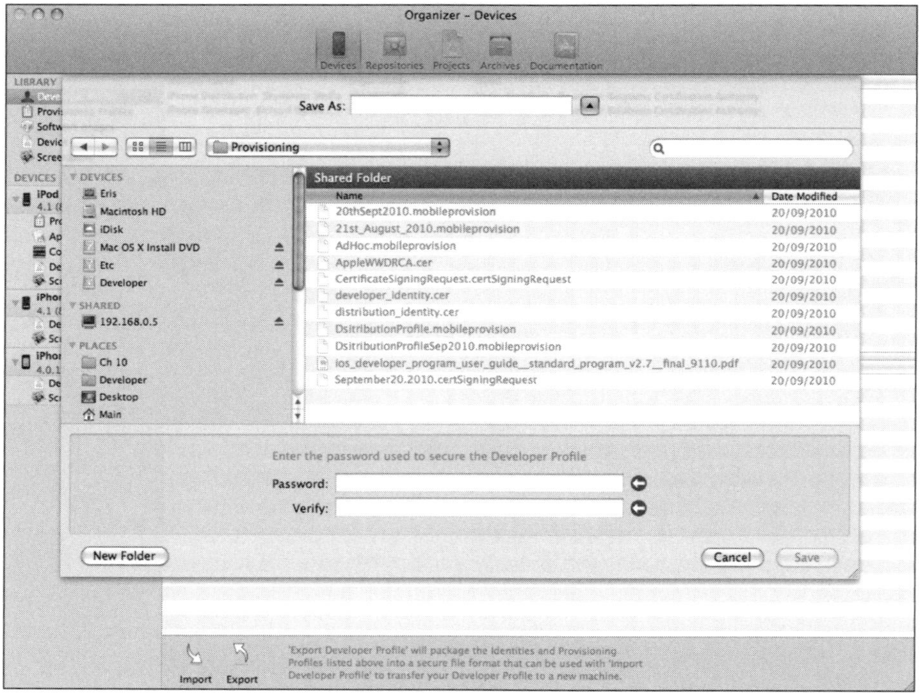

Figure 10.4 shows the Provisioning Profiles listing, which displays all available profiles.

The listing shows profile creation and expiry dates, and it highlights profiles that have expired or are about to expire. The device list at the bottom of the window indicates the device or devices on which the profile is installed.

You can right-click a profile and select options to delete it or to open a Finder window with the corresponding file. It's good practice to delete expired profiles to keep the list clean and up to date.

CAUTION

Distribution profiles can't be installed on devices. If you select a distribution profile in this window, the device list always displays a warning message.

Figure 10.4

Reviewing installed profiles with the Provisioning Profiles option

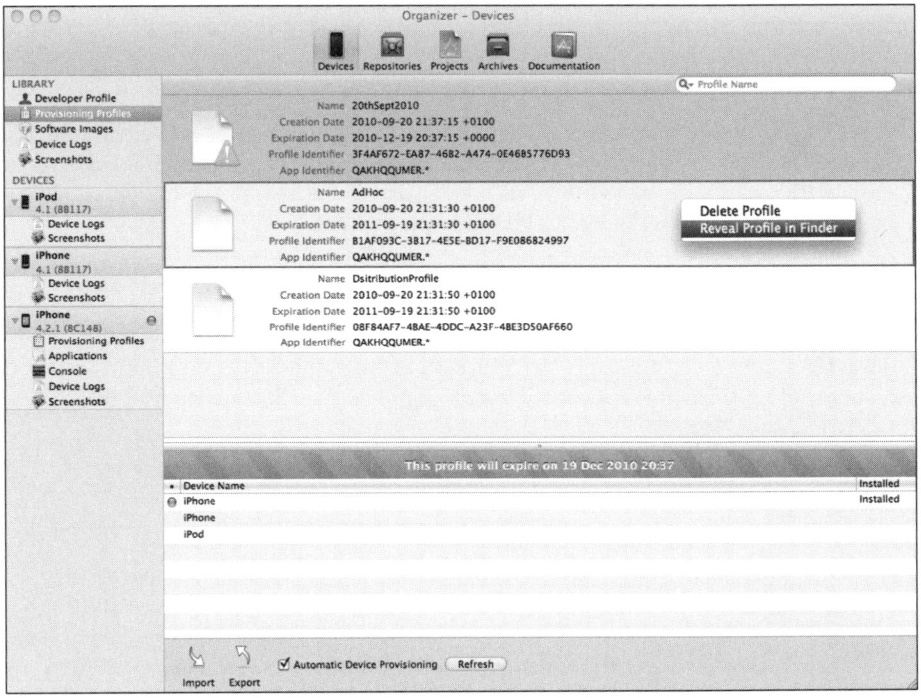

The most useful feature on this page is the Automatic Device Provisioning check box (and with it the Refresh button in the toolbar). You can use this to request an updated profile from Apple without having to manually create it in iTunes Connect, download it, and install it. For practical details, see Chapter 11.

CAUTION

The Import and Export options at the bottom of the window look identical to the ones in the Developer Profile page, but they are completely unrelated. You can use them to import and export individual profile files by hand.

Working with software images

As shown in Figure 10.5, the Software Images page shows the available versions of iOS for each device. When users update their devices with a new version, iTunes manages the process for them. But as a developer, you must test and run beta versions of iOS and manage updates manually.

The update process happens in three stages. First, you must locate the update file, download it, and import it into Xcode. You can then use the software version option on the device pages, described later, to install it on the device. To complete the process, sync the device in iTunes to restore your files and apps.

CAUTION

The update process usually works. Successful developers keep separate devices and use them exclusively for development. Less successful developers use one device and sync regularly. You often can restore to an older version and resync. If this doesn't work, you need to wipe the device, reinstall an older version of iOS, and try to resync again. It's not unusual to lose data when you update, so always sync beforehand.

Figure 10.5

Reviewing the available software images. Behind the scenes, this page is really just a list of firmware files. You can access it in Finder from a contextual right-click menu.

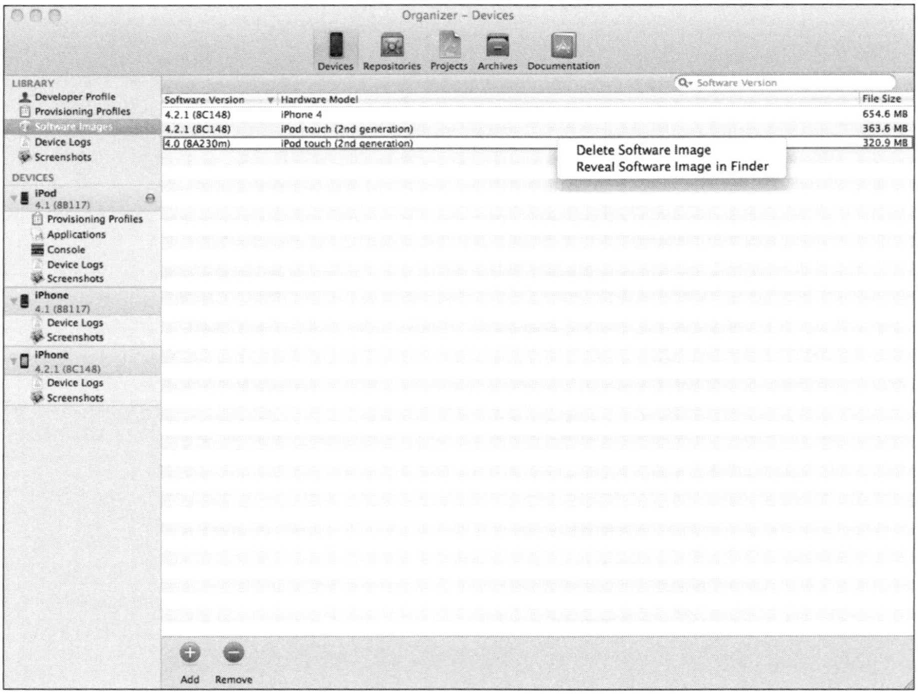

Finding and installing iOS updates

Public updates can be installed via iTunes in the usual way. But beta updates are reserved for developers, and you must download and install the files manually. You typically update device firmware whenever you download a new beta release of the SDK.

When update files are available, they're listed on the iOS Dev Center page. You must select the correct file for each type of device; for example, iPhone 4 firmware isn't compatible with an iPhone 3G, any iPad, or any iPod. To download a file, right-click it and select the Save As… (or equivalent) option in your browser. Firmware files have the `.ipsw` extension.

To import the file into Xcode, select the Add button at the bottom left of the main window. Navigate to the file, and select it to load it. This adds it to the list in this window but doesn't install it. Installation is a device-based process and is described below.

To remove the file from the list, use the Remove option. This deletes the file from Xcode's firmware folders and can't be undone. However, if you have a backup copy of the firmware file elsewhere on disk, you can always import it again.

T I P

Firmware files are big—from 300MB to 500MB. When you add a file, Xcode copies the original to a folder called `/Software Images`. This duplication wastes disk space. It's a good idea to move the original file to a backup server, if you have one, and delete it after Xcode imports it.

T I P

Beta files don't stay on the main developer pages for long. Apple keeps an archive of all previous iOS versions, including betas, GM (gold master) seeds, and finished releases. Unfortunately, there's no reliable static URL for these files. But you can find links to them by searching for "iOS x.y (beta) download", where x.y is the version number.

Using device logs

Device logs provide crash reports and information about memory errors. The list can also include user force-quit events, where the user kills an app deliberately, and watch-dog timeout events, where the OS kills an unresponsive app. The most recent logs are copied to Xcode whenever a device is connected.

Reading crash reports

A crash report (also known as a backtrace) is a context summary and a stack dump. The context includes information about the hardware and OS, and the stack dump is very similar to the real-time dumps available in Xcode's debugger.

Crash reports make it possible to collect crash information from apps that are being run and tested "live." Reports are recorded for every crash, anywhere. The device doesn't have to be connected to a Mac running the Xcode debugger.

C R O S S - R E F E R E N C E

Debugging is introduced in Chapter 15.

Figure 10.6 shows a typical example. The panel at the left is a list of crashes on the selected device. The panel at the right shows the details of each crash. In this example, the stack dump shows that the uSha application has crashed at the [UIView setText:] method. The stack dump doesn't include information about properties and variables, but if you scroll down the list, you can find a similar stack dump for each active thread. You can use these details to make educated guesses about useful breakpoint locations when you test the app with Xcode's debugger.

At the bottom of the report is a list of Binary Images, which includes the apps and libraries running at the time. This feature is a holdover from OS X debugging; you can use it to get information about crashes in plug-ins and libraries. It's less relevant to iOS debugging because the item at the top of the list is usually your app.

Figure 10.6

To make sense of a crash report stack dump, you should understand that events appear in reverse chronological order. The most recent event caused the crash, but earlier events may have prepared it.

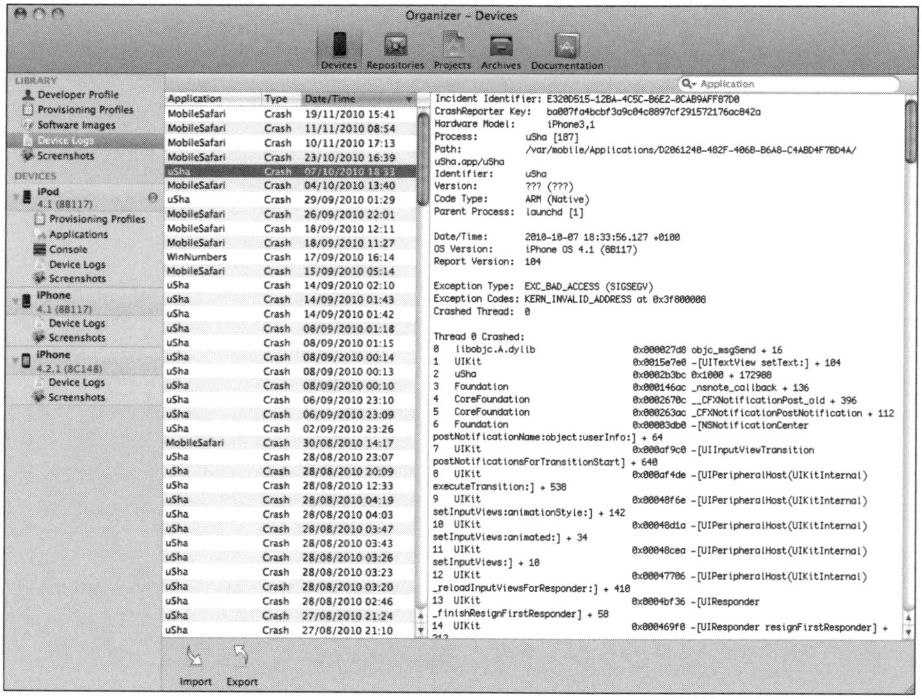

CAUTION

Crash dumps often list internal runtime system calls and undocumented internal Cocoa/Cocoa Touch methods. For example, you may know that objc_msgSend is part of the Objective-C runtime. But the [UIPeripheralHost...] calls internal methods to UIKit, and you won't find them in the documentation. This doesn't often matter, because the backtrace usually shows in your code the method that created a problem. But occasionally with beta code, the dump tells you that you've run into an internal bug, and you'll have to find a workaround until it's fixed.

Understanding low memory reports

Figure 10.7 shows a low memory report. Instead of a stack dump, the panel at the right shows processes and their memory usage. The report lists the application with the biggest memory footprint and includes a table of all loaded processes with a page count for each. A separate status field shows which apps were running and which were unloaded ("jettisoned").

Figure 10.7

Making sense of a low memory report, which is effectively just a process list

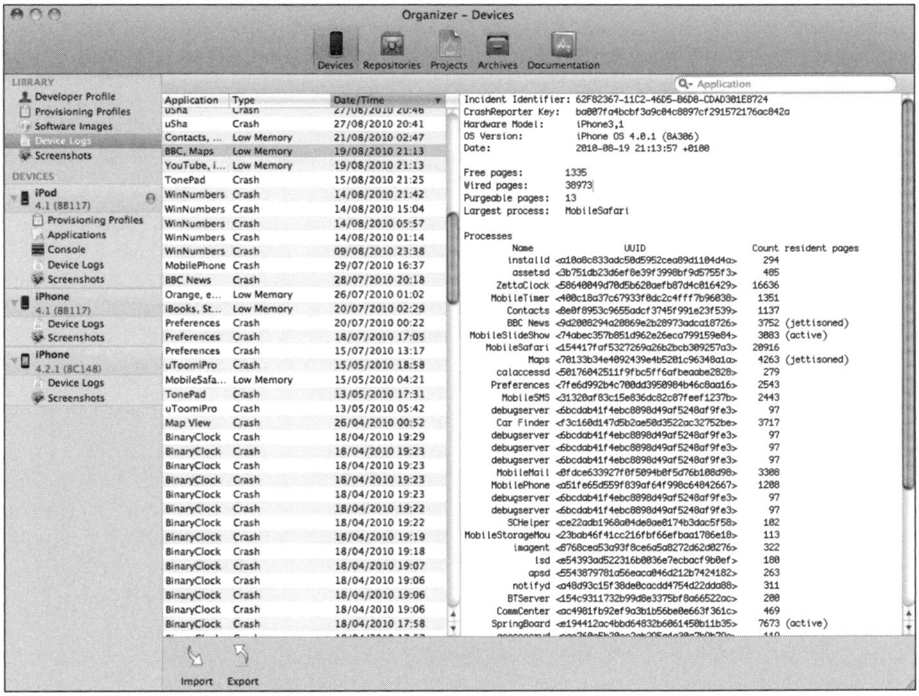

NOTE

Each app and process has a hex UUID, which is simply a long, random number. It doesn't contain useful debugging information.

Although the list doesn't appear very detailed, you can use it to check whether your apps have memory leaks. For example, the ZettaClock app (refer to Figure 10.7), a simple clock app, is using 16,636 memory pages.

Although Mobile Safari tripped the memory error and is using than 20,000 pages, ZettaClock contributed to the low memory and is likely to be leaking. With this information, you can use Xcode's other diagnostic tools to find and eliminate the leak.

Unfortunately, Apple's own apps may hog or leak memory, so memory errors aren't uncommon. But it's easy to use a report to see whether a native app is creating a problem or whether it's one of your apps.

Note that the dump shows only RAM—internal working memory separate from the main flash memory. The available RAM for each device is shown in Table 10.1.

N O T E

iOS supports limited paging. Read-only executables can be paged, but there's no swap file. The available RAM is the system maximum. In practice, as little as 20MB or so may be available to an app. To test memory effectively, use an older device with limited RAM.

Table 10.1 iOS Device Available RAM

Device	Available RAM
iPhone 1st generation	128MB
iPhone 3G	128MB
iPhone 3GS	256MB
iPhone 4	512MB
iPod Touch 1st generation	128MB
iPod Touch 2nd generation	128MB
iPod Touch 3rd generation	256MB
iPod Touch 4th generation	256MB
iPad 1st generation	256MB
iPad 2nd generation	512MB

Importing and exporting device logs

The import and export arrows at the bottom of the window make it possible to pass debugging information back to developers. This isn't a useful feature for solo developers. But team developers can export a crash event from Xcode to a file and share it by e-mail, upload it to a server, and so on. Importing a crash report from a file adds it to the list of current device logs.

Working with screenshots

The Screenshots feature is a convenient way to create, review, and export screenshots of active apps. It bypasses the image download features in iPhoto and iTunes and displays screenshots directly. It offers alternative functionality that overlaps with the standard iOS screenshot options. There's no "killer app" advantage; it does some of the same things in a slightly different way. Typically, you'll use both.

The Organizer's Screenshots feature appears in two locations, with a subtle difference. The main Screenshots option, shown in Figure 10.8, displays saved screenshots for all devices.

Each device has a separate Screenshots option, which includes a green New Screenshot button at the lower right of the page. Click this button to take a screenshot and add it to the display list. This feature is independent of the device's photo library; it doesn't display screenshots created with the standard iOS two-button click operation.

Figure 10.8

Use the Screenshots option to view the screenshot collection.

NOTE

If you're new to iOS, note that you can capture a screenshot manually by pressing and holding down a device's power button and then clicking the Home Button. When you trigger this feature, the screen flashes white and the speaker plays a photo shutter sound. Screenshots are added to the current photo roll, and they can be exported and viewed in iPhoto or in the iTunes image loader.

You can do the following in Screenshots using the icons along the bottom of the page:

- **Remove a screenshot from the list:** This deletes it from the display list and from disk.
- **Export a screenshot:** This saves it to a file location of your choice as an uncompressed PNG file.

- **Nominate the screenshot as an app's launch image:** The launch image appears after the application begins to load but before it runs. This is a simplified and less useful version of the equivalent feature in the Target Build Settings, which are discussed in more detail in Chapter 12.

- **Compare two screenshots to reveal differences:** The comparison applies a difference filter, with a variable tolerance. Color information is ignored, and differences appear white or gray. To select two shots for comparison, hold down the Option (⌥) key and select them with the mouse. Click the Compare check box to see a single combined view.

- **Make a new screenshot, as described above.**

You can access further features using a contextual right-click context menu, including the following (refer to Figure 10.8):

- **Save as Default Image:** This is identical to the Save as Launch Image feature.

- **Open Image with Finder:** This shows the image in Preview. If you have the PNG file type assigned to an editor, it runs the editor and loads the image.

- **Reveal Image in Finder:** This opens the Finder and displays the folder containing the image.

- **Delete Screenshot:** This deletes the image from the display list and from disk.

NOTE

A feature that's missing from the Screenshots page is the ability to upload images to iTunes Connect. (It would also be useful to view screenshots taken with the device itself, but you can't.) To use Screenshots in iTunes Connect, export them to a folder. It can be convenient to keep all PR material for iTunes Connect and supporting web pages in a single location.

Managing individual devices

Whenever you connect an iOS device, the Organizer automatically adds it to the device list shown in Figure 10.9. It also downloads the most recent logs from the device. Connected devices support a wide selection of options, including these:

- A device summary page
- A list of installed provisioning profiles
- A list of installed applications
- A Console dump
- A list of device logs
- A list of screenshots for the device

Figure 10.9

Use the Organizer to view key information about a connected device. You can view a simplified version of this page for disconnected devices, but most of the details in the full view aren't shown.

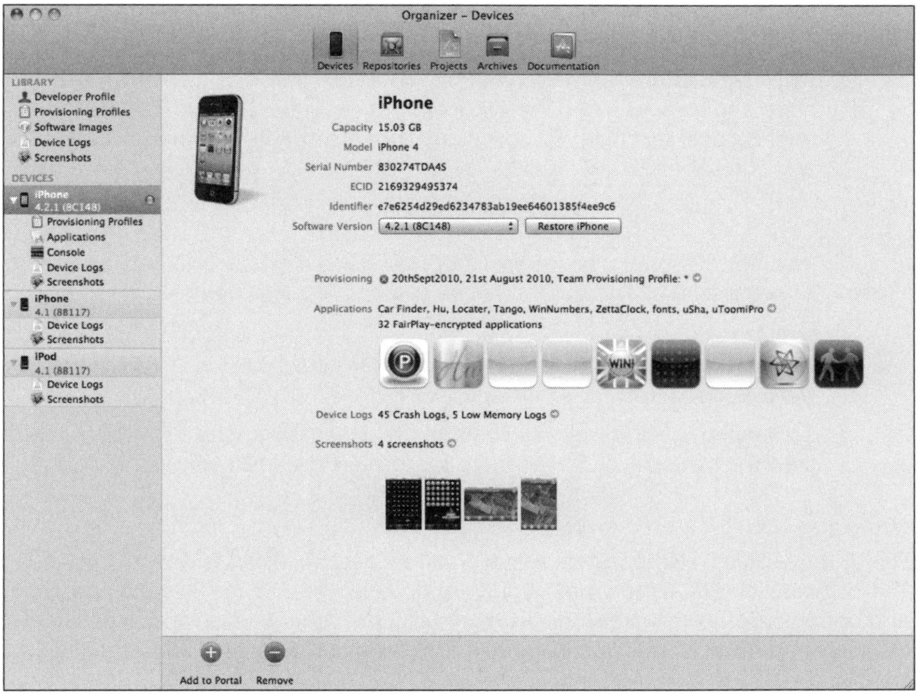

Using the device summary

The device summary displays a selection of useful information about a connected device, including the following:

- **Device type:** iPhone, iPod, or iPad.
- **Device model.**
- **ECID (Exclusive Chip Identification Number):** This is a unique serial number embedded in each device. Apple added ECIDs to iOS devices from the iPhone 3GS onward. The ECID is passed back to Apple's servers when you attempt a firmware restore or update. (The technology is supposed to prevent jailbreaking, but it was circumvented almost immediately.)
- **Identifier:** This is a long hex string and is another unique device identifier. This identifier is embedded in provisioning profiles and in apps downloaded from the app store and is used in the App Store DRM (Digital Rights Management) technology.

- **Software version:** The menu shows the version of iOS installed on the device. You can select other versions and install them by selecting the Restore iPhone button.
- **Provisioning:** This displays a summary of the installed provisioning profiles. A small red cross appears when profiles are out of date. Select the small gray arrow to view the separate Provisioning Profiles page, described later.
- **Applications:** This item lists your test apps. Use the small gray arrow to select the separate Applications page. The app icons appear under the list. The "FairPlay-encrypted applications" text tells you how many apps are installed in total, including test apps and other apps.

NOTE
FairPlay is the name of the DRM technology used to lock apps to a specific device. In theory, it prevents copying. In practice, it's easy to strip it, but apps will then only run on a device with an unlocked DRM and a customized open OS.

- **Device Logs:** This item displays a count of the available logs. To view them in the Device Logs, select the small gray arrow.
- **Screenshots:** This displays a count of the screenshots, with a small preview of each. To view the main device Screenshots page, select the small gray arrow.

Updating the software version

This option is linked to the Software Image feature described earlier. The menu shows the available software images. To add more, you must download the image files and add them using the Add option in Software Image. You also can select the Other Version option from the menu on this page and select a firmware file from disk. Importing the file here adds it to the list that appears on the Software Image page.

Select the Restore iPhone/iPod/iPad button to install the selected firmware. Although this option is labeled Restore, you can use this feature to install recent new firmware.

CAUTION
Always sync your device before changing the firmware. This doesn't guarantee that your contacts, installed apps, and other data will remain safe, but it does make it less likely that you'll lose data.

Using the Add to Portal feature

The two toolbar buttons on this page—Add to Portal and Remove—add and remove a device from the list stored in your account on the Provisioning Portal in iTunes Connect.

In previous versions of Xcode, you could add a device only by copying its identifier string and adding it by hand. Now you can use the Add to Portal feature to automate this process. When you select Add to Portal, Xcode sends the identifier to the portal, and the portal server adds it to your online device list. The server also generates and downloads the certificates and profiles used to provision the device. See Chapter 11 for more details.

N O T E
Ad Hoc—beta test—provisioning is usually done remotely, so you still need to know how to get a device identifier remotely and how to add it to the online device list by hand. For details, see Chapter 11.

Checking provisioning profiles

The device Provisioning Profiles page, shown in Figure 10.10, displays the profiles installed on the device. This list may not match the profiles shown in the more general Provisioning Profiles page in the Library.

Figure 10.10

Check the profiles installed on a device. You can remove expired profiles and install new profiles here.

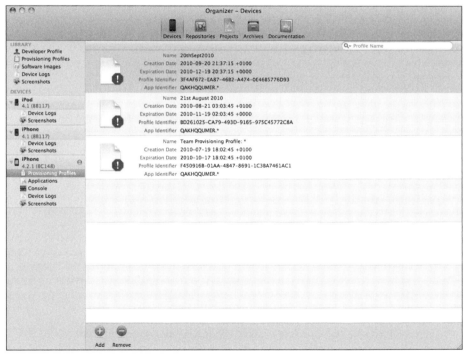

The device list shows the profiles in the device's file system. The general list shows the profiles installed in Xcode. Xcode generates and installs certain device profiles automatically, which is why the two lists are different.

On this page, you can install a profile created and downloaded from the Provisioning Portal. The Add button opens a file selector. Navigate to the file, and select it. It's copied to the device and added to the list.

The Remove button deletes the profile from the device. It's equivalent to the profile deletion feature in the device Settings, but it's easier to access because you can view all installed profiles at the same time.

Profiles aren't large files, but it's useful to delete expired profiles to avoid list clutter on the provisioning pages.

CROSS-REFERENCE

Provisioning is a very complex topic and is described in full in Chapter 11.

Managing applications

The Applications page, shown in Figure 10.11, displays the apps installed on the device. This list includes your own test apps and Apple/third-party apps. Each entry includes the following:

- The name
- The Bundle ID
- The version number
- The minimum OS version
- The icon (if there is one)

For your test apps, you set these details in the build settings, which are described in Chapter 12. You can use this page to check that you have set them correctly.

You have three options for app management:

- **Download:** This copies the files in an app's support directories—/Documents, / Library, and /tmp—to a location on your Mac's disk. You can use this option for debugging to check that files are being created and removed correctly, and to retrieve useful data created by the app.
- **Add:** This copies and installs a precompiled app. Xcode can install an app automatically after a build, so you don't need to use this option while testing. But you can use it to install app files created by other developers for testing, as long as they are supplied with a compatible provisioning profile. You also can use this option to reinstall prebuilt apps after a deletion without rebuilding them.
- **Remove:** This deletes the app from the device.

Figure 10.11

This is where you manage installed applications. This page isn't quite a key feature of Xcode—you can develop apps without it—but it does include useful options.

Viewing the Device Console

The Console page, shown in Figure 10.12, is a simplified iOS version of the OS X Console application. It collects and displays general system logs.

CAUTION

This console is *not* the same as the debugging console described in Chapter 15. The debugging console shows messages from one app. The Device Console shows messages from all apps and from iOS.

There isn't usually much of interest in the console log. Most of the device chatter is hardware-related and includes information about WiFi, battery, USB, and sleep events. You may find the details useful if you are developing hardware accessories, or if you are testing an app with NSLog calls outside the debugger. But aside from the curiosity value, there's little that helps with app debugging and isn't covered in more detail in the Device Logs.

Figure 10.12

Viewing the Device Console, which is just a copy of the main iOS log file

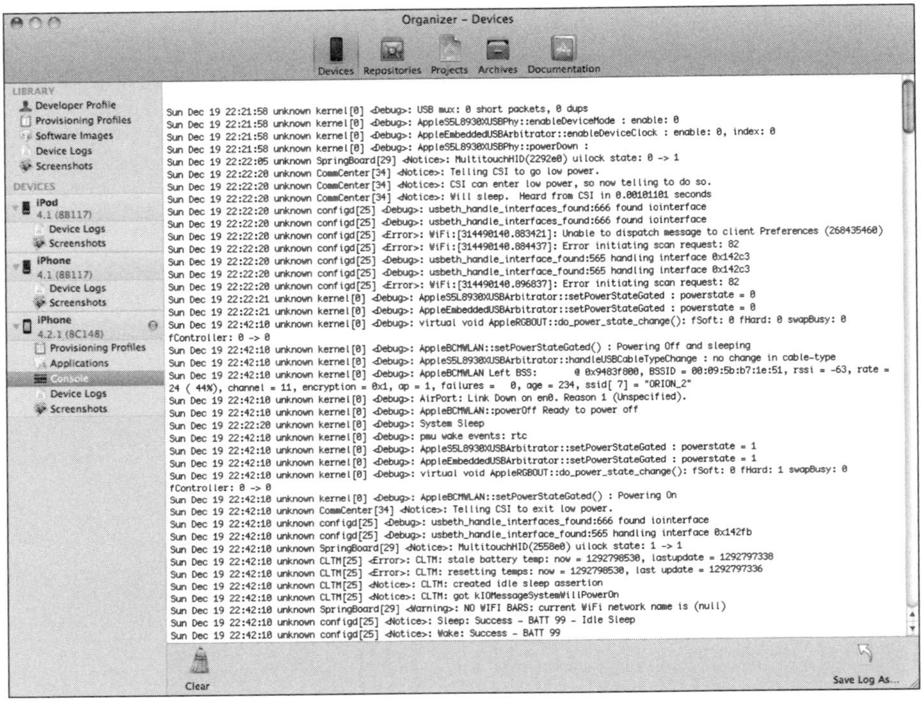

Using Device Logs and Screenshots

These features are identical to the Device Logs and Screenshots in the main Library window, with the minor differences that were described earlier in this chapter.

Working with Projects and Archives

The Organizer's Projects and Archives features include project management and archiving features that aren't available elsewhere in Xcode.

Managing Projects

The Projects window, shown in Figure 10.13, is a long list of recently opened projects with a number of extra features that include snapshot management and cleanup. This feature is a useful extra and can save you time and disk space. It's not a critical part of Xcode, but it can save time and make you more productive.

Figure 10.13

In the Project page, the list at the left is similar to but longer than the recent files list in Xcode's File menu.

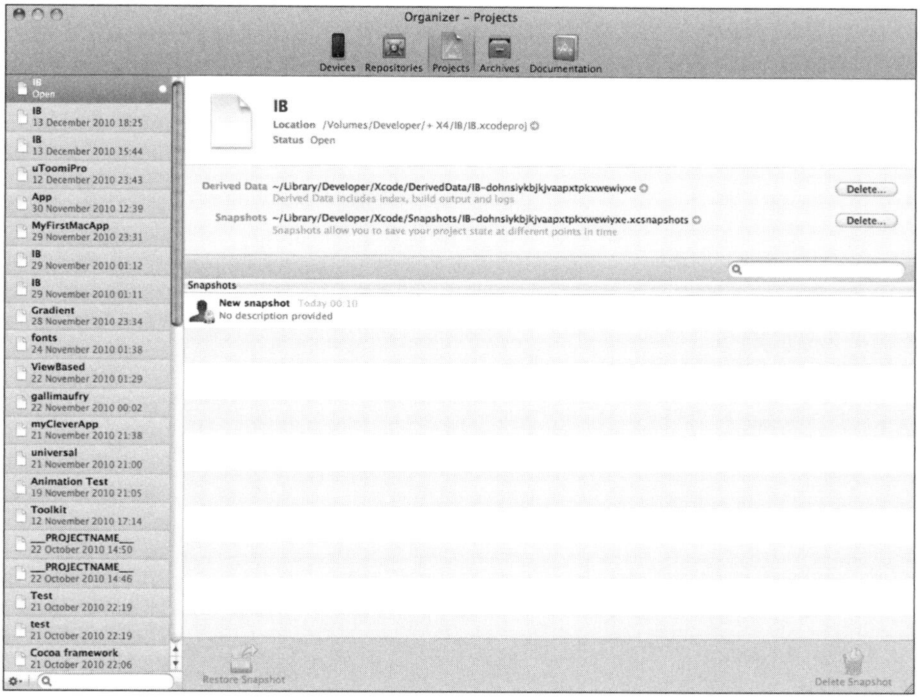

For example, it's often useful to open an older project in Xcode. The main recent files list includes 20 entries. The list on the Projects page grows indefinitely, which makes it a useful shortcut when you want to access older files without looking for them in Finder.

Each entry includes the following features:

- **Double-click to open:** Double-clicking any project in the list loads it into Xcode.
- **Derived Data review:** When you build a project, Xcode creates a collection of temporary files, which are called Derived Data and can take up significant disk space. The gray arrow to the right of Derived Data field for each project opens Xcode's temporary files folder and highlights the project.

TIP
You don't usually need to look inside the build folders. You do need to know where to find the built application, but you can reveal it by clicking the file in the Products group in the Symbol Navigator and using the Show in Finder... option.

- **Derived Data cleanup:** Temporary build files take up unnecessary space. When you complete a project, you can use the Delete option to remove them. This is *not* equivalent to the Product ⇨ Clean option in the main Xcode menu. Clean removes build-related files. Delete removes all other supporting files created by Xcode, including logs and indexes.

- **Snapshot management:** Project snapshots, if any, are listed in the lower part of the main area. You can restore a project to a snapshot (an older state) with the Restore Snapshot button at the lower left of the main area. You also can delete unneeded snapshots to save disk space. You cannot create snapshots here.

NOTE

Xcode 3 created derived data, including build files, in the project folder. Xcode 4 creates derived data in an independent folder. Before you delete a project from disk, use the Delete option in the Organizer to delete this data—otherwise it's never removed. Note that you can click the arrow next to the Derived Data path to open the relevant folder in Finder.

CROSS-REFERENCE

For information about creating and comparing snapshots, see Chapter 14.

Creating Archives

In spite of the name, the Archives feature, shown in Figure 10.14, has nothing to do with archiving or backups in the sense of keeping old copies of source code. In Xcode, an archive is a packaged, provisioned, and code-signed application build that can be sent to beta testers or uploaded to the App Store.

To create an archive, use the Product ⇨ Archive option in the main Xcode menu. Creating an archive adds the app to the list that appears at the left of this page. You can build an archive as often as you want. Each build adds a new entry to the list in the bottom half of the main area.

The buttons at the top left implement three archive-related features:

- **Validate:** This runs basic checks on an archive to confirm that it's suitable for the App Store, and it verifies that the contents have been code-signed correctly.

- **Share:** Use this option to create an Ad Hoc build that can be shared online or attached to an e-mail.

- **Submit:** This uploads the app to the App Store. You need to prepare a marketing description with supporting images and text before the App Store accepts an upload.

CROSS-REFERENCE

For more information about these features, see Chapters 12 and 13.

Figure 10.14

The Archive page, which has nothing to do with backups

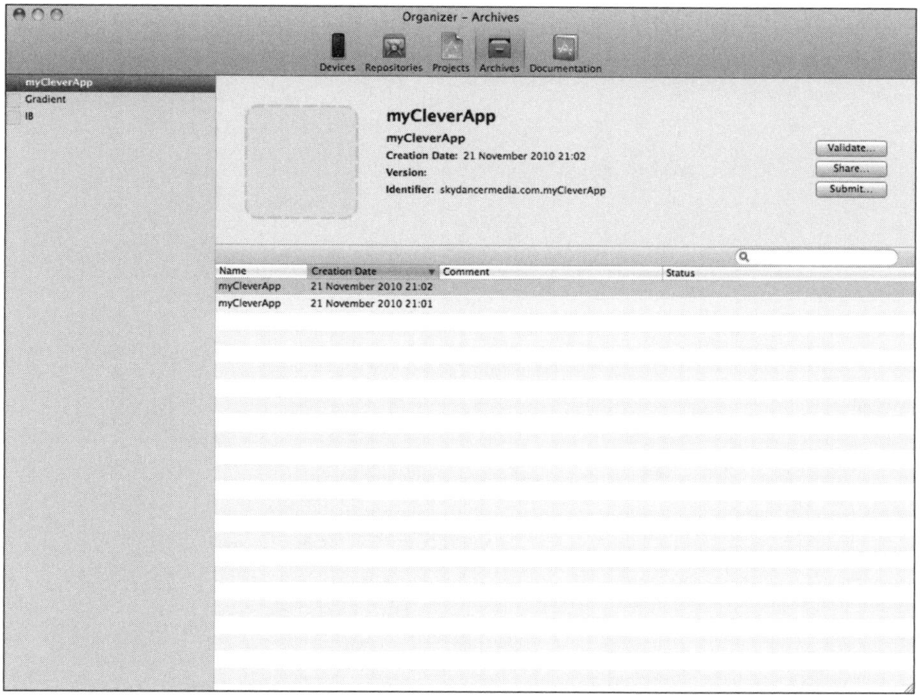

Summary

This chapter introduced the Organizer and described features that aren't covered elsewhere in this book. It explained how to add and manage hardware devices for testing, and how to receive debugging and support information from active devices. It sketched the key features used to implement automatic device provisioning and explained how to copy certificates and provisioning profiles between Macs. It also explored in more detail complex features such as device logs.

Finally, it introduced the Project and Archives pages, explored how to manage projects and their associated support files and snapshots, and explained how to use the Archive features to validate and share apps for deployment and testing.

Managing Certificates and Provisioning

P arts of the development process require secure access to Apple services, so Xcode includes built-in features that manage these. Security management is known as *provisioning*. Provisioning has been simplified in Xcode 4, but it remains a complex process. It can take a few hours to a day to create the initial files, certificates, settings, and permissions that allow app store development. After it's working, you can forget about provisioning for at least three months, because the system doesn't need further attention. After that time, some permissions must be updated regularly. But the update process is much simpler and quicker than the initial setup.

Understanding Provisioning

Provisioning is a set of permissions that allows you to do three things. When provisioning is working, you can do the following:

- **Test apps on iOS hardware:** This requires a Developer Certificate and a Development Provisioning Profile for each test device.
- **Upload apps to the App Store:** This requires a Distribution Certificate and a Distribution Provisioning Profile.
- **Distribute apps to beta testers by e-mail or through website downloads:** This requires both a Distribution Certificate and a separate Ad Hoc Distribution Provisioning Profile.

If provisioning isn't installed properly or your permissions have expired, some or all of the following will happen:

- Xcode won't build your app at all.
- Xcode won't allow you to install an app on an iOS device for testing.
- If the app is installed, it won't run.
- Existing test apps stop working when their permissions expire.
- iOS devices owned by beta testers won't run your test build.

In This Chapter

Understanding provisioning

Creating and installing certificates/identities for iOS development

Provisioning iOS devices

Provisioning for OS X development

Each profile and certificate is a file. In outline, provisioning has two components:

- **Personal developer details:** These files are called certificates or identities. They match an identity in your Mac's keychain, allowing Xcode to confirm that you are who you claim to be, and that you have the privileges needed to test apps on devices or upload them to the App Store.
- **Device details:** These files are called profiles. They allow a device to run test apps signed by a given developer.

Both certificates and profiles are files with embedded digital keys. The provisioning process would be much simpler if the files were created and installed in a standard way. Unfortunately, they aren't. Certificates are installed in your personal login keychain. Profiles are managed in Xcode. Both are created on the Provisioning Portal, but they need different and unrelated user input.

You can work through the provisioning process in two ways:

- **Manually:** The Apple developer website includes a profile manager area called the iOS Provisioning Portal, shown in Figure 11.1. To create provisioning files, you must upload information—such as a unique user key and various device identifier codes—to the portal. The portal generates the required files. You can then download them from the portal and install them in Xcode or in your keychain, as needed.
- **Automatically:** The device provisioning process has been automated in Xcode 4. Personal setup is still manual, but the part that manages test devices has been simplified. It can be as simple as a one-click operation.

This chapter introduces manual provisioning in detail, so you can work through the initial setup process and understand the requirements and options. Automated provisioning is described toward the end of the chapter.

You can develop apps for the iOS Simulator and for OS X without provisioning. You can also (for the time being) sell OS X apps independently of the App Store. But if you don't set up provisioning, you can't test apps on your own iOS hardware.

Note that even with provisioning, permissions are time-limited. After permissions expire, apps built for hardware testing stop working. You can renew their permissions only with a valid developer subscription. This means that any apps you create stop working after a time, unless you're a registered developer. To use your own apps indefinitely, you must upload them to the app store, have them accepted, give yourself a free gift certificate, and then "buy" the app with the certificate.

CROSS-REFERENCE
This chapter explains how to generate, download, and install the files used by the provisioning process. You need to make some changes to a project's build settings before you use these files to distribute projects, and this process is described in detail in Chapter 12. Don't try to submit your projects to the App Store until you've worked through that chapter.

Figure 11.1

A first look at the iOS Provisioning Portal

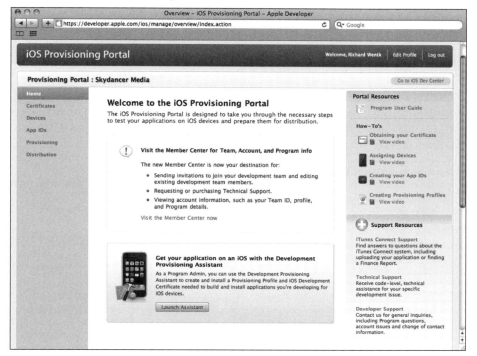

Introducing provisioning requirements

Before you can get started with provisioning, you need three items:

- **A digital identity:** This is a digital key file generated on your Mac and uploaded to the Provisioning Portal.

- **One or more device Uniform Device Identifiers (UDIDs):** These are long hex codes that uniquely define an iOS device. You can obtain them from beta testers, who can read them in iTunes, as described later in this chapter. Xcode also can display the UDID of your own local test devices.

- **An Application ID:** The App ID is an arbitrary string. You can use the same string for multiple applications, and you can use a generic star character as a wildcard. However, Apple services, such as Push Notification and In-App purchase, require apps with a unique ID.

Avoiding provisioning confusion

One source of confusion is Apple's imprecise jargon. You'll see certificates referred to as identities, and it's not clear how they differ from each other or from provisioning profiles.

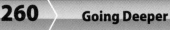

For simplicity, treat certificates and identities as if they're interchangeable. Technically, there are minor differences, but in practice you can ignore them. Both are associated with your personal identity.

Provisioning profiles manage device and app identity.

The key principle is code signing. When you build a project, Xcode includes a digital signature file. iOS hardware and the App Store both check that this signature is valid.

You might think this means that Xcode attaches a public key to your builds, but the process is much more complex, and it involves the interaction of your key, a master Apple key, software permissions, hardware access permissions, and app-specific permissions, included in a selection of different files.

You begin by generating a digital key, with public and private elements. You use the public key to create development and distribution certificates that include your key and add a further layer of permissions. Then you install the development and distribution certificates in your keychain. This also installs them in Xcode.

Xcode uses the two generated certificates as signing identities. This is because team development can support many separate identities for testing—one for each developer—but only a single identity for distribution.

Team management adds an extra level of complication to code signing. Apple's team management features allow lead developers to control which team members are allowed to test on hardware. They also limit distribution privileges to the team leader—also known as the team agent.

If you're a solo developer, the team management features are irrelevant because you're leader, agent, and contributing developer. Unfortunately, there's no way to bypass these extra features. So for solo developers, the provisioning process includes significant extra overhead you can't ignore.

To download the developer and distribution profiles, you upload your unique digital key as part of a Certificate Signing Request (CSR). The Provisioning Portal then asks the team manager (or you) to accept or decline the request.

If the request is accepted, the Portal generates the requested certificate, and you can download and install it. If the request is declined, nothing happens.

By default, debug builds are already set up to include the development profile. Release builds aren't, and you must modify the Xcode build settings to include your distribution profile before you can upload an app to the App Store.

CAUTION

The two profiles are mutually exclusive. You can sign a build with one or the other, but not both. This means you can't run a final distribution build on your own hardware or in the Simulator. Xcode is deliberately set up to make this impossible. This means there's no final preflight test for App Store app loads. You must debug and test your app, create an App Store build, and hope it works—because you can't run it to be sure.

One further source of confusion is an extra certificate, known as the WWDR (World Wide Developer Relations) intermediate certificate. You must download and install this certificate to guarantee that your developer and distribution certificates are valid. This isn't a difficult step, but it adds one more possible source of error.

Certificates are only part of the process. You also must create separate provisioning profiles to manage device and application permissions. Development provisioning profiles enable hardware testing in Xcode. When Xcode has a valid development certificate and a valid device provisioning profile for a device, you run and debug your code on that device.

Distribution provisioning profiles are used to control access to distribution channels. An App Store distribution profile gives you permission to upload an app to the store.

Ad Hoc distribution profiles enable beta distribution that bypasses the App Store and allows testers to load your beta builds into their devices using iTunes.

All provisioning profiles are locked to specific devices. You specify the supported devices when you create the profile. If a device doesn't have a profile that matches details embedded in a build, the app won't run.

Provisioning profiles are also locked to specific apps, through the App ID. You can specify a unique app name—and this is obligatory for access to Apple services including in-app purchase, push notification, or game center. If you don't need these special services, you can use a generic app name that includes a wildcard character and defines a suite of apps.

If the provisioning process seems complicated, it is. You don't need to understand the principles to use it, but you'll find it easier to work with if you do. Table 11.1 includes a summary of the key elements introduced so far.

TIP
For hardware testing, it's helpful to think of an App ID as a container for one or more device IDs.

Table 11.1 Provisioning Elements

Elements	Reports an Error If...
Public/private user key	An identity file generated from a digital key created on your Mac and stored in your keychain. It identifies you as a unique individual and allows Xcode to check and confirm your other permissions. The public element of the key is included in your certificates. The private element stays on your Mac and is used as a check.
WWDR certificate	An Apple-generated permissions file which confirms that you are an Apple developer, and that you're allowed to use Xcode for testing and development.

continued

Table 11.1 Continued

Elements	Reports an Error If...
Developer certificate/identity	A permissions file that signs an app build, and allows Xcode to create test builds for individual iOS devices. (Not needed for Simulator testing.)
Distribution certificate/identity	A permissions file that signs an app build and makes it possible to upload apps to the App Store—but *doesn't* allow local running or testing.
Development provisioning profile	A permissions file installed on one or more devices. It allows a specified developer to install and run test builds on those devices.
App Store distribution provisioning profile	A permissions file installed in Xcode. It allows an app or app suite to be uploaded to the App Store.
Ad Hoc distribution provisioning profile	A permissions file sent to beta testers with a beta build, which allows them to install and run that build. The profile includes a list of devices allowed to run the build.
App ID	An arbitrary string that identities an app, or a collection of apps from a single developer.
Device Identifier/UDID	A hex number that uniquely identifies an iOS device.
Certificate Signing Request (CSR)	A request uploaded to the portal by a developer requesting hardware testing or distribution build privileges.
Device list	A list of devices associated with a developer's account on the Provisioning Portal. The list is used to generate device profiles, developer profiles, and ad hoc profiles. Each profile is locked to one or more devices in the list.

Creating and Installing User Certificates

The easiest way to work through the provisioning process is to break it down into steps. Ignore your devices for now. Start by creating your development and distribution certificates, following the sequence below:

1. **Create a CSR on your Mac.**

2. **Upload the CSR to the Provisioning Portal to request a development certificate.**

3. **Approve the request. Download the development certificate.**

4. **Download the WWDR certificate, which is generated automatically with the development certificate.**

5. **Upload the CSR again to the Provisioning Portal to request a distribution certificate.**

6. **Approve the request. Download the distribution certificate.**

7. **Add all three certificates to your keychain.**

   This step installs the certificates in Xcode automatically.

Figure 11.2 summarizes these steps graphically.

Figure 11.2

How to generate and install development and distribution profiles

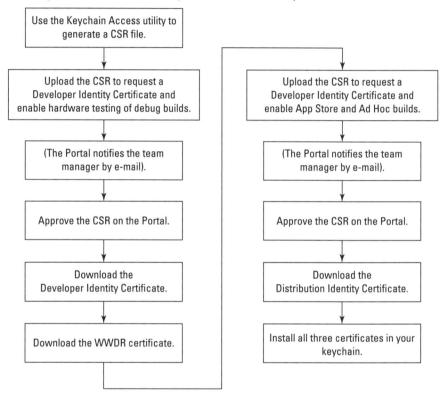

Creating a CSR

The CSR is a digital key (a series of numbers) that identities you as a unique individual. Technically, it uses a combination of public and private keys to identify you securely. The public key is included in the certificates generated by the iOS Provisioning Profile. The private key is stored in your Mac's keychain. Xcode combines the two keys to confirm your identity.

CAUTION

This system isn't as secure as it seems. If your Mac is stolen and your main system password is easy to guess, the stored keys and web passwords may include enough information for a skilled third party to impersonate you online. Although the key system is supposed to prevent app piracy, its relatively easy to strip out the keys from an app and distribute it illegally to users who have *jailbroken*—bypassed the security—in their iOS devices. It's more realistic to think of the key system as an access tool for Xcode than as an anti-piracy or anti-identity-theft measure.

To create a CSR, use your Mac's Keychain Access application. You can find it in `/Application/Utilities`. Select Keychain Access ⇨ Certificate Assistance ⇨ Request a Certificate From a Certificate Authority.

Enter the username and e-mail address you used when you registered as a developer. Leave the CA (Certificate Authority) Email Address field blank. Select the options labeled Saved to disk and Let me specify key pair information, as shown in Figure 11.3.

Figure 11.3

To create a CSR, enter your name and e-mail address and select the CSR options.

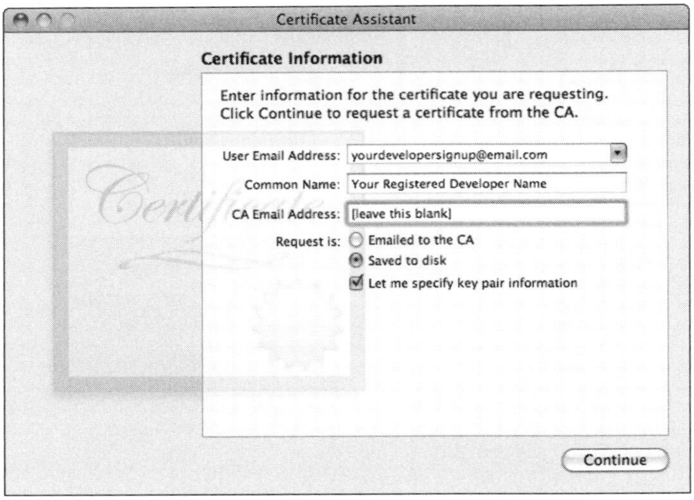

TIP

Before you start, create a folder or subfolder for files used in the provisioning process, so you know where they are. The default save location for the CSR file is the desktop, which may not be ideal.

CAUTION

You must keep a record of the details you enter here; they're essential if you move to another Mac.

Select the filename and save path on the next sheet, so the file is saved to your new `Provisioning` folder. Set the Key Size to 2048 bits and the Algorithm to RSA, as shown in Figure 11.4. When Keychain Access creates the certificate, it gives you the option of viewing its location in Finder. By default, the filename is CertificateSigningRequest.certSigningRequest. You need to know the location of this file for the next part of the process, where you upload the CSR to the iOS Provisioning Profile.

Figure 11.4

To create a CSR, set the Key Size and Algorithm.

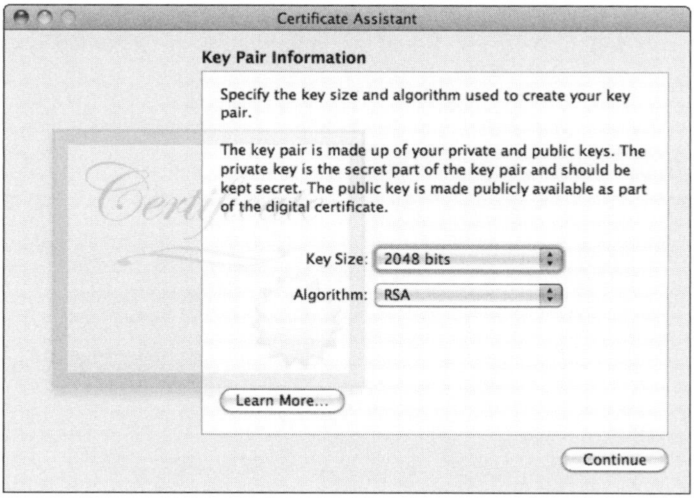

Uploading the CSR to the Provisioning Portal

Now that you have a file with a public key that identifies you, you must upload it to the Provisioning Portal. When you use the Portal to generate a certificate, the key is embedded in it, and Xcode uses it to confirm your build, testing, and distribution permissions.

NOTE

The CSR file created in the previous step is for upload only. Although the key inside the file is referenced by Xcode, the file itself isn't. When you need to re-provision from scratch—certificates expire after a year—it can be useful to keep a copy of the file, so you can skip the initial key generation step.

To convert a CSR file into a development or distribution certificate, follow these steps:

1. **On the Portal, select Certificates and then select either Development or Distribution.**

2. **Click the Request Certificate button.**

3. **Upload your CSR file.**

4. **Approve the request.**

Ignore the auto-generated e-mail message.

5. **Download the certificate.**

You must repeat this sequence for each of the two certificates: development and distribution. As a separate step, you also must download the WWDR certificate.

6. **Log in to your iOS developer account, and open the iOS Provisioning Profile. Select Certificates from the column at the left, and select Development from the tabs. Click the Request Certificate button at the right of the page.**

The first time you do this, the page should be similar to the one shown in Figure 11.5.

Figure 11.5

Getting ready to upload the CSR and generate a development certificate

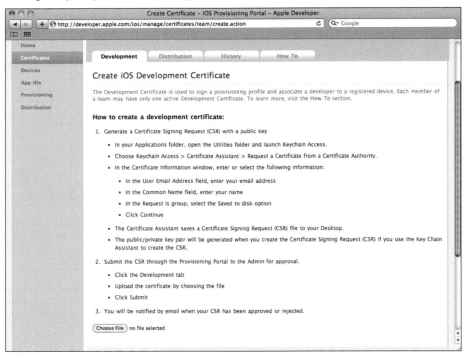

CAUTION

This page is visible only when you don't have a valid development certificate. You can't request another certificate if you already have one.

7. **Select the Choose File button at the bottom left, and navigate to the CSR file created in Step 6. Click Submit to confirm the file upload.**

The Portal auto-generates an e-mail informing you of the CSR. If you're a solo developer, ignore the e-mail; you're in the correct part of the Portal to approve the CSR.

The page should now look like the one shown in Figure 11.6. The Team Signing Requests area at the bottom of the page lists your CSR, and the two buttons at the bottom right of the page give you the choice to approve or reject the request.

8. **Select the check box under the Signing Requests tab to the top left of your name—it's not selected by default—and click Approve Selected.**

Figure 11.6

Approving the CSR

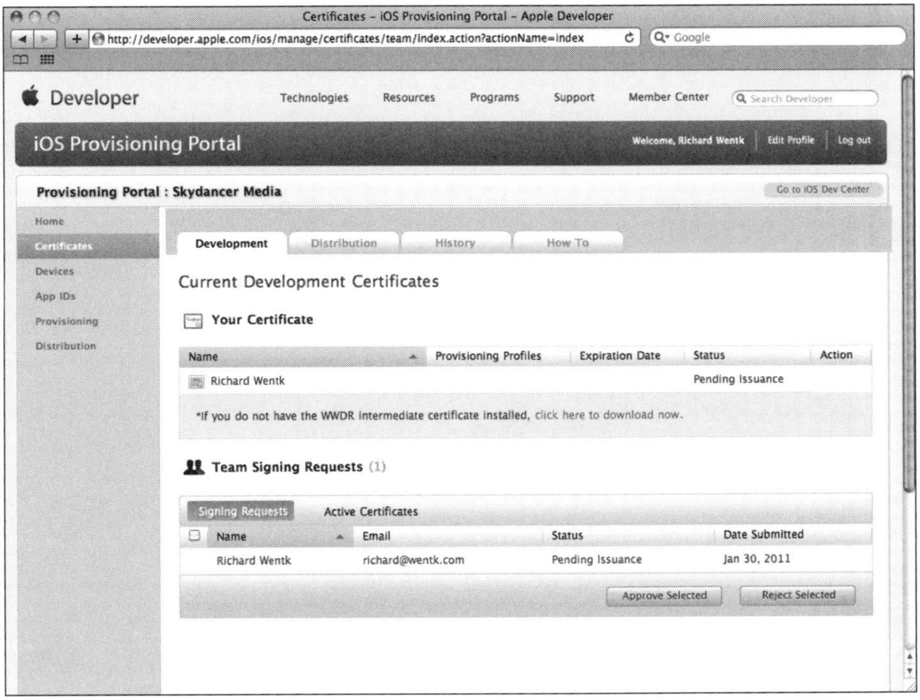

CAUTION

Traditionally, the Portal does something buggy at this point. Previously, the portal seemed to ignore the request, although if you refreshed the page you'd find that a certificate was generated correctly. At the time of writing, the Portal asks you to select a signing request, even though you've already selected one. If you click past the error and refresh the page, you find that a certificate is available for download. Future versions may or may not work correctly. Keep this in mind when using the Portal.

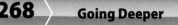

Creating and downloading a development certificate

When you refresh the page, you see that a new certificate has appeared, with two new buttons named Download and Revoke.

Revoke cancels the validity of a certificate. Download copies the certificate to your Mac, as shown in Figure 11.7. The file is named `developer_identity.cer`. If you're using Safari, the file appears in the standard downloads folder.

Figure 11.7

Downloading the development certificate

![Screenshot of the iOS Provisioning Portal showing the Certificates page with a Downloads window displaying developer_identity.cer]

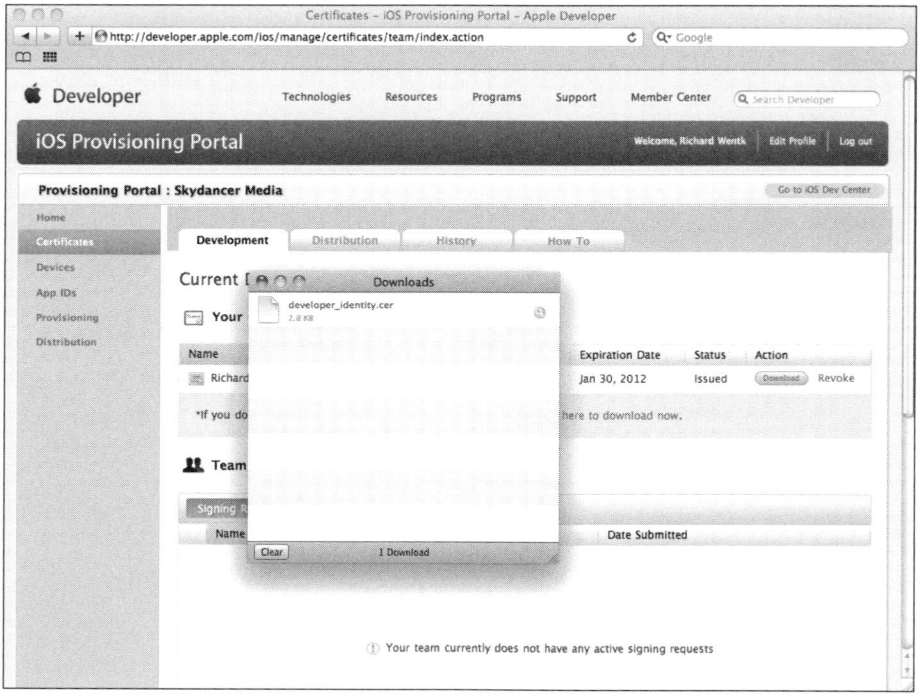

Next, download the Apple WWDR certificate from the link under the development certificate. Optionally, you can move the certificates from the default download folder to your provisioning folder.

Creating and downloading a distribution certificate

Click the Distribution tab on the same page, and repeat the process again. Click the Request Certificate Button, and upload your certificate.

You may be confused by the Pending Issuance message shown in Figure 11.8. If you're a solo developer, there are no Approve/Reject options on this page. So how do you get to the download screen? The answer is simple, but not obvious; you reload the page. You see the Download and Revoke options, as before, and you can download the distribution certificate in the same way. The file is named `distribution_identity.cer`.

Figure 11.8

Dealing with "Pending issuance"

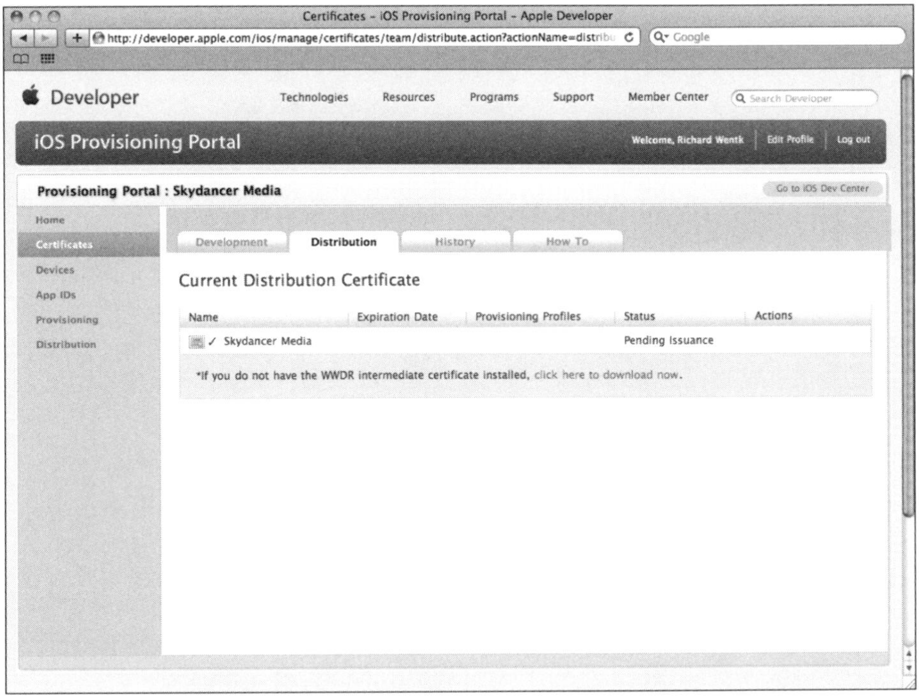

![Screenshot of Certificates – iOS Provisioning Portal – Apple Developer page showing the Distribution tab with a Current Distribution Certificate listing "Skydancer Media" with Status "Pending Issuance".]

N O T E
If you've signed up for the developer program as an incorporated business, the distribution certificate is labeled with your business name rather than your personal name. But it's still based on your personal public key.

Installing the certificates

To install each certificate, navigate to it in Finder and double-click it. Repeat this for all three certificates. Double-clicking a certificate launches the Keychain Assistant and confirms that the certificate has been added to your login Keychain. After you install the certificates, you should see all three in the Keychain, as shown in Figure 11.9.

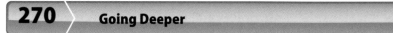

If you click the developer or distribution certificates, you see they include your private key. If you click the Keys category, you find the key installed there.

After installation, you can modify the Xcode build settings to create a distribution build for both Ad Hoc and App Store distribution, as described in Chapter 12. But you can't yet create a test build for a specific iOS device. To complete the process, you must create at least one device provisioning profile.

Figure 11.9

All three certificates are installed in your keychain. Xcode reads them from the keychain automatically.

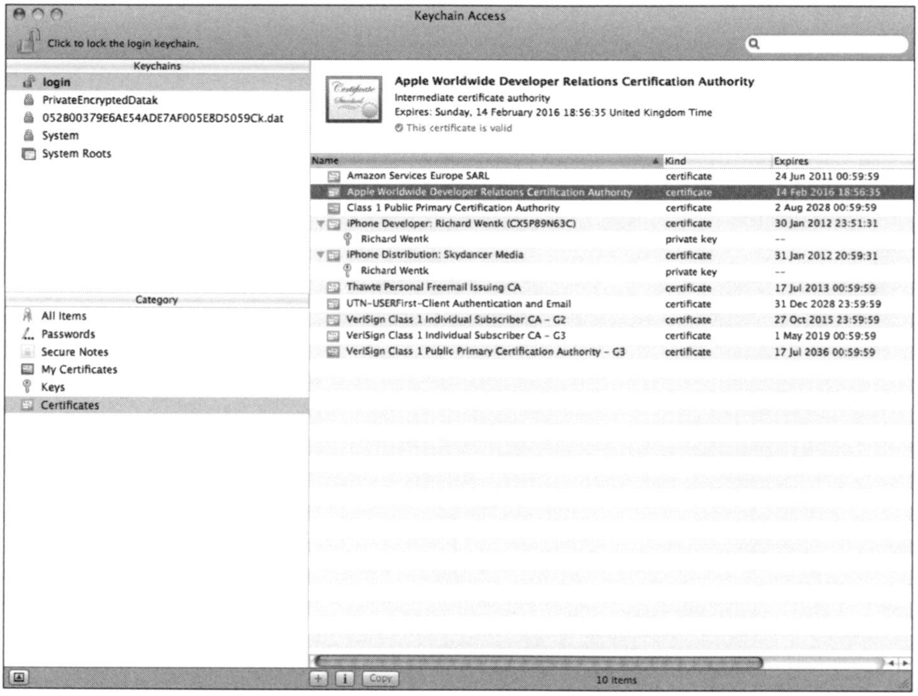

N O T E

The Certificates list includes a number of other certificates. These certificates aren't relevant to provisioning; they manage general online security. You can filter the list to show your own keys by selecting the My Certificates category. This filtered list doesn't include the WWDR certificate.

NOTE
By default, the certificates are valid for a year. When they expire, you must repeat the key generation and installation process. If you keep your original CSR file, you can reuse it, which is a good idea, because if you generate a new key, your key list becomes unnecessarily cluttered.

Provisioning Devices Manually

In addition to certificate generation, the Provisioning Portal also manages your test devices and creates downloadable provisioning profiles. For hardware testing, the provisioning profiles are the final stage in the security chain. When you install a profile on a device, iOS checks that the device is registered for testing, that you have permission to install and run test builds on it, and that the provisioning profile supports a specific App ID. All of these conditions must be true before iOS allows a test build to run on a device.

Figure 11.10 summarizes the device provisioning process. The steps are described in more detail here.

Figure 11.10

Generating and using device provisioning profiles to allow testing on specific devices

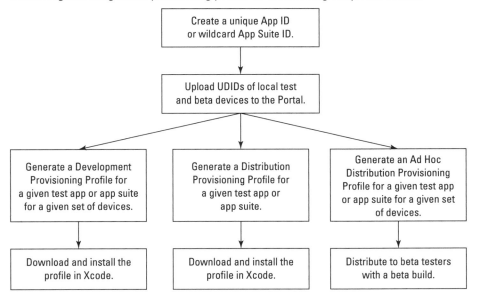

To generate device profiles, follow these steps:

1. **Create an app ID.**

   An App ID is embedded in every provisioning profile, so you must begin here.

2. **Upload at least one UDID to the Provisioning Portal, and use it to create a Device Provisioning Profile.**

3. **Install the device profile in Xcode.**

   You can now create a debug build and install that build on your chosen device, for live testing.

4. **Optionally, upload further UDIDs and update the Device Provisioning Profile to support these devices for your given App ID. Reinstall the updated profile in Xcode.**

   You can now create and run test builds on these other devices.

5. **Optionally, create an Ad Hoc Distribution Profile.**

   You can select some or all of the supported devices from your list of uploaded devices.

6. **Use the Build Archive feature and the Share feature in the Organizer to create an app for beta testers.**

   (This option is described in detail in Chapters 12 and 13.)

Steps 2 through 4 are now semi-automated for local test devices. But if you create ad hoc builds for beta testers, you must understand how to obtain their UDIDs, manage them on the Portal, and create a provisioning profile that includes them.

Creating an App ID

An App ID isn't just a string; it tags the app's bundle and controls access to various special services. A unique ID defines a single app. An ID that includes a wildcard defines a suite of apps.

- Unique IDs can be configured to give an app access to Apple's live services: in-app purchasing, push notification, and game center.
- Unique IDs also can be linked to specific hardware accessories.
- Keychain access in an iOS device gives all apps with a shared wildcard ID the same access privileges, so they can share passwords and other securely stored data.
- If you don't need to support special features or shared security, use a wildcard ID for convenience. You can use the same ID for all your apps.

CAUTION

Don't use a wildcard ID if your apps access the Keychain, unless you explicitly want to enable password sharing. If you create two apps with a common wildcard ID that store passwords, the passwords are shared automatically. This may not be the behavior you want.

The process as a whole sounds more complex than it really is. In previous versions of Xcode, you were forced to create the App ID manually. In later versions, including Xcode 4, the process has been automated and simplified, so now it mostly "just works."

To create a valid ID, follow these steps:

Creating a suite ID

1. **On the Portal, select App IDs.**

2. **Click the New App ID button at the top right, and fill in the fields as shown in Figure 11.11.**

   - **Description:** Type a string. This description is for your reference only, but it does appear elsewhere on the portal and in Xcode, so it's a good idea to keep it short, such as MyApp, AppOne, GameOne, and so on.

   - **Bundle Seed ID:** Leave this set to Generate New.

   - **Bundle Identifier (App ID Suffix):** You can either type * as a wildcard or com. domainname. *. Use the latter if your app will be exchanging data with other apps through URL schemes, UTIs, and other more advanced options. Use a single * for a simple self-contained app.

CROSS-REFERENCE

For a very short introduction to URL schemes, UTIs, and so on, see Chapter 17.

3. **Click the Submit button when you're finished.**

   The Portal immediately creates your new suite/wildcard ID and takes you back to the App ID page. The new ID appears at the bottom of the page. The 10-letter string defines the prefix.

CAUTION

There is no way—at all—to delete app IDs. After you create one, it stays in your account forever. So it's a good idea not to get too experimental with ID creation, because you won't be able to clean up the ID list later.

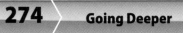

Figure 11.11

The Portal App ID settings for a wildcard/suite ID

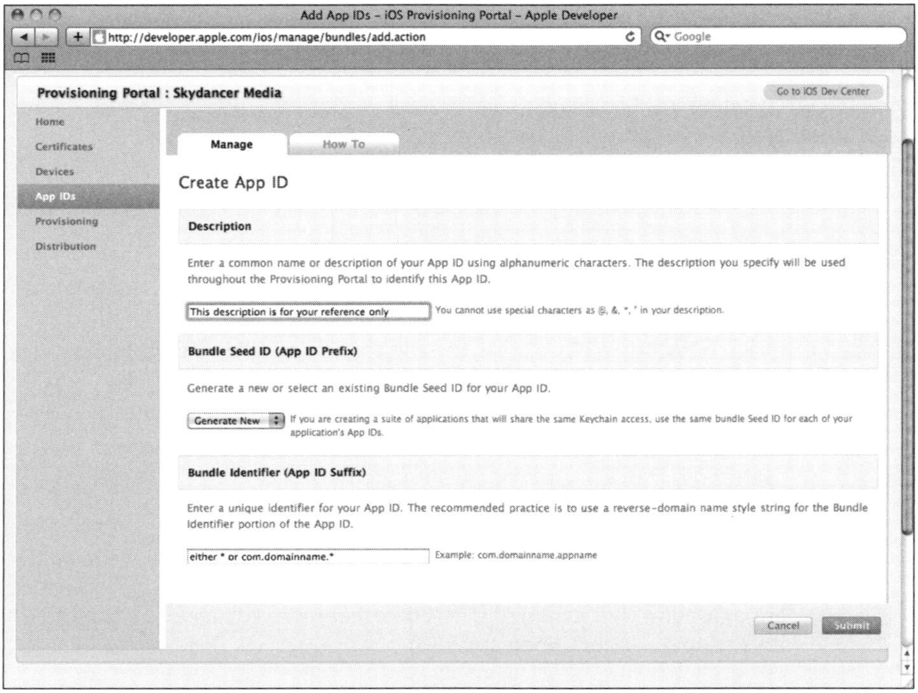

Creating a single ID

You can use a suite ID for general app development, as long as you understand the security restrictions described earlier. If you don't need the features of a unique app ID, skip the rest of this section and move straight to device provisioning.

To create a single ID that supports in-app purchase and other special services, repeat the process with some minor differences:

1. **Click the New App ID button again.**

2. **Enter another description.**

3. **Select the 10-letter suite ID from the Bundle Seed ID menu.**

4. **Type a unique app name into the Bundle Identifier box, as shown in Figure 11.12.**

   Don't type a wildcard; the name must be unique.

5. **Click Submit, and you see your new ID has been added to the list again.**

Figure 11.12

The Portal App ID settings for a unique ID

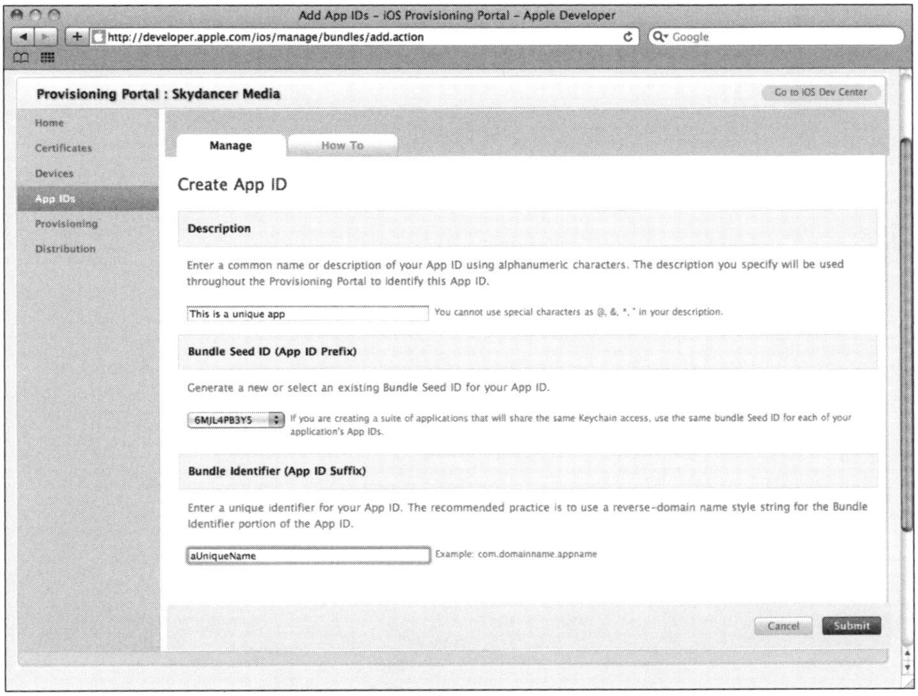

TIP

If you want a single App ID, why not skip straight to this step and type the reverse-domain string as the suffix immediately? Because sometimes you'll find you want a related suite ID. You can't create a suite ID from a single ID, but you can create a single ID from a suite ID. If you're *sure* you need a single unique ID, skip the first step and type the reverse-domain string right away.

Enabling other features

When you've created a wildcard/suite ID and a single app ID, the list at the bottom of the App IDs page should look similar to Figure 11.13. You can see that the extra features for the wildcard/suite ID are marked unavailable. Because this ID is generic, they're permanently disabled. If your app doesn't need them, you can skip the rest of this section.

However, they're enabled for the single ID. If you want to use in-app purchase or the game center, you don't need to do anything more—except write the code.

However, if you want your app to support push notification, you need to perform some further initialization, because the Configurable for Development and Configurable for Production options require two further certificates.

Figure 11.13

Reviewing the individual and wildcard/suite IDs on the Portal

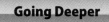

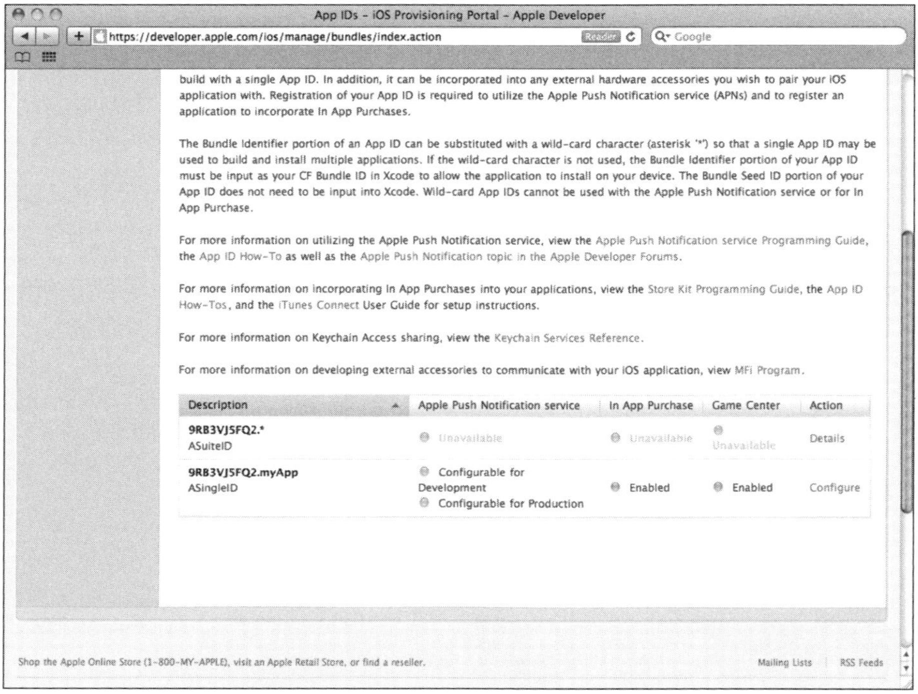

To create them, follow these steps:

1. Select the Configure button at the right of the ID.

2. You see the page shown in Figure 11.14.

3. Click the Configure button next to one of the certificates.

You're asked for a CSR file; you can use the same one from the earlier steps. (You did remember to save it, didn't you?)

4. When the Portal creates a certificate, download it.

5. Repeat for the other certificate.

Don't add these certificates to your keychain; they should be installed on your push notification server.

NOTE

Setting up a server is beyond the scope of this book, but the Portal page shown in the figure includes links to the relevant documentation.

Figure 11.14

Creating push notification server certificates

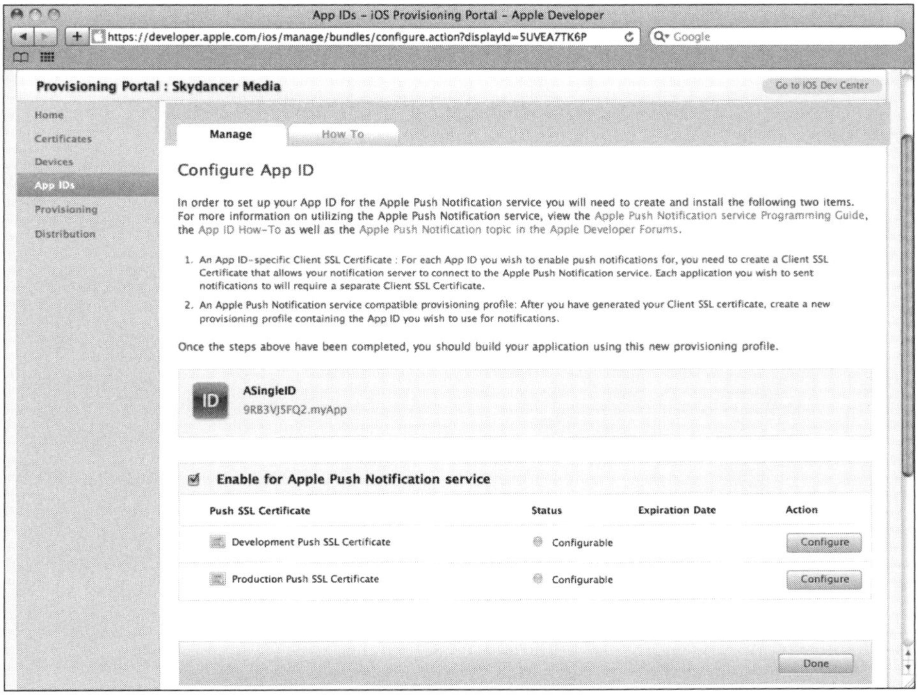

App IDs – iOS Provisioning Portal – Apple Developer

https://developer.apple.com/ios/manage/bundles/configure.action?displayId=5UVEA7TK6P

Provisioning Portal : Skydancer Media   Go to iOS Dev Center

Home
Certificates
Devices
App IDs
Provisioning
Distribution

| Manage | How To |

Configure App ID

In order to set up your App ID for the Apple Push Notification service you will need to create and install the following two items. For more information on utilizing the Apple Push Notification service, view the Apple Push Notification service Programming Guide, the App ID How-To as well as the Apple Push Notification topic in the Apple Developer Forums.

1. An App ID-specific Client SSL Certificate : For each App ID you wish to enable push notifications for, you need to create a Client SSL Certificate that allows your notification server to connect to the Apple Push Notification service. Each application you wish to sent notifications to will require a separate Client SSL Certificate.

2. An Apple Push Notification service compatible provisioning profile: After you have generated your Client SSL certificate, create a new provisioning profile containing the App ID you wish to use for notifications.

Once the steps above have been completed, you should build your application using this new provisioning profile.

ASingleID
9RB3VJ5FQ2.myApp

☑ **Enable for Apple Push Notification service**

Push SSL Certificate	Status	Expiration Date	Action
Development Push SSL Certificate	⊙ Configurable		[Configure]
Production Push SSL Certificate	⊙ Configurable		[Configure]

[Done]

Registering devices manually

Now that you have an App ID, you can start adding test devices. The portal includes support for manual device management. You must understand this option to create valid beta builds. For local device testing, Xcode includes a semi-automated option that simplifies provisioning. You still need to register your devices, but it's a quick process:

1. Find the Device ID/UDID.

2. Drag-select and copy it to the clipboard.

3. Add the UDID to the device list on the Portal.

Finding a Device ID in Xcode

With the new automated provisioning, you don't usually need to manage local devices manually. But for completeness, the details are included here:

1. **To find the UDID in Xcode, connect your device to your Mac, and launch Xcode.**

2. **Select Window⇨Organizer in the main Xcode menu to open the Organizer window.**

3. **Select the Devices tab, and click the Device with the green LED in the Devices list at the left.**

You see the screen shown in Figure 11.15. The field labeled Identifier is the UDID.

4. **Drag-select and copy the UDID from this field to your clipboard.**

Figure 11.15

Finding a UDID in the Organizer in Xcode is easy because the ID is highlighted.

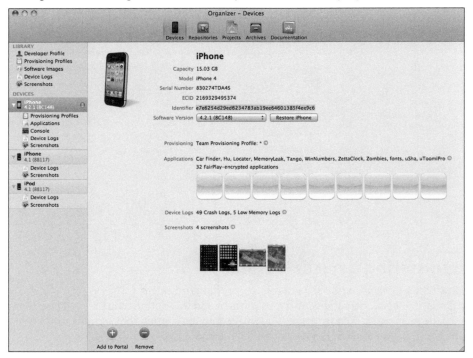

Finding a Device ID in iTunes

Your beta testers won't usually have Xcode installed. To get a UDID from your beta testers, ask them to connect a test device and launch iTunes. Selecting the device in the Devices list at the left brings up the display in Figure 11.16. To reveal the UDID, ask them to click the Serial Number field. They can then drag-select and copy the UDID and paste it into an e-mail.

Figure 11.16

Finding a UDID in iTunes

Adding a single UDID to the Portal

When you have a UDID, log in to the Portal and select the Devices tab. Click the Add Devices button near the top right. Enter an arbitrary device name—the name is for your reference only—and paste the UDID into the Device ID field, as shown in Figure 11.17. Click Submit. The device is registered and added to the Device List. You can now include it when you create device provisioning profiles.

TIP

If you're working as part of a large team, adding devices manually can be time-consuming. You can simplify the process with the iOS Configuration Utility application, which can be downloaded from the main iOS Developer Downloads page. Use the utility to register multiple devices locally. You can then export multiple UDIDs to a `.deviceids` file. Click Upload Devices on the Portal, and select the file to register every device in a single operation.

CAUTION

You can't register more than a hundred devices a year. Although the Portal includes a Remove Selected option that deletes devices, the deleted devices still count toward your allocation.

Figure 11.17

Adding a single device

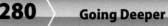

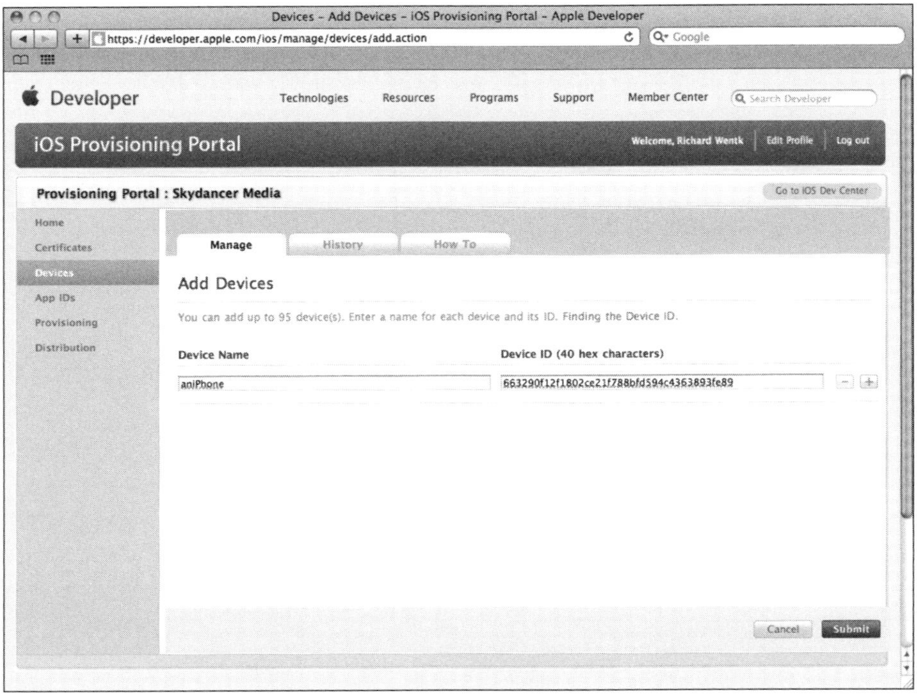

Creating a Development Provisioning Profile

After you have a development certificate, an App ID, and at least one registered device, you can create a Development Provisioning Profile, which allows test builds on that device.

To create a new profile:

1. On the Portal, select Provisioning from the list at the left.

2. Select Development and New Profile, and complete the options shown in Figure 11.18:

- **Profile Name:** This is arbitrary. It's a good idea to use the current date, so you can see how old a profile is when you're using it.

- **Certificates:** This field displays a check box for every registered developer in your team or a single check box with your name if you're a solo developer. Select the developer(s) who will be allowed to create test builds with the profile.

- **App ID:** Select an App ID for the profile. It's a good idea to use a suite/wildcard ID for testing.

- **Devices:** This field displays a check box for every registered device. Select one or more devices. Note that the profile is valid only for the devices you select here; unselected and unregistered devices can't be used for live testing.

Figure 11.18

Creating a Development Provisioning Profile

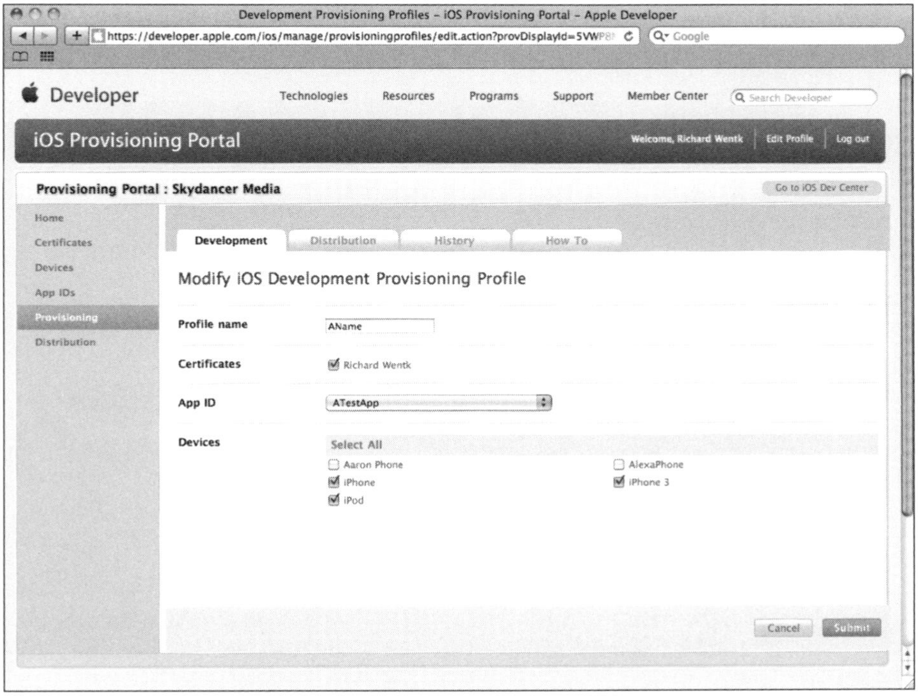

When you click Submit the Portal generates the file and lists it, as shown in Figure 11.19.

3. **Use the Download button to download the profile.**

You also can use the Edit button to make changes, but if you do, you have to download the profile again and install it in Xcode.

Figure 11.19

Downloading the provisioning profile

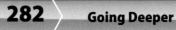

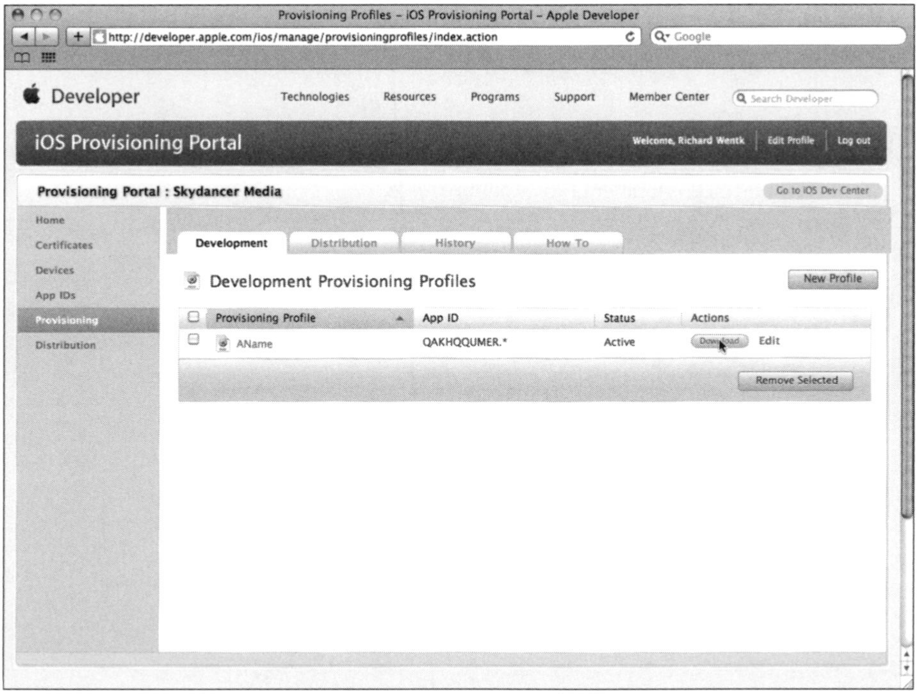

Installing the profile in Xcode

To install the profile in Xcode, navigate to it in Finder, open the Devices page in the Organizer, and drag the profile to the Provisioning Profiles item in the list at the top left, as shown in Figure 11.20. The file has the first name you gave it and the `.mobileprovision` extension.

TIP

You also can install a profile by dropping it onto the Xcode or iTunes icons in the dock.

Creating and running a device build

You can now create a new project in Xcode or load an existing one, and select the target device from the menu at the top left of the main Xcode toolbar. Click the Build button at the left of the toolbar.

The first time you create a test build, Xcode asks you to allow access to your keychain. Select the Always Allow option, and wait. Initially, the build is copied to device flash memory. From there, it's launched automatically and loaded into RAM, just like a standard app launch. This can take a minute or so. Eventually, the app runs. Subsequent builds launch more quickly.

Figure 11.20

Installing the profile in Xcode

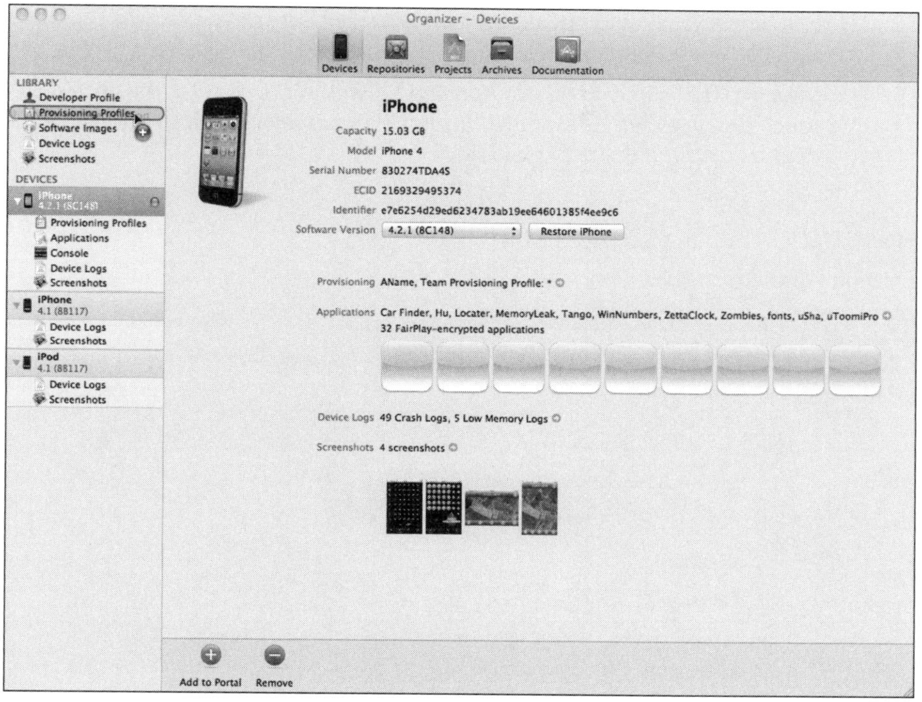

NOTE

Note that the profile exists in two places: in Xcode and on the device. Before the app is copied to the device, Xcode checks whether the profile has been installed. If it hasn't, it installs it automatically. After your first test build, open the Settings app in your device and select General and Profile. You can view the profile here, and you can delete it—but if you do, Xcode installs it again when you create a new test build.

CAUTION

Unlock your phone before a test build. If it's locked, Xcode can't unlock it automatically and can't install your test build.

Creating a Distribution Provisioning Profile

The steps for creating a distribution are similar to those needed for a development profile. On the Portal, select the Provisioning item from the list at the left and the Distribution tab. You see the screen in Figure 11.21. It's similar to the development profile screen, but the options are slightly different:

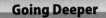
- **Distribution method:** Select App Store for final app store distribution profile, and select Ad Hoc for a beta distribution profile. The two choices are mutually exclusive.
- **Distribution certificate:** This is preset for you, with your distribution identity.
- **App ID:** This is identical to the App ID option for the development profile.
- **Devices:** This is grayed out for App Store distribution, because the profile isn't tied to specific devices. For Ad Hoc distribution, you can select devices from the list. Excluded devices can't run the beta build.

Figure 11.21

Creating a distribution build

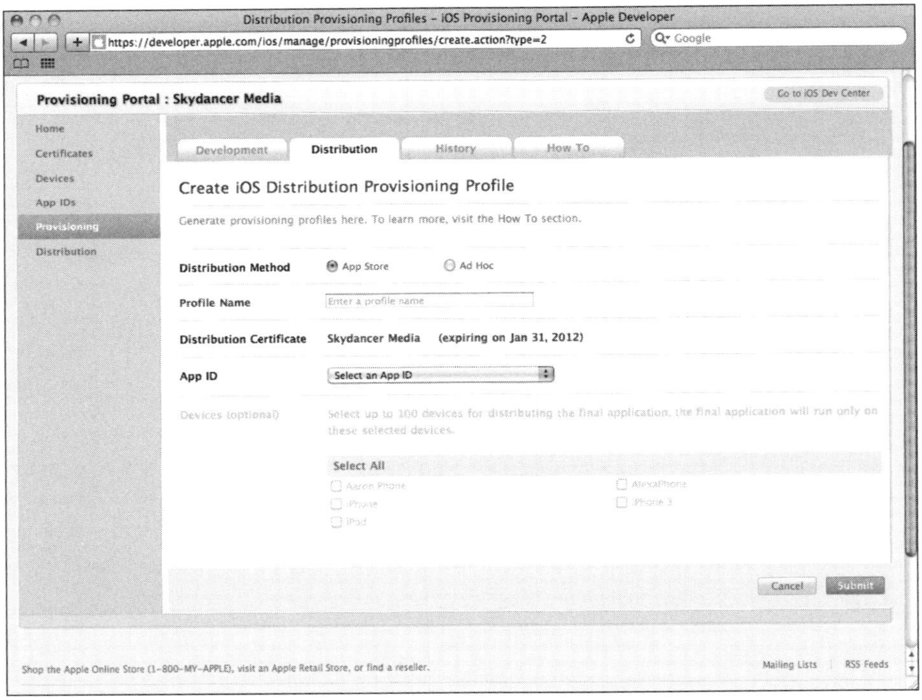

When you click the Submit button, the Portal creates a profile and displays a Download button. Download the profile, and drag it from the Finder to the Distribution Profiles item in the Xcode Organizer. This installs it in Xcode. You can now create a distribution build.

TIP

The final option in the list at the left on the Portal is called Distribution. It looks as if it might contain the resources needed to manage distribution, but it doesn't. It's really just a collection of documentation links with an unhelpful name. You can use it as a quick help reference, but it has no practical features for certification or provisioning.

CROSS-REFERENCE

You need to do some more work to create a distribution build in Xcode, because the Release build scheme doesn't use the distribution profile unless you tell it to. For details, see Chapter 12.

Automatic Provisioning

It would be a huge timesaver if the entire provisioning process were automated. Unfortunately, it isn't. Creating a CSR and generating and installing development, distribution, and WWDR certificates remains a manual process.

Creating an automatic device profile

But Xcode now includes an automated device provisioning feature, which does the following:

- Adds a device to the device list on the Portal
- Creates a wildcard App ID for testing
- Generates a development provisioning profile
- Downloads it to Xcode and installs it on the new device
- Downloads and installs existing developer and distribution certificates

It's important to know the limitations of automatic provisioning. It doesn't do the following:

- Generate public/private keys and a local identity
- Generate and install new developer and distribution certificates
- Download and install the WWDR certificate
- Generate or install an App Store distribution profile
- Generate or install an Ad Hoc distribution profile

To use automatic provisioning, follow these steps:

1. **Connect a device.**

2. **Open the Devices page in the Organizer, and wait for the device to be recognized.**

3. **Select the device.**

4. **Click the Add to Portal button at the bottom of the window.**

You're asked for your developer Apple ID and password, as shown in Figure 11.22. The rest of the process is automatic. When it completes, you see that a new development provisioning profile has been generated and installed in Xcode and on the device. You now create and run test builds on the device.

CAUTION
Automatic provisioning generates a custom App ID: Team Provisioning Profile.*. This is a wildcard/suite ID, so you can't use automatic provisioning to test game center, in-app purchase, or push technology apps. For these more advanced apps, you have to create a unique App ID and work through device provisioning by hand.

Figure 11.22

Automatic provisioning asks for your Portal login details.

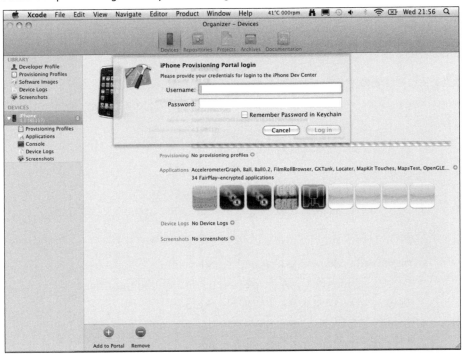

Refreshing a profile

Device profiles expire after three months. You can create a new automatic profile at any time by selecting the Devices tab, Provisioning Profiles at the top left of the Organizer, and clicking the Refresh button at the bottom of the window, as shown in Figure 11.23. You need to enter your Apple ID and password.

This creates a fresh profile with the current date, as shown in Figure 11.23. The profile uses the Team Provisioning Profile.* App ID.

CAUTION
There's no quick way to refresh a profile with a custom unique App ID; you must do this manually.

Figure 11.23

Creating a new profile with the Refresh feature

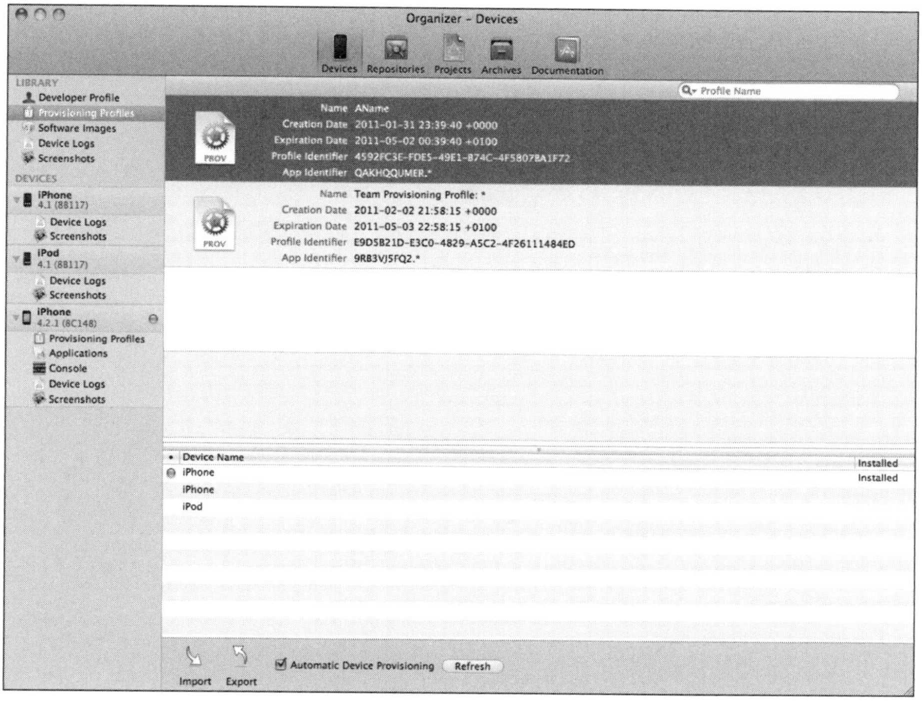

Moving between Macs

The other way to provision "automatically" is to use the new profile import/export option in Xcode. This works as you'd expect it to; it saves your provisioning information into a password-protected file that you can import into a copy of Xcode on a different Mac.

To accomplish this, follow these steps:

1. Select Devices and Developer Profile at the top left of the Organizer window, and click the Export button.

2. Type a filename, and give the same arbitrary password twice, as shown in Figure 11.24.

   Xcode asks to access your keychain and packages your complete collection of identities, certificates, and profiles into a file with the .developerprofile extension. You can use the equivalent Import button and the same password to import the profiles on the other Mac.

Figure 11.24

Copying the complete developer profile

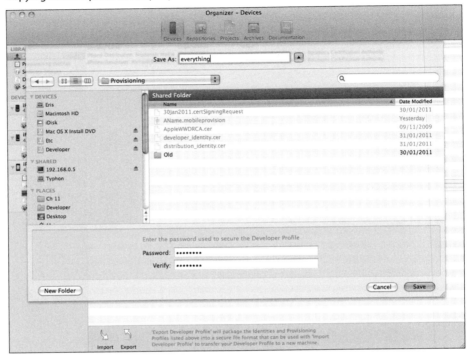

CAUTION

At the time of this writing, Xcode 4 fails to copy the WWDR certificate. This may be a bug, or it may deliberate. If you use this feature, keep in mind that you may need to install the WWDR on the other Mac manually.

Provisioning for OS X Distribution

So far, this chapter has discussed iOS provisioning. In 2010, Apple announced the Mac App Store and created a provisioning scheme for Mac developers, which is much simpler than its iOS equivalent.

You don't need to provision until your project is complete and ready to be submitted to the Mac App Store. You also don't need to provision if you distribute your project independently—for example, by selling it or making it available for free on a website. Provisioning is essential only for App Store submissions.

For Mac developers, the online Developer Certificate Utility is the equivalent of the iOS Provisioning Portal. There are no team development features and no separate device provisioning options: OS X projects run on the development Mac. However, developers must still begin by creating a CSR file with the Keychain Assistant. Developers who have created a CSR for iOS projects can use the same file for Mac distribution.

The Developer Certificate Utility appears as a link at the right of the main Mac Dev Center page under the Mac Developer Program header, as shown in Figure 11.25.

Figure 11.25

Here's the Developer Certificate Utility; as with all online Apple content, the location and design of this feature may change at any time.

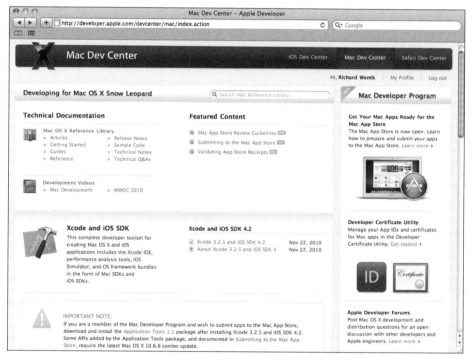

Understanding OS X provisioning

OS X provisioning has five components:

- **A CSR with a developer's public key.**
- **One or more unique App IDs:** The reverse-domain format is recommended.
- **The standard Apple WWDR certificate:** This is the same as the certificate used for iOS development. If you already have a copy, you don't need to install it again.

- **A Mac App Software Certificate:** This signs your application bundle.
- **A Mac Installer Package Certificate:** This is a separate signature file for the installer that wraps the bundle into an installable product that can be sold through the App Store.

There's no support for wildcard/suite App IDs, so you must create a unique App ID and two certificates for every project.

Provisioning in practice

The Developer Certificate Utility is shown in Figure 11.26. The first time you provision an OS X project, follow these steps:

1. **If you don't already have a CSR file, create it using the instructions earlier in this chapter.**

2. **Create a unique App ID using the Developer Certificate Utility.**

Figure 11.26

The Developer Certificate Utility is much simpler than the iOS equivalent.

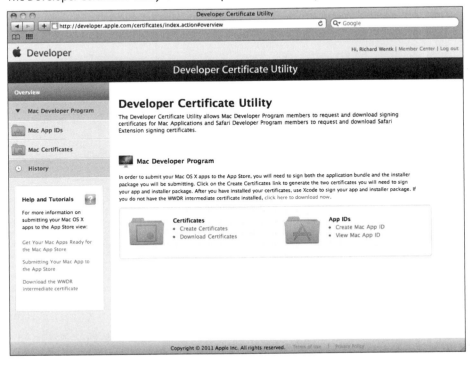

3. **Create the App Software certificate using the Developer Certificate Utility.**

This step uses your CSR file. Download the certificate, but don't install it yet, even though the Utility tells you to.

4. **Create an Installer Package certificate.**

This step uses the App ID. Download the certificate, but don't install it.

5. **If you don't already have the extra WWDR certificate, download it.**

6. **Install the certificates in your keychain.**

You can now use the certificates to create a distribution build with an installer package and upload the installer package to the App Store. The certificates are valid for a year, or until your developer subscription expires, whichever is shorter. They're not linked to a specific App ID, so you can use the same certificates for all your projects.

Creating an App ID

To create an App ID, follow these steps:

1. **Select the Create Mac App ID link, and fill in the two fields, as shown in Figure 11.27.**

2. **The name is an arbitrary string.**

3. **Use the reverse-domain scheme for the main App ID, such as** com.yourdomain-namegoeshere.yourappname**.**

N O T E

Your App ID must be unique on the App Store. Although the reverse-domain scheme isn't obligatory for App IDs, it's the best way to make sure your ID is unique. Other developers may use your chosen app name by accident, but if you prefix it with your domain name, uniqueness is guaranteed.

4. **Click the Confirm button at the lower right.**

You're asked to confirm the submission. When you click Submit, the App ID is added to the Utility.

T I P

You can use the View Mac App ID link to view a list of your App IDs. The list includes a Remove feature. To remove an ID, check the box next to an ID and click the Remove button at the lower right of the page.

Figure 11.27

Creating a Mac App ID

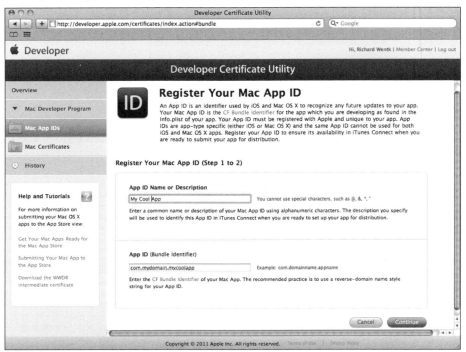

Creating distribution certificates

To create a pair of certificates, select the Create Certificates link on the Developer Certificate Utility page. You see the page shown in Figure 11.28. Leave both check boxes unchanged; you typically need to create both certificates.

Figure 11.28

Choosing the certificate types

Click past the page that explains the process, and you see the CSR submission page shown in Figure 11.29. Click the Choose File button, navigate to your CSR file, and select it.

Figure 11.29

Submitting your CSR file

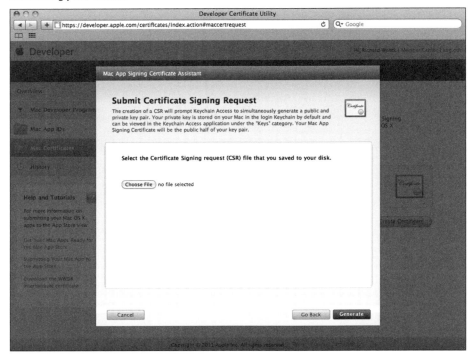

When you submit your CSR, the Mac App Signing Certificate is generated first. Click the Download button to copy it to your Mac, as shown in Figure 11.30. The file is called `mac_app_identity.cer`.

Figure 11.30

Downloading the App Signing Certificate

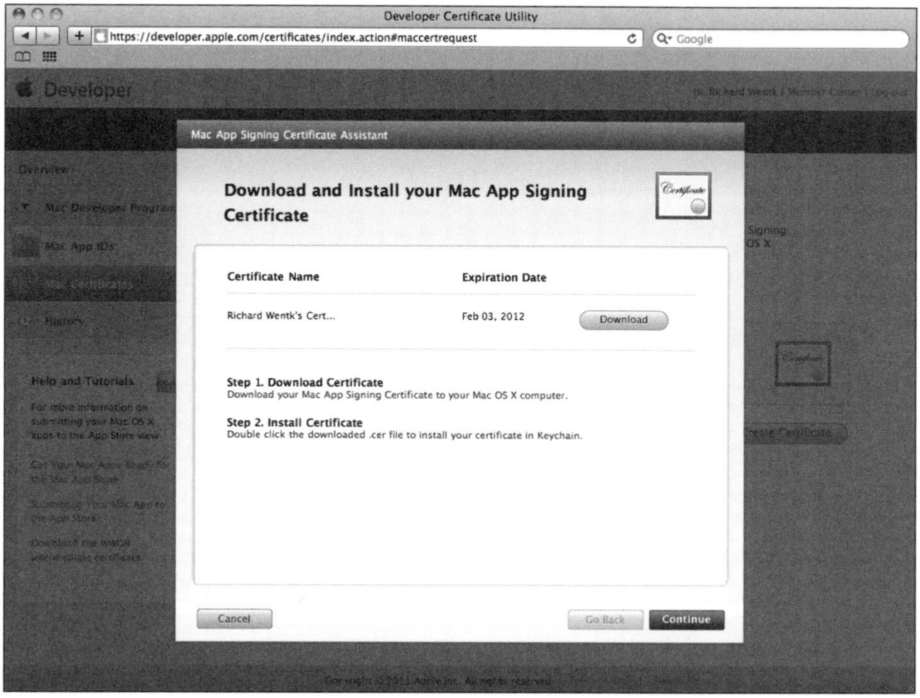

To generate the Installer Package Certificate, repeat the same steps: Upload your CSR, generate the certificate, and download it, as shown in Figure 11.31. If you're working in a team, you can use a separate team leader CSR for this step. The file is called `mac_installer_identity.cer`.

Figure 11.31

Downloading the Installer Package Certificate

 N O T E
Although it can take a few minutes to generate each certificate, you don't usually need to wait more than a few seconds.

To install the certificates, double-click them. Keychain Assistant loads automatically and adds the certificates to your login keychain, as shown in Figure 11.32. You can now set up Xcode to create a distribution build, as described in Chapter 12.

Figure 11.32

Adding the certificates

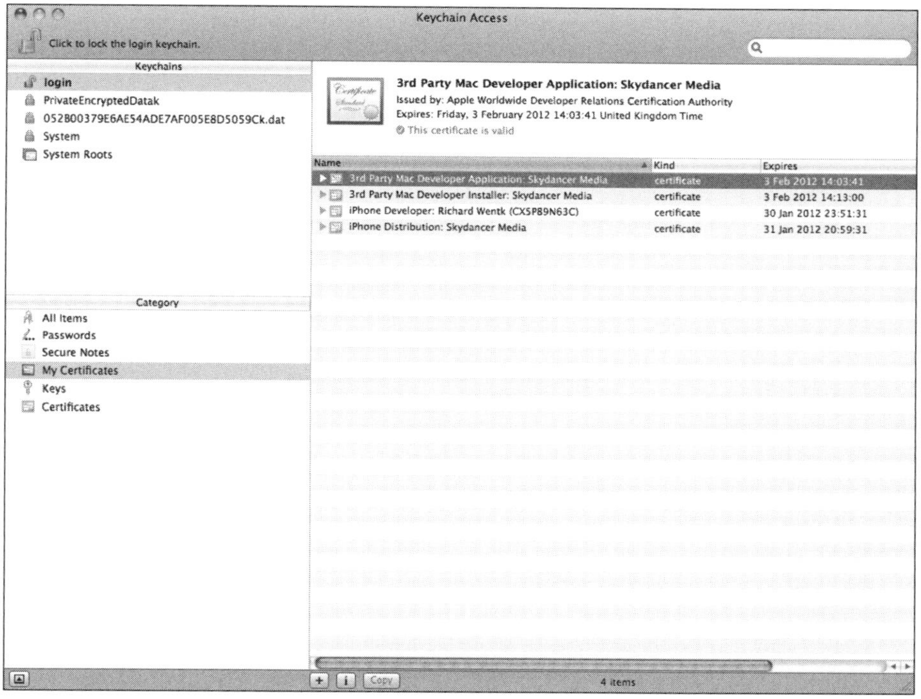

Summary

This chapter introduced provisioning, in theory and practice. It introduced the key concepts and components of provisioning and explained how to generate and install them.

I began by explaining iOS device provisioning and demonstrated how to begin the process by generating a CSR (Certificate Signing Request) file. I showed you how to embed the CSR into two key files: a development certificate that enabled hardware testing and a distribution certificate that enabled App Store uploads and beta distribution.

Next I worked through the device provisioning process step by step and explained how to create an App ID, how to register devices on the Provisioning Portal, and how to create device and install provisioning files both manually and automatically.

Finally I introduced the simpler system used for Mac App development and distribution and demonstrated how to generate and install the necessary files.

Working with Builds, Schemes, and Workspaces

12

So far in this book, builds have been treated as one-click processes, and projects have been treated as stand-alone collections of files.

But it's a key feature of Xcode that the build process is almost infinitely customizable. Instead of treating the build process as a black box that takes source files and converts them into an app, you can break the build process into steps, change the settings and outputs from each step, or even add completely new steps—for example, to create hybrid projects with code written in other languages.

You also can combine projects and files in various ways to create hybrid builds that share related code; for example, you can develop a framework and a project that tests it or uses it at the same time.

In Xcode 3, this kind of mixed build was difficult to manage. In Xcode 4, sharing code between projects has been simplified with a new workspace system that makes it easy to work on multiple related projects simultaneously.

This chapter outlines the key features of the Xcode 4 build system and introduces the editors and options that control the build process.

Chapter 13 introduces some practical examples of build customization and explores more advanced build control options.

In This Chapter

Getting started with the Xcode build system

Understanding settings and options

Editing schemes and build configurations

Managing schemes, build actions, and targets

Getting Started with the Xcode Build System

Although you can use the build system in a simple one-click way, the underlying technology is powerful, but complex. The default one-click option deliberately hides the complexity, but you must be familiar with its key elements before you can begin customizing builds.

Figure 12.1 is a first look at how Xcode builds are organized.

These are the key elements:

- **Projects:** A *project* is a collection of source files that you can select and change using the editing tools introduced earlier in this book.

- **Workspaces:** A *workspace* is a container for one or more projects. Previous versions of Xcode were project-based. However, developers often need to work with source files in a more open way. It's not unusual to use combinations of files from the same code base in multiple related projects. Workspaces make it easy to do this. All projects in a workspace share the same build space, and you can use Xcode's build features to define how the sources are combined. Potentially you can also build multiple projects with a single build operation.

- **Targets:** A *target* is a recipe for building the files in a project, and it defines its product—for example, an app or a framework. By default, a project includes a single target. You can add further targets, as needed. Note that a target doesn't have to be a finished app. You can also create targets that process code in other ways—for example, to run a selection of optional test macros to check that important features work correctly.

- **Products:** A *product* is the collection of files created by a target: an app, framework, test build, and so on.

Figure 12.1

The components of the Xcode build system

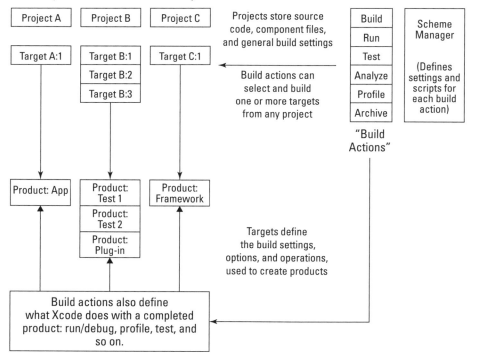

- **Build actions:** There are six standard actions, as shown in the figure. *Build actions* select one or more targets, build them, and then run them through further Xcode features. For example, the Run action loads the code into a runtime environment and

launches a debugger, and the Analyze action runs the code through an analyzer to
check for basic errors.

- **Scheme manager/editor:** A workspace can have one or more schemes, which are
  defined in the *scheme manager/editor.* You can use schemes to customize build
  actions; for example, the Run action in one scheme builds one target, but in another
  scheme, it builds every target in the workspace.

- **Scripts:** You can set up build actions to run pre-action and post-action *scripts,* which
  can play sounds, send e-mail messages, open alert boxes, copy files, and so on.

- **Settings and configurations:** Although not shown in the figure, *settings and configurations* define low-level options for compilation, linking, and packaging. They're introduced in more detail later in this chapter.

Even though Xcode 4 includes new simplified build management features, the relationship
between the different elements involved in a build isn't outstandingly intuitive. You may need
to read this chapter more than once before the relationships become clear.

NOTE

You don't need to understand the process in detail to create a simple App Store build, but some elements interact in
unexpected ways. You'll find it easier to use productively if you have a good understanding of the build system.

Creating and organizing a workspace

When you create a new project, you automatically create a workspace to hold it. For simple app
projects, you can ignore workspaces and simply save each new project as a stand-alone unit.
For more complex applications that hold multiple projects, you can use a workspace to group
related projects together.

The easiest way to use a workspace is to create an empty workspace and then add projects to it.
To create a blank workspace, select File ➪ New ➪ New Workspace from the main Xcode menu.
You can then add projects by right-clicking in the blank area at the bottom of the Project navi-
gator, and selecting New Project….

You also can add existing projects. Select Add Files…, navigate to an existing project's
.xcodeproj file, and select it.

CAUTION

This is useful for simple shared development, but this option doesn't support source control, so use it with care. For
more advanced source control options, see Chapter 14.

The workspace acts as an implied master group in the Project navigator. When you save your
new project for the first time, you can use the Group pop-up at the bottom of the dialog box to
control which group it's added to. The default is the new workspace, as shown in Figure 12.2.

You also can use this dialog box to define the project's save path in the usual way. Projects in a
workspace can be saved to any path; they don't have to be saved to the same folder.

Figure 12.2

When selecting a project's group in a workspace, the default selection is usually correct.

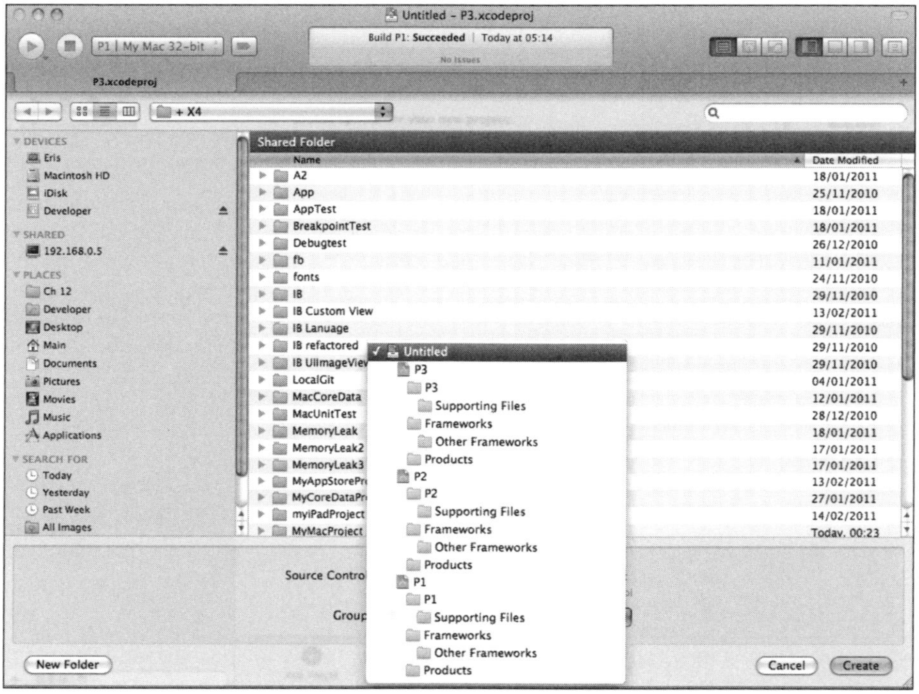

NOTE

You can nest projects and put a project inside another project's group. This isn't usually a useful thing to do; projects are easier to work with when each has its own group.

Working with projects and targets

A workspace is a container and has no build settings or options. It's effectively a master group that holds other items. Projects and targets do have build options—hundreds of them. Xcode includes a separate build editor to manage them, shown in Figure 12.3. To open this editor, select the project name at the top left of the Project navigator. A list of options appears at the right, as shown in the figure.

TIP

It may not be intuitively obvious that you need to click the project name to display the build editor. It's worth taking a few moments to fix this step in your mind to help you remember it later.

Figure 12.3

Navigating to the build editor. The project settings are shown by default.

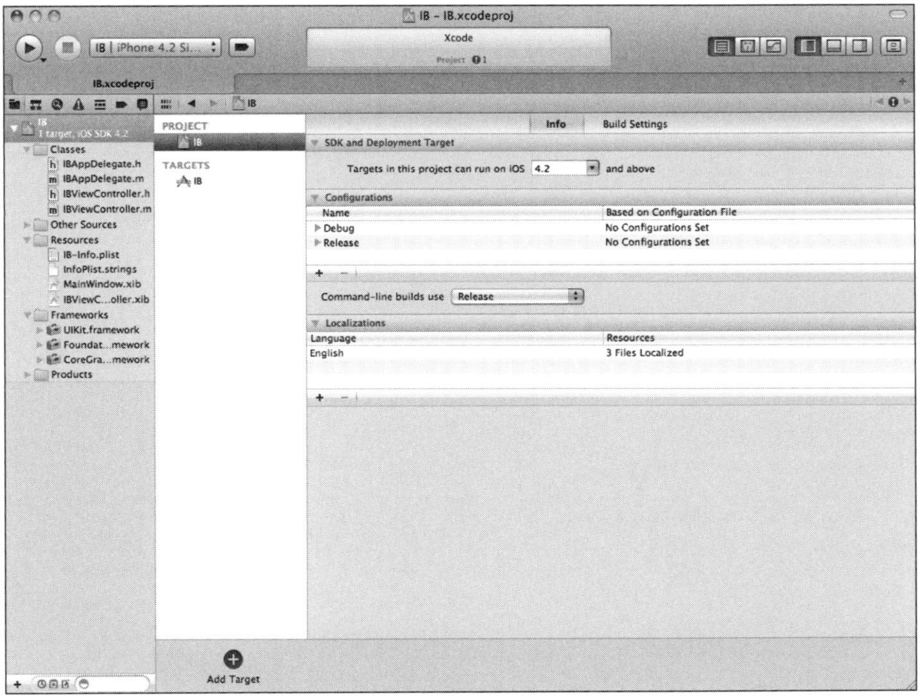

The build editor is complex. There are two items in the gutter area to the left of the options: the PROJECT and TARGETS headings. As you might expect, the project icon displays the options for the project as a whole, while each target icon displays options for each target. Select a target, and you'll see a longer list of tab options at the top of the window, as shown in Figure 12.4.

By default, each has project has one target. If you need to process a project's files in two or more ways, you can define multiple targets for a project—as you see in Chapter 17, where you work with projects that include two targets, one that creates a standard build and one that creates a specialized build to implement automatic code testing. For standard simple app projects, you can keep the default single target.

Figure 12.4

Navigating to the target build settings. The tabs at the top include extra items that aren't included in the project settings.

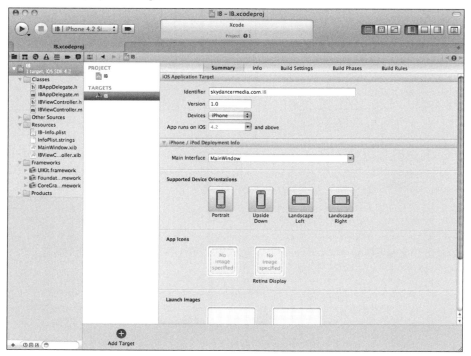

Understanding settings and options

There are five critical points to remember about projects and targets:

- Projects and targets can have separate build options.
- Build options are not the same as build *settings*.
- Build options include information needed to make a target, including selected artwork files, supported orientations, version numbers, property lists, and so on. They also include build settings.
- Build settings are a list of low-level compiler, linker, and packager switches.
- Target options override project options.

Xcode uses a priority hierarchy to calculate which settings and options to use when building a target. There's more information about this later in this chapter.

NOTE
In earlier versions of Xcode, you could also define an *executable*—a context in which a product would run. In Xcode 4, this option has been expanded and built into the new schemes feature, which is described later in this chapter.

Understanding the project options

If you select the project icon, you'll see two tabs:

- **Info:** This includes a minimum supported OS version, a list of configurations (selected build setting presets), and a summary of the files localized for specific languages. In practice, the Localizations option is essential for foreign language support, the Configurations option is useful to App Store build customization, and the SDK/Deployment/OS option is usually overridden by the target.

- **Build settings:** This is a long list with hundreds of compiler, linker, and deployment options that apply to the project as a whole. They can be overridden by the equivalent settings for each target.

Understanding the target options

If you select the target icon, or select one target if your project has many, you see five tabs with different options. Note that target options are independent. If your project has multiple targets, each has different options. These are the tabs you see:

- **Summary:** This includes basic build information, including an app version number, minimum OS, default nib, and so on. You must customize these settings to make a valid App Store build. These options are described in more detail in Appendix B.

- **Info:** This is a text-like list of options that control app launch. Again, you must customize these settings for an App Store build. Note that this list is a *plist*—an XML property list. Editing techniques and contents are described in Appendix B.

- **Build Settings:** At first sight, this list looks identical to the project build settings: It's another list of compiler, linker, and deployment options. The two lists are very similar, but there are some minor differences. Remember that these target build settings override the project build settings.

- **Build Phases:** The contents of this tab control the files that are processed and the order in which they're processed. Each phase defines the files and frameworks included in the build sequence. Here, you also can set dependencies to force a rebuild of a target when some related files are modified. For simple apps, you can ignore most of the features on this page, except for one: the option to include standard frameworks in your project.

- **Build Rules:** The rules define how files of each type are processed. Specifically, you can define or create custom scripts for each existing file type in the list, and you can add new file types of your own, with custom processing options. These advanced options aren't needed for simple apps; they become useful in more complex projects.

CROSS-REFERENCE

Build settings are introduced in this chapter. Build phases and rules are described in more detail in Chapter 13.

Exploring build settings

As mentioned earlier in this chapter, the build settings include every compiler, linker, and packager option. When you build a project, Xcode converts these settings into command-line switches and includes them in the compiler scripts. The full list of settings is very long and can seem intimidating. But in practice, you can leave most settings unchanged in a typical project.

To work with the build settings, select the Build Settings tab in the build options window. The settings appear in an editor, with four buttons that control the layout of the UI. The first two buttons control which settings are visible, and the second two control how they're displayed. The settings appear in a list or table, with group headings. These are the settings:

- **Basic:** This layout lists a small subset of the build settings, as shown in Figure 12.5. It's not the most useful subset, but it does include some important settings. The list of settings is fixed, so you can't create your own selection.

Figure 12.5

Within the basic build settings, the two most useful options are the Compiler Version and the Targeted Device Family.

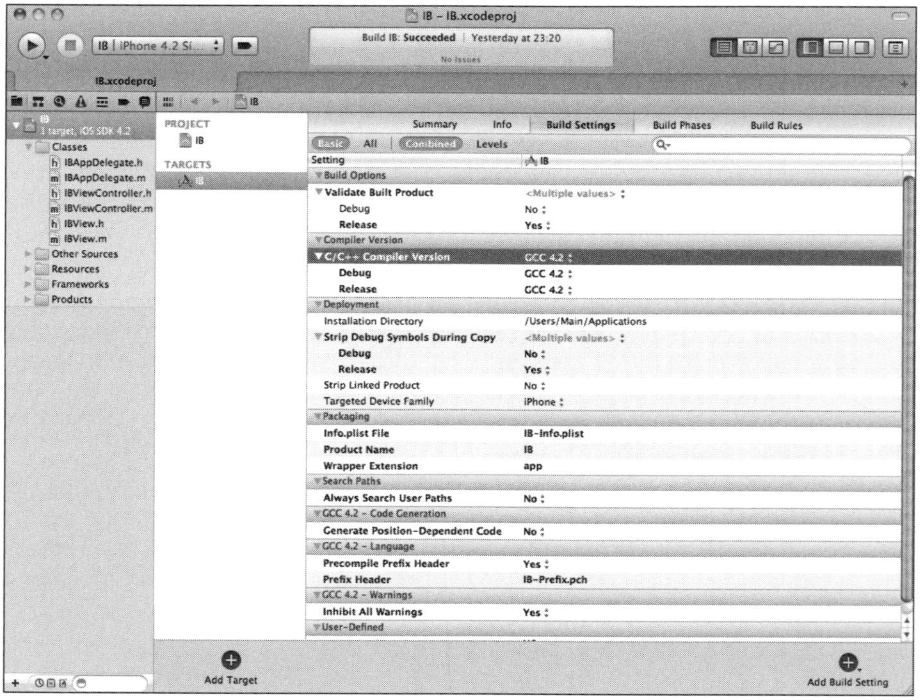

![Xcode build settings window screenshot showing the Build Settings tab with Build Options, Compiler Version, Deployment, Packaging, Search Paths, and other sections displayed]

- **All:** This layout lists every setting, as shown in Figure 12.6.
- **Combined:** Switches with multiple values appear as embedded menus. You can click a setting to select a different value.
- **Levels:** This is a complex view that illustrates how the settings cascade through various levels of defaults, as shown in Figure 12.7. This feature is explained below.

Figure 12.6

The complete list of settings is shown by the All button.

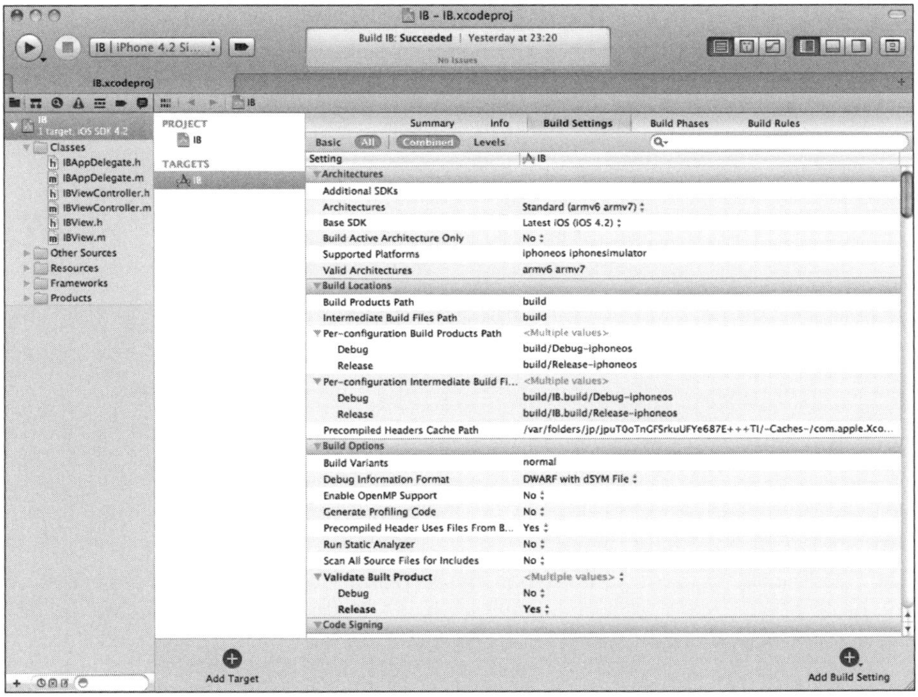

T I P
You can use the hide/reveal triangles in the group headings to hide the less useful settings and simplify the display.

T I P
If you open the Quick Help in the Utilities pane and select a build setting, you see a short but helpful description of the setting and the equivalent command-line switch. For more advanced customization, the settings are described in slightly (but not much) more detail in the official documentation, which has extra information about how some settings interact with others. Search for Build Setting Reference in the documentation in the Organizer.

Figure 12.7

The new Levels view shows multiple build settings in a single window.

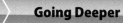

Understanding the Levels view

The Levels view has four columns when viewing target settings, and three columns when viewing project settings. It's not immediately obvious how this view works, but the design becomes clearer after you understand how it's organized.

There are two key points. The first is that Xcode build settings cascade through multiple levels of defaults. Each level overrides the previous level. When Xcode creates a build, it uses this table to find the settings with the highest priority and applies those to the build.

The order of priority flows from right to left. These columns are present:

- **OS default:** These are the standard default switches that apply when the other rows are empty.

- **Project settings:** This list shows the Project build settings. It's identical to the list you can view by selecting the PROJECT icon and All/Combined buttons under the Build Settings tab. These settings override the OS defaults. If a project has multiple targets, the settings apply to all of them.

- **Target settings:** This list shows the Target build settings for the current selected target. It's identical to the list you can view by selecting the All/Combined buttons. These settings override the project settings and the OS defaults. If your project has multiple targets, the settings in this column apply to the currently selected target. Other targets can have different settings.

- **Resolved:** These are the final calculated settings applied to the build. Because they're calculated from the other columns, you can't edit them.

Figure 12.8 illustrates how each level overrides the next. Levels with higher priority override those lower down the list.

The second key point is that *Xcode only stores the highest level setting needed to create an unambiguous resolution.*

If you scroll through the table, you'll see that many settings are left to their system defaults. There's no entry for either the project or the target. Because they're left empty, the resolved value is the same as the default.

This may seem like a trivial point, but in fact it's crucial. When you edit a target or project setting, you're not only modifying its value, *you're also adding a new entry to the settings table.*

Why does this matter? Consider the following sequence of actions:

1. You edit a project setting.

2. The setting has the highest priority, so it applies to all targets. You can change it repeatedly, and it's always applied.

3. Later on, you decide to edit that setting for one target.

4. The new target setting is applied as you'd expect.

5. You change the project setting again.

6. Because a target setting exists now, the new project setting *isn't applied to the target*. The target setting continues to override it.

As soon as you change a setting at the target level, you lock out all future project-level changes to that setting.

This is almost intuitive—but not quite. If you work exclusively in the Combined View, it can be difficult to understand what's happening, because sometimes changes you make are applied as you'd expect, and sometimes they aren't.

The Combined View doesn't illustrate the difference in priority between target and project settings. It also doesn't make it clear that if no target setting has been defined, a project setting can—confusingly—appear to override a target setting.

Figure 12.8

Build settings are arranged in levels. The diagram shows how levels with higher priority override lower levels.

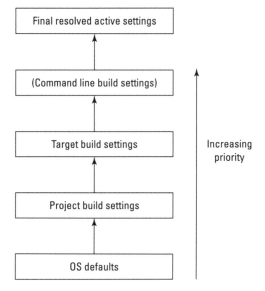

NOTE
Advanced developers who use the command-line tools can override all settings by hand. This is a specialized and advanced technique, included in the figure for completeness. It's not supported from Xcode directly.

The Levels view has some quirks:

- The two central columns aren't labeled. They include the project name and an icon, but there's no text to indicate that you're editing project and target settings.
- You can't edit the OS defaults or the Resolved column.
- There are some minor differences between the settings shown for a project and for a target.
- Both the target and project build settings include a Levels view. However, the version in the project settings doesn't include the target settings column.

As a simple working rule, if you're developing an app with a single target, it's easier to ignore the project settings and work exclusively at the target level. Use the Target Levels view to edit and confirm the settings you want to change. Ignore the project column entirely.

If your project has multiple targets, it's standard practice to make project-level settings. But beware of the target-level lock out described earlier. Once you add a target-level setting, there's no way to delete it. If you attempt to apply project-level changes, it always overrides them.

Note also that the empty rows in the project and target columns aren't really empty. If you select them, you see that you can edit them.

C R O S S - R E F E R E N C E
There's a more advanced guide to build settings in Chapter 13.

Working with Schemes and Build Configurations

Developers often need to customize builds for different purposes; for example, a test build for debugging is likely to have different build settings than a final App Store build. Xcode handles this in two ways.

Build configurations allow you to change a subset of build settings for a specific aim: debugging, release, and so on. Potentially, every build setting can hold a different value for each configuration. By default, most settings take a single value; only a small number are initialized with multiple values.

Schemes give you wider control. The key feature of schemes is that they define build actions that allow you to build your project for different purposes: testing and debugging, code analysis, archiving, and so on. Schemes include build configurations, but add other build and test options.

Getting started with build configurations

Switching configurations is a quick way to change a group of build settings in a single operation, as shown in Figure 12.9. When you select a configuration, Xcode automatically selects the corresponding values and applies them to the build. Single-valued settings remain constant.

In practice, this means that you can quickly customize a configuration to create a build for a specific aim—debugging, local testing, App Store release, Ad Hoc release, and so on—without having to create a separate independent list of build settings.

Conveniently, configurations include the settings needed to create useful debug and distribution builds. Less conveniently, these settings are scattered randomly throughout the full list of all build settings.

NOTE

Why not duplicate every build setting for a configuration? The practical reason is that the settings editor can display multiple values for different configurations. But duplicating every setting for all possible configurations would make the editor unwieldy and difficult to work with. In practice, most settings don't need to be modified, so most of the duplication would be unnecessary.

Figure 12.9

Most build settings have a single value. Settings included in a configuration file can take and display multiple values. The resolved value depends on which configuration is active.

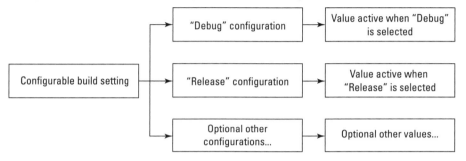

By default, each new project is created with two configurations: Debug and Release. You can create your own configurations by duplicating either or both of these and giving your new configuration a different name. You can then modify its settings and save it with your project.

To create a setting with multiple values, select it and click the reveal triangle at the far left. The setting opens to show a list of configurations. You can now set different values for each configuration.

The settings editor gives multiple values special treatment. It displays them with a `<Multiple Values>` tag, and the configuration settings appear in rows under it. Figure 12.10 illustrates this with an example of a key configuration setting for iOS projects: the Code Signing Identity.

NOTE

Configurations are project-specific. Configuration names and settings are part of a project. For more advanced configuration customization, see Chapter 13.

Figure 12.10

Viewing multiple configuration values for the Code Signing Identity setting

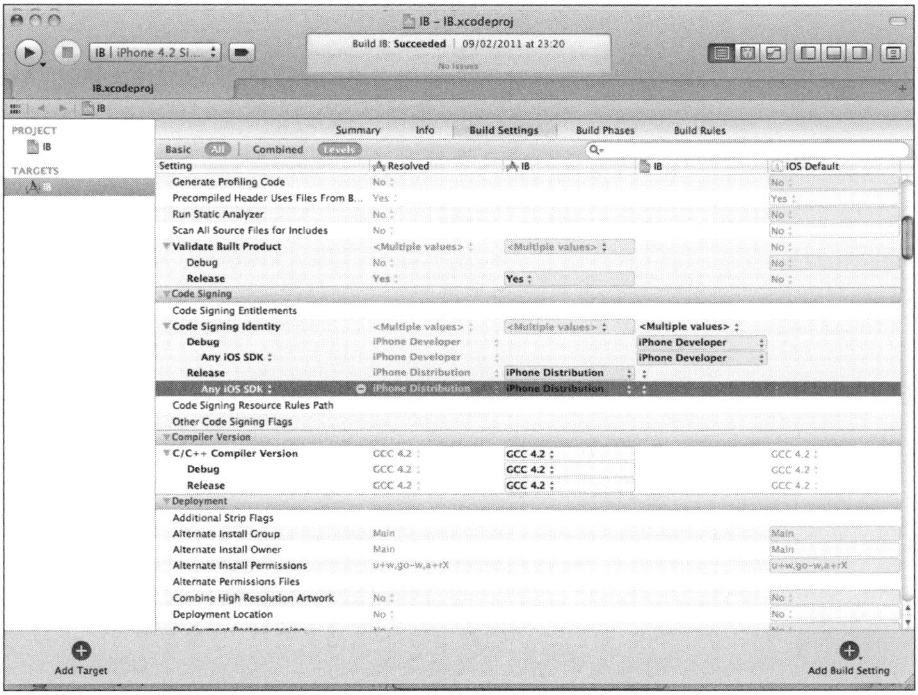

Table 12.1 lists every setting that defaults to multiple values. In practice, you can ignore most of them, because the essential differences can be summarized as follows:

- **Debug:** This configuration includes debug symbols—an appended list of strings and memory addresses used to display human-readable information in the debugger. On iOS, this configuration signs code with the Developer Identity so it can be tested on live hardware.

- **Release:** You can use this configuration as the basis of a build suitable for distribution — for example, Ad Hoc beta testing or App Store upload. But it typically has to be modified to achieve this. This configuration doesn't include debug symbols. On OS X, this configuration creates an app that can be run by double-clicking, but it doesn't include App Store distribution information and isn't wrapped in an installer package. On iOS, this configuration is useless without further customization. It doesn't create a build that you can upload to the App Store or e-mail to beta testers.

Table 12.1 Settings Included in a Configuration

Setting	Included in OS	Should be edited?	Notes
Build Active Architecture Only	OS X	Not usually	This specifies builds for 32-bit only, 64-bit only, or both architectures. For debug builds, this setting should match the hardware for debug builds on your test Mac. For distribution builds, it can enable or disable support for a specific architecture.
Code Signing Identity	iOS	Yes	For a distribution build, select the iPhone distribution identity created and downloaded in Chapter 11. For live hardware debug builds, the iPhone Developer identity is selected by default.
Per-Configuration Build Products Path	Both	No	This defines the file path to the intermediate build products.
Debug Information Format	OS X	No	This controls whether symbols are included with the build.
Validate Built Product	iOS	No	This enables an extra build validation pass. It should be enabled for final App Store distribution builds, but not for debugging.
Compiler Version	iOS	Optional	Optionally, you can select a different compiler for debug and distribution builds.
Strip Debug Symbols During Copy	Both	No	By default, this removes symbols from a distribution build.
Path to Link Map File	Both	No	This defines the file path to intermediate files generated by the linker.
Generate Position Dependent Code	OS X	No	By default, code is position-independent.
Optimization Level	Both	Not usually	You can experiment with this setting to trade off code size against performance.
Other C Flags	iOS	Not usually	Use this option to add custom compiler flags for C code.
Other C++ Flags	iOS	Not usually	Use this option to add custom compiler flags for C++ code.
Preprocessor Macros	Both	No	This enables the optional DEBUG preprocessor macro for debug builds.

Understanding schemes

Schemes take the various build options and configuration settings and wrap extra features around them.

By default, when you build a project, Xcode creates a test build that includes debugging symbols. It launches the debugger and attaches it to the active runtime automatically.

In Xcode, this sequence is one of six standard build actions—options that build and process targets in various ways. These are the standard actions:

- **Build:** Builds one or more targets—in other words, creates their products, but doesn't launch, process, or use them in any other way. This action is the master action. It's an essential first step and is performed automatically by all other actions. You also can run it manually with the Project ⇨ Build option in the main Xcode menu.
- **Run:** Builds and runs the app in the debugger. This is the default action, triggered when you click the big Run button in the main Xcode toolbar.
- **Test:** Builds and runs the unit testing features described in Chapter 17. If the project doesn't include a unit testing target, this action does nothing.
- **Profile:** Builds, launches the Instruments profiling and testing application described in Chapter 16, and loads the app into it.
- **Analyze:** Builds and runs the code analyzer described in Chapter 15. Although a full build may not be necessary for code analysis, Xcode runs the Build action anyway.
- **Archive:** Builds and packages an app ready for distribution, adding it to the Archive list in the Organizer (introduced in Chapter 10). This option is accessible only through the Product menu and isn't included in the toolbar pop-up.

The easy way to get started with schemes is to click and hold the master Build button at the top left of the Xcode toolbar. You see four of the actions in the pop-up list, as shown in Figure 12.11. You can select from the full list of actions under the Product header in the main Xcode menu.

You can use these build actions without changing them, but you also can customize them. At the very least, you should be familiar with the action options, because they interact with Xcode's main menu, build configurations, and build settings in ways that aren't obvious.

NOTE

You can't easily create your own custom build actions. The standard actions are hardwired into Xcode, and you can't extend or modify the list directly. Expert developers can create their own customized build scripts and run them from the command line, but this takes them out of the Xcode environment.

Figure 12.11

Selecting a build action from the toolbar

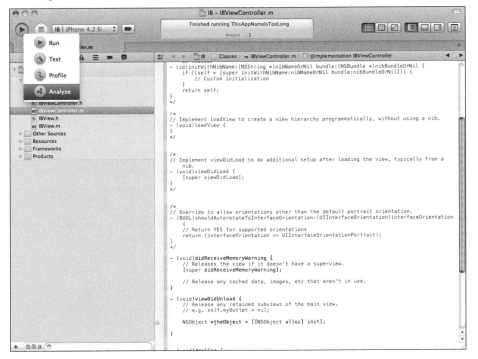

Editing schemes

Schemes define how each build action is customized, to define what happens before, during, and after each action. You also can set up each action to build a selection of targets.

Schemes are managed using Xcode's scheme editor/manager, which has separate dialog boxes for editing schemes and for managing them. You can use it to create a new scheme, edit an existing scheme, or manage a collection of schemes. Simple projects typically need a single scheme, so the edit option is the most useful.

You can access the editor/manager in two ways:

- The main Xcode Product menu header includes three scheme options at the bottom of the list.
- The same options appear at the bottom of the destination (platform) drop-down menu in the main Xcode toolbar, as shown in Figure 12.12.

Figure 12.12

The simple way to display the Scheme editor

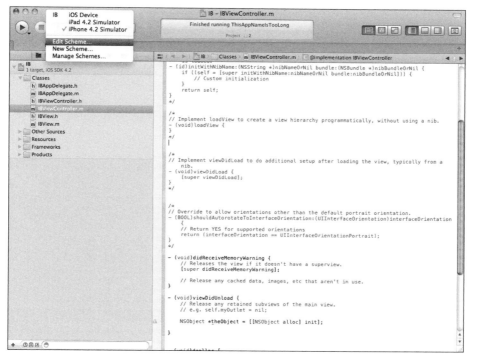

The editor is shown in Figure 12.13. It's a deceptively simple dialog box that hides some very powerful features. The five standard build actions are shown in a list at the left, with a special Build catch-all option that controls which actions are supported by the project. (The Build option is described in more detail later in this chapter.)

You can do the following in the editor:

- Click the reveal triangle to reveal a list of pre-action scripts, action options, and post-action scripts.
- Change the build action options under the Info tab in the pane on the right.
- For selected actions, you can set further customization options, including optional command-line arguments.
- For the Run action only, you also can enable extra low-level diagnostics and logging features.
- For the Build action only, you can include other possible targets and select the targets that are built by the other standard actions.
- Click the Manage Schemes button to open the Scheme Manager dialog box.

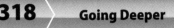

Figure 12.13

Using the Scheme editor

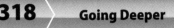

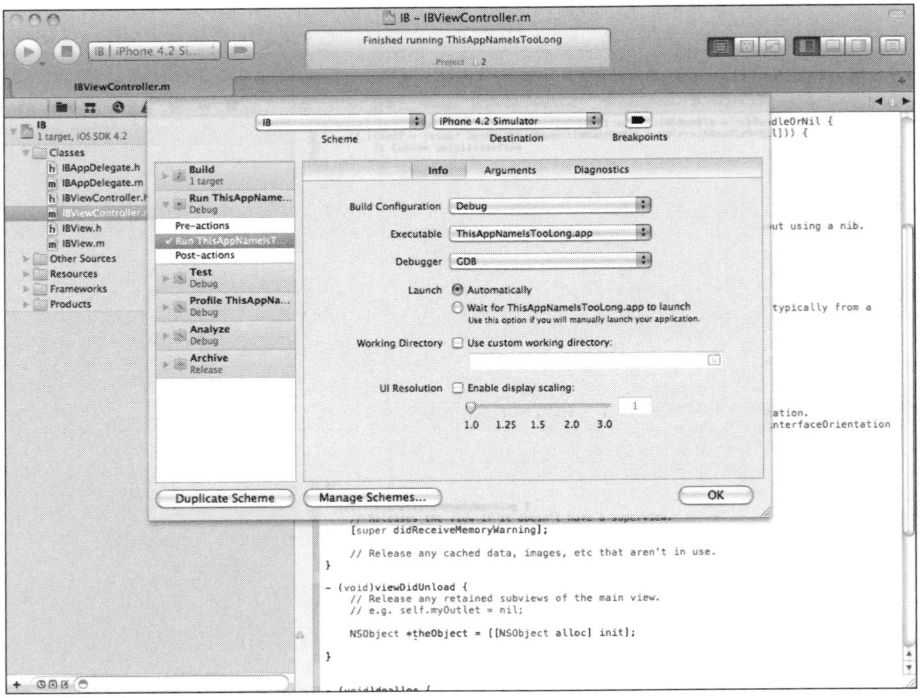

Each action has different options you can modify, although there's some overlap between them. The options control what happens after a build, what happens before and during the build run, and what happens after the run. By default, nothing happens before or after an action, but you can change this by adding custom scripts for each build action. The options also control other settings, including the build configuration used by the action.

Selecting a build configuration

This option is available for every action. Use the drop-down menu to select one of your project's build configurations. If you create a custom build configuration, it appears in the menu automatically.

Adding pre-action and post-action scripts

Each build action has six stages. The first three stages run the default build action. The last three define what Xcode does with the output from the build.

1. Xcode runs one or more pre-action script for the build, if defined.

2. The project runs the default build action: It compiles, links, copies, and otherwise processes the files to create one or more targets.

3. **Xcode runs one or more post-action scripts for the build, if defined.**

4. **The main action runs one or more optional pre-action scripts.**

5. **The main action performs its task—one or more built files is loaded into the debugger, analyzed, profiled, tested, and so on.**

6. **The main action runs one or more optional post-action scripts.**

You can use pre-action and post-action scripts for set-up and tear-down, messaging, and to trigger other arbitrary events. Scripts can be shell scripts or AppleScript code. You also can select a pre-written script that sends an e-mail message.

These are some possible applications of scripts:

- Playing a sound at the end of an automated test or debugging run
- Copying files generated during testing or debugging to another Mac, uploading them to a server, or e-mailing them
- Launching another application that uses the results of a test run
- Using the speech synthesizer to report test results from a run
- Bringing some other window to the front of the desktop

If you can write AppleScript, scripting is an immensely powerful feature for automated testing and test reporting.

NOTE

For information about AppleScript development, see the companion AppleScript Developer Reference title.

CAUTION

Note that scripting shouldn't be used for basic build control. If you need to set build switches, control which files are included in a project, or define how they're processed, use the Build Phases feature described in Chapter 13. Scripting is designed to control what happens after a build, not what happens during a build.

To add a pre-action or post-action script, select an action, click its reveal triangle to show the three optional stages, and select either the Pre-actions or Post-actions option. By default, you see a message telling you that no actions are defined. Click the + (plus) icon at the bottom left of the pane, and select either the New Run Script Action or New Send Email Action option, as shown in Figure 12.14.

For a scripted action, you can either type a script or drag and drop an existing script into the script pane. The example code in the figure plays one of the system sounds. You can add multiple independent scripts.

For an e-mail action, fill in the e-mail fields. The e-mail message is sent automatically when the script runs.

To remove an action, click the close box at the top left of the script's sub-pane, or select the action by clicking its title bar. Click the - (minus) icon at the bottom left of the pane to delete it.

Figure 12.14

Adding a couple of pre-action scripts

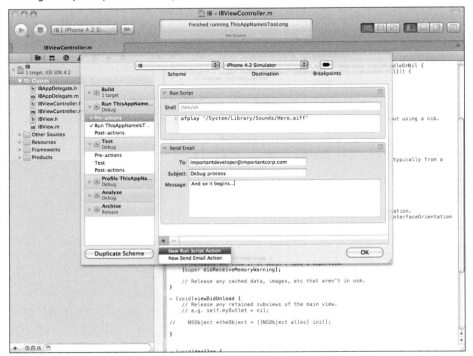

 NOTE
To clarify the terminology, scripted actions are optional and can be run before and after one of the five standard build actions, which are fixed.

Setting arguments and environment variables

The Run, Test, and Profile actions include an Arguments dialog box. You can use it to specify arguments and environment variables that are passed to your application when it launches, via the standard C language `argc/argv` placeholders. It's up to you to define what your application does with these variables. Click the + (plus) and - (minus) icons in the panes of the Arguments dialog box to add and remove items.

CAUTION

These are not build flags or switches. They're passed to your application, not to the compiler/linker.

Selecting a debugger

For OS X projects, you can override the debugger selected in the build configuration here. At the time of this writing, for iOS projects, the only debugger option shown here is GDB.

Setting Run action options

The Run action has some unique features. You can use the Executable menu to select which file is run. By default, this menu selects the app created by the build, but for more complex projects, such as testing a plug-in in a wrapper/master application, you can nominate some other file.

You also can select a custom working directory. This makes it easy to find files generated by the app and saved to its local file space, which is particularly useful for iOS projects.

For both the Run and Profile processes, you can scale the display with the UI Resolution option.

CAUTION

This feature works only on OS X projects. At the time of this writing, UI elements aren't always scaled consistently.

In the Arguments dialog box, you can add an optional list of modules with further debug symbols. This is a specialized feature used to include symbols from modules that may not be built into your project.

The Diagnostics dialog box enables specialized low-level diagnostic options. You can control memory management, enable logging for various events and exceptions, and allow your application to send messages to the debugger. Table 12.2 lists the options.

Table 12.2 Run Process Diagnostics Options

Setting	Notes
Memory management options	
Enable Scribble	Fill memory with $0xAA$ on allocation and $0x55$ on release.
Enable Guard Edges	Add guard pages before and after large allocations to prevent corruption from small overruns.
Enable Guard Malloc	Use the $libgmalloc$ library to monitor and report common memory errors.

continued

Table 12.2 Continued

Setting	Notes
Logging options	
Distributed Objects	Enable logging for `NSConnection`, `NSInvocation`, `NSDistantObject`, and `NSConcretePortCoder` objects.
Garbage Collection Activity	Log collection events, new region allocations, and weak reference manipulations.
Malloc Stack	Log the state of the stack during allocations and deallocations.
Compact Stack	Record compact stack logs during allocations and deallocations.
Log Exceptions	Log Objective-C runtime exceptions.
Log DYLD API	Log API calls to the dynamic-linker.
Log DYLD Libraries	Log library loads by the dynamic-linker.
Legacy/Debugger	
Stop on Debugger() and DebugStr()	Allow your code to call these routines to start the debugger with a message and send a SIGINT signal to the current process.

Setting Profile action options

The Profile action options are very similar to the Run process options. In fact, for the Arguments list, you can check the Use the Run action's options box to copy the arguments and environment variables from the Run action's settings.

The significant feature here is the Instrument option. You can use this to launch a default instrument automatically. This saves you having to select an instrument by hand.

CROSS-REFERENCE

For more about instruments and profiling, see Chapter 16.

Setting Archive process options

App Store and Ad Hoc distribution builds are described in detail later in this chapter. But as a preview, you typically either edit the standard Release configuration or make a copy. A key fact to remember is that if you create a copy for a distribution build, you must select the copy for the Archive action. Otherwise, the Archive action defaults to the standard Release configuration, which is likely to have incorrect settings.

Working with the Build action

The Build action has been left until last because it has some unusual features and a unique edit page.

Selecting common scripts

You can add pre-action and post-action scripts in the usual way. Because Build is the master action and is included automatically in the other actions, any scripts you add here are run by every action.

Selecting targets for each action

The editor also defines which targets are built by the other standard actions. The design of this editor isn't outstandingly intuitive, so it's worth taking the time to understand how to use it effectively.

As shown in Figure 12.15, targets are listed vertically at the left and the standard build actions are listed across the top. When you check a box under an action, it tells Xcode to build that target when you run that action.

Figure 12.15

Selecting the targets built by each action

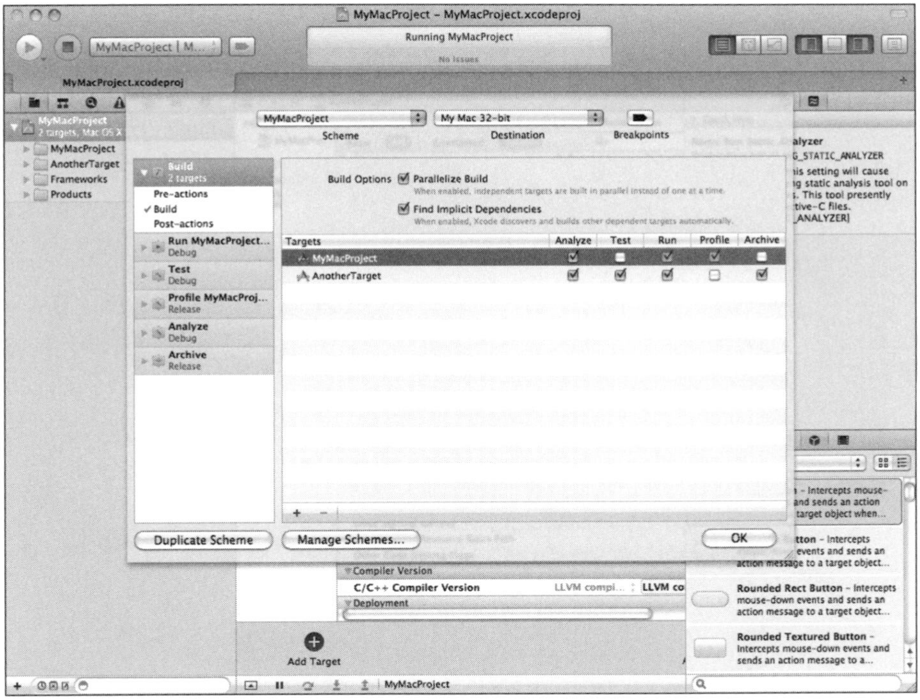

For example, with the settings in the figure, running Profile builds MyMacProject only. Running Test or Archive builds AnotherTarget only. Running Analyze builds both.

When you check the Parallelize Build box, Xcode builds independent targets in parallel. This isn't usually a timesaver on a single machine. But if you have more than one Mac, you can split the build process across a network, which is a timesaver, especially for complex projects.

The Find Implicit Dependencies tells Xcode to find and build dependent targets automatically.

Adding targets

Before you can select a target, you must add it. Unfortunately, when you create a new target in Xcode, it doesn't appear on this page automatically. You must add it manually before you can force a build action to build it.

To add a target, use the main build options pages shown earlier in this chapter. You can then add the target to this page by clicking the + (plus) icon near the bottom left and selecting the new target from the list, as shown in Figure 12.16.

Figure 12.16

Adding a target

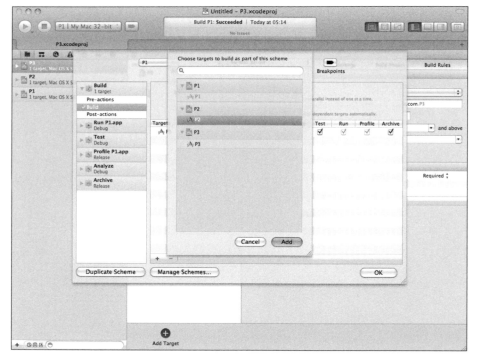

Note that if your workspace has multiple projects, you can select a target from any project in the workspace. This is the easiest way to create complex multi-target builds.

CAUTION
You can't create new targets for a project here; you can only add targets that were already created elsewhere in Xcode.

Understanding hidden effects

When there's a single target, enabling and disabling the actions has some erratic effects elsewhere in Xcode. With a single target, you can't disable the Run and Profile actions at all. If you disable Test and Archive, the corresponding options in the main Xcode menu become grayed out, so you can't select them. If you disable Analyze, the corresponding menu option isn't grayed out.

You can still select the actions with the pop-up menu shown earlier (refer to Figure 12.11), but if you do, you get an error message telling you that the action has been disabled.

Because none of these effects makes a great of deal of sense, it's easier to ignore this page when your project has a single target. The default settings leave every action enabled.

Managing schemes, build actions, and targets

By default, each project has a single scheme. But whenever you create a new target, Xcode 4 autocreates a new scheme for it.

There's almost limitless potential for confusion in this arrangement, because the UI doesn't make the distinction between schemes and targets clear. In fact, the new scheme and the new target have the same name.

To clarify the relationship, remember the following:

- The scheme menu selects schemes, not targets.
- In Xcode 4, you never build a target directly. Instead, you run a standard build action.
- The action defines which targets are built.
- A scheme can define separate multiple targets for each action.
- Before a scheme can build multiple targets, you have to add each target to the scheme by hand.

Figure 12.17 clarifies the anatomy of a scheme. The Build action is central because it's run by every other action, and it selects which targets are built by each action.

When you create a new target and Xcode autocreates a scheme for it, it enables all the build actions for it. This may or may not match your needs, depending on how your project is organized. For example, if you're creating a framework and building a test project around it, you're more likely to build both at the same time.

Figure 12.17

The anatomy of a scheme. The Build action is effectively a subroutine for the other actions. It also can be run independently.

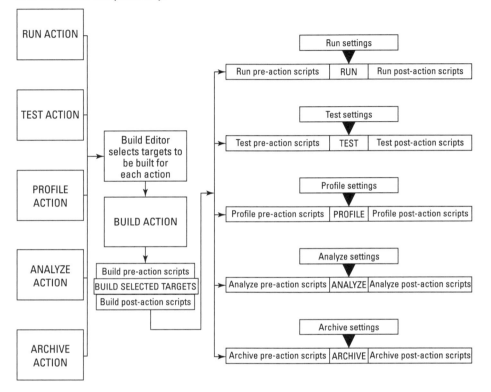

Often, to avoid possible confusion, it's useful to turn off autocreation and manage schemes manually. You can create them by hand as needed, or if you have multiple targets and need a scheme for each, you can click the Autocreate Schemes Now button.

It's also helpful to create and rename schemes for specific build and test events—for example, "Build All." Naming your schemes after your targets is likely to distract you, except for those relatively rare occasions when you have a project with multiple independent targets that you want to build separately.

The key point isn't that there's a right way and a wrong way to use schemes, but that you must understand the relationship among targets, schemes, and autocreation to work with multiple targets effectively.

Figure 12.18 shows the Manage Schemes dialog box. To disable autocreation, make sure the Autocreate schemes box at the top left is unchecked. To create a new scheme manually, select the + (plus) icon near the bottom left. You can choose to create a new scheme or duplicate an existing scheme. The - (minus) icon deletes a scheme. You can use the gear (action) icon to import and export schemes for reuse across other projects.

The final option is the container column, which defines whether the scheme is stored in a project or workspace. The advantage of storing a scheme in a project is that when you select the Shared option to the right of the Container column, everyone who is using that project can use the scheme also.

CAUTION

Sharing a scheme means that others can delete it or modify it without your permission.

Figure 12.18

Managing multiple schemes

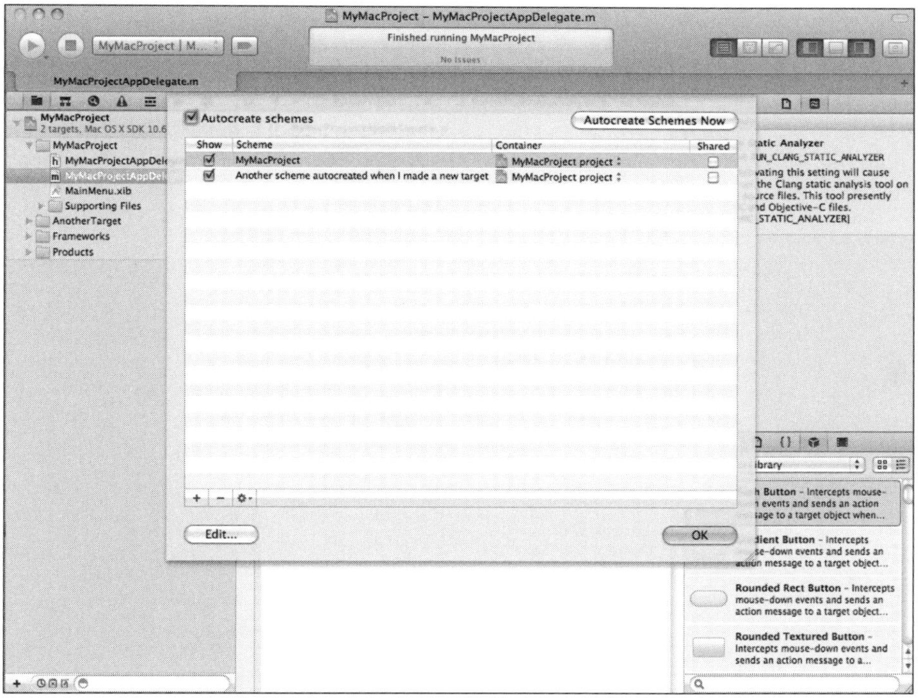

NOTE

Note that the scheme menu displays multiple destinations for each scheme. A *destination* is a platform—or more technically, an SDK. For example, an iOS scheme can select an iOS device, the iPhone Simulator, or the iPad Simulator as a destination. Destinations aren't stored or selected in a scheme, and you'll see that every scheme gives you the same platform choices. Typically, you select a scheme, then you select an SDK, and finally you select a build action, to create a build for that SDK.

Summary

This chapter introduced the Xcode build system. It outlined the relationship between workspaces, projects, targets, build actions, and schemes. It introduced build options and build settings, and it illustrated how settings are prioritized and how you can modify them in the build editor.

Next, it explained how build configurations define project-wide containers for a certain subset of build settings.

Finally, it examined build schemes, explored how schemes and build actions can be used to build different groups of targets, and explained how the build actions can then process products in various ways for debugging, code analysis, archiving, and so on.

Customizing Builds for Distribution and Advanced Development

Chapter 12 introduced the Xcode build system. This chapter introduces some useful examples of simple customization, explains how to create and distribute App Store and Ad Hoc builds, and introduces more advanced build customization techniques that work with build phases and build rules—the steps in the build sequence that define how individual files are processed.

NOTE
If you haven't read Chapter 12 yet, start there. The contents are a prerequisite for this chapter.

Introducing Common Basic Customizations

In This Chapter

Introducing common basic customizations

Creating App Store and Ad Hoc builds for iOS apps

Creating App Store builds for Mac apps

Working with advanced build techniques

Basic build customizations are very common. As you develop apps, you'll find that you typically need to perform the same customizations over and over. This section includes a selection of useful customizations. It isn't a definitive list, but it includes tasks that developers need to perform regularly that aren't highlighted in the official documentation. As you gain more experience, it's likely you'll extend this list with standard customizations of your own.

All require changes to the build options and build settings for projects and/or targets that were introduced in Chapter 12. They don't modify the build rules, which are introduced later in this chapter.

The customization process for iOS and OS X projects is recognizably similar. OS X and iOS projects have slightly different low-level compiler settings and noticeably different app-specific options under their respective Info tabs, but the settings are organized in the same way and appear in the same editor. Most of the customizations in this section are relevant to both platforms.

CAUTION

Be aware that some of the build settings and options interact with each other, while others may not do what you expect them to. These gotchas are listed in this section, with suggested workarounds.

Creating a build for testing and debugging

The debug/test build is the default in Xcode. So for iOS Simulator testing and OS X testing, you don't need to do any customization. Optionally, you can select the runtime platform using the pop-up menu at the top left of the main Xcode toolbar and customize other build settings as needed. But the defaults should create a build that can be debugged and launch it.

Selecting the Base SDK

The Base SDK is the version of the libraries and headers used to generate apps for a specific version of either iOS or OS X. Whenever a new version of either OS is released, Apple generates a new version of Xcode for developers with an updated SDK.

Early versions of Xcode 3 didn't handle this intelligently. When you loaded an old project or downloaded a project from a website, Xcode typically displayed an unhelpful "SDK missing" error message. Because Xcode couldn't find the original SDK, the project wouldn't build until you selected an updated SDK manually.

In Xcode 4, the project build settings include new automated Latest iOS and Latest Mac OS X options, as shown in Figure 13.1. If you save your projects with this setting and reload them into a later release of Xcode, they should select the most recent SDK automatically, even if it's different from the SDK used for the original project.

Note that projects saved with older versions of Xcode continue to show this error when you reload them. (This is a common error when you try to load a sample project downloaded from a developer's blog.)

To fix the problem, select the latest SDK manually in the build settings after loading the project.

NOTE

You may want to change this setting for final distribution builds, as described later.

Figure 13.1

Selecting the Latest OS option to ensure that projects always load with a current SDK

Setting the minimum supported OS version

With each new version of iOS and OS X, new functions, classes, and methods are added, and older elements are removed. Not all users upgrade to the most recent version of each OS, especially not those running OS X, who have to pay for upgrades. iOS users of older devices are typically limited to an older version of the OS.

It's often useful to create products that are compatible with an older version of the OS, but that also can run on newer versions. The minimum supported OS version is known as the *Deployment Target*. If a user tries to run the product on an older version, the loader displays an error message.

Understanding the SDK and the deployment target

Newcomers to Xcode are often confused by the relationship between the base SDK, the deployment target, and the OS version shown in the Simulator. The key point to understand is that the SDK defines the symbols and libraries that appear in the product. The deployment target is simply a number used by the loader to check OS compatibility.

CAUTION

Don't confuse the deployment target with the targets used in a project. The deployment target is an OS version. The build targets are processes and file specifications that create a product. For clarity, the deployment target could have been labeled the deployment OS, but unfortunately it wasn't.

The SDK supplied with any version of Xcode includes support for older versions of the OS, up to some arbitrary limit. For example, the iOS 4.3 SDK can build projects that run under iPhone OS 3.0 and later, but not iPhone OS 2.x and 1.x.

An often-repeated rule for selecting an SDK and deployment target is that you should always select the Latest OS SDK (as described earlier) and the most ancient supported deployment target. In practice, beta development complicates the requirements. Here's a more comprehensive guide:

- Select the Latest OS SDK for all development builds. With a beta SDK, you can use this option to experiment with new features.
- If you have a beta SDK installed, select the current public release of the OS—the version before the current beta—as the Base SDK for App Store distribution builds.
- Not all beta SDKs include this previous version. If you've installed a beta SDK and find the current public OS SDK is missing, you must use or reinstall a separate older copy of Xcode for distribution builds.
- Don't try to create a final production build with a beta version of the OS until the beta SDK is upgraded to a final GM (Gold Master) seed and Apple confirms this seed is suitable for production code. This usually happens just before public release.
- You can use a beta SDK for Ad Hoc test builds only if your testers have access to the equivalent beta versions of the OS for their devices. If they don't, which is often the case, select the previous public SDK as the active SDK. You can give them access, but some assembly is required. For details, see the Creating App Store and Ad Hoc builds section later in this chapter.
- The Simulator supports various older versions of the OS. You can use this option to partially test code for backward-compatibility.
- You also can test compatibility on real devices, if you have them. If you need to, you can use Xcode's Organizer to downgrade newer devices to older versions of the OS for testing. (Don't do this on devices you use personally; you're likely to lose data.)
- Set the deployment target as low as possible, for maximum backward-compatibility. This gives users the best chance of being able to buy and use your app.

A key point is that when you set the deployment target to an older version of the target OS, your code must test for OS-dependent features. Figure 13.2 illustrates this graphically.

In the figure, your app can run on any device with iOS 4.0 or later. The latest features from the iOS 4.3 SDK aren't available on devices with older versions of iOS, so your code must check they exist before it tries to use them. Your code will of course *compile* with the iOS 4.3 SDK—but when the deployment target is set to support older version of iOS, it won't *run* reliably on a range of supported OS versions unless you include versions-specific tests and code features.

Supporting multiple versions of an OS is non-trivial. It's also difficult to test in full. The only true test is to run the code on multiple devices, each of which has a different version of the OS—or on a single device multiple times, updating the installed OS each until every version has been tested.

N O T E

This can be lots of work. It's not unusual to test code on the oldest and newest supported OS, check by inspection that the code is likely to work on intermediate versions, and hope there are no surprises.

Figure 13.2

The most general view of SDK and deployment selection. Code must include tests to check for OS-dependent features that may not be available on a user's device. Missing features must be implemented with workarounds and fallbacks.

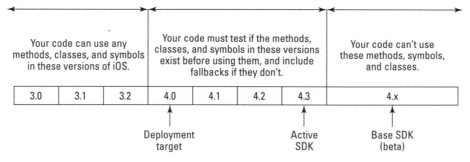

Common practical techniques for multi-OS support include the following:

- Using variations on the `respondsToSelector:` method to check whether methods are available
- Using `NSClassFromString` to check whether a class is supported
- Reading the supported system version from `UIDevice`
- Including conditional compilation elements to manually select OS-dependent code (This option is typically used to check for a platform—for example, OS X, the iOS Simulator, or an iOS device—during compilation. Don't use it to manage OS versions.)

T I P

For practical examples of multiple OS support with code, search for Using SDK-Based Development in the documentation. There's more about conditional compilation later in this chapter.

Setting the deployment target

You can set the deployment target in three ways:

- Select the deployment OS with the Deployment Target menu in the Project ⇨ Info tab, as shown in Figure 13.3.
- Select the deployment OS with the Deployment Target menu in the Target ⇨ Summary tab.
- Select the Deployment Target item in the build settings table for either the project or the target.

Figure 13.3

Selecting the Deployment Target. This feature appears in three places, but for single-target apps it's easiest to set it here.

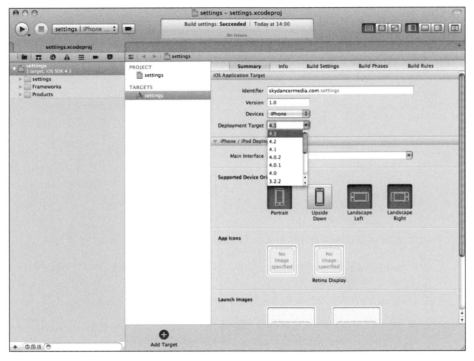

These options appear interchangeable, but they're subtly different. The first option creates a project build setting. The second creates a target build setting. The final option can create either a project or a target setting.

CROSS-REFERENCE

The differences between project and target settings and the interactions between them were introduced in Chapter 12. If you're not yet familiar with them, read that chapter before continuing—the differences are crucial.

For single-target iOS and OS X apps, use the target summary setting for simplicity and clarity. For more complex projects with multiple targets, it's up to you to select the option that works best in the context of the project.

Setting the Base SDK

There's exactly one way to set the Base SDK—it's included in the list of build settings, as shown in Figure 13.4. When you load a project created with an older version of Xcode and you see the "missing Base SDK" error, open the build settings and fix it by selecting the correct "Latest OS" option for your project and platform, as shown in the figure.

New projects should always have the Base SDK selected correctly, by default.

Figure 13.4

Using the Build Settings to set the Base SDK

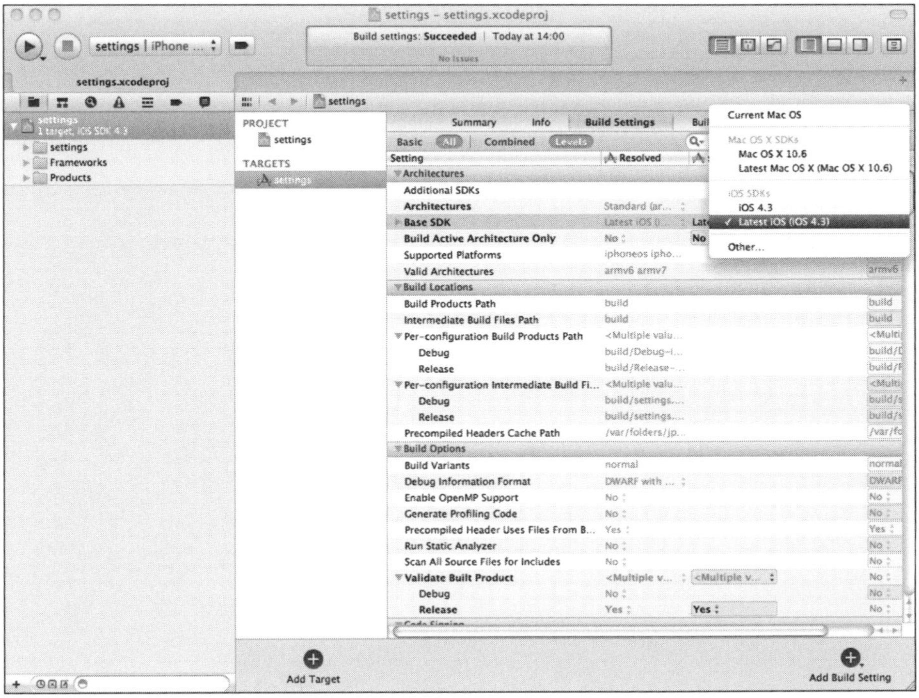

CAUTION

Note that Xcode allows you to select an iOS SDK for an OS X project, and vice versa. This is never a wise thing to do. Occasionally you can load an older Mac project and Xcode assumes it's an iOS project—and vice versa. So you may need to correct this by hand. Note also that you can set different SDKs for Release, Debug, and custom configurations. Very occasionally you may discover a practical need for this, but it's not a widely used feature.

Including a framework or library in a build

This topic was introduced in Chapter 5, but it's expanded here. To add a framework or library, follow these steps:

1. **Navigate to the Build Phases tab.**

2. **Open the Link Binary With Libraries item, as shown in Figure 13.5.**

3. **Click the + (plus) button at the bottom left of the item.**

Figure 13.5

Adding a framework to a target

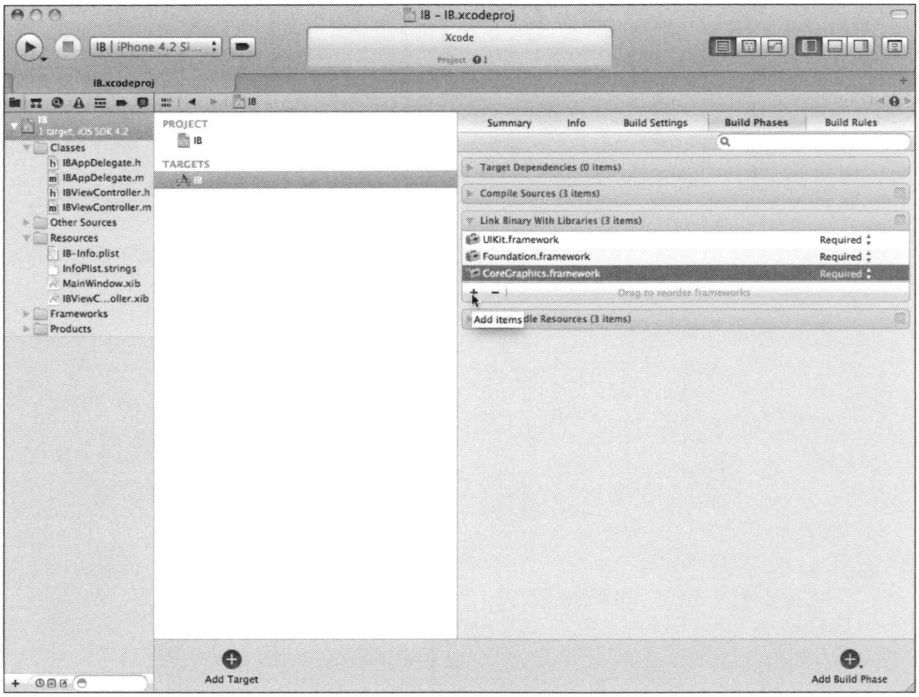

4. **Select the framework or library from the menu.**

5. **The framework is added to the Project navigator. To keep the project organized, drag it to the Frameworks group.**

Note that the list of frameworks is filtered by platform, so you can't add an iOS framework to an OS X project (or vice versa).

You can rearrange the compile order by dragging frameworks up and down the list, although this isn't usually necessary. You also can add an external non-Apple framework by selecting the Add Other option and navigating to the framework files. Use this option to add frameworks or libraries created by other developers.

Technically, you link against a framework. There are two options: Required and Optional.

A Required library must be present on the target platform and is loaded at launch with the rest of the application or product. If it isn't present, the application refuses to load.

Optional libraries are loaded only when they're referenced at runtime. This saves memory and creates a smaller initial product. But if the library isn't available, the application stalls or crashes. You can use the techniques introduced in the previous section—tests for classes and methods, conditional compilation, and so on—to create code that can handle optional libraries robustly.

Typically, you use the framework build option discussed here to add precompiled binaries with headers. But if you have a framework's source code, you can add the files to the project's sources using the Add Files option in the Project navigator. Third-party frameworks are often supplied as source code that you can add to your project, which may be a simpler option than trying to build and import the code as a stand-alone library.

Always remove frameworks from a finished project if they're not being used. For example, you might add one of the audio or graphics frameworks to experiment with it, decide that another framework is a better solution, but leave both in the build. Although this is an obvious point, it's easy to overlook it. When you finish development, check to see that every framework listed under Link Binary with Libraries is essential.

CAUTION
If you're used to framework management in Xcode 3, be aware that this feature is handled very differently in Xcode 4. The list of linked frameworks still appears in the Project navigator, but the right-click Add Framework option is no longer available.

TIP
It can be easier and quicker to add Apple frameworks using a different technique. Open the Frameworks group, right-click any of the existing frameworks, and select Show in Finder to view the default list of Apple frameworks. Each framework appears in a folder. To add a framework, drag its folder from Finder and drop it on the Frameworks group. Leave the Copy items option unchecked. Click Finish. The framework is added to your project, and it also appears in the Link Binary with Libraries list. (Don't forget to add an `#import` directive to include the headers in your code!)

Selecting a compiler

It's not immediately obvious that Xcode 4 includes two compilers for C family languages: the older GCC (Gnu Compiler Collection) and a newer LLVM (Low Level Virtual Machine) compiler. Each compiler has an associated debugger.

There are significant differences in speed, reliability, and debugger integration between the compilers. The LLVM compiler is more efficient and faster than GCC. The corresponding debugger is more tightly coupled with the source code than the Gnu Debugger, and it produces more informative error messages. But GCC has better optional support for other languages and can sometimes be a better choice for cross-platform projects.

To select a compiler, choose one of the three options from the Compiler Version menu in the Project build settings. These are your options:

- **GCC 4.2:** This uses the standard GCC compiler.
- **LLVM GCC 4.2:** This is a hybrid option that uses the old GCC frontend/parser and the new LLVM compiler. It gives faster compile times, especially on larger projects.
- **LLVM Compiler 2.0:** This is a somewhat experimental option. It selects the new Clang frontend/parser and the LLVM compiler. If you're used to GCC, you'll find that selecting this option generates new and unfamiliar—but more comprehensive and useful— errors and warnings.

NOTE

When a project has different targets, it's possible to select a different compiler for each target. While Xcode allows you to do this, it's not a common requirement. Note also that when you switch compilers, some of the switches and options displayed under the Build Settings tab change too. Because you don't usually need to fine-tune the default settings, you can leave these alone, but it's worth being aware that LLVM has a slightly smaller selection of options.

CROSS-REFERENCE

For more information about compiler technology, see Appendix C.

Controlling warnings

You can use the Warnings section toward the bottom of the full list of build settings to enable and disable specific warning messages, as shown in Figure 13.6.

The master switch is called Inhibit All Warnings. When this is enabled, the compiler ignores the other warning switches and suppresses all warnings, without exception. This is a dangerous option.

Most of the other options are self-explanatory, to varying degrees. For example, unused variables and unused values produce warnings by default. Unused functions don't. It's worth exploring the list to fine-tune the options to match your programming style.

Figure 13.6

Selecting warning messages

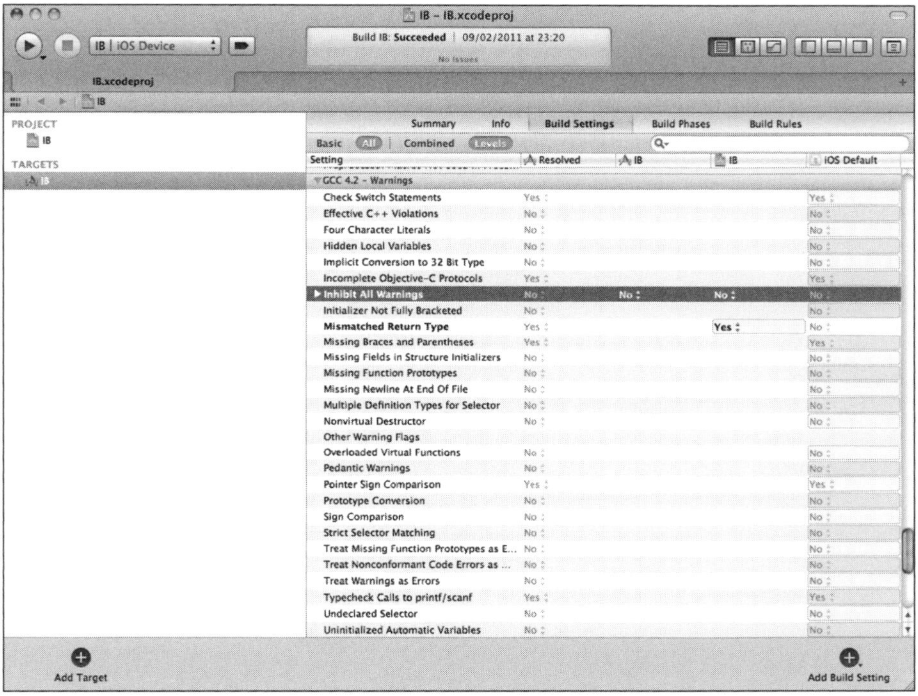

Disabling iOS PNG compression

By default, when you include PNG (Portable Network Graphics) image files in your project, the build process runs the art files through a PNG compression stage.

Unfortunately, Xcode's PNG compression isn't outstandingly efficient and may add unwanted transparency artifacts. You can minimize the size of the files by compressing them manually in an editor such as Adobe Photoshop or Fireworks. You can then tell Xcode to disable its compression and use the files as they are. (If you don't, you may find it makes precompressed files bigger.)

The compression setting is labeled Compress PNG Files. You can find it at the top of the Packaging heading in the Target Build Settings.

Changing an app's name before shipping

It's often useful to change the final production title for an app, to customize the name string that appears under the app icon in iOS or above the Dock in OS X.

There's no easy way to change the project's filenames or the project name as a whole. But you don't need to, because you can set the name independently using the Product Name setting in the Build Settings. You can find it halfway down under the Packaging header.

The default is a macro called $ (TARGET_NAME). You might assume this means that the target name is copied from the Target name. This is true, up to a point. But it's easier to edit the name directly, as shown in Figure 13.7. You can either single-click twice on the product name to edit the name in place. Or you can double-click to display the floating edit box shown in the figure.

Figure 13.7

Editing the product name. This setting changes the name that appears under/over the app in the Dock and in Springboard.

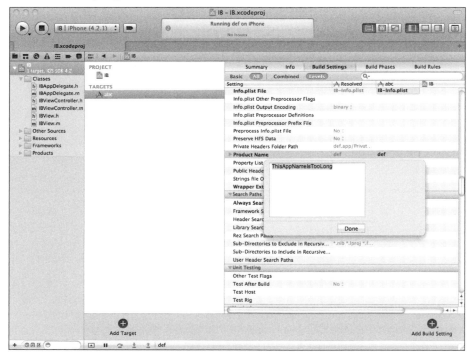

TIP

It's a good idea to keep iOS app names short, because Springboard truncates longer names with ellipses (...). Ten characters is a realistic maximum, but you may occasionally be able to squeeze in 11. You can test the truncation in the Simulator.

What if you want to edit the target name instead and force the product name to follow it? You can edit the target name by double-clicking it next to the icon in the gutter area to the left of the settings. If you leave the product name set to the default macro, it should follow suit.

Unfortunately, it doesn't. The product name field is copied to the target name only when the project loads. So to refresh the name, you have to close the project and load it again.

This is an obvious bug. It may or may not be fixed in future versions.

Creating App Store and Ad Hoc Builds

Now that you're familiar with the build system and with build customization, you can start to create builds for the App Store.

Xcode 4 includes a simplified building and packaging process that makes it easier to submit apps to the App Store and to create and distribute beta versions for testing. The process is simpler than it was in Xcode 3, but some assembly is still required.

The first time you submit an app, allow a day or two to work through each stage. The submission process isn't simple. It becomes easier with experience, but the best way to guarantee a successful first upload is to work through the stages carefully and methodically.

CAUTION
Before you can create an App Store or Ad Hoc, you must work through the provisioning process introduced in Chapter 11. If you haven't done this, do it now; it's a prerequisite for this section.

CAUTION
You must give iTunes Connect information about your bank account and tax details before you begin uploading a paid app. Work through this process well before you submit an app. International tax law is outside the scope of this book, but be aware that you may need to supply extra paperwork for certain territories; otherwise, income is taxed at source, although it may be possible to reclaim deductions later. Non-US individuals require an ITIN (Individual Taxpayer Identification Number) from the U.S. IRS to avoid deductions. It can take between three months and a year to obtain one.

Building and packaging an iOS project for the App Store

Debugging and testing an app is only the first stage of the App Store process. To sell it, you must package it and upload it, which takes significant extra work.

The packaging and uploading process has six steps:

1. **Start by preparing marketing and support materials.**

Technically, this isn't part of the build process, but you have to do it anyway before you create a final build.

2. **Create a modified Release build configuration.**

3. **Customize some of the build options in the new configuration.**

4. **Build the project as an archive.**

5. **Upload the marketing materials to iTunes Connect, and create an application record.**

6. **Validate the project archive to check for basic errors, and submit it to iTunes Connect.**

Preparing marketing and support materials
You need the following:

- **Standard Artwork files:** For a list, see Table 13.1. Preparing artwork isn't a trivial job; even if you have good design skills and aren't attempting a complex design, it can take half a day to a day to create every required file—longer to create every possible file. Professional developers often outsource this work to graphic designers. (This list includes essential artwork. Your project also may use its own separate artwork files for icons, sprites, and so on, but if it's finished, it should have those already.)

- **An SKU number (an arbitrary product code of your choice):** Every app must have a unique SKU.

- **Marketing text:** This can be up to 4000 words of compelling text to persuade iTunes customers that they need your app.

- **A list of search keywords, up to a maximum of 100 characters:** Your app appears in iTunes when users search for any of these words.

TIP
If you can't think of a suitably professional-looking SKU, you can prefix the code with a shortened version of your name or your company name, followed by the reversed date.

Table 13.1 Standard Artwork Files

Name	Size	Obligatory?	Notes
Icon.png	57 x 57	Yes	Springboard icon. iOS automatically adds the glass effect and rounds the corners. (Note that you can disable the glass effect by editing the project's info.plist file. See Table 13.2 and Appendix B for details.)
Default.png	320 x 480	Yes	iPhone and iPod touch loading screen. In theory, this should be a static copy of the default view, and splash screens aren't allowed. In practice, this rule isn't always applied.

Name	Size	Obligatory?	Notes
<arbitrary>	512 x 512	Yes	iTunes artwork file. In theory, this should be a high-resolution version of Icon.png, but some creative license is allowed.
Icon-72.png	72 x 72	Yes for iPad projects	Larger icon file for the iPad.
Default-iPad.png	768 x 1024	Yes for iPad projects	iPad loading screen.
Icon-small.png	29 x 29	Recommended	Smaller icon for the iOS Settings app.
Default@2x.png	640 x 960	Recommended	High resolution launch image for iOS devices with a retina display.
Icon@2x.png	114 x 114	Recommended	High-resolution icon for iOS devices with a retina display.
Icon-Small-50.png	50 x 50	No	iPad icon for Spotlight searches. The image includes a 2-pixel frame, so the safe area is 48 x 48 pixels.
<aDocumentType>.png	22 x 29	No	Icon for supporting document files.
Icon-Small@2x.png	58 x 58	No	High-resolution icon for Settings.
<aDocumentType>@2x.png	44 x 58	No	High-resolution icon for supporting document files.
<aDocumentType>-small.png	64 x 64	No	Small iPad document icon.
<aDocumentType>.png	320 x 320	No	Large iPad document icon.
Screenshots	Various	Yes	Between one and five screenshots of your app in action. You can grab these in the Organizer at your app's native resolution and export them as PNG files.

Although this list looks long, many of the images are optional, so you can get by with a more minimal selection. For the iPad, there are two default images rather than one: Default-Portrait.png and Default-Landscape.png. Optionally, you can add further default images to suit the LandscapeLeft, LandscapeRight, and PortraitUpsideDown orientations: Default-LandscapeLeft.png and so on. The default screen size is 1024 x 768, but you may need to remove 20 pixels from one edge when the status bar is visible.

All files except the screenshots should be added to the application in the Project navigator. For convenience, add them to the Resources group.

CAUTION

If you're having problems getting Xcode 4 to recognize PNG files during validation (see later in this section), try saving them with the Generic RGB color profile. The default is sRGB, and Xcode 4 sometimes doesn't accept files with this profile.

Creating a new build configuration

The build settings for an App Store release typically use a modified version of the default Release build configuration. You can create one in two ways:

- Modify the existing Release configuration in place.
- Make a copy, and use it for the final build.

The advantage of an in-place edit is that there's less other work to do. You can edit the existing Release configuration settings, and you're ready to build.

The advantage of creating a copy is that if you create further configurations—for example, for beta distribution—you can use the default Release configuration as a standard starting point. You also can save the configuration with the project and give it a useful name. When you're ready to release an updated version of the project, you can reuse your customized App Store configuration as is.

This example demonstrates how to use a separate file. Follow these steps:

1. **Select Project and the Info tab.**

2. **If the Configurations heading isn't open, click the reveal triangle to open it.**

3. **Click the + (plus) icon at the bottom of the subpane.**

4. **Select the Duplicate "Release" Configuration option from the floating menu, as shown in Figure 13.8.**

This creates a new configuration called Release copy.

5. **Single-click twice on the name, and type in a modified name, such as App Store.**

Customizing build settings and options

Preparing the build is a two-stage process. You can perform the steps in any order:

- Customize the build settings.
- Customize other build options.

Figure 13.8

Creating a new configuration for App Store builds by copying the default Release configuration

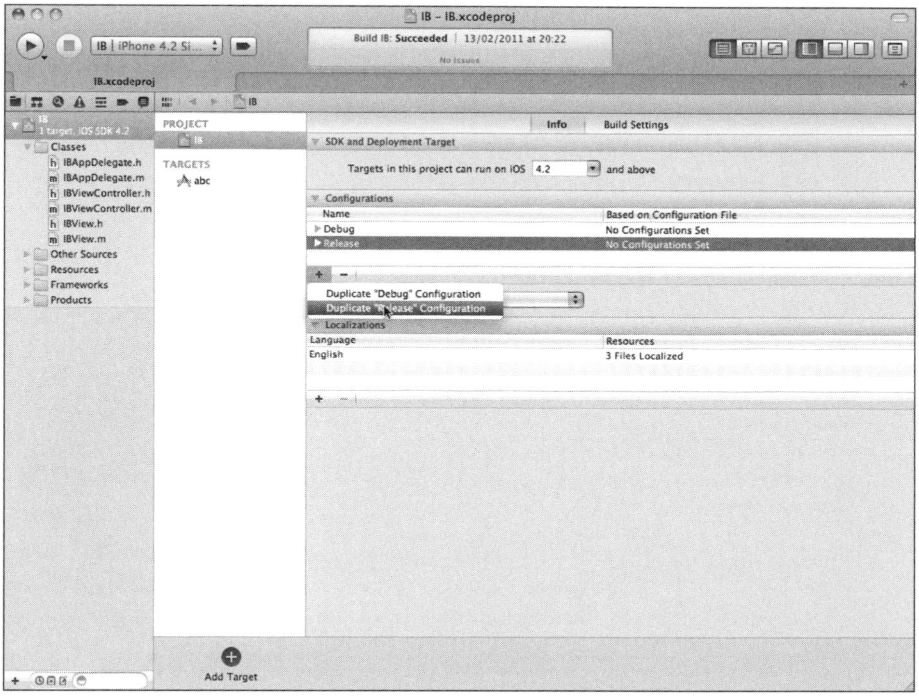

Customizing build settings

Select the app target, select the Build Settings tab, select the Combined view, and work through the list that follows.

Most items are configuration-specific, so if a setting appears with <multiple values>, click its reveal triangle and change the value next to the App Store configuration.

- **Base SDK:** This should have been set to the most recent public OS version during development. Double-check it anyway.
- **Validate Built Product:** Select Yes.

- **Code Signing Identity:** Select a valid distribution provisioning profile. You can use the default iPhone Distribution under the Automatic Profile Selector header, as shown in Figure 13.9. But be very careful: If you have multiple distribution profiles, it may select the wrong one or default to the last one used. Double-check that it really has selected the correct profile, which is usually the one you've named Distribution.
- **Strip Debug Symbols During Copy:** Select Yes.
- **Targeted Device Family:** Select the devices supported by your app.
- **iOS Deployment Target:** Set this to the oldest version of iOS supported by your app, as discussed earlier in this chapter.
- **Product name:** Set this to the final production name string, as discussed earlier.

Figure 13.9

Selecting the distribution profile in the build settings for the new App Store configuration

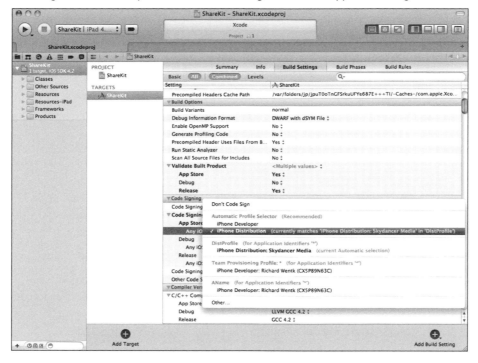

NOTE

You also can make these changes in the Levels view. The Combined view is simpler and less cluttered, especially on a smaller monitor.

Customizing other build options

Customizing the other options is a two-step process. Select the Summary tab, and make the following changes:

- **Version:** Set this to the current version number of your app.
- **Devices:** Ignore this; it copies its value from the Targeted Device Family build setting.
- **Main Interface:** Don't change this. (If you need to use this feature, set it during development and testing.)
- **Supported Device Orientations:** These options don't define the supported orientations; you do that in code in your view controllers. In theory, they define the orientations in which the app is allowed to launch. In practice, implementation is erratic and seems to vary between devices and different versions of iOS. So you need to experiment with these settings during development.
- **App icons:** Right-click each icon, and navigate to the icon files you prepared earlier, as shown in Figure 13.10, with the dimensions listed in Table 13.1 (57 x 57 for the required standard icon and 114 x 114 for the optional Retina Display icon).

Figure 13.10

Setting the Summary options for an iOS App

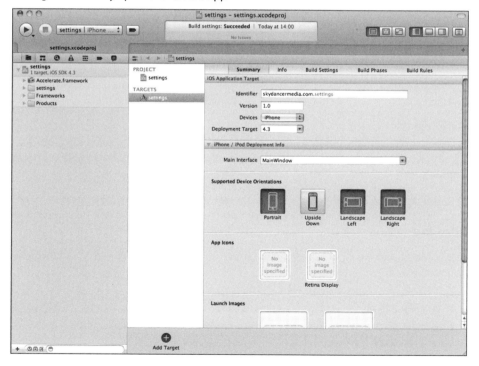

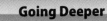

- **Launch Images:** Right-click each placeholder, and navigate to the default launch images you prepared earlier, with the dimensions in Table 13.1.
- **Other Images:** If your app is universal or iPad-only, add images for iPad support in the same way.

NOTE

It's likely you defined app icons and launch images during development. If so, you don't need to define them again.

Select the Info tab. You can typically leave the Custom iOS Target Properties unchanged; the Summary settings change some of them, and the default settings are usually correct.

Occasionally, you may want to add special features. Table 13.2 has a short list of the most useful optional keys. See Appendix B for more information about how to add, edit, and select the features on this page.

Table 13.2 Selected Optional iOS App Keys

Setting	Notes
Application does not run in background	Set YES to force the app to terminate immediately without running in the background.
Application supports iTunes file sharing	Set YES to enable access to saved files through iTunes
Icon already includes gloss effects	Set YES to disable the iOS glossy overlay.
Required background modes	Include at least one of audio, location, VoIP to allow the app to run in the background permanently

Building the project

You're almost (but not quite) ready to build the project. In Xcode 3, you built a project in the usual way, archived it manually in Finder, and manually uploaded the archive to iTunes Connect.

In Xcode 4, the Archive build action and the validation/submission features automate this process. You can do everything from Xcode without having to find the app package in Finder or using an external uploader.

By default, the Archive uses the Release configuration. You must change this before building. Follow these steps:

CAUTION

If you forget this step, the product is assigned your development certificate. Other very bad things may also happen, and your archive isn't valid.

1. **Select Product ⇨ Edit Scheme from the main Xcode menu.**

2. **Select the Archive action in the column at the left.**

3. **Select the App Store configuration from the Build Configuration menu, as shown in Figure 13.11.**

4. **Leave the Reveal Archive in Organizer option checked.**

5. **Select iOS Device as the Destination from the menu at the top of the dialog.**

6. **Make sure the Breakpoints button is deselected.**

Figure 13.11

Make sure that your new App Store configuration settings are applied when you build to archive/upload.

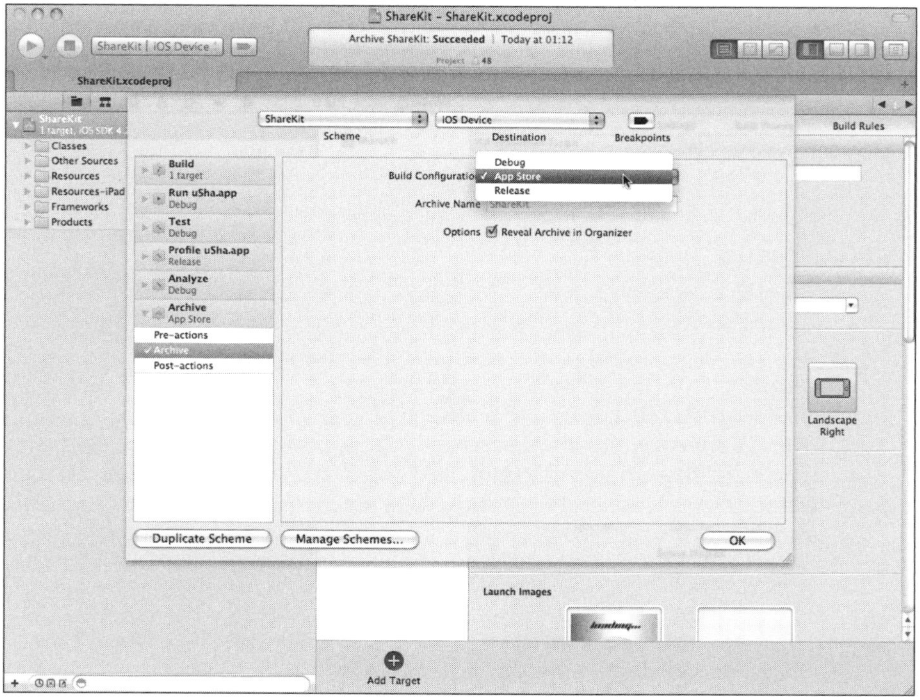

7. **Select Product ⇨ Archive from the main Xcode menu.**

This runs the Archive action and builds your app from scratch, which may take a while.

Eventually, the Archives window from the Organizer appears, as shown in Figure 13.12. But you can't submit the application yet; first, you must fill in the "paperwork" on iTunes Connect so that the App Store is ready for your app.

Figure 13.12

The Archive that appears in the Organizer is a packaged app that can be submitted to the App Store, but only after you've filled in some online "paperwork."

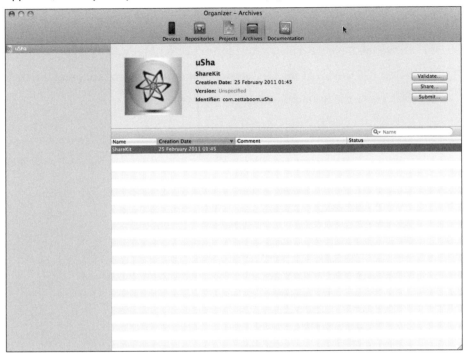

Uploading marketing and support materials

iTunes Connect works in almost exactly the opposite way you'd expect. Instead of uploading a binary and then adding marketing text and images for it, you upload the marketing materials first to create an application record. You then upload your archived app. It becomes the binary associated with the record.

NOTE
The way iTunes Connect works may seem counterintuitive, but it has a valid purpose. If your binary is rejected, the application record remains in place, and you don't have to reenter it when you resubmit. Similarly, when you upgrade your app to a new version, you can reuse the details you entered when you first submitted the app.

Follow these steps to upload your app:

1. Log in to the iOS Developer Portal, and select iTunes Connect from the list of items at the top right of the screen. (You can also access iTunes Connect directly at `itunesconnect.apple.com`.)

2. **Select Manage Your Apps.**

3. **Click Add New App at the top left.**

4. **Work your way through the "paperwork," the first page of which is shown in Figure 13.13, by filling in the fields, uploading artwork, answering questions about encryption technology and age ratings, and copying and pasting your marketing text.**

   Most of the options are straightforward. The most likely source of confusion is the Bundle ID option.

5. **Select the ID embedded in your distribution profile. If you have a single App ID, use it. If you have multiple IDs, select the last one you used when creating a certificate.**

   If you followed all the steps in Chapter 11, you should have an application record.

Figure 13.13

This is the first page of the "paperwork." Note the Bundle ID menu.

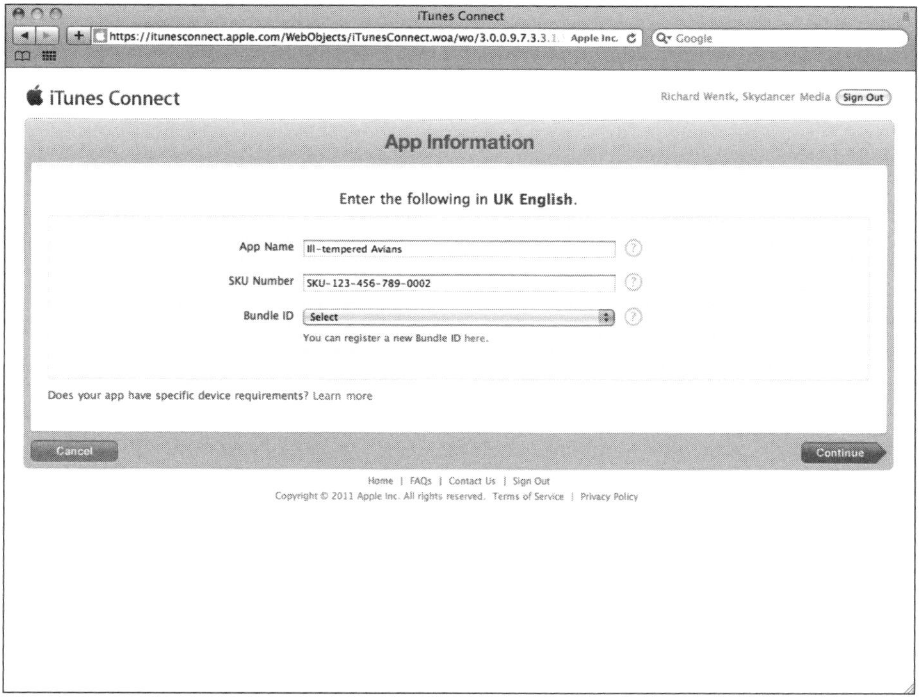

CROSS-REFERENCE

See Chapter 11 for a reminder about App IDs.

NOTE

You can repeat the process to create multiple app records in a single session. In fact, you can create as many records as you want. They aren't visible on the App Store until you upload a binary for each, and the record and binary are approved for sale.

Submitting an app to iTunes Connect

Eventually, your application record is complete. At the time of this writing, the final screen tells you to use an application called Application Loader to submit the binary. Whether Apple removes this screen in future, you can ignore it because Xcode 4 includes its own upload and packaging tools.

Submission is another two-stage process. The first step is app validation; it's optional but recommended. The second is submission/upload.

Validating an app

The internal details of the validation process are secret, but we know it checks for basic errors, including missing artwork, invalid package and bundle settings, and incorrect provisioning. Successful validation doesn't guarantee that your app will be accepted for sale, but it flags the most obvious errors that guarantee that Apple will reject it.

In the Organizer, select your archive (if it isn't already selected), and click the Validate button at the top right of the window. You are asked to log in with your developer name and password. Next, you see the dialog box shown in Figure 13.14.

The Application menu shows any application records that you haven't yet completed with a binary. Typically, there's a single item here—the last record you created.

The Identity menu should match the distribution identity you selected in the build settings before you built the app, as described earlier in this section.

Figure 13.14

Validating an app before upload

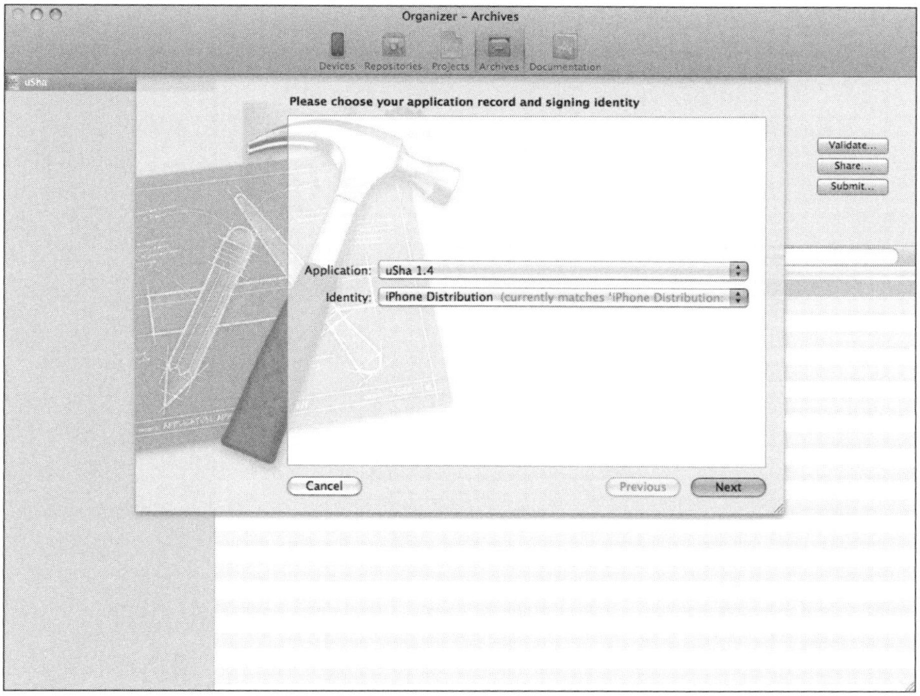

TIP

The menu is identical to the menu used to select an identity in the build settings. Make sure you select the same item in both.

Click Next. Xcode packages the app for upload and runs the validation checks. If validation fails, the dialog box lists one or more errors, as shown in Figure 13.15.

Figure 13.15

The Validate option displays a list of issues. There may be more than one.

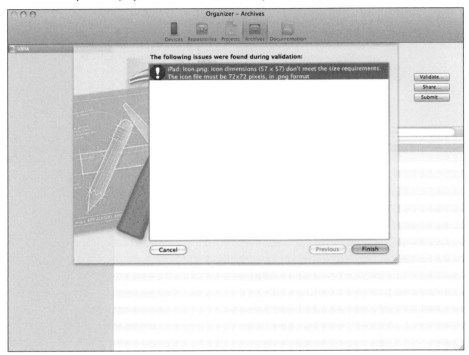

To fix validation errors, follow these steps:

1. **Delete the archive, unless you want to keep it, but typically, you don't.**

2. **Add or repair the items that are missing or incorrect.**

This may mean changing some of the items in the build summary/info pages. You don't usually need to modify the build settings.

3. **Create another archive build by selecting Product ⇨ Archive from the main Xcode menu.**

4. **Revalidate the new archive.**

Figure 13.16 shows a successful validation.

Figure 13.16

A successful validation means you're ready to submit the app.

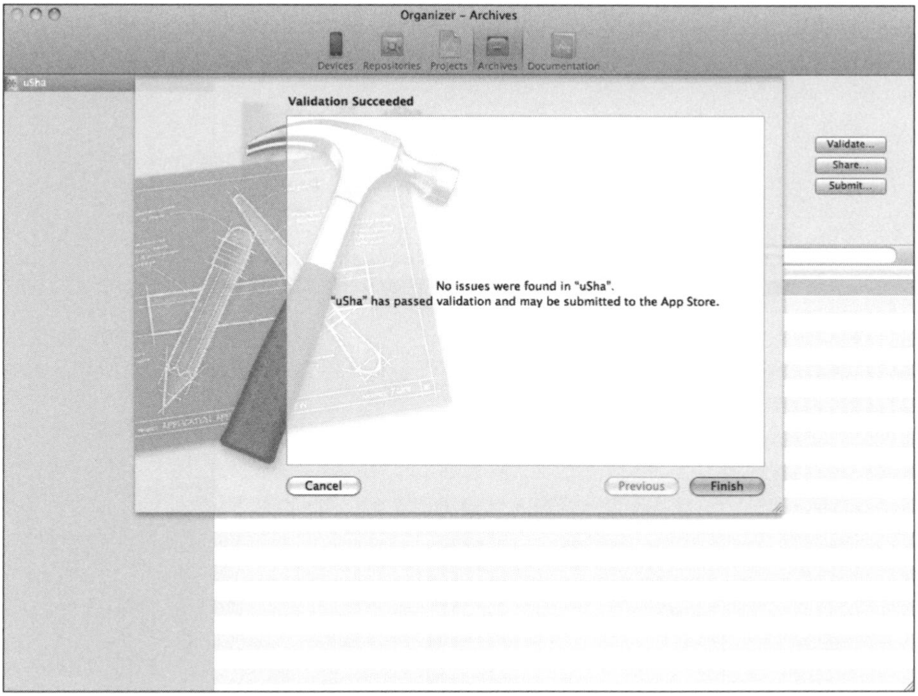

CAUTION

The validation process isn't completely robust, and sometimes apps fail for no reason. When there's a problem with iTunes Connect, you see cryptic error messages such as "Unable to extra package metadata." Obvious app problems are usually labeled accurately. It's a good idea to double-check everything, clean the build, and perhaps copy the files to a new folder before archiving and validating again. If you're sure your app is valid, you can sometimes submit it success-fully after a failed validation by clicking Submit three or four times until the upload is accepted.

Submitting an app

To submit an app, click the Submit button at the top right of the Organizer. The submission pro-cess is very similar to validation; you're asked to log in, and then the app is packaged. Instead of a validation pass, the package is uploaded, as shown in Figure 13.17.

Figure 13.17

A successful submission

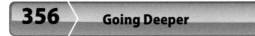

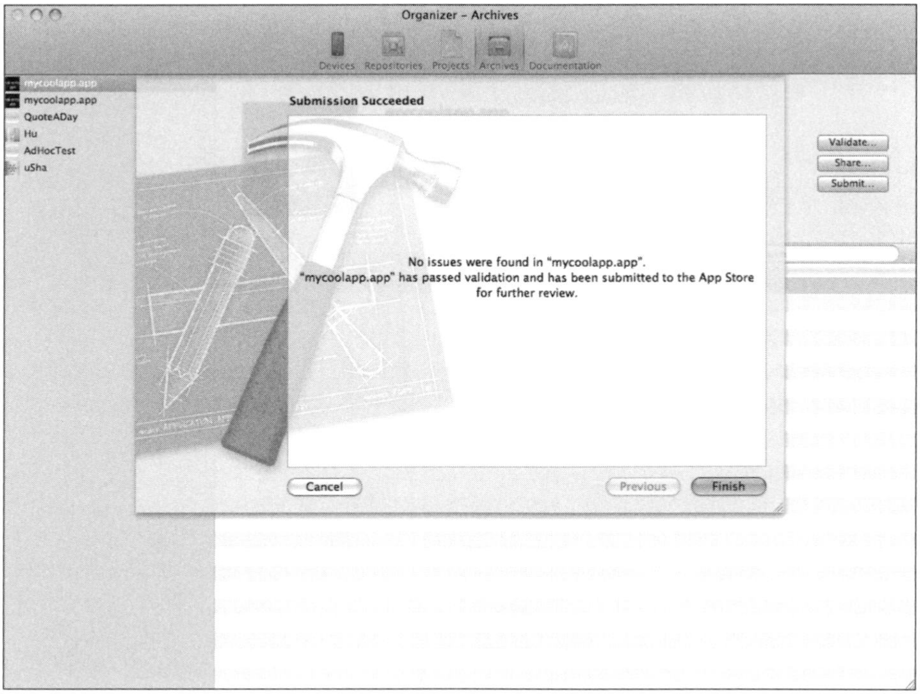

NOTE
In fact, submission includes another validation pass. But it's quicker to validate separately before submitting.

After submission, the app is added to the review queue. It typically takes one to two weeks for the app to reach the head of the queue, and a random duration that can last a day to a couple of months for the review process. Most apps go on sale within two weeks of submission.

iTunes connect displays status messages—Waiting For Review, and In Review—to let you see where the app is in the review process. When the review is complete, you'll receive an e-mail with notice of acceptance or rejection.

Deleting or hiding apps after submission

If you discover a problem with your binary after submission, select the app, select Binary Details, and click the Reject This Binary button at the top right. You can then repeat the submission process with a new binary. Note that you can't delete an app submission record while a binary is awaiting review.

If you want to delete an app after it's been accepted for sale, this is a complicated process. It's usually easier and quicker to remove an app from sale than to delete it completely. Select the app, click Rights and Pricing, select the Specific Stores link, and click the Deselect All button at the top right of the Rights and Territories list. This leaves its submission record on iTunes Connect so you can update it with a new version at a later date, but hides it from buyers on iTunes.

Creating and distributing an iOS Ad Hoc build

The build process for an Ad Hoc build that you can share with beta testers is similar to an App Store build. But there are differences. Before you create an Ad Hoc build, you must create a suitable distribution profile.

Creating and installing an Ad Hoc provisioning profile

For more details about provisioning, see Chapter 11. Figure 13.18 shows the settings for an Ad Hoc profile. Remember that you must do the following:

Figure 13.18

Creating an Ad Hoc profile

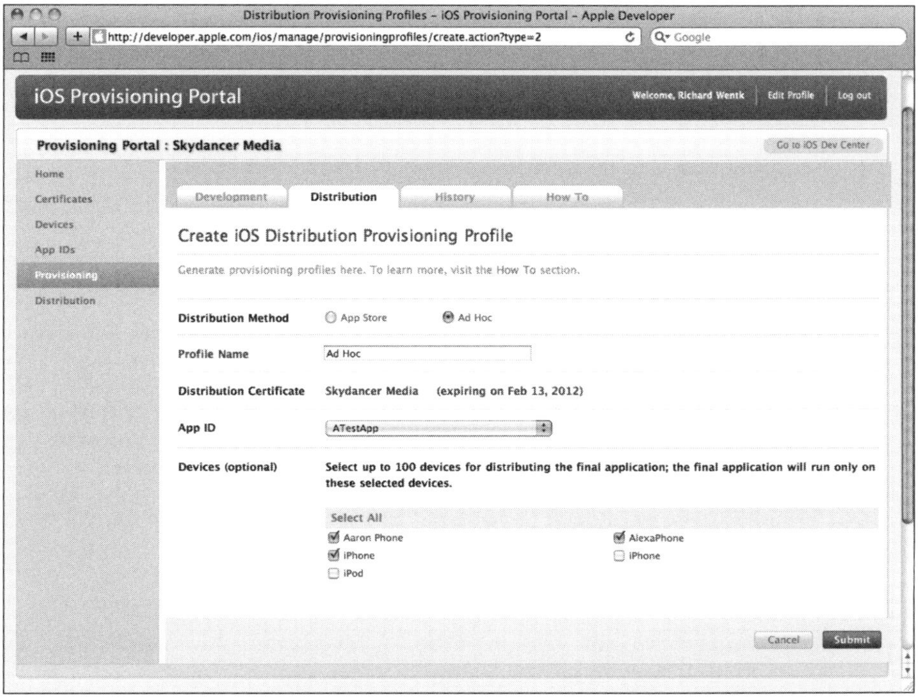

1. **Get the UDID of every supported device from each user, and add it to your device list.**

2. **Select the devices in the list that your testers will use.**

   Users can run the app only on the devices in the list.

3. **Pick a valid App ID for the profile or create a new one, and make a note of it for later.**

4. **Install the new profile by dragging it from Finder and dropping it onto the Provisioning Profiles item at the top left of the Devices window in the Organizer.**

   The new profile will have the `.mobileprovision` file extension.

T I P

After creating the new profile, don't forget to refresh the page on the portal to update its status from Pending to Active.

Creating an Ad Hoc build

Once you have an Ad Hoc profile, use the following steps to build your beta app:

1. **Create a new build configuration based on the default Release profile, and give it a new name, such as Ad Hoc.**

2. **Sign the app with the new Ad Hoc distribution profile in the build settings.**

   If you use the profile auto-selector, remember to double-check that this worked correctly and you're signing the build with the Ad Hoc profile. Modify other build settings as needed.

3. **Select the Ad Hoc Release configuration in the Archive Build Action.**

4. **Select the iOS Device option in the platform pop-up menu and build the archive with Product ➪ Archive.**

5. **In the Organizer, use the Share button to create a shareable app package with a .ipa suffix. Select the Ad Hoc profile from the Identity menu, and save the packaged app to a convenient location.**

6. **E-mail the file to testers, or upload it to a website and e-mail them a download link.**

7. **Testers use iTunes to install and run the app.**

8. **If the app is for a beta version of the OS, testers must be able to install that version on their devices before testing the app.**

Installing an Ad Hoc app with iTunes

To install an app, testers open iTunes and drag and drop the file onto the Library at the top left, as shown in Figure 13.19. Syncing the device with the Sync Apps option—testers may need to check the app in the app list manually—installs the app and automatically installs the embedded distribution profile.

Figure 13.19

Installing an Ad Hoc app with iTunes

N O T E

In earlier versions of Xcode, Ad Hoc distribution didn't work unless projects were built with an Entitlements.plist file, and the provisioning profile was supplied to testers with the app. These steps are no longer necessary, because the packaging process embeds a working profile and entitlements are managed automatically.

N O T E

If you're developing apps for a beta version of iOS or OS X, there's no legal way to supply beta copies of an OS update to testers who aren't registered developers. Illegal ways are discussed online, but they're outside the scope of this book.

Using Over the Air (OTA) distribution

In Xcode 3, enterprise developers had the option to create a package that could be down-loaded and installed directly on the device by clicking a web link in Safari. This is called Over the Air (OTA) distribution, and it creates a much smoother experience for testers.

OTA distribution uses a feature built into Safari (and only Safari) that allows the browser to vali-date a provisioning profile and install an app on any iOS device running iOS 4.0 and later.

Although it was introduced as an enterprise tool, all developers can use this feature, but the packaging process for creating the support files for an OTA app is moderately complex. In addi-tion to the `ipa` file, the link requires some basic HTML and a supporting `plist` manifest file with details of the app. Creating the HTML is easy, but creating the manifest `plist` is more challenging.

Xcode 4 doesn't support this feature for standard developers, but various commercial work-arounds are available. For example, diawi (`www.diawi.com`) is an ad-sponsored app that allows developers to upload test builds to its website and e-mail links to testers. TestFlight (`http://testflightapp.com`), shown in Figure 13.20, is a similar alternative. These options make OTA distribution almost as easy as drag and drop.

Figure 13.20

TestFlight: one way to create an OTA distribution for beta testers

Developers who don't want to entrust their files to a third party can use iOS BetaBuilder (`www.hanchorllc.com/category/ios-betabuilder/`) to create custom HTML and manifest files for distribution from their own web server. BetaBuilder loads an `ipa` file and generates supporting HTML and a manifest `plist` tied to a specific download URL. You can then upload the files to a server and e-mail testers the URL. At the time of this writing, a supporting app is being developed.

Note that although official enterprise OTA doesn't require device registration, standard developers must still register devices and include them in every Ad Hoc distribution profile.

C A U T I O N

Non-enterprise OTA isn't officially supported by Apple. The technology has been borrowed for non-enterprise use, and Apple may withdraw it without notice.

Creating a Mac App Store submission

A Mac submission is similar to an iOS submission, but somewhat simpler. Begin by creating an App Record on iTunes Connect, filling in the "paperwork" to create a binary slot. You then customize the app's settings, build it as archive, package it, and upload the binary.

Currently, there's no device registration or support for device-limited Ad Hoc distribution for testing. (This may change in the future.)

Finding iTunes Connect

At the time of this writing, there's no direct link to iTunes Connect on the front page of the Mac Dev Center. To open iTunes Connect, select the Get Your Mac Apps Ready for the Mac App Store link at the top right of the front page, and then click the Log in to iTunes Connect link at the bottom of the Set up Your iTunes Connect Account paragraph, shown in Figure 13.21.

Creating marketing and support materials

The "paperwork" for a Mac submission is very similar to an iOS submission. The promotional screenshot must have a resolution of 1280 x 800 or 1440 x 900 in `.jpeg`, `.jpg`, `.tiff`, or `.png` in the RGB color space with a resolution of 72dpi or better. In practice, this means you can run the app, set your Mac's display resolution to the required dimensions, and use Grab utility in `/Applications/Utilities` to capture the art as a `.tiff` file.

T I P

The artwork doesn't have to be an unedited screen grab. You also can create custom promotional artwork that captions or highlights important features of your app. This is pushing against the guidelines, but if the artwork isn't too heavy handed and promotional, there's a good chance it will be accepted.

Figure 13.21

There's no direct link to iTune Connect from the Mac Dev Center front page; you have to go through this intermediate page.

Creating an App ID and managing certificates

OS X apps don't support wildcard/suite IDs, so you must create a new ID for each app, following the steps described in Chapter 11.

App IDs aren't built into the Mac App Software Certificate or the Mac Installer Package Certificate, so you can reuse the same certificates for every app.

NOTE

When a user buys an app from the store, iTunes generates a receipt file that locks it to one specific Mac. Your app can validate this receipt to prevent piracy. This requires extra code; it's not automatic. Validation isn't part of the build process, but it's a good idea to add it and test it while developing. For details and sample code, see Validating App Store Receipts in the documentation.

Customizing the build for the App Store

You must do the following:

- Customize the build settings.
- Modify the build options: summary and info.

But you don't need to do these things:

- Create a new configuration. The default Release configuration can be used as is.
- Edit the default scheme. There's no need to select an updated configuration in the default settings for the Archive action.

Customizing the build settings

Click the project at the top of the project navigator, select the target, and click the Build Settings tab to open the settings editor. These are the critical settings:

- **Architectures:** Leave this set to Standard (32/64-bit Intel) for backward compatibility. For apps that are 64-bit only, including those that run under OS X 10.7 Lion, set this to 64-bit Intel.
- **Debug Information Format:** Check that this is set to DWARF with dSym File.
- **Code Signing Identity:** Set this to the identity that begins with 3rd Party Mac Developer Application, as shown in Figure 13.22.

Figure 13.22

Setting the code signing identity for a Mac app

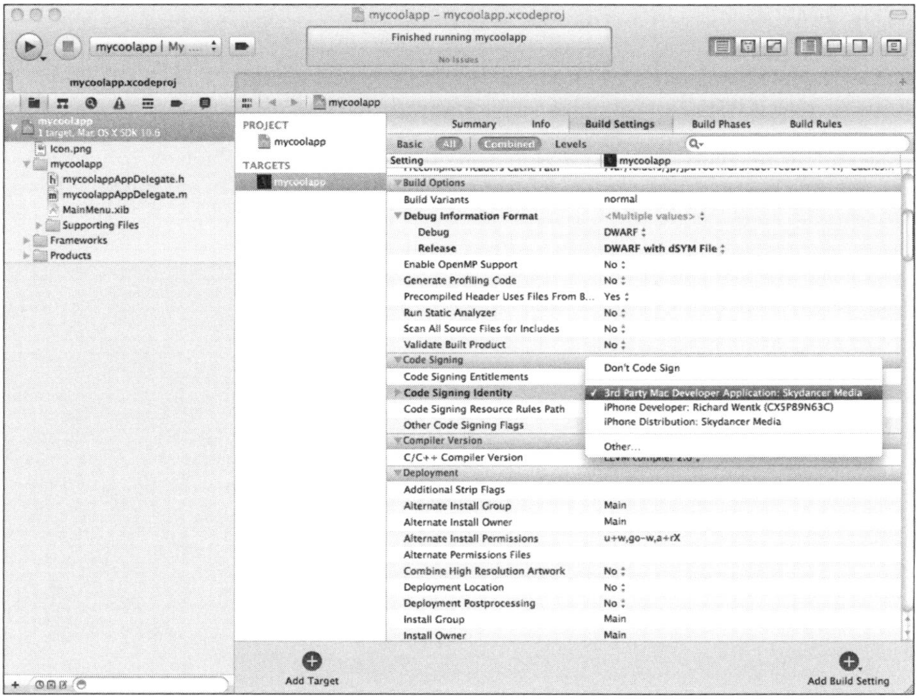

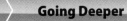

- **Product Name:** Optionally, you can change this to set the final production name.
- **Deployment Target:** Set the lowest supported version of OS X, as described earlier.

NOTE

After you set a code signing identity, you can continue to test and run the project on your Mac in the usual way. Unlike iOS code signing, Mac code signing doesn't prevent this. Receipt checking can complicate this, so disable receipt checking code until your final production build.

Creating the app icon file

Mac apps use a special multi-icon file with a `.icns` extension that stores multiple resolutions of the icon. There's only one way to create this file: Use the Icon Composer utility, which is supplied with Xcode 4. You can find it in `<Xcode 4 install folder>/Applications/Utilities`.

You have two options for icon design:

- Create a single 512 x 512 file in an image editor, and allow Icon Composer to create the other resolutions for you.
- Create separate files for other resolutions.

The required resolutions are 512 x 512, 256 x 256, 128 x 128, 32 x 32, and 16 x 16. Rescaling a single file usually creates poor results, but—depending the design of your icon—this may not matter.

A time-saving option is to create two resolutions: 512 x 512 and 32 x 32. Use Icon Composer to create the 256 x 256 and 128 x 128 resolutions from the larger file, and the 16 x 16 resolution from the smaller. For best results, create the smaller file independently. For example, if the icon includes text, retype the text in the smaller file with a smaller font size.

Save your source files as PNGs. Launch Icon Composer, and drag the files from Finder into the squares in the Icon Composer UI, as shown in Figure 13.23. When every square is filled, save the file with the `.icns` extension.

Figure 13.23

Creating an icon file with Icon Composer

Modifying the build options

On the Summary page, shown in Figure 13.24, you need to do the following:

- **Add the App Icon:** Right-click the Add Icon box and navigate to your new `.icns` file.
- **Select an Application Category:** Select one item from the menu. It must match the category in your submission record on iTunes Connect.
- **Ignore the Identifier:** Set it in the Info window instead.
- **Set a version number.**
- **Ignore the App Runs on Mac OS X menu:** This is overridden by the deployment target in the build settings.
- **Ignore the Main Interface**. If you changed this during development, don't change it again now.

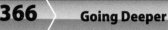

Figure 13.24

Preparing the target Summary settings

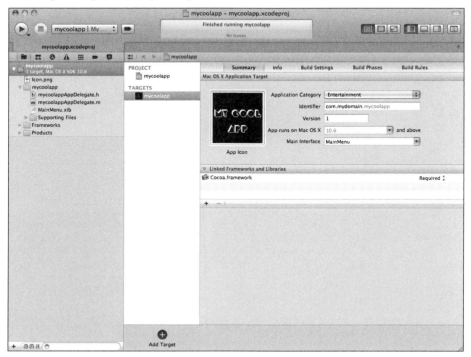

On the info page, shown in Figure 13.25, you need to do the following:

- **Set the Bundle Identifier:** This must match the string used as an App ID in your submission record. (See the Caution.)
- **Add a copyright notice:** Right-click in the Key list, select Add Row, and select Copyright (human readable) from the key list. Click the Value field to the right, and type your copyright text.

CAUTION

At the time of this writing, Xcode 4 defaults to a forward domain name on the target Info and Summary pages—in other words, your domain name appears as <yourdomain.com>. Reverse domain names—<com.yourdomain>—are considered standard, so you can manage this in two ways. One option is to create a matching, nominally incorrect App ID. The other is to edit this by hand to correct it. If you leave the PRODUCT_NAME macro unchanged, Xcode 4 successfully adds your product name to the bundle name. You can preview the name in the Identifier box on the target summary page. The critical point is that the Bundle Identifier *must* match the App ID you create for your project—although if you create a wildcard/suite ID, the product name itself is irrelevant.

Figure 13.25

Adding a copyright notice to the Info plist

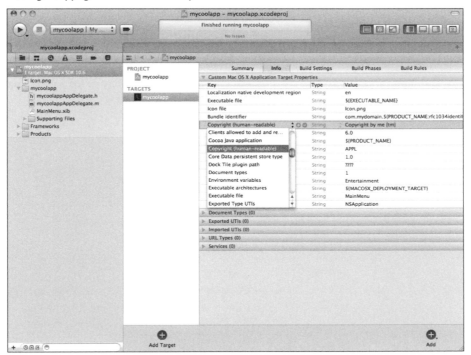

Building, testing, and validating the app

Follow these steps to build, test, and validate your app:

1. **Select Product ⇨ Archive to build the app and open the Organizer.**

You can use the Validate button to perform basic validation, as for an iOS app. You also must run a separate check to make sure your app will install correctly after it has been downloaded from the App Store.

2. **Select the Share button at the top right, and leave the default setting for Contents unchanged—for example, Mac OS X App Store Package** (.pkg)**, as shown in Figure 13.26.**

3. **Save the file to a location you can easily access from the command line, such as your root user directory.**

4. **Open Terminal, and type this code snippet:**

```
sudo installer -store -pkg <path-to-package> -target /
```

This runs the standard OS X installer in App Store mode, which forces it to check signatures and permissions. (If you double-click the app package it installs without these checks.) The app should install in your /Applications folder, where you can run it in the usual way.

5. **If validation and the installer test work correctly, click the Submit button to submit the app.**

6. **Log in, select an app record, and pick a signing identity, as for an iOS app.**

Figure 13.26

Checking installation with a store-compatible manual install

Working with Advanced Build Techniques

So far, the build process has been treated as a "black box" that does its job after it's initialized with a standard list of build settings. This is adequate for simpler apps, but for more complex projects, it can be useful to break apart the build process and customize it further.

Understanding the build process

In outline, the build process has four stages:

1. Preprocessor
2. Compiler
3. Linker
4. File copier and processor

The preprocessor makes working copies of the original source files, expanding `#include` directives to include the original headers, expanding macros (low-level reusable code snippets and definitions), and implementing *conditional compilation*. Conditional compilation uses directives such as `#if` and `#ifdef` to test compiler and system settings and select code according to their values.

Internally, the preprocessor is more complex than this simple description suggests, but a full introduction is outside the scope of this book. The key practical point is that you can use preprocessor directives to include and exclude code automatically according to various system, platform, and build settings.

The compiler converts the files generated by the preprocessor into machine code. The LLVM and GCC compilers do this in different ways, but the end result is identical—a file with the `.o` (object) extension. Projects that use source code in other languages can call an external compiler to produce compatible binaries.

Each source file in the project creates a separate object file. The linker combines them all into a single executable binary, resolves symbol references to a specific location in the binary, and checks that all references are present and correct. For example, if your code calls a framework, the linker checks that the framework is included. If it can't find the framework or the specific symbol in it, it can't complete its task and the build fails.

The file copier processes supporting files. Different file types are processed in different ways, according to set rules. For example, nib files are compacted, image files may be compressed, plists are processed using their own separate processor, and so on. All processed files are copied to the target's product folder. Some may be handed to the linker, so the point at which files are processed may vary.

The Xcode build system implements this scheme inside a customizable build manager. Each stage runs multiple shell scripts. You can add your own scripts to the default build sequence. Potentially, you can even replace the default scripts with your own custom-written alternatives, although this isn't a trivial job.

In practice, Xcode manages the build process through a combination of two elements:

- Build phases select and process files of a given type. You also can add phases that run arbitrary scripts. Build phases define when files are processed and when other scripted build events happen.
- Build rules define the scripts that control what happens to a file with a specific extension. They define how files are processed.

To customize a build fully you must know how to do the following:

- Access the standard build settings and environment variables in your code, so you can add conditional compilation features.
- Create your own custom build settings for use in conditional compilation.
- Create and manage build phases.
- Create and manage build rules.

Introducing conditional compilation

Conditional compilation is an automated process that literally includes and excludes lines of code from your source files. You create conditional code by surrounding it with preprocessor directives, which look similar to conventional C code but are prefixed with the # character.

Table 13.3 lists the standard conditional and unconditional directives.

Table 13.3 Conditional Compilation Directives

Macro	Meaning
#define	Sets the value of a token.
#if	Includes the following code if a conditional test is true. Conditional comparisons work only with integers. There's no way to compare a macro with a string or with the numeric value of a string.
#ifdef	Includes the following code if a token is defined.
#ifndef	Includes the following code if a token isn't defined.
#else	Includes the following code when the preceding test is false.
#elif	Combined #else #if for nested conditionals.
#endif	Ends the conditional test. Code after #endif is always included, in the usual way.
#include	Includes the following code unconditionally.
#import	The Objective-C equivalent of #include.
#warning	Prints a C string warning to the console. (Because this is a C directive, don't prefix the string with the Objective-C @ objectifier.)

Using conditional compilation

In theory, conditional compilation is very simple. A typical example looks like this:

```
#ifdef <some token>
        ...code to include...
#endif
```

The *token* is a general catch-all name for all the available settings, macros, environment variables, and user-defined flags and values. The challenge with conditional compilation is finding which tokens are available.

Compilers include a range of settings that are defined by the language, platform, compiler, and build. Some tokens are defined as macros and use a special format: their names are prefixed with a double underscore, and they may end with another double underscore. Users can define their own custom tokens as absolute values, references to other settings, or logical combinations of two or more settings.

CAUTION

Note that you can't compare strings in an #if directive, but you can compare tokens with numerical values. You can also check whether a specific token has been defined.

Table 13.4 lists a small selection of useful macros and platform settings.

Table 13.4 Useful Macros and Conditional Compilation Tokens

Macro	Meaning
__FILE__	The name of the current file as a C string constant
__LINE__	The current line number in a source file as a decimal integer
__DATE__	The date as a C string constant
__TIME__	The time as a C string constant
__OBJC__	True for an Objective-C project
TARGET_IPHONE_SIMULATOR	True when compiling for the Simulator
TARGET_OS_IPHONE	True when compiling for iOS, false for OS X

Having a single source for these tokens would be useful, but they're scattered across many different locations. For compiler-specific tokens, search online for "GCC preprocessor macros" and "LLVM preprocessor macros." For some of the Apple-specific tokens, search in Finder for the file TargetConditionals.h.

Creating custom tokens

Creating your own tokens is often useful—for example, you can add a token that's only defined when you select a custom configuration.

Note that it's a good idea to give your tokens a custom prefix; your initials are a popular option. Developers often add tokens to their code. If code is shared, simple names such as DEBUG and IPHONE can be defined in multiple locations, creating conflicts.

1. **Open a project with at least one custom configuration. Open the target build settings, and scroll down the Other C Flags entry under the Language settings, as shown in Figure 13.27.**

2. **Click the entry to show the different configuration options.**

3. **Click the name of your custom configuration, and click the small + icon that appears to the right.**

   This adds a new token to the build settings.

4. **Select Any Architecture | Any SDK from the floating menu at the left, and type** -DMY_TOKEN **into the value field at the right to define the name and the value of the token.**

   If you select a specific SDK or architecture, the token is defined only when that SDK is active.

   Figure 13.27

   Adding a custom token. In this example MY_TOKEN is only defined when the My Debug configuration is active.

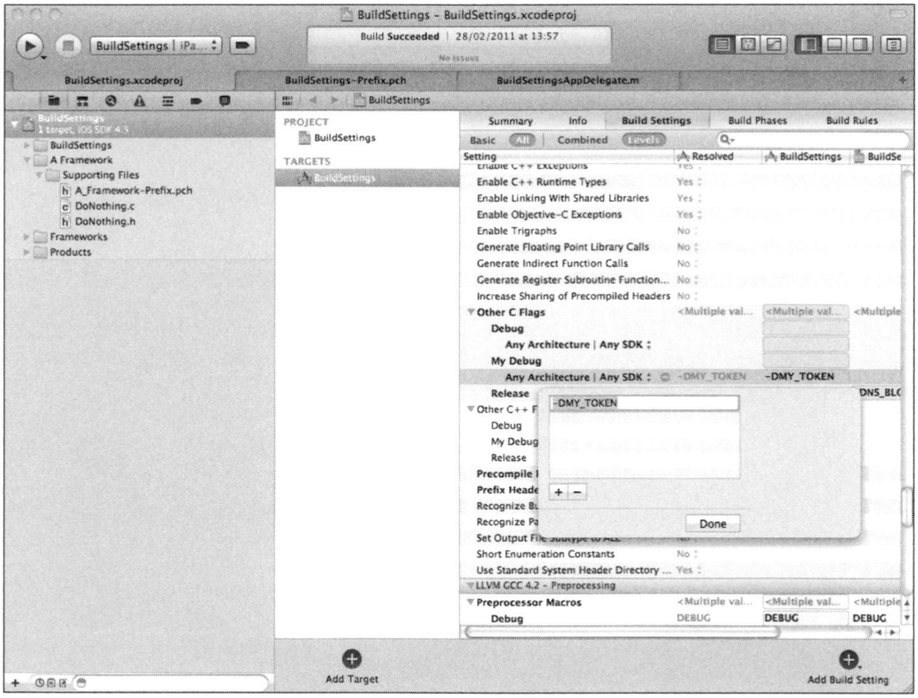

5. **If you need to add more tokens, repeat the process.**

You can define a value for the token by adding = (equal sign) followed by the value. The critical element that "tokenizes" your entry is the –D prefix.

You also can simply #define tokens in your project's -Prefix.pch file. They're available to every file in the project, and they override existing definitions.

TIP

The predefined token NS_BLOCK_ASSERTIONS=1 for the Release configuration is an example a token with a value. If you want to use #ifdef, it's enough to define the token without giving it a value. Use the more general <tokenname>=<value> only if you want to check a numeric value or use a string.

TIP

If you add #define NSLog to your project's -Prefix.pch file, all instances of NSLog are stripped from your code. This is a quick way to eliminate log messages when you no longer need them.

After you've defined MY_TOKEN correctly, you can use this conditional directive to include when the token is valid:

```
#ifdef MY_TOKEN
        <…code included if MY_TOKEN is defined…>
#endif
```

NOTE

You can also add tokens to the Preprocessing section. Add them in the same way, but don't prefix them with –D.

Converting build settings into tokens

You can convert any build setting into a token by wrapping it in a dollar sign and either brackets or curly braces. For example, to read the value of the SDKROOT build setting into your own custom SDK_ROOT token, use the following:

```
SDK_ROOT = $(SDKROOT)
```

You see that Xcode substitutes the real value immediately, so, for example, you may see this:

```
SDK_ROOT = iphoneos
```

Unfortunately, you can't do much with this because the value isn't treated as a C string. If you use `SDK_ROOT` anywhere, `iphoneos` is substituted by the preprocessor. The compiler then looks for a symbol called `iphoneos` and doesn't find it, because it isn't a true symbol.

You can, however, use this technique to read numerical build settings into your code. But don't forget (again) that these values are valid at compile-time only.

Conditional compilation is useful for language-, platform-, and target-dependent compilation, but using compile-time build settings to select runtime code is somewhat eccentric. A more useful alternative is to create scripts in the build phases and build rules to define how a build proceeds internally.

TIP

To find the name of any build setting, select it in the Build Settings editor, select Edit ⇨ Copy from the main Xcode menu, and paste the string into TextEdit. You can select multiple settings at the same time, as long as they don't take multiple configuration values. For a full list of build settings, see the Xcode Build Setting Reference in the documentation.

Understanding build phases and build rules

It's worth repeating that Xcode is simply a UI for a set of command-line scripts. The Build Phase and Build Rules tabs in the build editor define which scripts are run and what they do.

You can view the details of the build—the commands given at the command line and the output they generate—by selecting the Log navigator, selecting a completed build, and choosing All and All Messages in the toolbar at the top of the window. The default terse view shown in Figure 13.28 displays the commands in the order they were given. As you can see, the sequence in practice isn't as neat as the preprocess ⇨ compile ⇨ link ⇨ copy template given earlier.

If you right-click anywhere in the list and select Expand All Transcripts, you see the scripts for each stage. The long list of paths, steps, and compiler switches is difficult to read. In theory, you could copy and run each step in Terminal to create a complete build. In practice, you can't, because each new project uses a randomized file path for the build directory, which is in the project's derived data folder. You can find the location of this folder in the Projects page of the Organizer.

Working with build phases

The build phase system can seem complex when you encounter it for the first time, but in fact it's surprisingly easy to work with. To view the build phases editor, select the target build settings and click the Build Phases tab, as shown in Figure 13.29.

You can do the following:

- Manage target dependencies. (Use this option to control the order in which targets are compiled, so the targets are built in the correct sequence.)
- Add more files to the compile sources list.

- Add more libraries and frameworks to the Link Binary With Libraries list.
- Copy resource files to a product bundle.
- Add a custom build to do one of the following: copy files to the product, copy headers to the product, or run an arbitrary script.

Figure 13.28

Listing what happens during a build in the Log navigator

Build phases are most useful when working with multiple targets. For example, if your project has two targets, such as an app and a framework, you typically add the framework to the app's Target Dependencies and add the library it creates to the app's Link Binary with Libraries list as shown in Figure 13.29. Adding it to the link list guarantees that the compiled framework is included in the finished app. Depending on the details of the target, you can choose to compile its source files with the other app files or independently as part of its own target build sequence.

Figure 13.29

Exploring build phases

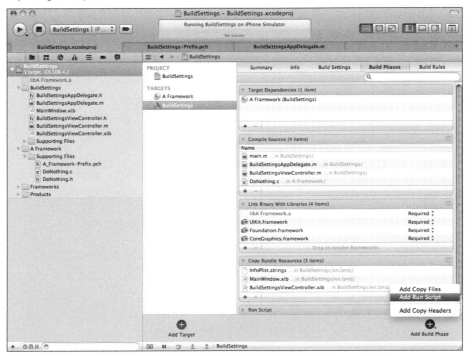

Getting started with scripts and macros

You can use the Run Script option to add customized scripted processing or support. Scripts can be written in any language that works from the command line, including AppleScript, Perl, Python, Ruby, and the standard UNIX shell, all of which are built into OS X.

Build setting macros allow you to access useful build settings in your script. The two default examples in Figure 13.30 show how to read the source and destination directories. A more complex script might loop through every file in the source directory, or select files with a specific extension and then process them in some way. Because scripts have access to environment variables and to other processes, the potential of custom scripting is almost limitless. For example, you can implement or import complete source management tools and add them here, or back up some or all of the files in your build to a remote server.

To remove a script or build phase, click the cancel icon at the top right. You can rearrange the order in which build phases are run by dragging them up and down the list. The Target Dependencies are fixed, but every other phase can be moved.

Figure 13.30

Creating a new build phase begins with an empty custom script. Note that the input and output directories are taken from the build settings and filled in for you.

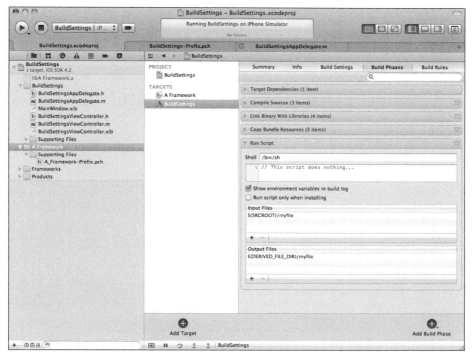

C A U T I O N

Rearranging build phases can create nonsensical results; for example, placing the compile phase after the link phase is rarely useful.

Creating a simple example of a build phase

It's often useful to copy extra resources such as a font file to a bundle. Both OS X and iOS can access fonts from an application bundle. You can use this feature to guarantee that your choice of fonts is available to your app.

While it's possible to add fonts using the standard Add Files... option in Xcode, a custom build phase gives you control over your app bundle's folder structure. You can use a build phase to copy items from any location in your Mac to a folder inside the app.

Figure 13.31 shows one example of a Copy Files build phase. The settings shown in the figure create a folder called /fonts inside the app bundle's /Resources folder, and copy a font file to it from a shared project art directory. The Destination pop-up menu gives you more other powerful choices, including an absolute path option that can install resources to any disk location on a Mac.

Figure 13.31

Using a Copy Files build phase to add a font resource to a project.

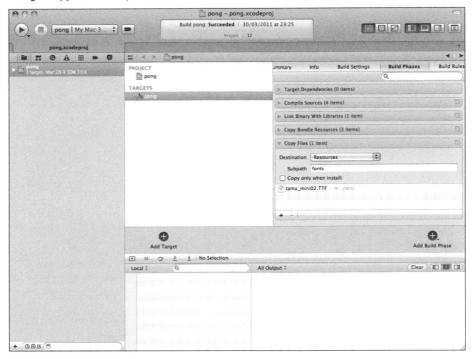

Figure 13.32 shows the result—the fonts folder is added to the bundle. You can now add a key called Application fonts resource path (`ATSApplicationFontsPath`) to the project's Info plist, and add standard code to load and use the font in the usual way. OS X treats the font as if it were included in a Mac's standard `/fonts` folder, but it's not accessible to most users, and can't easily be copied.

Figure 13.32

The /fonts folder added to the bundle, with the copied font

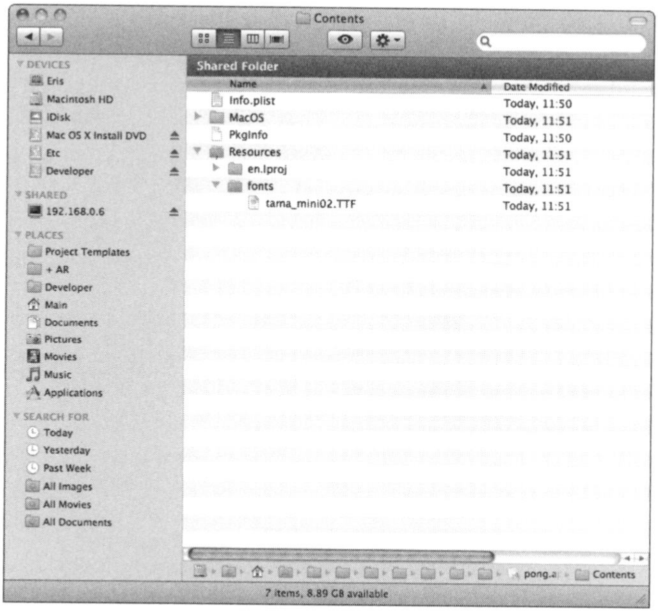

Creating build rules

To view the default build rules, select a target and click the Build Rules tab at the top right. The list shown in Figure 13.33 is the same for every target. It includes a list of file types and names the commands that can process them. The commands are at the lowest level of the Xcode build system; they're utilities that copy, compile, and process files in various ways, and they're scattered around various /usr/bin directories throughout the /Developer directory.

Figure 13.33

The default build rules

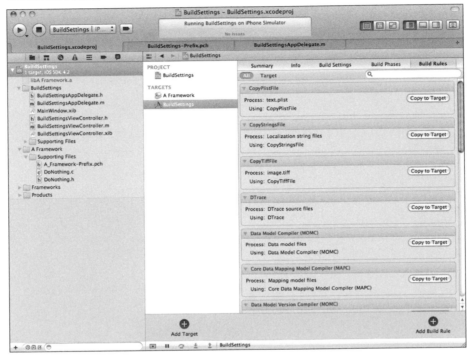

You can customize the existing rules by clicking the Copy to Target button. This opens the pane shown in Figure 13.34. Use the Process menu to select a file type. You can choose from a standard selection of types, or you can select Source files with names matching: and type the extension in the box to the right. Each of the standard rules defaults to one type. If you select a custom script, the default script stub includes a relevant build setting that points you to the directory holding the associated files. You can modify any of these default options in your script, as needed.

Use the Using box to select a processing action. You can select from another list of standard options or select the Custom script option to create your own scripted processor. The script editor is identical to the one for build phases, and it can use the same selection of languages supported by the shell.

Note that build rules are target-specific.

NOTE
You may be unfamiliar with some of the file types and processes in the menus. Many are highly specialized, and you're unlikely to use them.

Figure 13.34

The build rules use the same scripting options as the build phases. (You can get as creative as you want here.)

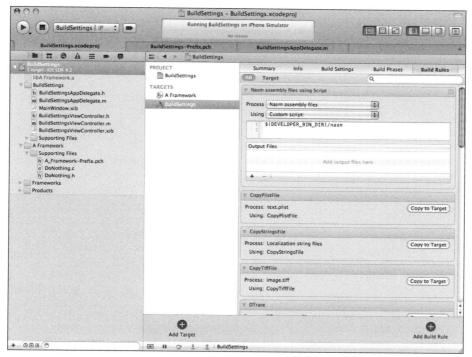

TIP
You can speed up complex builds with many files and targets by using the Distributed Builds feature in the Xcode Preferences, which spreads the build process across multiple Macs. Install Xcode on every Mac, open Preferences, select Distributed Builds, Authenticate, and check both boxes. Repeat for other Macs, and select Refresh. Launch Xcode, and repeat the process on other Macs. The Distributed Builds dialog should find the other Macs automatically and distribute builds to them.

Summary

This chapter explored practical build customization. It began with a list of common simple customization tasks that used modified build settings to control some small part of the build process.

Next, it worked methodically through the steps needed to create distribution builds for the App Store and for Ad Hoc beta testing.

Finally, it introduced the low-level features of the build system, and it sketched how build phases and build rules can be used to create complex, fully customized builds that support multiple targets and dependencies and non-standard file types.

Using Version Control

Development isn't always a smooth process, and sometimes it's necessary to abandon code that isn't working and restore a project to a previous state. It also can be useful to compare older and newer versions and to use tools that manage development across a team.

Managing code in these ways is known as *version control* or *source control management* (SCM). Several version control tools are built into Xcode. They're not obligatory, so you can ignore them, but this isn't recommended. At a minimum, you can manage versions manually in Finder. But you also can use the more powerful tools that are new to Xcode 4.

Using Manual Version Control

The easiest way to manage versions is to duplicate and rename project folders in Finder, as shown in Figure 14.1. Each folder should contain stable or nearly stable code with a consistent set of features. The code should build cleanly.

Create a copy before you begin to add new versions. If it's obvious that the next version must be abandoned, you can mark it by giving the folder a unique name—perhaps one that includes the word "abandoned"—and starting again with a new copy.

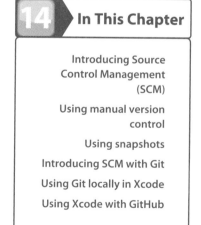

Figure 14.1

Manual version control is simple and easy to use, but limited.

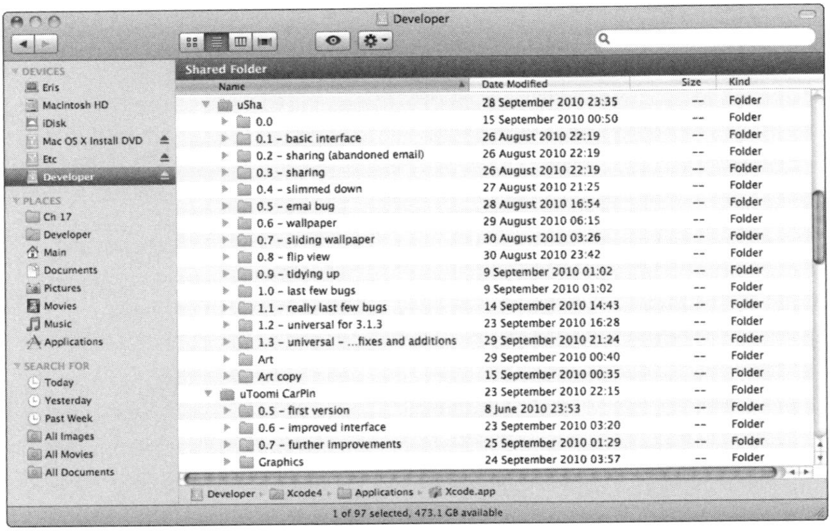

Manual version control is ideal for simple, self-contained projects, such as apps. It's not recommended for more complex projects, such as frameworks. And it should never be used for a collaborative development. You can rely on manual management if you're a solo developer. Don't use it if you need to share your work or if your code must be linked into another project.

The advantages of manual control include the following:

- **Simple and clear no-fuss management:** Each version is separate and clearly marked. If you need to backtrack, you can.
- **Easy backups:** You can copy folders to a backup server manually or allow Time Machine to manage them.
- **Robust persistence:** Combined with backups, multiple copies mean that your work is less likely to be lost if a disk crashes. Files in a project are discrete and easy to access.

The disadvantages include the following:

- **No change logs:** You can use the Unix `diff` family of command-line utilities to compare files manually. But you can only do this manually in Terminal, not in the Xcode editor.
- **No support for constant file locations:** If your files are accessed from another project, you must keep the directory name constant, and this solution isn't practical.

- **No simple rollback:** You can't see a record of edits, and you can't compare different versions of a file or restore it to a previous state.

- **No collaborative development:** Although it's possible to use informal schemes to check out code for editing, there's no easy way to integrate changes created by a team into a single code base.

Although manual version control is extremely primitive, it can be worth considering if you're new to Xcode development and don't yet want to learn how to use a professional solution such as Git, described below. It's a practical solution for simple projects, and it won't distract you with further learning while you're trying to master the rest of Xcode and Cocoa.

Using Snapshots

A snapshot is a simple semi-automated solution for source control. You can take a snapshot of your project at any point with the File ⇨ Create Snapshot menu option in the main Xcode menu. A snapshot records the state of the files in the project, and snapshots are listed in the Organizer. You can restore a project to an earlier state by restoring the snapshot.

As an example, create a new OS X Cocoa application following these steps:

1. **Save your new OS X Cocoa application as SnapshotExample.**

2. **Use the Create Snapshot option to save a snapshot of its initial state.**

   Figure 14.2 shows the new snapshot dialog box.

3. **You can give each snapshot a title and an optional description.**

N O T E

In a real project, you don't usually need to save the initial default state of the application, because you can always re-create the default as a new project. But occasionally, it can be useful to keep the initial state as a starting point when you're experimenting.

4. **Add some code.**

   For an initial demonstration, it can be as simple as a single comment line.

5. **Create another snapshot, and give it a different title and description.**

6. **Open the Organizer window.**

   You open the Organizer window by selecting the filing cabinet icon near the top right of the Xcode window.

Figure 14.2

Creating a new snapshot, with a name and description

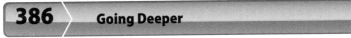

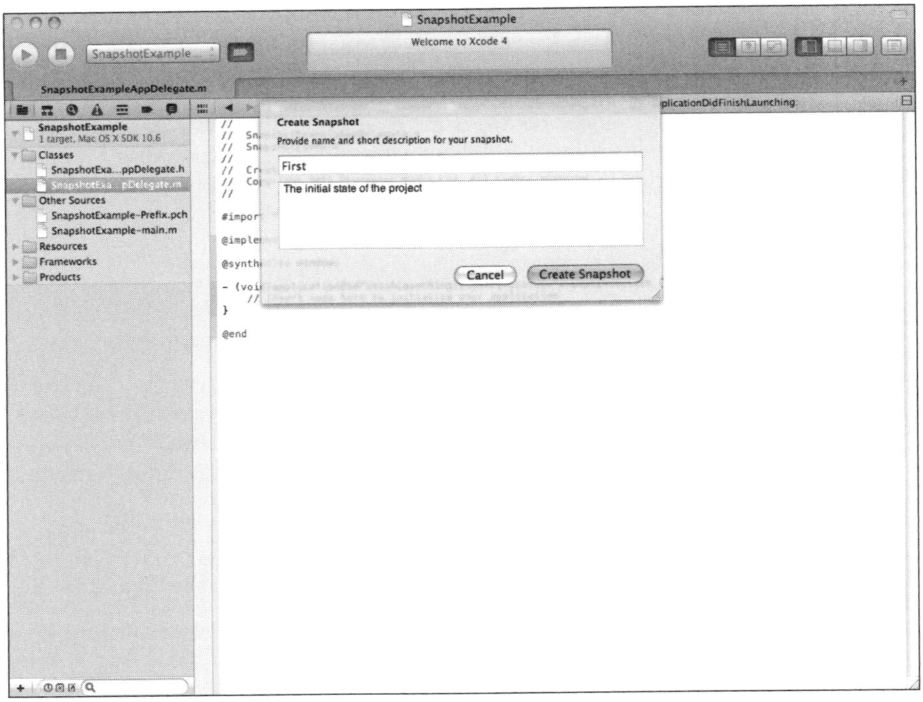

7. **Select the Projects icon at the top of the window.**

You should see a display similar to the one shown in Figure 14.3. The new SnapshotExample project appears at the top of the list at the left of the window. A list of snapshots for the projects appears in the pane at the bottom of the window.

The snapshot list can become cluttered, so you can delete individual snapshots by selecting the Delete Snapshot icon at the bottom right of the window. You also can restore a project to an earlier state by selecting a snapshot and using the Restore Snapshot option. You'll see a preview window, shown in Figure 14.4, which highlights the changes between the selected snapshot and the preceding snapshot.

CAUTION

There's no undo option for deleted snapshots; after they're gone, they're gone. And note that changes are incremental. The preview window doesn't show the changes between the first version of the project and the snapshot. Instead, it shows the changes between the current and previous snapshots.

Figure 14.3

Viewing a project's snapshots

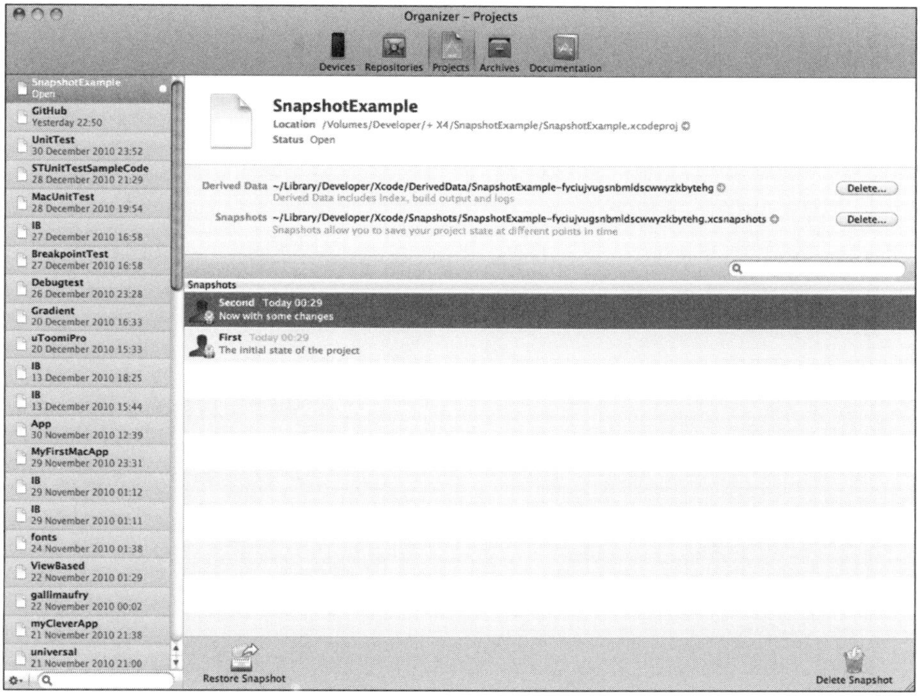

TIP

Xcode can create snapshots automatically before every bulk edit, such as a refactoring operation or a find-and-replace. Select File ➯ Project Settings or File ➯ Workspace settings to open a preferences dialog, click the Snapshots tab, and check the Create snapshot of project before mass-editing operations box. You can also define a custom location for the snapshots. Note that this feature is *on* by default.

You might expect the snapshot to restore the project to its earlier state, but it doesn't. Instead, a Restore dialog box appears and asks you to specify a folder on disk. The old state of the project is written to the folder. To reload the state, close the current project and reload the old version from the folder you specified. This separate save requirement makes the snapshot option clumsy. It implements minimal version control, but it's not very elegant or sophisticated.

Figure 14.4

Viewing the restore options

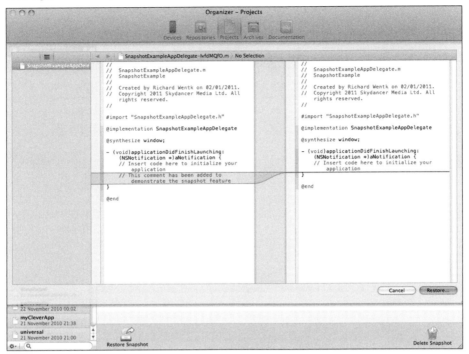

Working with Source Control

Xcode supports two source control systems—Subversion and Git—which can track changes to files, and support collaborative development. Source control adds the following features to Xcode:

- **Open development:** You can allow other developers to work with you on projects.
- **Edit logging:** You can see how files have developed over time, and how code has been added, changed, or removed.
- **Change control:** You can accept or discard changes made by you or by other developers.
- **Blame logging:** Changes are tagged with the ID of the developer who made them.
- **Project branching:** You can create parallel to support independent development of different features, or to split projects to allow branches to develop in different directions.
- **Remote server backup:** Server-based source control stores code on a remote server, so you're less likely to lose it in an accident.

Subversion and Git have significant differences. Although Subversion is supported in Xcode, Git is integrated more tightly. You can create and manage a project that supports Git from the Xcode UI without using the command line. Certain advanced Git features are only available at the command line, but you can use Git successfully without them.

In contrast, you must use command-line access to set up Subversion for a project. After set-up, many basic features are also available in the UI. Subversion requires an external server. Git can be used locally, and it can also support server-based development.

CAUTION

Git and Subversion are part of the command-line utilities that are installed with Xcode. To use them, check the System Tools box when you install Xcode. If you don't do this, they're not available.

Understanding Git

Source control tools work with a repository or repo—a database configured to manage the files in a project. A key benefit of professional source control is that the contents of a repo can be kept on a single Mac or shared, either on a private server or online. It's possible to copy, or clone, repositories to duplicate them across multiple Macs. Online storage with a service such as GitHub (github.com) gives you "free" backups—a remote copy of your source code is always available—and also supports collaborative development.

Repositories can store either incremental changes to files or complete files. Subversion stores incremental changes. Git stores complete files; in fact, it always works with a complete local version of the entire project. This makes it more robust than Subversion, at the cost of extra disk space and download/upload times. Because code files are usually small, the time penalty isn't usually significant. Because Git doesn't need to merge and update files, it can feel more responsive.

To use Git, you create a repository, either locally using Xcode or manually on a remote server, and then add and edit files in the usual way. After each significant edit, you commit the changes. This creates a complete snapshot of the project and adds copies of any modified or added files to the repository.

Commits don't have to proceed in a linear order. You can create a new branch to experiment with code or work on certain features independently. Branches can develop independently, or they can be merged together.

If you work with Git locally, version control is automatic. Git tracks your commits, and you can use a new Xcode feature called the Version Editor to view and compare the changes to each file as the project develops.

CAUTION
When you make commits you're updating multiple files at the same time. There's no automated way to revert a single file to an earlier state without also changing other files that were committed at the same time. However, you can use simple manual copy/paste to copy an old version of a file from the Version Editor into the main code editor and then create a new commit with the old contents of the file.

If you use a remote server, the process becomes more complex. To use Git remotely, collaborators need to supply a name, an e-mail address, and a public key for security. If you are managing a Git project, you can review and accept or decline commits supplied by other developers.

When you work with an online repo, you can clone a project—copy the current version from the server to your Mac—to work on it independently and then perform a push to merge your changes back into the source. The lead developer can then review the changes and accept or delete them. When you work collaboratively, Git and Xcode include author information with all commits, making it easy to see who is responsible for changes. You can also update a project to refresh the version you're editing with the most recent changes without creating a new copy.

NOTE
Git is a complex system with many features and options, but it's well documented. This chapter introduces Git in Xcode, but it isn't a complete Git primer on collaborative development with GitHub. For full documentation, see the free ProGit book available at `progit.org/book`, the official command summaries at `gitref.org`, and the GitHub help at `help.github.com`.

Using Git locally

You can use Git locally for simple project versioning. Simple versioning doesn't require a remote server, advanced Git skills, or command-line management, and it uses GUI features that are built into Xcode. This example demonstrates how to create a local repository and how to use the Version Editor to review changes to the files in a project. The edits in this sample project are trivial, but they're sufficient to illustrate how you can use the Version Editor to manage code as you work.

CAUTION
The Xcode implementation of Git leaves out many of the features and concepts that are used when working with the command line or with existing popular Mac Git tools such as GitX (`gitx.frim.nl`). For example, Xcode doesn't support explicit file staging. If you've used Git from the command line in other contexts, you'll find that the Xcode implementation is simpler and less powerful, but still adequate for basic SCM.

Creating a project with Git support

Git support is optional and available for both OS X and iOS projects. Use the File ➪ New Project option in the main Xcode menu to create a new project (this example uses an OS X project called LocalGit) and check the Source Control box, as shown in Figure 14.5.

Figure 14.5

Creating a project with Git support

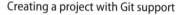

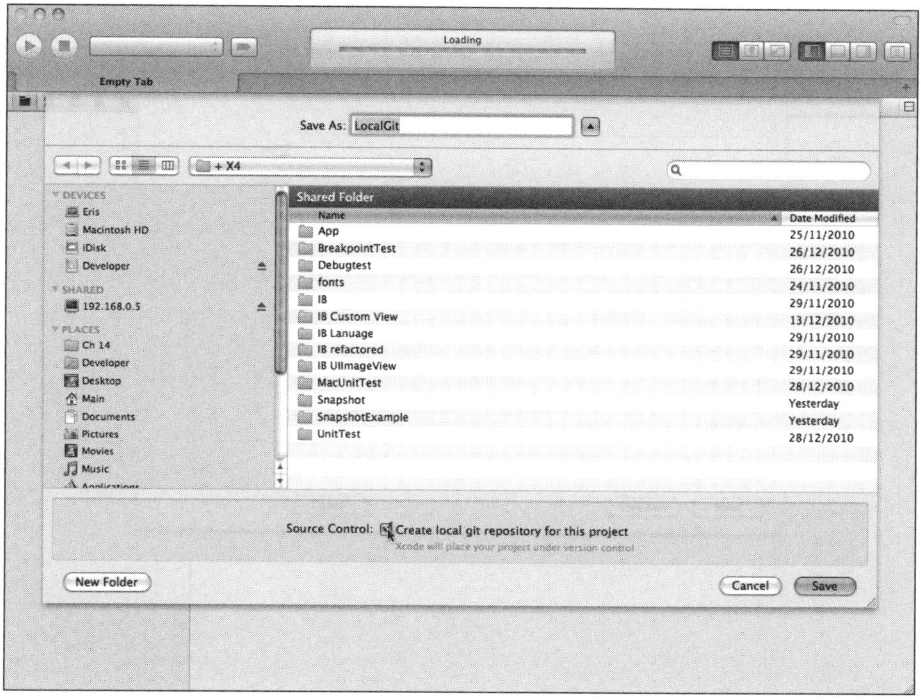

Xcode creates the project in the usual way. If you open the project's folder on disk, you see the standard collection of files. However, if you open the Organizer and select the Repositories tab, you see that a repository has been created for the project, as shown in Figure 14.6. Whether you're working locally or online, this repository view lists all the repositories managed by Git. Whenever you create a new project with Git support, a new repository is added to the list.

Notice that the project already includes the following:

- **The project name:** This is defined when you create the project.
- **The repository type:** This is either Git or Subversion.
- **The location:** For a local project, this is the folder on disk that contains the source. For a remote project, this is a special URL that links to the repository on the remote server.
- **An initial commit:** The first commit for the project is created automatically and includes the initial default files. You can use the reveal triangle to view the file list.
- **A timestamp:** The time and date of each commit is recorded.

- **A *hash*:** The `faa5b77c734f` tag in the figure is a random number generated to give the commit a unique identifier. Each new commit has a new hash. If you work exclusively in Xcode, you can ignore the hash tags. If you work at the command line, you can use the tags to specify a commit when you want to modify it, clone it, delete it, and so on.

Figure 14.6

Reviewing the project repository in the Organizer

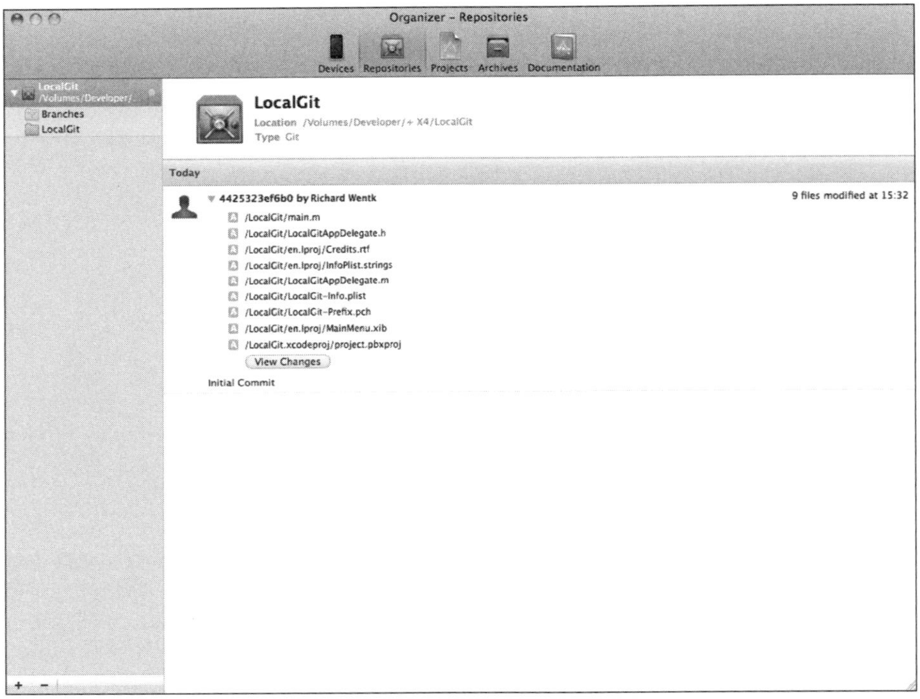

Inside the repository you'll see two other items:

- **A Branches item:** Initially, this shows a single item called Master. If you create further branches, they appear here.
- A **<ProjectName> folder:** This shows the current state of the project on disk. When you add files to a project, they appear in this folder. They don't appear in Root until you commit the project.

Editing a project with Git support

Git support is transparent, so you can develop a project in the usual way while Git is active.

Try this example:

1. **Add an extra Objective-C class to the project by right-clicking the <ProjectName> group in the Project Navigator and selecting New File.**

2. **Create a new subclass of** NSObject **and save it with the default MyClass name.**

3. **Make a small, but obvious, change to the original** LocalGitAppDelegate.m **file.**

The example shown in Figure 14.7 has been extended with a single comment.

4. **Save the edited file with File ⇨ Save.**

Note the icons that appear next to certain files after you save them. The M stands for "modified" and indicates that a file has been changed since the last commit. The A stands for "added." These icons are added by the Git system, and only appear when a project uses Git.

Figure 14.7

When you modifying a project with Git support, modified files are tagged automatically.

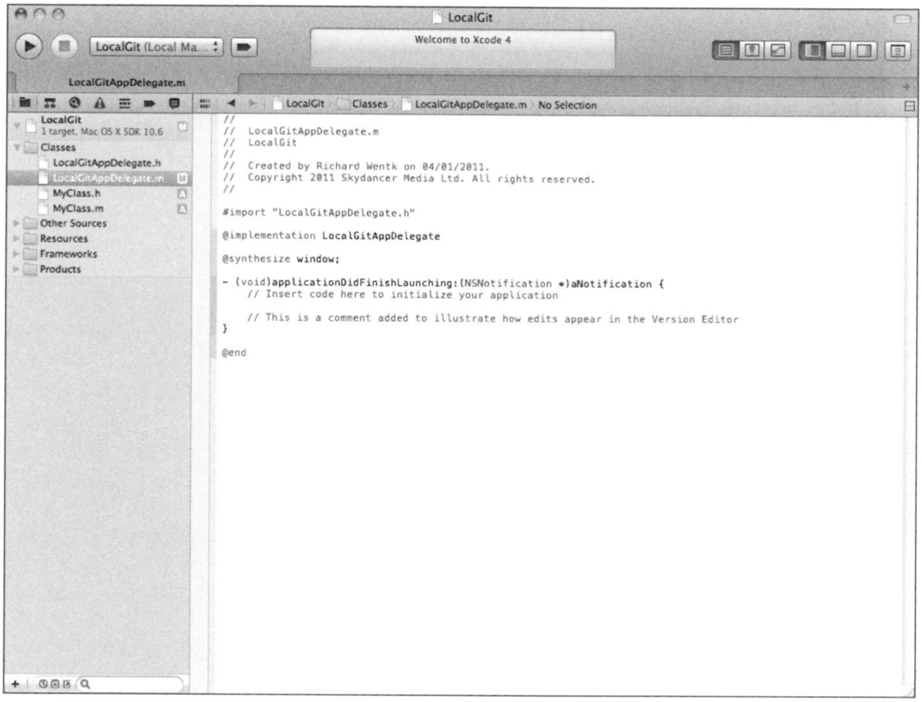

NOTE

Edits are tracked by Git, but builds aren't. Git is a source control system, not a binary control system, and it doesn't care if your project builds successfully. It tracks changes to the project source files only. You can make edits that break a build, and Git tracks them faithfully whenever files are saved.

Committing changes

To create a new commit, select File ➪ Source Control ➪ Commit from the main Xcode menu. You see the dialog box shown in Figure 14.8. It shows a list of modified or added files at the top left and a comparison window called the Version Editor—the new Xcode tool for exploring and comparing different versions of a file.

At the bottom of the window is a blank line for descriptive text about the commit. Note that *Xcode forces you to add a comment for each commit.* If you don't edit this line, you can't complete the commit.

Figure 14.8

Creating a commit. Xcode's new Version Editor displays and compares current and previous versions of a file.

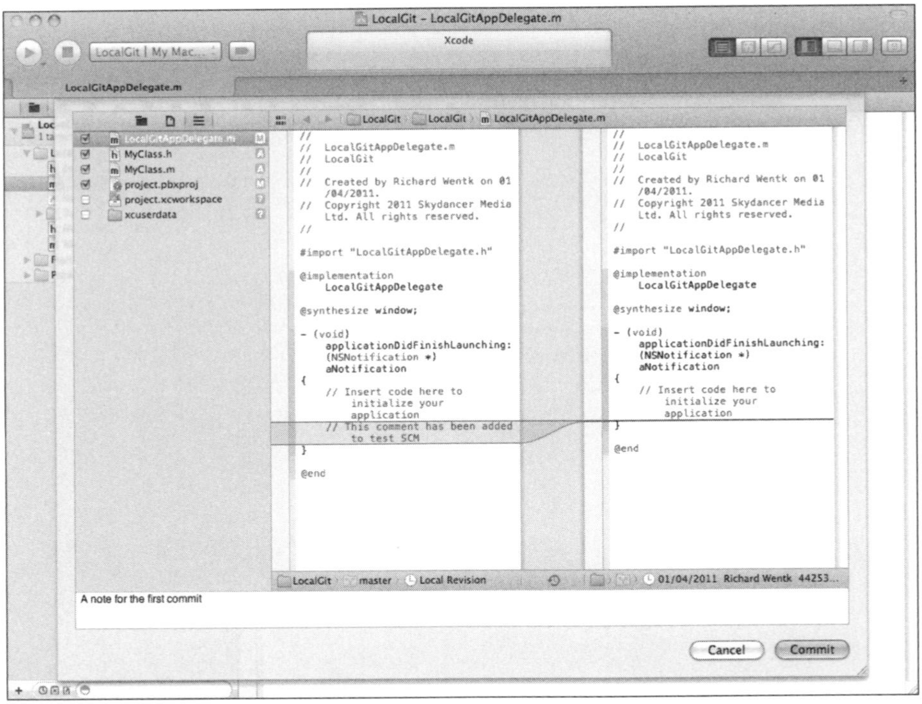

CAUTION

If you don't have the main editor selected—which is likely, if you're looking at the Organizer—the source control menu options are grayed out.

The comment has been highlighted in the Version Editor. The highlighting in the view at the left tells you how each file has changed since the last commit, compared to the previous version shown at the right.

In this example, the changes in each file are trivial, but in a working project, the highlighted areas are more extensive. Added files don't yet have changes, so the same version is shown in both views.

After a commit, the M and A icons disappear from the Project Navigator until you make further changes.

To practice the commit process and create further changes, add a few more comment lines to any of the files and commit after each line. Don't forget to save the file after each edit.

Open the Organizer, select the Repositories icon, and you should see a history list similar to the one in Figure 14.9, showing every commit for the project. Each commit has an author, a hash, the commit description, and a timestamp.

You can click the reveal triangle next to each commit to show a list of modified files. Click View Changes to open a version display.

You can hide the history list with the icon at the lower left, or you can change its height by dragging the bar at the top. If you've made changes after a commit, you can use the Commit button at the bottom left of this page to make a new one. You can also open the local project and select files from the list at the top to see the last commit in which they were added or modified.

This page in the Organizer is designed to give you an overview of the files and commits in a project. *It's not an editor, and it doesn't link to an editor.*

This is counterintuitive. You might expect to be able to manage changes here—but you can't. To compare versions and check a time line of commits, use the Version Editor. It's a feature of the main Xcode editor.

Figure 14.9

Reviewing the history list in the Organizer after multiple commits

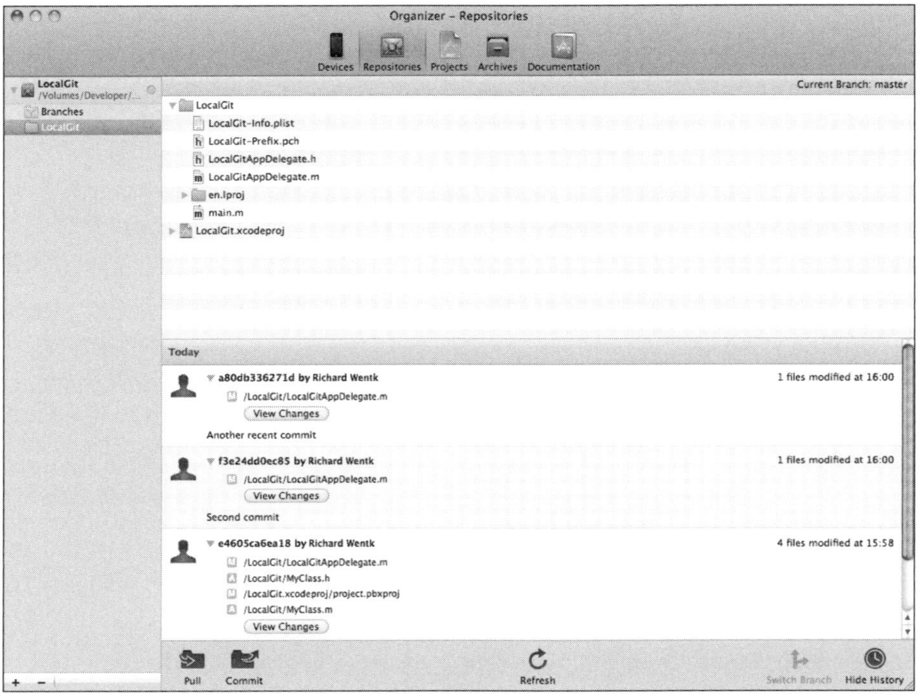

Using the comparison view in the Version Editor

By default, the Version Editor, shown in Figure 14.10, provides a double comparison window for a given file. To load the editor, select the icon near the top right, as shown in the figure.

You can view the state of the file at any commit in either window. There's no implied before or after in the left and right views. The two selections are independent. If they're different, the editor highlights the changes.

Figure 14.10

Loading the Version Editor to compare versions

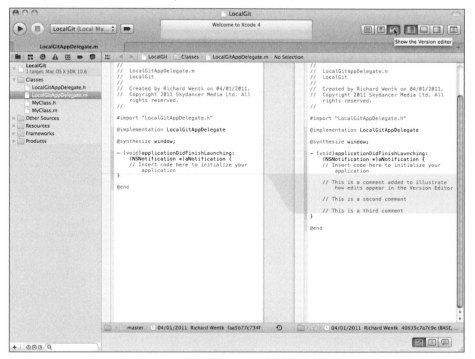

There are various ways to view a commit. If you click the jump bar near the bottom of the window, you see a pop-up menu with a list of commits arranged in chronological order, as shown in Figure 14.11.

It's important to understand that the most recent edit is at the *top* of this list, and the oldest initial commit is at the *bottom*.

The nomenclature for revisions isn't intuitive, so it's explained below:

- **Unsaved revision:** This version has been edited, but not saved.
- **Local revision:** The version has been edited and saved, but not committed.
- **<Entries with time stamp, name and hash>:** These versions have been committed. It's worth repeating that the most recent version is at the top of the list, marked (BASE, HEAD). The oldest initial commit is at the bottom of the list.

Figure 14.11

Selecting commits from the jump bar menu

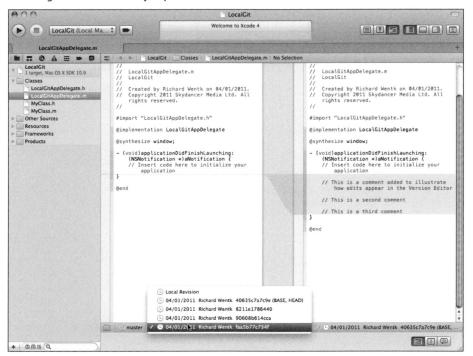

Selecting any commit loads the corresponding state of the file into the viewer window. The left and right windows use an identical system, so you can view any commit in either. To view the commits for a different file, select it in the Project Navigator in the usual way.

Instead of a list, you can display a time line—similar to a Time Machine time line—with a list of commits between the two views. Select the clock/curved arrow icon in the gutter between the two jump bars. You see the display shown in Figure 14.12. Each "button" in the time line indicates a commit. Older versions appear at the top of the list, so the initial commit is always the first one from the top. Empty commit slots at the top of the list appear in a darker gray.

The buttons are animated and expand as you mouse over them. Although you can click a button to select a commit, it's not always clear in which window your selection will appear. To select a commit in a specific window, click in the gap to the right or left of the button. The triangle indicator for that window moves to the commit you selected, and the corresponding version of the file is loaded and displayed. The base version at the bottom of the list is the last commit. The local version is the last version after editing and is identical to the Local Revision in the jump bar menus.

CAUTION

Arguably, the time line list is upside down. The initial commit is the top item, and the most recent edit appears at the bottom of the time line. Whichever orientation makes more sense to you, it's important to understand that the commits in the jump bar menu *are listed in the opposite order to the time line.*

Figure 14.12

Selecting versions using the new time line feature

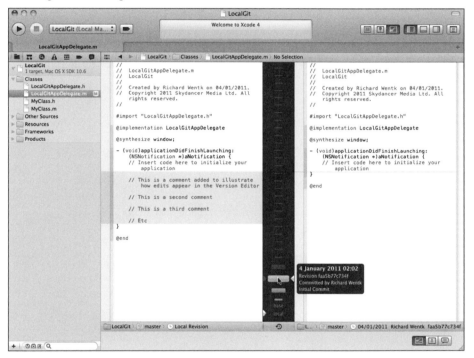

CAUTION

Version comparisons are for display only; when you view a version in the Version Editor, the file doesn't change in the main editor. There's no single-click option for reverting a project to a previous commit. You can revert to an earlier commit manually from the command line using the `git revert` command, but you can revert individual files in Xcode only by copying a version from the Version editor, pasting the old code into the main code editor, and creating a new commit. If the project has multiple files, you must do this for all of them, but you can simplify this with branches, as described later in this chapter.

Using the Blame view

The Version Editor includes two further views. You can select them using the icons at the bottom right of the window. The Blame view, shown in Figure 14.13, is primarily used for team development, but if you're working solo, you can use it to view a list of changes to a file. Each commit is listed at the right of the file in a view that includes time, date, and author information, and it's linked to one or more lines of source at the left. If you select a commit with one of the small gray arrows, it's loaded into the left window of the Version Editor, and the preceding commit is loaded into the right.

Figure 14.13

Using the Blame view to list changes to a single file, with the name of the author of each change

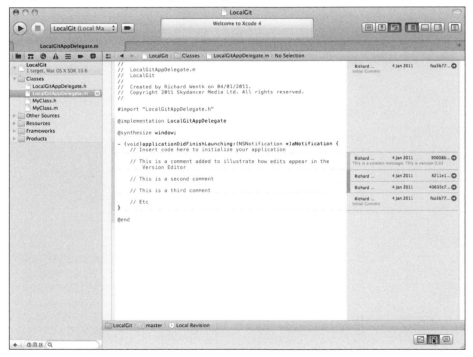

Using the Log view

The Log view, shown in Figure 14.14, is a blend of the code view and the commit list in the Organizer. The code editor appears at the left, and a simple list of commits appears at the right. You can load a commit into the Version editor by selecting its gray arrow.

Figure 14.14

Using the Log view

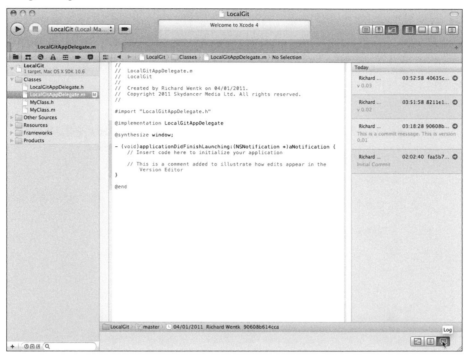

Branching a project

A branch is a parallel development track. When you create a branch, Git copies the current project and creates an independent version. Editing one branch leaves other branches unchanged. When you select a branch, Xcode loads the files from that branch and displays them for editing.

It's important to understand that you can only edit one branch at a time. When you select a different branch, Xcode loads *all* of the files from that branch. Changing branches can literally switch the contents of every file in a project.

This can be a useful thing. But there are a couple of potential gotchas to be aware of:

- The editor doesn't give you any indication of which branch is being edited. The Organizer is the *only* way to see which branch is active.

- The editor doesn't include branch switching. Again, you can only switch branches in the Organizer.

Because of these limitations, branch management can seem more like an afterthought than an essential part of the development process. This is unfortunate, because it can be a very powerful and useful tool.

In a team context, branching is often used for independent development of unrelated features. Branching allows each team or individual to work with a fixed version of the code that surrounds the feature they're working on.

As a solo developer, you can use branching for version management. If you create a branch for each version instead of using the commit system to manage versions, you can restore every file in the project to an earlier state quickly and easily, by selecting its branch.

Because it can be so useful, it's worth taking the time to experiment with branching. For a simple example, follow these steps:

1. **Add a few more lines of comments or code to the project App Delegate.**
2. **Open the Repositories page in the Organizer.**
3. **Select Branches.**
4. **Click the Add button near the bottom right.**

    You'll see the dialog box shown in Figure 14.15.

Figure 14.15

Creating a new branch

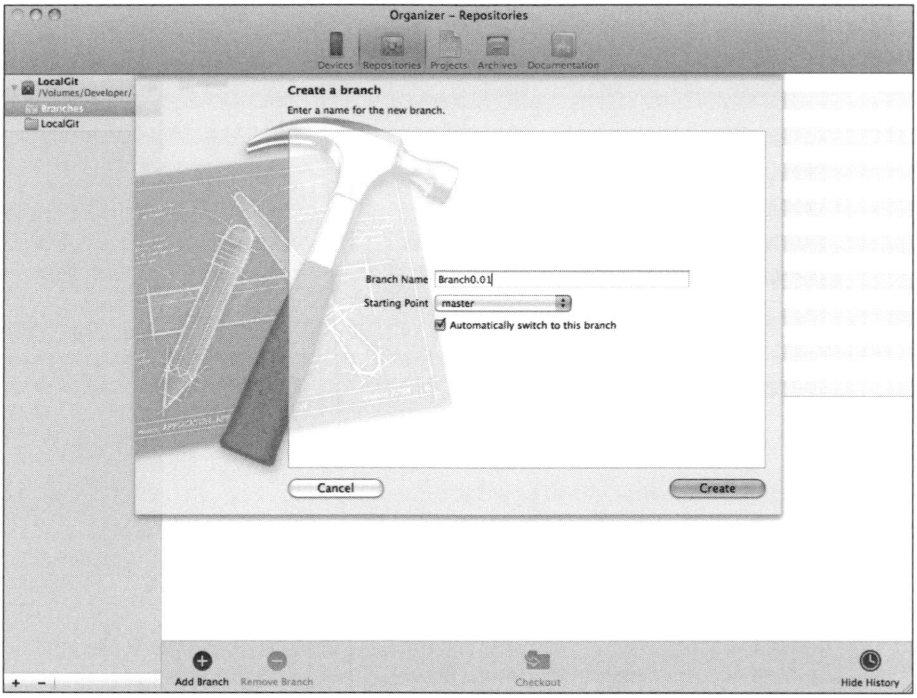

5. **Enter a name for your branch.**

   Spaces aren't allowed.

6. **Check the Automatically switch to this branch box.**

7. **Select Create.**

   This adds a new branch to the list.

8. **Commit the changes to the new branch.**

9. **In the Organizer, click the Branches folder at the top right,**

   You see that your new branch has been added to the list. If you edit the code, only the current branch is affected. The old Master branch doesn't change.

10. **To switch between branches, select the project folder under Branches and click the Switch Branch icon near the bottom right.**

    A dialog box with a menu of branches appears, as shown in Figure 14.16. When you select a branch here, the code for the branch appears in Xcode's main editor.

Figure 14.16

Although it's not obvious from this dialog box, selecting a branch loads its files into the main editor.

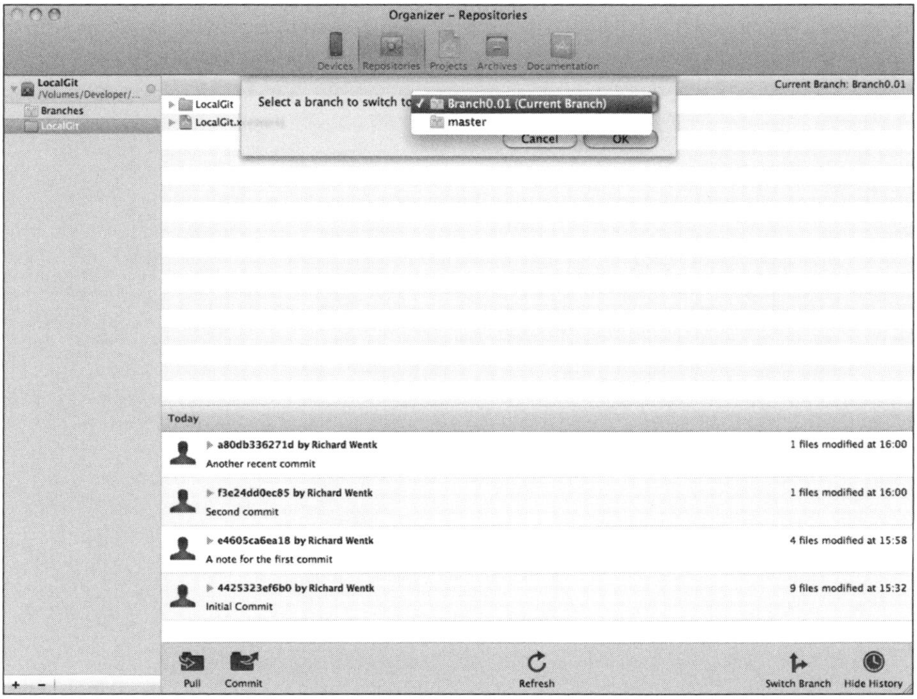

CAUTION
Note that selecting branches in the Branches folder *doesn't* load them into the editor. You must click the Switch Branches icon to change branches.

Merging branches

To merge branches, begin by using the Organizer to switch to the branch you want to use as a merge destination. This is often, but not always, the original Master branch.

Next, pick a branch as a merge source. Select File ⇨ Source Control ⇨ Merge, and choose a branch from the menu in the dialog. The code in this branch is merged into the destination branch.

After the merge, this branch remains unchanged—the changes happen only in the destination.

Xcode displays the Version Editor, as shown in Figure 14.17. A preview of the merged code is shown at the right.

Figure 14.17

Although it's not obvious from this dialog box, selecting a branch loads its files into the main editor.

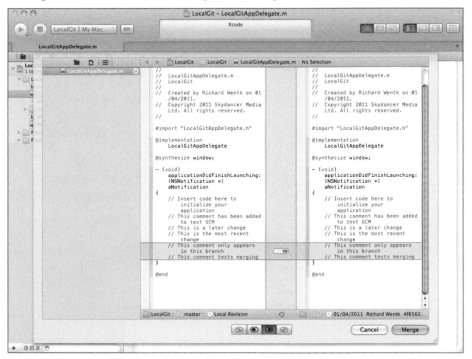

Every difference in every file is highlighted. The gutter area includes a switch icon. You can use the switch buttons at the bottom of the window to select the differences. The switches are on by default, but you can turn them off to exclude a change. You can also use the switches to resolve conflicts.

Note that you can't toggle the switches by clicking them directly in the gutter. You can only change their state by clicking the button bar at the bottom of the window.

CAUTION

At the time of writing, merging isn't working correctly but is likely to be fixed soon. As a workaround, you can use Git's command-line merge option. For details see the Git manual. A link is listed near the end of this chapter.

Using Xcode with GitHub

Although it's possible to create a custom remote server for use with Git, the GitHub website at github.org shown in Figure 14.18, has become a popular choice for development teams and solo developers who use Git. In theory, the differences between local and remote development should be minor, because Git handles both situations in a similar way. In practice, remote development requires significant extra effort when creating a new project.

Figure 14.18

A first look at github.org

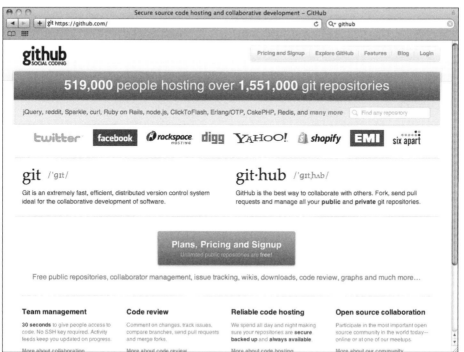

GitHub is optional. If you're working solo, you can develop locally without using GitHub at all. But it's a simple and accessible solution for team development. GitHub features include the following:

- **Free public collaborative development:** By default, GitHub projects are open and public, so anyone can download your code and add their own commits. This is a good thing for open-source projects, but unhelpful for proprietary development.

- **Monthly payment plans for private team development:** Privacy on GitHub, which includes the ability to hide your projects from the public and only open them to select developers, costs from $7 to $200, depending on the number of repositories and developers. Open free accounts are limited to 300MB of disk space. Paid accounts offer more.

- **Easy online access:** You can exchange commits and updates wherever there's an Internet connection. You also can work offline and upload changes when you reconnect.

- **Easy downloads:** Your projects can be packaged automatically into a single archive to make it easy for third parties to download them.

- **Project support tools:** These include a Wiki server for documentation, a bug tracker for bug reporting, and the ability to link to a separate project web page.

- **"Free" backups:** Code is stored securely on commercial servers, with a robust backup policy.

These are the chief practical differences between local and GitHub development:

- **Security:** You must set up a username, password, and access key.

- **Updates:** You should update (download) a file or a complete project before you change it. This guarantees that your version of the project includes the latest commits from other developers.

- **Push commands:** You must use the command line to update local commits to the GitHub server.

- **Location:** Instead of a disk location, the project is referenced using a remote server URL.

Creating a GitHub account

It's very easy to create a new free GitHub account. GitHub asks for a username, an e-mail address, and a password. You don't need to give any other details.

On GitHub, your username, e-mail address, and password are essential parts of the online access process. They do more than log you in to the site, so you need them later when you create a user identity for Git on your Mac.

Optionally, you can add public contact information and other personal information to your account, but these details aren't necessary for basic repo management.

TIP
If you have an account with an existing online service such as gravatar or WordPress, you can use your existing login details. GitHub shares login information with all services that use the Automattic service. See `automattic.com` for more details.

Creating a public key

Git communicates with GitHub via ssh (Secure Shell), which is a secure low-level protocol for data transfers between devices. Before you can use ssh, you need to define and upload a binary key that signs communication between your Mac and the GitHub server and makes it possible for GitHub to confirm your identity. Creating a key is a slightly complex process, but you only need to do it once. Follow these steps:

1. **Open Terminal.**

2. **Type** cd ~/.ssh**.**

3. **If there's no such file or directory, skip to Step 5.**

4. **If the directory exists, you may want to back up the contents to another directory using the** cp **command. After you have a backup, delete the directory.**

5. **Type** ssh-keygen -t rsa -C "youremail@address.com"**. The e-mail address must match the one you use as a GitHub login.**

6. **Type Return when asked for a filename to save to the default location.**

7. **Use a good password for the key, and enter it twice.**

   The ssh keygen utility creates a key and saves it to two files: id_rsa, which is the private key you don't share with anyone, and id_rsa.pub, which is the public key file you need to copy to GitHub.

8. **Type** cat ~/.ssh/id_rsa.pub | pbcopy**.**

   This copies the public part of the key to the clipboard.

9. **Open your browser, and log in to GitHub.**

10. **Click Account Settings.**

11. **Select SSH Public Keys from the menu at the left.**

12. **Select Add another public key, and paste the key into the Key box, as shown in Figure 14.19.**

13. **Select Add key.**

    The key is now installed.

N O T E

You can use the edit option to change your key later. This isn't usually a good idea, unless you start the key-making process from scratch. If the key on your Mac doesn't match the key used by GitHub, you won't be able to access your source code.

Setting up a Git username and e-mail

In addition to the key, Git and GitHub require a username and e-mail. These are unencrypted. Although you can give each repository a separate contact name and e-mail, it's much simpler to set these globally for all repositories. You need to make these settings only once.

Figure 14.19

Defining your public key

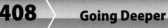

In Terminal, type the following:

```
git config --global user.name "<your name>"
git config --global user.email <your@emailaddress>
```

Creating a remote repository on GitHub

Creating a remote repository is a very simple process; follow these steps:

1. **Log in to GitHub.**

2. **Select Dashboard.**

3. **Select Create a Repository from the list of items at the left, as shown in Figure 14.20.**

4. **Type a name.**

   It's a good idea, for obvious reasons, to use the project name. When you click the Create Repository button, GitHub adds the repository to your account.

5. **Click your account name to see a list of repositories.**

NOTE

It would be convenient if you could create a new GitHub repository by duplicating the existing Git repository on your Mac with a single command. Unfortunately, you can't do this. You *must* create a new repository on GitHub first, and then copy files to it manually. The GitHub name must match the name of your local repository.

Figure 14.20

Creating a new online repository

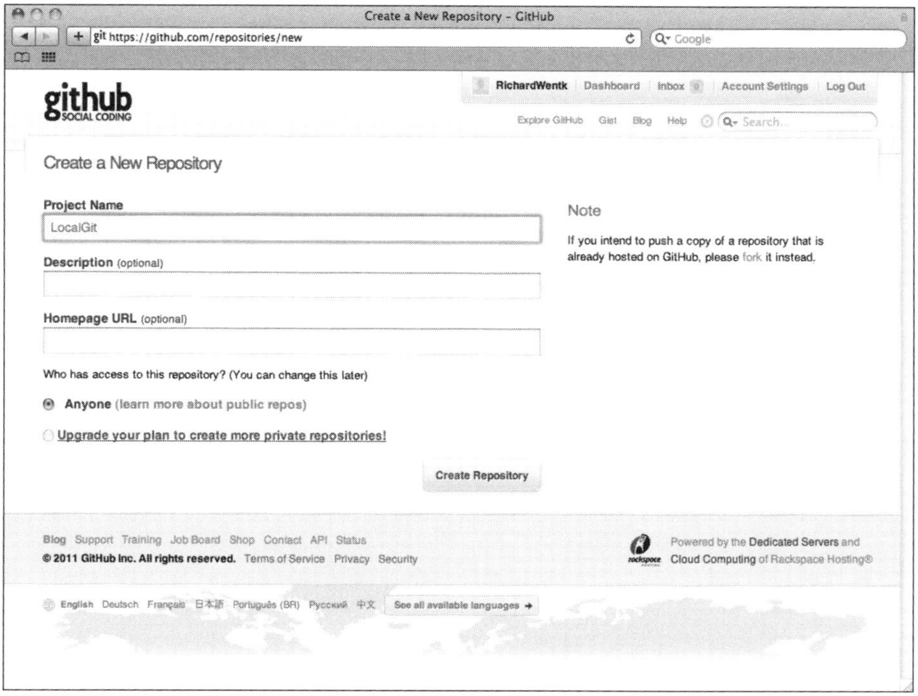

Copying a local Git repository to GitHub

After you have an online repository, you can tell Git to copy your project files to it. Eventually Xcode 4 will include UI support for this operation. At the time of writing, it's easier to perform it from the command line.

In Terminal, `cd` to the project directory with the original source. For example, if the directory is /MyProjectsX4/LocalGit type:

```
cd MyProjects/X4/LocalGit
```

Next, tell Git that you'll be using the remote repository. Type on a single line:

```
git remote add <RepositoryName> git@github.com:<YourGitHubUser
    Name>/<RepositoryName>.git
```

To copy the files, type this:

```
git push <RepositoryName> --all
```

The --all switch copies all branches, including the master. Figure 14.21 shows the result. The branches are listed under the SwitchBranches option at the left, and commits for the active branch appear in a list beneath the main menu. You can select the Source menu item at the top left and drill down through the source code to view.

Figure 14.21

Review the online repository after copying. For clarity, a few more commits were added to this project before it was uploaded. Note how the commit comments you type into Xcode are copied to GitHub.

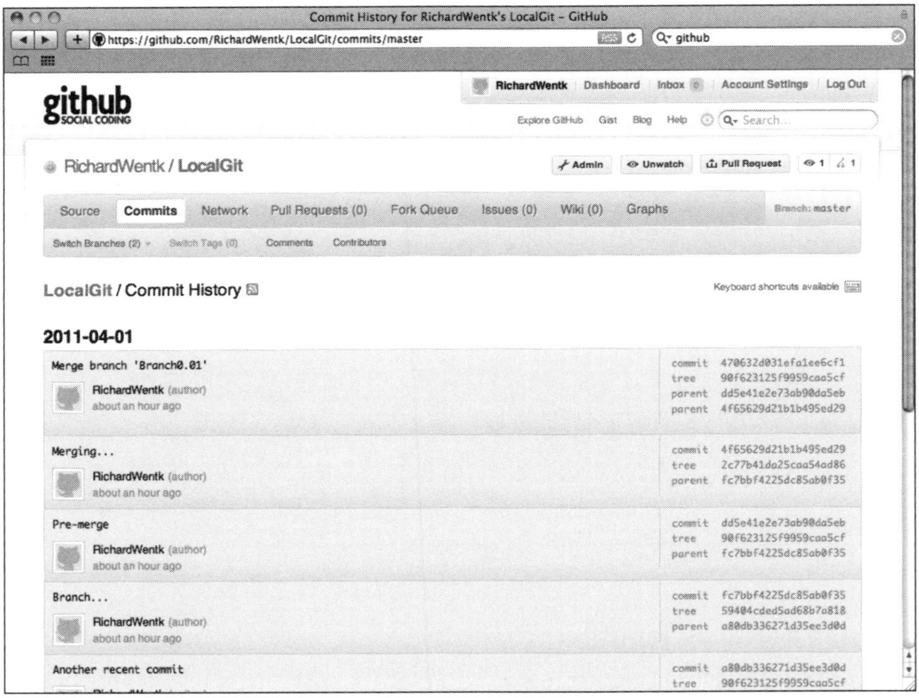

CAUTION

If you're familiar with Git on other platforms, you may be used to typing origin for remote repo access and push commands, instead of <RepositoryName>. Sometimes this works. Sometimes it confuses Xcode. You need to experiment with the most recent version of Xcode to find the best name.

Working with a GitHub repository

C A U T I O N

At the time of writing online repository support remains extremely buggy, with persistent crashes and error messages. Some of the features only work if you ignore the errors and attempt them twice. Xcode 4 should improve as it matures, but *don't* use these features with valuable production code until you've experimented with them and confirmed their reliability. The following examples are believed correct at the time of writing, but features and operations may change in the future.

After you create an online repository, the local repository is no longer needed, so you can select it in the Repositories page in the Organizer, and use the Delete key to delete it. Note that this doesn't delete the project itself—it simply removes the list of source changes.

You can now replace the original local repository with a version that also supports GitHub. In the Repository Page in the Organizer, click the "+" icon at the lower left. Select the Add Repository option. You'll see the dialog in Figure 14.22.

Figure 14.22

Creating a new online repository

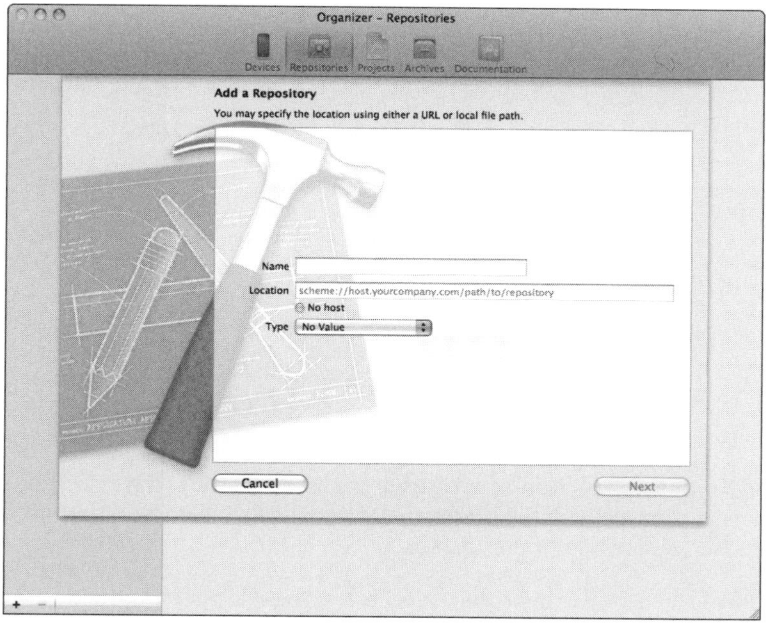

The two important fields here are the Name and the Location. Set the name to match the repository name. To find the location, select your repository on GitHub, select Source, and click the HTTP box in the middle of the page. This box displays a URL for the repository.

Copy the URL—it's shown in Figure 14.23—and paste it into the Location field in the dialog. Note that you can also use the SSH URL scheme, but the HTTP URL is easier to work with.

Xcode recognizes that this is a Git repository automatically and sets the Type menu to Git. If you're online—and you need to be—you should see the Host is reachable label next to a green light.

Figure 14.23

Copying the location URL for the repository from GitHub

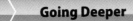

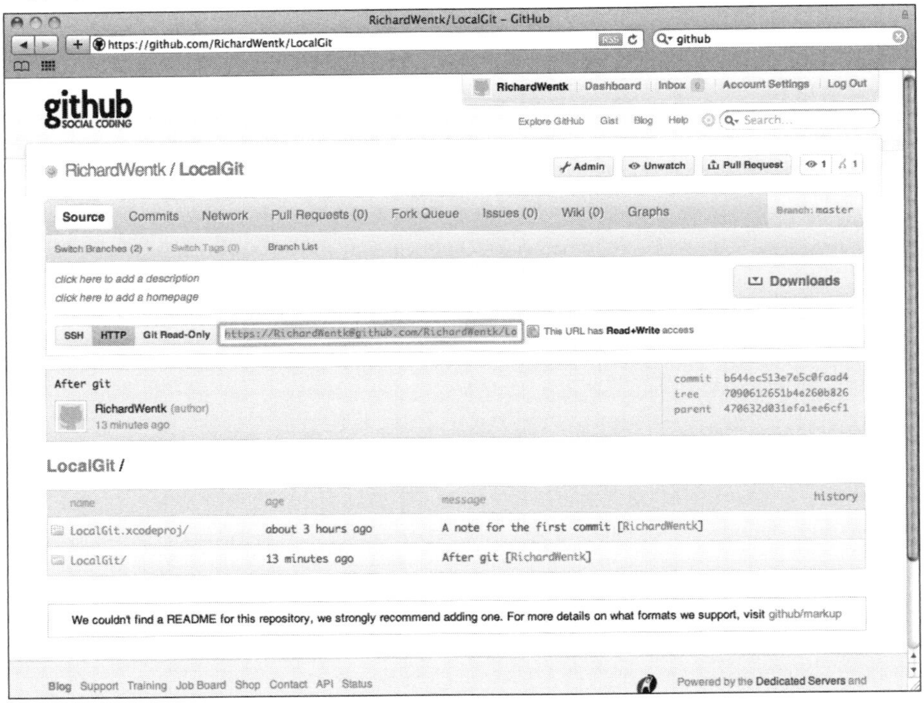

Click Add to add the online repository. It appears in the list at the left of the Repositories Organizer page. Select it, type your GitHub password into the Password field, and select a branch to download, as shown in Figure 14.24.

Click Clone to download a local copy of the code. Create a new folder for the code. (Xcode doesn't let you overwrite an existing folder.) Click Open when asked to open the cloned project in Xcode.

You should now have a complete copy of the original project, with all of the commits you made locally.

Figure 14.24

Selecting a branch to download

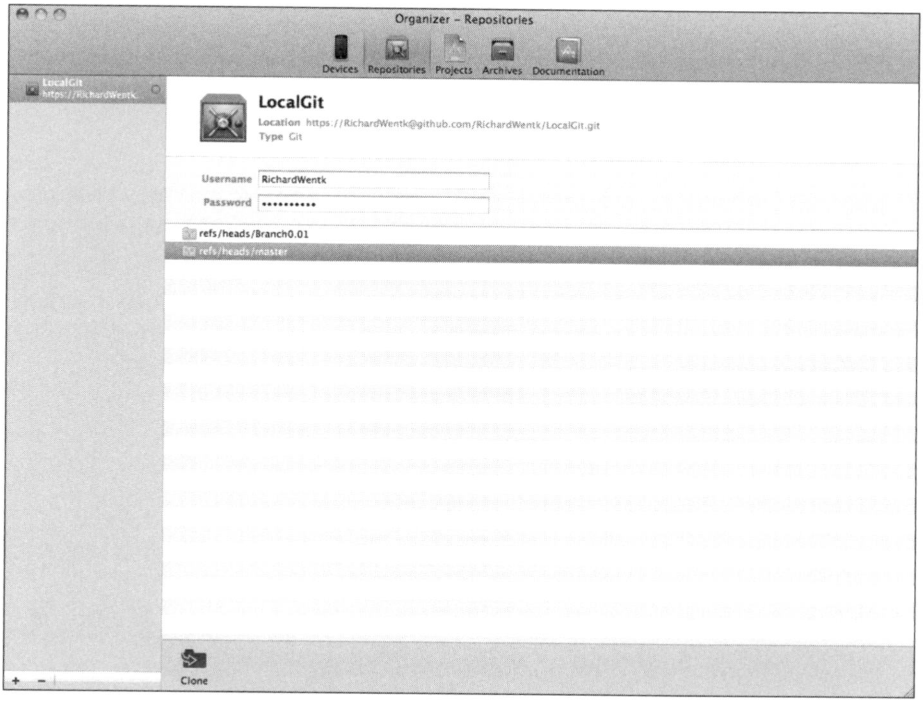

Further local commits remain local. To copy them to the GitHub repository, select File ➪ Source Control ➪ Push.

You can also update a repository from the command line by typing:

```
git push <RepositoryName>  --all
in Terminal.
```

Using Git from the command line

The examples in this chapter should be enough to get you started with Git. Git includes more advanced features such as an ignore file, which tells Git to leave one or more files out of the update process, and various filtering options. You also can integrate existing Subversion projects with Git, although this isn't entirely straightforward.

You can access these features only from the command line. A full list of Git commands is outside the scope of this book. For details, see the documentation referenced earlier in this chapter. A full set of Git man pages is available at `www.kernel.org/pub/software/scm/git/docs/git.html`.

TIP

For more information about SCM with Git and Subversion, see the Managing Versions of Your Project guide in the Xcode 4 documentation. It includes the command-line options needed to work with Subversion.

Summary

This chapter introduced source control and demonstrated how to manage source files in Xcode. It sketched a manual method for simple version and file management. It also introduced the Xcode snapshot feature and illustrated it with a simple example.

It explored the new Git features built into Xcode, with an introduction to the Git source control utility and to the new Version Editor tool. Finally, it demonstrated how to integrate local Git features with the popular GitHub site for team development and remote backups.

Creating Fast and Reliable Code

Getting Started with Code Analysis and Debugging

The Xcode toolchain includes a powerful suite of code analysis, code correction, and debugging tools. Some run outside the main Xcode editor and are introduced in the following chapters. This chapter discusses features that are built into Xcode itself: the code analyzer, tips and issues, the debugging area, and a selection of other options in the Project Navigator that are dedicated to debugging.

With these features, you can perform the following tasks:

- Check your code for issues as you type
- View tips that can help you correct issues
- Analyze code to reveal more complex issues
- Log messages to a window called the *console* while your application is running—typically to provide live diagnostic information
- View the console output from previous runs
- Pause execution at any point in the code with one or more *breakpoints*
- Add *conditional breakpoints* that pause the code when a specified condition is true
- Step through the code line by line or method by method
- View object properties and list their contents at a breakpoint
- Monitor the state of active threads
- Trigger external events at breakpoints, including sounds or scripts

In This Chapter

Using the console

Working with breakpoints

Using the Variables View

Using breakpoint actions

Working with command-line debugging

The Xcode debugging tool is a windowed frontend to an open-source command-line debugger called GDB (GNU Project Debugger.) GDB adds extra low-level options such as direct hex dumps of memory, object listings, and hundreds of other features. You can access these features by typing commands into the Console window. GDB is a huge, complex tool, and these advanced features are optional. You can be productive and efficient without them, but it's useful to know that they're available.

NOTE
GDB and the Debugger support very advanced options, such as remote debugging, that are outside the scope of this book. The definitive guide to the debugger's features is the Xcode Debugging Guide in the documentation. You can find the latest version online. The URL changes regularly, so search for the name.

NOTE
Future versions of Xcode will default to an alternative low-level debugger called LLDB (Low Level Debugger). You can select LLDB manually in Xcode in a project's build settings. LLDB is somewhat faster than GDB, but currently there are few other obvious differences. Eventually LLDB will expand to allow advanced scripted debugging. Because it's still a work in progress, it isn't discussed further here.

Checking and Analyzing Code

It's more productive to get code right as you type than it is to fix it later. To help you achieve this, Xcode 4 checks code and reports issues as you edit.

Checking code as you enter it

This feature is enabled automatically. It begins working as soon as you start typing. Questionable code is underlined or marked with a tiny arrow, and warning or error icons appear in the gutter to the left of the code. If you open the Issue navigator, you can see longer descriptions of each issue, as shown in Figure 15.1.

NOTE
The issues checker is identical to the code parser used during a build. It flags the same errors and generates the same error messages, but it runs in the background and parses your code as you edit.

The issues checker is reasonably intelligent, but it can be slow. A lag of a few seconds isn't unusual, and on larger files the lag can be 10 seconds or more. It doesn't understand partial edits, so it reports errors that only exist because you haven't finished typing a complete line of code.

The faster your Mac, the more you can rely on this feature. Unfortunately, it's less useful on slower hardware. Because of the lag, issues can continue to be flagged after you've fixed them. In extreme cases, you can waste time trying to fix code that's correct, as the parser plays catch-up with your most recent edit. Xcode can also miss errors because of lag.

This is a powerful feature, but you should treat it with care. Don't assume it's infallible—it isn't.

Figure 15.1

Xcode has flagged two errors in this line of code—a missing delimiter, and a misspelled class name.

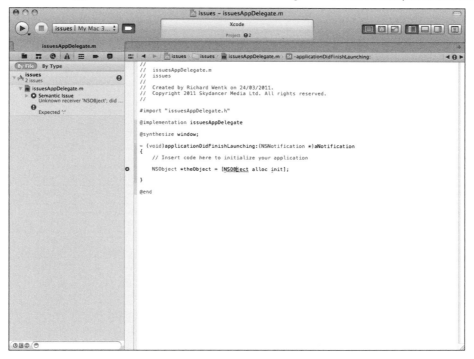

CAUTION

Xcode 4 displays a warning whenever you call a method before it's defined. This is a feature of Objective-C—the compiler does a single pass and always flags unresolved method references, even if they're resolved later. Unfortunately this makes it difficult to tell the difference between bad code that attempts to call a nonexistent method and calls to valid methods that are defined lower in the implementation. You can avoid these messages by adding valid method names to a category declaration at the start of an implementation, but this isn't often done.

Using Fix-It code tips

If you click on an issue flag in the gutter, Xcode may suggest a possible fix, as shown in Figure 15.2. To accept the fix, double-click the blue fix-it suggestion. The Fix-It feature is good at catching obvious errors, but it isn't a full expert system and lacks awareness of certain common code idioms. For example it's confused by the

```
...self = [super init]...
```

assignment which is often used in class initialization code. It assumes this code is a mistyped conditional and suggests a fix accordingly.

Experienced developers will find it easy to tell the difference between helpful and misleading fix-it suggestions. Newcomers should be aware that this feature isn't a substitute for writing good code, and that some of its suggestions may not fix code that isn't working. It's ideal for fixing various minor issues, but it isn't a comprehensive teaching or training tool.

Figure 15.2

Using the Fix-It feature

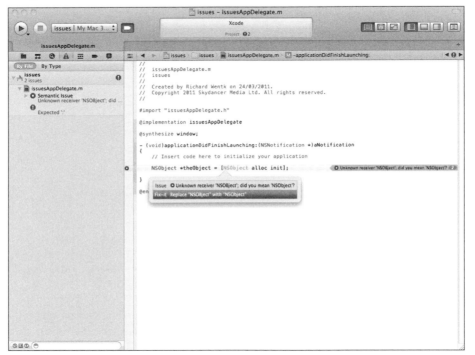

NOTE

If Xcode can't suggest a Fix-It tip, it displays a short issue summary instead. Fix-It tips are only available for a subset of all possible issues. Don't be surprised if Xcode doesn't offer one.

Using the Static Code Analyzer

Xcode 4 includes a Static Code Analyzer designed to flag deeper issues, such as errors in code logic and memory management. It's particularly useful for the latter, and is very good at finding and highlighting code that's likely to leak.

To analyze your code, select Product ➪ Analyze in the main Xcode menu. Xcode builds the project and adds an extra analysis pass. Issues are reported in the code and in the Issues navigator with blue highlights, as shown in Figure 15.3. The highlighting is sophisticated enough to display execution logic and variable dependency chains.

Figure 15.3

Issues appear with blue highlights.

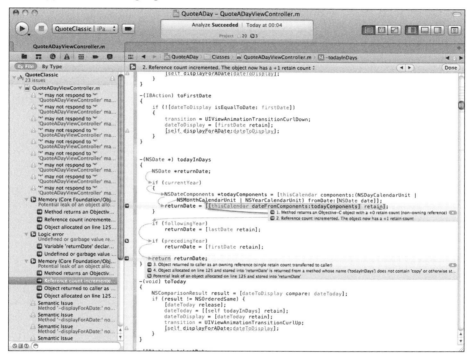

NOTE

The Analyzer displays likely issues. It doesn't suggest fixes for them—but the issue descriptions are often detailed enough to hint at what needs to be fixed.

Getting Started with Debugging

The Issues navigator and the Static Analyzer are good for finding basic syntactical errors and simple logical errors. But bugs are often more complex, and don't appear until you run the code. The Xcode 4 debugger includes a selection of tools for checking code *as it runs*.

The debugger appears in its own area, which is hidden by default. To display it, click the middle icon of the three near the top left of the Xcode window. You also can select View⇨ Show Debug Area in the main Xcode menu. The debug area appears at the bottom of the screen, under the code editor. There are three active panes:

- **A mini-toolbar:** The buttons are used with breakpoints. You can use them to single-step or restart execution after a pause.

- **A hierarchical object viewer called the *Variables View,* in the pane at the left:** The viewer displays an object as a tree that can be expanded to show its contents. Like the toolbar, this pane is used when working with breakpoints to examine objects and check their contents.

- **The *console window,* in a pane at the right:** The console displays messages from the application and the OS.

You can choose to show either or both of these panes with the three buttons above the console. Or you can resize the entire area by clicking and dragging the line under the toolbar—the area is usually too small, by default—and move the split point between the left and right panes by clicking and dragging it.

TIP

In Xcode 3, the debugger appeared in a separate floating window. You can emulate this by opening a new tab, displaying and resizing the debug area until it fills the editor window, and tearing it off. It's useful to have code visible at the same time as you use the debugger. But the split-pane design can feel awkward, especially on a smaller monitor.

Optionally, you can display the Navigator area at the left. Figure 15.4 shows a typical combined view of the display at a breakpoint, with the Debug Navigator, the code editor showing the location of the breakpoint, and the two debug area panes at the bottom of the screen.

TIP

If you need to run an application full-screen you can place a smaller version of the debugger window in front of it by selecting Product⇨ Window Behavior⇨ Xcode in Front. When Xcode hits a breakpoint, the window expands to show a larger version of the debugger window.

Figure 15.4

The Debug Navigator at the left of the debug area is optional. You can hide it to maximize the code view.

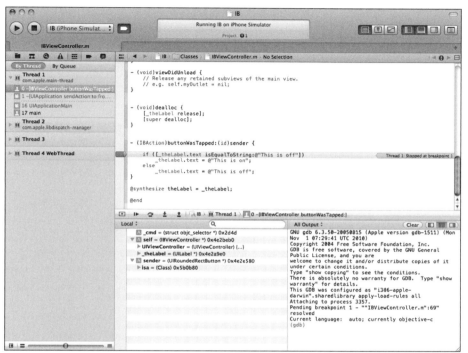

Using the Console

The console is a text output terminal, equivalent to UNIX's stdout (the standard output file), which is typically routed to a display rather than written to disk. It displays four kinds of messages:

- **System generated messages:** Console messages include time stamps and other supporting information that is generated automatically.

- **Custom messages, created with** NSLog **or** printf **statements in your code:** Use custom messages to check program flow, dump information about object properties, and monitor variable values.

- **System generated warnings:** These are rare. A very small number of Cocoa classes generate text to report errors or warnings. Beta OS versions are more likely to generate warnings than production versions.

- **Crash dumps:** These are also known as a backtraces and stack dumps, and they list the messages and events that led to the crash.

You can choose some or all of these messages with the output selection menu at the top left of the console. These are your options:

- **All Output:** Displays all messages
- **Debugger Output:** Displays system messages, crash reports, and error messages
- **Target Output:** Displays messages from your application

You also can use the Clear button to clear the console of all output.

Creating custom messages

You can write a message to the console by including a call to `printf` anywhere in your code. For example,

```
printf("This is a message");
```

writes `This is a message` to the console. All of the standard `printf` formatting features are supported.

If you are writing Objective-C rather than C or C++, the `NSLog` function is more comprehensive. It includes additional formatting and output options that aren't available in `printf`, at the cost of slightly clumsier syntax. For example, to write a text string, you must prefix it with Objective-C's @ "objectification" feature:

```
NSLog(@"This is a message");
```

`NSLog` supports the standard `printf` formatting features and adds a new one—the `%@` option, which displays information about an object. Table 15.1 summarizes the most useful options.

Table 15.1 Useful NSLog Format Options

Option	Used for
%i or %d	signed int
%u	unsigned int
%f	float/double
%x or %X	int as hexadecimal
%p	memory address (similar to %x, with a standard $0x$ prefix)
%zu	size_t
%@	object
\r	new line

For example, to display the value of an integer use:

```
NSLog(@"Int value is: %i", someInt);
```

To dump information about an object, use:

```
NSLog(@"%@", someObject);
```

Note that the first @ prefixes the format and output string; the second @ selects the format.

This object logging feature has special properties. It runs a method called description on the object being logged. Different objects implement description in different ways. For example, data collection objects such as NSArray and NSDictionary dump their contents as text. For other objects, description defaults to the object's class name and memory address.

NOTE

description isn't always listed in class reference documentation. The easiest way to discover what this method does is by experimenting.

TIP

Every message in the console appears with a date and time stamp. The time is specified to the nearest millisecond. You can sometimes use this information to check performance.

Using custom messages

You can add custom messages anywhere in your code. Figure 15.5 shows a log message added to the application didFinishLaunchingWithOptions: method in the app delegate of a typical iOS project. This method runs once when the application loads. The console logs the message, as shown in the figure.

You can use this technique to log events—for example, by writing a message to confirm when a method is called. You also can use messages to list variables and values, display loop counts, and so on.

Unlike breakpoints, messages don't interrupt execution. They're usually faster and more informative than breakpoints when you want to check a sequence of events, but they don't give you the option of exploring memory or checking conditional execution.

CAUTION

Be careful about using messages in loops. There's nothing to stop you writing from a message on every repeat of a loop, but this may generate hundreds or thousands of messages. It's good practice to use messages more selectively. Don't forget that you can surround log messages with custom code to create conditional logging. For example, you might log only every tenth or hundredth iteration of a loop.

CAUTION

NSLog is slow, and you certainly don't want to include it in production code. You can comment out all NSLog statements by hand, but it's easier to include a single line with #define NSLog in the project's .pch file. This redefines NSLog to a null feature and eliminates it from the project. You can comment out this line to re-enable logging if you need to continue debugging.

Figure 15.5

Adding an NSLog message to send output to the console

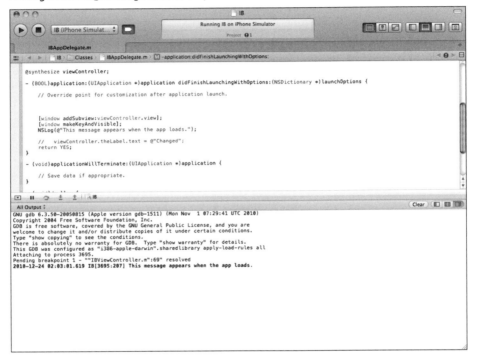

Understanding crashes

When an application crashes, the console appears automatically and displays a series of diagnostic messages that can help you discover the cause of the crash.

Your projects will crash accidentally often enough. But as an exercise that illustrates how Xcode handles crash event, you can create a crash deliberately. Add the following line to the `application didFinishLaunchingWithOptions:` method of the app delegate of an iOS project, such as the IB project from Chapter 7:

```
[window thisWillCrash];
```

The window object has no method called thisWillCrash, so the app crashes when it tries to execute this line.

Figure 15.6 shows the result. If it's not already visible, the Debug Navigator appears automatically at the top left. The message that caused the crash is highlighted in black. Internal messages associated with the crash are shown in a lighter gray.

Figure 15.6

Displaying a crash event

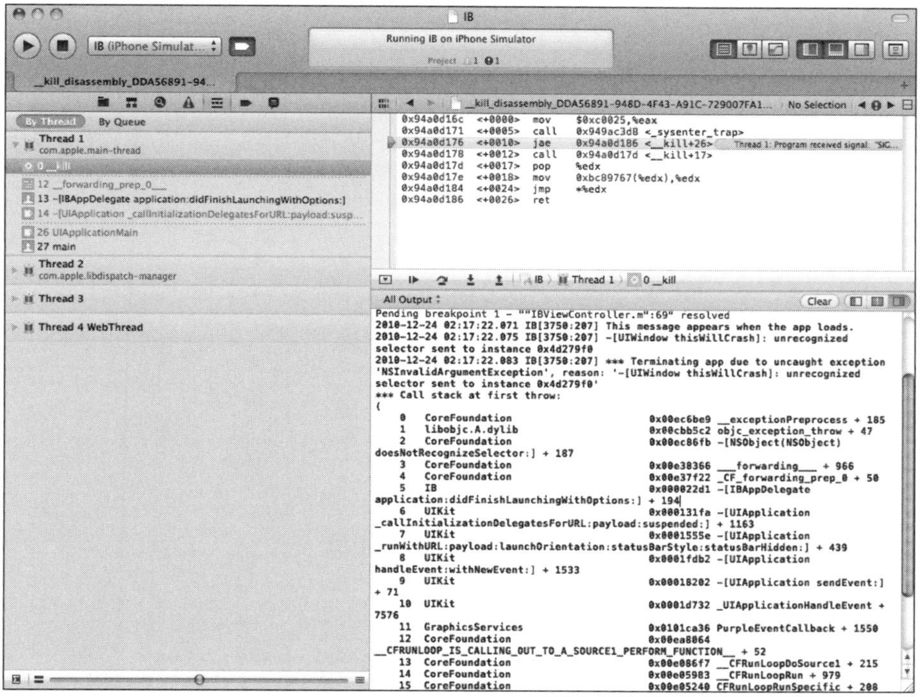

You can see immediately that the crash occurred within the `application didFinish LaunchingWithOptions:` method of the `IBAppDelegate` object. In a larger project, this gives you enough information to find the file with the bug.

The top pane shows a disassembly of the code around the crash point. This is rarely useful. iOS apps trap crash events, and this code is usually part of the iOS crash handler. Because it's in assembler and internal to iOS, you can usually ignore it. If the crash happens in a less controlled way, and you're skilled with assembler, you may be able to extract useful information from this listing. But it's usually easier and more productive to use Xcode's other debugging tools.

The bottom pane shows the backtrace/stack dump. This is a more detailed version of the message list shown in the Debug Navigator.

Figure 15.7 shows a clearer view, with the Debug Navigator hidden to expand the bottom pane and make the backtrace easier to read. The console lists a reason for the crash:

"unrecognized selector sent to instance 0x4d278f0". This tells you that the object at that address received a method call it couldn't execute.

NOTE

OS X applications don't always display a backtrace when they crash. Backtrace availability seems sporadic, and depends partly on the reason for the crash and partly on the version of the OS. When no backtrace is available the console displays a simple error description with no other information. Note also that unlike an iOS application, an "unrecognized selector" exception *doesn't* crash a Mac app.

Figure 15.7

A clearer view of the crash event, with the Debug Navigator hidden

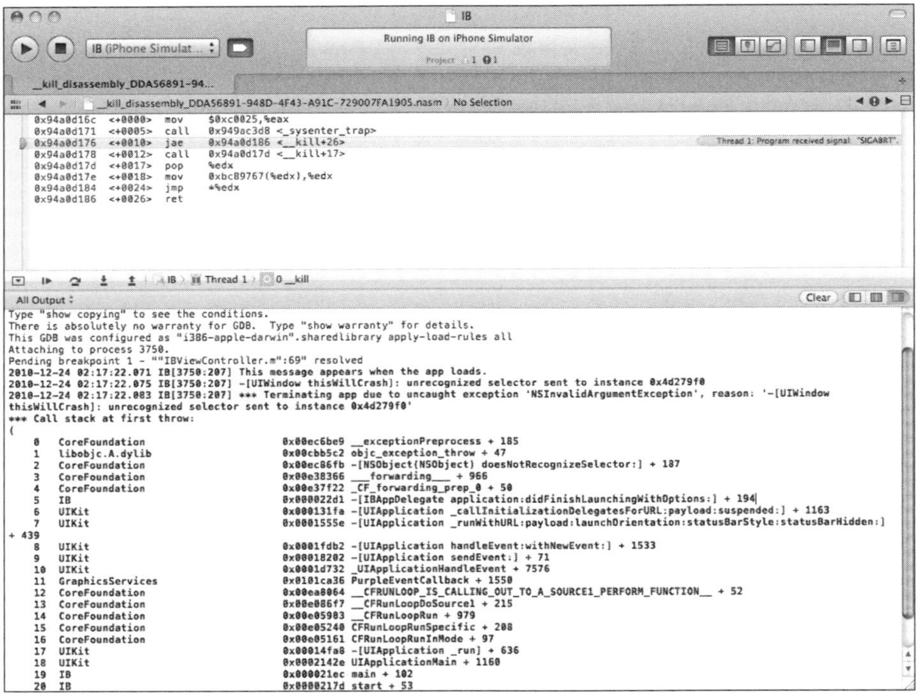

The next line includes supplementary information. In this example, it includes the object and the method that caused the crash. The extra information shown here depends on the type of crash and the objects associated with it.

The backtrace is a chronological list of messages and events that led to the crash, with the most recent events at the top. The last few messages are usually internal to the OS. To find the event in your code that caused the problem, look down the second column until you find the name of your app. The event to the right triggered the crash. Previous events may have contributed to it.

The list is usually "noisy": Lots of detail is available about internal OS objects and messages that may not be described in the documentation. Typically, you can ignore most of the noise and concentrate on the event in your code that created a problem. When you fix a bug in your code, you usually find that the surrounding OS features work correctly.

CAUTION

Crash dumps aren't always as straightforward as this. If your app has serious memory errors, it may stop without displaying any crash information at all. You can usually rely on a backtrace for useful hints. But sometimes you get nothing at all, and the only way to find a problem is to use breakpoints. *Very* occasionally, you may get internal OS crashes that you can't fix. This is most obvious with beta OS versions, but it does happen—extremely rarely—with production code. When an OS object crashes, it's likely you initialized it incorrectly. But sometimes the OS itself is buggy, and you have to work around the problem in some other way.

Viewing multiple logs

You can use the Log Navigator shown in Figure 15.8 to compare the console output from different runs. Each build and debug run adds a new entry to the list at the left. Clicking a Build entry displays build information, including errors and warnings. Clicking a Debug entry displays the console output from that run.

Figure 15.8

Viewing a list of logs in the Log Navigator: Debug logs display console output. Build logs display build results.

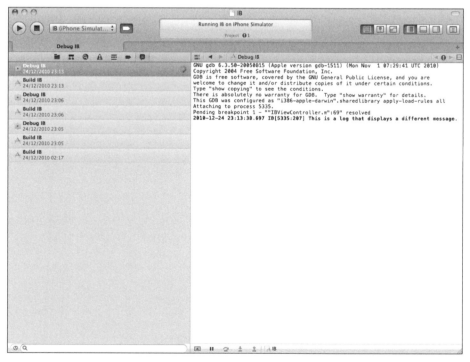

For example, the log message added earlier has been modified, and the most recent Debug entry shows the modified text. Although it's not illustrated in the figure, clicking the earlier Debug entry shows the original console output from the example earlier in this chapter.

Sessions aren't saved with the project, and the list of entries and their contents is cleared when you close a project.

TIP

You can drag-select the contents of the Console and use the right-click context menu to copy them. You also can use the main Xcode File ⇨ Save As… menu option to write the entire log to a text file.

Working with Breakpoints

A *breakpoint* is a deliberate pause in your code. When Xcode encounters a breakpoint, it stops and drops into a special breakpoint mode. You can use this mode to view memory, list objects and their contents, and step through the code line by line.

Breakpoint debugging is very powerful, but relying on it can slow you down. For maximum productivity, use breakpoint debugging selectively, and don't assume that it's a reliable solution for every possible problem. For example, if you don't manage memory correctly in an iOS app, memory errors can happen at almost any point in your code. Single-step debugging can show you that an object or property has incorrect or null contents, but it won't show you which line of code released it prematurely.

Working with simple breakpoints

To explore breakpoints, create a very simple application as a test bed. Use File ⇨ New in Xcode to create a new OS X Cocoa Application and save it as BreakpointTest. Add a simple counter loop to the end of the `applicationdidFinishLaunching:` method in the App Delegate:

```
for (int i = 0 ; i< 10; i++) {
    NSLog(@"Count: %i", i);
}
```

The code counts from 0 to 9 and logs each increment to the console. Open and resize the console window, and then build and run the application. The result should look like Figure 15.9.

When you run the code, the count completes almost instantly. With a breakpoint, it's possible to step through the loop manually and check what happens at each repeat.

Figure 15.9

Logging a very simple counter to the console

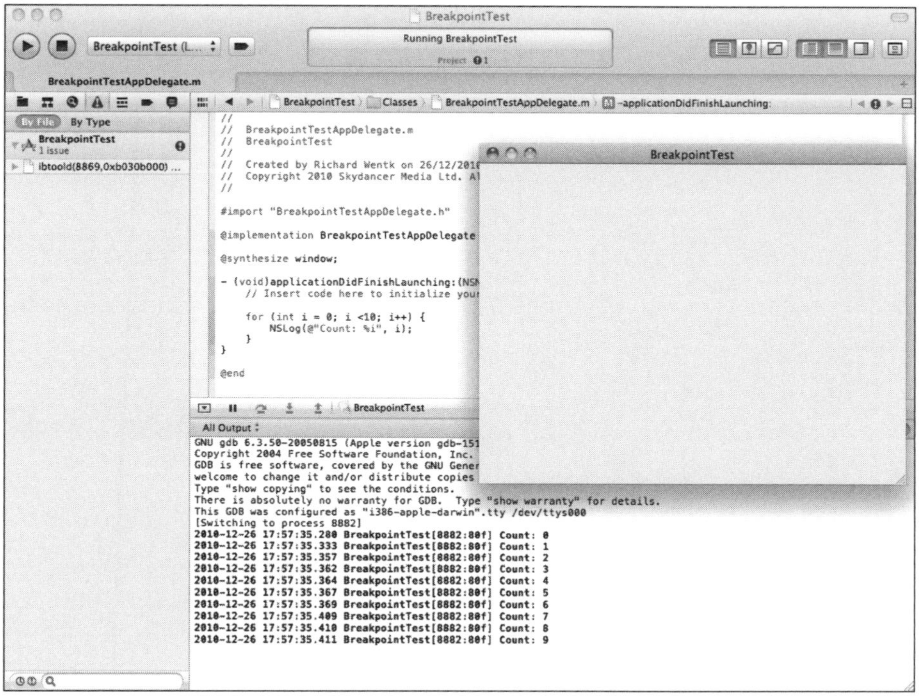

Inserting a breakpoint

To insert a breakpoint, click in the gutter area to the left of the `for...` line, as shown in Figure 15.10. An arrow indicator appears in the gutter. Note that the debug mode button—the arrow to the right of the Stop icon in the toolbar at the top left of Xcode—is selected and highlighted automatically. This tells you that Xcode is running in debug mode and that breakpoints are active.

CAUTION

Be careful not to click in the shaded area to the right of the gutter. The shaded area controls the code folding feature described in Chapter 10. It hides the code instead of adding a breakpoint, which isn't what you want here.

Figure 15.10

Inserting a breakpoint

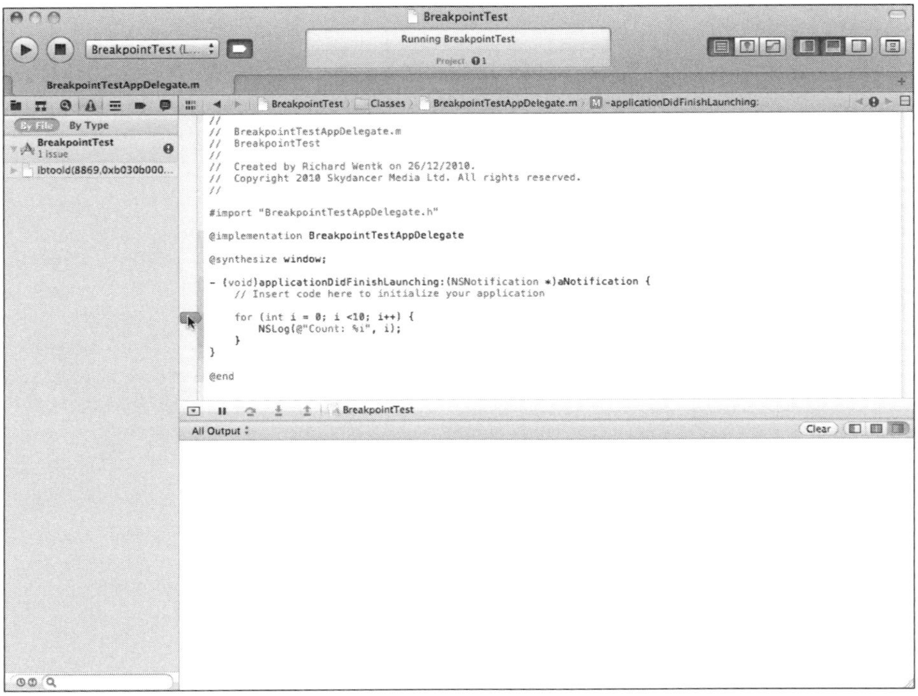

Build and run the application again. This time the run pauses automatically at the breakpoint, with the display shown in Figure 15.11. The breakpoint is highlighted in the code editor, the Debug Navigator appears at the left, and the Variables View appears at the bottom of the screen. You can now use the Variables View, described in more detail later, to examine objects, or you can continue to step through the code by hand.

Continuing after a breakpoint

When Xcode pauses at a breakpoint, you can use the toolbar to control how execution continues. The buttons have the following functions:

- **Show/Hide Debug area:** Click this to show or hide the debugging area at the bottom of the screen. This option is equivalent to the show/button in the toolbar at the top right of Xcode.

- **Continue:** Click this to run the application from the point at which it paused. It continues to run until it's terminated or it encounters a breakpoint.

- **Step Over:** This executes the current line and stops at the next. This is equivalent to the single-step option in other debuggers.

● **Step Into:** This steps into a method or function. By default, Xcode runs a method or function without stepping into it; you see the result, but you can't step through each line of the code. Use this option when you want to examine what happens inside the method or function.

● **Step Out:** This steps out of the current method or function—in other words, it runs to the end or returns—and then it steps in the calling function or method. If there is no calling function or method, this option steps out to an assembly listing of the OS internals.

Figure 15.11

Examining the state of the application at a breakpoint

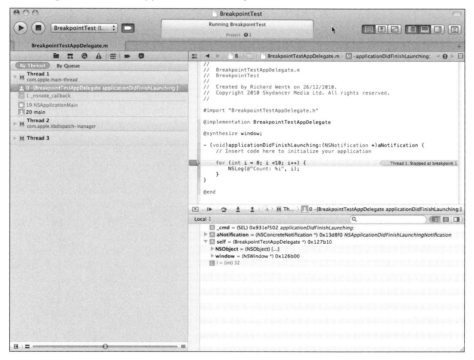

In this example, use the Step Over button to continue the count manually. You see the code cycling between the first line of the `for...` loop and the second line. The value of the `i` loop counter increases with each repeat.

When `i` is 9 on the last repeat, the final Step Over takes you to the end of the method. If you Step Over again, you see an assembly listing of the method dispatch code in the Objective-C runtime. This is OS internal code. Although you can continue stepping through it statement by statement, this isn't usually a useful thing to do.

Enabling and disabling breakpoints

You can disable an individual breakpoint by clicking its gutter arrow, which becomes translucent. A disabled breakpoint remains in place but is ignored by Xcode. (It also keeps its settings, which are described below.)

You can also disable all breakpoints by clicking the main Debug arrow at the top left of Xcode. This turns off debug mode globally. As before, all breakpoints remain in memory, and they are saved as part of the project. But when Debug Mode is disabled globally, Xcode ignores them.

TIP
You can click any breakpoint and drag it to move it.

Using the Variables View

Figure 15.12 shows the Variables View expanded to full screen size. The view shows a list of objects in the application, with disclosure triangles next to each. Clicking a triangle reveals an object's contents, including named properties. Where relevant, properties may have associated memory addresses or literal values. The current object—the one in which the breakpoint was triggered—is labeled `self`.

Standard system objects such as the app delegate, windows, and views have very complex hierarchies. In the figure, you can see that the app delegate's `window` object includes a long list of properties. Many of the items in this list are objects in their own right and have further subproperties that you can explore.

Because the view is unfiltered, it can be difficult to find useful details. As a general rule, you can ignore internal properties and objects unless you have a good reason to check them. In this example, all the properties of `window` are irrelevant. But in a more complex project, you might want to check the `_delegate, _initialFirstResponder` or `_frame` properties to see if `window` is being initialized correctly.

TIP
You can also view the contents and structure of an object by hovering the mouse cursor over it. A yellow box appears with reveal triangles that can drill down through the object hierarchy. This can be a *very* useful debugging tool.

Figure 15.12

Exploring the contents of an object with the Variables View

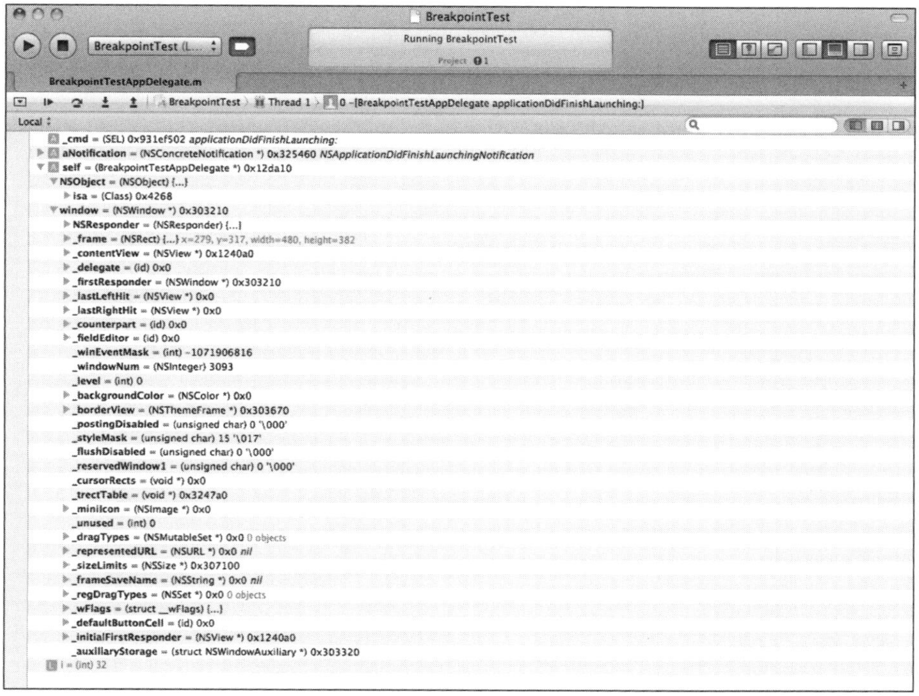

NOTE

System object instance variables are typically prefixed with an underscore character. They may not be listed in the documentation. Examining them can give you useful insights into how system objects are organized and how they work with each other.

The useful detail in this example is the i = (int) 32 entry at the bottom of the window. This is a placeholder for the i loop counter, which hasn't yet been initialized. Use the Step Over button to step through the loop. You see the value is initialized to 0 and incremented on each repeat. Figure 15.13 shows how the value is updated in the Variables View before the log message prints it to the Console.

Figure 15.13

A typical combined debugging session that combines information from the Variables View with messages on the console

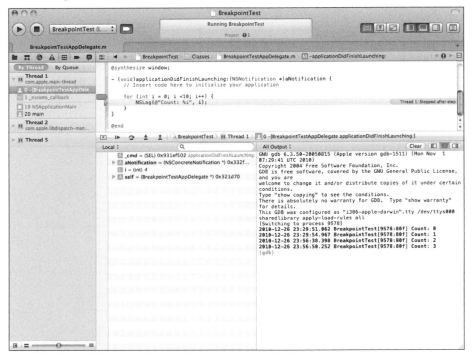

TIP

You don't need to use the right-click contextual menu to display the edit box for a variable. As a shortcut, you can simply double-click the value.

Working with values

The Variables View isn't just a passive display. Right-click a variable to show the menu illustrated in Figure 15.14. You can use the options here to enable and disable data formatting and type information and to edit values by hand. For example, select the Edit Value option as shown in the figure, and type 0 into the box that appears next to the i variable. This resets the counter without restarting the application. You can now repeat the count from the beginning.

Figure 15.14

Using the right-click menu to edit a value "live" after a breakpoint

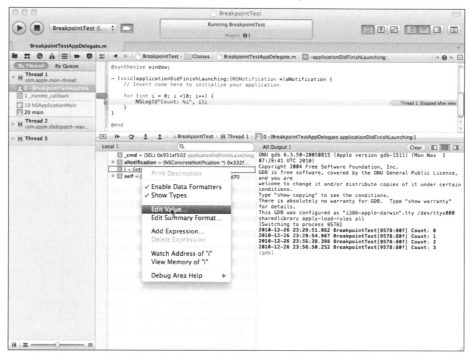

Using expressions

You can add your own items to the Variables View using *expressions*. An expression is an extra customized listing of an object, property, or variable. You can use expressions to extract properties and values from objects, so you don't have to drill down the hierarchy to find them. Expressions can contain standard C, C++, and Objective-C code, but they don't require the semicolon terminator. Expressions must be prefixed with a cast to define the type.

Figure 15.15 shows a sample expression. Right-click anywhere in the Variables View, select Add Expression, enter the following string, and click Save.

```
(NSString *) [window description]
```

You see a new entry in the view, which shows the result of running the `description` method on the `window` object. For a different result, replace `window` with `aNotification`. You'll see information about the initial notification that is posted when the application completes its startup sequence.

Expressions can be challenging but powerful. The syntax required to display a certain value or property can become complex, and you often need to rely on trial and error before you find the correct answer. But if you can master expressions, you can make your debugging sessions significantly more productive. You can review the most important properties and variables at a glance, without having to open other objects to reveal them.

Figure 15.15

Creating a custom expression to display a value of interest

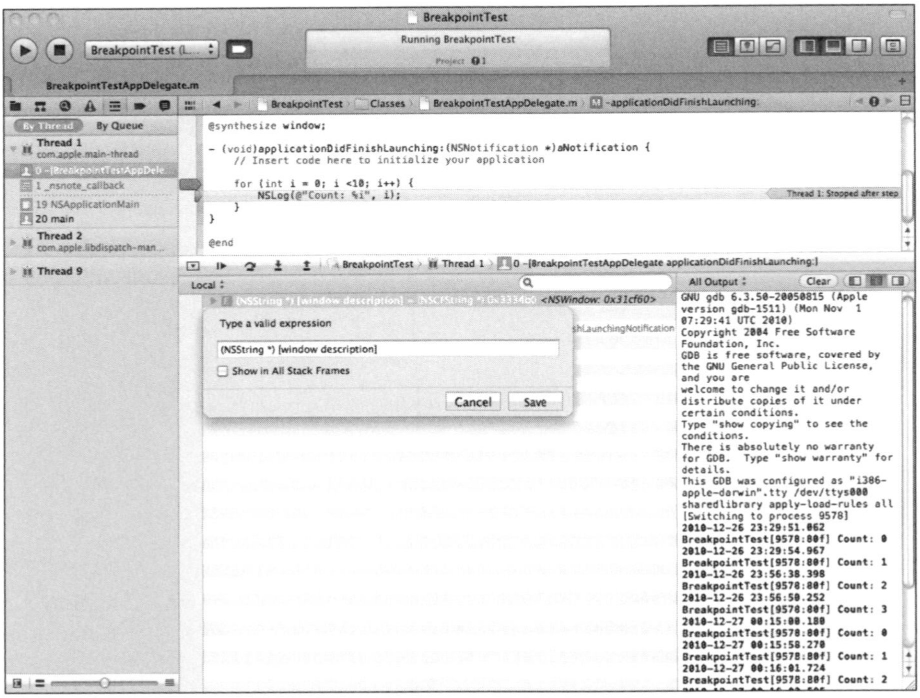

Using data formatters

Every item that appears in the Variables View is formatted, and the formatting information is set by a *data formatter*. All the standard data types have predefined formatters. In practice, these define extra details that may be unnecessary. Uncheck the Enable Data Formatters option in the right-click contextual menu to hide these details, leaving a shorter summary of the key information.

You can also customize the formatting for certain data types. Use the Edit Summary Format option to display a dialog box with an editable field that defines the formatting. Formatters are similar to expressions, but the syntax is more complex and more general. A formatter is enclosed between curly brackets and usually includes a type cast. It may also include one or more macro placeholders to represent input data and a format reference that selects one of four display options. Table 15.2 summarizes the key options.

Table 15.2 Variable View Reference Options and Macros

Option	Used for
n	Shows the variable name
v	Value
t	Type
s	Summary
%apath.to.avalue%	Dot syntax key path for `apath.to.avalue`
$VAR	Variable value
$ID	Variable identifier
$PARENT	Structure or object containing the variable

For example, this line of code runs the standard Objective-C `sel_getName` function on the selected variable and outputs the description as a summary string:

```
{(char *) sel_getName($VAR)}:s
```

Data formatters can create some very sophisticated effects. You have almost total freedom to select and combine data from any object in your application and to display it as you choose. However, the programming cost can be substantial. Custom data formatters are best reserved for more complex projects where Xcode's other features can't display data in a useful way.

TIP

You can define your own custom data formatters and import them into Xcode. The process is moderately complex, but you need to do it only once. You can then reuse the formatters in any project. For details, see the Viewing Variables and Memory section of Xcode Debugging Guide in the documentation.

Adding watchpoints

A watchpoint is loosely related to a breakpoint, but it's triggered when a variable is modified. Use the Watch Address of… option in the right-click contextual menu to create a watchpoint, as shown in Figure 15.16. There's no way to add a watchpoint using the code editor.

When the watchpoint is triggered, Xcode logs a message to the console and highlights the line of code that modified the variable in the code editor. Messages list the values of the variable before and after the watchpoint was triggered.

CAUTION

There's no way to delete a watchpoint manually. A watchpoint is deleted automatically when execution moves beyond the scope of the watched variable. This is strange behavior and not entirely helpful; for better or worse, watchpoints are only loosely related to breakpoints. Internally, they modify the stack. This means system calls are likely to crash if you set a watchpoint for a local stacked variable, because this operation modifies the stack.

Figure 15.16

Creating and using a watchpoint

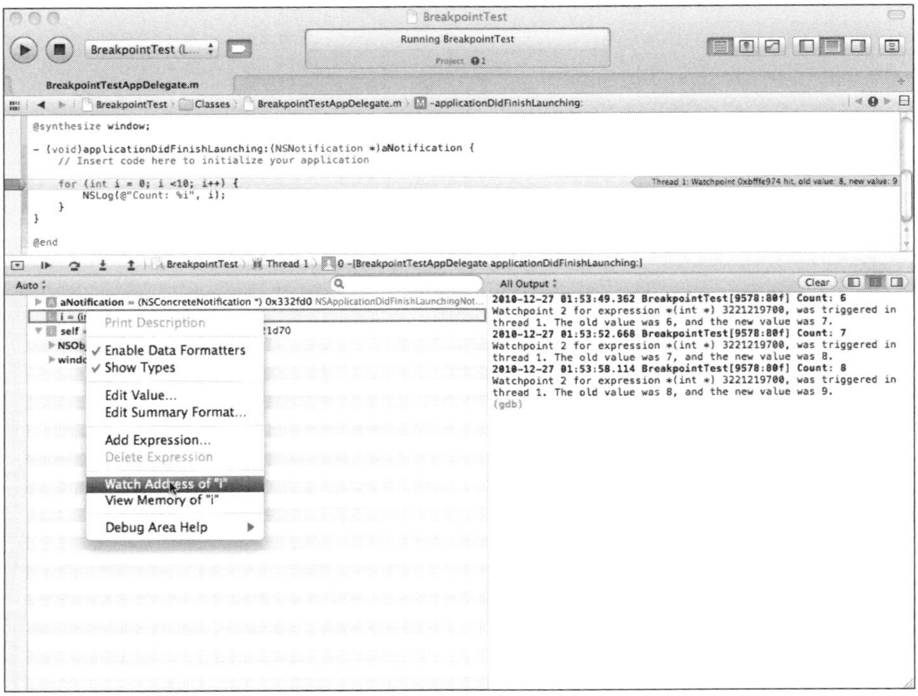

![Screenshot of Xcode showing a watchpoint being created via a context menu with the "Watch Address of 'i'" option highlighted, alongside debug output showing watchpoint triggers.]

Viewing and editing memory

You can use the View Memory of… option in the menu to display a hex memory dump, as shown in Figure 15.17. The dump appears in the editor area and starts with the address of the selected variable. You can rearrange the display to show various byte groupings and dump lengths. Hex dumps can be useful when working with text or with byte-level buffers. But unless you can read raw hexadecimal and convert it to code in your head, other applications are limited.

The display includes an editor, and you can edit, insert, or delete individual bytes by hand. This is a powerful but dangerous low-level feature. Used indiscriminately, it can destroy a build, but it is sometimes useful to tweak byte-level features for testing.

Figure 15.17

Viewing and editing raw hex in memory

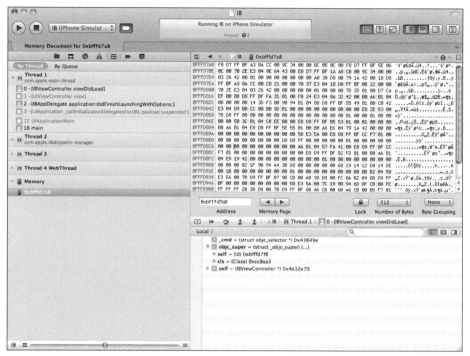

Using advanced breakpoint features

Breakpoints include a selection of optional advanced features. You can use these to create conditional breakpoints, which are triggered selectively, and to trigger actions (external events).

Editing breakpoints

To access the more advanced features, right-click a breakpoint to display a right-click contextual menu. The following options are available:

- **Edit Breakpoint:** This displays the dialog box described later in this chapter.
- **Disable Breakpoint:** This is equivalent to clicking a breakpoint to disable it, as described earlier.
- **Delete Breakpoint:** This removes the breakpoint, with all existing settings.
- **Reveal in Breakpoint Navigator:** This opens the Breakpoint Navigator and highlights the breakpoint.

Creating conditional breakpoints

You can create a conditional breakpoint in two ways. Follow these steps for your first option:

1. **Delete the original breakpoint at the loop initialization point.**

2. **Add a new breakpoint at the line with the** NSLog **statement.**

3. **Right-click the breakpoint, and select the Edit Breakpoint option.**

4. **Set the Ignore value to 5, as shown in Figure 15.18.**

5. **Build and run the application.**

   The breakpoint is ignored the first five times the code runs through the loop, and it isn't triggered until the sixth repeat. This option is ideal for simple delayed breakpoints where you know in advance how many times a loop or method will be executed.

Figure 15.18

Creating a delayed conditional breakpoint

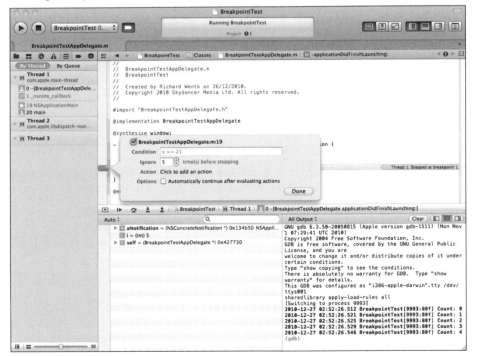

You can create a similar result by resetting the ignore count to zero and entering i == 5 into the Condition box. In this simple example, this creates exactly the same outcome. But the Condition box is far more flexible. You can reference any variable that is in scope and use any valid code as a conditional.

For example, if you replace `i == 5` with `aNotification`, the breakpoint is triggered whenever `aNotification` is non-zero. In this example, the condition is always true. In a more complex application, `aNotification` might follow some other feature or event. You can use this feature to add intelligence to your debugging, creating conditions that reference values in distant but related objects.

Triggering actions at breakpoints

The Actions feature is one of the more powerful options in the debugger. You can use it to trigger almost any event at a breakpoint. For example, you can:

- Run an AppleScript
- Send the debugger a text command
- Log a message to the console or speak it as text
- Run a UNIX shell command
- Play a sound

You can combine actions without limit, adding and deleting them with the +/- buttons. You can also run multiple scripts simultaneously or run a script at the same time as you run a shell command.

For example, select the AppleScript option from the Action menu and type the following:

```
display dialog "Breakpoint %B, Count: %H"
```

Check the Automatically continue after evaluating actions box. Select Done and then build and run the application.

NOTE

The %B option lists the breakpoint location, which is typically the method name and a line number. The %H option lists the number of times the breakpoint has been triggered.

You won't see the alert shown in Figure 15.19, because your application has focus. This is a drawback of the action system; some features don't work unless you can force focus or the action doesn't need it.

For this simple example, force focus manually by clicking anywhere in the Xcode window to bring the alert to the front. Click OK or Cancel, and watch the count increment. With a more sophisticated script, you could force focus from the script code and create a delayed loop that displayed the alert for a short period before continuing execution.

Actions are almost infinitely customizable. They're limited only by your imagination and scripting skills. A key point is that you don't have to use them for manual debugging. You can use actions to create complex automatic testing tools that can respond to external events, log code paths, and list variable values to log files. You can run tests remotely, posting the results by e-mail or uploading them to a web server. These advanced options are specialized, and describing them in detail is outside the scope of this book. But it's important to understand that after you include actions, your debugging options become much more open-ended and creative.

Figure 15.19

Using simple scripting to create a custom breakpoint alert

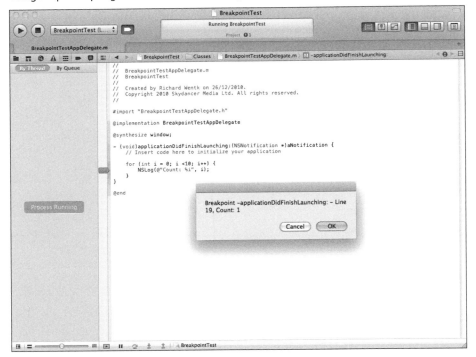

Using the Breakpoint Navigator

The Breakpoint Navigator, shown in Figure 15.20, displays a list of all breakpoints in the project. You can use this list to simplify breakpoint management. You can enable, disable, and delete breakpoints in a single window without having to find and edit the corresponding file. The options in the right-click menu are similar to those available for a single breakpoint, with a couple of additions:

- **Move Breakpoints To:** Use this to group breakpoints. You can enable and disable every breakpoint in a group with a single menu selection. There are three groups: Project, User, and <project name>. By default all breakpoints are in the <project name> group. There's no way to create further custom groups. But you can command-click any number of breakpoints to create a single manual multiple selection.

- **Share Breakpoints:** Use this option to export breakpoints to a file that can be shared with other developers.

Figure 15.20

Working with the Breakpoint Navigator

![Screenshot of Xcode Breakpoint Navigator with a context menu showing Edit Breakpoint, Disable Breakpoints, Share Breakpoints, Delete Breakpoints, and Move Breakpoints To submenu with Project, User, and BreakpointTest options]

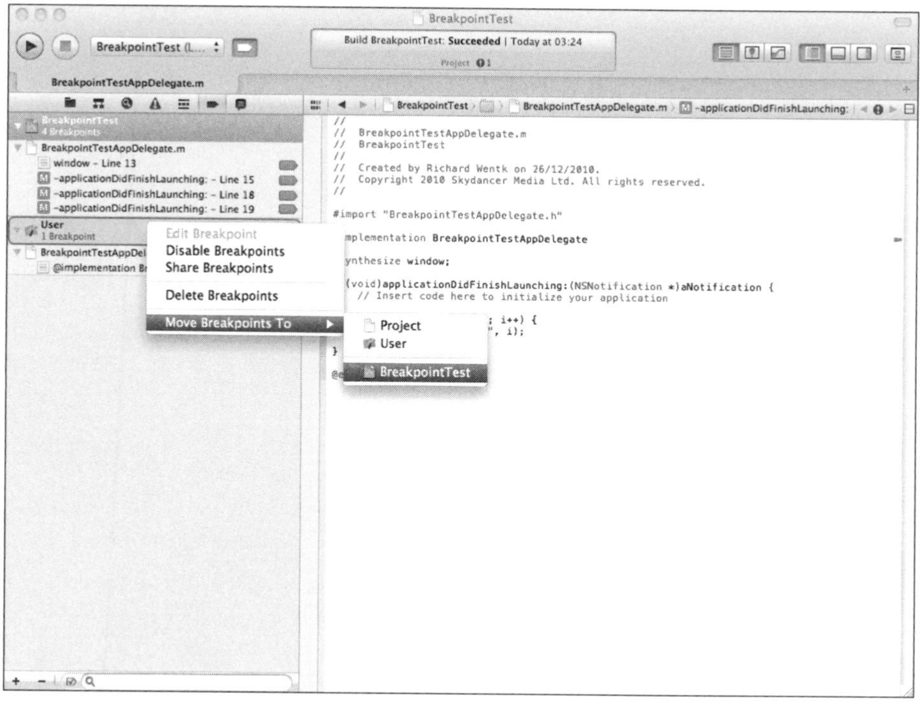

Debugging multiple threads

Debugging becomes more complex when an application has multiple parallel threads. Breakpoints suspend execution in a single thread, but other threads continue to run. It can be useful to suspend them so other events don't interfere as you step through your application. Figure 15.21 illustrates the Debug Navigator's thread display. To suspend a thread, right-click it and select the Suspend Thread option from the menu.

CAUTION

The lowest few threads in the display are usually system threads. Xcode lets you suspend system threads, but unless you have a very good reason for stopping OS threads, it's better to leave them running.

Figure 15.21

Suspending a thread in the Debug Navigator

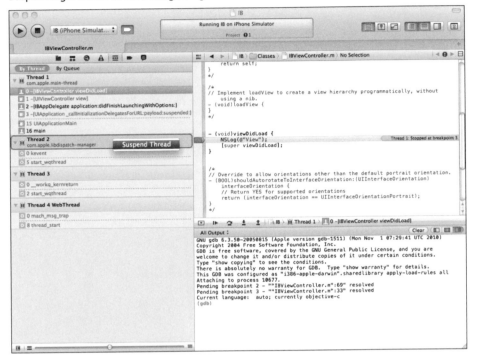

Working with Command-Line Debugging

The (gdb) text at the bottom of the console window is a command-line prompt. You can enter text commands to the GDB debugger to reveal details that can't be accessed with the standard debugging tools.

The complete list of GDB commands includes hundreds of entries, and it's unlikely that any Xcode user has ever memorized them all. Many commands are legacy features left over from GDB's origins. Although interesting, they're not essential if you're working with a high-level language such as Objective-C. Others can provide useful insights. Table 15.3 shows a small selection.

Figure 15.22 shows an example of GDB command-line control. The help command lists the main command groups, and the backtrace command displays a stack dump. Note that standard breakpoints support GDB commands. You can type in a command as a breakpoint action, and GBD prints the output to the console. Use this feature to print extra information about objects without using NSLog or to modify test conditions. For example, one breakpoint can set or delete another automatically.

Table 15.3　Selected Useful GDB Commands

Command	Used for
help	Lists the main GDB command groups. You also can use help <command> to get information about a specific command.
po	An abbreviation for "print object." Runs the description method on a specified object and displays the result in the console.
backtrace	Prints a backtrace to the console. The output is similar to a crash backtrace, but it lists events and messages before the current breakpoint.
set variable	Evaluates any expression and assigns it to a variable. You also can change the GDB prompt with set prompt <string>.
print	Lists the result of evaluating any expression.
info symbol <address>	Gives you information about the symbol at memory location <address>.
info task	Displays a list of threads and gives a status summary of each.
info breakpoints	Lists the current breakpoints with status information and a hit count for each.

Figure 15.22

Using the GBD command line

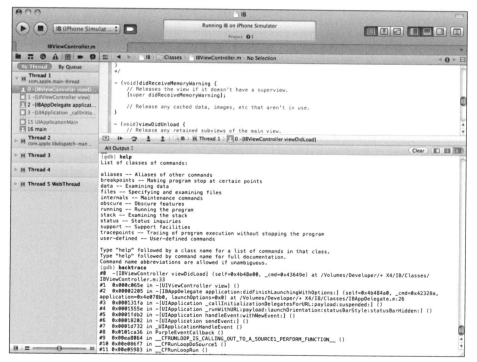

TIP
You can use the up and down arrows to scroll through a list of typed commands. For example, to repeat a command without retyping it, tap the up arrow key followed by the Return key.

Summary

This chapter introduced Xcode's Debug area. It explored the features of the console, introduced the Variables View, and explained how to use it to modify and track variables, view their contents, and list and edit memory.

It discussed Xcode's simple breakpoint features; demonstrated how to create, edit, and delete breakpoints; and explained how to step through code line by line, monitoring variables and results.

It introduced more advanced breakpoint features, including conditional breakpoints and actions.

Finally, it listed some of the more useful command-line options available in the underlying GDB debugging environment, explained how to explore the rest, and demonstrated how command-line options provide extra debugging options that aren't included in the main graphic debugging environment.

Testing Code with Instruments

D ebugging is ideal for low-level line-by-line fault finding. But it's often useful to take a wider view of application performance—for example, to identify performance bottlenecks, monitor processor loading, and check for memory leaks.

The Xcode toolchain includes a powerful and comprehensive helper application called Instruments, used for general testing and profiling. Instruments is a general purpose time line–based test rig that supports a selection of instruments—plug-in test probes that monitor some feature or performance metric.

NOTE
The name of the test application is Instruments, with a capital I. The individual test plug-ins are instruments, with a small i.

You can combine multiple instruments to create a custom test rig, save the rig for use with other applications, and save the results of every test run for comparison with other runs. Instruments supports both iOS and OS X applications, but each OS supports a slightly different selection of instruments.

These are the key benefits of Instruments:

- **A time line:** You can graph and compare the output of multiple instruments simultaneously and watch supporting charts and tables.
- **Live testing:** You can interact with an application and monitor how user events affect its performance.
- **Overall system profiling:** Some instruments monitor how an application affects system resources as a whole and how other applications or processes compete with it.
- **A comprehensive library of instruments:** You can monitor performance in almost every possible way.
- **Automated testing:** You can play back scripted events to drive your application.
- **Simultaneous parallel testing:** You can track and monitor multiple instruments in the same application; on OS X, you can monitor multiple applications simultaneously.

- **Test recording:** Instruments creates a record of each run on separate tracks. You can save the record and reload it to compare it with other runs.

- **Customized instruments:** Advanced developers can create their own instruments.

Beginning with Instruments

Instruments runs in an independent window, as shown in Figure 16.1. You can launch it in two ways:

- Select Product ⇨ Profile in the main Xcode menu to build a project and load it into Instruments. By default, Instruments is automatically attached to (set up to profile) the current project. The monitored application is called the target.

- Launch Instruments independently from Finder or the Dock. Instruments is in the main Xcode /Developer/Applications directory. When you launch Instruments manually, you must attach it to a target yourself. Usually, the target is your project, but you can monitor any running process, with some limitations, described later in this chapter.

Figure 16.1

A first view of Instruments, showing one instrument out of the many that are available

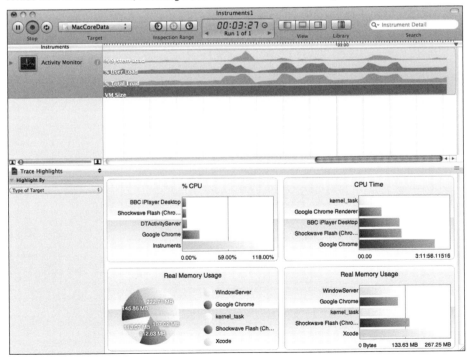

Understanding Instruments

Instruments is a multi-track recorder for system events and statistics, similar to a music or video recorder.

Each instrument records data of one type—object allocations, processor load, user events, and so on—on a separate lane, or data track. When you start a test run, Instruments initializes each lane and begins to fill it with statistics collected from the target. Instruments remembers the results of each test run, and you can review each recording while Instruments is paused.

Many instruments include filters, and you can use them to include or exclude certain event sub-types. For example, when monitoring object and memory allocations, you can exclude all low-level `malloc` events to simplify the display and make it easier to monitor object-level events of interest.

In addition to the time line view, most instruments display various statistics as they're collected. Statistics may appear as tables, charts, lists, or other summaries.

NOTE

Instruments is huge and complex, almost as complex as Xcode. A detailed breakdown of every element would fill this book. Most features can be understood with educated guesswork and experimentation. This chapter doesn't list every feature, but it does outline how you can get started with Instruments so you can begin to explore it for yourself and start working with the tools that you're most likely to find useful.

Exploring the Instruments UI

Figure 16.2 shows a more typical working view of the Instruments UI, this time showing the Allocations instruments, which monitors objects in memory. The design follows the standard OS X guidelines, with a selection area at the top left, an active area in the middle, and a view at the right that can display supporting information. The active area is split into a time line view at the top and a detail pane the bottom. A toolbar at the top of the window controls the main application features.

The selection area is called the instruments pane and includes a list of all instruments used in a trace. Each instrument has a reveal triangle that shows the results of previous runs and an information icon that reveals extra options for fine-tuning a recording.

The time line view is called the track pane. You can use a slider at the bottom of the instruments pane to expand the scale of the track pane.

The detail pane fills the bottom of the display. It includes a selection area at the left that can fine-tune and filter the information that's displayed and a display pane in the bottom middle that displays the information that has been selected.

The extended detail pane at the right shows optional further detail that supports the information in the detail pane. In the figure, the extended detail pane shows a stack trace.

Creating Fast and Reliable Code

Figure 16.2

Looking in more detail at the Allocations instrument

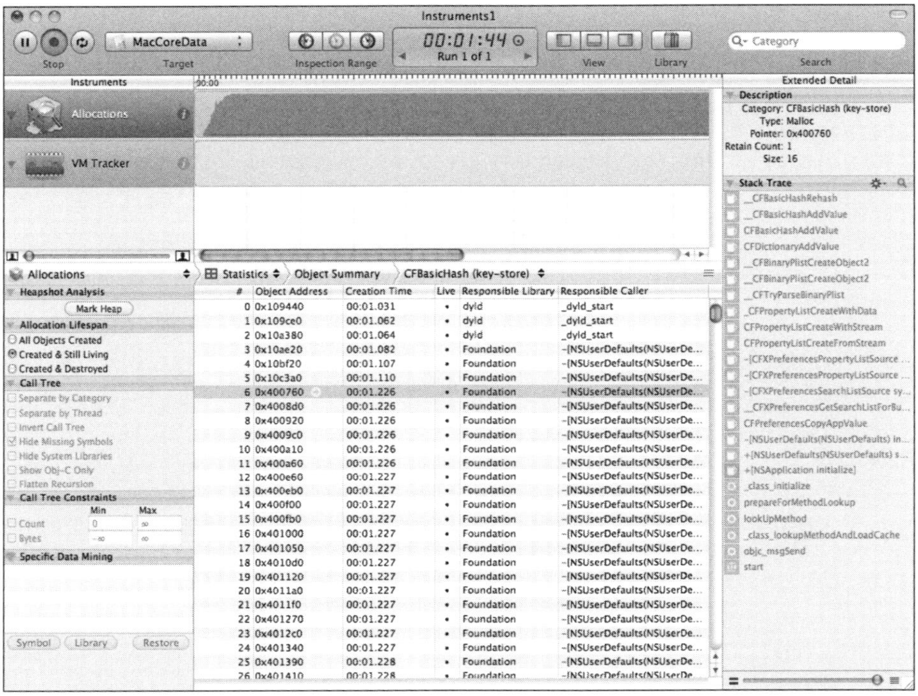

You can see there's an immense amount of detail in the display. The Allocations instrument (refer to Figure 16.2) literally lists every object in memory. You can monitor the creation and destruction of specific class instances and view stack traces for each creation event. You can also get more general statistics about created and destroyed objects, the total memory footprint of the application, and so on. Not all instruments display this much detail; others are simpler summaries of less complex application states.

CAUTION

Some features work at a low level, so you need a basic understanding of Cocoa and OS X/iOS internals to get the most from certain instruments. You can use Instruments without this knowledge, but you will miss the more powerful and productive features.

NOTE

Because some instruments literally modify the OS kernel as it's running, you may be asked for your OS X username and password before they grant low-level access. The kernel changes are transparent and temporary.

Introducing the toolbar

The toolbar includes the most important controls and is visible unless you hide it using the button at the top right. The features in the toolbar are described in the following sections.

Record, pause, and loop control

The large Record button begins and ends recording. While recording, the label changes from Record to Stop. If you're recording an instrument that manages UI events, the label changes to Drive and Record.

CAUTION

When you profile an application, you first select one or more instruments for a run, as described later in this chapter. Instruments then pauses while the instruments are loaded, and eventually it begins recording automatically. If you're profiling your project from Xcode, don't click the Record button while nothing seems to be happening. Instruments begins recording when it's ready. If you're profiling some other existing process, you need to start the recording manually.

The Pause button pauses recording. The timer shown in the main time indicator stops, and Instruments stops collecting data. In fact, the timer continues to run, and if you click the pause button again, you see that a gap has appeared in the recording, as shown in Figure 16.3. This isn't an essential feature, and typically you can ignore it. But occasionally, you may want to change application settings or interact with the application without recording the results.

Figure 16.3

Creating gaps in the recording with the Pause button

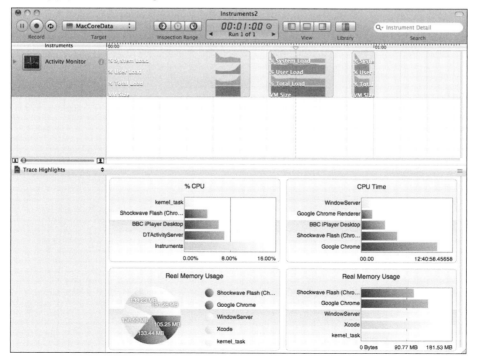

The Loop button toggles between playing a track once and repeating it. You can use this feature with recordings of UI events to create multiple test runs from the same user actions.

The target menu

Use the target pop-up to select the process or processes to be recorded. When you profile a project from Xcode, your project is pre-selected for you here. But you can profile any running process by attaching Instruments to it, as shown in Figure 16.4.

Manual attaching is more limited than project profiling. For example, system applications such as iTunes, Front Row, DVD Player, and QuickTime are deliberately cloaked from Instruments, and you can't collect data from them. Some instruments rely on debug symbol tables. Most applications don't include these, so you can't profile or test them at a low level.

Figure 16.4

When you are attaching to a process, the pop-up shows all running processes, including ones you won't usually want to profile.

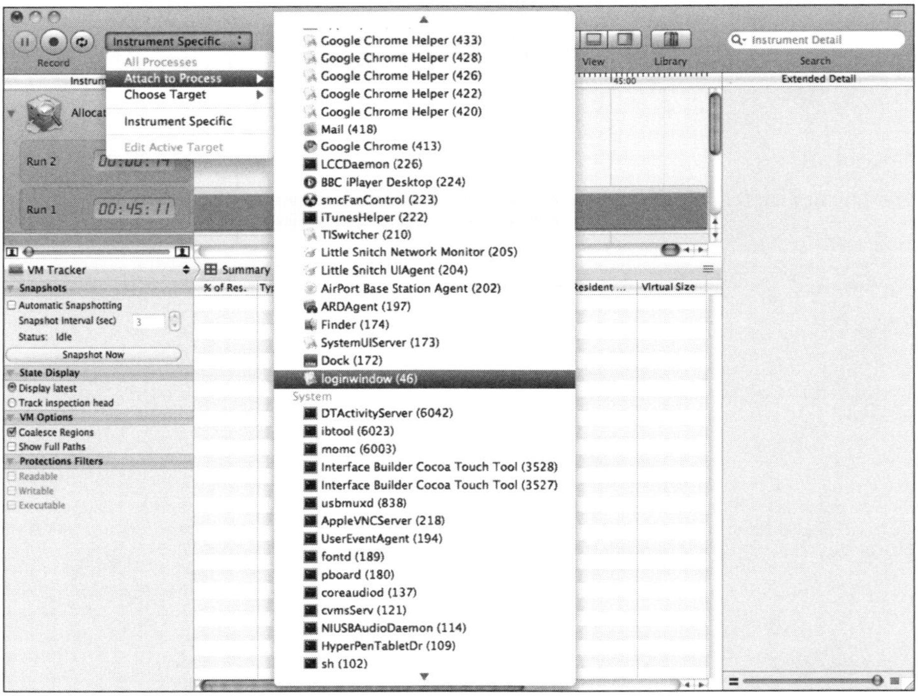

Like many features in Instruments, the target menu has hidden depths, and you can make very specific selections. Figure 16.5 shows the Edit Active Target sub-option in the target menu. You can define the environment variables for the target, add new variables and launch arguments, and select one of the possible consoles for the application.

Figure 16.5

Working with target settings

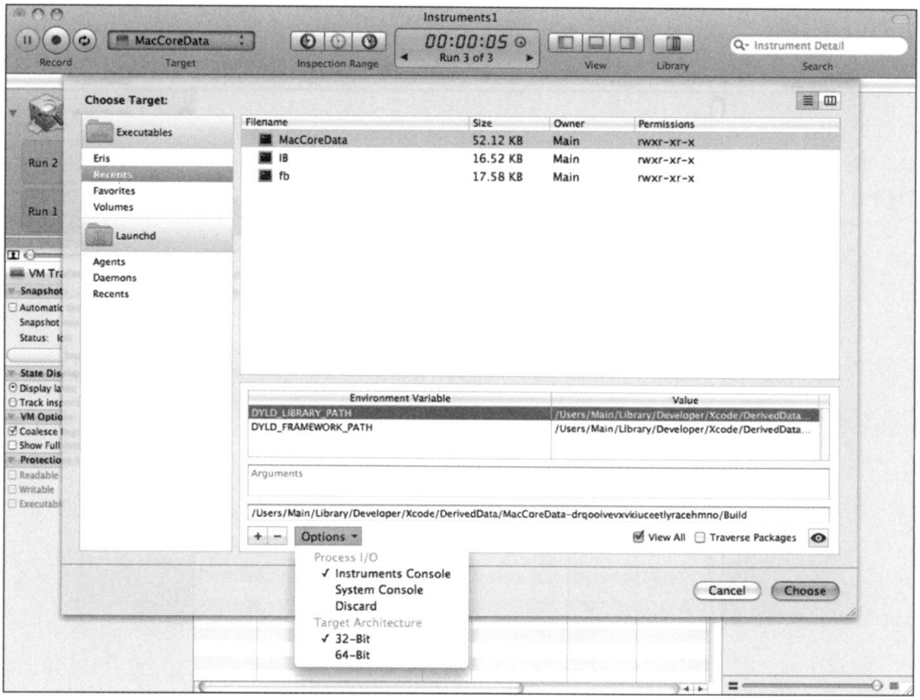

![Instruments1 window showing the Choose Target dialog]

TIP

The Agents and Daemons views are useful because they collect default plists for each system item in a single, easily accessible location. To view the defaults, select a daemon or agent from the list and click the eye icon at the bottom right of the dialog box. You see a text XML dump of the plist, with the keys and values in the dictionary. To edit the plist, double-click it. Xcode opens a new plist editor window. For more about editing plists, see Appendix B.

The inspection range

Use the three inspection range buttons to set the start and end time of the display. To set the start time, drag the position cursor in the time line (described later) to your chosen start point and click the leftmost range button. To set the end time, repeat for the rightmost button. To clear the range, click the middle button.

The inspection range doesn't affect the time line. It doesn't zoom to fill the screen, and it doesn't modify the position cursor. However, it sometimes affects the statistics that are chosen and displayed elsewhere in Instruments.

The time/run control

This shows the elapsed time in a recording. You can use the arrows under the time display to select different runs. The clock/run icon to the right of the time digits toggles the display between the current recording position and the current cursor time.

The view selector

The three view buttons display and hide the various possible panes. You can view as much detail as possible, or you can hide everything except the time line display, as shown in Figure 16.6. It's more usual to run Instruments with the left and lower panes showing.

Figure 16.6

Use the view selector to hide all information except the track lanes. This isn't often useful, but occasionally you may want to maximize the number of visible tracks, to simplify multiple comparisons.

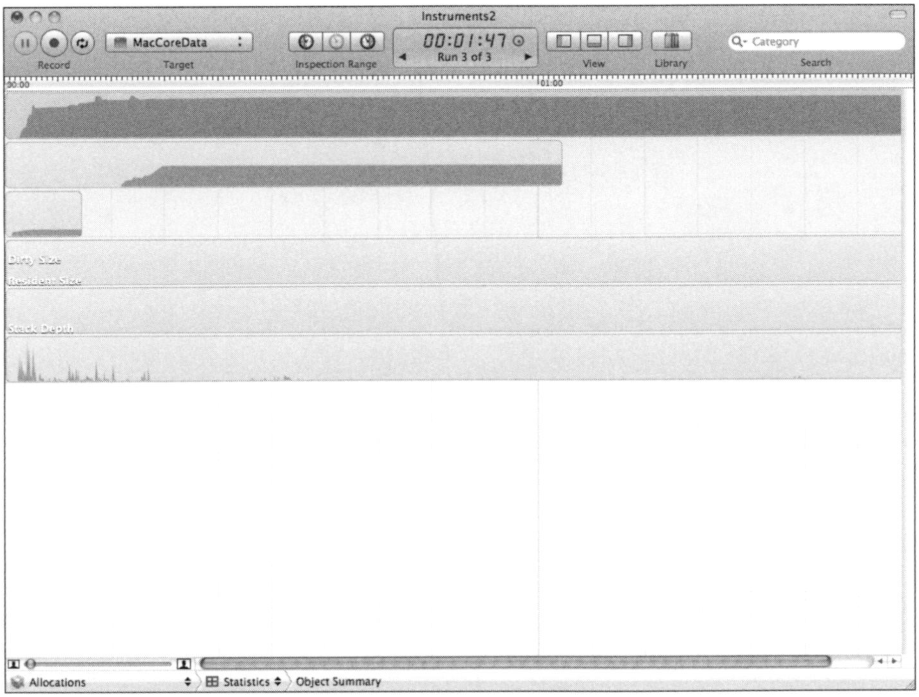

The library button

This button toggles display of the instrument library—a floating window that lists all available instruments, as shown in Figure 16.7. You can use the gear icon at the bottom left of the window to show a menu with various display options. The Library menu at the top of the window displays a list of instrument groups. You can use the library to create your own instrument collections, saving them as *templates*—instrument collections that profile related application elements.

Figure 16.7

Use the Library's view options to save space on smaller monitors. The large icons are impressively detailed, but they waste space on a smaller monitor.

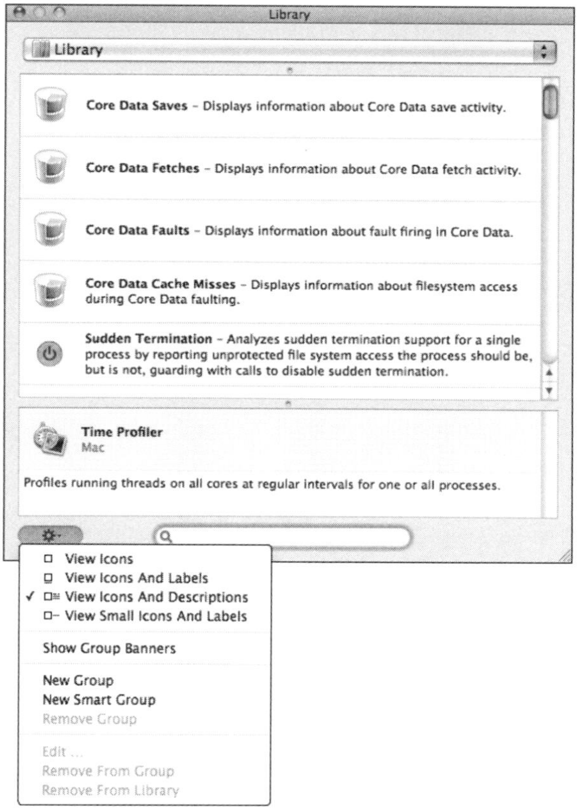

NOTE

Only instruments that match the current project platform are shown; in other words, only Mac-compatible instruments appear for an OS X project, and only iOS compatible instruments appear for an iOS project. There are significant differences between the instruments supported on each.

The search field

You can use the search field to add another set of filters to the information in the detail pane. Search operations depend on the data produced by an instrument, so searches are context-dependent.

Figure 16.8 shows how you can filter the output of the allocations instrument to show only `CFArray` items. In your own projects, you can use this feature to monitor your own custom objects while hiding all other activity. It's easy to overlook the search field, but it can be a very powerful way to filter a flood of data to a trickle of precisely targeted useful statistics.

Figure 16.8

Use the search field to filter the output of the allocations instrument, reducing hundreds of items to just two.

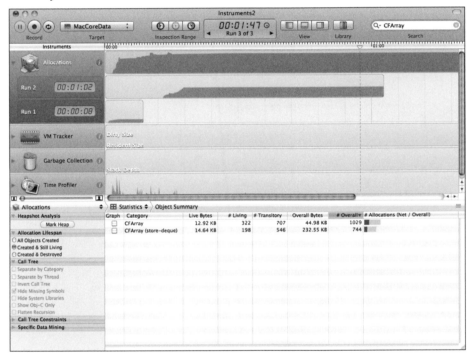

Getting Started with Instruments

Instruments has some quirks, and the easiest way to become familiar with them is to experiment with a practical profiling project—one that monitors memory events in an iOS app.

Memory management in iOS can be challenging, and Instruments includes tools that can monitor memory and report on crashes. Although Instruments has many possible applications, memory profiling is one of the most useful. If you develop for iOS, Instruments can save you time and help you create apps that are robust and don't leak memory.

Creating a leaky test app

To demonstrate this in practice, you need to create an app that deliberately leaks memory. Instruments monitors the leak so you can see how allocations and leaks are graphed and summarized as statistics. Follow these steps:

1. **Create a new Window-based iOS project in Xcode with File ➪ New Project.**

Don't include unit tests or Core Data.

2. **Save the project as MemoryLeak.**

3. **Modify the start of MemoryLeakAppDelegate.m so it matches the following listing:**

```
@implementation MemoryLeakAppDelegate

@synthesize window;

- (BOOL)application:(UIApplication *)application didFinishLaunchi
  ngWithOptions:(NSDictionary *)launchOptions
{
    // Override point for customization after application launch.

    [self.window makeKeyAndVisible];

    NSTimer *theTimer =
    [NSTimer scheduledTimerWithTimeInterval:1.0
                                     target:self
                                   selector:@selector(timerDo)
                                   userInfo:nil
                                    repeats:YES];
    return YES;
}

- (void) timerDo {
    NSObject *theLeak = [[NSObject alloc] init];
}
```

This code creates a timer that repeats once per second. The `timerDo` timer handler method creates a new object called `theLeak`, which is never released. When the pointer is overwritten, the memory is lost and becomes a leak.

If you build and run the project, as shown in Figure 16.9, the app appears to work. The window has no UI elements and does nothing. But the app doesn't crash, and there's no indication that it's leaking memory. If you leave it running for long enough, it eventually causes an iOS memory error. But because `theLeak` is a small object, it's difficult to distinguish the leak from other possible crash events, unless you monitor memory directly.

Figure 16.9

There's no way to tell from the Simulator or from the build messages in the editor that this app is leaking memory.

Profiling an app with Instruments

Loading a project into Instruments is known as *profiling*. The process is the same for OS X and iOS projects. The simplest version has the following steps:

1. **Make sure the project builds with no errors.**

2. **Select the Product ➪ Profile option in the main Xcode menu.**

3. **Wait while Xcode creates a special profiling build.**

You see the usual Build Succeeded message at the end of this step.

4. **Wait again while Xcode loads and launches Instruments automatically.**

You don't need to launch Instruments manually when profiling.

5. **Select a trace template.**

A template includes one or more instruments with predefined settings, and it's designed to collect and display information about specific issues or runtime values.

6. **Wait while Instruments initializes the instrument.**

7. **Optionally, authenticate with your standard OS X user password if asked to.**

Not all instruments require this step.

8. **Wait again while Instruments completes its initialization.**

This can take a few seconds. Instruments appears to do nothing, and your Mac may become slow or unresponsive until initialization completes.

9. **Begin monitoring the app, using the instrument you selected.**

The time line begins scrolling with a graphical display, and the details pane shows dynamic statistics. Depending on the instrument, you can modify the display to zoom in or out, select or hide certain statistics, reveal further details, and so on.

10. **At the end of a run, select the Stop button at the top left.**

You can now scroll through the time line to review the graph.

This process seems simple, but there are a few hidden complications. Not all templates are available on all platforms. When Instruments launches, it offers a slightly different selection for OS X, iOS Simulator, and iOS hardware projects.

Note also that the startup delay is variable and inconsistent. When you load Instruments for the first time, it can take up to a minute before the time line displays useful information. iOS projects usually take longer than OS X projects, because it can take a while for the Simulator or a device to load and run an app. Instruments needs extra initialization time on top of this delay. Generally, startup isn't an instant process, and there's an ambiguous period after launch where it may not be clear if everything is running correctly. (It usually is.)

TIP

You can delay recording and time line updates by selecting File ⇨ Record Options in the main Instruments menu. The options dialog box includes a start delay option, a time limit option, and a deferred display check box that disables data processing and display until the end of a run, minimizing the live processing overhead. Delay times can be set in seconds, milliseconds, microseconds, or nanoseconds. (You won't often use the last option.)

CAUTION

In the first release of Xcode, Instruments sometimes fails to attach itself automatically to the iOS Simulator if you select Product ⇨ Profile. If this happens, attach manually instead.

Note that although you can scroll along the time line graph manually, Instruments doesn't necessarily keep a record of the statistics gathered at every point. Typically, the statistics remain frozen with the values they had at the end of the run. Although it would be useful to replay statistics manually, Instruments doesn't support this.

Selecting a trace template

To explore this process in practice, select the Project ➪ Profile menu option in Xcode to create a profile build and launch Instruments.

Figure 16.10 shows the Trace Template selection dialog box. Because this project is running in the iOS Simulator, Instruments has pre-selected the relevant iOS Simulator Instruments. The All option at the top left displays all available templates. You can filter them by selecting the Memory, CPU, and File System groups.

Figure 16.10

Selecting a template from the standard list

For this example, select the Leaks template. Click Profile. Wait while Instruments launches and initializes. Eventually, you see the display in Figure 16.11. The Leaks template includes two instruments: Allocations and Leaks.

Figure 16.11

A first look at the Leaks template

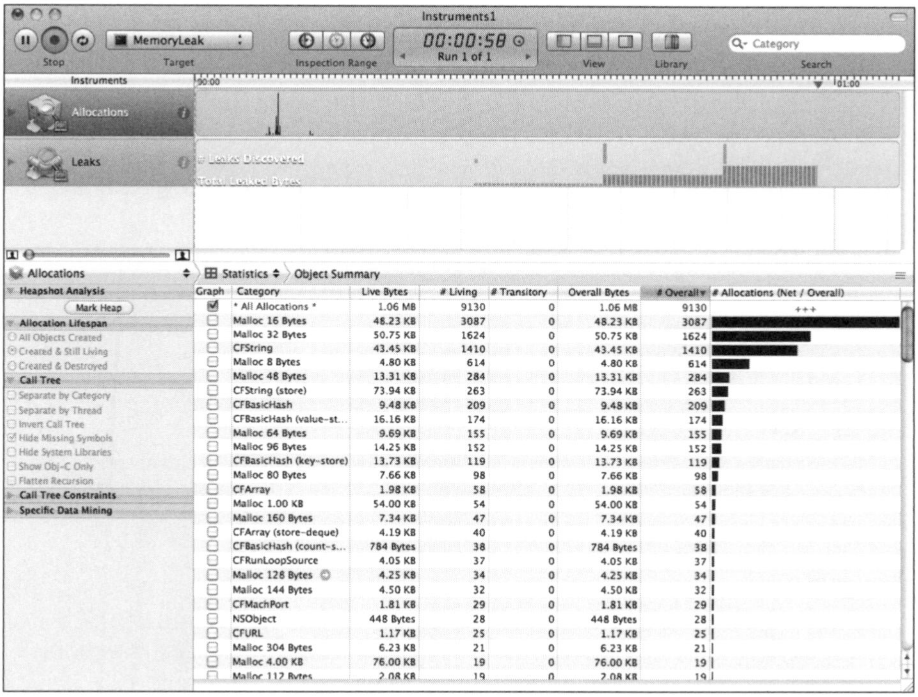

Understanding the time line

After the display is updating regularly, you can begin reviewing the output to see how it offers insights into the behavior of the app.

There are two areas of activity. The time line area shows an initial flurry of allocation events when the app launches and a steadily increasing series of events in the Leaks lane. The statistics show a much more comprehensive—and difficult to understand—list of information, which is described in more detail later.

The Leaks graph provides a clear indication that the app is leaking. But note that the graph doesn't exactly mirror the leak activity. You might expect the leak count to grow steadily, but by default, the graph is sampled every 10 seconds, so the leaks time line displays a summary view.

TIP

In fact, you can change the sampling time to force the graph to update more frequently. For smaller apps the cost is a small performance hit. Select the Leaks instrument, and change the value in the box in the Sampling Options configuration under the Instruments list. The initial 10 second default is excessively long for many applications. As apps use more memory, the performance hit becomes more obvious, so use this feature with care.

Generally, the time line is best used for quick broad-brush overviews of app activity. It's not a precise diagnostic tool, but it does give you enough information to check whether more detailed investigation is necessary.

Getting started with the statistics

The statistics in the detail pane are the key to using Instruments productively. Where the time line provides an overview, the statistics provide extremely detailed information.

At first sight, the Allocations statistics may look complex, but the display is simply a list of all objects created by your app, with an associated instance count, and the instrument is literally monitoring and counting every object in memory.

A combined All Allocations summary at the top of the list counts the total number of objects and lists the total memory used. You can click each column header (Category, Live Bytes, # Living, and so on) to sort the list in various ways and to highlight aspects of the data.

NOTE

If you can't see the display shown in Figure 16.11, select the Allocations instrument at the top left of the time line pane and select Statistics and Object Summary using the menus under the time line.

NOTE

Allocations displays all objects and all low-level memory allocations. Many of the objects in the list aren't documented, because they are internal to the OS and are created and released at a low level. Typically, when you create a standard Cocoa object, the allocation code runs a number of low-level allocations and creates various other low-level structures and objects. Allocations lists them all separately.

As the app runs, you see that both the # Living and the # Overall counts for the All Allocations summary increase by one every second. The # Living column counts objects that are allocated and active. The # Overall column is a running total for the app, and it includes objects that have been released. Because our leaky app doesn't release any objects, the two numbers are identical. In a real project, the two numbers diverge almost immediately.

CAUTION

Occasionally, you find that Apple's own iOS and OS X objects are leaking memory. When this happens, Instruments shows it clearly. But don't forget that in the application, the objects are organized in a hierarchy and not a linear list, and OS objects may leak memory at the `malloc` level. If your code is doing nothing while memory allocations are increasing, you're likely dealing with a genuine OS bug. You may not be able to see which object is causing the problem, because Allocations is reporting the problem as a low-level leak.

Monitoring specific objects

The unfiltered object list includes objects created behind the scenes by the OS. You don't usually need to monitor these, so instruments includes a powerful selection of filtering options that can help you focus on some objects while hiding others.

Use these options to show objects with specific names. Functionally, the various filters overlap, and there's usually more than one way to pick out individual objects from the list. It's up to you to choose the approach that works for you.

Selecting objects with the category list

Select the Category column header to sort the object list alphabetically. Scroll down to find the NSObject entry, as shown in Figure 16.12. If you monitor this entry while the app is running, you see that its # Living and # Overall count both increase steadily.

Figure 16.12

Using the Category column to list objects alphabetically

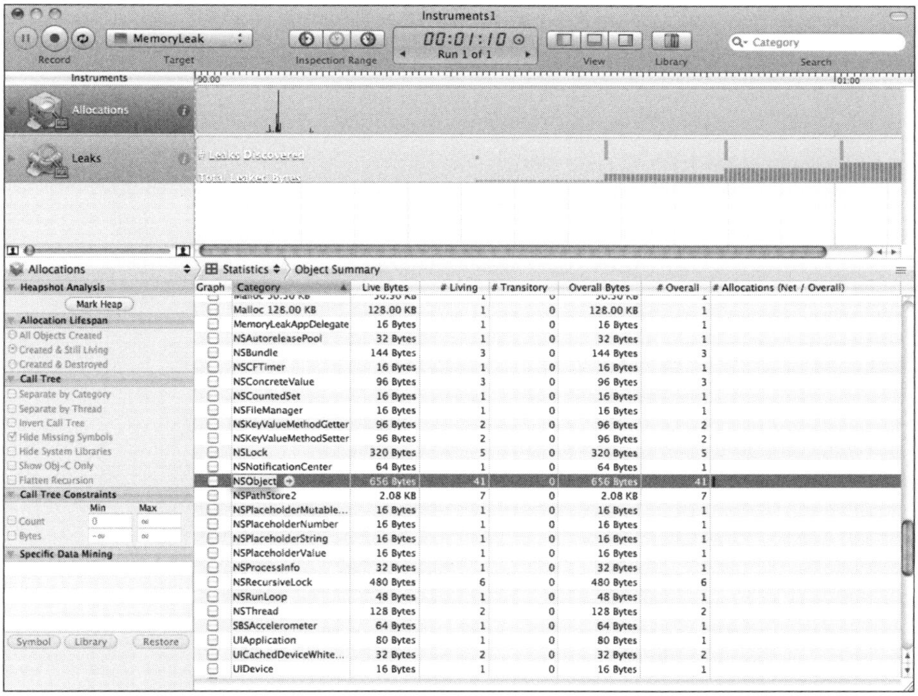

Selecting objects with the search field

Figure 16.13 shows an alternative solution. Type one or more class names into the search field at the top right of the Instruments window, select the magnifying glass icon, and choose Matches Any. The main list is filtered to show the object names you entered. Use this approach when you want to monitor a small number of related objects.

Figure 16.13

Selecting objects with the search field

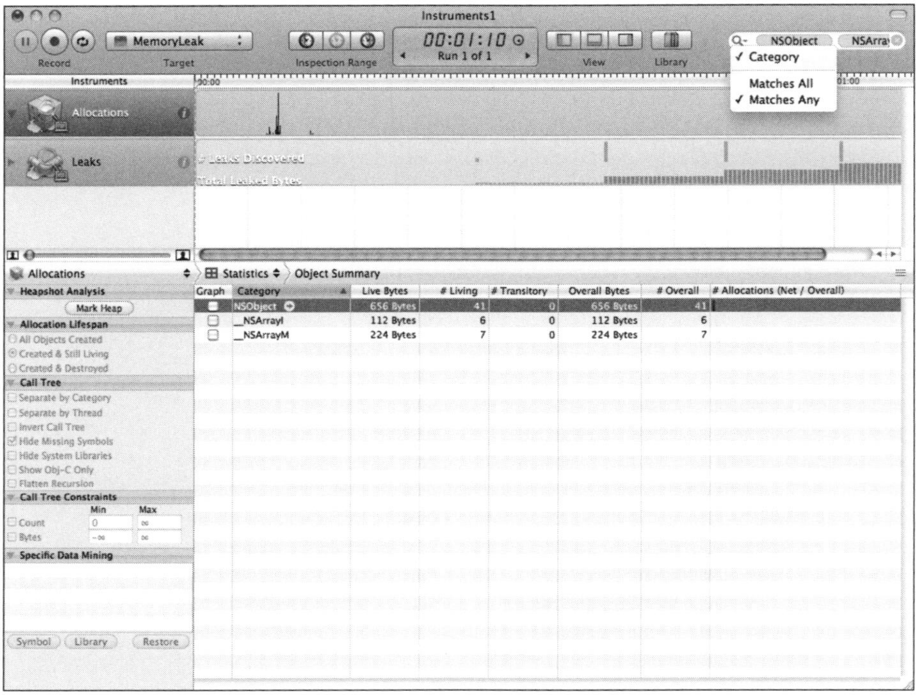

CAUTION

There may be a difference between internal system object names and official documented object names. In Figure 16.13, you can see that searching for **NSArray** displays two related internal system objects that implement **NSArray** internally. These objects aren't mentioned in the documentation, but ideally you should know enough about Cocoa to understand what they do from the search context. This applies only when you're monitoring Cocoa and other system objects. Your own custom objects should have unique and unambiguous searchable names.

Listing object allocation events

When you select an object, you can click the detail arrow that appears to its right to reveal a list of allocation events, as shown in Figure 16.14. The list includes an address, time stamp, and context for every allocation.

You can see from this list that the app is generating multiple NSObject allocations. Because all of them are live, it's not releasing them. Most of them are created in the timerDo method in the app delegate.

Figure 16.14

Listing objects of a single class with their associated allocation times, addresses, and the application/
library and method in which the allocation occurred

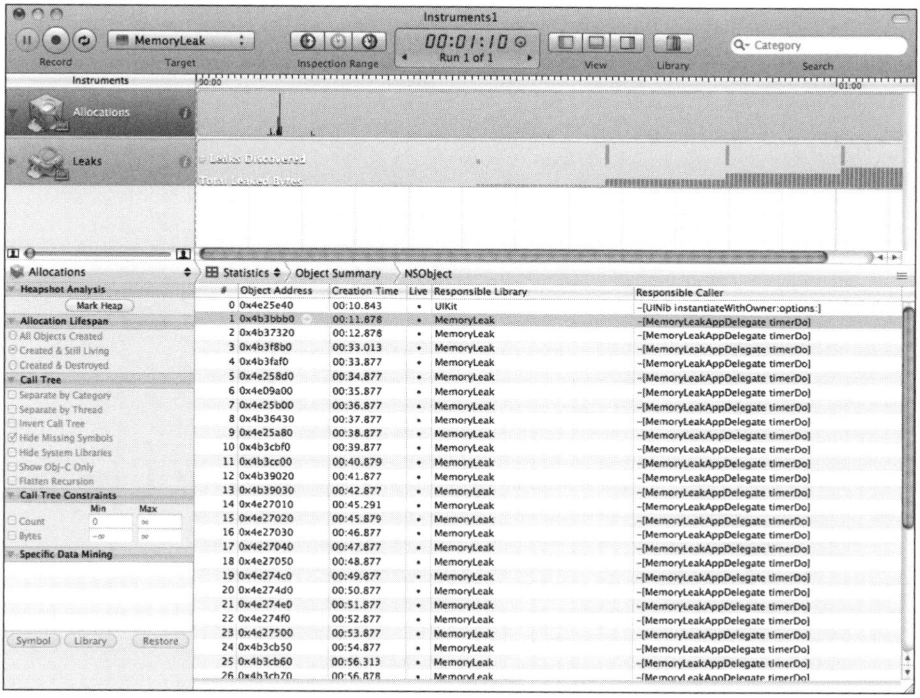

In a real project, this kind of information can give you useful debugging hints, but even more
detail is available. If you select the detail triangle next to an allocation event, you see the display
shown in Figure 16.15. The critical column here is RefCt, which is the object's reference count.

The object view in the Allocations instrument is the only way to get a reliable reference count.
Conveniently, you can view the counts of multiple objects simultaneously. This can be a life-
saver on projects with memory issues, because it gives you an X-ray of the app's memory
events. You can interact with the app while it's running and monitor an object to check whether
it's being allocated and released correctly.

CAUTION

Don't forget that Cocoa may not release objects immediately after they receive a `release` or `autorelease`
message. Depending on the context, some other object may be retaining your target object. Or it may simply take
Cocoa a short while to run the release or autorelease code. However Cocoa handles an object, you can monitor it with
Instruments.

Figure 16.15

Looking at a single object allocation to view the reference count

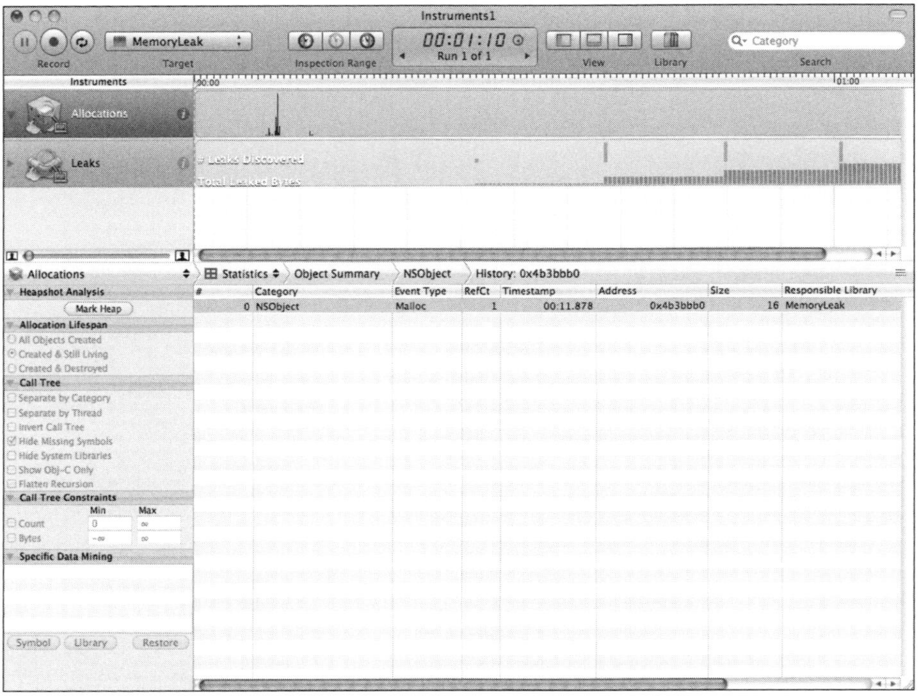

Viewing an allocation event stack trace

A related powerful option gives you precise information about the event that created an object. Select an allocation event, and click the extended detail icon in the toolbar—the one at the right of the group of three labeled View.

You should see the display in Figure 16.16. The stack trace lists the events that preceded the allocation. You can display further information in the trace; for example, you can list the Cocoa and OS libraries by name, highlight user and system events with different icons, and display file links to your source code.

The latter is an extremely useful option, but because it's buried so deeply, it's easy to overlook. Use the menu (refer to Figure 16.16) to enable every display option. Scroll down to item 5—the item that lists the allocation event in your code, marked with the head-and-shoulders user icon. Double-click the file link to the left of the icon.

Figure 16.16

Viewing an allocation stack trace

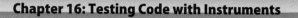

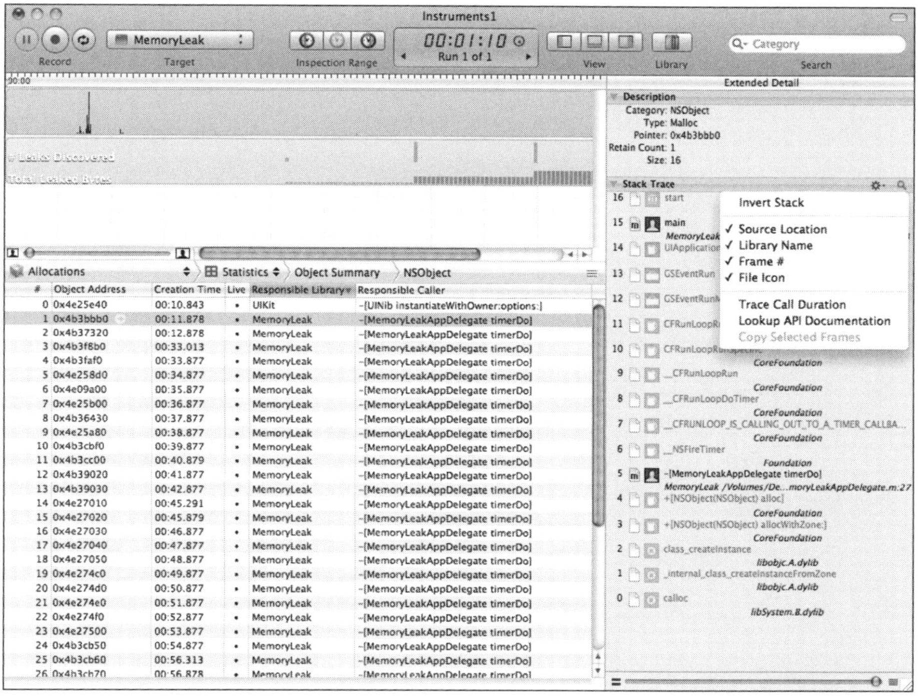

Viewing code from a stack trace

Instruments loads the source code and highlights the line associated with the event, as shown in Figure 16.17. You can immediately see where the object was allocated.

For an object that's still active—one with a retain count greater than zero and that hasn't been released from memory—the reference count display in Figure 16.15 shows the most recent memory management event. You can use the source code link feature in Figure 16.17 to find the code associated with that event.

N O T E

You can use this feature to monitor system objects. But if you try to jump into the source code, you see a short assembly listing, because naturally you cannot view or change the original system files.

Figure 16.17

Bringing it back to the source code

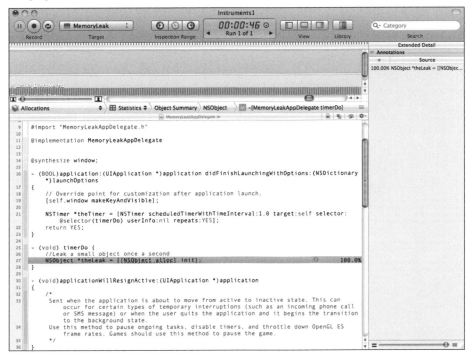

Using the Leaks instrument

The Leaks instrument, shown in Figure 16.18, is a version of Allocations designed to display leak events only. The UI and features are similar—you can drill down to show source code in the same way—but only leak events are listed.

You can use either Allocations or Leaks to find leaky code. But because Leaks displays leaks without the clutter of surrounding allocations, it's a more efficient way to find and debug leak events.

Figure 16.18

Using Leaks to view leak events without other allocations

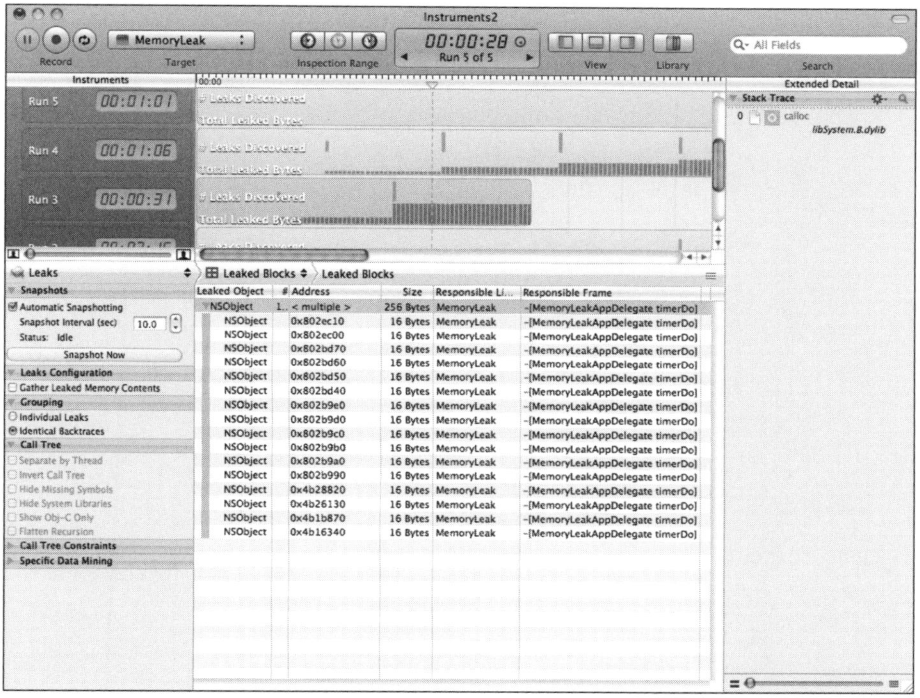

Managing zombies

Unfortunately, there's no way to view objects that have been freed; after they're gone, they're gone, and they no longer appear in any of the statistics. When you release an event and send a message to it, it becomes a *zombie*—an undead object that haunts memory and tries to eat your Mac or iPhone's brain. Because manual memory management is so tricky, Instruments include a special zombie monitoring tool to help you capture zombies before they get out of hand.

To illustrate this, the next example uses bad code to deliberately create a zombie and demonstrate how Instruments can highlight its location. Create a new Window-based iOS application, or modify the one you made earlier, changing the code in the app delegate to this listing:

```
#import "ZombiesAppDelegate.h"

@implementation ZombiesAppDelegate

NSObject *theZombie;

@synthesize window;

- (BOOL)application:(UIApplication *)application didFinishLaunchi
    ngWithOptions:(NSDictionary *)launchOptions
{
    [self.window makeKeyAndVisible];
    NSTimer *theTimer =
    [NSTimer scheduledTimerWithTimeInterval:1.0
                                     target:self
                                   selector:@selector(timerDo)
                                   userInfo:nil
                                    repeats:YES];

    theZombie = [[NSObject alloc] init];
    [theZombie release];

    return YES;
}

- (void) timerDo {
    NSLog (@"Tick");
    [theZombie release];
}
```

The code creates an instance of NSObject and releases it immediately. The timer handler includes a duplicate release event. If you build and run this app without profiling it in Instruments, it crashes because the second release creates a zombie.

Figure 16.19 shows the result. You can see that the app crashed. But other than the EXC_BAD_ACCESS, which can be caused by various issues, there's nothing to suggest why it crashed.

NOTE
If you have some experience with iOS, you may know that the absence of a stack trace or console report often suggests a memory error. But there's nothing here to tell you where the error is located.

Figure 16.19

In this unhelpful crash report, Xcode doesn't give anything away about the cause of the crash.

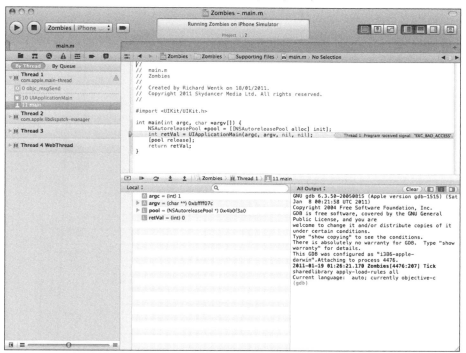

To use the zombies feature, follow these steps:

1. **Select Product ⇨ Profile in the main Xcode menu.**

2. **Choose the Zombies instrument, as shown in Figure 16.20.**

CAUTION

In iOS, the Zombies instrument is available only in the Simulator. It isn't included in the templates for an iOS device.

3. **Wait for Instruments to load, and begin recording.**

4. **Authenticate when asked to.**

The test app crashes almost immediately, and it can take a while for Instruments to catch up. Don't worry if you see the spinning beach ball while this happens; Instruments is working toward a useful display.

Figure 16.20

Selecting the Zombies instrument

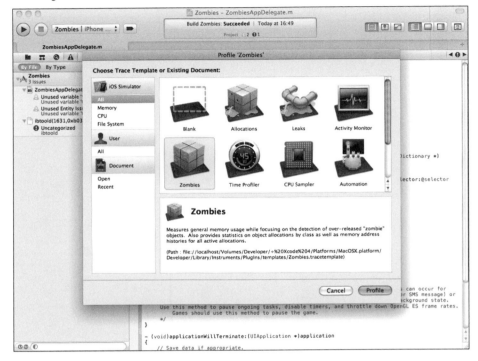

Eventually, you see the display in Figure 16.21. The zombie event is tagged with a small red flag at the top of the time line and a floating pop-up that includes a short summary of the zombie event. The detail pane shows the history of the object and the reference count history of the history. In this example, the reference count history is very simple: The object is created, released, and released again. In a practical project, this history can be longer and more complex.

If you open the extended detail pane, you can see a stack trace for each event, as shown in the figure. Note that the Responsible Library and Responsible Caller fields are blank in the history table and that the stack trace doesn't include source code links. It would be useful if this information were available, but unfortunately it disappears when an object is released, and the zombies display doesn't include it. Instead, you have to work back from the hints you're given. For example, you might search the code for NSObject release events and monitor each event with a breakpoint.

Usually, there's just a single zombie event, because the app crashes immediately after it encounters one. It's possible, under special circumstances, to have more than one, and the Zombies instrument displays multiple red flags on the time line. You can view the contents of each by clicking it and using the Done button to hide the pop-up dialog box when finished.

Figure 16.21

Catching a zombie

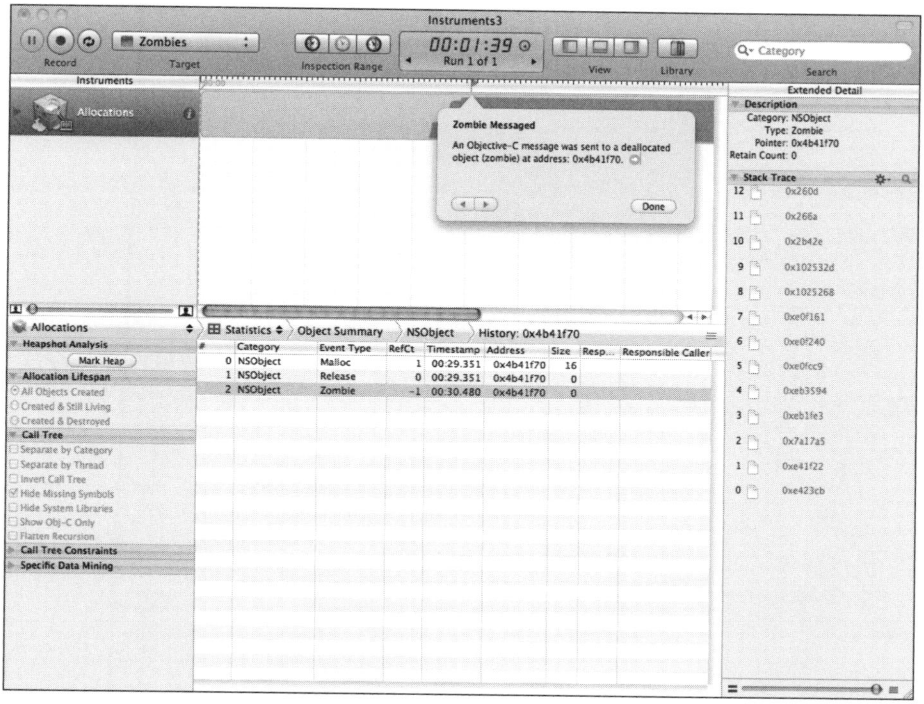

Exploring the detail pane

When you've finished exploring zombies, note that the Allocations instrument can display even more information in the detail pane. The default view in the detail pane is called the Statistics view. But the pane can display allocation data in other ways. You can select the other options, described later, using the menu above the detail pane, as shown in Figure 16.22. Here's what's available:

- **Call Trees:** This displays a complete list of nested function and method calls. Use it with the Mark Heap feature, described later, to display a calling context for an active method. You also can view the complete call tree of the entire application. This gives you a very detailed view of the events in your app, but it's so detailed that it's rarely useful.

- **Object List:** This is a simple linear list of objects that can be sorted by memory address, category (name, for example), creation time, size, library, and calling context. It's identical to the object list introduced earlier.

- **Heapshots:** This creates a simple summary snapshot of heap (total memory) use. Click the Mark Heap button at the left to measure the heap. The Heap Growth column displays the difference between the current and previous heap sizes.

● **Console:** This displays a console window to monitor text output. You can select the application console or the main system console.

Figure 16.22

Selecting other types of displays in the detail pane

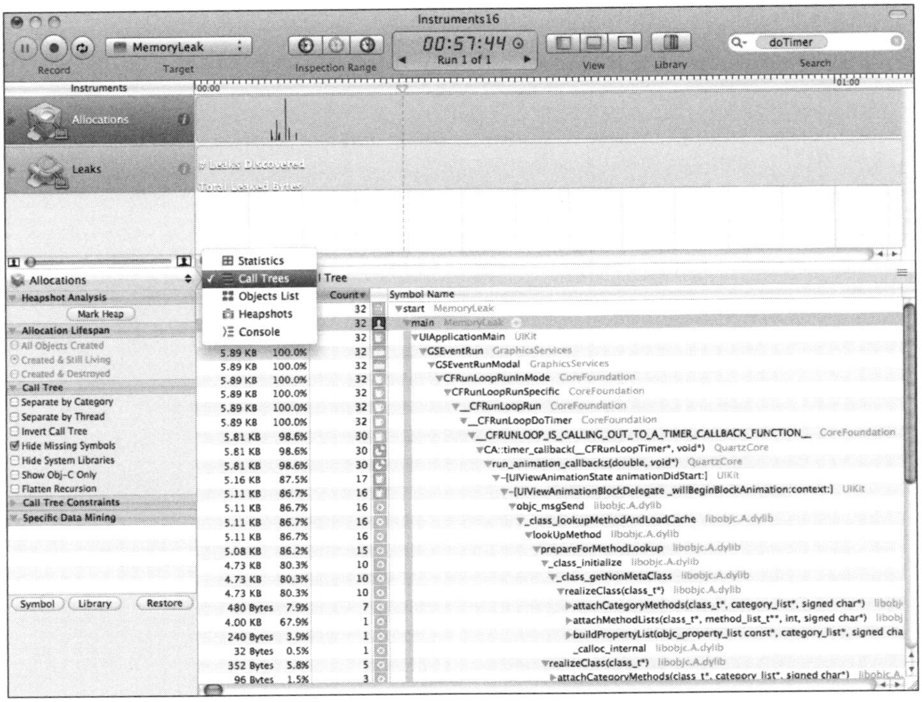

Modifying instrument settings

When you load a template, the instruments it contains are initialized with default settings. You can modify these settings before or after a run by clicking the small information (i) icon at the right of the instrument to show an Inspector dialog box, as shown in Figure 16.23. Each instrument displays a different set of options. Some options are available for many instruments.

The settings inspector is easy to overlook, but it includes powerful features. Some common settings include the following:

● **Target:** By default, this matches the process or thread that Instruments is monitoring. Some instruments allow you to select a different process or thread with this menu, to enable simultaneous monitoring across multiple applications.

● **Launch Configuration:** These are general settings for the instrument.

- **Track Display - Zoom:** The Zoom option changes the vertical height of the time line. You can use it to emphasize the data from one instrument or to highlight activity at the lower scale of the display.

- **Track Display - Style and Type:** The Style and Type options can show cumulative or activity-summary views of the data. The Overlay type displays different runs on a single graph, while the Stacked type (which is preferred) displays a series of strips with the same vertical scale.

Figure 16.23

Changing instrument settings with the inspector

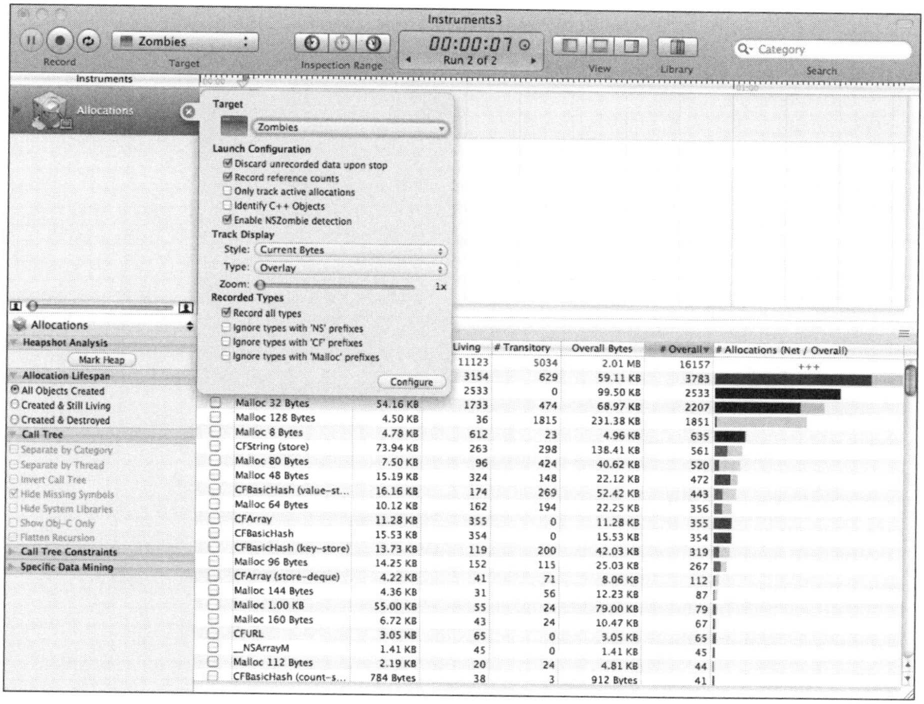

For the Allocations instrument, the remaining settings are unique. The Launch Configuration options for the Allocations instrument include a selection of check boxes. Most are self-explanatory. For example, the Record reference counts option does what you'd expect it to; if you uncheck the box, the instrument doesn't record reference counts.

TIP

Note that Enable NSZombie detection turns on the zombie monitoring feature introduced earlier. There is no separate Zombies instrument; zombie detection is built into the Allocations instrument, and you can enable or disable it here. It's important to remember this if you create your own templates; otherwise, you'll look for a Zombies instrument and wonder why there isn't one.

The Recorded Types option enables crude but useful filtering of the objects list in the detail pane. Events tagged with Malloc are typically low-level system events, and they can clutter up the display, so it's often useful to ignore them. CF (Core Foundation) objects are slightly more complex, but they're still relatively low level. NS objects are Cocoa objects.

CAUTION

Your custom objects are considered Cocoa objects. If you don't record NS objects, Instruments ignores them, even though their names may not begin with NS. But on iOS, objects that begin with UI *aren't* ignored. Also, you can set the Recorded Types options to filter out everything. If you do this, you'll see an empty yellow time line with a warning message.

If you click the Configure button at the bottom right of the inspector, it spins around to show the view in Figure 16.24. By default, this dialog box repeats the record/ignore options from the previous view, but you can use the add/remove icons under the table to add your own prefix strings for customized filtering. Most instruments include the Configure option, but as with the main settings, every instrument displays a different set of features on the flip view.

Figure 16.24

The other side of the inspector. Not all instruments implement this flip view feature. Each instrument displays different options.

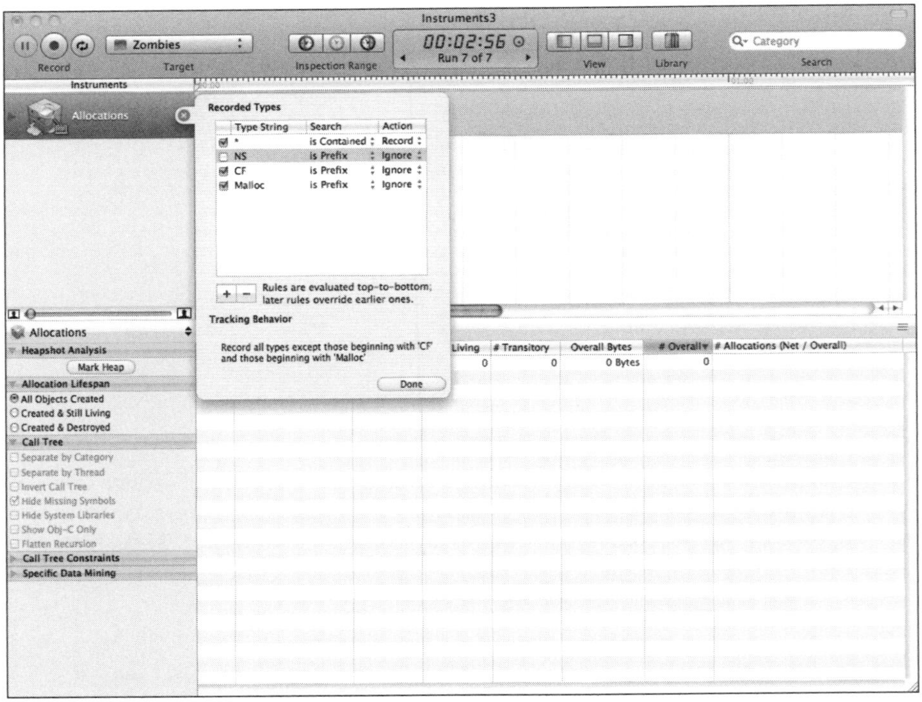

Comparing different runs

To monitor a new run, click the Record button to stop a run, and click it again to begin recording. By default, you see a new set of tracks in the time line, and the description string under the main time counter changes to "Run N of N", where N is the total number of runs.

To compare different runs, click the reveal triangle at the left of an instrument. The time line displays each run on a different track, as shown in Figure 16.25. Selecting each run in the time line displays its final statistics in the detail view. You can also select runs by clicking the forward/back arrows on each side of the "Run N of N" text in the time counter.

Figure 16.25

Comparing different runs

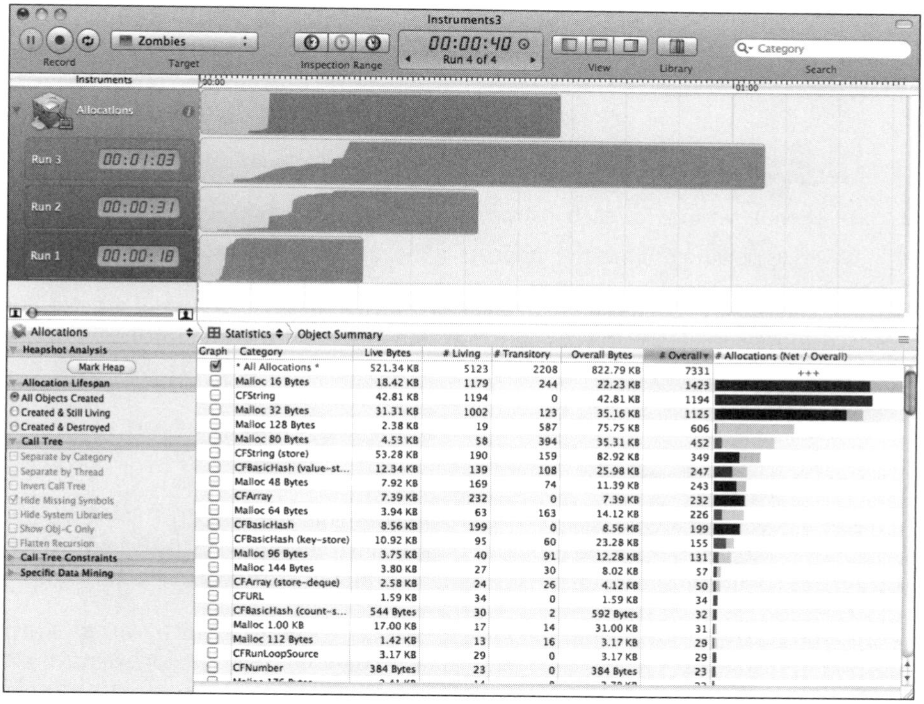

CAUTION

Although each run in this example is identical because they all use the same zombies test app, you can see from the graphs how different the timing can be. Instruments must share Mac resources with other applications, including Xcode and the Simulator. The time taken to launch an app and begin recording events can vary dramatically. Generally, you can't rely on profiling for interactive time-critical monitoring, at least not for the first minute or so of each run.

Saving and loading runs

To save a run, select File⇨Save As from the Instruments menu. The current run is saved to a .trace file, with all the current settings and data. You can reload a trace with File⇨Open. After loading, you can record further runs. They're added to the data in the usual way. The original runs aren't deleted or modified. You can then resave the new file with a new name or overwrite the original.

Working with Instruments and Templates

You can use the templates to get started with Instruments. But to customize the testing with your own preferred mix of instruments, you must understand the difference between instruments, documents, and templates.

Understanding templates

The standard templates have three elements:

- One or more instruments
- Default settings for each instrument
- An appealing graphic that appears in the standard template list on launch

The default templates are designed to create a selection of standard useful profiles. But you can create custom templates, with your own selection of instruments and settings. When you save a template, it's added to the user library. You can select one of the standard icons for the template when you save it.

Creating a template

To create a new template, select File⇨New in Instruments and select the Blank template. Click the Library button, and drag and drop one or more instruments from the list onto the Instruments column at the left of the Instruments window, as shown in Figure 16.26.

Go through each instrument, and change the settings to useful defaults. You can add multiple copies of the same instrument to the template with different settings. For example, you might add two copies of the CPU Monitor instrument and use the Configure options to display two different statistics in the time line, such as PhysicalMemoryUsed and PhysicalMemoryFree.

CAUTION

Make sure you select only the instruments that match your target platform.

Figure 16.26

Creating a custom template

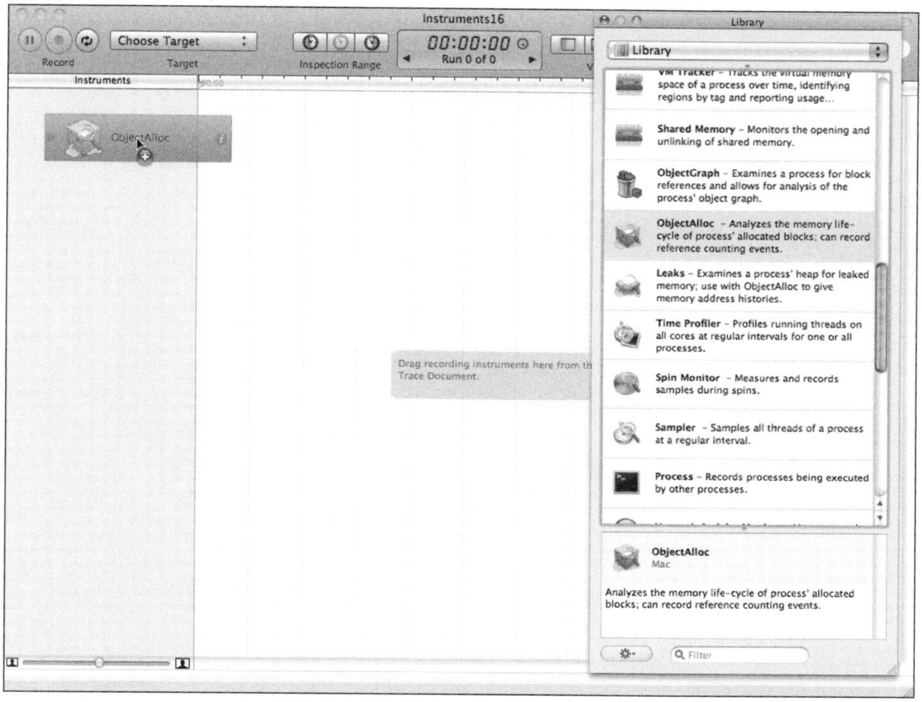

If you want to monitor different threads and processes in each track, set the Target menu in the toolbar to Instrument Specific. You can then select the targets for each instrument when the template loads.

Finally, use the File ⇨ Save as Template option in the main Instruments menu to save the new template. Click the triangle at the bottom right of the Icon box to select one of the standard icons. Give the template a memorable name.

As shown in Figure 16.27, when you create a new Instruments document, the saved template appears in the User section of the template list. To delete a custom template from the list, navigate to the path shown in the template description in Finder, and delete the file by hand.

TIP

The Library window includes a terse description for each instrument in the list. You can find more information about each instrument, with selected extra details about parameters and settings, in the documentation under Tools & Languages ⇨ Performance Analysis Tools ⇨ Instruments User Guide ⇨ Built-in Instruments.

Figure 16.27

Loading a custom template

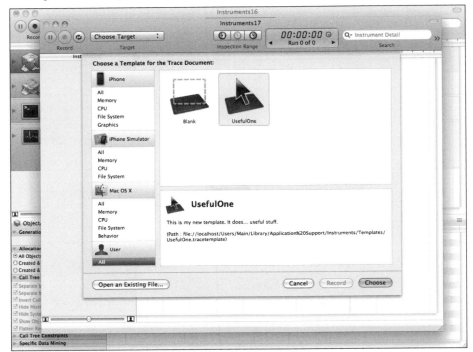

Creating custom instruments

You can create custom instruments to monitor OS features and other events that aren't included in the standard library. Instruments uses a technology called DTrace, which is outlined below. But you can create simple custom event monitors without understanding DTrace.

Select Instrument ➪ Build New Instrument to display the custom instrument dialog box, shown in Figure 16.28. If you understand DTrace and the D scripting language, you can fill in the DATA, BEGIN, and END fields with custom code.

For a simple event monitor, you can enter a library and function name in the probe fields and select one or more parameters to monitor in the Record the following data: box. A more detailed primer on creating custom instruments is beyond the scope of this book. A basic outline is included in the documentation at Tools & Languages ➪ Performance Analysis Tools ➪ Instruments User Guide ➪ Creating Custom Instruments with DTrace.

Figure 16.28

The custom instrument dialog box

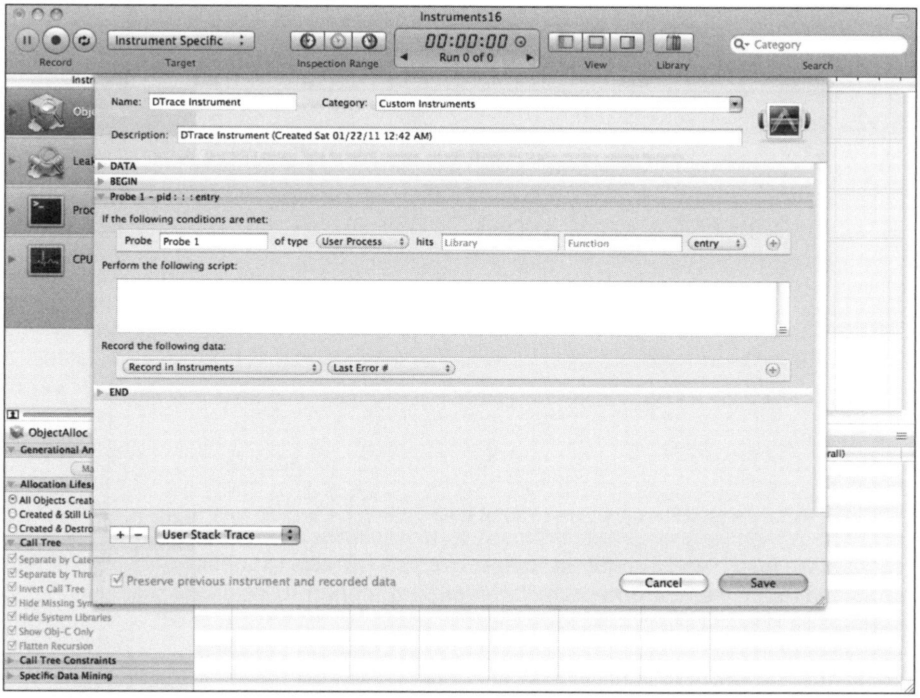

DTrace and Instruments

Internally, Instruments is based on a technology called DTrace. Originally developed by Sun Microsystems (now Oracle) to help debug kernel and application issues in Solaris, DTrace was made available under a free Common Development and Distribution License (CDDL) and ported to various Unix systems. Instruments, effectively, is a GUI for DTrace, with a selection of pre-written scripts for monitoring useful performance features. Because DTrace works at the kernel level and modifies running code, it requires kernel level privileges.

DTrace scripts are written in a custom programming language called D. The syntax of D is very similar to C, but the program structure has more in common with the acronymically named AWK language invented by Alfred Aho, Peter Weinberger, and Brian Kernighan.

Internally, DTrace uses a selection of providers, or access points, that are patched into key parts of the kernel. For example, a provider called `objc` reports information about Objective-C objects in user space. `syscall` reports on system calls in the kernel. `fbt` (function boundary tracing) reports kernel functions. Each provider can be monitored by one or more probes that report on provider-level events.

continued

continued

You can access DTrace from the command line in Terminal with the `dtrace` command. For example, the following dumps a list of active probes:

```
sudo dtrace -l
```

Instruments works by adding a custom action to each probe, which runs when the probe "fires"—in other words, when some relevant event triggers it. You can script your own actions, although you need to have some understanding of each probe and its options.

You don't need to use or understand DTrace to use Instruments, but it can be useful to incorporate DTrace

features into command-line development. A full introduction to the scripting syntax is outside the scope of this book. Default scripts are available in /usr/bin. In Terminal, type the following to see a list of scripts that you can reverse-engineer:

```
grep -l DTrace /usr/bin/*
```

More information is available at `wikis.sun.com/display/DTrace/Documentation`.

Although this kind of low-level exploration of DTrace is better suited to experienced programmers than beginners, it can give almost everyone some insights into how DTrace can be used to monitor application and process activity.

Working with UIAutomation

It's often useful to send a sequence of test events to an app to check the UI for various possible errors and fail states. Instruments includes an Automation script player that can read a set of automation and test events from a file and send them as actions to an iOS app.

Test scripts are written in JavaScript and use the `UIAutomation` class. UIKit objects have a library of associated `UIAutomation` objects that can receive automation events. You can find the full list of objects in the UI Automation Reference Collection in the Xcode documentation.

Test scripts can be simple, or extremely complex. It's up to you to decide how you want to test your UI. The following example is very simple indeed, but illustrates the process of testing and can be expanded to create a more sophisticated test suite.

It's tempting to leave testing to the end of the development cycle, but it can be more productive to develop your test script as you develop. Testing adds some overhead, but if you combine automated testing with the unit testing described in Chapter 17 you can create a useful test suite that exercises the key features of your project and helps ensure that features aren't broken by updates and bug fixes.

TIP

Most UI objects are subclasses of `UIAElement`. The documentation for `UIAElement` lists the messages you can send to objects as you test them. It's a good place to start when you begin using `UIAutomation`. (If you look at the object subclasses themselves, you won't find much of interest.)

NOTE

The Automation instrument is only available on iOS. For OS X, Instruments includes a simple UI recorder that can capture and replay user actions.

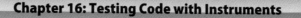

Setting up objects to support automation

The UI automation system doesn't use outlets or links. Objects are referenced in two ways:

- Views can be accessed through the application's view tree. With the correct code, views "just work."
- UI elements must be modified in IB.

To include an object in testing, select in IB and modify it as listed here and shown at the right of Figure 16.29:

- Make sure the Accessibility box is checked. (For many objects, Accessibility is on by default.)
- Give the object a unique name in its Label field.

The figure shows a very simple example with a single text field. A real UI is likely to have a longer list of UI elements, and you must repeat both steps for all of them.

Figure 16.29

Setting up a UI object to support test automation

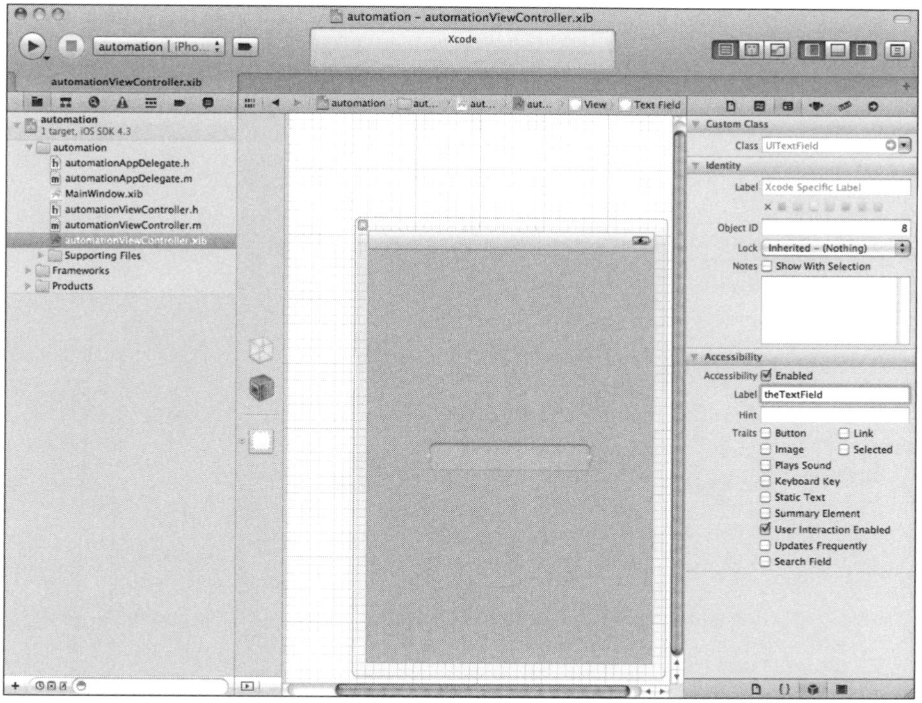

CAUTION

Don't enable accessibility for container views. If you do, automation can't find the UI elements inside them.

Creating a test script

In Xcode 3, you could load a script before launching the Automation instrument. It's possible Xcode 4 will restore the same approach at some point in the future, but at the time of writing scripts are managed in a less elegant and intuitive way.

The easiest way to create a test script is to create an empty file with a .js extension using an editor such as TextEdit. You can save the file anywhere. Your project directory is a good location because it guarantees you'll be able to find it later. Optionally you can include some test code in the file, but you'll be editing this file later within Instruments, so it's convenient to leave the file blank until you do that.

NOTE

Even though Automation files can be loaded into Instruments and saved in a project directory, they're not part of the project's code base. You can't edit them with the main Xcode editor, and there's no reason to add them to a build.

Launching the Automation instrument

Select Product ➪ Profile and choose the Automation instrument, as shown in Figure 16.30.

Figure 16.30

Selecting the Automation instrument

At the time of writing this launches the instrument, and immediately begins recording—nothing. No script is selected, so Automation simply fills the time line with a blank rectangle.

Click the Stop button to stop the run. Wait while Instruments resets itself, then select the Choose Script option from the menu, as shown in Figure 16.31. Click Choose Script again and navigate to your script file in the file selector to load it.

N O T E

The first time you select the Choose Script menu, it has one item in it—the Choose Script option. Whenever you load a script, it's added to the list to this menu, so you don't have to navigate to it again.

Figure 16.31

Loading an automation script

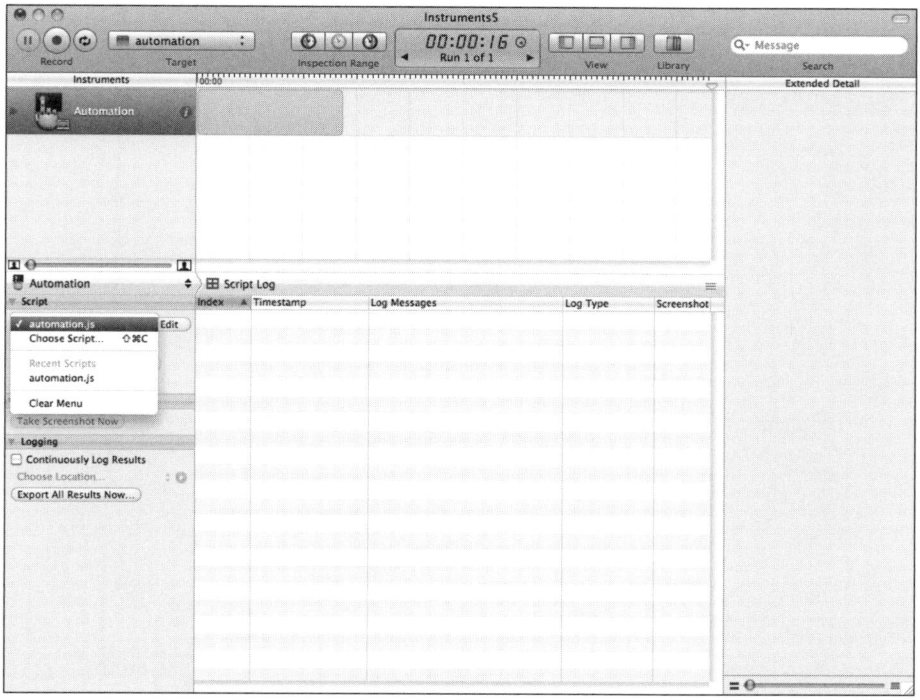

Editing an Automation script

Select Product ➪ Profile and choose the Automation instrument, as shown in Figure 16.30.

Click the Edit button and an edit window appears as shown in Figure 16.32. This window is part of the Dashcode widget editor described in Appendix A. It includes keyword highlighting for

JavaScript and a script selection menu. But it's less sophisticated than the Xcode editor and lacks most of Xcode's features, including code completion, syntax checking, and automated indentation.

Even though it's limited, it's built into the Automation instrument; this makes it more convenient than an external editor.

Figure 16.32

Editing an automation script

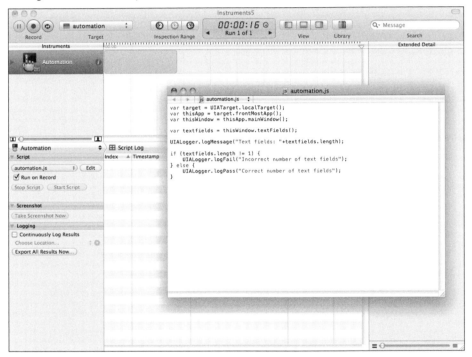

Getting started with Automation scripting

Automation scripting is related to the Document Object Model (DOM) used to access the features of web pages. Like Objective-C, it uses objects and accessors, but the syntax is somewhat different. You don't need to create classes in your code, because they already exist.

Initializing the script

Scripts typically start with the following boilerplate code:

```
var target = UIATarget.localTarget();
var thisApp = target.frontMostApp();
var thisWindow = thisApp.mainWindow();
```

You can then use the object types listed in the documentation for `UIAElements` to return arrays of UI elements. For example:

```
var textfields = thisWindow.textFields();
```

returns an array of textfields. You can then access the textfields by the name you set in IB

```
textfields.["aNameSetInIB"]…
```

or by the standard numerical subscript

```
textfields[0]…
```

The `length` function returns the number of items in an array.

Generating input events

You can set values for UI events by accessing their value property. For example

```
textFields["username"].setValue("Mr Anonymous");
```

You can also automate button taps using the `tap()` function. For example

```
myButtons["okButton"].tap();
```

An extended version of the same code can tap buttons on the built-in keyboard. For example

```
app.keyboard().elements().["go"].tap();
```

taps the Go button.

If your application needs to wait after an event, use

```
target.delay(timeInSeconds);
```

Logging output

To log events and values, use calls to `UIALogger`, which displays messages in the script log window under the time line. `UIALogger` has various message levels, which force messages to appear in different colors. For example

```
UIALogger.logFail ("Something bad happened.");
```

appears on the console in red.

Creating test scripts

Testing typically follows these steps:

1. Preset some UI elements with test values.

2. Perform an operation, sometimes using a button tap.

3. Pause if necessary.

4. Read return values and generate messages for pass/fail conditions or general reporting.

You can, of course, include various paths through the test sequence, depending on the test results.

Figure 16.33 shows a trivial example that runs a very simple test. In this example the code is unlikely to fail, because the number of text fields is fixed. But in a more complex test it can be useful to report the number of items in a UI. For example, you can report the number of cells in a table view after loading data from a remote source.

Figure 16.33

The output from a very simple test script

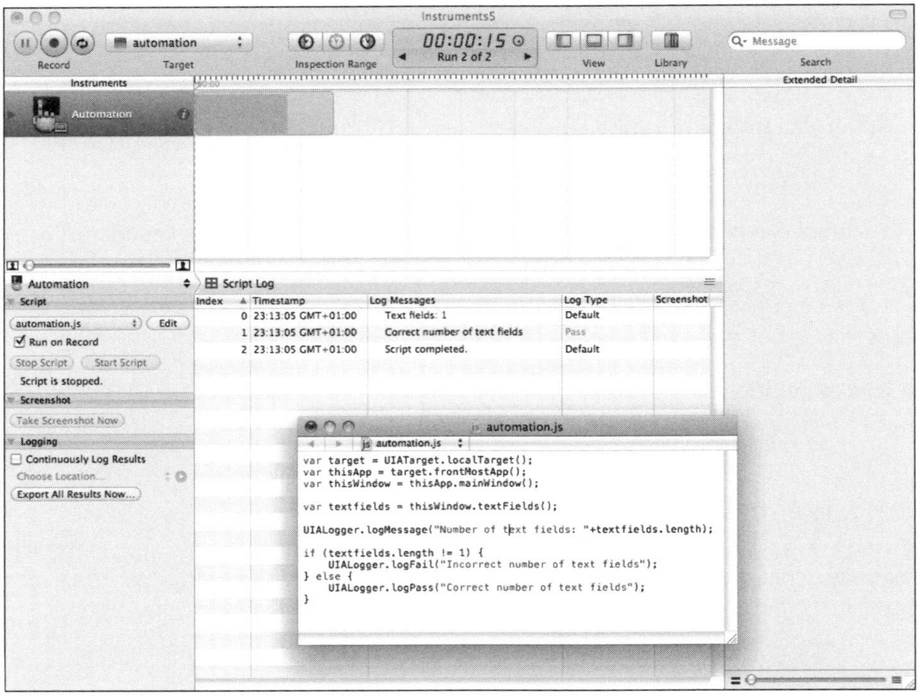

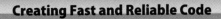

CAUTION
Scripts can be unpredictable, and features may not work as expected. It's a good idea to review the many online examples of scripting created by other developers before you begin creating your own. At the time of writing, scripting remains somewhat buggy.

Summary

This chapter introduced Instruments and explained how they can be used to aid debugging, testing, and performance profiling. It began by demonstrating how to launch Instruments when profiling a simple test app, and it outlined the key UI features.

Next, it delved in some detail into the Allocations and Leaks instruments, explored how to use them to monitor and debug memory problems in an active application, and explained how to look for lines of code that might be causing memory issues.

It introduced the Zombies template, explained how it was related to the Allocations instrument, and showed how to manage instrument settings and display options.

It demonstrated how to create and use custom templates for your own projects and touched briefly on creating custom instruments for advanced low-level monitoring and debugging.

Finally it introduced the Automation instrument and explained how you can use it to create automated test sequences for UIs.

17

Creating Unit Tests

U nit testing is a powerful software engineering technique that's supported in Xcode. This chapter outlines the technique so you can understand the theory behind unit testing, and it explains how to use unit testing in practice.

Introducing Unit Testing

You can test software in many ways, and software engineering has evolved formal processes that can simplify design and improve project efficiency.

Software can fail in five ways:

- The conceptual model for the user interface is misleading, incorrect, or inconsistent. If typical users make wrong assumptions about the software, the developer has made wrong assumptions about how users think and how they expect the software to work. Failures at this level may not be critical, but they frustrate users and waste their time.

- The UI is fragile. Common and inevitable user errors—such as whitespace in text, null entries, misspellings or invalid characters, or accidental mouse clicks—cause the application to fail.

- The UI or underlying model isn't secure. Deliberate hacking attempts can open an application's internal features to outsiders in an uncontrolled way.

- The underlying logic is flawed. Code may contain incorrect assumptions about interfaces, contracts, and processing requirements.

- The underlying logic is fragile. Memory or file errors, API inconsistencies and bugs, and other method-driven issues create crashes or other problems. Failures can be complex and cumulative; a feature works until a problem occurs, and then a dependent feature appears to fail at some point later. The dependencies may not be obvious.

NOTE
In software engineering a *contract* is an explicitly defined interface between two elements. The two elements are designed to exchange information in a certain way, and the contract defines the details of the exchange—specifically the data format, timing, and sequence of the exchange.

Unit testing is designed to help with some of these problems but isn't a solution for all of them. Philosophically, unit testing is closer to method and function testing than sequence testing. To use unit testing successfully, code should have clearly defined interfaces and predictable outputs.

A key benefit of unit testing is that if a bug is easy to reproduce, it's easy to test for it. Creating a test guarantees that future bug fixes don't reintroduce problems. Unit testing can help make these *regression errors* less likely.

Another benefit is that with minor modifications, test code can be used as example code in documentation, to illustrate how features are designed to work.

You also can use unit testing as a design aid. If you test as you go, you can catch logical inconsistencies and overly complex contracts before you implement them. Potentially, you can use test code to sketch how a feature should work before you implement the code for the feature.

In spite of the advantages, unit testing remains controversial. There's an approximate consensus that unit testing is most effective in collaborative projects with a well-defined API. Solo programmers are more likely to have an overview of their project than group developers, so objective testing of elements can sometimes be more of a distraction than a benefit. As interaction becomes more GUI-driven and open-ended, unit testing code can become so large that it rivals the size of the main application, and the return on the time and effort invested becomes smaller.

For all applications, unit testing is most effective when combined with intensive beta testing and formal bug tracking. The most robust production regime combines beta testing, unit testing, and aggressive defensive coding that anticipates and codes around likely input errors.

Understanding Unit Testing in Xcode

In outline, you can do the following with unit testing:

- Compare returned values from a method or function with expected values
- Check that objects are created and initialized correctly
- Confirm that error conditions throw an exception
- Repeat tests any number of times
- Create composite test sequences that run various tests in order
- Select tests depending on the results of previous tests

When you create a new iOS or OS X project, you can choose to add unit testing features. Xcode automatically adds the features—in fact, it adds a separate target that implements unit testing—and initializes them. However, the initialization isn't comprehensive, and extra work is required before you can begin adding test code. The work isn't described in the official documentation, but it is listed below.

In detail, the unit testing package includes the following:

- **A framework called SenTest:** The framework manages the testing and creates error reports. You must add custom code for each feature or case you want to test.

- **A set of test macros:** The macros are designed to check for possible error conditions and report them during a build.

- **A separate test bundle:** To run your tests, build the bundle. Errors are reported during the build.

- **A test class, which is part of the bundle:** You add custom test code to this class and include macros to check for error conditions and report them. This custom code runs automatically during a build. Each test method in the class is called a *test case*.

- **A unit test application:** This runs automatically behind the scenes, triggered by a script, and does the heavy lifting required for the unit testing process. You don't have to run it by hand.

If you're new to unit testing, you may find the process counterintuitive. You might expect unit testing to be a runtime process, like debugging, but it isn't. In fact, you run unit tests by building your project in a special way. The build process runs your test code, and errors appear in the build log. They're not logged to the console like runtime errors.

You must understand that the test build is independent of the standard release/debug builds. It's possible for a release/debug build to complete with no errors, even though a test build reports multiple bugs.

A standard build reports basic compilation and linking errors. Your test build adds further checks for logical consistency, predictable output, and other error conditions. It's up to you to define these checks, to add custom test code to implement them, and to define the format and content of the error messages that report them.

The testing framework gives you the tools to build tests, but it doesn't recommend specific tests, include any default tests, or suggest useful testing strategies. Until you add test case code, a test build does nothing. So it's also up to you to decide which features should be tested, how they should be tested, and how complex and exhaustive the testing process should be.

CAUTION

If your test code includes logical errors, the testing process itself fails. Keep tests as simple as possible, and build more complex tests from simple tests that are known to work. This won't guarantee that your tests are valid, but it's more likely to be useful and manageable than a complex, intricate test system that's difficult to understand.

NOTE

The test framework is called `SenTest` in the test code. You may see it described as `OCUnit` in the Apple documentation. Technically, `OCUnit` is the Objective-C variant of `SenTest`. In practice, the two names are interchangeable.

Creating a Simple Unit Test Project

To create a project that includes unit testing, follow these steps:

1. **Use File ⇨ New Project to create a new project.**

Check the unit testing options before you save the project. This creates a standard project with extra test build features that include a build bundle and a test class.

2. **Develop your project, modifying the standard project classes and adding new classes in the usual way.**

3. **For each feature you want to test, add test case code to the test class file.**

4. **Initialize Xcode's settings to make sure the test code runs as it should.**

5. **Optionally, you can use standard debugging tools to verify the test code.**

6. **Whenever you need to test the project, select the test build and build it.**

If the test build fails, correct the bugs in the project code.

7. **When the project is complete, build a release version in the usual way.**

Because the test code exists in a separate bundle, it isn't linked into a standard release build.

Because unit testing is open-ended, the example described in the rest of this chapter illustrates how to create a single simple test case for a single trivial class; it's a very basic math operation in a math framework. Although the framework and the test code are trivial, you can easily expand this example to meet the needs of a real project.

NOTE

This example illustrates how to create unit test for an iOS project. The unit testing process for iOS and OS X projects is similar enough to be considered identical.

NOTE

If your project uses Core Data, you can include it in the usual way. Core Data features and unit testing features are unrelated. You can add either, neither, or both to a project.

Creating a new project that supports unit testing

For both Xcode and iOS projects, the unit testing option appears as a check box, as shown in Figure 17.1. For this example, create a new Navigation-based project and check the box. Save the project as UnitTest.

CAUTION

Although you can add unit testing to an existing project, it's not a simple process. It's more efficient to include unit testing when you create a new project. If you don't use the test features, they won't get in your way, but they'll be ready if you need them.

Figure 17.1

Creating a new project that supports unit testing

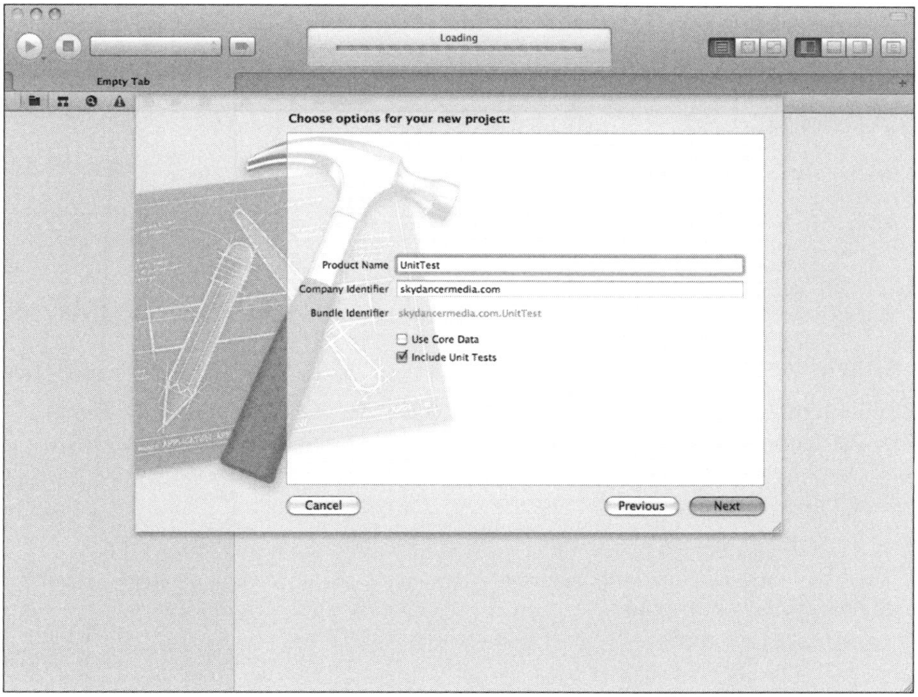

Xcode automatically adds unit testing features to the project, as shown in Figure 17.2. You'll find a new product bundle with the suffix `Tests.octest`, a new target with the Tests suffix, and a new class called Tests with a standard header and implementation file.

Figure 17.2

Exploring the new test features

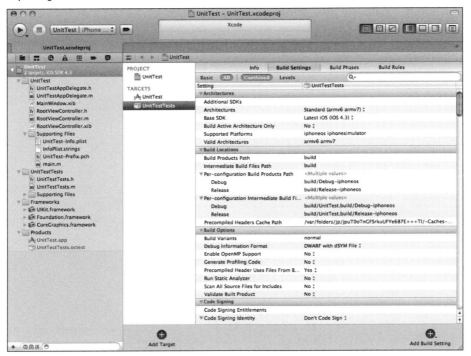

Although these features are included in the project, testing isn't enabled. To enable it, select the Tests target and view the Build Settings. Scroll down to the Unit Testing switches, and make sure Test After Build is set to Yes, as shown in Figure 17.3.

CAUTION

Make sure you enable testing for the test target, not for the main build. Optionally, scroll up to the Linking switches. You'll see `-framework SenTestingKit` added to the Other Linker Flags field. In earlier versions of Xcode, you had to set this switch manually, but this is no longer necessary in Xcode 4.

Figure 17.3

Enabling testing. Testing is disabled if this switch is set to No, even during test builds.

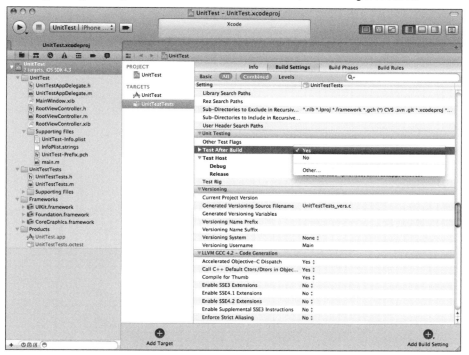

Creating a class for testing

Testing doesn't modify your main source code. It's an external process, and it leaves your main build code unchanged.

For this example, create a new class called `MathMachine` to hold some basic math code. Right-click the UnitTest group in the Project Navigator, select New File, choose the Objective-C class option, and set it to be a subclass of `NSObject`. Save the file as `MathMachine`. Xcode adds a header and implementation file to the Classes group in the usual way.

NOTE

Because this project is called UnitTest, the UnitTest group holds the main source code. The unit testing code is in the UnitTestTests group. In a project with a different name such as ProjectX, the unit testing code would be in ProjectXTests—and so on.

MathMachine is going to unleash the power of gigahertz computing by adding together two integers—`inputA` and `inputB`—and storing them in a property called `sumAB`. Add the following code to the header file, as shown in Figure 17.4:

```
#import <Foundation/Foundation.h>

@interface MathMachine : NSObject {

    int inputA;
    int inputB;
    int sumAB;
}

@property int inputA;
@property int inputB;
@property int sumAB;

-(id) initWithSum: (int) inA and: (int) inB;

@end
```

This defines the MathMachine class with some supporting properties. It also creates a single method called initWithSum:.

Figure 17.4

Creating a new class to add a pair of integers

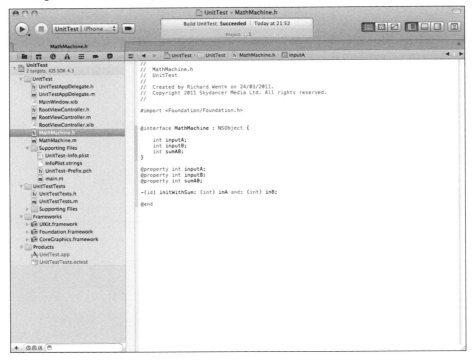

Add the following code to the implementation file, as shown in Figure 17.5:

```
@implementation MathMachine

@synthesize inputA;
@synthesize inputB;
@synthesize sumAB;

-(id) initWithSum:(int)inA and:(int)inB
{
    if (self = [super init]) {
        self.inputA = inA;
        self.inputB = inB;
        self.sumAB = inA + inB;
    }

    return self;
}

}

@end
```

Figure 17.5

Implementing the initialization and addition method

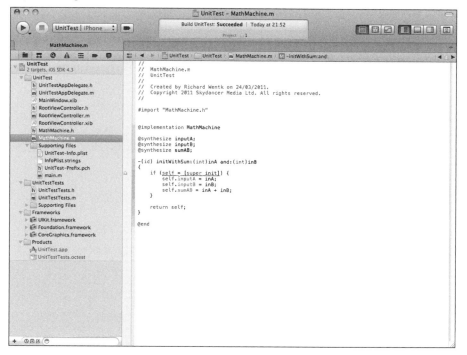

NOTE

If you're new to Objective-C and Cocoa, this may seem like a lot of code for a simple operation. In fact, most of this code creates a new class and defines one possible custom initialization method. Although this is a long-winded idiom, it's standard for Objective-C and Cocoa classes. In a real math framework, the class would be extended with many more properties and many other initialization and processing methods.

Creating a test case

Now that the project includes something to test, you can add the code to test it. Tests are defined as individual methods in the `<ProjectName>Tests` class. The name of each method *must* start with `test`. Methods that begin with any other string are ignored.

Each method is called a *test case*. As explained earlier, it's up to you to create test code that exercises the features of your target class in the most logical and comprehensive way. In practice, this requires three steps:

1. **Define the inputs to the test and the results they should generate.**

2. **Add a test case method to the** `Tests` **class header.**

Depending on your test code, you may need to define the inputs and expected results as constants.

3. **Implement the test method in the Tests implementation file.**

Use *assert macros,* described below, to implement the tests and report errors.

4. **Optionally, add set-up and tear-down code around the test.**

The Tests implementation file includes predefined `setUp` and `tearDown` methods to hold this optional code. You can create and release test objects in these methods, or you can build `alloc` and `release` calls directly into each test case. The best solution depends on the test requirements.

Defining test inputs and results

Figure 17.6 shows the header of the test class. You can see two predefined inputs, `kA` and `kB`, and a predefined expected sum, named `kExpectedSum`. The `testMathMachineSum` method runs the test that compares them. Here's the code:

```
#import <SenTestingKit/SenTestingKit.h>

#define kA 1
#define kB 1
#define kExpectedSum 2


@interface UnitTestTests : SenTestCase {
@private
```

```
    }

-(void) testMathMachineSum;

@end
```

The `#define` statements and the `testMathMachineSum` method have been added. The other parts of the file are created with the project. Note that the method doesn't take parameters, and there are no semicolons after the #define directives.

This example is trivial. In a more realistic test case, the relationship between the expected result and the inputs would be less obvious. It might rely on a series of object allocations and other complex operations. Potentially, you could predefine an array holding a sequence of input events in the `setUp` method and sequence through the array in the test code implementation. Inputs and expected results might be downloaded as a file from a remote server and created by other members of a development team.

Figure 17.6

Defining test inputs, an expected value, and a test method

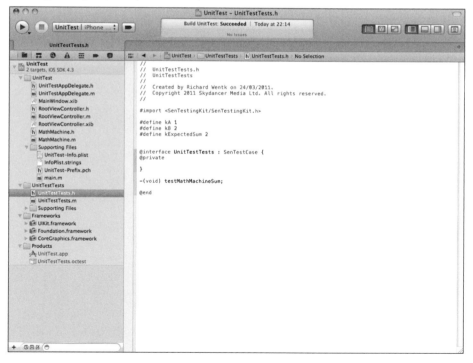

The key point isn't that the test is simple, but that the relationship between the test inputs and the expected output is well defined and predictable. The point of testing is to confirm that this relationship is reliable and that the code being tested reproduces it on demand.

The test code itself can use any standard Cocoa/Cocoa Touch and OS X/iOS features in any combination. You can even generate inputs and results dynamically using independent code that is known to work.

Creating test code

By default, the test implementation file includes a single testExample method that prints a "Unit tests are not implemented yet…" message. To create a test, delete this method and add the code shown in Figure 17.7 and listed below. The code creates an instance of the MathMachine class, initializing it with the initWithSum: method. It runs an assert macro to check whether the expected sum is the same as the sum returned by the method. Finally, it releases the instance. The two %i parameters are part of the macro. The first displays the expected value, the second the value returned by the test method.

NOTE

The alloc and release code could go into the setUp and tearDown methods. This example is deliberately self-contained for simplicity. In a more complex example, you can often improve clarity by keeping set-up, test, and tear-down code separated.

```
#import "UnitTestTests.h"
#import "MathMachine.h"


@implementation UnitTestTests

- (void)setUp {
    [super setUp];

    //Set up code here
}

- (void)tearDown {
    // Tear-down code here.

    [super tearDown];
}

-(void) testMathMachineSum
{
```

```
    MathMachine *testMathMachine =
    [[MathMachine alloc] initWithSum: kA and: kB];

    STAssertTrue(testMathMachine.sumAB == kExpectedSum,
    @"Sum incorrect. Expected %i, got %i",
    kExpectedSum, testMathMachine.sumAB);

    [testMathMachine release];
    }
    @end
```

Figure 17.7

Implementing a test method

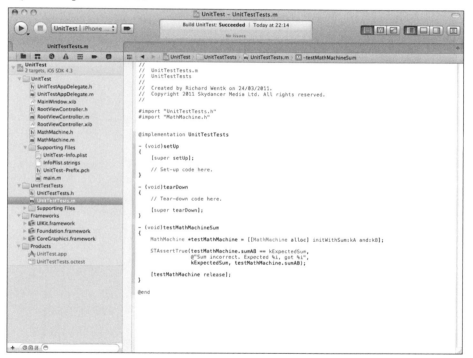

Understanding STAssert macros

The core of the test is in the line that begins STAssertTrue. This is one of the special macros included in the test framework. The full list is shown in Table 17.1.

Table 17.1 OCUnit Assert Macros

Macro	Reports an error if...
STAssertNil(a1, message, <parameters>)	a1 is not nil.
STAssertNotNil(a1, message, <parameters>)	a1 is nil.
STAssertTrue(expression, message, <parameters>)	expression does not evaluate to true.
STAssertFalse(expression, message, <parameters>)	expression does not evaluate to false.
STAssertEqualObjects(a1, a2, message, <parameters>)	a1 is not equal to a2. Both must be Objective-C objects.
STAssertEquals(a1, a2, message, <parameters>)	a1 is not equal to a2. Both must be C scalar values.
STAssertEqualsWithAccuracy(a1, a2, accuracy, message, <parameters>)	a1 and a2 are not within the stated accuracy. Used to compare floats and doubles, allowing for small rounding errors.
STAssertThrows(expression, message, <parameters>)	expression does not throw an exception.
STAssertThrowsSpecific(expression, specificException, message, <parameters>)	expression does not throw an exception of the specificException class.
STAssertThrowsSpecificNamed(expression, specificException, aName, message, <parameters>)	expression does not throw an exception of the specificException class with aName.
STAssertNoThrow(expression, message, <parameters>)	expression throws an exception.
STAssertNoThrowSpecific(expression, specificException, message, <parameters>)	expression throws an exception of the specificException class.
STAssertNoThrowSpecificNamed(expression, specificException, aName, message, <parameters>)	expression throws an exception of the specificException class with aName.
STAssertTrueNoThrow(expression, message, <parameters>)	expression is false or throws an exception.
STAssertFalseNoThrow(expression, message, <parameters>)	expression is true or throws an exception.
STFail(message, <parameters>)	Always.

The macro syntax is unusual compared to standard Objective-C, so it's worth breaking it apart element by element. To create a test using the macro, you must include the following:

- An `STAssert` macro from the table
- A conditional expression to implement the test, which may take multiple parameters
- An error string, which optionally can contain standard `printf/NSLog` parameter placeholders with formatting codes
- The parameters to be logged, if there are any

In the example code, the elements look like this:

- `STAssertTrue`. Test if the following conditional evaluates to true. Write an error to the build log if it doesn't.
- `testMathMachine.sumAB == kExpectedSum`. This is the conditional that implements the test. It checks whether the expected sum constant matches the sum returned by the `initWithSum:` method in the previous line.
- `@"Sum incorrect. Expected %i, got %i"`. This is the text of the message that appears in the build log when the test fails. It takes two integer parameters.
- `kExpectedSum, testMathMachine.sumAB`. These two parameters are reported in the message. If the test fails, the current value of the parameters is logged as part of the message.

When you create test code, you must select a macro from the table, add a suitable expression, and fill in the message and parameter details as needed. Without a test macro, your test code does nothing.

You can test for multiple error conditions by including multiple macros in a single test method. You can and should include multiple independent test methods. In a real example, each test case method should test a specific feature in your code. When you add a new feature or correct a bug, add a corresponding test case. You can also use these macros to generate messages that confirm when tests have been passed.

TIP
The `assert` macro syntax is used throughout development in many environments. If this is your first encounter with it, it can seem unintuitive because `assert` assumes negative logic and does the opposite of what you'd expect it to in English. It checks a condition and logs an error if the condition *isn't* true. When you use these macros, it can be helpful to think of "assert" as equivalent to "test if."

Running tests

When you save the code, the tests are almost ready to run. But Xcode requires one final step before it can run a test build successfully.

By default, classes that are being tested aren't included in the test bundle. If you try to run a test build, Xcode can't find the headers or the code for them.

To fix this, select the UnitTestTests target, as shown in Figure 17.8. Select the Build Phases tab, and open the Compile Sources pane. Click the + triangle to add a new source, and select the MathMachine.m file, as shown in the figure. This adds the source file to the build and ensures that the test framework can see the class you're trying to test.

When you are testing multiple classes, you must add them all. Add UI management classes such as view controllers only if they're referenced in the classes that are being tested.

Figure 17.8

Adding the code to be tested to the test build

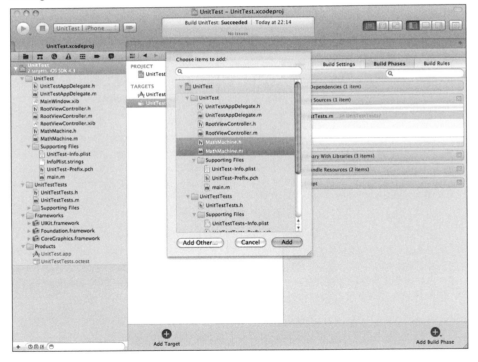

Optionally, if you have multiple versions of Xcode installed, you can choose to run a specific version of the OCUnit testing package, as shown in Figure 17.9. The package is run as a script. The default selects the standard system script, which should be suitable for most projects. The modified default shown in the figure selects the most recent version. You may also need to do this if Xcode can't find the standard script, so it's worth knowing that this option exists.

Figure 17.9

Selecting the test script using the Run Script option in the Build Phases. You don't usually need to do this, but it is worth knowing how to change this option in case you want to customize the process.

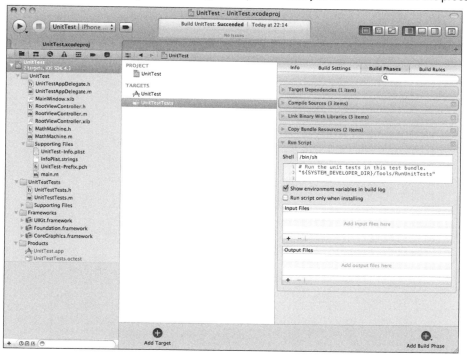

You can now run your first test build. Select Product ⇨ Test from the main Xcode menu, as shown in Figure 17.10. Xcode runs the testing script on both targets. You should see a Build Succeeded message. The project passes the build test with no errors.

Figure 17.10

Select the test build. The initial build should be successful.

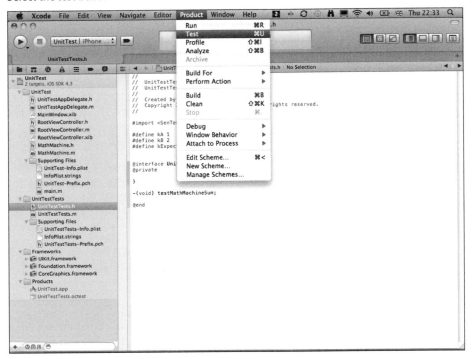

To see what happens when a build fails, open the MathMachine.m file and change

```
self.sumAB = inA + inB;
```

to

```
self.sumAB = inA - inB;
```

Clearly, this won't add two numbers correctly. Build the test again, and you should see the output shown in Figure 17.11. The test case for the sum operation reports that the sum is incorrect. The error message uses the text and parameters you added to the test code.

Figure 17.11

This time the test failed. The unit testing code generated an error message to tell you which test raised an error.

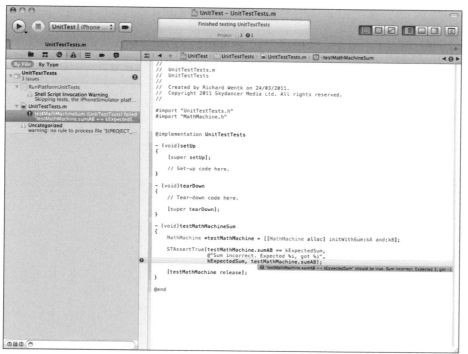

Note again that testing isn't like a normal build or debug session. The error appears in the test case code, not in the class is being tested. In fact it appears—with some redundancy—under the code that defines the error. And it's reported in the Issue Navigator as an issue with the test bundle, not the main target.

This shouldn't be surprising, but it is unusual compared to a standard Xcode build, and it's worth keeping the differences in mind when you work with the SenTest test framework.

TIP

SenTest/OCUnit is ideal for Objective-C tests, but alternatives are available. For C++, it's worth exploring the alternative googletest framework available from `code.google.com/p/googletest/`. The framework isn't trivially easy to integrate into Xcode, but it offers expert developers a richer feature set and wider community support.

TIP
Don't forget that you can use the UI Automation feature in Instruments to exercise a UI. UI Automation is a different system, but the two test systems can work well together. You can use unit tests to check basic code logic and then exercise the UI to ensure that it manages user events correctly.

Summary

This chapter introduced the SenTest/OCUnit unit testing framework. It explained some of the theory behind unit testing and demonstrated how to prepare a project for unit testing and set up Xcode so the unit testing features work correctly.

It illustrated the essential features of the test process with a simple example test case and summarized the key STAssert macros used to create test code.

Finally, it showed how to run the test code and how to find and interpret the messages it generates.

Appendixes

Using Xcode's Tools and Utilities

X code 4 is bundled with an exceptional collection of tools and utilities. These extras are easy to miss. They're not built into the main Xcode application, and many are sparsely documented. This is unfortunate, because the tools offer developers significant extra creative possibilities, finer control over app development and packaging, and advanced testing and customization features.

A full user guide for every tool would double the size of this book, so this appendix summarizes the key features of each tool. Interested readers can find more detailed information in Apple's official documentation and in online discussions.

NOTE
The online URL for the tools and utilities is currently `http://developer.apple.com/library/mac/#documentation/MacOSX/Conceptual/OSX_Technology_Overview/Tools/Tools.html`.

Finding the Tools and Utilities

Figure A.1 shows how the tools and utilities appear in `/Developer/Applications`. Some of the tools—Dashcode, Quartz Composer, and Instruments—are placed at the same level as Xcode in the `/Applications` folder to draw attention to them. The remaining tools are grouped into folders.

In This Appendix

Understanding tools and utilities

Introducing Dashcode

Getting started with Quartz Composer

Introducing the other tools

Working with the utilities

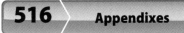

Figure A.1

Finding Xcode's external tools and utilities

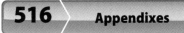

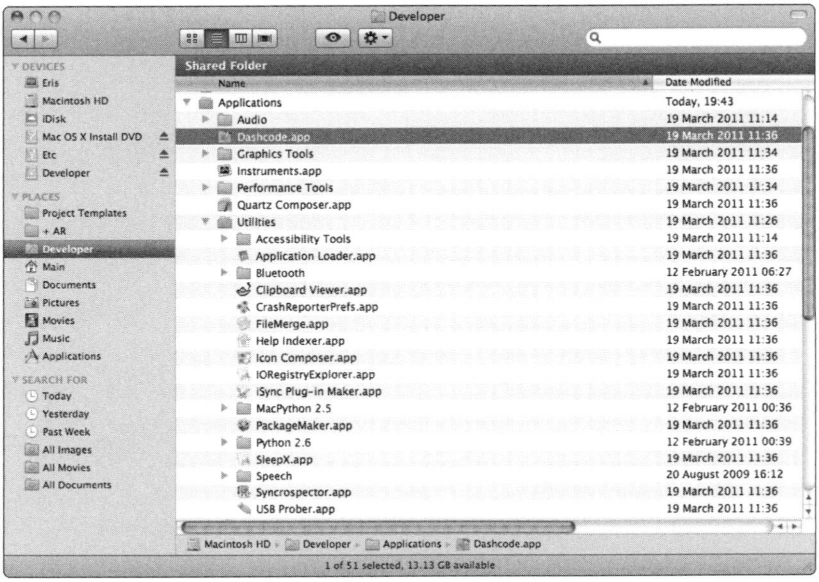

Understanding the Top-Level Tools

The Instruments tool is described in detail in Chapter 16. The remaining two tools are Dashcode, a widget editor used to create mini-apps for the OS X Dashboard, and Quartz Composer.

Introducing Dashcode

Dashcode, shown in Figure A.2, supports Apple's Dashboard technology. Dashboard was introduced in OS X 10.4 Tiger, adding an alternate desktop that can be populated with small, simple applications known as *widgets*. Widgets are written in a combination of HTML, CSS, and JavaScript, using Apple's WebKit framework.

Dashcode was released with OS X 10.5 Leopard and is a widget design and coding tool. Apple worked hard to support widget technology by promoting its own widgets and creating a sales and promotion page for third-party developers. For a year or so, some developers made significant sums from widget sales.

Figure A.2

Dashcode's design and layout tools and the code editor have obvious similarities to Xcode.

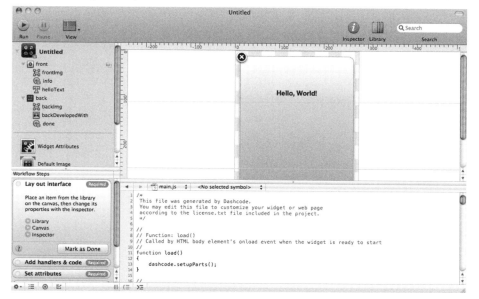

But technically, widget technology is hampered by the ease with which anyone with a copy of Dashcode can open a widget and extract the graphics and source code. Apple's focus soon switched to the iPhone and iOS apps.

With the arrival of OS X Apps in OS X 10.7 Lion, widgets have become a legacy technology. Although app and widget technology doesn't overlap perfectly—widgets are designed to be small and self-contained, while OS X Apps are designed to run full-screen—the market for widget sales has almost disappeared. New developers are being encouraged toward app development for OS X.

NOTE

For practical information about widget editing and creation with Dashcode, see the Cocoa Developer Reference companion title to this book.

Getting started with Quartz Composer

Quartz Composer, shown in Figure A.3, is a sophisticated tool that can create static image filters and complex animations, including screen savers. As the name suggests, it uses the Quartz image generation and processing libraries built into OS X, but you don't need to know anything about Quartz to use Composer successfully.

Figure A.3

A simple Quartz Composer project can create sophisticated animated effects.

Composer is the video- and image-filtering equivalent of a music synthesizer. Developers link together *compositions* from a library of objects—known as *patches*—that create and transform graphics, video, and supporting parameter information.

A composition is a set of objects with defined connections. The connections are made visually with virtual patch cords that link patch input and output parameters, which appear as terminals on each visible object. To make a connection, drag a cord from an output terminal on one object to an input terminal on another.

The library is feature-rich, with hundreds of patches. Some patches perform simple operations such as basic arithmetic or simple time-varying control of animation parameters. Others work at an intermediate level. For example, the audio splitter patch splits an audio stream into a set of frequency-filtered bins that can be used to build an audio visualizer. A few create very complex effects that you can drop into your own compositions.

The patching system includes a macro feature that can hide the internal complexity of a composition and make it reusable as a new patch called a *clip*. Clips can be nested almost indefinitely.

Quartz Composer includes a selection of application templates, listed in Table A.1. Most templates include sample compositions that you can modify and extend.

Table A.1 Selected Important Compiler Settings

Application/Template	Notes
Basic composition	A blank composition with a frame store timer.
Graphic animation	An open-ended animation template that can create 2D and 3D moving backgrounds. The animations can be used in Mac applications such as Keynote.
Graphic transition	A template for customized transition effects that can be used in Final Cut Pro.
Image filter	A template for image filter effects that can be used in Mac applications such as iChat and iPhoto.
Music visualizer	A sound-to-animation template that takes frequency bin information from iTunes or a live audio input and converts it into color and movement.
RSS visualizer	A template that can parse and display RSS feeds, converting them into plain text and/or sophisticated animations.
Screen saver	A screen saver template. The sample project copies the screen and rotates the colors in the copied image.
Mesh filter	A composition that modifies a 3D mesh. This is an advanced effect use in OpenCL development.

CAUTION

Compositions saved to either `/Library/Screen Savers` or `/Library/Compositions` become available to other applications. You may need to modify file permissions before you can save files to these folders from within Quartz Composer. Also note that the link between iTunes and a Quartz Composer visualizer patch starts to work properly only after you select one of the existing visualizers in iTunes. If you don't select an existing visualizer and run it in iTunes, the visualizer template appears to do nothing.

Using Quartz Composer with Xcode

Under the hood, Quartz Composer creates Quartz library calls, which in turn are compiled to OpenGL instructions that run on a Mac's graphics card. Composer is much easier to work with than either Quartz or OpenGL. As a visual development tool with instant feedback, it's more productive and creative than the others.

You can develop for Quartz Composer visually, or you can access a code level which is closely associated with two Quartz Composer player objects: `QCView` and `QCRenderer`. On the Mac, Xcode includes a Quartz Composer plug-in application template. You can use this to create your own patches. You can also add a selection of Quartz Composer objects to your own applications from the library in IB, as shown in Figure A.4. The list includes a patch controller that can connect parameters in a composition to custom code, a player view, a parameter view, and a composition picker.

Figure A.4

Use IB to add a QCView object to the standard Mac application template.

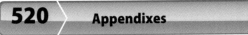

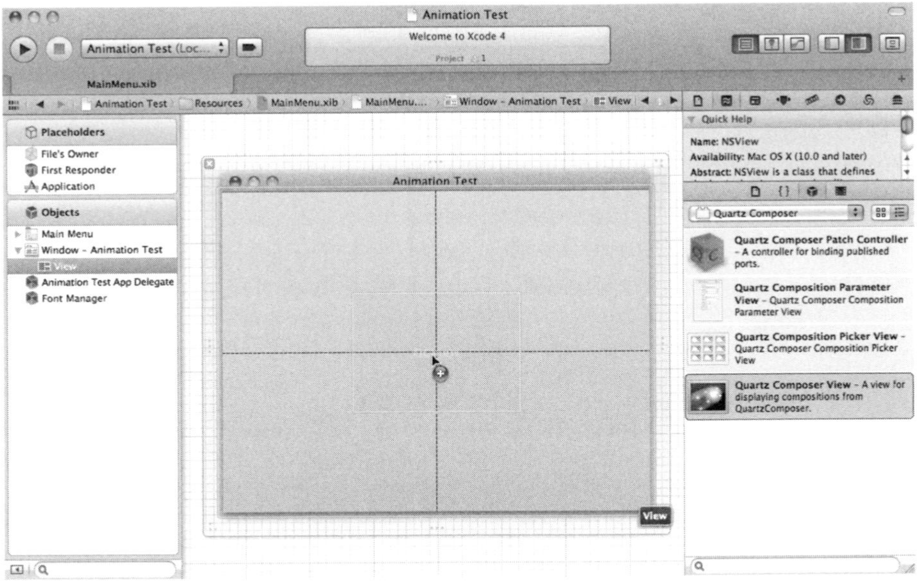

Quartz Composer is very powerful and can create complex and rich video effects with little effort. Unfortunately, it remains poorly documented, and support for the API and the visual editor is minimal. However, if you have an interest in visual effects, it can be worth persevering with the documentation, which is currently at `developer.apple.com/graphicsimaging/quartzcomposer`. Searching for third-party examples elsewhere online is also worth the effort. There aren't many, but the ones that exist can help fill in some of the background detail missing in the official documentation.

NOTE

Currently, Quartz Composer is available only on OS X. It's not supported on iOS.

Working with the Other Tools

The remaining tools are a grab bag of utilities and extras. None is essential. Some can be very useful, but others seem to be lingering for historical reasons.

Introducing the audio tools

The `/Developer/Applications/Audio` folder includes two tools: HALLab and AULab. HALLab (Hardware Abstraction Layer Lab), shown in Figure A.5, displays information about audio hardware and drivers. You can use it to test audio drivers and report on the status of the default system drivers.

AULab (Audio Unit Lab) is a host application for audio units. If you don't own a separate sequencer application such as Logic, you can use AULab to host and test AU plug-ins.

Figure A.5

The HALLab interface is minimal, but you can use it to check the operation of audio drivers and their related hardware.

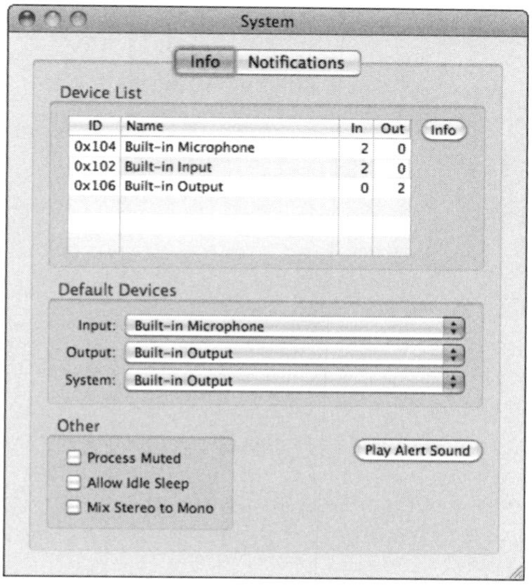

Introducing the graphics tools

The graphics tools include three groups of applications: Quartz and Quartz Composer support, OpenGL support, and general graphics.

General graphics tools

There are two general graphics tools. Pixie is a floating magnifying window. Anything under the window is magnified by a factor between 1X and 12X, depending on Pixie's settings. You can lock movement horizontally or vertically. Pixie is useful for general magnification of app windows and includes a capture feature that can save the magnified image to disk.

Core Image Fun House, shown in Figure A.6, is a filter preview tool. You can test the effects of the standard Core Image filters on a small selection of images. You can also stack filters to create combined effects and use this tool to test custom filters.

Figure A.6

The results of using a couple of Core Image filters on the standard wolf image

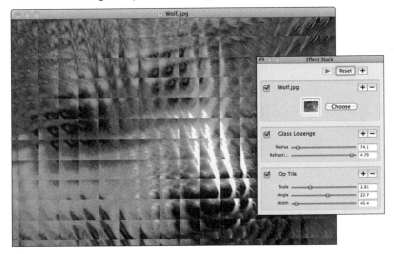

Quartz graphics tools

The two Quartz graphics tools are Quartz Composer Visualizer and Quartz Debug.

Quartz Visualizer is a more sophisticated version of the Viewer tool built into Quartz Composer, with improved network support. You can use it to test local compositions and run them remotely.

Quartz Debug is a reporting and control tool that monitors frame rates and CPU loads. You can use it to enable or disable a minimal selection of hardware acceleration options.

OpenGL graphics tools

The OpenGL Driver Monitor, shown in Figure A.7, displays a fanatically comprehensive list of information about OpenGL events. To use it, click the Parameters button at the lower right of the window and select one or more driver parameters from the slide-out list. The results report the status of the OpenGL subsystem as a whole.

Figure A.7

Track system-wide OpenGL events and parameters with the OpenGL Driver Monitor.

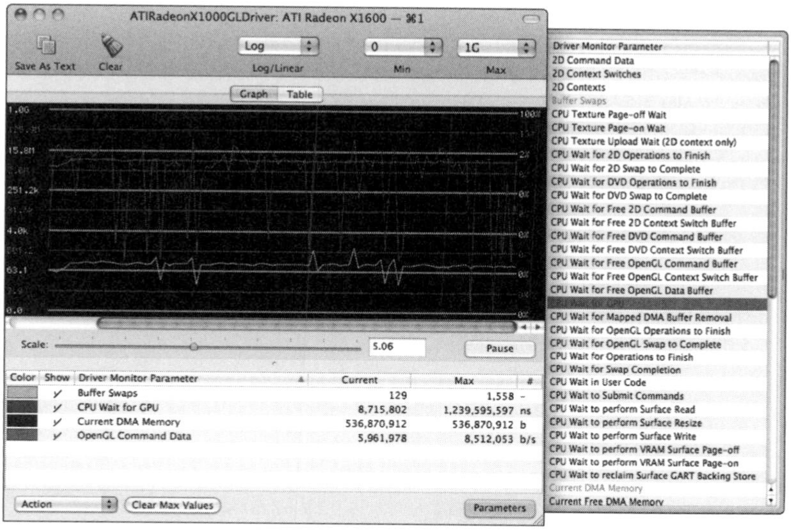

The OpenGL Profiler tool is the app-specific equivalent. You can attach it to any application and use it to monitor a selection of graphics-related information. Initial set-up can be slightly tricky, and you may need to log out of your Mac and login again before this tool works correctly.

The OpenGL Shader Builder is a development and test environment for custom shader code. It provides a generic run-time environment for shader testing, with a simple editor for development. Although you can develop shader code directly in Xcode, OpenGL Shader Builder includes a selection of simple test shapes with basic but useful texture loading and selection.

Introducing the performance tools

There are two performance tools. The Quartz Debug tool is a direct alias for the Quartz Debug tool in the /Graphics Tools folder.

Spin Control reports hang events that display the Spinning Beachball of Death. To use Spin Control, launch it and leave it running. Check it when an application hangs. Spin Control can give you hints about what the application was doing at the time.

Working with the Utilities

The utilities are grouped together in `/Developer/Applications/Utilities`. The collection is a grab bag of assorted mini-applications. It's well worth your time to become familiar with the full list, because a few of the utilities fill in features that are missing elsewhere in OS X. Rather than listing the utilities alphabetically, the sections below collect them into related groups.

Device and hardware support utilities

With the utilities in this group, you can probe and test the I/O and hardware features of your Mac:

- The Bluetooth Diagnostics Utility counts dropped packets and checks for other Bluetooth issues. Less usefully, it also prepares a diagnostics report and uploads it to Apple's Bluetooth engineering team.

- Bluetooth Explorer lists active devices and logs discovery attempts. Devices can be interrogated to reveal a detailed set of low-level Bluetooth parameters; tested to show connection quality.

- The Packet Logger shows raw byte-level Bluetooth packet data. All three Bluetooth utilities are in the `/Applications/Utilities/Bluetooth` folder.

- IORegistryExplorer lists detailed information about a Mac's hardware registry, which can be useful when working with the I/O Kit OS X framework.

- iSync Plug-in maker is a tool for building and testing plug-ins that handle specific features in a hardware device, typically a cell phone. For more information, search for the iSync Plug-in Maker User Guide in the documentation.

- USB Prober monitors the USB subsystem. You can list the USB parameters and settings of each USB port and device, find the associated kernel extensions, review the USB devices listed in the IORegistry, and monitor USB events with a logger.

Application and OS support utilities

These utilities provide extra support for debugging, resource creation, and application management:

- Application Loader is used to upload apps to the App Store. You define sales information for an app in iTunes Connect and then run Application Loader to locate and copy the app to the store's review queue.

- CrashReporterPrefs, shown in Figure A.8, can create detailed crash reports for both user and system processes. This isn't helpful if you're debugging in Xcode, but it can be useful if you're testing an application in a live environment.

- FileMerge can compare—'diff'—and merge the contents of files or directories. The file merge is ASCII-only, and the tool doesn't understand application-specific file formats. Anyone migrating from Windows can use this tool to recreate the directory-merge behavior, which is the default in Windows Explorer but isn't implemented in Finder.

- Help Indexer creates an index for a help file. For more information about supporting your application with help files, search for the Apple Help Programming Guide in the documentation.

- Icon Composer is a tool for creating and editing OS X icon files. The feature set is very basic, but it includes preview options that aren't available in standard image editors.

- Package Maker is a key utility that wraps an installer around any OS X application. You can add binaries and other elements to the installer package, specify an organization name, and customize the interface.

- SleepX schedules sleep and hibernate cycles. This can be useful for testing, but you also can use this app to wake up your Mac automatically at certain times.

- Syncrospector is a debugger and monitoring tool for the OS X synchronization engine. You can view a history of sync sessions and check the sync database. For more details, search the documentation for the Sync Services Tutorial. Alternative third-party examples are available online.

Figure A.8

Setting the Crash Reporter Preferences with CrashReporterPref is easy; this isn't a sophisticated application.

Language support utilities

Some utilities are designed to work with other languages. Previous versions of Xcode included templates for Java and Python applications. Apple no longer supplies these templates, but you can still use the Build Applet utility to convert Python code into stand-alone applications. Two versions are included: one for MacPython and one for the standard version of Python.

MacPython includes OS X features and supports the optional PyObjC package, which gives full access to the Cocoa libraries from Python. Standard Python is the default OS-independent version of Python.

NOTE

Early beta versions of Xcode 4 included corresponding tools for creating Java applications from Java code. Apple is scaling down its Java support, and these tools weren't included in the final release.

Accessibility utilities

The accessibility utilities test an application's support for accessibility features. The two main utilities are in the /Applications/Utilities/Accessibility Tools folder. The speech synthesizer editors are in /Applications/Utilities/Speech.

- Accessibility Inspector reports accessibility attributes and actions when you roll the mouse cursor over the controls in an application's UI.
- Accessibility Verifier checks for mistakes in an application's accessibility information.
- Repeat After Me can improve the performance and legibility of the standard OS X speech synthesizer. This application includes a PDF manual.
- SRLanguageModeler supports custom language model design for the speech synthesizer.

Introducing the Command-Line Tools

Most of the features of Xcode are duplicated at the command-line level. If you prefer to work with pipes, processes, and raw text, you can use all the tools that are standard in any BSD (Berkley Software Distribution) UNIX distribution. Xcode adds a selection of other tools that are specific to OS X development. The tools can compare and process text files; automate events under the control of Python, Perl, Ruby, or Java code; and provide low-level information about memory use and the Mac's hardware.

The complete list of tools is very long. Many are highly specialized, and some are obsolete. Because most of the useful features are also available in Xcode, a full description is outside the scope of this book. However, hardware developers should review the list in Apple's Tools documentation (available at the URL listed earlier in this appendix) because some of the kernel and I/O level tools can only be accessed from the command line.

N O T E

Unlike the other tools and utilities mentioned in this appendix, the Command-Line Tools aren't installed by default. To install them, check the "UNIX Development" box when you install Xcode.

Summary

This appendix listed the tools and utilities that are bundled with Xcode but aren't built into the main application. It explored Dashcode and Quartz Composer and listed the audio, graphics, and performance monitoring tools. Finally, it introduced the full set of supporting utilities and briefly summarized each one.

Working with Other Editors

Xcode includes a number of other built-in editors and supports links to external editors.

Editing plists

Plists (or property lists) define application settings. When you create a new iOS or OS X app, Xcode automatically creates a file called `info.plist`, prefixed with the app name—for example, `myApp-info.plist`.

This file includes important app settings—the name of the nib file loaded on launch, the application icon, version number, and so on—which are discussed later in this appendix. You can also create your own separate custom plists for your own use—for example, to define application preferences.

Plist editing is more complex than it looks. Xcode 4 has a number of non-obvious features that can simplify the editing process, if you know they exist and understand how to use them.

Understanding plists

Internally, a plist is an XML file saved with the `.plist` extension. The content is a standard Cocoa `NSDictionary`. It holds a hierarchy of named key objects that either store a single value or hold an array or dictionary object with its own contents.

If you're new to iOS and OS X, think of a key/value pair as an entity with two components: a key, which is a name string, and a value, which can be a simple or complex object.

Simple values are one of the following: a string, a number, a date, a Boolean, and a general data field.

Container objects are arrays or dictionaries.

An array stores values in strict sequential order and can be accessed with either a numerical or enumerated index. Array items typically appear with a number, such as Item 0, Item 1, and so on. Non-contiguous numbering isn't allowed.

A dictionary is more free-form and is used as a more general, but slower, key/value container.

Container objects can be nested. An item in an array can be a string, a Boolean, and another array. This second array can contain a date and a dictionary. The dictionary may contain one or more further collections and so on, creating a hierarchical data structure.

Plists are typically used for application initialization of launch settings and user preferences. Although they can be arbitrarily complex, they're not designed for generic data storage. Some plists are standardized with specific keys and content formats. When you edit these in Xcode, you can only add keys from a fixed set of options. The formatting of the key values is preset.

Other plists are optional and freeform. It's up to you to design their formatting and content.

It can take some time to master plist editing, so it's good practice to experiment with it before you need to use it professionally.

Getting started with plist editing

Although Xcode includes a general purpose plist editor, it also includes features that simplify the editing of certain kinds of plists.

Four options are available:

- To edit any plist included in a project bundle, select it in Xcode, as shown in Figure B.1. This loads the file into Xcode's plist editor window.

- For simplified access to the main application settings plist—the info.plist file—you can use two editors built into the project build settings. These editors can be used only to modify this one file.

- To edit another plist—for example, one of the standard OS X plists used to define the preferences for other applications—double-click it in Finder. After you install Xcode, it becomes the default editor for all plists. A floating editor window appears, as shown in Figure B.2. This editor is identical to the plist editor in Xcode. If the plist is part of an Xcode project, the project isn't loaded.

- You can edit a plist as raw text in TextEdit, as shown in Figure B.3. Right-click the plist in Finder, select Open With ⇨ Other…, and select TextEdit.app in the Applications window.

CAUTION

In Xcode, you don't need to save a plist file by hand. If you edit the same file in multiple Xcode editors, you see that any change in any editor is instantly duplicated in every editor. The file is saved automatically when you build or quit a project, like a source code file. This applies only to Xcode. Edits made in TextEdit must be saved in the usual way. It's a bad idea to open a file in Xcode and TextEdit at the same time.

Figure B.1

Editing a project plist in Xcode is the easiest way to work with plists.

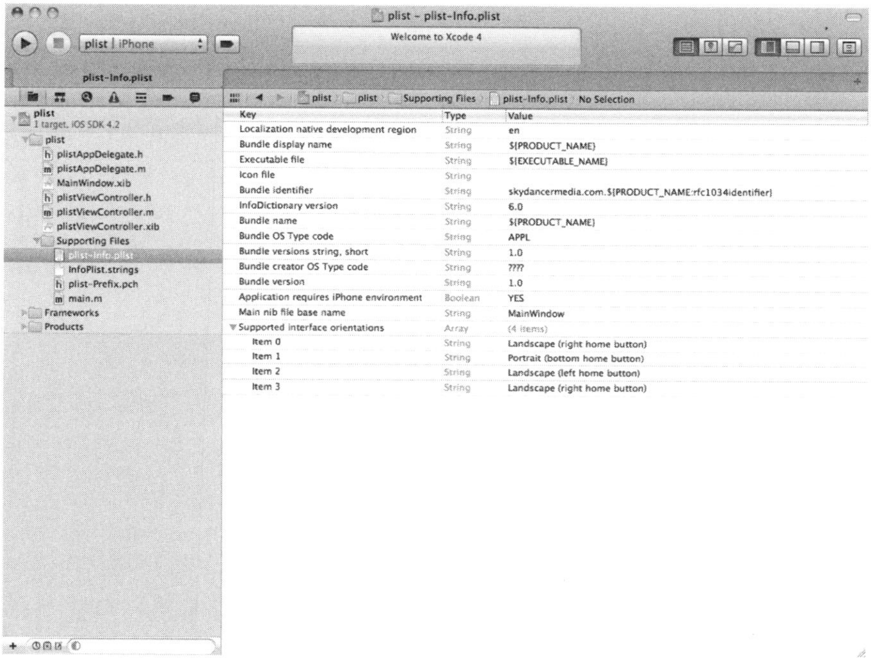

Figure B.2

Loading a plist into the Xcode editor as a stand-alone file launches Xcode, if it's not already running. If the plist is part of a project bundle, the rest of the project isn't loaded.

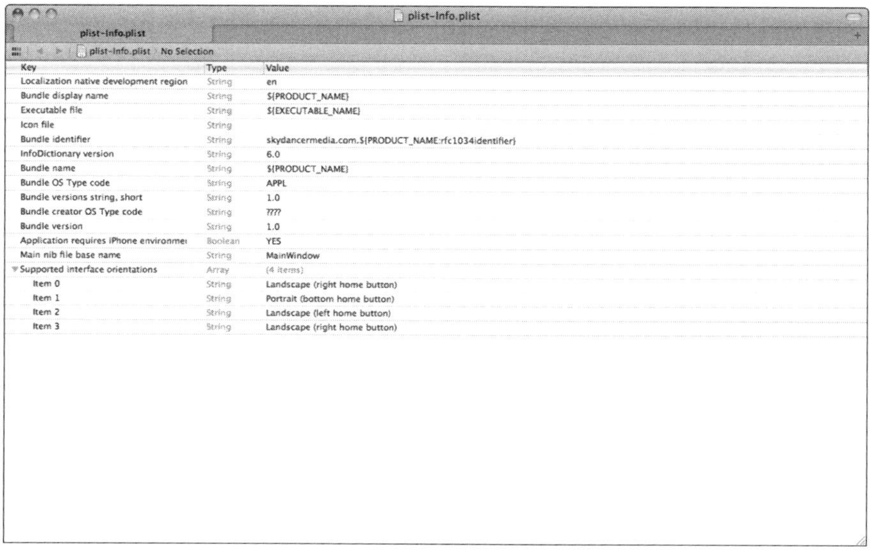

Figure B.3

Using TextEdit, you can make changes to the text and resave the file, but the contents must be formatted correctly.

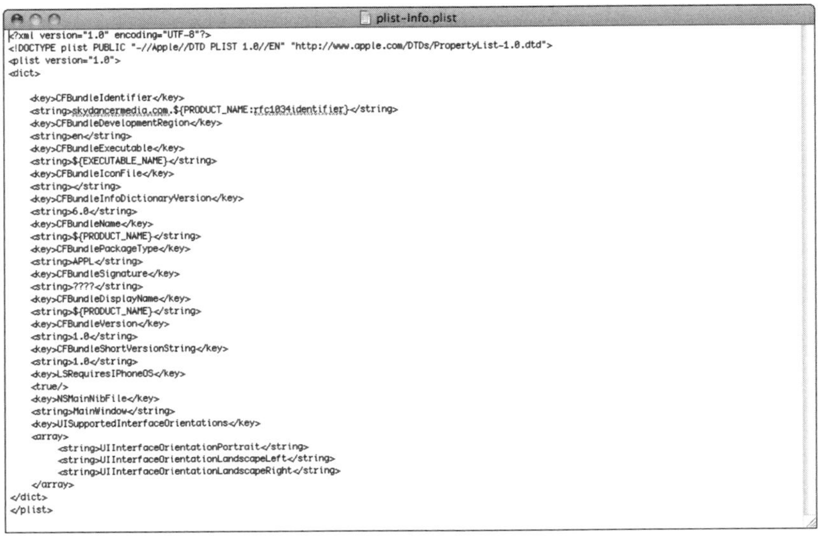
plist-Info.plist

```
<?xml version="1.0" encoding="UTF-8"?>
<!DOCTYPE plist PUBLIC "-//Apple//DTD PLIST 1.0//EN" "http://www.apple.com/DTDs/PropertyList-1.0.dtd">
<plist version="1.0">
<dict>

    <key>CFBundleIdentifier</key>
    <string>skydancermedia.com.${PRODUCT_NAME:rfc1034identifier}</string>
    <key>CFBundleDevelopmentRegion</key>
    <string>en</string>
    <key>CFBundleExecutable</key>
    <string>${EXECUTABLE_NAME}</string>
    <key>CFBundleIconFile</key>
    <string></string>
    <key>CFBundleInfoDictionaryVersion</key>
    <string>6.0</string>
    <key>CFBundleName</key>
    <string>${PRODUCT_NAME}</string>
    <key>CFBundlePackageType</key>
    <string>APPL</string>
    <key>CFBundleSignature</key>
    <string>????</string>
    <key>CFBundleDisplayName</key>
    <string>${PRODUCT_NAME}</string>
    <key>CFBundleVersion</key>
    <string>1.0</string>
    <key>CFBundleShortVersionString</key>
    <string>1.0</string>
    <key>LSRequiresIPhoneOS</key>
    <true/>
    <key>NSMainNibFile</key>
    <string>MainWindow</string>
    <key>UISupportedInterfaceOrientations</key>
    <array>
        <string>UIInterfaceOrientationPortrait</string>
        <string>UIInterfaceOrientationLandscapeLeft</string>
        <string>UIInterfaceOrientationLandscapeRight</string>
    </array>
</dict>
</plist>
```

Editing info.plist project settings in Xcode

Every project includes a `<projectname>-info.plist` file that stores application settings. The settings are chosen from a list of standard keys. When you create a new Xcode project, `info.plist` file appears in the project's Supporting Files group. If you import a project created with an older version of Xcode, the info.plist file usually appears in the Resources group.

Understanding the application settings

When your app launches, one of the first things it does is load this `info.plist` file. It reads the keys and values from the file to find paths to the app's initial nib file and other support resources, to define runtime features such as the OS platform and multitasking options, to enable or disable graphics options such as anti-aliasing and the gloss look on iOS springboard icons, and so on.

The full list of keys that can be included in the file is long and is grouped under five headings:

- **Launch Services:** These keys define low-level architecture-specific options.
- **OS X:** These miscellaneous keys are specific to OS X apps.
- **UIKit:** These miscellaneous keys are specific to iOS apps and the iOS UI.
- **Core Foundation:** These keys for either or both platforms define application house-keeping and set-up features.
- **Cocoa:** These keys define Cocoa initialization options and Cocoa support features.

N O T E
A brief introduction to each key is available in the documentation in the Information Property List Key Reference document.

By default, the `info.plist` file includes a minimal selection of essential keys. You can and should set the values of some of these keys by hand; otherwise, your app won't be accepted for sale.

The other keys are less critical. If they're included in the default `info.plist`, you can leave their settings unchanged. If they're not included in the default file, you can usually ignore them.

Occasionally, you may want to add a key by hand to enable a non-standard feature. For example, you can use the optional `UIFileSharingEnabled` key to allow a user to access files created by the app through iTunes. Including the `UIPrerenderedIcon` key and setting the value to YES disables the iOS shine effect for the app's icon in Springboard. Adding other keys adds other corresponding features.

The `info.plist` editors include features for editing the default keys and for adding optional new keys.

Introducing the application settings editors

Editing the `info.plist` file is a critical part of app development. This file gets preferential treatment in Xcode, so there are three ways to edit it:

- You can select it in the Project Navigator and edit it with the standard plist editor, which is described later in this chapter.
- In the project build settings, you can use a simplified Summary editor to display and change selected important settings, as shown in Figure B.4.
- Also in the project build settings, you can use a more comprehensive Info editor, as shown in Figure B.5. This editor is similar to the standard Xcode plist editor, but it adds some extra features.

To use the editors in the build settings, select the project name at the top left in Project Navigator, select the project under TARGETS, and choose either the Summary or the Info tab at the top of the build settings window.

CAUTION

It's important to understand that these editing options all edit the same file.

Figure B.4

When you view the Summary settings, there's nothing to indicate that when you change these settings, you're editing the `info.plist` file, but you are—immediately and permanently.

Figure B.5

The more comprehensive Info editor is similar to the standard Xcode plist editor, but it has added fields to set an optional document type and UTI (Uniform Type Identifier) and URL scheme keys. The iOS and OS X versions of this file include slightly different contents, but they are recognizably similar and can be edited in the same ways.

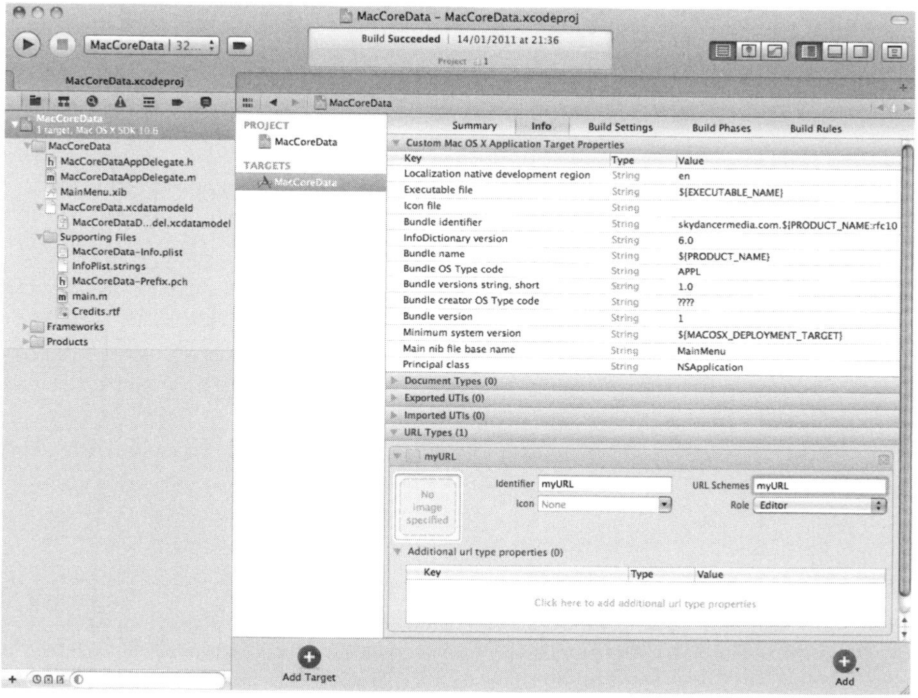

Changing settings with the Summary editor

The Summary settings editor is a collection of buttons, menus, and text fields used to define the basic key values needed for App Store acceptance. For simplicity, this editor hides many of the keys in the file. To view and edit them, use one of the other editors.

Although the meanings of the settings may not be obvious, the UI features are Mac-standard and simple enough to be self-explanatory. Changing any setting immediately updates the corresponding value in the app's `info.plist` file. The settings are listed in Table B.1.

Table B.1 Key Application Settings

Setting	iOS/OS X	Notes
Identifier	Both	Defines the application name. Set automatically from the project filename. Can be edited manually, but this isn't usually necessary.
Application category	OS X only	Sets the category in the App Store from a menu of standard options.
Version	Both	App version number. Uses the standard major.minor numbering format—for example, 1.2. The numbers are arbitrary.
Devices	iOS only	Defines an app as iPhone-only, iPad-only, or Universal.
App runs on...	Both	Selects the minimum compatible OS version. Code must support this version. Newer OS versions can optionally be supported with soft linking and conditional OS-specific code.
Main interface	Both	The initial nib file loaded with the application. Usually left unchanged.
Supported device orientation	iOS only	A group of buttons that selects various orientations. Portrait is mandatory for the iPhone, but other orientations are optional. All orientations are mandatory for the iPad.
App icon(s)	Both	Defines the icon file that appears on the Dock or Springboard. Must be a png. Right-click an empty icon box to select a file with Finder. See the platform documentation for information about the required pixel dimensions.
Launch images	iOS only	Defines the image that appears while the app is loading. See the documentation for information about pixel dimensions for each platform.

Changing settings with the Build Info editor

Unlike the Summary editor, which lists selected highlights from a project's `info.plist` file, the Build Info editor lists every key and value in the entire file. It's very similar to the standard plist editor described later in this chapter, but it includes four extra options: Document Types, Exported UTIs, Imported UTIs, and URL Types. The OS X version adds one further option called Services. These options add standard keys to the plist that define optional document type, URL scheme, and services support for an application.

Adding optional keys

To add an optional key, follow the steps below:

1. **Right-click an existing row.**

You can select any row as long as it isn't a multi-valued type; for example, the Type field isn't Array or Dictionary.

2. **Select Add Row from the floating menu.**

3. **Select a key from the floating list, as shown in Figure B.6.**

4. **Click the Value field to edit the key.**

Value editing depends on the value type and is described later in this chapter, in the description of the general plist editor.

Figure B.6

Adding one of the optional keys to the `info.plist` file

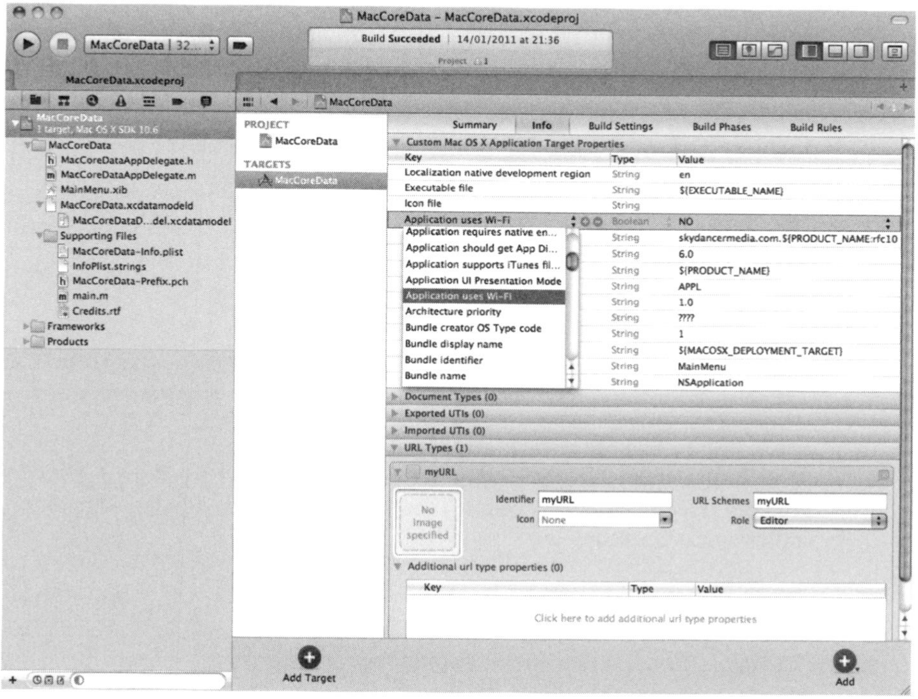

To remove a key, select its row and click the - (minus) icon to the left of the Type field.

A few caveats apply to key editing. Some keys are valid only on one platform; for example, it makes no sense to specify the Application requires iPhone environment key for an OS X app. But the key list is the same for iOS and OS X projects, and there's nothing to stop you from adding an invalid key to the project settings. Results are unpredictable; the OS may ignore the key, or it may crash your app.

Don't assume that the keys work as advertised, because some don't. For example in iOS 4.2, you can set the Status bar is initially hidden key for an iOS app, but unless you add extra supporting code to your app's `applicationDidFinishLaunching:` method, the status bar is still visible after launch. Generally, explicit initialization code is more reliable than the start-up keys. It's good practice to experiment with a key to make sure that it works correctly.

Finally, do read the Information Property List Key Reference. This reference is buried in the doc-sets, and it's difficult to find unless you know it exists. Without it, you won't know which keys are available or what they do, and the start-up options and settings will remain inexplicable and mysterious.

Adding support for documents, URL schemes, and services

In addition to generic start-up options, experienced iOS and OS X developers and programmers can add further optional keys to define how an app uses file types, URL schemes, and services.

In iOS and OS X, a URL scheme is a system that links an application to a certain URL launch string. In the same way that the http:// string always opens a web page, you can define custom strings here that can launch your apps from some other app.

A UTI can define your app as an editor or viewer for a custom file type.

Services on OS X are similar but more advanced features that can define an application as a pro-vider or consumer of Services; these are optional external options that appear in every major application under the "Application Name" ⇨ Services menu entry.

NOTE
For more information about UTIs, search the documentation for Uniform Type Identifiers. For information about URL schemes, search for the Apple URL Scheme Reference document. For information about Services, see the Services Implementation Guide.

These optional keys appear in a list at the bottom of the Info editor. Figure B.6 includes a simple example. In a practical application, more set-up would be needed, with extra support code to implement this feature.

Creating new plists

The app's `info.plist` file is created for you and its keys are fixed and standardized, but you can add further custom plists for your own use and add arbitrary keys to them to suit the needs of your app. Here's how:

1. **Right-click the Supporting Files group, and select New File.**

   For iOS and OS X, select Resource and then Property List.

2. **Select Next, and save the file with a useful name.**

On iOS only, you can create a unique kind of plist known as a *settings bundle*. This is identical to a standard empty plist, but you can use it to store and manage application preferences. The iOS preferences system is complex and outside the scope of this book. But in this context, the `settings.bundle` file can be edited in the plist editor in the same way as a standard plist; the editor ignores the unusual name.

Using the general Xcode plist editor

The main Xcode plist editor is similar to the Info editor in the Build settings, but it lacks the UTI, document, file type, and services options.

In fact, the `info.plist` is just one of a number of default plist file types. In the Summary and Info editors, the plist file type is fixed. In the general plist editor, you can select an alternative plist type. This doesn't change the contents or the format of the file, but it does replace the standard list of optional keys with one of a number of other lists.

Depending on the application, you can use these alternative key lists to save time when entering new keys. Or you can ignore them and create your own unique key list.

To select a file type, right-click anywhere in the edit area, select Property List Type, as shown in Figure B.7. Select one of the options from the sub-menu. For a customized key list, Unique is the best choice.

Figure B.7

When you set the plist type, this doesn't modify the file type; it selects between the different sets of default keys that appear while editing.

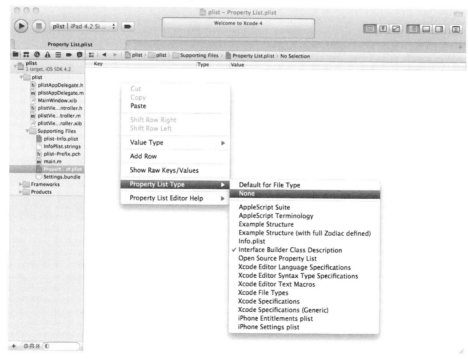

NOTE
These options are not all properly documented. The easiest way to find out what each file type does is to select it, select one or more of the default keys, and search for them in the documentation. Most options are aimed at intermediate to expert developers.

After you set the type, you can edit the list in the following ways:

- **Add a new key:** Right-click an existing single-value key, and select Add Row. Either select the key name from the default list or edit the default New Item name.
- **Change or select the key type:** Right-click the key, and select one of the types from the Value Type sub-options.
- **Delete a key:** Select the key, and use the Cut option in the right-click menu or press the Delete key.
- **View the raw key name:** For keys associated with Cocoa and other OS constants and parameters, you can view the key names by right-clicking and selecting Show Raw Keys/Values. This shows the key as a name—for example, CFBundleIconFile—instead of a text description. This can be useful when you're looking for key names in the documentation.
- **Edit a value:** Value editing depends on the key type. See Table B.2 for details.

Note that if you're creating a completely customized plist, it's up to you to decide if arrays or dictionaries are the best containers for the data. If you're editing any of the standard predefined key lists, the type is defined by the standard values and can't be edited.

CAUTION
Note that if there are no single-value keys in the list, if you try to add a new key, you get a new key/value pair in one of the multi-value items. The workaround is to make a copy of the multi-value item and edit it as needed, rather than trying to add it from scratch.

Table B.2 Key Value Editing

Key Type	Single/Multi-Value	Editing Operation
Boolean	Single	Double-click and use the menu to select YES or NO.
Data	Single	Double-click and enter an XML data value—for example, a string with arbitrary contents—between the angle brackets. The format and meaning of the data type is context-dependent.
Date	Single	Double-click and enter a date and time string. Dates are checked for validity before the edit is confirmed.
Number	Single	Double-click to enter an integer or floating-point number in string form. Invalid entries (text) are set to zero.
String	Single	Double-click value to enter a new string.
Array	Multi	Use the + and - icons to add and remove key/value pairs. Set the type for each and edit as above. Use the reveal triangle to view the hierarchy.
Dictionary	Multi	Use the + and - icons to add and remove key/value pairs. Set the type for each and edit as above. Use the reveal triangle to view the hierarchy.

Editing Core Data Files

In addition to an updated plist editor, Xcode 4 also includes a revised editor for Core Data files. Core Data is an optional data management framework included in both iOS and OS X. Although the concepts used in Core Data are simple, the English words used to describe them are complicated, and elements of the API are also more complex than they need to be. This can make Core Data seem more intimidating than it really is.

Understanding Core Data

Core Data has three main elements, supported by three optional elements:

- **A managed object context:** This is a complicated way to say "a container for objects."
- **One or more entities:** An entity is an object that holds data.
- **One or more attributes in each entity:** An attribute is a key/value pair. The key is a name string, and the values are one of a set of standard supported types: integers of various lengths, decimal numbers, floats, doubles, strings, Booleans, and so on.
- **Optionally, entities can have relationships:** A relationship references one entity from another. References can be bidirectional. They can be one-to-one, linking entities directly, or one-to-many, with multiple cross-links. Core Data's support for one-to-many relationships is limited.
- **Optionally, entities can include one or more predefined fetch requests:** A fetch request is an operation that returns objects or selected object attributes, such as the highest or lowest value.
- **Optionally, each fetch request can include one or more predicates:** These are specific search filters.

Although Core Data isn't a full relational database, it's often used for general data management. Typical applications include media collections and contact databases. For example, to manage a library, you might create a Book entity and add attributes to store the title, year of publication, author, and so on. You can then call standard Core Data code to add an instance of the Book entity for each book in the library, call other code to list all books with a specific author, and so on.

Entities, attributes, relationships, and other details are defined in a data model file, with the .xcadatamodel extension.

When you create a new project, you can include Core Data by ticking the Use Core Data option, as shown in Figure B.8. This option generates a blank data model file that you can expand with your own entity designs.

The data model becomes "live" with only supporting code. The Core Data templates include minimal set-up and tear-down code, but you must add further code to access and modify the data.

NOTE
This section is a brief practical introduction to the Core Data model editor but isn't a complete guide to Core Data development. For an introduction to practical Core Data programming and more information about creating and using entities, relationships, fetch requests, and predicates in practice, see the companion Cocoa Developer Reference title.

Figure B.8

Creating a Core Data project for OS X. iOS projects include the same feature.

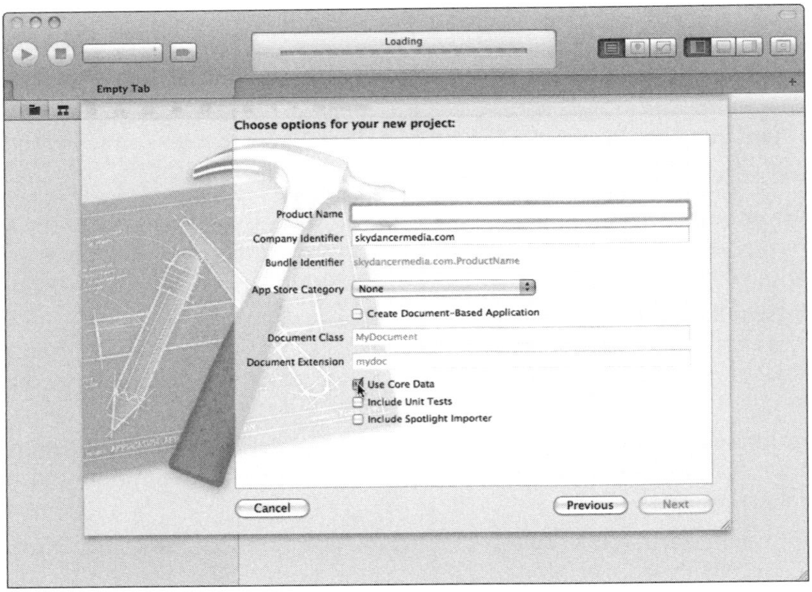

Introducing the data model editor

The data model editor appears when you select a data model file in the Project Navigator, as shown in Figure B.9. The default file is empty.

CAUTION
File selection is somewhat counter-intuitive. The data model file appears inside a container file with the `.xcadata modeld` extension. To load the editor, click this file's reveal triangle and select the `.xcadatamodel` file inside it. The `.xcadatamodeld` container file can, in theory, contain more than one data model file. Even if there's only one, you must select it to edit it.

A key feature of the editor is the Editor Style option at the bottom right of the window. You can use this feature to toggle between the default table view and a graph view, as shown in Figure B.10. When the file is empty, the graph view shows a blank editing area with a graph paper background.

The table view is designed for quick summary overviews of the entities in the file. The graph view shows entities and relationships visually. The table view is easier to work with when the data model is busy, with many entities. The graph view is better suited for simpler models with a smaller number of entities, and it provides a more intuitive visual guide to entity relationships.

Figure B.9

A first look at the Core Data editor, with an empty default data model file

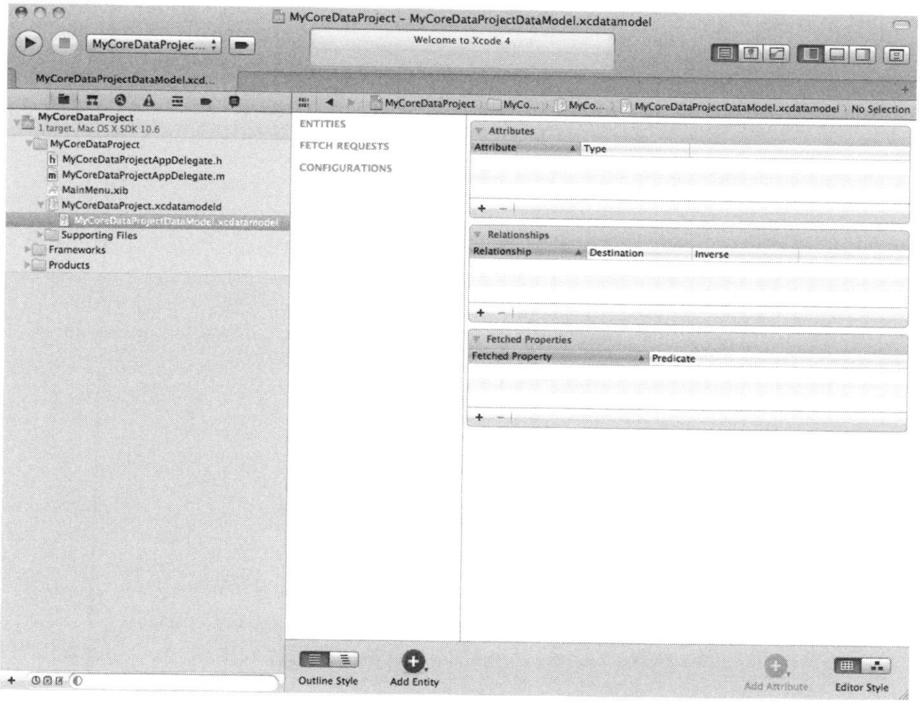

Figure B.10

A first look at the graph editor

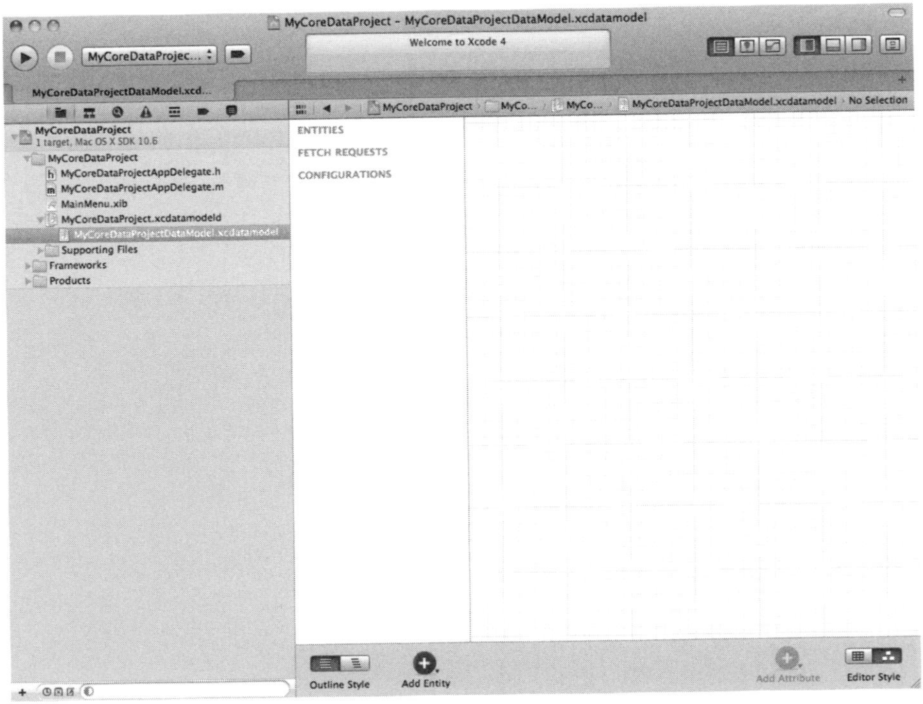

Creating a simple data model

As a very simple example of a data model, you'll add a couple of entities with a handful of attributes and create a relationship between them.

To create an entity, follow these steps:

1. **Begin in the table editor, and click the Add Entity button near the bottom left of the window, as shown in Figure B.11.**

    A new entity appears in the Entities list at the top left.

2. **Give the entity a name such as Entity1.**

NOTE

As soon as you create an entity, a new configuration named Default appears under the Configurations header. You can select the Default configuration to view a list of entities in the file with associated class names. By default, each entity is an instance of Cocoa's `NSManagedObject` class. In a more complex project, you can subclass entities to customize them with special features, but you can use Core Data successfully without subclassing.

Figure B.11

Creating a new entity

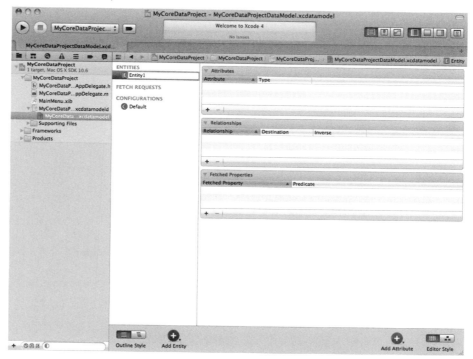

CAUTION

Entity names cannot contain spaces or special characters. Only letters, digits, and underscores are allowed. Names must begin with a letter.

To add attributes, follow these steps:

1. **Click the + button at the bottom of the Attributes pane, and type a name.**

2. **Left-click (not right-click) in the Type column to set the type.**

Figure B.12 shows an entity with three attributes.

3. **To remove an attribute, click the − button.**

CAUTION

Although you can modify entities and attributes at any time, if your project has a data collection, you need to *reversion* the data. Reversioning is a complex topic outside the scope of this book; in outline, you must create a new extended data model and then merge the existing data with it. If you change the data model and re-import an existing data collection, Core Data crashes. It's good practice to finalize the design of the entities, attributes, and relationships in a data model before you begin working with live data.

Figure B.12

Adding attributes

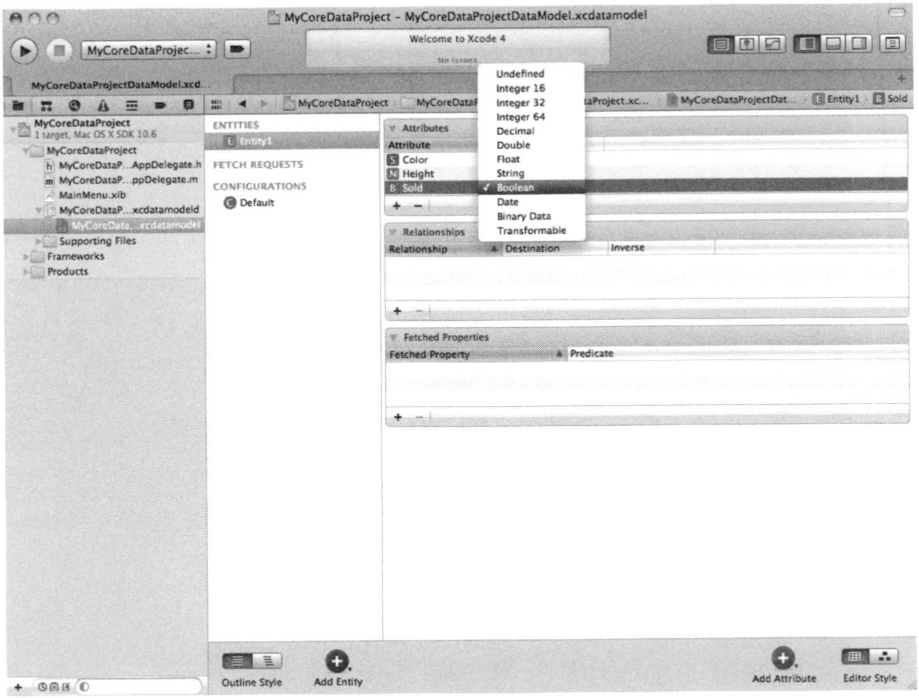

To create relationships, follow these steps:

1. **Add another entity, and add a property.**

Name this Entity2.

2. **Select Entity1 again, and click the + button in the Relationship pane.**

You'll see a new relationship called "relationship."

3. **Left-click under the Destination header to select Entity2 as a destination, as shown in Figure B.13.**

This creates a simple one-way link between Entity1 and Entity2.

4. **Select Entity2.**

You'll see the relationship in the Relationships pane.

5. **Select Entity1 as a destination and select relationship again under the Inverse header.**

These steps create a mutual two-way link between Entity1 and Entity2. In your code, you can use the relationship to share data between Entity1 and Entity2.

Figure B.13

Creating relationships

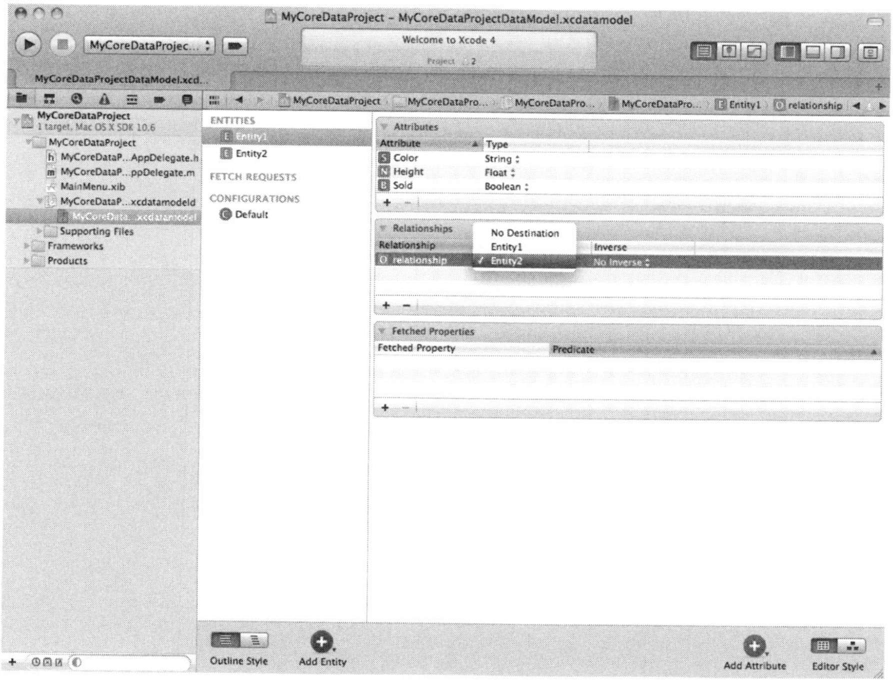

Using the graph editor

Select the graph editor to view the entities and their relationship visually, as shown in Figure B.14. The graph view is notional. The contents of each entity and the arrows that indicate relationships are significant. You can move entities by dragging them. Entity positions on the graph aren't important, so you can rearrange them for clarity. You also can add an attribute by selecting an entity and clicking the Add Attribute button near the bottom right of the editor.

Figure B.14

Viewing entities and relationships in the graph editor

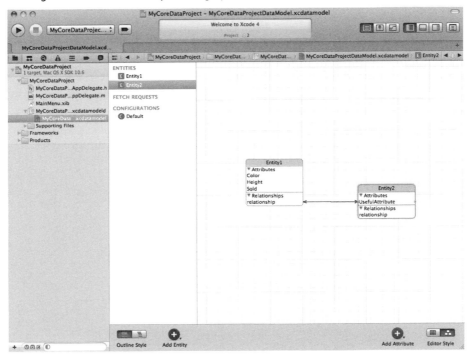

TIP

Arrowheads include information about relationship. A one-way relationship has a single arrowhead at one end. Two-way relationships have an arrowhead at each end. To-many relationships have double arrowheads. Note that you can have a one-way to-many relationship; this appears as a double arrowhead at one end, while the other end of the link has no arrowhead.

Using other options

You can add fetched properties in the Fetched Properties by clicking the + button. To add a predicate filter rule, click twice under the Predicate header and type the predicate as a string.

When the data model editor is selected in Xcode, a number of menu items become available under the main Xcode menu Editor header. Some options duplicate the buttons in the main editor; for example, the Add Entity menu item duplicates the Add Entity button.

However, this menu includes unique options that lack corresponding buttons:

- **Add Configuration.**
- **Add Fetch Request:** This defines a fetch request used to read data from records that match a selected entity type and also match an optional list of attribute conditions. Figure B.15 shows an example.
- **Create** NSManagedObject **subclass:** Use this option to create a customized version of one or more of your entities, with extra code features. By default, each entity is an instance of NSManagedObject. This class provides basic read, search, and write options for an entity. If your entity needs to do more—for example, it might need to interact with the rest of your application whenever data is accessed—this option creates code files for a subclass.
- **Import:** Use this option to import an existing data model from a saved file.
- **Create Model Version and Convert to Versioned Model:** Use these options to manage multiple versions of a model file and convert data between versions.

CAUTION

Xcode 3 included a useful UI generator feature. To create an OS X UI from a Core Data model, you could select every entity in the graph editor and drag and drop the objects into an Interface Builder document. The resulting file created an application with a working UI and basic search and editing feature. No extra code was needed. This feature isn't yet implemented in Xcode 4, but it may appear in later versions.

Using external editors

In Xcode 3, you could define the external editors used to open supporting files such as text, graphics, audio, and so on. Currently, Xcode 4 has no equivalent.

In Xcode 4, selecting an item, right-clicking, and selecting the Open With External Editor menu option loads the default editor or viewer for that file type. To open a file with some other editor, select the Show in Finder option, right-click the file, and use Finder's Open With option.

Figure B.15

You can define arbitrary fetch requests in code, but it can be easier to define standard requests in the model editor. You can then load them and use them as needed.

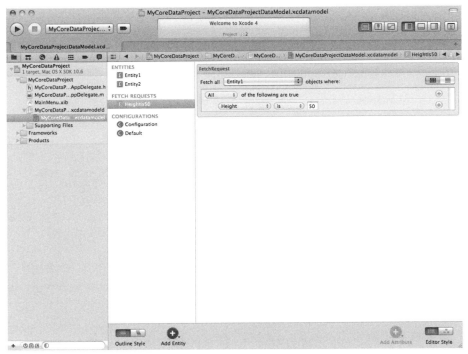

Summary

This appendix introduced plists and four different ways to edit them. It explained how a project's `info.plist` file gets special treatment in Xcode in the project's build settings. It also demonstrated how to use the main Xcode plist editor to edit other plist files.

Next, it sketched the key features of Core Data and explained how to use Xcode's new Core Data model editor. Finally, it ended with a brief note about using external editors for other file types.

Understanding Compiler Technology

One of the biggest changes between Xcode 3 and Xcode 4 is almost completely invisible. Xcode 4 begins a move away from the GCC (GNU Compiler Collection) frontend and code generator to a new compiler technology called LLVM (Low Level Virtual Machine). This small change has big implications for the future of Xcode and has influenced the design of some of the new features in Xcode 4.

Figure C.1 shows the two main components of a compiler. The parser/frontend reads source code written in a given language and converts it into an intermediate list of instructions. This is called *intermediate form* (IF) code. IF code uses a simplified set of virtual instructions that represents the essential operations and variables in the source in a machine- and language-independent way. IF code also includes a flow graph that optimizes the order in which instructions are processed. Variables may also be rearranged to optimize access.

The code generator module converts the IF code into machine-specific binary. It performs further optimizations that use the specific features of each target processor—for example, managing registers—to create a binary that is as efficient as possible. Most compilers, including Xcode, create binaries with an .o (object file) extension.

The *linker,* not shown in the figure, resolves variable references across different object files and collects them into a single executable binary. For example, if you define a variable called myNumber in one file, the linker fixes the location of myNumber in the binary and ensures that every reference anywhere in the project accesses that location.

Code parsing and code generation technology are still being researched and developed. Linker technology is largely a solved problem and typically "just works."

In This Appendix

NOTE
A complete set of compiler tools that includes an editor, one or more language frontends, a code generator, and a debugger is sometimes called a *tool chain*.

Figure C.1

The compiler revealed. IF code uses a simplified virtual instruction set that isn't implemented on any specific CPU.

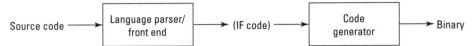

Introducing GCC

Earlier versions of Xcode used GCC modules for both the parser and the code generator. GCC, shown in Figure C.2, is a core project managed by the Free Software Foundation (FSF.) GCC is free in the sense that it can be freely modified and developed by anyone; it's also free in the sense that it costs nothing.

Figure C.2

The GCC website at gcc.gnu.org includes information about updates, language support, and a mission statement.

Initially, Xcode was designed as a runtime wrapper and code editor built around GCC. When the user clicks the Run icon, Xcode runs GCC in the background, collects its warnings and error messages, and displays them in Xcode's Build Results window. You can edit Xcode files directly with a text editor and run GCC directly from the command line in Terminal. But most developers find it easier and more productive to use a window-based editing environment because it offers extra features such as code completion and error marking.

Xcode's debugger is a wrapper for GDB, the GCC debugging tool. Xcode translates messages and user actions into text commands that are sent to GDB, and it converts GDB's responses into windowed output.

GCC has the advantage of an established code base and wide support for languages outside the C family. While Xcode doesn't support languages such as ADA and Fortran directly, you can add plug-ins to Xcode that make it possible to use Xcode's editor to write code in languages other than C and its descendants. Although this is a minority interest, languages such as Fortran are still used in scientific computing.

However, over time GCC has become a legacy project. Development is run by volunteers. Some features and Xcode plug-ins have become abandonware and are no longer compatible with current versions of Xcode. For example, Figure C.3 shows the current state of GCC's Fortran plug-in.

Figure C.3

Like many projects run by volunteer developers, interest in maintaining GCC add-ons wanes after a project has been completed successfully.

GCC has other disadvantages. Parts of the codebase date back to the 1980s, and compiler technology in the second decade of the 21st century is significantly more advanced. Put simply, GCC is inefficient and old-fashioned. It compiles code slowly and produces slow code.

GCC 4.0 is now considered a legacy compiler and is no longer supported in Xcode. GCC 4.2 is still available for backward compatibility. GCC 4.5 is the most recent version of GCC, but it will not be supported in future versions of Xcode.

Moving to LLVM

LLVM, whose project website is shown in Figure C.4, is an updated set of compiler tools that uses recent compiler research to speed up compilation times and create faster binaries. LLVM began as a research project at the University of Illinois at Urbana-Champaign under Vikram Adve and Chris Lattner. In 2005, Apple hired Lattner and created a team to develop LLVM in Xcode and also for Apple's internal R&D.

Figure C.4

Current versions of Xcode still support GCC for backward compatibility. Future versions will move to LLVM exclusively.

Like GCC, LLVM's source code is open, and it is a collaborative development project. But unlike GCC, LLVM is released under a version of the BSD (Berkeley Software Distribution) license that allows proprietary use.

In spite of the name, LLVM does not attempt to implement a virtual machine—a complete abstract model computer. Instead, it uses the most recent academic research to create fast, efficient, and highly optimized code. The LLVM code generator module is compatible with the IF code generated by GCC. This makes it possible to use GCC as a familiar frontend while using LLVM for final code output.

Introducing Clang

Clang is a C-family frontend that is paired with LLVM and tightly integrated with it. Clang parses Objective-C code much more quickly than GCC—up to three times faster in some tests. It also includes extra features that are starting to influence the editing and debugging of C++ and Objective-C in Xcode.

A key benefit of Clang is parser modularity. The GCC C-family frontend is self-contained and designed to run in batch mode. Effectively, it runs as a single closed process that converts source code into IF code.

Clang is more advanced and can be run interactively to parse expressions on demand. It also includes a static code analysis tool that can highlight possible bugs. Both features improve the performance and usefulness of the LLDB (Low Level Debugger) tool, which is included in LLVM as an advanced alternative to GDB Internally. Clang has been developed as a series of libraries and modules that can be used individually or together. Advanced users can customize and extend some or all of the features, or use them interactively with other languages—for example, using commands generated by Python or Java to manage code and control compilation.

Like LLVM, Clang is an open collaborative project. The website is shown in Figure C.5.

These are some of the other benefits of Clang:

- **Very fast and memory-efficient code parsing:** This makes large projects more practical on basic hardware.

- **Improved context-aware error messages and error correction:** Compared to GCC, Clang attempts to guess developer intentions and can correct code automatically.

- **Code profiling with bug finding:** For example, Clang can report possible memory errors in iPhone code.

- **Unified support for C, Objective-C, C++, and Objective-C++:** Clang provides a single parser for all C-family languages, making it easier to mix code in a project. It also aims to support all the major variants, including dialects and unusual features.

- **Interactive debugging:** LLDB includes the key features of the Clang parser, allowing you to include complex expressions in debugging statements or to generate complex expressions in Python or Java to control the debugger.

Figure C.5

The Clang website at clang.llvm.org introduces the key features of Clang and evangelizes its benefits.

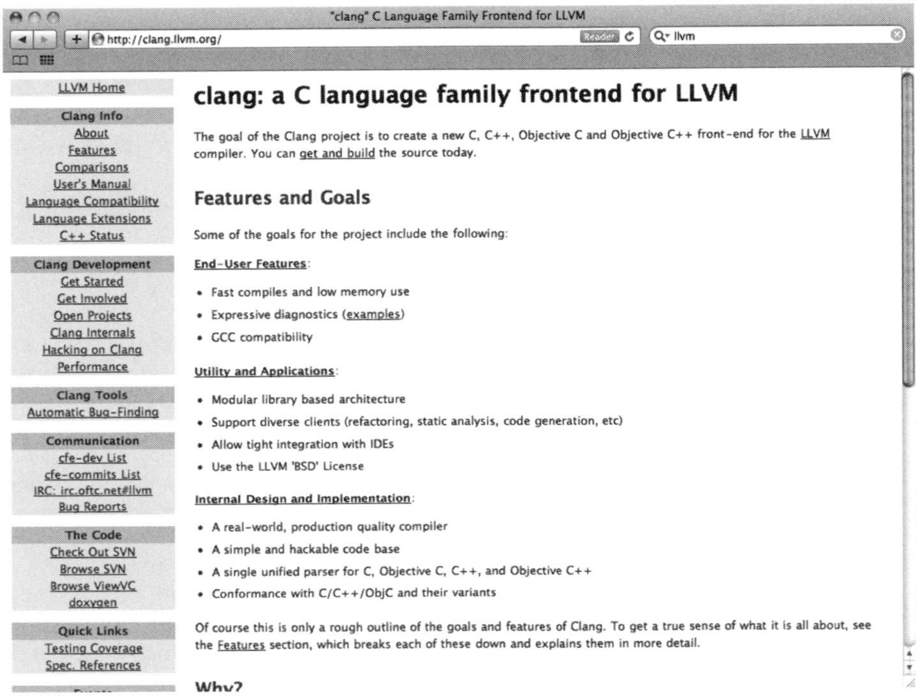

Selecting a Compiler

Xcode 4 defaults to a hybrid compiler named LLVM GCC 4.2. This uses the LLVM optimizer and code generator with the GCC 4.2 frontend. Although this isn't the speediest or most efficient option, it is the most reliable.

The LLVM Compiler 2.0 option selects the LLVM code generator and Clang frontend. For the moment, this remains an experimental option. Clang is still being developed and doesn't support the full range of extensions and other specialized features in GCC. This is unlikely to cause problems in most iPhone projects, but it may occasionally be an issue for OS X developers.

NOTE

For a current list of incompatibilities, see the C Language Features section toward the bottom of the Clang User Manual at `clang.llvm.org/docs/UsersManual.htm`.

To select a compiler manually, select the Project Navigator in the left pane and click the Project item at the top left of the pane, as shown in Figure C.6. Next, select Build Settings and find the Compiler Version. Click the arrows to display a pop-up menu with a list of compilers.

Figure C.6

When selecting a compiler, keep in mind that the LLVM GC 4.2 default remains the best choice for now, but you can experiment with LLVM 2.0 to see if you can improve build times and execution speeds.

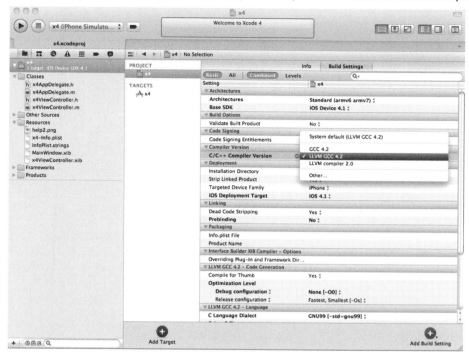

NOTE

If your project has multiple targets, you can select different compilers for each. This isn't usually a useful thing to do. Rarely you may run into a compiler bug that requires a downgrade from LLVM to GCC—but this happens so infrequently it's unlikely you'll encounter this issue.

When you select a compiler, the items under it are updated with compiler-specific options. If you select Basic in the line under the Build Settings tab, you can view the most critical compiler options. For iPhone development, you can typically leave these unchanged. For OS X development, select All to see all compiler settings and then scroll down, as shown in Figure C.7.

Although the list seems dauntingly long, only a handful of settings may need to be modified, as shown in Table C.1. Chapters 12 and 13 introduced key build settings for projects and targets. But you also may want to customize the compiler settings, for example by controlling which warnings appear by modifying the Warnings options. Removing some warnings is dangerous, and selecting the option to Inhibit All Warnings is very dangerous indeed. But many warnings are a matter of personal taste, and you can use this section to show warnings that are disabled by default as well as disabling warnings that may not be useful to you.

Figure C.7

Select All to see the full list of compiler options. Each compiler displays a different list, but most of the settings can be left unchanged.

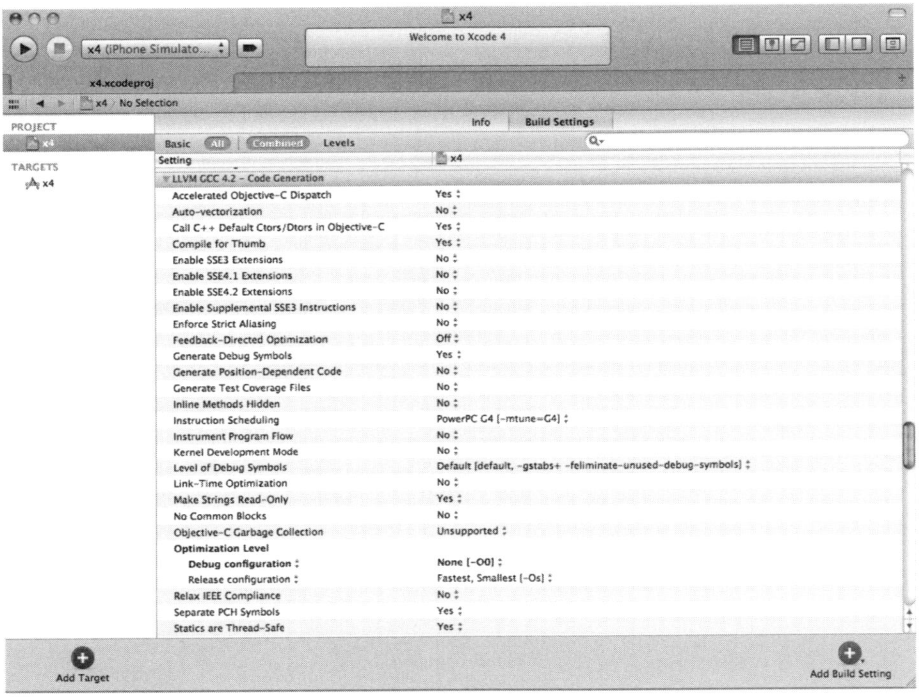

Table C.1 Selected Important OR USEFUL Compiler Settings

Setting	Application
Enable SSE3 Extensions Enable Supplemental SSE3 Extensions Enable SSE4.1/4.2 Extensions	Enable when using the vDSP and BLAS features in the Accelerate framework in OS X. (Note: SSE4 extensions are supported only on selected Intel processors, but the Accelerate framework creates conditional code that uses them if they are available.)
Objective-C Garbage Collection	Enable to turn on garbage collection on OS X. (Note: This is off by default.)
Enable AltiVec extensions	Enable when compiling legacy binaries for PPC processors with AltiVec acceleration.

Summary

This appendix introduced the essential features of compiler technology and listed the new compiler choices available in Xcode 4. It explored key features of the new technologies, explained how to change the default compiler, and listed the most important settings to consider when developing for OS X.

Index

Notes

Everything You Need to Craft Killer Code for Apple Applications

Whether you are a seasoned developer or just getting into the Apple platform, Wiley's Developer Reference series is perfect for you. Focusing on topics that Apple developers love best, these well-designed books guide you through the most advanced and very latest Apple tools, technologies, and programming techniques. With in-depth coverage and expert guidance from skilled authors who are proven authorities in their fields, the Developer Reference series will quickly become your indispensable Apple development resource.

The Developer Reference series is available wherever books are sold.

The books you read to succeed.

Get the most out of the latest software and leading-edge technologies with a Wiley Bible—your one-stop reference.

978-0-470-55419-7

978-0-470-56813-2

978-0-470-50909-8

978-0-470-55481-4

WILEY
Now you know.
wiley.com